BIBLIOGRAPHY
OF
BIBLIOGRAPHIES
IN
AMERICAN LITERATURE

BIBLIOGRAPHY
OF
BIBLIOGRAPHIES
IN
AMERICAN LITERATURE

BY CHARLES H. NILON

R.R. BOWKER COMPANY
New York & London 1970

Published by R.R. Bowker Co. (A Xerox Company)
1180 Avenue of the Americas, New York, N.Y. 10036
Copyright © 1970 by Xerox Corporation

Standard Book Number: 8352-0259-3

Library of Congress Catalog Card Number: 73-103542

Printed and Bound in the United States of America

CONTENTS

IV

ANCILLARY

PREFACE

I began work informally on this bibliography several years ago, in order to provide for Professor Lewis Sawin and myself a working knowledge of the quantity of bibliography that had been produced in American literature and some sense of the varieties of bibliographical forms that were in common use. We needed this information in beginning to plan the pattern of our efforts in the Integrated Bibliography Pilot Study, Cooperative Project 2,189, in which we sought to determine how the computer might be used in the selection, sorting, storage and retrieval of bibliographical data. At a conference called to evaluate our progress in the study, I made a brief report on the state of the bibliography of American literature before a group of consultants, including Eric H. Boehm of the American Bibliographical Center; John H. Broderick of the Library of Congress; I. Rotkin of the Harry Diamond Laboratories; H. F. Arader of IBM; Arlin Turner of the Duke University English faculty; James Woodress, the editor of *American Literary Scholarship;* and T. W. Ziehe of the Rand Corporation. As a result of discussion with them and of Professor Sawin's and my interests, I began a survey of American literary bibliography which has resulted in this bibliography of bibliographies.

Initially, I made a list of the sources in which I might find bibliographies of American literature. For this purpose I checked the *Library of Congress Catalog*, the *Cumulative Book Index*, the volumes of the *Annual Bibliography of English Language and Literature*, the PMLA bibliographies and such generally used tools in American literature as:

BESTERMAN, THEODORE. *A World Bibliography of Bibliographies.*
BLANCK, JACOB. *Bibliography of American Literature.*
EVANS, CHARLES. *American Bibliography.*
GOHDES, CLARENCE. *Bibliographical Guide to the Study of the Literature of the United States.*
KENNEDY, ARTHUR G., and DONALD B. SANDS. *A Concise Bibliography for Students of English.*
LEARY, LEWIS G. *Articles in American Literature.*
QUINN, ARTHUR HOBSON. *The Literature of the American People.*
SABIN, JOSEPH. *The Dictionary of Books Relating to America.*
SPILLER, ROBERT ERNEST, et al. *Literary History of the United States.*
TRENT, WILLIAM P., et al. *Cambridge History of American Literature.*
WOODRESS, JAMES. *Dissertations in American Literature.*

In compiling the bibliography I have used bibliographical and critical journals and bibliographical lists from special libraries and presses; examined literary histories and bibliographical and critical studies; included sale and exhibition catalogs; surveyed standard foreign language bibliographies; and examined bibliographies in ancillary fields, such as book publishing and American history. Generally, I have used the resources of the library of the University of Colorado.

I hope that the bibliographies represented here, although provisional, are sufficiently complete to be of service to libraries, students of American literature and others who may choose to use them. I hope also that in supplements and revisions many of the bibliographies that are not included in this edition may be listed.

The work cited in an entry in this bibliography is usually a list. Some of the works are books or essays that are bibliographical tools or studies and that treat bibliographical problems. In many instances it was not possible to examine the work that an entry represents. Because the entries were taken from a variety of sources, they varied considerably in form, accuracy, and completeness. When I found an entry that was not a complete bibliographical citation, I completed it whenever possible by examining the book or article that it described. When that was not possible, I used other sources for this purpose. For descriptions of books I accepted for accuracy and completeness the *Library of Congress Catalog* and the *Cumulative Book Index* listings, although I am certain that some of my entries are different in their content from the listings in these works. Generally, I have tried to conform to the practices of the *Annual Bibliography of English Language and Literature* and the *PMLA* Bibliography where matters of form are concerned.

One note is appropriate. All sections of this work list entries alphabetically by authors' names — with two exceptions. These are the first two sections of Part One: Bibliography. Section 1, Basic American Bibliography, is arranged chronologically, according to historical time periods covered by works cited. Section 2, Library of Congress and National Union Catalogs, is arranged chronologically within four topical areas comprised by LC and National Union materials: authors, imprints, subjects and manuscript collections.

I hope I have fulfilled Mr. Theodore Besterman's definition, "a bibliography is a list of books arranged according to some permanent principle," and that most of the practices in this bibliography will not confuse the reader. I think of this bibliography as an ordered list of bibliographies and bibliographical tools that provide information on particular authors, works and topics. The list may be used as a starting point by a person who wants bibliographical information on a particular author or subject in American literature. To some extent the number of entries listed on a particular author, work or topic will suggest to the user the quantity and character of bibliographical information that is available in the area of his interest. I feel also that a tool of this sort is useful in that, in a limited way, it performs a task of information retrieval by bringing to the attention of the user certain older, perhaps dated or unfashionable works that are not usually listed in the contemporary sources. Many such works have historical, aesthetic and critical value.

In addition to materials that have to do with American literature in its several phases, some tools are listed for the study of American history, the history of publishing and printing in America, biography, newspapers and other subjects. These ancillary entries may make the bibliography of some modest value, not only to the student of American literature, but to students in American studies and American civilization. The work may be of interest to the student who is interested in the history of ideas as an appropriate approach to literature.

The entries in this bibliography are not cross indexed. Each entry is listed as a full citation in each category in which it seemed appropriate to have it appear.

I acknowledge with grateful thanks the contribution and interest of a good number of people without which this work could not have been done. I am particularly grateful to the four graduate students who have worked at different times as my research assistants: Mr. Robert Cherry, Mr. Eugene Cunnar, Mr. Gordon Eriksen and Miss Carole FitzSimmons. They typed the cards, verified entries, and made corrections on the first draft of this work. In many ways the bibliography is their book. I am grateful too for the grant-in-aid from the University of Colorado Council on Research and Creative Work which helped reimburse my assistants and purchase supplies. I am indebted to the gentlemen whose names are mentioned in the first paragraph of this preface for their interest in bibliography and for my discussions with them. The interest and willingness to help with the project that was shown me by Professor Clarence Gohdes and Professor Lewis Sawin are courtesies that I deeply appreciate. The University of Colorado Library has provided me a study, the use of its resources and much valuable assistance from its staff. My wife, Nancy Nilon, who is head of the Reference Department of the University of Colorado Library, has assisted me graciously in many ways with the project. I am grateful also to my graduate students who have known about the project and have wished me well in doing it and to my editors, Mr. John N. Berry, III and Robert A. Landau, for their interest and faith in the completed project.

Charles H. Nilon
Boulder, Colorado
August 1, 1970

LIST OF ABBREVIATIONS

The following abbreviations for journals, after the style of the Publications of the Modern Language Association (PMLA) and Modern Humanities Research Association (MHRA) bibliographies, are used in the entries in this work:

AA	American Archivist	EAL	Early American Literature
ABC	American Book Collector	EALN	Early American Literature
AC	American Collector		Newsletter
AHQ	Arkansas Historical Quarterly	EJ	English Journal
		ELT	English Literature in
AHR	American Historical Review		Transition (1800-1920)
		ESQ	Emerson Society
AJS	American Journal of Sociology		Quarterly
		GaR	Georgia Review
AL	American Literature	HAB	Harvard Alumni Bulletin
AS	American Speech	HAHR	Hispanic American Historical Review
BA	Books Abroad		
BAASB	British Association for American Studies Bulletin	HC	Hollins Critic
		HLB	Harvard Library Bulletin
BALA	Bulletin of the American Library Association	HLQ	Huntington Library Quarterly
BB	Bulletin of Bibliography	IJHP	Iowa Journal of History and Politics
BBr	Books at Brown		
BC	Book Collector	IUB	Indiana University Bookman
BNYPL	Bulletin of the New York Public Library		
		JAAC	Journal of Aesthetics and Art Criticism
CCC	College Composition and Communication	JAF	Journal of American Folklore
CE	College English	JAMS	Journal of the American Musicological Society
CFQ	California Folklore Quarterly		
		JQ	Journalism Quarterly
CLC	Columbia Library Columns	KSHSR	Kentucky State Historical Society Review
CLQ	Colby Library Quarterly Colophon		
CRL	College and Research Libraries	LCQJ	Library of Congress Quarterly Journal
CWH	Civil War History	LCUP	Library Chronicle of the University of Pennsylvania
DULN	Duke University Library Notes		
		LCUT	Library Chronicle of the University of Texas
EA	Etudes Anglaises		

LJ	Library Journal
LQ	Library Quarterly
MD	Modern Drama
MFS	Modern Fiction Studies
MLJ	Modern Language Journal
MLN	Modern Language Notes
MLR	Modern Language Review
MP	Modern Philology
MVHR	Mississippi Valley Historical Review
NCHR	North Carolina Historical Review
NDQ	North Dakota Quarterly
N&Q	Notes and Queries
NLB	Newberry Library Bulletin
NMQ	New Mexico Quarterly
Notes	Music Library Association Notes
NYFQ	New York Folklore Quarterly
NYH	New York History
NYHSB	New York Historical Society Bulletin
NYHSQ	New York Historical Society Quarterly
PAAS	Proceedings of the American Antiquarian Society
PAPS	Proceedings of the American Philosophical Society
PBSA	Papers of the Bibliographical Society of America
PCSM	Publications of the Colonial Society of Massachusetts
PMHB	Pennsylvania Magazine of History and Biography
PMHS	Proceedings of the Massachusetts Historical Society
PMLA	Publications of the Modern Language Association of America
PULC	Princeton University Library Chronicle
PW	Publishers' Weekly

QJS	Quarterly Journal of Speech
RR	Romantic Review
SA	Studi Americani (Roma)
SAB	South Atlantic Bulletin
SAQ	South Atlantic Quarterly
Sat R	Saturday Review
SB	Studies in Bibliography
SLM	Southern Literary Messenger
SP	Studies in Philology
SRev	Southwest Review
SR	Studies in Romanticism
SS	Scandinavian Studies
TCL	Twentieth Century Literature
THQ	Tennessee Historical Quarterly
TLS	Times Literary Supplement
TQ	Texas Quarterly
TSB	Thoreau Society Bulletin
TSLL	Texas Studies in Literature and Language
UKCR	University of Kansas City Review
URKC	University Review (Kansas City)
URLB	University of Rochester Library Bulletin
VMHB	Virginia Magazine of History and Biography
WMH	Wisconsin Magazine of History
WMQ	William and Mary Quarterly
WR	Western Review
WSCL	Wisconsin Studies in Contemporary Literature
WWR	Walt Whitman Review
YULG	Yale University Library Gazette
ZAA	Zeitschrift fur Anglistik und Amerikanistik (Berlin Ost)

I

BIBLIOGRAPHY

1. BASIC AMERICAN BIBLIOGRAPHIES

EVANS, CHARLES. *American Bibliography: A Chronological Dictionary of All Books, Pamphlets and Periodical Publications Printed in the United States of America from the Genesis of Printing in 1639 down to and Including the Year 1800, with Bibliographical and Biographical Notes,* 14 Vols. Chicago: privately printed for the author by Blakely Press, 1903.

WATERS, WILLARD O. "American Imprints, 1648–1797, in the Huntington Library, Supplementing Evans' American Bibliography." *HLQ,* III (1933), 1–95.

Addition to Charles Evans' *American Bibliography,* 1903.

ADAMS, THOMAS R. "American Imprints before 1801 in the University of Pennsylvania Library and Not in Evans." *LCUP,* XXII (1956), 41–57.

Addition to Charles Evans' *American Bibliography,* 1903.

NEW YORK PUBLIC LIBRARY, RARE BOOK DIVISION. *Checklist of Additions to Evans' American Bibliography,* compiled by Lewis M. Stark and Maud D. Cole. New York: New York Public Library, 1960, 122 pp.

Addition to Charles Evans' *American Bibliography,* 1903.

SHAW, RALPH R., and RICHARD H. SHOEMAKER, comps. *American Bibliography: A Preliminary Checklist, 1801–1819,* 22 Vols. New York: The Scarecrow Press, 1958–1966.

ROORBACH, ORVILLE AUGUSTUS, comp. *Bibliotheca Americana: Catalogue of American Publications, Including Reprints and Original Works from 1820–1852, together with a List of Periodicals in the United States.* New York: O. A. Roorbach, 1849, 357 pp.

Supplement: O. A. Roorbach Jr., 1855, 220 pp. Covers October 1852–May 1855.

Supplement: Wiley and Halsted, 1858, 256 pp. Covers May 1855–March 1858.

Supplement: 1861, 162 pp. Covers March 1858–January 1861.

Also: P. Smith, 1939, 652 pp. Includes supplements.

SHOEMAKER, RICHARD H., comp. *A Checklist of American Imprints, 1820– .* New York: The Scarecrow Press, 1964– .

Intended to supplement Orville Augustus Roobarch's *Bibliotheca Americana,* 1849. To date four volumes have been issued covering 1820–1823.

KELLY, JAMES. *The American Catalogue of Books . . . Published in the United States from January, 1861, to January . . . 1871 . . . ,* 2 Vols. New York: J. Wiley and Sons, 1866–1871.

Also: P. Smith, 1938.

The Annual American Catalogue, 1869–1909, 25 Vols. New York: Publishers' Weekly, 1870–1910.

The American Catalogue: Author and Title Entries of Books in Print and for Sale (Including Reprints and Importations) July 1, 1876–Dec. 31, 1910, 15 Vols. New York: publisher varies, 1886–1911.

The United States Catalog: Books in Print, 1899–1928. Minneapolis and New York: H. W. Wilson Co., 1899–1928.

Addition to Charles Evans' *American Bibliography,* 1903. Superseded by *The Cumulative Book Index,* 1898– , formerly considered a supplement.

The Cumulative Book Index, 1898– . Minneapolis: H. W. Wilson Co., 1898–

Monthly, 1898–1911; bi-monthly, 1912–1915; monthly except February, August and December since 1916. Cumulated in various multi-year segments. Published in Minneapolis, 1898–1913; White Plains, 1914–1917; and New York, 1917 to date.

2. LIBRARY OF CONGRESS AND NATIONAL UNION CATALOGS

A Catalog of Books Represented by Library of Congress Printed Cards Issued to July 31, 1942, 167 Vols. Ann Arbor: J. W. Edwards, Inc., 1942.

A Catalog of Books Represented by Library of Congress Printed Cards Issued August 1, 1942 – December 31, 1947, 42 Vols. Ann Arbor: J. W. Edwards, Inc., 1948.

The Library of Congress Author Catalog, 1948–1952, 24 Vols. Ann Arbor: J. W. Edwards, Inc., 1953.

The National Union Catalog: A Cumulative Author List, 1953–1957, 28 Vols. Ann Arbor: J. W. Edwards, Inc., 1958.

The National Union Catalog: A Cumulative Author List, 1958–1962, 54 Vols. New York: Rowan and Littlefield, Inc., 1963.

The National Union Catalog: A Cumulative Author List, 1963–1967, 67 Vols. Ann Arbor: J. W. Edwards, Inc., 1969.

Monthly issues and quarterly and annual cumulations have appeared regularly since 1967.

The National Union Catalog, Pre-1956 Imprints. London and Chicago: Mansell, 1968–

A collation of Library of Congress materials with those of all other American libraries for the period before the National Union Catalog began in 1956. To comprise 610 volumes.

The National Union Catalog: 1952–1955 Imprints, 30 Vols. Ann Arbor: J. W. Edwards, Inc., 1955.

Library of Congress Catalog: Books: Subjects, 1950–1954, 20 Vols. Ann Arbor: J. W. Edwards, Inc., 1955.

Library of Congress Catalog: Books: Subjects: A Cumulative List of Works Represented by Library of Congress Printed Cards, 1955–1959, 21 Vols. Paterson, New Jersey: Pageant Books, Inc., 1960.

Library of Congress Catalog: Books: Subjects: A Cumulative List of Works Represented by Library of Congress Printed Cards, 1960–1964, 25 Vols. Ann Arbor: J. W. Edwards, Inc., 1965.

Library of Congress Catalog: Books: Subjects, 1965, 3 Vols. Washington, 1966.

Quarterly and annual cumulations have appeared since 1965.

The National Union Catalog of Manuscript Collections, 1959–1961. Ann Arbor: J. W. Edwards, Inc., 1962, 1,061 pp.

The National Union Catalog of Manuscript Collections, 1962. Hamden, Connecticut: The Shoe String Press, Inc., 1964, 532 pp.

The National Union Catalog of Manuscript Collections, Index, 1959–1962. Hamden, Connecticut: The Shoe String Press, Inc., 1964, 732 pp.

The National Union Catalog of Manuscript Collections, 1963–1964. Washington, 1965, 500 pp.

The National Union Catalog of Manuscript Collections, 1965, and Index, 1963–1965. Washington, 1966, 701 pp.

The National Union Catalog of Manuscript Collections, 1966, and Index, 1963–1967. Washington, 1967, 920 pp.

The National Union Catalog of Manuscript Collections, 1967, and Index, 1967. Washington, 1968, 525 pp.

3. OTHER BASIC BIBLIOGRAPHIES

A.L.A. Catalog. Chicago: American Library Association, 1926, 1,295 pp.

Supplement: 1926–1931, 330 pp.

Supplement: 1932–1936, 357 pp.

Supplement: 1937–1941, 306 pp.

Supplement: 1942–1949, 448 pp.

BIBLIOGRAPHICAL SOCIETY OF AMERICA. *The Bulletin of the Bibliographical Society of America,* 4 Vols. Chicago: Univ. of Chicago Press, 1907–1912.

I covers 1907–1909, others annual.

The Papers of the Bibliographical Society of America. New York: Bibliographical Society of America, 1904– .

BIBLIOGRAPHICAL SOCIETY OF CHICAGO. *Yearbook,* 4 Vols. Chicago: n.p., 1899-1900 – 1902-1903.

No more published. The society reorganized in 1904 as the Chicago chapter of the Bibliographical Society of America.

BLANCK, JACOB. *Bibliography of American Literature,* 5 Vols. New Haven: Yale Univ. Press, 1955–1969.

To date I–V (A–Long) have been issued.

_____. "The Bibliography of American Literature." *PW,* CXXXVIII (Nov. 17, 1945), 2,242–2,273; CLII (Nov. 22, 1947), 2,409–2,411.

_____, ed. *Merle Johnson's American First Editions,* 4th edition, revised and enlarged. Waltham, Massachusetts: Mark Press, 1965, 553 pp.

RICHARDSON, LYON N. "On Using Johnson's *American First Editions* and Other Sources." *AL,* IX (January 1938), 449–455.

COLLISON, ROBERT LEWIS. *Bibliographies, Subject and National: A Guide to Their Contents, Arrangement and Use.* New York: Hafner Publishing Co., 1951, 184 pp.

DIAZ, ALBERT JAMES, ed. *Guide to Microforms in Print.* Washington: Microcard Editions, Inc., 1961, 72 pp.

DOWNS, ROBERT BINGHAM, ed. *Union Catalogs in the United States.* Chicago: American Library Association, 1942, 393–402.

GERSTENBERGER, DONNA, and GEORGE HENDRICK. *Directory of Periodicals Publishing Articles in English and American Literature and Language.* Denver: Alan Swallow, 1959, 178 pp.

Second Directory . . . : 1965, 151 pp.

GOHDES, CLARENCE. *Bibliographical Guide to the Study of the Literature of the U.S.A.* Durham: Duke Univ. Press, 1959, 102 pp.

IRELAND, NORMA OLIN. *An Index to Indexes: A Subject Bibliography of Published Indexes.* Boston: F. W. Faxon, 1942, 107 pp.

LIBRARY OF CONGRESS, PROCESSING DEPARTMENT. *Monthly Checklist of State Publications.* Washington, 1910–

Bound into annual volumes and indexed.

New Serial Titles: A Union List of Serials Newly Received by North American Libraries. Washington, 1953–

From the title page: *"New Serial Titles* appears in twelve monthly issues and in annual cumulations which have been in turn cumulated over five- or ten-year periods."

NORTHUP, CLARK SUTHERLAND. *A Register of Bibliographies of the English Language and Literature.* New York: Hafner Publishing Co., 1962, 507 pp.

Originally published in 1925 as part of the *Cornell Studies in English.* Includes various American authors and topics, such as Negro literature, printing and publishing and local literature.

REUSS, JEREMIAH DAVID. *Alphabetical Register of All the Authors Actually in Great-Britain, Ireland, and in the United Provinces of North-America, with a Catalogue of Their Publications from the Year 1770 to the Year 1790.* Berlin and Stettin: Nicolai, 1791.

Supplement: 1804. Covers 1790–1803.

SABIN, JOSEPH. *Bibliography of Bibliography . . .: Being an Alphabetical Catalogue of the Most Important Works Descriptive of the Literature of Great Britain and America.* New York: J. Sabin and Sons, 1877, 150 pp.

From the preface: "Based on Part 1 ('Bibliography') of J. Power's *Handy Book about Books,* 1870; revised and enlarged . . .Originally issued in parts . . . as a supplement to the *American Bibliopolist,* V–IX, 1873– 1877."

——————. *Bibliotheca Americana Dictionary of Books Relating to America from Its Discovery to the Present Time,* 29 Vols. Amsterdam: N. Israel, 1961.

An important reprint of the classic work in American bibliography. Contains more than 100,000 books described and collated by Joseph Sabin, Wilberforce Eames and R. W.

G. Vail. Originally published 1868– 1936.

TRÜBNER, NIKOLAUS. *Trübner's Bibliographical Guide to American Literature: Being a Classified List of Books in All Departments of Literature and Science, Published in the United States . . . during the Last Forty Years,* with introduction, notes, three appendices and index. London: Trübner, 1855, 140 pp.

VAN PATTEN, NATHAN. *An Index to Bibliographies and Bibliographical Contributions to the Work of American and British Authors, 1923–1932.* Palo Alto: Stanford Univ. Press, 1934, 324 pp.

4. GENERAL BIBLIOGRAPHIES

ALTICK, RICHARD DANIEL, and ANDREW WRIGHT. *Selective Bibliography for the Study of English and American Literature.* New York: Macmillan, 1960, 138 pp.

2nd edition: 1963, 149 pp.

3rd edition: 1967, 152 pp.

AMERICAN COUNCIL OF LEARNED SOCIETIES DEVOTED TO HUMANISTIC STUDIES. *Catalogue of Current Bibliographies in the Humanistic Sciences.* Washington: American Council of Learned Societies Devoted to Humanistic Studies, 1931, 73 pp.

AMERICAN FOUNDATION FOR THE BLIND. *Directory of Periodicals of Special Interest to the Blind in Braille and Inkprint,* compiled by Helga Lende. New York: American Foundation for the Blind, 1933, 58 pp.

3rd edition: 1938, 66 pp.

"Anglo-French and Franco-American Studies: A Bibliography." *RR.*

Bibliography appears annually in either April or October issue, 1939–1948.

BAGINSKY, PAUL BEN, comp. *German Works Relating to America, 1493–1800: A List Compiled from the Collections of the New York Public Library.* New York: New York Public Library, 1942, 232 pp.

BEÉCHE, GREGORIO MIGUEL PASCUAL DE. *Bibliografía Americana,* edited by Benjamin Vicuña Mackenna. Valparaiso: Mercurio, 1879, 829 pp.

BLACK, GEORGE F. "List of Works in the New York Public Library Relating to Witchcraft in the United States." *BNYPL,* XII (September 1908), 658–675.

BLANCK, JACOB. *"BAL* Addenda." *PBSA,* LV (1st Quart. 1961), 46–47.

Addenda to entries for Ambrose Bierce and Mary H. Catherwood.

_____. "A Calendar of Bibliographical Difficulties." *PBSA,* XLIV (1st Quart. 1955), 1–18.

BOBBITT, M. R. "A Bibliography of Etiquette Books Published in America before 1900." *BNYPL,* LI (December 1947), 687–720.

BOON, EDWARD P. *Catalogue of Bibliographical Pamphlets.* New York, 1878, 597 pp.

Sold by Leavitt, Strebeigh and Co., 1878.

_____. *Catalogue of Books and Pamphlets Principally Relating to America.* New York, 1870, 601 pp.

Sold by Leavitt, Strebeigh and Co., May 16, 1870.

BRADLEY, I. S. "Bibliographies Published by Historical Societies of the United States." *PBSA,* I (1907), 146–157.

The Braille Review: A Monthly List of Braille Publications, etc. London: The British and Foreign Blind Association, 1903–1916.

BRITISH MUSEUM, DEPARTMENT OF PRINTED BOOKS. "America," in *Catalogue of Printed Books,* 393 Parts in 95 Vols. London: W. Clowes and Sons, 1881–1900, II, Part 5, 156–174.

BROCKHAUS, FREIDRICH ARNOLD. *Bibliothèque Américaine.* Leipzig: F. A. Brockhaus, 1861, 133 pp.

CANNONS, HARRY GEORGE TURNER. *Classified Guide to 1700 Annuals, Directories, Calendars, and Year Books.* New York: H. Wilson Co., 1923, 220 pp.

CARR, H. J. "Index to Some Recent Reference Lists." *LJ,* VIII (February 1883), 27.

CARRIERE, JOSEPH M., et al. "Anglo-French and Franco-American Studies: A Bibliography." *French American Review,* II (October-December 1949), 214–232; III (April-September 1950), 94–119.

CARTER, PAUL J., and GEORGE K. SMART, comps. *Literature and Society, 1961–1965: A Selective Bibliography.* Coral Gables: Modern Language Association and Univ. of Miami Press, 1967, 160 pp.

Univ. of Miami Publications in English and American Literature, No. 9.

CLAPP, JANE. *International Dictionary of Literary Awards.* New York: Scarecrow Press, 1963, 545 pp.

"Current Bibliography." *European Association for American Studies Newsletter,* 1955–

Includes translations and critical studies. Not confined to literature.

CUSHING, WILLIAM. *Initials and Pseudonyms: A Dictionary of Literary Disguises.* New York: T. Y. Crowell, 1885, 602 pp.

Interleaved copy of pioneer American work, listing some 12,000 initials and pseudonyms, plus index of true authors.

2nd series: 1888, 314 pp.

DENNY, REUEL, and MARY L. MEYERSOHN. "A Preliminary Bibliography on Leisure." *AJS,* LXII (May 1957), 602–615.

DICKINSON, ASA DON. *The Best Books of the Decade, 1936–1945: Another Clue to the Literary Labyrinth.* New York: H. W. Wilson Co., 1948, 295 pp.

DOUGLAS, GEORGE WILLIAM. *The American Book of Days . . . ,* revised edition. New York: H. W. Wilson Co., 1948, 719 pp.

DOWNS, ROBERT BINGHAM, and FRANCES B. JENKINS, eds., *Bibliography, Current State and Future Trends.* Urbana: Univ. of Illinois Press, 1967, 611 pp.

Illinois Contributions to Librarianship, No. 8.

Appeared originally in the January and April 1967 issues of *Library Trends.*

DOWNS, ROBERT BINGHAM, et al. *American Library Resources: A Bibliographical Guide.* Chicago: American Library Association, 1951, 428 pp.

Lists some published checklists of local holdings of newspapers and magazines. Includes numerous catalogs of newspapers and of holdings of individual libraries.

Supplement: 1962, 226 pp. Covers 1950–1961.

EARLE, ALICE MORSE. *Two Centuries of Costume in America,* 2 Vols. New York: Macmillan, 1903.

FESSLER, AARON L. "Selective Bibliography of Literary Censorship in the United States." *BB,* XX (May-August 1952), 188–191.

Lists essays, books dealing with past and present controversy over literary censorship.

FLANAGAN, JOHN T. "American Literary Bibliography in the Twentieth Century." *Library Trends,* XV (January 1967), 550–572.

FLETCHER, W. I., and R. R. BOWKER. "Bibliographies, American and English," in *Annual Literary Index,* 1892–1904. New York: Publishers' Weekly, 1893–1905.

Issued annually. Continued in *Annual Library Index,* 1905–1910, and in *American Literary Annual,* 1911–1918.

FORD, PAUL LEICESTER. *Check List of Bibliographies, Catalogues, Reference Lists, and Lists of Authorities of American Books and Subjects.* Brooklyn: n.p., 1889, 64 pp.

––––––––––. "Reference List to Bibliographies, Catalogues, and Reference Lists on America." *LJ,* XIII (February–October 1888), 37–40, 82–86, 135–139, 174–179, 244–248, 289–291.

GOFF, FREDERICK R. *The Primordia of Bishop White Kennet: the First English Bibliography on America.* Washington: Pan American Union, 1960, 275 pp.

GRANNISS, RUTH S. "Series of Books about Books." *The Colophon,* ns I (Spring 1936), 549–564.

HACKETT, ALICE PAYNE. *60 Years of Best Sellers, 1895–1955.* New York: R. R. Bowker Co., 1956, 223–229.

HARLOW, NEAL. "The Well-Tempered Bibliographer." *PBSA,* L (1st Quart. 1956), 28–39.

HARRISSE, HENRY, "Bibliographies Relating to America" in *Bibliotheca Americana Vetustissima,* New York: G. P. Philes, 1866, x.

HART, JAMES D. *Oxford Companion to American Literature,* 4th edition. New York: Oxford Univ. Press, 1965, 991 pp.

_____. *The Popular Book: A History of America's Literary Taste.* New York: Oxford Univ. Press, 1950, 289–300.

HAWLEY, EDITH J. ROSSWELL. "Literary Geography: A Bibliography." *BB,* X (April 1918), 34–38; (July 1918), 58–60; (October 1918), 76; (January 1919), 93–94; (April 1919), 104–105.

Also: *Bulletin of Bibliography Pamphlet,* No. 25.

HERZBERG, MAX J. *The Reader's Encyclopaedia of American Literature.* New York: Crowell, 1962, 1,290 pp.

HOFFMAN, HESTER R., ed., *Bessie Graham's Bookman's Manual: A Guide to Literature,* 6th edition. New York: R. R. Bowker Co., 1948, 785 pp.

HOLMES, ABRIEL. *Annals of America . . . ,* 2nd edition, 2 Vols. Cambridge: Hilliard and Brown, 1829, I, ix-xvi.

JOSEPHSON, AKSEL GUSTAV SALOMON. *Bibliographies of Bibliographies, Chronologically Arranged, with Occasional Notes and an Index.* Chicago: Bibliographical Society of Chicago, 1901, 45 pp.

KINNEY, MARY RAMON. *Bibliographical Style Manuals: A Guide to Their Use in Documentation and Research.* Chicago: Association of College and Reference Libraries, 1953, 21 pp.

ACRL Monographs, No. 8.

KOGAN, BERNARD. "Current Sourcebooks." *CCC,* XIII (May 1962), 41–46.

LANE, WILLIAM COOLIDGE. *Index to Recent Reference Lists, 1884–1890.* Cambridge: Library of Harvard Univ., 1885–1891.

These lists also appear in *Harvard Bulletin,* 1886–1891.

LEARY, LEWIS. *Articles on American Literature, 1900–1950.* Durham: Duke Univ. Press, 1954, 336–340.

"Bibliography, Special."

_____. "Bibliographical and Textual Studies and American Literary History." *TQ* III (Summer 1960), 160–166.

LEIDY, W. PHILIP. *A Popular Guide to Government Publications,* 2nd edition. New York: Columbia Univ. Press, 1963, 291 pp.

LEISY, ERNEST E. "Materials for Investigations in American Literature." *SP,* XXIII (January 1926), 90–115.

LIBRARY OF CONGRESS. *Check List of Collections of Personal Papers in Historical Societies, University and Public Libraries, and Other Learned Institutions in the United States.* Washington, 1918, 87 pp.

_____. *Some Bibliographies Which List Works Published in the United States during the War Years.* Washington, 1947, 4 pp.

LIBRARY OF CONGRESS, DIVISION OF BIBLIOGRAPHY. *List of References on Women in Literature.* Washington, 1922, 3 leaves.

LIBRARY OF CONGRESS, GENERAL REFERENCE AND BIBLIOGRAPHY DIVISION. *Current National Bibliographies,* compiled by Helen F. Conover. Washington, 1955, 132 pp.

LINDER, HAROLD LE ROY. *The Rise of Current Complete National Bibliography.* New York: The Scarecrow Press, 1959, 290 pp.

Chapter VI, "The United States from 1846 to 1891," identifies and describes particular bibliographies, its focus historical.

Literary and Library Prizes, 5th edition. New York: R. R. Bowker Co., 1963, 280 pp.

MacARTHUR, JAMES, ed. *The Bookman: Literary Year-Book, 1898.* New York: Dodd, Mead and Co., 1898, 263 pp.

No more published.

McCLELLAN, ELISABETH. *Historic Dress in America,* 2 Vols. Philadelphia: George W. Jacobs and Co., 1904.

MALCLES, LOUISE NOËLLE. *Les Sources du Travail Bibliographique.* Geneva: E. Droz, 1950–

Issued annually.

MARSHALL, THOMAS F., and GEORGE K. SMART, comps., *Literature and Society, 1956–1960: A Selective Bibliography.* Coral Gables: Modern Language Association and Univ. of Miami Press, 1962, 71 pp.

Univ. of Miami Publications in English and American Literature, No. 4.

MARSHALL, THOMAS F., GEORGE K. SMART and LOUIS J. BUDD, comps. *Literature and Society, 1950–1955: A Selective Bibliography.* Coral Gables: Modern Language Association and Univ. of Miami Press, 1956, 57 pp.

Univ. of Miami Publications in English and American Literature, No. 2.

MATSON, HENRY. *References for Literary Workers, with Introductions to Topics and Questions for Debate.* Chicago: A. C. McClurg and Co., 1893, 582 pp.

3rd edition: 1897, 582 pp.

MINTO, JOHN, comp. *Reference Books: A Classified and Annotated Guide to the Principal Works of Reference.* London: Library Association, 1929, 356 pp.

MÖNNIG, RICHARD. *Amerika und England im Deutschen, Österreichischen und Schweizerischen Schrifttum der Jahre 1194–1949.* Stuttgart: W. Koklhammer Verlag, 1951, 259 pp.

MORRISON, HUGH ALEXANDER, ed. "A Bibliography of the Official Publications of the Confederate States of America." *PBSA,* III (1908), 92–132.

MOSHER, FREDERIC J., and ARCHER TAYLOR. *The Bibliographical History of Anonyma and Pseudonyma.* Chicago: printed for the Newberry Library by the Univ. of Chicago Press, 1951, 288 pp.

Contains a bibliography and classified guide to dictionaries and other lists of anonyma and pseudonyma.

MUNSELL, JOEL. *Catalogue of American and Foreign Books in Bibliography and Other Departments of Literature, . . . Rare Works Relating to*

Printing, Voyages and Travels.
Albany: J. Munsell, 1857, 74 pp.

NATIONAL COUNCIL OF WOMEN
OF THE UNITED STATES. *The
One Hundred Best Books by Ameri-
can Women during the Past Hundred
Years, 1833–1933.* Chicago: Asso-
ciated Authors Service, 1901, 317 pp.

"The New Bibliography of American
Literature." *LJ,* LXIX (June 5,
1944), 549–550.

O'NEILL, EDWARD HAYES.
"Plans for a Bibliography of American Literature." *AL,* XI (March
1939), 81–83.

PATTEE, FRED LEWIS. "Anthologies of American Literature before
1861." *The Colophon,* Part 16
(1934), no pagination.

An annotated list.

PEET, L. H. *Who's the Author? A
Guide to the Authorship of Novels,
Stories, Speeches, Songs, and General
Writings of American Literature.*
New York: Crowell, 1901, 317 pp.

POWELL, JOHN HARVEY. *The
Books of a New Nation: United States
Government Publications, 1774–
1814.* Philadelphia: Univ. of Pennsylvania Press, 1957, 170 pp.

PRINCETON UNIVERSITY,
LIBRARY. "One Hundred Notable
American Books." *PULC,* XIX
(Winter 1958), 87–91.

PUTNAM, HERBERT. "Bibliographic Bureaus." *LJ,* XXII (September
1897), 409–413; (October 1897),
450–452.

RICHARDS, ROBERT FULTON.
*Concise Dictionary of American
Literature.* New York: Philosophical
Library, 1955, 253 pp.

Student edition: Ames, Iowa: Littlefield, Adams, 1956.

ROBINSON, WILLIAM H., LTD.,
LONDON. *Books Relating to America.* London: F. Juckes, Ltd.,
printers, 1933, 116 pp.

Catalog No. 41.

SCHWARTZ, JACOB. *1100 Obscure
Points: The Bibliographies of 25
English and 21 American Authors.*
London: published by the Ulysses
Bookshop, 1931, 95 pp.

SHERA, JESSE H. "The Beginnings
of Systematic Bibliography in America, 1647–1799," in *Essays Honoring
Lawrence C. Wroth.* Portland,
Maine: Anthoensen Press, 1951,
263–278.

Contains tables listing book catalogs
published in America, social libraries
established in New England, and a
chronological listing of innovations
in American bibliographic work.

SILVER, ROLLO G. "Problems in
Nineteenth-Century American Bibliography." *PBSA,* XXXV (1st Quart.
1941), 35–47.

SMITH, LESTER W. "Writings on
Archives, Current Records, and
Historical Manuscripts." *AA,* XIX
(October 1956), 337–369.

SPAETH, JOHN DUNCAN ERNST,
and JOSEPH E. BROWN. *American
Life and Letters: A Reading List.*
Princeton: Princeton Univ. Press,
1934, 62 pp.

STODDARD, ROGER E. "Oscar
Wegelin, Pioneer Bibliographer of
American Literature." *PBSA,* LVI
(2nd Quart. 1962), 237–247.

TAYLOR, ARCHER. *A History of
Bibliographies of Bibliographies.*

New Brunswick, New Jersey: Scare-crow Press, 1955, 147 pp.

TAYLOR, ARCHER, and BARTLETT JERE WHITING, comps. *A Dictionary of American Proverbs and Proverbial Phrases, 1820–1880.* Cambridge: Belknap Press of Harvard Univ. Press, 1958, xiii–xxii.

U.S.A. Book News, January 1946–January 1947. New York: R. R. Bowker Co., 1947.

Labelled I, but no more volumes published.

UNITED STATES, DEPARTMENT OF INTERIOR, BUREAU OF EDUCATION. "List of Printed Catalogues of Public Libraries in the United States, Arranged by Date of Publication" in *Public Libraries in the United States of America.* Washington, 1876, 576–622.

UNITED STATES, SUPER-INTENDENT OF DOCUMENTS. *Checklist of United States Public Documents, 1789–1909,* 3rd edition, revised. Washington, 1911, 1,740 pp.

United States Quarterly Book Review, 12 Vols. Washington, 1945–1956.

VALLEE, LEON. *Bibliographie des Bibliographies,* 2 Vols. Paris: E. Terquem, 1883–1887.

Includes supplement.

WILSON, H. W. COMPANY. *Essay and General Literature Index.* New York: H. W. Wilson Co., 1900–

Issued annually since 1965; earlier issues covered larger time spans.

II

AUTHORS

1. 17TH CENTURY

ALEXANDER, WILLIAM

SLAFTER, EDMUND FARWELL. *Sir William Alexander and American Colonization.* Boston: The Prince Society, 1873, 119.

BAXTER, RICHARD

LEARY, LEWIS. *Articles on American Literature, 1900–1950.* Durham: Duke Univ. Press, 1954, 18.

BRADFORD, WILLIAM

LEARY, LEWIS. *Articles on American Literature, 1900–1950.* Durham: Duke Univ. Press, 1954, 25.

MUNBY, A. N. L. "Elias Burling, *A Call to Back-Sliding Israel,* New York, 1964: An Unrecorded Tract Printed by William Bradford." *SB,* XIV (1961). 251–253.

SPILLER, ROBERT ERNEST, et al. *Literary History of the United States,* 2 Vols. New York: Macmillan, 1962, 412–414. Supplement, 84.

TAYLOR, WALTER FULLER. *A History of American Letters,* with bibliographies by Harry Hartwick. Boston: American Book Co., 1936, 471–472.

Subsequent editions entitled: *The Story of American Letters.*

TRENT, WILLIAM PETERFIELD, et al. *Cambridge History of American Literature,* 4 Vols. New York: G. P. Putnam's Sons, 1917–1921, I, 383.

BRADSTREET, ANNE

BUCHANAN, CHARLES. "Colonial Manuscript Back Home." *LJ,* LXXXI (Jan. 15, 1956), 148–149.

LEARY, LEWIS. *Articles on American Literature, 1900–1950.* Durham: Duke Univ. Press, 1954, 25–26.

SPILLER, ROBERT ERNEST, et al. *Literary History of the United States,* 2 Vols. New York: Macmillan, 1962, 414–415. Supplement, 84.

SVENDSEN, J. KESTER. "Anne Bradstreet in England: A Bibliographical Note." *AL,* XIII (March 1941), 63–65.

TAYLOR, WALTER FULLER. *A History of American Letters,* with bibliographies by Harry Hartwick. Boston: American Book Co., 1936, 474–475.

Subsequent editions entitled: *The Story of American Letters.*

THOMAS, DANTE, comp. "Anne Bradstreet: An Annotated Checklist." *EAL,* III (Winter 1968), 217–240.

WEGELIN, OSCAR, comp. "A List of Editions of the Poems of Anne Bradstreet, with Several Additional

Books Relating to Her." *ABC*, IV (July 1933), 15—16.

COOPER, THOMAS

HUBBELL, JAY B. *The South in American Literature, 1607—1900.* Durham: Duke Univ. Press, 1954, 927—928.

COTTON, JOHN

HUBBELL, JAY B. *The South in American Literature, 1607—1900.* Durham: Duke Univ. Press, 1954, 928—929.

LEARY, LEWIS. *Articles on American Literature, 1900—1950.* Durham: Duke Univ. Press, 1954, 59.

SPILLER, ROBERT ERNEST, et al. *Literary History of the United States,* 2 Vols. New York: Macmillan, 1962, 455—457.

TRENT, WILLIAM PETERFIELD, et al. *Cambridge History of American Literature,* 4 Vols. New York: G. P. Putnam's Sons, 1917—1921, I, 386—390.

TUTTLE, JULIUS H. "Writings of Rev. John Cotton," in *Bibliographical Essays: A Tribute to Wilberforce Eames.* Cambridge: Harvard Univ. Press, 1924, 363—380.

COTTON, JOHN (OF ACQUIA CREEK)

LEARY, LEWIS. *Articles on American Literature, 1900—1950.* Durham: Duke Univ. Press, 1954, 60.

DULANY, DANIEL

HUBBELL, JAY B. *The South in American Literature, 1607—1900.* Durham: Duke Univ. Press, 1954, 931.

D'URFEY, THOMAS

BISWANGER, RAYMOND A., JR. "Thomas D'Urfey's 'Richmond Heiress' (1693): A Bibliographical Study." *SB*, V (1953), 169—178.

ELIOT, JOHN

EAMES, WILBERFORCE. "Discovery of a Lost Cambridge Imprint: John Eliot's *Genesis,* 1655." *PCSM*, XXXIV (1943), 11—12.

FRANCIS, CONVERS. *The Life of John Eliot: The Apostle of the Indians.* New York: Harper, 1849, 357 pp.

LEARY, LEWIS. *Articles on American Literature, 1900—1950.* Durham: Duke Univ. Press, 1954, 79.

SPILLER, ROBERT ERNEST, et al. *Literary History of the United States,* 2 Vols. New York: Macmillan, 1962, 486—488.

TRENT, WILLIAM PETERFIELD, et al. *Cambridge History of American Literature,* 4 Vols. New York: G. P. Putnam's Sons, 1917—1921, I, 390—393.

WINSHIP, GEORGE P. "The Eliot Indian Tracts," in *Bibliographical Essays: A Tribute to Wilberforce Eames.* Cambridge: Harvard Univ. Press, 1924, 179—192.

GOOKIN, DANIEL

LEARY, LEWIS. *Articles on American Literature, 1900—1950.* Durham: Duke Univ. Press, 1954, 121.

HARRIS, BENJAMIN

LEARY, LEWIS. *Articles on American Literature, 1900—1950.* Durham: Duke Univ. Press, 1954, 125.

HOOKER, THOMAS

EMERSON, EVERETT H. "Notes on the Thomas Hooker Canon." *AL,* XXVII (January 1956), 554–555.

Corrections of the checklists now in print.

LEARY, LEWIS. *Articles on American Literature, 1900–1950.* Durham: Duke Univ. Press, 1954, 144.

SPILLER, ROBERT ERNEST, et al. *Literary History of the United States,* 2 Vols. New York: Macmillan, 1962, 568–569. Supplement, 140.

TRENT, WILLIAM PETERFIELD, et al. *Cambridge History of American Literature,* 4 Vols. New York: G. P. Putnam's Sons, 1917–1921, I, 395–397.

WALKER, GEORGE L. *Thomas Hooker: Preacher, Founder, Democrat,* with a bibliography by J. Hammond Trumball. New York: Dodd, Mead and Co., 1891, 184–195.

HUBBARD, WILLIAM

ADAMS, RANDOLPH G. "Hubbard's Narrative, 1677." *The Colophon,* ns I (Winter 1936), 456–457.

——————. "William Hubbard's 'Narrative,' 1677: A Bibliographical Study." *PBSA,* XXXIII (1939), 25–39.

LEARY, LEWIS. *Articles on American Literature, 1900–1950.* Durham: Duke Univ. Press, 1954, 150.

JOSSELYN, JOHN

LEARY, LEWIS. *Articles on American Literature, 1900–1950.* Durham: Duke Univ. Press, 1954, 171.

LEE, RICHARD

LEARY, LEWIS. *Articles on American Literature, 1900–1950.* Durham: Duke Univ. Press, 1954, 178.

LEE, SAMUEL

LEARY, LEWIS. *Articles on American Literature, 1900–1950.* Durham: Duke Univ. Press, 1954, 178.

MASON, JOHN

LEARY, LEWIS. *Articles on American Literature, 1900–1950.* Durham: Duke Univ. Press, 1954, 201.

MATHER, COTTON

HOLMES, THOMAS JAMES. *Cotton Mather: A Bibliography of His Works,* 3 Vols. Cambridge: Harvard Univ. Press, 1940.

——————. "Cotton Mather and His Writings on Witchcraft." *PBSA,* XVIII (1924), 31–59.

——————. "The Mather Bibliography." *PBSA,* XXXI (1937), 57–76.

——————. "The Mather Collection at Cleveland." *The Colophon,* Part 14 (1933), no pagination.

JONES, M. B. "Some Bibliographical Notes on Cotton Mather's *The Accomplished Singer."* *PCSM,* XXVIII (1935), 186–193.

KITTREDGE, G. L. "Some Lost Works of Cotton Mather." *PMHS,* XLV (1912), 418–477.

LEARY, LEWIS. *Articles on American Literature, 1900–1950.* Durham: Duke Univ. Press, 1954, 202–203.

MANIERRE, WILLIAM R., II. "A Description of 'Paterna': The Unpublished Autobiography of Cotton Mather." *SB,* XVIII (1965), 183–205.

MATHER, COTTON. *Manductio ad Ministerium: Directions for a Candidate of the Ministry,* reproduced from the original edition, Boston, 1726, with bibliographical notes by Thomas J. Holmes and Kenneth B. Murdock. New York:published for the Facsimile Text Society by Columbia Univ. Press, 1938, unnumbered pages at beginning of volume.

MURDOCK, KENNETH BALLARD, ed. *Selections from Cotton Mather.* New York: Harcourt, Brace and World, 1926, lxi-lxiii.

SIBLEY, JOHN LANGDON. *Biographical Sketches of Graduates of Harvard University,* 3 Vols. Cambridge: Harvard Univ. Press, 1873–1885, III, 42–158.

Continued as: SHIPTON, CLIFFORD K., ed. *Sibley's Harvard Graduates: Biographical Sketches of Those Who Attended Harvard College.*

SPILLER, ROBERT ERNEST, et al. *Literary History of the United States,* 2 Vols. New York: Macmillan, 1962, 640–644. Supplement, 164.

TAYLOR, WALTER FULLER. *A History of American Letters,* with bibliographies by Harry Hartwick. Boston: American Book Co., 1936, 476–478.

Subsequent editions entitled: *The Story of American Letters.*

TRENT, WILLIAM PETERFIELD, et al. *Cambridge History of American Literature,* 4 Vols. New York: G. P. Putnam's Sons, 1917–1921, I, 407–425.

MATHER, INCREASE

CADBURY, HENRY JOEL. "Harvard College Library and the Libraries of the Mathers." *PAAS,* L (April 1940), 20–48.

HOLMES, THOMAS JAMES, comp. *Increase Mather: A Bibliography of His Work,* 2 Vols. Cleveland: printed by Harvard Univ. Press for William Gwinn Mather, 1931, 711 pp.

A descriptive bilbiography. 500 copies printed.

LEARY, LEWIS. *Articles on American Literature, 1900–1950.* Durham: Duke Univ. Press, 1954, 203–204.

PEDEN, WILLIAM, ed. *Testimony against Prophane Customs,* with a bibliographical note by Lawrence Starkey. Charlottesville: Univ. of Virginia Press for the Tracy W. McGregor Library, 1953, 57–59.

SIBLEY, JOHN LANGDON. *Biographical Sketches of Graduates of Harvard University,* 3 Vols. Cambridge: Harvard Univ. Press, 1873–1885, I, 410–470.

Continued as: SHIPTON, CLIFFORD K., ed. *Sibley's Harvard Graduates: Biographical Sketches of Those Who Attended Harvard College.*

SPILLER, ROBERT ERNEST, et al. *Literary History of the United States,* 2 Vols. New York: Macmillan, 1962, 644–646. Supplement, 164.

TAYLOR, WALTER FULLER. *A History of American Letters,* with bibliographies by Harry Hartwick. Boston: American Book Co., 1936, 475–476.

Subsequent editions entitled: *The Story of American Letters.*

TRENT, WILLIAM PETERFIELD, et al. *Cambridge History of American Literature,* 4 Vols. New York: G. P. Putnam's Sons, 1917–1921, I, 398–407.

MATHER (MINOR MATHERS)

HOLMES, THOMAS JAMES, comp. *The Minor Mathers: A List of Their Works.* Cambridge: Harvard Univ. Press, 1940, 238 pp.

MATHER, NATHANAEL

LEARY, LEWIS. *Articles on American Literature, 1900–1950.* Durham: Duke Univ. Press, 1954, 204.

MATHER, RICHARD

LEARY, LEWIS. *Articles on American Literature, 1900–1950.* Durham: Duke Univ. Press, 1954, 204.

TRENT, WILLIAM PETERFIELD, et al. *Cambridge History of American Literature,* 4 Vols. New York: G. P. Putnam's Sons, 1917–1921, I, 397–398.

MORTON, NATHANIEL

LEARY, LEWIS. *Articles on American Literature, 1900–1950.* Durham: Duke Univ. Press, 1954, 219.

MORTON, THOMAS

LEARY, LEWIS. *Articles on American Literature, 1900–1950.* Durham: Duke Univ. Press, 1954, 219.

PASTORIUS, FRANCIS DANIEL

LEARY, LEWIS. *Articles on American Literature, 1900–1950.* Durham: Duke Univ. Press, 1954, 231.

SPILLER, ROBERT ERNEST, et al. *Literary History of the United States,* 2 Vols. New York: Macmillan, 1962, 683–684.

PENN, WILLIAM

BLUM, HERMAN. *William Penn, 1644–1728: New Light Thrown on the Quaker Founder of Pennsylvania Through Heretofore Unpublished Documents in the Blumhaven Library . . . .* Philadelphia: Blumhaven Library and Gallery, 1950, 48 pp.

Catalog of an exhibition of holograph letters and autograph documents.

HULL, WILLIAM ISAAC. *Eight First Biographies of William Penn in Seven Languages and Seven Lands.* Swarthmore, Pennsylvania: Swarthmore College, 1936, 154 pp.

Swarthmore College Monographs on Quaker History, No. 3.

LEARY, LEWIS. *Articles on American Literature, 1900–1950.* Durham: Duke Univ. Press, 1954, 233–234.

SPENCE, MARY KIRK. *William Penn: A Bibliography.* Harrisburg: Pennsylvania Historical Commission, 1932, 19 pp.

Pennsylvania Historical Commission Bulletin, No. 1.

SPILLER, ROBERT ERNEST, et al. *Literary History of the United States,* 2 Vols. New York: Macmillan, 1962, 687–689. Supplement, 178.

ROWLANDSON, MARY

LEARY, LEWIS. *Articles on American Literature, 1900–1950.* Durham: Duke Univ. Press, 1954, 265.

VAIL, ROBERT WILLIAM GLEN-
ROIE. *The Voice of the Old Frontier.*
Philadelphia: Univ. of Pennsylvania
Press, 1949, 90—466.

SANDYS, GEORGE

BOWERS, FREDSON, and RICHARD
BEALE DAVIS. "George Sandys: A
Bibliographical Catalogue of Printed
Editions in England to 1700."
BNYPL, LIV (April 1950), 159—
181; (May 1950), 223—244; (June
1950), 280—286.

DAVIS, RICHARD BEALE.
"Early Editions of George Sandys'
'Ovid': The Circumstances of
Production." *PBSA,* XXXV (4th
Quart. 1941), 225—276.

———————. "Two New Manu-
script Items for a George Sandys
Bibliography." *PBSA,* XXXVII
(3rd Quart. 1943), 215—222.

LEARY, LEWIS. *Articles on American Literature, 1900—1950.* Durham: Duke Univ. Press, 1954, 267—
268.

SHEPARD, THOMAS

LEARY, LEWIS. *Articles on American Literature, 1900—1950.* Durham: Duke Univ. Press, 1954, 272.

SPILLER, ROBERT ERNEST, et al.
Literary History of the United States,
2 Vols. New York: Macmillan, 1962,
718—719.

SMITH, JOHN

HUBBELL, JAY B. *The South in
American Literature, 1607—1900.*
Durham: Duke Univ. Press, 1954,
961—962.

LEARY, LEWIS. *Articles on American Literature, 1900—1950.* Durham:
Duke Univ. Press, 1954, 275.

SMITH, JOHN. *The True Travels,
Adventures, and Observations of
Captain John Smith . . . ,* with an
introduction by John Gould Fletcher
and a bibliographical note by
Lawrence C. Wroth. New York:
Rimington and Hooper, 1930, 71—
80.

SPILLER, ROBERT ERNEST, et al.
Literary History of the United States,
2 Vols. New York: Macmillan,
1962, 725—727. Supplement, 191.

TAYLOR, WALTER FULLER. *A
History of American Letters,* with
bibliographies by Harry Hartwick.
Boston: American Book Co., 1936,
470—471.

Subsequent editions entitled: *The
Story of American Letters.*

TRENT, WILLIAM PETERFIELD,
et al. *Cambridge History of American Literature,* 4 Vols. New York:
G. P. Putnam's Sons, 1917—1921, I,
380—382.

STEENDAM, JACOB

LEARY, LEWIS. *Articles on American Literature, 1900—1950.* Durham:
Duke Univ. Press, 1954, 277.

STRACHEY, WILLIAM

HUBBELL, JAY B. *The South in
American Literature, 1607—1900.*
Durham: Duke Univ. Press, 1954,
962—963.

LEARY, LEWIS. *Articles on American Literature, 1900—1950.* Durham:
Duke Univ. Press, 1954, 283.

TAYLOR, EDWARD

HOFFMANN, CAROL A. "Edward Taylor: A Selected Bibliography." *BB,* XXII (January-April 1961), 85–87.

JOHNSON, THOMAS H., ed., *The Poetical Works of Edward Taylor.* New York: Rockland Editions, 1939, 229–231.

LEARY, LEWIS. *Articles on American Literature, 1900–1950.* Durham: Duke Univ. Press, 1954, 286.

SIBLEY, JOHN LANGDON. *Biographical Sketches of Graduates of Harvard University,* 3 Vols. Cambridge: Harvard Univ. Press, 1873–1885, II, 410–412.

Continued as: SHIPTON, CLIFFORD K., ed. *Sibley's Harvard Graduates: Biographical Sketches of Those Who Attended Harvard College.*

SPILLER, ROBERT ERNEST, et al. *Literary History of the United States,* 2 Vols. New York: Macmillan, 1962, 740–741. Supplement, 196–197.

TAYLOR, JOHN

HUBBELL, JAY B. *The South in American Literature, 1607–1900.* Durham: Duke Univ. Press, 1954, 963–964.

TRENT, WILLIAM PETERFIELD, et al. *Cambridge History of American Literature,* 4 Vols. New York: G. P. Putnam's Sons, 1917–1921, II, 478–479.

TOMPSON, BENJAMIN

JANTZ, HAROLD STEIN. *The First Century of New England Verse.* Worcester, Massachusetts: American Antiquarian Society, 1944, 292 pp.

MILLER, PERRY, and THOMAS H. JOHNSON, eds. *The Puritans.* New York: American Book Co., 1938, 785–834.

SIBLEY, JOHN LANGDON. *Biographical Sketches of Graduates of Harvard University,* 3 Vols. Cambridge: Harvard Univ. Press, 1873–1885, II, 109–111.

Continued as: SHIPTON, CLIFFORD K., ed. *Sibley's Harvard Graduates: Biographical Sketches of Those Who Attended Harvard College.*

WARD, NATHANIEL

DEAN, JOHN WARD. *A Memoir of the Rev. Nathaniel Ward . . .*Albany: J. Munsell, 1868, 168–177.

LEARY, LEWIS. *Articles on American Literature, 1900–1950.* Durham: Duke Univ. Press, 1954, 298.

SPILLER, ROBERT ERNEST, et al. *Literary History of the United States,* 2 Vols. New York: Macmillan, 1962, 751–752.

TRENT, WILLIAM PETERFIELD, et al. *Cambridge History of American Literature,* 4 Vols. New York: G. P. Putnam's Sons, 1917–1921, I, 390.

WROTH, LAWRENCE COUNSELMAN, ed. *The Simple Cobler of Aggawam in America, (1647).* New York: Scholars' Facsimiles and Reprints, 1937, v-vii.

WHITE, JOHN

LEARY, LEWIS. *Articles on American Literature, 1900–1950.* Durham: Duke Univ. Press, 1954, 303.

WIGGLESWORTH, MICHAEL

GREEN, SAMUEL ABBOTT. "The

Day of Doom." *Massachusetts Historical Society Publications,* 2nd Series, IX (1895), 269–275.

——————. *Michael Wigglesworth: The Earliest Poet among Harvard Graduates, with Some Bibliographical Notes on His 'Day of Doom.'* Boston: Massachusetts Historical Society, 1895, 7 pp.

JONES, MATT B. "Michael Wigglesworth's *Meat Out of the Eater." YULG,* V (January 1931), 45–47.

——————. "Notes for a Bibliography of Michael Wigglesworth's *Day of Doom* and *Meat Out of the Eater." PAAS,* XXXIX (April 1929), 77–84.

LEARY, LEWIS. *Articles on American Literature, 1900–1950.* Durham: Duke Univ. Press, 1954, 319–320.

SIBLEY, JOHN LANGDON. *Biographical Sketches of Graduates of Harvard University,* 3 Vols. Cambridge: Harvard Univ. Press, 1873–1885, I, 283–286; II, 531.

Continued as: SHIPTON, CLIFFORD K., ed. *Sibley's Harvard Graduates: Biographical Sketches of Those Who Attended Harvard College.*

SPILLER, ROBERT ERNEST, et al. *Literary History of the United States,* 2 Vols. New York: Macmillan, 1962, 773–774. Supplement, 208.

TAYLOR, WALTER FULLER. *A History of American Letters,* with bibliographies by Harry Hartwick. Boston: American Book Co., 1936, 475.

Subsequent editions entitled: *The Story of American Letters.*

WILLIAMS, ROGER

CHAPIN, HOWARD MILLAR. *List of Roger Williams' Writings.*

Providence: Preston and Rounds Co., 1918, 7 pp.

LEARY, LEWIS. *Articles on American Literature, 1900–1950.* Durham: Duke Univ. Press, 1954, 321.

SPILLER, ROBERT ERNEST, et al. *Literary History of the United States,* 2 Vols. New York: Macmillan, 1962, 774–776. Supplement, 208–209.

TAYLOR, WALTER FULLER. *A History of American Letters,* with bibliographies by Harry Hartwick. Boston: American Book Co., 1936, 473–474.

Subsequent editions entitled: *The Story of American Letters.*

TRENT, WILLIAM PETERFIELD, et al. *Cambridge History of American Literature,* 4 Vols. New York: G. P. Putnam's Sons, 1917–1921, I, 393–395.

WINTHROP, ADAM

LEARY, LEWIS. *Articles on American Literature, 1900–1950.* Durham: Duke Univ. Press, 1954, 324.

WINTHROP, JOHN

LEARY, LEWIS. *Articles on American Literature, 1900–1950.* Durham: Duke Univ. Press, 1954, 324.

SPILLER, ROBERT ERNEST, et al. *Literary History of the United States,* 2 Vols. New York: Macmillan, 1962, 782–783. Supplement, 212–213.

TAYLOR, WALTER FULLER. *A History of American Letters,* with bibliographies by Harry Hartwick. Boston: American Book Co., 1936, 472–473.

Subsequent editions entitled: *The Story of American Letters.*

TRENT, WILLIAM PETERFIELD, et al. *Cambridge History of American Literature,* 4 Vols. New York: G. P. Putnam's Sons, 1917–1921, I, 383.

2. 18TH CENTURY

ADAMS, ABIGAIL

LEARY, LEWIS. *Articles on American Literature, 1900–1950.* Durham: Duke Univ. Press, 1954, 3.

ADAMS, JOHN (1704-1740)

LEARY, LEWIS. *Articles on American Literature, 1900–1950.* Durham: Duke Univ. Press, 1954, 6.

ADAMS, JOHN

ADAMS, CHARLES F., ed. *The Works of John Adams,* 10 Vols. Boston: Little, Brown and Co., 1850–1856.

ANDERSON, PAUL RUSSELL, and MAX HAROLD FISCH, eds. *Philosophy in America from the Puritans to James, with Representative Selections.* New York: D. Appleton Century Co., Inc., 1939, 213.

LEARY, LEWIS. *Articles on American Literature, 1900–1950.* Durham: Duke Univ. Press, 1954, 6–7.

SPILLER, ROBERT ERNEST, et al. *Literary History of the United States,* 2 Vols. New York: Macmillan, 1962, 377–379. Supplement, 72–73.

ADAMS, SAMUEL

DARGAN, MARION. *Guide to American Biography: Part 1, 1607–1815.* Albuquerque: Univ. of New Mexico Press, 1949, 83–94, 97–98.

ADAMS, SAMUEL HOPKINS

GERSTENBERGER, DONNA, and

YALE, ELIHU

LEARY, LEWIS. *Articles on American Literature, 1900–1950.* Durham: Duke Univ. Press, 1954, 330.

GEORGE HENDRICK. *The American Novel, 1789–1959: A Checklist of Twentieth Century Criticism.* Denver: Alan Swallow, 1961, 8.

ALLEN, ETHAN

ANDERSON, PAUL RUSSELL, and MAX HAROLD FISCH, eds. *Philosophy in America from the Puritans to James, with Representative Selections.* New York: D. Appleton Century Co., Inc., 1939, 165–166.

LEARY, LEWIS. *Articles on American Literature, 1900–1950.* Durham: Duke Univ. Press, 1954, 9–10.

ALSOP, RICHARD

LEARY, LEWIS. *Articles on American Literature, 1900–1950.* Durham: Duke Univ. Press, 1954, 10–11.

AMES, NATHANIEL

LEARY, LEWIS. *Articles on American Literature, 1900–1950.* Durham: Duke Univ. Press, 1954, 11.

ANDRÉ, JOHN

STOCKBRIDGE, J. C. "Bibliography of John André." *Magazine of American History,* VIII (January 1882), 61.

BAILEY, JACOB

LEARY, LEWIS. *Articles on American Literature, 1900–1950.* Durham: Duke Univ. Press, 1954, 16.

BARLOW, JOEL

BLANCK, JACOB. *Bibliography of American Literature,* 5 Vols. New Haven: Yale Univ. Press, 1955–1969, I, 169–184.

BRIDGEWATER, DOROTHY W. "The Barlow Manuscripts in the Yale Library." *YULG,* XXXIV (October 1959), 57–63.

HOWARD, LEON. *The Connecticut Wits.* Chicago: Univ. of Chicago Press, 1943, 421–424.

LEARY, LEWIS. *Articles on American Literature, 1900–1950.* Durham: Duke Univ. Press, 1954, 17–18.

LIBRARY OF CONGRESS, DIVISION OF BIBLIOGRAPHY. *Joel Barlow, 1754–1812: A Bibliographical List.* Washington, 1935, 26 leaves.

SPILLER, ROBERT ERNEST, et al. *Literary HIstory of the United States,* 2 Vols. New York: Macmillan, 1962, 396–398. Supplement, 80.

TODD, CHARLES BURR. *Life and Letters of Joel Barlow, Ll.D.: Poet, Statesman, Philosopher,* with extracts from his works and hitherto unpublished poems. New York: G. P. Putnam's Sons, 1886, 289–294.

ZUNDER, THEODORE ALBERT. *The Early Days of Joel Barlow.* New Haven: Yale Univ. Press, 1934, 308–311.

BARTRAM, JOHN

BARNHART, JOHN HENDLEY. "Bartram Bibliography." *Bartonia: Proceedings of the Philadelphia Botanical Club,* XII-A ([Special Mid-Year Issue] 1931), 51–55.

LEARY, LEWIS. *Articles on American Literature, 1900–1950.* Durham: Duke Univ. Press, 1954, 18.

SPILLER, ROBERT ERNEST, et al. *Literary History of the United States,* 2 Vols. New York: Macmillan, 1962, 398–399. Supplement, 80–81. ·

BARTRAM, WILLIAM

BARNHART, JOHN HENDLEY. "Bartram Bibliography." *Bartonia: Proceedings of the Philadelphia Botanical Club,* XII-A ([Special Mid-Year Issue] 1931), 55–67.

FAGIN, NATHAN BRYLLION. *William Bartram: Interpreter of the American Landscape.* Baltimore: Johns Hopkins Press, 1933, 205–215.

LEARY, LEWIS. *Articles on American Literature, 1900–1950.* Durham: Duke Univ. Press, 1954, 18.

SPILLER, ROBERT ERNEST, et al. *Literary History of the United States,* 2 Vols. New York: Macmillan, 1962, 398–399. Supplement, 80–81.

BATWELL, DANIEL

LEARY, LEWIS. *Articles on American Literature, 1900–1950.* Durham: Duke Univ. Press, 1954, 18.

BELKNAP, JEREMY

BLANCK, JACOB. *Bibliography of American Literature,* 5 Vols. New Haven: Yale Univ. Press, 1955–1969, I, 185–191.

LEARY, LEWIS. *Articles on American Literature, 1900–1950.* Durham: Duke Univ. Press, 1954, 19.

BENEZET, ANTHONY

LEARY, LEWIS. *Articles on Ameri-*

can Literature, 1900–1950. Durham: Duke Univ. Press, 1954, 21.

BEVERLY, ROBERT

HUBBELL, JAY B. *The South in American Literature, 1607–1900.* Durham: Duke Univ. Press, 1954, 917.

LEARY, LEWIS. *Articles on American Literature, 1900–1950.* Durham: Duke Univ. Press, 1954, 21.

WRIGHT, LOUIS B. "Beverley's History . . . of Virginia (1705): A Neglected Classic." *WMQ*, 3rd Series, I (January 1944), 49–64.

BOLTON, NATHANIEL

LEARY, LEWIS. *Articles on American Literature, 1900–1950.* Durham: Duke Univ. Press, 1954, 23.

BOONE, DANIEL

MINER, WILLIAM HARVEY. *Daniel Boone: Contribution Toward a Bibliography of Writings Concerning Daniel Boone.* New York: Dibdin Club, 1901, 32 pp.

BOUCHER, JONATHAN

DARGAN, MARION. *Guide to American Biography: Part 1, 1607–1815.* Albuquerque: Univ. of New Mexico Press, 1949, 110–111.

HUBBELL, JAY B. *The South in American Literature, 1607–1900.* Durham: Duke Univ. Press, 1954, 918.

LEARY, LEWIS. *Articles on American Literature, 1900–1950.* Durham: Duke Univ. Press, 1954, 23–24.

BRACKENRIDGE, HUGH HENRY

BLANCK, JACOB. *Bibliography of American Literature,* 5 Vols. New

Haven: Yale Univ. Press, 1955–1969, I, 261–268.

————————, ed. *Merle Johnson's American First Editions,* 4th edition, revised and enlarged. Waltham, Massachusetts: Mark Press, 1965, 58–59.

GERSTENBERGER, DONNA, and GEORGE HENDRICK. *The American Novel, 1789–1959: A Checklist of Twentieth Century Criticism.* Denver: Alan Swallow, 1961, 20.

HEARTMAN, CHARLES FREDERICK. *A Bibliography of the Writings of Hugh Henry Brackenridge Prior to 1825.* New York: privately printed, 1917, 37 pp.

LEARY, LEWIS. *Articles on American Literature, 1900–1950.* Durham: Duke Univ. Press, 1954, 24–25.

NEWLIN, CLAUDE MILTON. *The Life and Writings of Hugh Henry Brackenridge.* Princeton: Princeton Univ. Press, 1932, 309–322.

————————, ed. *Modern Chivalry,* with introduction, chronology and bibliography by Claude M. Newlin. New York: American Book Co., 1937, xlii-xliv.

SPILLER, ROBERT ERNEST, et al. *Literary History of the United States,* 2 Vols. New York: Macmillan, 1962, 411–412. Supplement, 84.

TRENT, WILLIAM PETERFIELD, et al. *Cambridge History of American Literature,* 4 Vols. New York: G. P. Putnam's Sons, 1917–1921, I, 526.

BRADFORD, ANDREW

LEARY, LEWIS. *Articles on American Literature, 1900–1950.* Durham: Duke Univ. Press, 1954, 25.

BRAY, THOMAS

LEARY, LEWIS. *Articles on American Literature, 1900–1950.* Durham: Duke Univ. Press, 1954, 26.

BREINTNALL, JOSEPH

LEARY, LEWIS. *Articles on American Literature, 1900–1950.* Durham: Duke Univ. Press, 1954, 26.

BROWN, WILLIAM HILL

BLANCK, JACOB. *Bibliography of American Literature,* 5 Vols. New Haven: Yale Univ. Press, 1955–1969, I, 310–311.

BROWN, WILLIAM HILL. *The Power of Sympathy,* reproduced from the first edition with a bibliographical note by Milton Ellis, 2 Vols. New York: Facsimile Text Society, 1937.

GERSTENBERGER, DONNA, and GEORGE HENDRICK. *The American Novel, 1789–1959: A Checklist of Twentieth Century Criticism.* Denver: Alan Swallow, 1961, 24.

LEARY, LEWIS. *Articles on American Literature, 1900–1950.* Durham: Duke Univ. Press, 1954, 29.

BUCKMINSTER, JOSEPH

TRENT, WILLIAM PETERFIELD, et al. *Cambridge History of American Literature,* 4 Vols. New York: G. P. Putnam's Sons, 1917–1921, II, 530.

BUCKMINSTER, JOSEPH STEVENS

TRENT, WILLIAM PETERFIELD, et al. *Cambridge History of American Literature,* 4 Vols. New York: G. P. Putnam's Sons, 1917–1921, II, 531.

BYLES, MATHER

LEARY, LEWIS. *Articles on American can Literature, 1900–1950.* Durham: Duke Univ. Press, 1954, 34.

SIBLEY, JOHN LANGDON. *Biographical Sketches of Graduates of Harvard University,* 3 Vols. Cambridge: Harvard Univ. Press, 1873–1885, VII, 490–493.

Continued as: SHIPTON, CLIFFORD K., ed. *Sibley's Harvard Graduates: Biographical Sketches of Those Who Attended Harvard College.*

BYRD, WILLIAM

BEATTY, RICHMOND CROOM. *William Byrd of Westover.* Boston: Houghton Mifflin Co., 1932, 225–229.

HUBBELL, JAY B. *The South in American Literature, 1607–1900.* Durham: Duke Univ. Press, 1954, 919–921.

LEARY, LEWIS. *Articles on American Literature, 1900–1950.* Durham: Duke Univ. Press, 1954, 34–35.

PAINE, GREGORY LANSING, ed. *Southern Prose Writers: Representative Selections,* with introduction, bibliography and notes. New York: American Book Co., 1947, cxxvi-cxxvii.

SPILLER, ROBERT ERNEST, et al. *Literary History of the United States,* 2 Vols. New York: Macmillan, 1962, 429–431. Supplement, 88.

TAYLOR, WALTER FULLER. *A History of American Letters,* with bibliographies by Harry Hartwick. Boston: American Book Co., 1936, 479.

Subsequent editions entitled: *The Story of American Letters.*

TRENT, WILLIAM PETERFIELD, et al. *Cambridge History of American Literature,* 4 Vols. New York: G. P. Putnam's Sons, 1917–1921, II, 504.

CARROLL, CHARLES
(OF CARROLLTON)

HUBBELL, JAY B. *The South in American Literature, 1607–1900.* Durham: Duke Univ. Press, 1954, 923.

CARVER, JONATHAN

BOURNE, EDWARD G. "The Travels of Jonathan Carver." *AHR,* XI (January 1906), 287–302.

KELLOGG, LOUISE P. "The Mission of Jonathan Carver." *WMH,* XII (December 1928), 127–145.

LEE, JOHN THOMAS. "Captain John Carver: Additional Data." *Proceedings of the State Historical Society of Wisconsin,* LX (1912), 87–123.

CHAUNCY, CHARLES

CLARKE, JOHN. *A Discourse, Delivered at the First Church in Boston, February 15, 1787, at the Interment of the Rev. Charles Chauncy, D.D. . . .* Boston: privately printed, 1787, 32–34.

FORD, PAUL LEICESTER. *Bibliotheca Chaunciana: A List of the Writings of Charles Chauncy.* Brooklyn: privately printed, 1884, 35 leaves.

FOWLER, WILLIAM CHAUNCEY. *Memorials of the Chaunceys, Including President Chauncy, His Ancestors and Descendants.* Boston: H. W. Dutton and Sons, 1858, 305–336.

SIBLEY, JOHN LANGDON. *Biographical Sketches of Graduates of Harvard University,* 3 Vols. Cambridge: Harvard Univ. Press, 1873–1885, VI, 461–467.

Continued as: SHIPTON, CLIFFORD K., ed. *Sibley's Harward Graduates: Biographical Sketches of Those Who Attended Harvard College.*

CHURCH, BENJAMIN

LEARY, LEWIS. *Articles on American Literature, 1900–1950.* Durham: Duke Univ. Press, 1954, 43.

COBBETT, WILLIAM

LEARY, LEWIS. *Articles on American Literature, 1900–1950.* Durham: Duke Univ. Press, 1954, 55.

COLDEN, CADWALLADER

ANDERSON, PAUL RUSSELL, and MAX HAROLD FISCH, eds. *Philosophy in America from the Puritans to James, with Representative Selections.* New York: D. Appleton Century Co., Inc., 1939, 101.

KEYS, ALICE MAPELSDEN. *Cadwallader Colden: A Representative Eighteenth Century Official . . . .* New York: Columbia Univ. Press, 1906, 389 pp.

WROTH, LAWRENCE COUNSELMAN. *An American Bookshelf, 1755.* Philadelphia: Univ. of Pennsylvania Press, 1934, Appendix 10.

COLMAN, BENJAMIN

LEARY, LEWIS. *Articles on American Literature, 1900–1950.* Durham: Duke Univ. Press, 1954, 56.

COOKE, EBENEZER

HUBBELL, JAY B. *The South in American Literature, 1607–1900.* Durham: Duke Univ. Press, 1954, 926.

LEARY, LEWIS. *Articles on American Literature, 1900–1950.* Durham: Duke Univ. Press, 1954, 56.

CRÈVECOEUR, ST. JEAN DE

LEARY, LEWIS. *Articles on American Literature, 1900–1950.* Durham: Duke Univ. Press, 1954, 64.

RICE, HOWARD CROSBY. "The American Farmer's Letters, with a Checklist of the Different Editions.' *The Colophon,* Part 18 (1934), no pagination.

_____. *Le Cultivateur Américain: Étude sur l'Oeuvre de Saint John de Crevecoeur.* Paris: H. Champion, 1933, 263 pp.

SPILLER, ROBERT ERNEST, et al. *Literary History of the United States,* 2 Vols. New York: Macmillan, 1962, 461–462. Supplement, 102.

TAYLOR, WALTER FULLER. *A History of American Letters,* with bibliographies by Harry Hartwick. Boston: American Book Co., 1936, 479–480.

Subsequent editions entitled: *The Story of American Letters.*

DAVIES, SAMUEL

HUBBELL, JAY B. *The South in American Literature, 1607–1900.* Durham: Duke Univ. Press, 1954, 930.

DAVIS, JAMES

LEARY, LEWIS. *Articles on American Literature, 1900–1950.* Durham: Duke Univ. Press, 1954, 67.

DAWSON, WILLIAM

DAWSON, WILLIAM (attributed to). *Poems on Several Occasions, by a*

Gentleman of Virginia, edited by Earl Gregg Swem. New York: reprinted for C. F. Heartman, 1920, 30 pp.

Also: *Poems . . . ,* reproduced from the edition of 1736, with a bibliographical note by Ralph L. Rusk. Facsimile Text Society, 1930.

LEARY, LEWIS. *Articles on American Literature, 1900–1950.* Durham: Duke Univ. Press, 1954, 67.

DAY, MAHLON

LEARY, LEWIS. *Articles on American Literature, 1900–1950.* Durham: Duke Univ. Press, 1954, 67.

DEARBORN, BENJAMIN

LIPPENCOTT, MARGARET E. "Dearborn's Musical Scheme." *NYHSQ,* XXV (October 1941), 134–142.

DENNIE, JOSEPH

BLANCK, JACOB. *Bibliography of American Literature,* 5 Vols. New Haven: Yale Univ. Press, 1955–1969, II, 438–442.

ELLIS, MILTON, ed. *The Lay Preacher.* New York: Scholar Facsimiles and Reprints, 1943, x.

LEARY, LEWIS. *Articles on American Literature, 1900–1950.* Durham: Duke Univ. Press, 1954, 68.

SPILLER, ROBERT ERNEST, et al. *Literary History of the United States,* 2 Vols. New York: Macmillan, 1962, 464–465. Supplement, 104.

DICKINSON, JOHN

LEARY, LEWIS. *Articles on American Literature, 1900–1950.* Durham: Duke Univ. Press, 1954, 71.

SPILLER, ROBERT ERNEST, et al. *Literary History of the United States,* 2 Vols. New York: Macmillan, 1962, 470–472. Supplement, 107.

TAYLOR, WALTER FULLER. *A History of American Letters,* with bibliographies by Harry Hartwick. Boston: American Book Co., 1936, 486–487.

Subsequent editions entitled: *The Story of American Letters.*

DICKINSON, JONATHAN

ANDREWS, EVANGELINE WALKER, and CHARLES McLEAN ANDREWS, eds. *Jonathan Dickinson's Journal* . . . . New Haven: Yale Univ. Press, 1945, 162–196.

LEARY, LEWIS. *Articles on American Literature, 1900–1950.* Durham: Duke Univ. Press, 1954, 71.

DIGGES, THOMAS ATWOOD

GERSTENBERGER, DONNA, and GEORGE HENDRICK. *The American Novel, 1789–1959: A Checklist of Twentieth Century Criticism.* Denver: Alan Swallow, 1961, 56.

LEARY, LEWIS. *Articles on American Literature, 1900–1950.* Durham: Duke Univ. Press, 1954, 71.

DILWORTH, THOMAS

VAIL, ROBERT WILLIAM GLEN-ROIE. "Checklist of Thomas Dilworth's 'A New Guide to the English Tongue.' " *PAAS,* ns XLIII (October 1933), 267–269.

DOUGLASS, WILLIAM

WROTH, LAWRENCE COUNSEL-MAN. *An American Bookshelf, 1775.* Philadelphia: Univ. of Pennsylvania Press, 1934, 176–177.

DUCHÉ, JACOB

LEARY, LEWIS. *Articles on American Literature, 1900–1950.* Durham: Duke Univ. Press, 1954, 75.

DUNLAP, WILLIAM

BLANCK, JACOB. *Bibliography of American Literature,* 5 Vols. New Haven: Yale Univ. Press, 1955–1969, II, 506–518.

COAD, ORAL SUMNER, ed. *False Shame and Thirty Years: Two Plays.* Princeton: Princeton Univ. Press, 1940, xi–xiv.

——————. *William Dunlap: A Study of His Life and Works.* New York: The Dunlap Society, 1917, 284–302.

HALLINE, ALLAN GATES. *American Plays.* New York: American Book Co., 1935, 752–753.

LEARY, LEWIS. *Articles on American Literature, 1900–1950.* Durham: Duke Univ. Press, 1954, 76.

SPILLER, ROBERT ERNEST, et al. *Literary History of the United States,* 2 Vols. New York: Macmillan, 1962, 478–480.

TRENT, WILLIAM PETERFIELD, et al. *Cambridge History of American Literature,* 4 Vols. New York: G. P. Putnam's Sons, 1917–1921, I, 496–499.

WEGELIN, OSCAR. *A Bibliographical Checklist of the Plays and Miscellaneous Writings of William Dunlap, 1766–1839.* New York: C. F. Heartman, 1916, 14 leaves.

DWIGHT, TIMOTHY

BLANCK, JACOB. *Bibliography of American Literature,* 5 Vols. New

Haven: Yale Univ. Press, 1955–1969, II, 519–530.

CHAPIN, CALVIN. *A Sermon Delivered, 14th January, 1817, at the Funeral of the Rev. Timothy Dwight, D.D.* . . . . New Haven: Maltby, Goldsmith and Co., T. G. Woodward, Printer, 1817, 34–35.

DEXTER, FRANKLIN BODWITCH. *Biographical Sketches of the Graduates of Yale College,* 5 Vols. New York: Henry Holt and Co., 1885–1919, III, 326–333.

HOWARD, LEON. *The Connecticut Wits.* Chicago: Univ. of Chicago Press, 1943, 416–418.

LEARY, LEWIS. *Articles on American Literature, 1900–1950.* Durham: Duke Univ. Press, 1954, 76–77.

SPILLER, ROBERT ERNEST, et al. *Literary History of the United States,* 2 Vols. New York: Macmillan, 1962, 480–481. Supplement, 110.

STILLINGER, JACK. "Dwight's *Triumph of Infidelity*: Text and Interpretation." *SB,* XV (1962), 259–266.

TRENT, WILLIAM PETERFIELD, et al. *Cambridge History of American Literature,* 4 Vols. New York: G. P. Putnam's Sons, 1917–1921, II, 533–534.

EDWARDS, JONATHAN

ANDERSON, PAUL RUSSELL, and MAX HAROLD FISCH, eds. *Philosophy in America from the Puritans to James, with Representative Selections.* New York: D. Appleton Century Co., Inc., 1939, 81–82.

FAUST, CLARENCE H., and THOMAS HERBERT JOHNSON, eds. *Jonathan Edwards: Represen-*

tative Selections, with introduction, bibliography and notes. New York: American Book Co., 1935, cxix–cxlii.

HOPKINS, SAMUEL. *Life and Character of Jonathan Edwards.* Boston: printed and sold by S. Kneeland, 1765, 98 pp.

JOHNSON, THOMAS HERBERT, comp. *The Printed Writings of Jonathan Edwards, 1703–1758: A Bibliography.* Princeton: Princeton Univ. Press, 1940, 148 pp.

LEARY, LEWIS. *Articles on American Literature, 1900–1950.* Durham: Duke Univ. Press, 1954, 77–79.

RICE, HOWARD C., JR. "Jonathan Edwards at Princeton: With a Survey of Edwards Material in the Princeton University Library." *PULC,* XV (Winter 1954), 68–69.

SPILLER, ROBERT ERNEST, et al. *Literary History of the United States,* 2 Vols. New York: Macmillan, 1962, 481–485. Supplement, 110–111.

TAYLOR, WALTER FULLER. *A History of American Letters,* with bibliographies by Harry Hartwick. Boston: American Book Co., 1936, 480–483.

Subsequent editions entitled: *The Story of American Letters.*

TRENT, WILLIAM PETERFIELD, et al. *Cambridge History of American Literature,* 4 Vols. New York: G. P. Putnam's Sons, 1917–1921, I, 426–438.

WINSLOW, OLA ELIZABETH. *Jonathan Edwards, 1703–1758: A Biography.* New York: Macmillan, 1940, 373–393.

EVANS, LEWIS

WROTH, LAWRENCE COUNSEL-MAN. *An American Bookshelf, 1755.* Philadelphia: Univ. of Pennsylvania Press, 1934, 148–166.

EVANS, NATHANIEL

LEARY, LEWIS. *Articles on American Literature, 1900–1950.* Durham: Duke Univ. Press, 1954, 96.

FLYNT, HENRY

LEARY, LEWIS. *Articles on American Literature, 1900–1950.* Durham: Duke Univ. Press, 1954, 104.

FOSTER, HANNAH WEBSTER

BLANCK, JACOB. *Bibliography of American Literature,* 5 Vols. New Haven: Yale Univ. Press, 1955–1969, III, 211.

BOLTON, CHARLES KNOWLES. *The Elizabeth Whitman Mystery at the Old Bell Tavern in Danvers.* Peabody, Massachusetts: Peabody Historical Society, 1912, 147–155.

GERSTENBERGER, DONNA, and GEORGE HENDRICK. *The American Novel, 1789–1959: A Checklist of Twentieth Century Criticism.* Denver: Alan Swallow, 1961, 97.

LEARY, LEWIS. *Articles on American Literature, 1900–1950.* Durham: Duke Univ. Press, 1954, 104.

TRENT, WILLIAM PETERFIELD, et al. *Cambridge History of American Literature,* 4 Vols. New York: G. P. Putnam's Sons, 1917–1921, I, 534.

FRANKLIN, BENJAMIN

ADAMS, RANDOLPH G. "Notes and Queries." *The Colophon,* ns II (Autumn 1937), 602–608.

Various bibliographical notes and critical judgments of the Franklin manuscripts, biographies and editions.

AMERICAN PHILOSOPHICAL SOCIETY, LIBRARY (PHILADELPHIA). *Calendar of the Papers of Benjamin Franklin in the Library of the American Philosophical Society,* compiled by Isaac Minis Hays. Philadelphia: printed for the American Philosophical Society, 1908, 399–546.

ANDERSON, PAUL RUSSELL, and MAX HAROLD FISCH, eds. *Philosophy in America from the Puritans to James, with Representative Selections.* New York: D. Appleton Century Co., Inc., 1939, 129–130.

BEST, JOHN HARDIN, ed. *Benjamin Franklin on Education.* New York: Bureau of Publications, Teachers College, Columbia Univ., 1962, 18–21.

BRIDGEWATER, DOROTHY W. "Notable Additions to the Franklin Collection." *YULG,* XX (October 1945), 21–28.

CONWAY, ELEANOR. "Dr. Abeloff's Franklin Collection." *NYHSQ,* XXVI (July 1942), 65–66.

CRANE, VERNER W. "Certain Writings of Benjamin Franklin on the British Empire and the American Colonies." *PBSA,* XXVIII (1934), 1–27.

CURTIS PUBLISHING COMPANY. *The Collection of Franklin Imprints in the Museum of the Curtis Publishing Company, with a Short-Title Check List of All the Books, Pamphlets, Broadsides, etc., Known to Have Been Printed by Benjamin Franklin,* compiled by William J. Campbell. Philadelphia: Curtis Publishing Co., 1918, 333 pp.

DARGAN, MARION. *Guide to American Biography: Part I, 1607–1815.* Albuquerque: Univ. of New Mexico Press, 1949, 51–55.

DE PUY, HENRY FARR. *A Bibliography of the English Colonial Treaties with the American Indians, Including a Synopsis of Each Treaty.* New York: printed for the Lenox Club, 1917, 109 pp.

DODD, MEAD AND COMPANY. *Books Printed by Benjamin Franklin, Born January 17, 1706, for Sale by Dodd, Mead and Co.* New York: Dodd, Mead and Co., 1906, 29 pp.

EDDY, GEORGE SIMPSON. "Ramble through the Mason-Franklin Collection." *YULG,* X (April 1936), 65–90.

──────────. "A Work Book of the Printing House of Benjamin Franklin and David Hall, 1759–1766." *BNYPL,* XXXIV (August 1930), 575–589.

FAŸ, BERNARD. *Bernard Fay's Franklin: The Apostle of Modern Times.* Boston: Little, Brown and Co., 1929, 517–533.

──────────. *The Two Franklins: Fathers of American Democracy . . . .* Boston: Little, Brown and Co., 1933, 363–377.

FORD, PAUL LEICESTER. *Franklin Bibliography: A List of Books Written by or Relating to Benjamin Franklin.* Brooklyn: n.p. 1889, 538 pp.

500 copies printed.

FORD, WORTHINGTON CHAUNCY. *List of Benjamin Franklin Papers in the Library of Congress.* Washington, 1905, 322 pp.

The General Magazine and Historical Chronicle, for All the British Plantations in America, published by Benjamin Franklin, reproduced from the original edition, Philadelphia, 1741, with a bibliographical note by Lyon N. Richardson. New York: Facsimile Text Society, 1938, 426 pp.

GROLIER CLUB (NEW YORK). *Catalogue of an Exhibition Commemorating the 200th Anniversary of the Birth of Benjamin Franklin.* New York: DeVinne Press, 1906, 100 pp.

HAGEDORN, RALPH K. *Benjamin Franklin and Chess in Early America: A Review of the Literature.* Philadelphia: Univ. of Pennsylvania Press, 1958, 92.

HAYS, ISAAC MINIS. *The Chronology of Benjamin Franklin . . . .* Philadelphia: American Philosophical Society, 1904, 32 pp.

LEARY, LEWIS. *Articles on American Literature, 1900–1950.* Durham: Duke Univ. Press, 1954, 105–111.

LIBRARY OF CONGRESS, DIVISION OF MANUSCRIPTS. *List of Benjamin Franklin Papers in the Library of Congress.* Washington, 1905, 322 pp.

"List of Works in the New York Public Library by or Relating to Benjamin Franklin." *BNYPL,* X (January 1906), 29–83.

LIVINGTON, LUTHER S. *Franklin and His Press at Passy: An Account of the Books, Pamphlets, and Leaflets Printed There, Including the Long-lost 'Bagatelles.'* New York: The Grolier Club, 1914, 216 pp.

MOTT, FRANK LUTHER, and CHESTER E. JORGENSON, eds. *Benjamin Franklin: Representative Selections,* with introduction, bibliography and notes. New York: American Book Co., 1936, cli–clxxxviii.

MUGRIDGE, DONALD H."Scientific Manuscripts of Benjamin Franklin." *LCQJ,* IV (August 1947), 12–21.

Formerly *Library of Congress Quarterly Journal of Current Acquisitions.*

OSWALD, JOHN CLYDE. *Benjamin Franklin in Oil and Bronze.* New York: W. E. Rudge, 1926, 58 pp.

PENNSYLVANIA, UNIVERSITY, LIBRARY. *Benjamin Franklin and Winston Churchill: An Exhibition Celebrating the Bicentennial of the University of Pennsylvania Library, May 8–June 15, 1951.* Philadelphia: Wm. F. Fell Co., 1951, 55 pp.

PHILBRICK, FRANCIS S. "Notes on Early Editions and Editors of Franklin." *PAPS,* XCVII (No. 5, 1953), 525–564.

SHIPLEY, J. B. "Franklin Attends a Book Auction." *PMHB,* LXXX (January 1956), 11–36.

SPILLER, ROBERT ERNEST, et al. *Literary History of the United States,* 2 Vols. New York: Macmillan, 1962, 507–515. Supplement, 123–126.

STEVENS, BENJAMIN FRANKLIN, comp. *B. F. Stevens' Facsimiles of Manuscripts in European Archives Relating to America, 1773–1783,* 24 Portfolios. London: photographed and printed by Malby and Sons, 1889–1895.

From the introduction to the index: "The Facsimiles are almost wholly of unpublished manuscripts." Issued only to subscribers.

STEVENS, HENRY. *Benjamin Franklin's Life and Writings: A Bibli-*

ographical Essay on the Stevens' Collection of Books and Manuscripts Relating to Doctor Franklin. London: Messrs. Davy and Sons, 1881, 48 pp.

TAYLOR, WALTER FULLER. *A History of American Letters,* with bibliographies by Harry Hartwick. Boston: American Book Co., 1936, 484–486.

Subsequent editions entitled: *The Story of American Letters.*

TRENT, WILLIAM PETERFIELD, et al. *Cambridge History of American Literature,* 4 Vols. New York: G. P. Putnam's Sons, 1917–1921, I, 442–452.

FRANKLIN, WILLIAM

LEARY, LEWIS. *Articles on American Literature, 1900–1950.* Durham: Duke Univ. Press, 1954, 111.

FRENEAU, PETER

LEARY, LEWIS. *Articles on American Literature, 1900–1950.* Durham: Duke Univ. Press, 1954, 111.

FRENEAU, PHILIP

AXELRAD, JACOB. *Philip Freneau: Champion of Democracy.* Austin: Univ. of Texas Press, 1967, 437–459.

BLANCK, JACOB. *Bibliography of American Literature,* 5 Vols. New Haven: Yale Univ. Press, 1955–1969, III, 244–256.

——————, ed. *Merle Johnson's American First Editions,* 4th edition, revised and enlarged. Waltham, Massachusetts: Mark Press, 1965, 192–193.

CLARK, HARRY HAYDEN, ed. *Major American Poets.* New York: American Book Co., 1936, 781–782.

FRENEAU, PHILIP. *Letters on Various Interesting and Important Subjects,* with an introduction and bibliographical note by Harry Hayden Clark. New York: Scholars' Facsimiles & Reprints, 1943, vi.

LEARY, LEWIS. *Articles on American Literature, 1900–1950.* Durham: Duke Univ. Press, 1954, 111–113.

——————. "Philip Freneau in Charleston: Checklist of Freneau's Contributions to Charleston's Newspapers, 1785–1806." *South Carolina Historical and General Magazine,* XLII (July 1941), 89–98.

——————. *That Rascal Freneau: A Study in Literary Failure.* New Brunswick: Rutgers Univ. Press, 1941, 418–480.

——————. "An Uncollected Item in the Bibliography of Philip Freneau." *AL*, VI (November 1934), 331–334.

PALTSITS, VICTOR HUGO. *The American Village: A Poem by Philip Freneau.* Providence: [Standard Printing Co.], 1906, 55–69.

Facsimile reproduction of the original edition published in 1772. 100 copies printed.

——————. *A Bibliography of the Separate and Collected Works of Philip Freneau, together with an Account of His Newspapers.* New York: Dodd, Mead and Co., 1903, 111 pp.

PATTEE, FRED LEWIS. "Bibliography of Freneau." *Bibliographer,* I (January 1902), 90–106.

SPILLER, ROBERT ERNEST, et al. *Literary History of the United States,* 2 Vols. New York: Macmillan, 1962, 517–520. Supplement, 126–127.

TAYLOR, WALTER FULLER. *A History of American Letters,* with bibliographies by Harry Hartwick. Boston: American Book Co., 1936, 490–491.

Subsequent editions entitled: *The Story of American Letters.*

THOMAS, OWEN P. "Philip Freneau: A Bibliography." *New Jersey Historical Society Publications,* LXXV (July 1957), 197–205.

TRENT, WILLIAM PETERFIELD, et al. *Cambridge History of American Literature,* 4 Vols. New York: G. P. Putnam's Sons, 1917–1921, II, 522.

GALLOWAY, JOSEPH

KUNTZLEMAN, OLIVER CHARLES. *Joseph Galloway, Loyalist.* Philadelphia: Temple Univ. Press, 1941, 175–184.

GODFREY, THOMAS

LEARY, LEWIS. *Articles on American Literature, 1900–1950.* Durham: Duke Univ. Press, 1954, 121.

QUINN, ARTHUR HOBSON. *A History of the American Drama from the Beginning to the Civil War,* revised edition. New York: F. S. Crofts and Co., 1943, 404.

SPILLER, ROBERT ERNEST, et al. *Literary History of the United States,* 2 Vols. New York: Macmillan, 1962, 533–534.

GRIDLEY, JEREMY

LEARY, LEWIS. *Articles on American Literature, 1900–1950.* Durham: Duke Univ. Press, 1954, 123.

HAMILTON, ALEXANDER

ALY, BOWER. *The Rhetoric of*

Alexander Hamilton. New York: Columbia Univ. Press, 1941, 199–213.

BRIDENBAUGH, CARL, ed. *Gentleman's Progress: The Itinerarium of Dr. Alexander Hamilton, 1744.* Chapel Hill: Univ. of North Carolina Press, 1948, 201–253.

FORD, PAUL LEICESTER. *Bibliotheca Hamiltoniana: A List of Books Written by or Relating to Alexander Hamilton.* New York: printed for the author by The Knickerbocker Press, 1886, 165 pp.

————————. *A List of Editions of "The Federalist."* Brooklyn: n.p., 1886, 25 pp.

Reprinted from the author's *Bibliotheca Hamiltoniana . . . .* New York: printed for the author by The Knickerbocker Press, 1886, Part 1, 13–35.

HAMILTON, ALEXANDER, JOHN JAY and JAMES MADISON. *The Federalist,* edited by Henry Cabot Lodge. New York: G. P. Putnam's Sons, 1888, xxv–xlii.

HUBBELL, JAY B. *The South in American Literature, 1607–1900.* Durham: Duke Univ. Press, 1954, 934.

LEARY, LEWIS. *Articles on American Literature, 1900–1950.* Durham: Duke Univ. Press, 1954, 124.

LODGE, HENRY CABOT, ed. *The Works of Alexander Hamilton,* 11 Vols. New York: G. P. Putnam's Sons, 1904, XI, xxi–xl.

PRESCOTT, FREDERICK C., ed. *Alexander Hamilton and Thomas Jefferson: Representative Selections,* with introduction, bibliography and notes. New York: American Book Co., 1934, lxxiii–lxxvi.

SPILLER, ROBERT ERNEST, et al. *Literary History of the United States,* 2 Vols. New York; Macmillan, 1962, 536–540. Supplement, 131–132.

TAYLOR, WALTER FULLER. *A History of American Letters,* with bibliographies by Harry Hartwick. Boston: American Book Co., 1936, 489–490.

Subsequent editions entitled: *The Story of American Letters.*

HASTINGS, SARAH

LEARY, LEWIS. *Articles on American Literature, 1900–1950.* Durham: Duke Univ. Press, 1954, 128.

HENRY, PATRICK

DARGAN, MARION. *Guide to American Biography: Part 1, 1607–1815.* Albuquerque: Univ. of New Mexico Press, 1949, 97–98.

HUBBELL, JAY B. *The South in American Literature, 1607–1900.* Durham: Duke Univ. Press, 1954, 937.

HOLCROFT, THOMAS

COLBY, ELBRIDGE. "A Bibliography of Thomas Holcroft." *BNYPL,* XXVI (June 1922), 455–492; (August 1922), 664–686; (September 1922), 765–787.

HOLMES, ABIEL

LEARY, LEWIS. *Articles on American Literature, 1900–1950.* Durham: Duke Univ. Press, 1954, 142.

HOPKINS, LEMUEL

LEARY, LEWIS. *Articles on American Literature, 1900–1950.* Durham: Duke Univ. Press, 1954, 144.

HOPKINS, SAMUEL

LEARY, LEWIS. *Articles on American Literature, 1900–1950.* Durham: Duke Univ. Press, 1954, 144.

TRENT, WILLIAM PETERFIELD, et al. *Cambridge History of American Literature,* 4 Vols. New York: G. P. Putnam's Sons, 1917–1921, II, 536–537.

HOPKINSON, FRANCIS

HASTINGS, GEORGE EVERETT. *The Life and Works of Francis Hopkinson.* Chicago: Univ. of Chicago Press, 1926, 481–496.

LEARY, LEWIS. *Articles on American Literature, 1900–1950.* Durham: Duke Univ. Press, 1954, 144.

SPILLER, ROBERT ERNEST, et al. *Literary History of the United States,* 2 Vols. New York: Macmillan, 1962, 569–571. Supplement, 140.

HUMPHREYS, DAVID

HOWARD, LEON. *The Connecticut Wits.* Chicago: Univ. of Chicago Press, 1943, 419–420.

LEARY, LEWIS. *Articles on American Literature, 1900–1950.* Durham: Duke Univ. Press, 1954, 150.

SPILLER, ROBERT ERNEST, et al. *Literary History of the United States,* 2 Vols. New York: Macmillan, 1962, 577.

HUTCHINSON, THOMAS

DEANE, CHARLES. *A Bibliographical Essay on Governor Hutchinson's Historical Publications.* Boston: privately printed, 1857, 30 pp.

LEARY, LEWIS. *Articles on American Literature, 1900–1950.* Durham: Duke Univ. Press, 1954, 151.

MAYO, LAWRENCE SHAW. "Thomas Hutchinson and His 'History of Massachusetts-Bay.'" *PAAS,* ns XLI (October 1931), 321–339.

IMLAY, GILBERT

LEARY, LEWIS. *Articles on American Literature, 1900–1950.* Durham: Duke Univ. Press, 1954, 151.

IREDELL, JAMES

HUBBELL, JAY B. *The South in American Literature, 1607–1900.* Durham: Duke Univ. Press, 1954, 938.

JEFFERSON, THOMAS

ADAMS, RANDOLPH GREENFIELD. *Three Americanists: Henry Harrisse, Bibliographer; George Brinley, Book Collector; Thomas Jefferson, Librarian.* Philadelphia: Univ. of Pennsylvania Press, 1939, 101 pp.

ANDERSON, PAUL RUSSELL, and MAX HAROLD FISCH, eds. *Philosophy in America from the Puritans to James, with Representative Selections.* New York: D. Appleton Century Co., Inc., 1939, 190–191.

BOYD, JULIAN PARKS. *The Declaration of Independence: The Evolution of the Text as Shown in Facsimiles of Various Drafts by Its Author....* Princeton: Princeton Univ. Press, 1945, 46 pp.

FORD, PAUL LEICESTER, ed. *The Writings of Thomas Jefferson,* 10 Vols. New York: G. P. Putnam's Sons, 1892–1899, I.

Includes the best bibliography of Jefferson's *Notes on the State of Virginia* (1784–1785). Also contains a list of printed works.

HIRSCH, RUDOLF. "Notes and Queries." *The Colophon,* ns III (Winter 1938), 134—139.

HUBBELL, JAY B. *The South in American Literature, 1607—1900.* Durham: Duke Univ. Press, 1954, 939—940.

JOHNSTON, RICHARD HOLLAND. *A Contribution to a Bibliography of Thomas Jefferson.* Washington, 1905, 74 pp.

Reprinted from the Jefferson Memorial Edition of Jefferson's Writings. 30 copies printed.

LEARY, LEWIS. *Articles on American Literature, 1900—1950.* Durham: Duke Univ. Press, 1954, 167—170.

LIPSCOMB, ANDREW ADGATE, and ALBERT LELLERY BERGH, eds. *The Writings of Thomas Jefferson,* 20 Vols. Washington, 1903, XX.

O'NEAL, WILLIAM B., comp. "A Checklist of Writings on Thomas Jefferson as an Architect." *Bibliographical Society of the University of Virginia, Secretary's News Sheet,* No. 43 (September 1959), 1—18.

PAINE, GREGORY LANSING, ed. *Southern Prose Writers: Representative Selections,* with introduction, bibliography and notes. New York: American Book Co., 1947, cxxxii—cxxxiii.

PEDEN, WILLIAM HARWOOD. *Some Aspects of Jefferson Bibliography* .... Lexington, Virginia: Journalism Laboratory Press, Washington and Lee Univ., 1941, 22 pp.

350 copies printed.

PETERSON, MERRILL D., comp. *Thomas Jefferson: A Profile.* New York: Hill and Wang, 1967, 261—262.

PRESCOTT, FREDERICK C., ed. *Alexander Hamilton and Thomas Jefferson: Representative Selections,* with introduction, bibliography and notes. New York: American Book Co., 1934, lxxvi—lxxix.

RANDALL, DAVID A. "'Dukedom Large Enough': III. Thomas Jefferson and The Declaration of Independence." *PBSA,* LVI (4th Quart. 1962), 472—480.

SPILLER, ROBERT ERNEST, et al. *Literary History of the United States,* 2 Vols. New York: Macmillan, 1962, 595—602. Supplement, 149—152.

THURLOW, CONSTANCE E., and FRANCIS L. BERKELEY JR., comps. *The Jefferson Papers of the University of Virginia,* with an appended essay by Helen D. Bullock on the papers of Thomas Jefferson. Charlottesville: published for the Univ. of Virginia Library with assistance from the Research Council of the Richmond Area University Center, 1950, 355 pp.

Univ. of Virginia Bibliographical Series, No. 8.

TOMPKINS, HAMILTON BULLOCK. *Bibliotheca Jeffersoniana: A List of Books Written by or Relating to Thomas Jefferson.* New York: G. P. Putnam's Sons, 1887, 187 pp.

350 copies printed.

VERNER, COOLIE. *A Further Checklist on the Separate Editions of Jefferson's Notes on the State of Virginia.* Charlottesville: Bibliographical Society of the Univ. of Virginia, 1950, 26 leaves.

_____. "Mr. Jefferson Distributes His *Notes*: A Preliminary Checklist of the First Edition." *BNYPL,* LVI (April 1952), 159—186.

JOHNSON, SAMUEL

ANDERSON, PAUL RUSSELL, and
MAX HAROLD FISCH, eds. *Philosophy in America from the Puritans
to James, with Representative Selections.* New York: D. Appleton Century
Co., Inc., 1939, 54.

LEARY, LEWIS. *Articles on American Literature, 1900–1950.* Durham:
Duke Univ. Press, 1954, 171.

TRENT, WILLIAM PETERFIELD, et
al. *Cambridge History of American
Literature,* 4 Vols. New York: G. P.
Putnam's Sons, 1917–1921, I, 439–
440.

JOHNSON, SAMUEL (1704-1784)

LEARY, LEWIS. *Articles on American Literature, 1900–1950.* Durham:
Duke Univ. Press, 1954, 171.

JOHNSON, THOMAS

HUBBELL, JAY B. *The South in
American Literature, 1607–1900.*
Durham: Duke Univ. Press, 1954,
940.

KALM, PETER

BENSON, A. B. "Peter Kalm's
Writings on America: A Bibliographical Review." *SS,* XII (May 1933),
89–98.

KEIMER, SAMUEL

LEARY, LEWIS. *Articles on American Literature, 1900–1950.* Durham:
Duke Univ. Press, 1954, 172.

KNIGHT, SARAH KEMBLE

LEARY, LEWIS. *Articles on American Literature, 1900–1950.* Durham:
Duke Univ. Press, 1954, 173.

LADD, JOSEPH BROWN

HUBBELL, JAY B. *The South in
American Literature, 1607–1900.*
Durham: Duke Univ. Press, 1954,
942–943.

LEARY, LEWIS. *Articles on American Literature, 1900–1950.* Durham:
Duke Univ. Press, 1954, 174.

_____. "The Writings of
Joseph Brown Ladd." *BB,* XVIII
(January-April 1945), 131–133.

LEE, ARTHUR

HUBBELL, JAY B. *The South in
American Literature, 1607–1900.*
Durham: Duke Univ. Press, 1954,
944.

LEARY, LEWIS. *Articles on American Literature, 1900–1950.* Durham:
Duke Univ. Press, 1954, 178.

LEE, RICHARD

LEARY, LEWIS. *Articles on American Literature, 1900–1950.* Durham:
Duke Univ. Press, 1954, 178.

LEWIS, RICHARD

HUBBELL, JAY B. *The South in
American Literature, 1607–1900.*
Durham: Duke Univ. Press, 1954,
947.

LEARY, LEWIS. *Articles on American Literature, 1900–1950.* Durham:
Duke Univ. Press, 1954, 179–180.

LINN, JOHN BLAIR

LEARY, LEWIS. *Articles on American Literature, 1900–1950.* Durham:
Duke Univ. Press, 1954, 186.

_____. "The Writings of
John Blair Linn (1777–1804)."
BB, XIX (September-December
1946), 18–19.

LIVINGSTON, WILLIAM

SPILLER, ROBERT ERNEST, et al. *Literary History of the United States,* 2 Vols. New York: Macmillan, 1962, 618–619. Supplement, 159.

LODOWICK, CHRISTIAN

LEARY, LEWIS. *Articles on American Literature, 1900–1950.* Durham: Duke Univ. Press, 1954, 186.

MADISON, JAMES

BRANT, IRVING. *James Madison: The Virginia Revolutionist,* Indianapolis: Bobbs-Merrill Co., 1941, 401–450.

BURNS, EDWARD McNALL. *James Madison: Philosopher of the Constitution.* New Brunswick: Rutgers Univ. Press, 1938, 201–206.

HUBBELL, JAY B. *The South in American Literature, 1607–1900.* Durham: Duke Univ. Press, 1954, 948–949.

LEARY, LEWIS. *Articles on American Literature, 1900–1950.* Durham: Duke Univ. Press, 1954, 199.

SCOTT, JAMES BROWN, ed. *James Madison's Notes of Debate in the Federal Convention of 1787 . . . .* New York: Oxford Univ. Press, American Branch, 1918, xvii–xviii.

SPILLER, ROBERT ERNEST, et al. *Literary History of the United States,* 2 Vols. New York: Macmillan, 1962, 636–638. Supplement, 163.

MASON, GEORGE

HUBBELL, JAY B. *The South in American Literature, 1607–1900.* Durham: Duke Univ. Press, 1954, 949.

MATHER, SAMUEL

LEARY, LEWIS. *Articles on American Literature, 1900–1950.* Durham: Duke Univ. Press, 1954, 204.

MAXWELL, WILLIAM

HUBBELL, JAY B. *The South in American Literature, 1607–1900.* Durham: Duke Univ. Press, 1954, 949–950.

LEARY, LEWIS. *Articles on American Literature, 1900–1950.* Durham: Duke Univ. Press, 1954, 204.

MAYHEW, JONATHAN

TRENT, WILLIAM PETERFIELD, et al. *Cambridge History of American Literature,* 4 Vols. New York: G. P. Putnam's Sons, 1917–1921, I, 440–441.

MAYLEM, JOHN

LEARY, LEWIS. *Articles on American Literature, 1900–1950.* Durham: Duke Univ. Press, 1954, 204.

WROTH, LAWRENCE C. "John Maylem: Poet and Warrior." *PCSM,* XXXII (1937), 87–120.

MORGAN, JOSEPH

SCHLATTER, RICHARD, ed. *The History of the Kingdom of Basaruah and Three Unpublished Letters, New York, 1715.* Cambridge: Harvard Univ. Press, 1946, 23–28.

MORTON, SARAH WENTWORTH

LEARY, LEWIS. *Articles on American Literature, 1900–1950.* Durham: Duke Univ. Press, 1954, 219.

TRENT, WILLIAM PETERFIELD, et al. *Cambridge History of American*

Literature, 4 Vols. New York: G. P. Putnam's Sons, 1917–1921, I, 538.

MUNFORD, ROBERT

HUBBELL, JAY B. *The South in American Literature, 1607–1900.* Durham: Duke Univ. Press, 1954, 950–951.

LEARY, LEWIS. *Articles on American Literature, 1900–1950.* Durham: Duke Univ. Press, 1954, 220.

MURRAY, JUDITH SARGENT

LEARY, LEWIS. *Articles on American Literature, 1900–1950.* Durham: Duke Univ. Press, 1954, 221.

OAKES, URIAN

SIBLEY, JOHN LANGDON. *Biographical Sketches of Graduates of Harvard University,* 3 Vols. Cambridge: Harvard Univ. Press, 1873–1885, I, 173–185.

Continued as: SHIPTON, CLIFFORD K., ed. *Sibley's Harvard Graduates: Biographical Sketches of Those Who Attended Harvard College.*

ODELL, JONATHAN

LEARY, LEWIS. *Articles on American Literature, 1900–1950.* Durham: Duke Univ. Press, 1954, 224.

OGLETHORPE, JAMES EDWARD

LEARY, LEWIS. *Articles on American Literature, 1900–1950.* Durham: Duke Univ. Press, 1954, 224.

OTIS, JAMES

LEARY, LEWIS. *Articles on American Literature, 1900–1950.* Durham: Duke Univ. Press, 1954, 228.

SPILLER, ROBERT ERNEST, et al. *Literary History of the United States,* 2 Vols. New York: Macmillan, 1962, 672–673.

PAINE, THOMAS

CLARK, HARRY HAYDEN, ed. *Thomas Paine: Representative Selections,* with introduction, bibliography and notes. New York: American Book Co., 1944, cxxv–cli.

GIMBEL, RICHARD. *Thomas Paine: A Bibliographical Check List of 'Common Sense,' with an Account of Its Publication.* New Haven: Yale Univ. Press, 1956, 124 pp.

_____. "Thomas Paine Fights for Freedom in Three Worlds." *PAAS,* ns LXX (October 1960), 387–492.

LEARY, LEWIS. *Articles on American Literature, 1900–1950.* Durham: Duke Univ. Press, 1954, 228–230.

SPILLER, ROBERT ERNEST, et al. *Literary History of the United States,* 2 Vols. New York: Macmillan, 1962, 674–678. Supplement, 175.

TAYLOR, WALTER FULLER. *A History of American Letters,* with bibliographies by Harry Hartwick. Boston: American Book Co., 1936, 487–489.

Subsequent editions entitled: *The Story of American Letters.*

WOODRESS, J. L., JR. "The 'Cold War' of 1790–1791: Documented by a Collection of Eighteenth-Century Pamphlets in the Duke University Library." *DULN,* XX (July 1948), 7–18.

PENHALLOW, SAMUEL

LEARY, LEWIS. *Articles on Ameri-*

can Literature, 1900−1950. Durham: Duke Univ. Press, 1954, 233.

PETERS, SAMUEL ANDREW

LEARY, LEWIS. *Articles on American Literature, 1900−1950.* Durham: Duke Univ. Press, 1954, 234.

PLUMMER, JONATHAN

LEARY, LEWIS. *Articles on American Literature, 1900−1950.* Durham: Duke Univ. Press, 1954, 235.

POYDRAS, JULIEN

LEARY, LEWIS. *Articles on American Literature, 1900−1950.* Durham: Duke Univ. Press, 1954, 254.

PRINCE, THOMAS

LEARY, LEWIS. *Articles on American Literature, 1900−1950.* Durham: Duke Univ. Press, 1954, 254.

SIBLEY, JOHN LANGDON. *Biographical Sketches of Graduates of Harvard University,* 3 Vols. Cambridge: 1837−1885, V, 361−368.

Continued as: SHIPTON, CLIFFORD K., ed. *Sibley's Harvard Graduates: Biographical Sketches of Those Who Attended Harvard College.*

PROUD, ROBERT

LEARY, LEWIS. *Articles on American Literature, 1900−1950.* Durham: Duke Univ. Press, 1954, 254.

QUINCY, JOSIAH

TRENT, WILLIAM PETERFIELD, et al. *Cambridge History of American Literature,* 4 Vols. New York: G. P. Putnam's Sons, 1917−1921, II, 475−476.

RALPH, JAMES

LEARY, LEWIS. *Articles on American Literature, 1900−1950.* Durham: Duke Univ. Press, 1954, 255.

RAMSEY, DAVID

LEARY, LEWIS. *Articles on American Literature, 1900−1950.* Durham: Duke Univ. Press, 1954, 255.

RIVINGTON, JAMES

HEWLETT, LEROY. "James Rivington, Loyalist Printer, Publisher, and Bookseller of the American Revolution, 1724−1802: A Biographical-Bibliographical Study." Unpublished doctoral dissertation, Univ. of Michigan, 1958.

ROGERS, ROBERT

LEARY, LEWIS. *Articles on American Literature, 1900−1950.* Durham: Duke Univ. Press, 1954, 264.

ROWSON, SUSANNA HASWELL

BLANCK, JACOB, ed. *Merle Johnson's American First Editions,* 4th edition, revised and enlarged. Waltham, Massachusetts: Mark Press, 1965, 449−450.

HALSEY, FRANCIS WHITING. *Charlotte Temple: A Tale of Truth.* New York: Funk and Wagnalls, 1905, xci−cix.

LEARY, LEWIS. *Articles on American Literature, 1900−1950.* Durham: Duke Univ. Press, 1954, 265.

NASON, ELIAS. *A Memoir of Mrs. Susanna Rowson.* Albany: J. Munsell, 1870, bibliographical footnotes.

TRENT, WILLIAM PETERFIELD, et al. *Cambridge History of American Literature,* 4 Vols. New York: G. P. Putnam's Sons, 1917−1921, I, 539.

VAIL, ROBERT WILLIAM GLEN-
ROIE, comp. "Susanna Haswell Rowson, the Author of *Charlotte Temple*:
A Bibliographical Study." *PAAS,*
ns XLII (April 1932), 47–160.

RUSH, BENJAMIN

LEARY, LEWIS. *Articles on American Literature, 1900–1950.* Durham:
Duke Univ. Press, 1954, 265.

SCHAW, JANET

HUBBELL, JAY B. *The South in
American Literature, 1607–1900.*
Durham: Duke Univ. Press, 1954,
958.

SEABURY, SAMUEL

LEARY, LEWIS. *Articles on American Literature, 1900–1950.* Durham:
Duke Univ. Press, 1954, 270.

SECOMB, JOHN

TRENT, WILLIAM PETERFIELD, et
al. *Cambridge History of American
Literature,* 4 Vols. New York: G. P.
Putnam's Sons, 1917–1921, II, 509.

SEWALL, SAMUEL

LEARY, LEWIS. *Articles on American Literature, 1900–1950.* Durham:
Duke Univ. Press, 1954, 271.

SIBLEY, JOHN LANGDON. *Biographical Sketches of Graduates of
Harvard University,* 3 Vols. Cambridge: Harvard Univ. Press, 1873–
1885, II, 360–364.

Continued as: SHIPTON, CLIF-
FORD K., ed. *Sibley's Harvard
Graduates: Biographical Sketches of
Those Who Attended Harvard College.*

SPILLER, ROBERT ERNEST, et al.
Literary History of the United States,

2 Vols. New York: Macmillan, 1962,
717–718. Supplement, 189.

TAYLOR, WALTER FULLER. *A
History of American Letters,* with
bibliographies by Harry Hartwick.
Boston: American Book Co., 1936,
478–479.

Subsequent editions entitled: *The
Story of American Letters.*

SHAW, JOHN

HUBBELL, JAY B. *The South in
American Literature, 1607–1900.*
Durham: Duke Univ. Press, 1954,
958.

SMITH, ELIHU HUBBARD

LEARY, LEWIS. *Articles on American Literature, 1900–1950.* Durham:
Duke Univ. Press, 1954, 275.

SMITH, SAMUEL STANHOPE

LEARY, LEWIS. *Articles on American Literature, 1900–1950.* Durham:
Duke Univ. Press, 1954, 276.

SMITH, WILLIAM

DELAFIELD, MATURIN L. "William Smith, the Historian." *Magazine
of American History,* VI (June 1881),
418–439.

GEGENHEIMER, ALBERT FRANK.
*William Smith: Educator and Church-
man, 1727–1803.* Philadelphia: Univ.
of Pennsylvania Press, 1943, 228–
230.

LEARY, LEWIS. *Articles on American Literature, 1900–1950.* Durham:
Duke Univ. Press, 1954, 276.

SMITH, HORACE WEMYSS. *Life
and Correspondence of the Rev. William Smith, D.D. . . . ,* 2 Vols.
Philadelphia: Ferguson Brothers and
Co., 1880.

SMITH, WILLIAM MOORE

LEARY, LEWIS. *Articles on American Literature, 1900–1950.* Durham: Duke Univ. Press, 1954, 276.

SPROAT, ANN DENNIS (NANCY)

EMERY, ALICE SPROAT. "Nancy Sproat and Her Little Books for Good Children." *BNYPL,* LV (August 1951), 367–385.

STERLING, JAMES

LEARY, LEWIS. *Articles on American Literature, 1900–1950.* Durham: Duke Univ. Press, 1954, 280.

STILES, EZRA

LEARY, LEWIS. *Articles on American Literature, 1900–1950.* Durham: Duke Univ. Press, 1954, 281.

TRENT, WILLIAM PETERFIELD, et al. *Cambridge History of American Literature,* 4 Vols. New York: G. P. Putnam's Sons, 1917–1921, II, 539.

STITH, WILLIAM

ROBINSON, MORGAN POITAUX. "A Complete Index to Stith's *History of Virginia." Virginia State Library Bulletin,* V (No. 1, 1912), 10–18.

STOCKTON, AUNIS BOUDINOT

LEARY, LEWIS. *Articles on American Literature, 1900–1950.* Durham: Duke Univ. Press, 1954, 281.

STODDARD, SOLOMON

LEARY, LEWIS. *Articles on American Literature, 1900–1950.* Durham: Duke Univ. Press, 1954, 282.

TAYLOR, AMOS

McCORISON, MARCUS ALLEN.

"Amos Taylor: A Sketch and Bibliography." *PAAS,* ns LXIX (April 15, 1959), 37–55.

TENNEY, TABITHA GILMAN

TRENT, WILLIAM PETERFIELD, et al. *Cambridge History of American Literature,* 4 Vols. New York: G. P. Putnam's Sons, 1917–1921, I, 544.

TRUMBULL, JOHN

COWIE, ALEXANDER. *John Trumbull: Connecticut Wit.* Chapel Hill: Univ. of North Carolina Press, 1936, 215–223.

DEXTER, FRANKLIN BOWDITCH. *Biographical Sketches of the Graduates of Yale College,* 5 Vols. New York: Henry Holt and Co., 1885–1919, III, 254–257, 720.

HOWARD, LEON. *The Connecticut Wits.* Chicago: Univ. of Chicago Press, 1943, 413–415.

LEARY, LEWIS. *Articles on American Literature, 1900–1950.* Durham: Duke Univ. Press, 1954, 295.

SPILLER, ROBERT ERNEST, et al. *Literary History of the United States,* 2 Vols. New York: Macmillan, 1962, 748–740. Supplement, 200.

VAIL, ROBERT WILLIAM GLENROIE. "Report of the Librarian: John Trumbull Checklist." *PAAS,* XLIV (October 1934), 231–233.

TUCKER, NATHANIEL

HUBBELL, JAY B. *The South in American Literature, 1607–1900.* Durham: Duke Univ. Press, 968–969.

LEARY, LEWIS. *Articles on American Literature, 1900–1950.* Durham: Duke Univ. Press, 1954, 295.

_____. "The Published Writings of Nathaniel Tucker, 1750–1807." *BB,* XX (January-April 1950), 5–6.

TUCKER, ST. GEORGE

HUBBELL, JAY B. *The South in American Literature, 1607–1900.* Durham: Duke Univ. Press, 1954, 968–969.

LEARY, LEWIS. *Articles on American Literature, 1900–1950.* Durham: Duke Univ. Press, 1954, 295.

TRENT, WILLIAM PETERFIELD, et al. *Cambridge History of American Literature,* 4 Vols. New York: G. P. Putnam's Sons, 1917–1921, II, 479.

TYLER, ROYALL

GILMAN, MARCUS DAVIS. *The Bibliography of Vermont.* Burlington: printed by the Free Press Association, 1897, 251–255.

HALLINE, ALLAN GATES. *American Plays.* New York: American Book Co., 1935, 751–752.

LEARY, LEWIS. *Articles on American Literature, 1900–1950.* Durham: Duke Univ. Press, 1954, 296.

SPILLER, ROBERT ERNEST, et al. *Literary History of the United States,* 2 Vols. New York: Macmillan, 1962, 749–750.

TRENT, WILLIAM PETERFIELD, et al. *Cambridge History of American Literature,* 4 Vols. New York: G. P. Putnam's Sons, 1917–1921, I, 545.

WARREN, MERCY OTIS

LEARY, LEWIS. *Articles on American Literature, 1900–1950.* Durham: Duke Univ. Press, 1954, 298.

WASHINGTON, GEORGE

BAKER, WILLIAM SPOHN. *Bibliotheca Washingtoniana; A Descriptive List of the Biographies and Bibliographical Sketches of George Washington.* Philadelphia: R. M. Lindsay, 1889, 184 pp.

BRYAN, WILLIAM ALFRED. *George Washington in American Literature, 1775–1865.* New York: Columbia Univ. Press, 1952, 247–269.

FITZPATRICK, JOHN CLEMENT. *Calendar of the Correspondence of George Washington . . . with the Officers,* 4 Vols. Washington, 1915.

_____, ed. *The Writings of George Washington from the Original Manuscript Sources, 1745–1799,* prepared under the direction of the United States George Washington Bicentennial Commission, 39 Vols. Washington, 1931–1944.

General index in the two final volumes.

GRIFFIN, APPLETON PRENTISS CLARK, comp. *A Catalogue of the Washington Collection in the Boston Athenaeum.* Cambridge: Harvard Univ. Press, 1897, 577 pp.

HARASZTI, Z. "Washington Bicentennial Exhibit." *More Books,* VII (April 1932), 79–97.

Description of an exhibition of Washingtoniana of nearly 300 items including books, maps, broadsides, original letters and manuscripts.

HUBBELL, JAY B. *The South in American Literature, 1607–1900.* Durham: Duke Univ. Press, 1954, 969.

HUGHES, RUPERT. *George Washington,* 3 Vols. New York: W.

Morrow and Co., 1926–1930, I, 565–572, 675–683; III, 796–810.

LEARY, LEWIS. *Articles on American Literature, 1900–1950.* Durham: Duke Univ. Press, 1954, 299.

SPILLER, ROBERT ERNEST, et al. *Literary History of the United States,* 2 Vols. New York: Macmillan, 1962, 752–755. Supplement, 200–202.

STILWELL, M. B. "Checklist of Eulogies and Funeral Orations on the Death of George Washington." *BNYPL,* XX (May 1916), 403–450.

WELLS, WILLIAM CHARLES

HUBBELL, JAY B. *The South in American Literature, 1607–1900.* Durham: Duke Univ. Press, 1954, 970.

WHEATLEY, PHILLIS

HEARTMAN, CHARLES FREDERICK. *Phillis Wheatley (Phillis Peters): A Critical Attempt and a Bibliography of Her Writings.* New York: printed for the author, 1915, 44 pp.

91 copies printed.

LEARY, LEWIS. *Articles on American Literature, 1900–1950.* Durham: Duke Univ. Press, 1954, 302.

WHITEFIELD, GEORGE

LEARY, LEWIS. *Articles on American Literature, 1900–1950.* Durham: Duke Univ. Press, 1954, 303.

TRENT, WILLIAM PETERFIELD, et al. *Cambridge History of American Literature,* 4 Vols. New York: G. P. Putnam's Sons, 1917–1921, I, 441–442.

WILLIAMS, WILLIAM

LEARY, LEWIS. *Articles on American Literature, 1900–1950.* Durham: Duke Univ. Press, 1954, 322.

WISE, JEREMIAH

LEARY, LEWIS. *Articles on American Literature, 1900–1950.* Durham: Duke Univ. Press, 1954, 325.

WISE, JOHN

LEARY, LEWIS. *Articles on American Literature, 1900–1950.* Durham: Duke Univ. Press, 1954, 325.

SIBLEY, JOHN LANGDON. *Biographical Sketches of Graduates of Harvard University,* 3 Vols. Cambridge: 1873–1885, II, 440–441.

Continued as: SHIPTON, CLIFFORD K., ed. *Sibley's Harvard Graduates: Biographical Sketches of Those Who Attended Harvard College.*

SPILLER, ROBERT ERNEST, et al. *Literary History of the United States,* 2 Vols. New York: Macmillan, 1962, 783–784. Supplement, 213.

TRENT, WILLIAM PETERFIELD, et al. *Cambridge History of American Literature,* 4 Vols. New York: G. P. Putnam's Sons, 1917–1921, I, 425.

WOOLMAN, JOHN

GUMMERE, AMELIA MOTT. *The Journal and Essays of John Woolman.* New York: Macmillan Co., 1922, 610–630.

LEARY, LEWIS. *Articles on American Literature, 1900–1950.* Durham: Duke Univ. Press, 1954, 328.

SPILLER, ROBERT ERNEST, et al. *Literary History of the United States,*

2 Vols. New York: Macmillan, 1962, 787–788. Supplement, 215–216.

TAYLOR, WALTER FULLER. *A History of American Letters,* with bibliographies by Harry Hartwick. Boston: American Book Co., 1936, 483–484.

Subsequent editions entitled: *The Story of American Letters.*

TOLLES, FREDERICK B. "John Woolman's List of 'Books Lent.'" *Bulletin of Friends Historical Association,* XXXI (Autumn 1942), 72–81.

WHITNEY, JANET. *John Woolman: American Quaker.* Boston: Little, Brown and Co., 1942, 435–440.

ZENGER, JOHN PETER

LEARY, LEWIS. *Articles on American Literature, 1900–1950.* Durham: Duke Univ. Press, 1954, 330.

ZUBLY, JOHN JOACHIM

HUBBELL, JAY B. *The South in American Literature, 1607–1900.* Durham: Duke Univ. Press, 1954, 974.

3. 19TH CENTURY

ABBOTT, JACOB

LEARY, LEWIS. *Articles on American Literature, 1900–1950.* Durham: Duke Univ. Press, 1954, 3.

TRENT, WILLIAM PETERFIELD, et al. *Cambridge History of American Literature,* 4 Vols. New York: G. P. Putnam's Sons, 1917–1921, II, 527.

WEBER, CARL JEFFERSON, comp. *A Bibliography of the Published Writings of Jacob Abbott, Based Primarily upon the Abbott Collection in the Colby College Library . . . .* Waterville, Maine: Colby College Press, 1948, 155 pp.

Colby College Monograph, No. 14.

ABBOTT, LYMAN

LEARY, LEWIS. *Articles on American Literature, 1900–1950.* Durham: Duke Univ. Press, 1954, 3.

ADAMS, HENRY

ADAMS, JAMES TRUSLOW. *Henry Adams.* New York: A. and C. Boni, Inc., 1933, 213–229.

BAYM, MAX ISAAC. "The 1858 Catalogue of Henry Adam's Library." *The Colophon,* ns III (Autumn 1938), 483–489.

––––––––––––––. *The French Education of Henry Adams.* New York: Columbia Univ. Press, 1951, 329–347.

BLANCK, JACOB. *Bibliography of American Literature,* 5 Vols. New Haven: Yale Univ. Press, 1955–1969, I, 1–11.

––––––––––––––, ed. *Merle Johnson's American First Editions,* 4th edition, revised and enlarged. Waltham, Massachusetts: Mark Press, 1965, 3–5.

GERSTENBERGER, DONNA, and GEORGE HENDRICK. *The American Novel, 1789–1959: A Checklist of Twentieth Century Criticism.* Denver: Alan Swallow, 1961, 7.

HOCHFIELD, GEORGE. *Henry Adams: An Introduction and Interpretation.* New York, 1967, 145–147.

Part of the *American Authors and Critics Series,* begun in 1961, and purchased by Holt, Rinehart and Winston from Barnes and Noble. The nine original and three new volumes were issued under the Holt imprint in January 1967.

JORDY, WILLIAM H. *Henry Adams: Scientific Historian.* New Haven: Yale Univ. Press, 1952, 291–317.

LEARY, LEWIS. *Articles on American Literature, 1900–1950.* Durham: Duke Univ. Press, 1954, 3–6.

LE CLAIR, ROBERT CHARLES. *Three American Travellers in England: James Russell Lowell, Henry Adams, Henry James.* Philadelphia: Univ. of Pennsylvania Press, 1945, 216–219.

MILLER, RICHARD F. "Henry Adams as a Reformer." Unpublished doctoral dissertation, Univ. of Washington, 1947.

SAMUELS, ERNEST. *Henry Adams: The Middle Years, 1877–1891.* Cambridge: Harvard Univ. Press, 1958, 489–497.

——————. *The Young Henry Adams.* Cambridge: Harvard Univ. Press, 1948, 353–362.

SPILLER, ROBERT ERNEST, et al. *Literary History of the United States,* 2 Vols. New York: Macmillan, 1962, 373–377. Supplement, 71–72.

STEVENSON, ELIZABETH. *Henry Adams: A Biography.* New York: Macmillan, 1955, 387–405.

TAYLOR, WALTER FULLER. *A History of American Letters,* with bibliographies by Harry Hartwick. Boston: American Book Co., 1936, 567–569.

Subsequent editions entitled: *The Story of American Letters.*

ADAMS, HERBERT B.

VINCENT, JOHN MARTIN. "Herbert B. Adams," in *American Historical Association Annual Report, 1901.* Washington, 1902, 197–210.

ADAMS, JOHN QUINCY

LEARY, LEWIS. *Articles on American Literature, 1900–1950.* Durham: Duke Univ. Press, 1954, 7.

TRENT, WILLIAM PETERFIELD, et al. *Cambridge History of American Literature,* 4 Vols. New York: G. P. Putnam's Sons, 1917–1921, II, 468–469.

ADAMS, OSCAR FAY

BLANCK, JACOB. *Bibliography of American Literature,* 5 Vols. New Haven: Yale Univ. Press, 1955–1969, I, 12–19.

AINSWORTH, WILLIAM HARRISON

LOCKE, HAROLD. *A Bibliographical Catalogue of the Published Novels and Ballads of William Harrison Ainsworth.* London: Elkin Mathews, 1925, 68 pp.

AKERS, ELIZABETH

LEARY, LEWIS. *Articles on American Literature, 1900–1950.* Durham: Duke Univ. Press, 1954, 8.

ALCOTT, AMOS BRONSON

BLANCK, JACOB. *Bibliography of American Literature,* 5 Vols. New Haven: Yale Univ. Press, 1955–1969, I, 20–26.

DINWIDDIE, SHIRLEY W., and RICHARD L. HERRNSTADT.

"Amos Bronson Alcott: A Bibliography." *BB*, XII (April 1954), 64–67; (August 1954), 92–96.

LEARY, LEWIS. *Articles on American Literature, 1900–1950*. Durham: Duke Univ. Press, 1954, 8.

SPILLER, ROBERT ERNEST, et al. *Literary History of the United States*, 2 Vols. New York: Macmillan, 1962, 381–382. Supplement, 75.

TRENT, WILLIAM PETERFIELD, et al. *Cambridge History of American Literature*, 4 Vols. New York: G. P. Putnam's Sons, 1917–1921, I, 547.

ALCOTT, LOUISA MAY

BLANCK, JACOB. *Bibliography of American Literature*, 5 Vols. New Haven: Yale Univ. Press, 1955–1969, I, 27–45.

——————, ed. *Merle Johnson's American First Editions*, 4th edition, revised and enlarged. Waltham, Massachusetts: Mark Press, 1965, 12–15.

GERSTENBERGER, DONNA, and GEORGE HENDRICK. *The American Novel, 1789–1959: A Checklist of Twentieth Century Criticism*. Denver: Alan Swallow, 1961, 8–9.

GULLIVER, LUCILE. *Louisa May Alcott: A Bibliography*. Boston: Little, Brown and Co., 1932, 71 pp.

LEARY, LEWIS. *Articles on American Literature, 1900–1950*. Durham: Duke Univ. Press, 1954, 8–9.

ROSTENBERG, LEONA. "Some Anonymous and Pseudonymous Thriilers of Louisa M. Alcott." *PBSA*, XXXVII (2nd Quart. 1943), 131–140.

SPILLER, ROBERT ERNEST, et al. *Literary History of the United States*,

2 Vols. New York: Macmillan, 1962, 383–384. Supplement, 75.

WILSON, CARROLL ATWOOD. *Thirteen Author Collections of the Nineteenth Century and Five Centuries of Familiar Quotations*, edited by Jean C. S. Wilson and David A. Randall, 2 Vols. New York: privately printed for Scribner, 1950, I, 1–16.

ALDEN, HENRY MILLS

LEARY, LEWIS. *Articles on American Literature, 1900–1950*. Durham: Duke Univ. Press, 1954, 9.

ALDRICH, THOMAS BAILEY

BARTLETT, FRANCIS. *A Catalogue of the Works of Thomas Bailey Aldrich Collected by Francis Bartlett*. N.p.: privately printed, 1898, no pagination.

BLANCK, JACOB. *Bibliography of American Literature*, 5 Vols. New Haven: Yale Univ. Press, 1955–1969, I, 46–77.

——————, ed. *Merle Johnson's American First Editions*, 4th edition, revised and enlarged. Waltham, Massachusetts: Mark Press, 1965, 16–19.

CARY, RICHARD. "Thomas Bailey Aldrich Writes to an English Eccentric." *CLQ*, Series III (August 1954), 244–253.

GERSTENBERGER, DONNA, and GEORGE HENDRICK. *The American Novel, 1789–1959: A Checklist of Twentieth Century Criticism*. Denver: Alan Swallow, 1961, 9.

GOMME, G.J.L. "T.B. Aldrich and 'Household Words.'" *PBSA*, XLII (1st Quart. 1948), 70–72.

GREENSLET, FERRIS. *The Life of Thomas Bailey Aldrich*. Boston:

Houghton Mifflin Co., 1908, 261–
292.

LEARY, LEWIS. *Articles on American Literature, 1900–1950.* Durham:
Duke Univ. Press, 1954, 9.

NORTH, E. D. "A Bibliography of
the Original Editions of the Works of
Thomas Bailey Aldrich." *Book
Buyer,* XXII (May 1901), 296–303.

SHERMAN, FREDERIC FAIR-
CHILD. *A Check List of First
Editions of the Works of Thomas
Bailey Aldrich.* New York: privately
printed, 1921, 16 pp.

SPILLER, ROBERT ERNEST, et al.
Literary History of the United States,
2 Vols. New York: Macmillan, 1962,
384–386. Supplement, 76.

TRENT, WILLIAM PETERFIELD, et
al. *Cambridge History of American
Literature,* 4 Vols. New York: G. P.
Putnam's Sons, 1917–1921, II, 618;
IV, 644–646.

WARD, ANNETTE PERSIS, comp.
*Annotated List of the Works of
Thomas Bailey Aldrich.* New York:
Church of the Ascension, Parish Lib-
rary, 1907, 7 pp.

WINSHIP, GEORGE P. "The
Aldrich Collection of Books." *HAB,*
XII (1920), 852–854.

WOODRESS, JAMES, et al. *American Literary Scholarship: An Annual.*
Durham: Duke Univ. Press, 1963,
129–130.

ALGER, HORATIO

ALGER, HORATIO, JR. *The Young
Miner: or, Tom Nelson in California,*
with an introduction and bibliographical note by John Seelye. San Francisco: Book Club of California, 1965,
187 pp.

450 copies printed.

GERSTENBERGER, DONNA, and
GEORGE HENDRICK. *The American Novel, 1789–1959: A Checklist
of Twentieth Century Criticism.*
Denver: Alan Swallow, 1961, 9–10.

LEARY, LEWIS. *Articles on American Literature, 1900–1950.* Durham:
Duke Univ. Press, 1954, 9.

MAYES, HERBERT R. *Alger: A
Biography without a Hero.* New
York: Macy-Masius, 1928, 239–241.

*ALLEN, ELIZABETH ANN
(CHASE) AKERS*

BLANCK, JACOB. *Bibliography of
American Literature,* 5 Vols. New
Haven: Yale Univ. Press, 1955–1969,
I, 78–87.

WINTERICH, JOHN T. "Elizabeth
Akers and the Unsubstantial
Character of Fame." *The Colophon,*
Part 15 (1933), no pagination.

The authorship of "Rock Me to
Sleep" and others.

ALLEN, JAMES LANE

BLANCK, JACOB. *Bibliography of
American Literature,* 5 Vols. New
Haven: Yale Univ. Press, 1955–1969,
I, 88–95.

––––––––––, ed. *Merle Johnson's
American First Editions,* 4th edition,
revised and enlarged. Waltham, Massachusetts: Mark Press, 1965, 23–24.

GERSTENBERGER, DONNA, and
GEORGE HENDRICK. *The American
Novel, 1789–1959: A Checklist of
Twentieth Century Criticism.* Denver:
Alan Swallow, 1961, 10–11.

KNIGHT, GRANT COCHRAN.
James Lane Allen and the Genteel

Tradition. Chapel Hill: Univ. of North Carolina Press, 1935, 288–304.

LEARY, LEWIS. *Articles on American Literature, 1900–1950.* Durham: Duke Univ. Press, 1954, 10.

PAINE, GREGORY LANSING, ed. *Southern Prose Writers: Representative Selections,* with introduction, bibliography and notes. New York: American Book Co., 1947, cxxiii–cxxiv.

SPILLER, ROBERT ERNEST, et al. *Literary History of the United States,* 2 Vols. New York: Macmillan, 1962, 386.

TOWNSEND, JOHN WILSON. *James Lane Allen: A Personal Note.* Louisville: Courier-Journal Job Printing Co., 1928, 149 pp.

100 copies printed.

ALLEN, WILLIAM

SPRAGUE, WILLIAM BUELL. *A Discourse Delivered in the First Congregational Church . . . on the Sabbath Immediately Succeeding the Funeral of the Rev. William Allen . . . .* Albany: C. Van Benthuysen and Sons, 1868, 32 pp.

ALLSTON, WASHINGTON

BLANCK, JACOB. *Bibliography of American Literature,* 5 Vols. New Haven: Yale Univ. Press, 1955–1969, I, 96–102.

BROOKS, VAN WYCK. *The Dream of Arcadia: American Writers and Artists in Italy, 1760–1915.* New York: Dutton, 1958, bibliographical footnotes.

HUBBELL, JAY B. *The South in American Literature, 1607–1900.* Durham: Duke Univ. Press, 1954, 915–916.

LEARY, LEWIS. *Articles on American Literature, 1900–1950.* Durham: Duke Univ. Press, 1954, 10.

ALMQUIST, JONAS LUDWIG

LEARY, LEWIS. *Articles on American Literature, 1900–1950.* Durham: Duke Univ. Press, 1954, 10.

ANDERSON, ALEXANDER

DUYCKINCK, EVERT AUGUST, comp. *A Brief Catalogue of Books Illustrated with Engravings by Dr. Alexander Anderson.* New York: Thompson and Moreau, printers, 1885, 42 pp.

ARP, BILL (see SMITH)

ARTHUR, TIMOTHY SHAY

GERSTENBERGER, DONNA, and GEORGE HENDRICK. *The American Novel, 1789–1959: A Checklist of Twentieth Century Criticism.* Denver: Alan Swallow, 1961, 15.

ATWATER, CALEB

LEARY, LEWIS. *Articles on American Literature, 1900–1950.* Durham: Duke Univ. Press, 1954, 14.

AUDUBON, JOHN JAMES

AUDUBON, JOHN JAMES. *Delineations of American Scenery and Character,* with an introduction by Francis Hobart Herrick. New York: G. A. Baker and Co., 1926, vii–viii.

BLANCK, JACOB, ed. *Merle Johnson's American First Editions,* 4th edition, revised and enlarged. Waltham, Massachusetts: Mark Press, 1965, 31–32.

HERRICK, FRANCIS HOBART. *Audubon the Naturalist: A History of*

His Life and Time, 2 Vols. New York: D. Appleton-Century Co., 1917, II, 401–456.

Contains a list of "Familiar Letters," II, 415–417.

2nd edition: 1938, II, 401–461.

LEARY, LEWIS. *Articles on American Literature, 1900–1950.* Durham: Duke Univ. Press, 1954, 14–15.

LYMAN ALLYN MUSEUM (NEW LONDON). *John J. Audubon Centennial Exhibition.* New London: printed for the Lyman Allyn Museum 1951, no pagination.

SPILLER, ROBERT ERNEST, et al. *Literary History of the United States,* 2 Vols. New York: Macmillan, 1962, 390–392. Supplement, 78–79.

AUSTIN, BENJAMIN

LEARY, LEWIS. *Articles on American Literature, 1900–1950.* Durham: Duke Univ. Press, 1954, 15.

AUSTIN, JANE GOODWIN

BLANCK, JACOB. *Bibliography of American Literature,* 5 Vols. New Haven: Yale Univ. Press, 1955–1969, I, 12–19.

——————, ed. *Merle Johnson's American First Editions,* 4th edition, revised and enlarged. Waltham, Massachusetts: Mark Press, 1965, 33–34.

AUSTIN, WILLIAM

TRENT, WILLIAM PETERFIELD, et al. *Cambridge History of American Literature,* 4 Vols. New York: G. P. Putnam's Sons, 1917–1921, II, 503.

BACON, DELIA SALTER

BLANCK, JACOB. *Bibliography of American Literature,* 5 Vols. New Haven: Yale Univ. Press, 1955–1969, I, 110–112.

LEARY, LEWIS. *Articles on American Literature, 1900–1950.* Durham: Duke Univ. Press, 1954, 16.

BAGBY, GEORGE WILLIAM

BLANCK, JACOB. *Bibliography of American Literature,* 5 Vols. New Haven: Yale Univ. Press, 1955–1969, I, 113–115.

HUBBELL, JAY B. *The South in American Literature, 1607–1900.* Durham: Duke Univ. Press, 1954, 916.

KING, JOSEPH LEONARD, JR. *Dr. George William Bagby: A Study of Virginian Literature, 1850–1880.* New York: Columbia Univ. Press, 1927, 189–193.

LEARY, LEWIS. *Articles on American Literature, 1900–1950.* Durham: Duke Univ. Press, 1954, 16.

TRENT, WILLIAM PETERFIELD, et al. *Cambridge History of American Literature,* 4 Vols. New York: G. P. Putnam's Sons, 1917–1921, II, 503.

BAIRD, SPENCER FULLERTON

GOODE, GEORGE BROWN. *The Published Writings of Spencer Fullerton Baird.* Washington, 1883, 377 pp.

Bulletin of the National Museum, No. 20.

BAKER, WILLIAM MUMFORD

LEARY, LEWIS. *Articles on American Literature, 1900–1950.* Durham: Duke Univ. Press, 1954, 16.

BALDWIN, JOSEPH GLOVER

BLANCK, JACOB. *Bibliography of American Literature,* 5 Vols. New Haven: Yale Univ. Press, 1955–1969, I, 116–117.

HUBBELL, JAY B. *The South in American Literature, 1607–1900.* Durham: Duke Univ. Press, 1954, 916–917.

LEARY, LEWIS. *Articles on American Literature, 1900–1950.* Durham: Duke Univ. Press, 1954, 16.

McDERMOTT, JOHN FRANCIS. "Baldwin's 'Flush Times of Alabama and Mississippi,' A Bibliographical Note." *PBSA,* XLV (3rd Quart. 1951), 251–256.

PAINE, GREGORY LANSING, ed. *Southern Prose Writers: Representative Selections,* with introduction, bibliography and notes. New York: American Book Co., 1947, cxxiv–cxxv.

TRENT, WILLIAM PETERFIELD, et al. *Cambridge History of American Literature,* 4 Vols. New York: G. P. Putman's Sons, 1917–1921, II, 503–504.

BANCROFT, GEORGE

BANCROFT, GEORGE. "Lists of Letters and Documents Dealing with American Affairs, Seventeenth and Eighteenth Centuries, Bancroft's Memoranda . . . ." Unpublished manuscript, Bancroft Collection, New York Public Library, 250 pp.

BLANCK, JACOB. *Bibliography of American Literature,* 5 Vols. New Haven: Yale Univ. Press, 1955–1969, I, 118–138.

HOWE, MARK ANTHONY DE WOLFE. *The Life and Letters of George Bancroft,* 2 Vols. New York: C. Scribner's Sons, 1908, II, 329–341.

LEARY, LEWIS. *Articles on American Literature, 1900–1950.* Durham: Duke Univ. Press, 1954, 16–17.

NYE, RUSSEL BLAINE. *George Bancroft: Brahmin Rebel.* New York: A.A. Knopf, 1944, 324–340.

SABIN, JOSEPH F. *The Library of the Late Hon. George Bancroft: A Sketch of the Historical Manuscripts, Memoranda Concerning the Books and Pamphlets.* New York: n.p., 1891?, 101 pp.

SPILLER, ROBERT, ERNEST, et al. *Literary History of the United States,* 2 Vols. New York: Macmillan, 1962, 394–395. Supplement, 79.

BANCROFT, HUBERT HOWE

LEARY, LEWIS. *Articles on American Literature, 1900–1950.* Durham: Duke Univ. Press, 1954, 17.

BANGS, JOHN KENDRICK

BANGS, FRANCIS H. "John Kendrick Bangs, Humorist of the Nineties." *YULG,* VII (January 1933), 53–76.

BLANCK, JACOB. *Bibliography of American Literature,* 5 Vols. New Haven: Yale Univ. Press, 1955–1969, I, 139–161.

——————, ed. *Merle Johnson's American First Editions,* 4th edition, revised and enlarged. Waltham, Massachusetts: Mark Press, 1965, 39–42.

LEARY, LEWIS. *Articles on American Literature, 1900–1950.* Durham: Duke Univ. Press, 1954, 17.

BANNISTER, NATHANIEL HARRINGTON

LEARY, LEWIS. *Articles on American Literature, 1900–1950.* Durham: Duke Univ. Press, 1954, 17.

BARKER, JAMES NELSON

BLANCK, JACOB. *Bibliography of American Literature,* 5 Vols. New Haven: Yale Univ. Press, 1955–1969, I, 162–168.

MUSSER, PAUL HOWARD. *James Nelson Barker.* Philadelphia: Univ. of Pennsylvania Press, 1929, 211–223.

SPILLER, ROBERT ERNEST, et al. *Literary History of the United States,* 2 Vols. New York: Macmillan, 1962, 395–396.

BARR, AMELIA

LEARY, LEWIS. *Articles on American Literature, 1900–1950.* Durham: Duke Univ. Press, 1954, 18.

BARTLETT, ROBERT

LEARY, LEWIS. *Articles on American Literature, 1900–1950.* Durham: Duke Univ. Press, 1954, 18.

BAUM, L. FRANK

BAUM, L. FRANK. *L. Frank Baum, The Wonderful Wizard of Oz: An Exhibition of His Published Writings in Commemoration of the Centenary of His Birth,* May 16, 1856. New York: Grosset and Dunlap, 1956, 50 pp.

BEADLE, ERASTUS

LEARY, LEWIS. *Articles on American Literature, 1900–1950.* Durham: Duke Univ. Press, 1954, 19.

BECKFORD, WILLIAM

YALE UNIVERSITY, LIBRARY. *William Beckford of Fonthill, Writer, Traveller, Collector, Caliph, 1760–1844: A Brief Narrative and Catalogue of an Exhibition,* by Howard B. Gotlieb. New Haven: Yale Univ. Library, 1960, 100 pp.

BEECHER, HENRY WARD

ABOTT, LYMAN. *Henry Ward Beecher.* Boston and New York: Houghton Mifflin Co., 1903, xvii–xxxviii.

CROCKER, LIONEL GEORGE. *Henry Ward Beecher's Art of Preaching.* Chicago: Univ. of Chicago Press, 1934, 132–138.

HIBBEN, PAXTON. *Henry Ward Beecher: An American Portrait.* New York: The Press of the Readers Club, 1942, 317–350.

LEARY, LEWIS. *Articles on American Literature, 1900–1950.* Durham: Duke Univ. Press, 1954, 19.

SPILLER, ROBERT ERNEST, et al. *Literary History of the United States,* 2 Vols. New York: Macmillan, 1962, 400–401. Supplement, 81.

TRENT, WILLIAM PETERFIELD, et al. *Cambridge History of American Literature,* 4 Vols.

New York: G.P. Putnam's Sons, 1917–1921, II, 528–530.

BEECHER, LYMAN

LEARY, LEWIS. *Articles on American Literature, 1900–1950*. Durham: Duke Univ. Press, 1954, 19.

TRENT, WILLIAM PETERFIELD, et al. *Cambridge History of American Literature*, 4 Vols. New York: G.P. Putnam's Sons, 1917–1921, II, 530.

BELLAMY, EDWARD

AARON, DANIEL, and HARRY LEVIN. *Edward Bellamy*. Schenectady: Union College Press, 1968, 23–27.

BLANCK, JACOB. *Bibliography of American Literature*, 5 Vols. New Haven: Yale Univ. Press, 1955–1969, I, 192–196.

——————, ed. *Merle Johnson's American First Editions*, 4th edition, revised and enlarged. Waltham, Massachusetts: Mark Press, 1965, 45.

GERSTENBERGER, DONNA, and GEORGE HENDRICK. *The American Novel, 1789–1959: A Checklist of Twentieth Century Criticism.* Denver: Alan Swallow, 1961, 16–17.

LEARY, LEWIS. *Articles on American Literature, 1900–1950*. Durham: Duke Univ. Press, 1954, 20.

MORGAN, ARTHUR ERNEST. *Edward Bellamy.* New York: Columbia Univ. Press, 1944, 421–439.

Columbia Studies in American Culture, No. 15.

SPILLER, ROBERT ERNEST, et al. *Literary History of the United States,* 2 Vols. New York: Macmillan, 1962, 401–403. Supplement, 81–82.

BENJAMIN, PARK

BLANCK, JACOB. *Bibliography of American Literature,* 5 Vols. New Haven: Yale Univ. Press, 1955–1969, I, 197–207.

LEARY, LEWIS. *Articles on American Literature, 1900–1950*. Durham: Duke Univ. Press, 1954, 21.

TAFT, KENDALL B., ed. *Minor Knickerbockers: Representative Selections,* with introduction, bibliography and notes. New York: American Book Co., 1947, cxxviii.

BENNETT, EMERSON

BLANCK, JACOB. *Bibliography of American Literature,* 5 Vols. New Haven: Yale Univ. Press, 1955–1969, I, 208–215.

LEARY, LEWIS. *Articles on American Literature, 1900–1950*. Durham: Duke Univ. Press, 1954, 21.

BENNETT, JAMES GORDON

LEARY, LEWIS. *Articles on American Literature, 1900–1950*. Durham: Duke Univ. Press, 1954, 21.

TRENT, WILLIAM PETERFIELD, et al. *Cambridge History of American Literature,* 4 Vols. New York: G.P. Putnam's Sons, 1917–1921, II, 521–522.

BENTON, THOMAS HART

TRENT, WILLIAM PETERFIELD, et al. *Cambridge History of American Literature,* 4 Vols. New York: G.P. Putnam's Sons, 1917–1921, II, 469–470.

BIDDLE, NICHOLAS

LEARY, LEWIS. *Articles on American Literature, 1900–1950.* Durham: Duke Univ. Press, 1954, 21.

BIERCE, AMBROSE (GWINNETT)

BLANCK, JACOB. *Bibliography of American Literature,* 5 Vols. New Haven: Yale Univ. Press, 1955–1969, I, 216–227.

───────────, ed. *Merle Johnson's American First Editions,* 4th edition, revised and enlarged. Waltham, Massachusetts: Mark Press, 1965, 53–55.

GREANDER, M. E. "Au coeur de la vie: A French Translation of Ambrose Bierce." *Boston Univ. Studies in English, I* (Winter 1956), 237–241.

LEARY, LEWIS. *Articles on American Literature, 1900–1950.* Durham: Duke Univ. Press, 1954, 21–22.

McWILLIAMS, CAREY. *Ambrose Bierce: A Biography.* New York: A. and C. Boni, 1929, 337–346.

SPILLER, ROBERT ERNEST, et al. *Literary History of the United States,* 2 Vols. New York: Macmillan, 1962, 404–406. Supplement, 82–83.

STARRETT, VINCENT. *Ambrose Bierce: A Bibliography.* Philadelphia: The Centaur Bookshop, 1929, 117 pp.

TRENT, WILLIAM PETERFIELD, et al. *Cambridge History of American Literature,* 4 Vols. New York: G.P. Putnam's Sons, 1917–1921, II, 618.

BIRD, ROBERT MONTGOMERY

BLANCK, JACOB. *Bibliography of American Literature,* 5 Vols. New Haven: Yale Univ. Press, 1955–1969, I, 228–234.

───────────, ed. *Merle Johnson's American First Editions,* 4th edition, revised and enlarged. Waltham, Massachusetts: Mark Press, 1965, 56.

FOUST, CLEMENT. *Life and Dramatic Works of Robert Montgomery Bird.* New York: Knickerbocker Press, 1919, 161–167.

GERSTENBERGER, DONNA, and GEORGE HENDRICK. *The American Novel, 1789–1959: A Checklist of Twentieth Century Criticism.* Denver: Alan Swallow, 1961, 18.

HALLINE, ALLAN GATES. *American Plays.* New York: American Book Co., 1935, 754–755.

HARRIS, RICHARD. "From the Papers of R.M. Bird: The Lost Scene from News of the Night." *LCUP,* XXVI (Fall–Winter 1958), 1–12.

───────────. "A Young Dramatist's Diary: The Secret Records of R.M. Bird." *LCUP,* XXV (Fall–Winter 1959), 8–24.

LEARY, LEWIS. *Articles on American Literature, 1900–1950.* Durham: Duke Univ. Press, 1954, 22.

SPILLER, ROBERT ERNEST,
et al. *Literary History of the
United States,* 2 Vols. New York:
Macmillan, 1962, 406–407.
Supplement, 83.

TRENT, WILLIAM PETERFIELD,
et al. *Cambridge History of
American Literature,* 4 Vols.
New York: G.P. Putnam's Sons,
1917–1921, I, 493–494.

WILLIAMS, CECIL B., ed.
Nick of the Woods, with introduction, chronology and bibliography.
New York: American Book Co.,
1939, lxvi–lxxv.

BLAIR, FRANCIS

LEARY, LEWIS. *Articles on
American Literature, 1900–1950.*
Durham: Duke Univ. Press,
1954. 23.

BLEECKER, ANTHONY

TAFT, KENDALL B., ed.
*Minor Knickerbockers: Represen-
tative Selections,* with introduction,
bibliography and notes. New York:
American Book Co., 1947,
cxxviii.

BOKER, GEORGE HENRY

BLANCK, JACOB. *Bibliography of
American Literature,* 5 Vols.
New Haven: Yale Univ. Press,
1955–1969, I, 235–250.

BRADLEY, EDWARD SCULLEY.
*George Henry Boker: Poet
and Patriot.* Philadelphia: Univ.
of Pennsylvania Press, 1927,
343–355.

LEARY, LEWIS. *Articles on
American Literature, 1900–1950.*
Durham: Duke Univ. Press,
1954, 23.

SPILLER, ROBERT ERNEST,
et al. *Literary History of the
United States,* 2 Vols. New York:
Macmillan, 1962, 408–409.

TAYLOR, GEORGE H. "Check
List to the Writings by and about
George H. Boker." *ABC,* V (Decem-
ber 1934), 372–374.

BONAPARTE, CHARLES JOSEPH

LIBRARY OF CONGRESS,
MANUSCRIPT DIVISION.
*Charles Joseph Bonaparte: A
Register of His Papers in the
Library of Congress.* Washington,
1958, 20 pp.

BONER, JOHN HENRY

TRENT, WILLIAM PETERFIELD,
et al. *Cambridge History of
American Literature,* 4 Vols.
New York: G.P. Putnam's Sons,
1917–1921, II, 589.

BONNEY, EDWARD

REED, DORIS M. "Edward
Bonney, Detective." *IUB,* II
(November 1957), 5–17.

BORRENSTEIN, DAVID A.

MILLER, GEORGE J. "David A.
Borrenstein: A Printer and Publisher at Princeton, N.J.,
1824–1828," *PBSA,* XXX
(1936), 1–56.

BOUCICAULT, DION

LEARY, LEWIS. *Articles on
American Literature, 1900–1950.*
Durham: Duke Univ. Press,
1954, 24.

WALSH, TOWNSEND. *The
Career of Dion Boucicault.*
New York: Dunlap Society,
1915, 220–224.

300 copies printed.

BOWDITCH, NATHANIEL

PICKERING, JOHN. *Eulogy on Nathaniel Bowditch, Ll. D. . . . .* Cambridge: Harvard Univ. Press, 1838, 94.

YOUNG, ALEXANDER. *A Discourse on the Life and Character of the Hon. Nathaniel Bowditch . . . .* Boston: C.C. Little and J. Brown, 1838, 116–117.

BOWLES, SAMUEL

TRENT, WILLIAM PETERFIELD, et al. *Cambridge History of American Literature,* 4 Vols. New York: G.P. Putnam's Sons, 1917–1921, II, 522.

BOYESEN, HJALMER HJORTH

BLANCK, JACOB. *Bibliography of American Literature,* 5 Vols. New Haven: Yale Univ. Press, 1955–1969, I, 251–260.

GERSTENBERGER, DONNA, and GEORGE HENDRICK. *The American Novel, 1789–1959: A Checklist of Twentieth Century Criticism.* Denver: Alan Swallow, 1961, 20.

LEARY, LEWIS. *Articles on American Literature, 1900–1950.* Durham: Duke Univ. Press, 1954, 24.

SPILLER, ROBERT ERNEST, et al. *Literary History of the United States,* 2 Vols. New York: Macmillan, 1962, 410–411. Supplement, 83.

BRACKENRIDGE, HENRY MARIE

LEARY, LEWIS. *Articles on*

American Literature, 1900–1950. Durham: Duke Univ. Press, 1954, 24.

BRADBURY, JOHN

LEARY, LEWIS. *Articles on American Literature, 1900–1950.* Durham: Duke Univ. Press, 1954, 25.

BRADFORD, JOHN

LEARY, LEWIS. *Articles on American Literature, 1900–1950.* Durham: Duke Univ. Press, 1954, 25.

BRAINARD, JOHN GARDINER CALKINS

BLANCK, JACOB. *Bibliography of American Literature,* 5 Vols. New Haven: Yale Univ. Press, 1955–1969, I, 269–274.

BRANN, W. C.

LEARY, LEWIS. *Articles on American Literature, 1900–1950.* Durham: Duke Univ. Press, 1954, 26.

BREITMAN, HANS (See *LELAND*)

BREVOORT, HENRY

TAFT, KENDALL B., ed. *Minor Knickerbockers: Representative Selections,* with introduction, bibliography and notes. New York: American Book Co., 1947, cxxviii–cxxix.

BRIGGS, CHARLES FREDERICK

BLANCK, JACOB. *Bibliography of American Literature,* 5 Vols. New Haven: Yale Univ. Press, 1955–1969, I, 275–278.

BROOKS, CHARLES TIMOTHY

BLANCK, JACOB. *Bibliography of American Literature,* 5 Vols. New Haven: Yale Univ. Press, 1955–1969, I, 279–297.

VIRGINIA, UNIVERSITY, LIBRARY. *The Barrett Library: Charles Timothy Brooks: A Checklist of Printed and Manu- script Works* . . . . Charlottesville: Univ. of Virginia Press, 1960, 9 pp.

BROOKS, JAMES GORDON

TAFT, KENDALL B., ed. *Minor Knickerbockers: Represen- tative Selections,* with introduction, bibliography and notes. New York: American Book Co., 1947, cxxix.

BROOKS, MARIA GOWEN

BLANCK, JACOB. *Bibliography of American Literature,* 5 Vols. New Haven: Yale Univ. Press, 1955–1969, I, 298–301.

LEARY, LEWIS. *Articles on American Literature, 1900–1950.* Durham: Duke Univ. Press, 1954, 27.

BROOKS, NOAH

LEARY, LEWIS. *Articles on American Literature, 1900–1950.* Durham: Duke Univ. Press, 1954, 27.

BROOKS, PHILLIPS

LEARY, LEWIS. *Articles on American Literature, 1900–1950,* Durham: Duke Univ. Press, 1954, 27.

BROWN, ALICE

LEARY, LEWIS. *Articles on*

American Literature, 1900–1950. Durham: Duke Univ. Press, 1954, 28.

TRENT, WILLIAM PETERFIELD, et al. *Cambridge History of American Literature,* 4 Vols. New York: G.P. Putnam's Sons, 1917–1921, II, 618–619.

BROWN, CHARLES BROCKDEN

BLANCK, JACOB. *Bibliography of American Literature,* 5 Vols. New Haven: Yale Univ. Press, 1955–1969, I, 302–309.

––––––––––, ed. *Merle Johnson's American First Editions,* 4th edition, revised and enlarged. Waltham, Massachu- setts: Mark Press, 1965, 66.

CLARK, DAVID LEE. *Charles Brockden Brown: Pioneer Voice of America.* Durham: Duke Univ. Press, 1952, 334–341.

GERSTENBERGER, DONNA, and GEORGE HENDRICK. *The Ameri- can Novel, 1789–1959: A Checklist of Twentieth Century Criticism.* Denver: Alan Swallow, 1961, 21–24.

GREEN, DAVID BONNELL. "Charles Brockden Brown, America's First Important Novelist: A Checklist of Biography and Criticism." *PBSA,* LX (3rd Quart. 1966), 349–363.

JUST, WALTER. *Die romantische Bewegung in der amerikanischen Literatur: Brown, Poe, Hawthorne: ein Beïtrag sur Geschicte der Romantik.* Berlin: Mayer and Muller, 1910, 91–93.

LEARY, LEWIS. *Articles on Ameri- can Literature, 1900–1950.* Durham: Duke Univ. Press, 1954, 28–29.

MARCHAND, ERNEST, ed. *Ormand,* with introduction, chronology and bibliography. New York: American Book Co., 1937, xlvii–li.

SPILLER, ROBERT ERNEST, et al. *Literary History of the United States,* 2 Vols. New York: Macmillan, 1962, 417–419. Supplement, 85.

"Supplement to the Guide to the Manuscript Collections in the Historical Society of Pennsylvania." *PMHB,* LXVII (January 1944), 98–111.

TAYLOR, WALTER FULLER. *A History of American Letters,* with bibliographies by Harry Hartwick. Boston: American Book Co., 1936, 491–492.

Subsequent editions entitled: *The Story of American Letters.*

TRENT, WILLIAM PETERFIELD, et al. *Cambridge History of American Literature,* 4 Vols. New York: G. P. Putnam's Sons, 1917–1921, I, 527–528.

WARFEL, HARRY REDCAY. *Charles Brockden Brown: American Gothic Novelist.* Gainesville: Univ. of Florida Press, 1949, 239–243.

WILEY, LULU RUMSEY. *The Sources and Influence of the Novels of Charles Brockden Brown.* New York: Vantage Press, 1950, 364–381.

BROWNE, CHARLES FARRAR (ARTEMUS WARD)

BLANCK, JACOB. *Bibliography of American Literature,* 5 Vols. New Haven: Yale Univ. Press, 1955–1969, I, 312–324.

LEARY, LEWIS. *Articles on American Literature, 1900–1950.* Durham: Duke Univ. Press, 1954, 29.

SEITZ, DON C. *Artemus Ward: A Biography and Bibliography.* New York: Harper and Brothers, 1919, 319–338.

SPILLER, ROBERT ERNEST, et al. *Literary History of the United States,* 2 Vols. New York: Macmillan, 1962, 419–420. Supplement, 86.

TRENT, WILLIAM PETERFIELD, et al. *Cambridge History of American Literature,* 4 Vols. New York: G. P. Putnam's Sons, 1917–1921, II, 504.

BROWNE, JOHN ROSS

LEARY, LEWIS. *Articles on American Literature, 1900–1950.* Durham: Duke Univ. Press, 1954, 29.

BROWNE, WILLIAM HAND

LEARY, LEWIS. *Articles on American Literature, 1900–1950.* Durham: Duke Univ. Press, 1954, 29.

BROWNELL, HENRY HOWARD

BLANCK, JACOB. *Bibliography of American Literature,* 5 Vols. New Haven: Yale Univ. Press, 1955–1969, I, 325–330.

BROWNELL, WILLIAM CRARY

BROWNELL, GERTRUDE HALL. *William Crary Brownell: An Anthology of His Writings.* New York: C. Scribner's Sons, 1933, 383 pp.

FLETCHER, FRANK. "A Bibliography of William Crary Brownell (1851–1928)." *BB,* XX (January–April 1953), 242–244.

LEARY, LEWIS. *Articles on American Literature, 1900–1950.* Durham: Duke Univ. Press, 1954, 29.

SPILLER, ROBERT ERNEST, et al. *Literary History of the United States,* 2 Vols. New York: Macmillan, 1962, 420–421.

BROWNSON, ORESTES A.

LEARY, LEWIS. *Articles on American Literature, 1900–1950.* Durham: Duke Univ. Press, 1954, 29–30.

MAYNARD, THEODORE. *Orestes Brownson: Yankee, Radical, Catholic.* New York: Macmillan Co., 1943, 433–443.

MICHEL, VIRGIL GEORGE. *The Critical Principles of Orestes A. Brownson.* Washington: Catholic Univ. of America, 1918, 103–106.

SCHLESINGER, ARTHUR MEIER, JR. *Orestes A. Brownson.* Boston: Little, Brown and Co., 1939, 299–305, bibliographical footnotes.

SPILLER, ROBERT ERNEST, et al. *Literary History of the United States,* 2 Vols. New York: Macmillan, 1962, 421–422. Supplement, 86.

WEGELIN, OSCAR. "An Early Iowa Playwright." *NYHSQ,* XXVIII (April 1944), 42–44.

BRUCE, DAVID

LEARY, LEWIS. *Articles on American Literature, 1900–1950.* Durham: Duke Univ. Press, 1954, 30.

BRYAN, DANIEL

HUBBELL, JAY B. *The South in American Literature, 1607–1900.* Durham: Duke Univ. Press, 1954, 918–919.

LEARY, LEWIS. *Articles on American Literature, 1900–1950.* Durham: Duke Univ. Press, 1954, 30.

BRYANT, WILLIAM CULLEN

ARNOLD, W. H. *First Editions of Bryant, Emerson, Hawthorne, Holmes, Longfellow, Lowell, Thoreau, Whittier.* Jamaica, New York: Marion Press, 1901, varying pagination.

1,200 copies printed.

BLANCK, JACOB. *Bibliography of American Literature,* 5 Vols. New Haven: Yale Univ. Press, 1955–1969, I, 331–384.

_____, ed. *Merle Johnson's American First Editions,* 4th edition, revised and enlarged. Waltham, Massachusetts: Mark Press, 1965, 67–70.

CLARK, HARRY HAYDEN, ed. *Major American Poets.* New York: American Book Co., 1936, 788–792.

HERRICK, A. H. "Chronology of a Group of Poems by W. C. Bryant." *MLN,* XXXII (March 1917), 180–182.

LEARY, LEWIS. *Articles on American Literature, 1900–1950.* Durham: Duke Univ. Press, 1954, 30–32.

McDOWELL, TREMAINE, ed. *William Cullen Bryant: Representative Selections,* with introduction, bibliography and notes. New York: American Book Co., 1935, lxxiii–lxxxii.

SHIPMAN, C. "The Principal Editions of Bryant's Works (1808–1847)." *Bibliographer,* II (1903), 388–399.

SPILLER, ROBERT ERNEST, et al. *Literary History of the United States,* 2 Vols. New York: Macmillan, 1962, 422–427. Supplement, 86–87.

SPIVEY, HERMAN E. "Manuscript Resources for the Study of William Cullen Bryant." *PBSA,* LXIV (3rd Quart. 1950), 254—268.

TAYLOR, WALTER FULLER. *A History of American Letters,* with bibliographies by Harry Hartwick. Boston: American Book Co., 1936, 499—501.

Subsequent editions entitled: *The Story of American Letters.*

TRENT, WILLIAM PETERFIELD, et al. *Cambridge History of American Literature,* 4 Vols. New York: G. P. Putnam's Sons, 1917—1921, I, 517—525.

VOSS, THOMAS H. *William Cullen Bryant: An Annotated Checklist of the Exhibit Held in the Mullen Library of the Catholic University of America, October 30—November 10, 1967.* Washington: Mullen Library, 1967, 18 pp.

WAKEMAN, STEPHEN H. *The Stephen H. Wakeman Collection of Books of Nineteenth Century American Writers: The Property of Mrs. Alice L. Wakeman, First Editions, Inscribed Presentation and Personal Copies, Original Manuscripts and Letters of Nine American Authors.* New York: American Art Association, 1924, Items 1—155.

WOODRESS, JAMES, et al. *American Literary Scholarship: An Annual.* Durham: Duke Univ. Press, (1964), 126—130; (1965), 149—153; (1966), 136—139.

BULFINCH, THOMAS

LEARY, LEWIS. *Articles on American Literature, 1900—1950.* Durham: Duke Univ. Press, 1954, 32.

BUNNER, HENRY CUYLER

BLANCK, JACOB. *Bibliography of American Literature,* 5 Vols. New Haven: Yale Univ. Press, 1955—1969, I, 385—399.

_____, ed. *Merle Johnson's American First Editions,* 4th edition, revised and enlarged. Waltham, Massachusetts: Mark Press, 1965, 73—75.

LEARY, LEWIS. *Articles on American Literature, 1900—1950.* Durham: Duke Univ. Press, 1954, 32.

TRENT, WILLIAM PETERFIELD, et al. *Cambridge History of American Literature,* 4 Vols. New York: G. P. Putnam's Sons, 1917—1921, II, 544, 619.

BURDETTE, ROBERT JONES

BLANCK, JACOB. *Bibliography of American Literature,* 5 Vols. New Haven: Yale Univ. Press, 1955— 1969, I, 400—412.

BURRITT, ELIHU

LEARY, LEWIS. *Articles on American Literature, 1900—1950.* Durham: Duke Univ. Press, 1954, 33.

BURROUGHS, JOHN

BLANCK, JACOB. *Bibliography of American Literature,* 5 Vols. New Haven: Yale Univ. Press, 1955—1969, I, 433—448.

_____, ed. *Merle Johnson's American First Editions,* 4th edition, revised and enlarged. Waltham, Massachusetts: Mark Press, 1965, 79—81.

LEARY, LEWIS. *Articles on American Literature, 1900—1950.* Durham: Duke Univ. Press, 1954, 33—34.

SPILLER, ROBERT ERNEST, et al. *Literary History of the United States,* 2 Vols. New York: Macmillan, 1962, 427–428. Supplement, 87–88.

BUSHNELL, HORACE

LEARNED, H. B. *Horace Bushnell, The Spirit in Man: Sermons and Selections,* Centenary edition. New York: Scribner, 1903, 445–473.

LEARY, LEWIS. *Articles on American Literature, 1900–1950.* Durham: Duke Univ. Press, 1954, 34.

BUTLER, WILLIAM HOWARD ALLEN

BLANCK, JACOB. *Bibliography of American Literature,* 5 Vols. New Haven: Yale Univ. Press, 1955–1969, I, 449–459.

LEARY, LEWIS. *Articles on American Literature, 1900–1950.* Durham: Duke Univ. Press, 1954, 34.

BUTTERWORTH, HEZEKIAH

LEARY, LEWIS. *Articles on American Literature, 1900–1950.* Durham: Duke Univ. Press, 1954, 34.

CABLE, GEORGE WASHINGTON

BIKLE, LUCY LEFFINGWELL (CABLE), ed. *George W. Cable: His Life and Letters.* New York: C. Scribner's Sons, 1928, 303–306.

BLANCK, JACOB. *Bibliography of American Literature,* 5 Vols. New Haven: Yale Univ. Press, 1955–1969, II, 1–14.

——————, ed. *Merle Johnson's American First Editions,* 4th edition, revised and enlarged. Waltham, Massachusetts: Mark Press, 1965, 92–93.

GERSTENBERGER, DONNA, and GEORGE HENDRICK. *The American Novel, 1789–1959: A Checklist of Twentieth Century Criticism.* Denver: Alan Swallow, 1961, 28–29.

HUBBELL, JAY B. *The South in American Literature, 1607–1900.* Durham: Duke Univ. Press, 1954, 921–922.

LEARY, LEWIS. *Articles on American Literature, 1900–1950.* Durham: Duke Univ. Press, 1954, 36–37.

PAINE, GREGORY LANSING, ed. *Southern Prose Writers: Representative Selections,* with introduction, bibliography and notes. New York: American Book Co., 1947, cxxvii–cxxviii.

SPILLER, ROBERT ERNEST, et al. *Literary History of the United States,* 2 Vols. New York: Macmillan, 1962, 433–434. Supplement, 89–90.

TAYLOR, WALTER FULLER. *A History of American Letters,* with bibliographies by Harry Hartwick. Boston: American Book Co., 1936, 543–544.

Subsequent editions entitled: *The Story of American Letters.*

TRENT, WILLIAM PETERFIELD, et al. *Cambridge History of American Literature,* 4 Vols. New York: G. P. Putnam's Sons, 1917–1921, II, 619.

CALHOUN, JOHN CALDWELL

HUBBELL, JAY B. *The South in American Literature, 1607–1900.* Durham: Duke Univ. Press, 1954, 922–923.

PAINE, GREGORY LANSING, ed. *Southern Prose Writers: Representative Selections,* with introduction, bibliography and notes. New York: American Book Co., 1947, cxxix.

SPILLER, ROBERT ERNEST, et al. *Literary History of the United States,* 2 Vols. New York: Macmillan, 1962, 435—436. Supplement, 90—91.

TRENT, WILLIAM PETERFIELD, et al. *Cambridge History of American Literature,* 4 Vols. New York: G. P. Putnam's Sons, 1917—1921, II, 470.

WILTSE, CHARLES MAURICE. *John C. Calhoun, Nationalist, 1782—1828.* Indianapolis: Bobbs-Merrill Co., 1944, 443—453.

CALVERT, GEORGE HENRY

BLANCK, JACOB. *Bibliography of American Literature,* 5 Vols. New Haven: Yale Univ. Press, 1955—1969, II, 15—24.

LEARY, LEWIS. *Articles on American Literature, 1900—1950.* Durham: Duke Univ. Press, 1954, 38.

TOMPKINS, HAMILTON BULLOCK. *Bibliography of the Works of George Henry Calvert.* Newport, Rhode Island: privately printed, 1900, 15 pp.

30 copies printed.

CAMPBELL, BARTLEY

LEARY, LEWIS. *Articles on American Literature, 1900—1950.* Durham: Duke Univ. Press, 1954, 38.

CAREY, MATTHEW

BRADSHER, EARL LOCKRIDGE. *Mathew Carey, Editor, Author and Publisher: A Study in American Literary Development.* New York:

Columbia Univ. Press, 1912, 136—139.

Columbia Univ. Studies In English.

LEARY, LEWIS. *Articles on American Literature, 1900—1950.* Durham: Duke Univ. Press, 1954, 38.

CARITAT, HOCQUET

LEARY, LEWIS. *Articles on American Literature, 1900—1950.* Durham: Duke Univ. Press, 1954, 38.

CARLETON, WILL

LEARY, LEWIS. *Articles on American Literature, 1900—1950.* Durham: Duke Univ. Press, 1954, 38.

WOODRESS, JAMES, et al. *American Literary Scholarship: An Annual.* Durham: Duke Univ. Press, (1964), 126—130.

CARLETON, WILLIAM McKENDREE

BLANCK, JACOB. *Bibliography of American Literature,* 5 Vols. New Haven: Yale Univ. Press, 1955—1969, II, 25—41.

CARMAN, BLISS

BLANCK, JACOB. *Bibliography of American Literature,* 5 Vols. New Haven: Yale Univ. Press, 1955—1969, II, 42—76.

——————, ed. *Merle Johnson's American First Editions,* 4th edition, revised and enlarged. Waltham, Massachusetts: Mark Press, 1965, 96—102.

LEARY, LEWIS. *Articles on American Literature, 1900—1950.* Durham: Duke Univ. Press, 1954, 38.

MORSE, WILLIAM INGLIS. *Bliss Carman: Bibliography, Letters, Fugitive Verses, and Other Data.* Windham, Connecticut: Hawthorn House, 1941, 86 pp.

SHEPARD, ODELL. *Bliss Carman.* Toronto: McClelland and Stewart, 1923, 171–184.

A checklist of first editions of the works of Bliss Carman, compiled by Frederic F. Sherman, with revisions and additions by R. H. Hathaway.

SHERMAN, FREDERIC FAIRCHILD. *A Check List of First Editions of the Works of Bliss Carman.* New York: privately printed, 1915, 16 pp.

CARRYL, GUY WETMORE

BLANCK, JACOB. *Bibliography of American Literature,* 5 Vols. New Haven: Yale Univ. Press, 1955–1969, II, 77–80.

CARUTHERS, WILLIAM ALEXANDER

BLANCK, JACOB. *Bibliography of American Literature,* 5 Vols. New Haven: Yale Univ. Press, 1955–1969, II, 81–82.

DAVIS, CURTIS CARROLL. *Chronicler of the Cavaliers: A Life of the Virginia Novelist, Dr. William A. Caruthers.* Richmond: Dietz Press, 1953, 521–547.

GERSTENBERGER, DONNA, and GEORGE HENDRICK. *The American Novel, 1789–1959: A Checklist of Twentieth Century Criticism.* Denver: Alan Swallow, 1961, 31.

HUBBELL, JAY B. *The South in American Literature, 1607–1900.*

Durham: Duke Univ. Press, 1954, 923–924.

LEARY, LEWIS. *Articles on American Literature, 1900–1950.* Durham: Duke Univ. Press, 1954, 39.

TRENT, WILLIAM PETERFIELD, et al. *Cambridge History of American Literature,* 4 Vols. New York: G. P. Putnam's Sons, 1917–1921, I, 529.

CARY, ALICE

BLANCK, JACOB. *Bibliography of American Literature,* 5 Vols. New Haven: Yale Univ. Press, 1955–1969, II, 83–96.

CARY, PHOEBE

BLANCK, JACOB. *Bibliography of American Literature,* 5 Vols. New Haven: Yale Univ. Press, 1955–1969, II, 97–106.

CATHERWOOD, MARY HARTWELL

BLANCK, JACOB. *Bibliography of American Literature,* 5 Vols. New Haven: Yale Univ. Press, 1955–1969, II, 107–116.

GERSTENBERGER, DONNA, and GEORGE HENDRICK. *The American Novel, 1789–1959: A Checklist of Twentieth Century Criticism.* Denver: Alan Swallow, 1961, 36.

LEARY, LEWIS. *Articles on American Literature, 1900–1950.* Durham: Duke Univ. Press, 1954, 40–41.

PRICE, ROBERT. "Mary Hartwell Catherwood: A Bibliography." *Journal of the Illinois State Historical Society,* XXXIII (March 1940), 68–77.

CATLIN, GEORGE

MINER, WILLIAM HARVEY. "Bibliography of Catlin's Works." *Proceedings and Collections of the Wyoming Historical and Geological Society,* XXI (1927–1929), 83–97.

CAWEIN, MADISON JULIUS

BLANCK, JACOB. *Bibliography of American Literature,* 5 Vols. New Haven: Yale Univ. Press, 1955–1969, II, 117–128.

LEARY, LEWIS. *Articles on American Literature, 1900–1950.* Durham: Duke Univ. Press, 1954, 41.

CHAMBERS, ROBERT WILLIAM

GERSTENBERGER, DONNA, and GEORGE HENDRICK. *The American Novel, 1789–1959: A Checklist of Twentieth Century Criticism.* Denver: Alan Swallow, 1961, 36.

HORNBERGER, THEODORE. "American First Editions at Texas University: Robert William Chambers (1865–1933)." *LCUT,* II (Spring 1947), 193–195.

LEARY, LEWIS. *Articles on American Literature, 1900–1950.* Durham: Duke Univ. Press, 1954, 41.

CHANDLER, ELIZABETH MARGARET

LEARY, LEWIS. *Articles on American Literature, 1900–1950.* Durham: Duke Univ. Press, 1954, 41.

CHANNING, WILLIAM ELLERY (1780-1842)

FOSTER, W. E. "Reference List on William Ellery Channing." *LJ,* V (April 1880), 112.

LEARY, LEWIS. *Articles on American Literature, 1900–1950.* Durham: Duke Univ. Press, 1954, 41.

SPILLER, ROBERT ERNEST, et al. *Literary History of the United States,* 2 Vols. New York: Macmillan, 1962, 438–439. Supplement, 92–93.

TRENT, WILLIAM PETERFIELD, et al. *Cambridge History of American Literature,* 4 Vols. New York: G. P. Putnam's Sons, 1917–1921, I, 547–548.

CHANNING, WILLIAM ELLERY (1818-1901)

BLANCK, JACOB. *Bibliography of American Literature,* 5 Vols. New Haven: Yale Univ. Press, 1955–1969. II, 129–133.

LEARY, LEWIS. *Articles on American Literature, 1900–1950.* Durham: Duke Univ. Press, 1954, 41–42.

McGILL, FREDERICK T. *Channing of Concord: A Life of William Ellery Channing II.* New Brunswick: Rutgers Univ. Press, 1967, 209–214.

CHEEVER, GEORGE BARRELL

LEARY, LEWIS. *Articles on American Literature, 1900–1950.* Durham: Duke Univ. Press, 1954, 42.

CHILD, FRANCIS JAMES

LEARY, LEWIS. *Articles on American Literature, 1900–1950.* Durham: Duke Univ. Press, 1954, 42.

CHILD, LYDIA MARIA FRANCIS

BLANCK, JACOB. *Bibliography of American Literature,* 5 Vols. New Haven: Yale Univ. Press, 1955–1969, II, 134–156.

GERSTENBERGER, DONNA, and GEORGE HENDRICK. *The American Novel, 1789–1959: A Checklist of Twentieth Century Criticism.* Denver: Alan Swallow, 1961, 37.

LEARY, LEWIS. *Articles on American Literature, 1900–1950.* Durham: Duke Univ. Press, 1954, 42.

TRENT, WILLIAM PETERFIELD, et al. *Cambridge History of American Literature,* 4 Vols. New York: G. P. Putnam's Sons, 1917–1921, I, 529.

WHITTIER, JOHN GREENLEAF, ed. *Letters of Lydia Maria Child,* with a biographical introduction by John G. Whittier and an appendix by Wendell Phillips. Boston: Houghton Mifflin, 1883, 280 pp.

CHIVERS, THOMAS HOLLEY

BLANCK, JACOB. *Bibliography of American Literature,* 5 Vols. New Haven: Yale Univ. Press, 1955–1969, II, 157–159.

_____, ed. *Merle Johnson's American First Editions,* 4th edition, revised and enlarged. Waltham, Massachusetts: Mark Press, 1965, 107.

DAMON, SAMUEL FOSTER. *Thomas Holley Chivers: Friend of Poe,* with selections from his poems. New York: Harper and Brothers, 1930, 283–288.

HUBBELL, JAY B. *The South in American Literature, 1607–1900.* Durham: Duke Univ. Press, 1954, 924.

LEARY, LEWIS. *Articles on American Literature, 1900–1950.* Durham: Duke Univ. Press, 1954, 42–43.

SPILLER, ROBERT ERNEST, et al. *Literary History of the United States,* 2 Vols. New York: Macmillan, 1962, 440–441. Supplement, 93.

WOODRESS, JAMES, et al. *American Literary Scholarship: An Annual.* Durham: Duke Univ. Press, (1964), 136–138.

CHOATE, RUFUS

TRENT, WILLIAM PETERFIELD, et al. *Cambridge History of American Literature,* 4 Vols. New York: G. P. Putnam's Sons, 1917–1921, II, 470.

CHOPIN, KATE (KATHERINE) O'FLAHERTY

BLANCK, JACOB. *Bibliography of American Literature,* 5 Vols. New Haven: Yale Univ. Press, 1955–1969, II, 160–161.

GERSTENBERGER, DONNA, and GEORGE HENDRICK. *The American Novel, 1789–1959: A Checklist of Twentieth Century Criticism.* Denver: Alan Swallow, 1961, 37.

LEARY, LEWIS. *Articles on American Literature, 1900–1950.* Durham: Duke Univ. Press, 1954, 43.

RANKIN, DANIEL S. *Kate Chopin and Her Creole Stories.* Philadelphia: Univ. of Pennsylvania Press, 1932, 318 pp.

TRENT, WILLIAM PETERFIELD, et al. *Cambridge History of American Literature,* 4 Vols. New York: G. P. Putnam's Sons, 1917–1921, II, 619.

CLARK, LEWIS GAYLORD

TAFT, KENDALL B., ed. *Minor Knickerbockers: Representative Selections,* with introduction, bibliography and notes. New York: American Book., 1947, cxxix–cxxx.

TRENT, WILLIAM PETERFIELD, et al. *Cambridge History of American Literature,* 4 Vols. New York: G. P. Putnam's Sons, 1917–1921, II, 504.

CLARK, WILLIS GAYLORD

BLANCK, JACOB. *Bibliography of American Literature,* 5 Vols. New Haven: Yale Univ. Press, 1955–1969, II, 162–168.

LEARY, LEWIS. *Articles on American Literature, 1900–1950.* Durham: Duke Univ. Press, 1954, 43.

TAFT, KENDALL B., ed. *Minor Knickerbockers: Representative Selections,* with introduction, bibliography and notes. New York: American Book Co., 1947, cxxx.

CLARKE, JAMES FREEMAN

LEARY, LEWIS. *Articles on American Literature, 1900–1950.* Durham: Duke Univ. Press, 1954, 43.

CLARKE, McDONALD

BLANCK, JACOB. *Bibliography of American Literature,* 5 Vols. New Haven: Yale Univ. Press, 1955–1969, II, 169–172.

TAFT, KENDALL B., ed. *Minor Knickerbockers: Representative Selections,* with introduction, bibliography and notes. New York: American Book Co., 1947, cxxx–cxxxi.

WOODRESS, JAMES, et al. *American Literary Scholarship: An Annual.* Durham: Duke Univ. Press, (1964), 126–130.

CLAY, HENRY

BRIGANCE, WILLIAM NORWOOD, ed. *A History and Criticism of American Public Address,* 3 Vols. New York: McGraw-Hill, 1943, II, 635–638.

MAYO, BERNARD. *Henry Clay: Spokesman of the New West.* Boston: Houghton Mifflin, 1937, 527–548.

POAGE, GEORGE RAWLINGS. *Henry Clay and the Whig Party.* Chapel Hill: Univ. of North Carolina Press, 1936, 279–283.

SPILLER, ROBERT ERNEST, et al. *Literary History of the United States,* 2 Vols. New York: Macmillan, 1962, 441–442. Supplement, 93–94.

TRENT, WILLIAM PETERFIELD, et al. *Cambridge History of American Literature,* 4 Vols. New York: G. P. Putnam's Sons, 1917–1921, II, 471.

CLEMENS, SAMUEL L. (MARK TWAIN)

ANDERSON, FREDERICK. "Twain Papers: A Fount of Biographical Studies." *Manuscripts,* XI (Fall 1959), 14–15.

ASSELINEAU, ROGER. *The Literary Reputation of Mark Twain from 1910 to 1950: A Critical Essay and a Bibliography.* Paris: Didier, 1954, 67–226.

BALDANZA, FRANK. *Mark Twain: An Introduction and Interpretation.* New York, 1967, 141–146.

Part of the *American Authors and Critics Series,* begun in 1961, and purchased by Holt, Rinehart and Winston from Barnes and Noble. The nine original and three new volumes were issued under the Holt imprint in January 1967.

BELLAMY, GLADYS CARMEN. *Mark Twain as a Literary Artist.* Norman: Univ. of Oklahoma Press, 1950, 337–382.

BENSON, IVAN. *Mark Twain's Western Years.* Palo Alto: Stanford Univ. Press, 1938, 165–174.

Bibliography of Mark Twain's contributions to Nevada and California newspapers and magazines, 1861–1866.

BLANCK, JACOB. *Bibliography of American Literature,* 5 Vols. New Haven: Yale Univ. Press, 1955–1969, II, 173–254.

_____. "In Re *Huckleberry Finn.*" *The New Colophon,* III (1950), 153–159.

_____, ed. *Merle Johnson's American First Editions,* 4th edition, revised and enlarged. Waltham, Massachusetts: Mark Press, 1965, 110–115.

BLISS, WALTER. *Twainiana Notes from the Annotations of Walter Bliss,* edited by Frances M. Edwards. Hartford: The Hobby Shop, 1930, 24 pp.

BRANCH, EDGAR M. "A Chronological Bibliography of the Writings of Samuel Clemens to June 8, 1867." *AL,* XVIII (May 1946), 104–159.

BRASHEAR, MINNIE MAY. *Mark Twain: Son of Missouri.* Chapel Hill: Univ. of North Carolina Press, 1934, 264–284.

_____. "Mark Twain's Juvenilia." *AL,* II (March 1930), 25–53.

BRASHEAR, MINNIE MAY, and ROBERT M. RODNEY, eds. *The Art, Humor, and Humanity of Mark Twain,* with an introduction by Edward Wagenknecht. Norman: Univ. of Oklahoma Press, 1959, 411–417, bibliographical footnotes.

BROWNELL, GEORGE HIRAM. "About Twain in Periodicals." *Twainian,* I (October 1939), 4–5.

BUFFALO PUBLIC LIBRARY. Huckleberry Finn: *A Descriptive Bibliography of the* Huckleberry Finn *Collection at the Buffalo Public Library,* compiled by Lucile Adams. Buffalo: Buffalo Public Library, 1950, 39 pp.

CONSIGIO, CARLA. "Nota bibliografica su la fortuna di Mark Twain in Italia." *SA,* IV (1958), 198–208.

DE VOTO, BERNARD. *Mark Twain's America.* Boston: Little, Brown and Co., 1932, 323–334.

DODD AND LIVINGSTON. *Mark Twain: Autograph Manuscripts and First Editions.* New York: Dodd and Livingston, 1911, 14 pp.

FONER, PHILIP SHELDON. *Mark Twain: Social Critic.* New York: International Publishers, 1958, 323–330.

GERSTENBERGER, DONNA, and GEORGE HENDRICK. *The American Novel, 1789–1959: A Checklist of Twentieth Century Criticism.* Denver: Alan Swallow, 1961, 236–250.

HEMMINGHAUS, EDGAR HUGO. *Mark Twain in Germany.* New York: Columbia Univ. Press, 1939, 147–164.

Covers 1874–1937. Extensive bibliography.

HENDERSON, ARCHIBALD. *Mark Twain.* London: Duckworth, 1911, 215–230.

Bibliography of writings on Mark Twain, September 1869 – September 1910.

HUBBELL, JAY B. *The South in American Literature, 1607–1900.* Durham: Duke Univ. Press, 1954, 924–925.

JOHNSON, MERLE DE VORE. *A Bibliography of the Works of Mark Twain, Samuel Langhorne Clemens: A List of First Editions in Book Form and of First Printings in Periodicals and Occasional Publications of His Various Literary Activities,* revised edition. New York and London: Harper and Brothers, 1935, 287 pp.

——————. *Catalogue of First and Other Editions of the Writings of Mark Twain, Samuel Langhorne Clemens, and of Lafcadio Hearn.* New York: American Art Association, 1914, no pagination.

LEARY, LEWIS. *Articles on American Literature, 1900–1950.* Durham: Duke Univ. Press, 1954, 43–55.

LIBRARY OF CONGRESS, DIVISION OF BIBLIOGRAPHY. *List of Writings by Mark Twain Translated into Certain Foreign Languages.* Washington, 1939, 14 leaves.

LIVINGSTON, LUTHER SAMUEL. *The Works of Mark Twain (Samuel Langhorne Clemens): The Description of a Set of First Editions of His Books.* New York: Dodd and Livingston, 1911, 3–63.

75 copies printed.

LONG, EUGENE HUDSON. *Mark Twain Handbook.* New York: Hendricks House, 1958, 454 pp.

LORCH, FRED. "Mark Twain's Early Nevada Letters." *AL,* (January 1939), 486–488.

MARTIN, MRS. ALMA BORTH. *A Vocabulary Study of* The Gilded Age. Webster Groves, Missouri: Mark Twain Society, 1930, 52–54.

MOBLEY, LAWRENCE E. "Mark Twain and the *Golden Era.*" *PBSA,* LVIII (1st Quart. 1964), 8–23.

MORSE, WILLARD SAMUEL. *A Check List of the Mark Twain Collection Assembled by the Late Willard S. Morse,* prepared by Ellen K. Shaffer and Lucille S. J. Hall. Los Angeles: offered for sale by Dawson's Book Shop, 1942, 92 leaves.

Collection given to Yale Univ. Library.

PAINE, ALBERT BIGELOW. *Mark Twain: A Biography.* New York: Harper and Brothers, 1912, 1674–1684.

Also: 1935.

PATTEE, FRED LEWIS, ed. *Mark Twain: Representative Selections,* with introduction, bibliography and notes. New York: American Book Co., 1935, liii–lxi.

"Recent Acquisitions." *PULC,* XII (Summer 1951), 217–218.

Announces the acquisition of the Thomas L. Leeming Collection of Mark Twain, consisting of the manuscript of *The $1,000,000 Bank Note* and choice first editions.

SCOTT, ARTHUR LINCOLN, ed. *Mark Twain: Selected Criticism.* Dallas: Southern Methodist Univ. Press, 1967, 286–289, bibliographical footnotes.

SMITH, HENRY NASH, ed. *Mark Twain: A Collection of Critical Essays.* Englewood Cliffs, New Jersey: Prentice Hall, 1963, 179.

——————. *Mark Twain: The Development of a Writer.* Cambridge: Belknap Press of Harvard Univ. Press, 1962, 189–208.

——————, ed. *Mark Twain of* the Enterprise: *Newspaper Articles and Other Documents, 1862–1864.* Berkeley: Univ. of California Press, 1957, 209–234.

——————. *Mark Twain's Fable of Progress: Political and Economic Ideas in* A Connecticut Yankee. New Brunswick, New Jersey: Rutgers Univ. Press, 1964, 109–116.

SMITH, HENRY NASH, and WILLIAM McGIBSON, eds. *Mark Twain–Howells' Letters: The Correspondence of Samuel L. Clemens and William D. Howells, 1872–1910,* 2 Vols. Cambridge: Harvard Univ. Press, 1960, I, xxi–xxv.

SPILLER, ROBERT ERNEST, et al. *Literary History of the United States,* 2 Vols. New York: Macmillan, 1962, 442–450. Supplement, 94–97.

STOVALL, FLOYD, et al. *Eight American Authors: A Review of Research and Criticism.* New York: W. W. Norton and Co., 1963, 319–363, 451–458.

TAYLOR, WALTER FULLER. *A History of American Letters,* with bibliographies by Harry Hartwick. Boston: American Book Co., 1936, 545–549.

Subsequent editions entitled: *The Story of American Letters.*

TRENT, WILLIAM PETERFIELD, et al. *Cambridge History of Ameri-*

can Literature, 4 Vols. New York: G. P. Putnam's Sons, 1917–1921, IV, 635–639.

TROXELL, GILBERT McCOY. "Samuel Langhorne Clemens, 1835–1910." *YULG,* XVIII (July 1943), 1–5.

WAGENKNECHT, EDWARD CHARLES. *Mark Twain: The Man and His Work.* New Haven: Yale Univ. Press, 1935, 279–290.

WECTER, DIXON. *Sam Clemens of Hannibal.* Boston: Houghton Mifflin Co., 1952, 317–322.

WOODRESS, JAMES, et al. *American Literary Scholarship: An Annual.* Durham: Duke Univ. Press, (1963), 53–63; (1964), 50–61; (1965), 57–68; (1966), 48–64.

COBB, JOSEPH B.

HUBBELL, JAY B. *The South in American Literature, 1607–1900.* Durham: Duke Univ. Press, 1954, 925.

LEARY, LEWIS. *Articles on American Literature, 1900–1950.* Durham: Duke Univ. Press, 1954, 55.

COLWELL, STEPHEN

CAREY, HENRY CHARLES. *A Memoir of Stephen Colwell.* Philadelphia: H. C. Baird, 1872, 33–35.

CONWAY, MONCURE DANIEL

HUBBELL, JAY B. *The South in American Literature, 1607–1900.* Durham: Duke Univ. Press, 1954, 925–926.

LEARY, LEWIS. *Articles on American Literature, 1900–1950.* Durham: Duke Univ. Press, 1954, 56.

COOKE, JOHN ESTEN

BEATY, JOHN OWEN. *John Esten Cooke, Virginian.* New York: Columbia Univ. Press, 1922, 164–168.

BLANCK, JACOB. *Bibliography of American Literature,* 5 Vols. New Haven: Yale Univ. Press, 1955–1969, II, 255–265.

_____, ed. *Merle Johnson's American First Editions,* 4th edition, revised and enlarged. Waltham, Massachusetts: Mark Press, 1965, 121–122.

GERSTENBERGER, DONNA, and GEORGE HENDRICK. *The American Novel, 1789–1959: A Checklist of Twentieth Century Criticism.* Denver: Alan Swallow, 1961, 39.

HUBBELL, JAY B. *The South in American Literature, 1607–1900.* Durham: Duke Univ. Press, 1954, 926–927.

LEARY, LEWIS. *Articles on American Literature, 1900–1950.* Durham: Duke Univ. Press, 1954, 56.

PAINE, GREGORY LANSING, ed. *Southern Prose Writers: Representative Selections,* with introduction, bibliography and notes. New York: American Book Co., 1947, cxxix–cxxx.

WEGELIN, OSCAR. "A Bibliography of the Separate Writings of John Esten Cooke." *AC,* I (December 1925), 96–99.

Also: Metuchen, New Jersey: printed for Charles F. Heartman, 1925, 20 pp.

COOKE, PHILIP PENDLETON

ALLEN, JOHN DANIEL. *Philip Pendleton Cooke.* Chapel Hill: Univ. of North Carolina Press, 1942, 106–120.

HUBBELL, JAY B. *The South in American Literature, 1607–1900.* Durham: Duke Univ. Press, 1954, 927.

LEARY, LEWIS. *Articles on American Literature, 1900–1950.* Durham: Duke Univ. Press, 1954, 56.

COOKE, ROSE TERRY

BLANCK, JACOB. *Bibliography of American Literature,* 5 Vols. New Haven: Yale Univ. Press, 1955–1969, II, 266–275.

DOWNEY, JEAN. "Rose Terry Cooke: A Bibliography." *BB,* XXI (May–August 1955), 159–163; (September–December 1955), 191–192.

GERSTENBERGER, DONNA, and GEORGE HENDRICK. *The American Novel, 1789–1959: A Checklist of Twentieth Century Criticism.* Denver: Alan Swallow, 1961, 39.

LEARY, LEWIS. *Articles on American Literature, 1900–1950.* Durham: Duke Univ. Press, 1954, 56.

TRENT, WILLIAM PETERFIELD, et al. *Cambridge History of American Literature,* 4 Vols. New York: G. P. Putnam's Sons, 1917–1921, II, 619–620.

COOLBRITH, INA

LEARY, LEWIS. *Articles on American Literature, 1900–1950.* Durham: Duke Univ. Press, 1954, 56.

COOPER, JAMES FENIMORE

BARBA, PRESTON ALBERT. *Cooper in Germany.* Bloomington:

Univ. of Indiana Press, 1914, 93—104.

German translations of Cooper's works.

BLANCK, JACOB. *Bibliography of American Literature*, 5 Vols. New Haven: Yale Univ. Press, 1955—1969, II, 276—310.

_____. "The Bibliography of American Literature: James Fenimore Cooper." *PW*, CLI (Feb. 1, 1947), B83—B84.

Bibliographical notes on *The Heidenmauer* and *Home as Found*.

_____ed, *Merle Johnson's American First Editions*, 4th edition, revised and enlarged. Waltham, Massachusetts: Mark Press, 1965, 123—127.

BROOKS, VAN WYCK. *The Dream of Arcadia: American Writers and Artists in Italy, 1760—1915.* New York: Dutton, 1958, bibliographical footnotes.

CLYMER, WILLIAM BRANFORD SHUBRICK. *James Fenimore Cooper.* Boston: Small, Maynard and Co., 1900, 146—149.

COLUMBIA UNIVERSITY, LIBRARY. *An Exhibition of First Editions of James Fenimore Cooper, Gift of Leonard Kebler.* New York: Columbia Univ. Library, 1946, 5 pp.

COOPER, JAMES FENIMORE. *Satanstoe*, with introduction, chronology and bibliography by Robert E. Spiller and Joseph D. Coppock. New York: American Book Co., 1937, xxxiii—xli.

DEKKER, GEORGE. *James Fenimore Cooper: The American Scott.* New York: Barnes and Noble, 1967, bibliographical footnotes.

Also: *James Fenimore Cooper: The Novelist.* London: Routledge and K. Paul.

GERSTENBERGER, DONNA, and GEORGE HENDRICK. *The American Novel, 1789—1959: A Checklist of Twentieth Century Criticism.* Denver: Alan Swallow, 1961, 40—47.

LEARY, LEWIS. *Articles on American Literature, 1900—1950.* Durham: Duke Univ. Press, 1954, 56—59.

LOUNSBURY, THOMAS RAYNESFORD. *James Fenimore Cooper.* Boston: Houghton, 1883, 290—299.

NEW YORK STATE HISTORICAL ASSOCIATION. "James Fenimore Cooper Centennial Exhibition." *NYH*, XXXII (October 1951), 474—487.

SPILLER, ROBERT ERNEST, ed. *James Fenimore Cooper: Representative Selections*, with introduction, bibliography and notes. New York: American Book Co., 1936, lxxxix—cii.

SPILLER, ROBERT ERNEST, and PHILLIP C. BLACKBURN, comps. *A Descriptive Bibliography of the Writings of James Fenimore Cooper.* New York: R. R. Bowker Co., 1934, 268 pp.

500 copies printed.

SPILLER, ROBERT ERNEST, et al. *Literary History of the United States*, 2 Vols. New York: Macmillan, 1962, 450—455. Supplement, 97—98.

TAYLOR, WALTER FULLER. *A History of American Letters*, with bibliographies by Harry Hartwick. Boston: American Book Co., 1936, 495—499.

Subsequent editions entitled: *The Story of American Letters.*

TRENT, WILLIAM PETERFIELD, et al. *Cambridge History of American Literature,* 4 Vols. New York: G. P. Putnam's Sons, 1917–1921, I, 530–534.

WALKER, WARREN S. *James Fenimore Cooper: An Introduction and Interpretation.* New York, 1967, 127–133.

Part of the *American Authors and Critics Series,* begun in 1961, and purchased by Holt, Rinehart and Winston from Barnes and Noble. The nine original and three new volumes were issued under the Holt imprint in January 1967.

WOODRESS, JAMES, et al. *American Literary Scholarship: An Annual.* Durham: Duke Univ. Press, (1963), 110–112; (1964), 111–113; (1965), 129–133; (1966), 115–118.

COOPER, SUSAN AUGUSTA FENIMORE

BLANCK, JACOB. *Bibliography of American Literature,* 5 Vols. New Haven: Yale Univ. Press, 1955–1969, II, 311–315.

LEARY, LEWIS. *Articles on American Literature, 1900–1950.* Durham: Duke Univ. Press, 1954, 59.

COTTER, JOSEPH S.

LEARY, LEWIS. *Articles on American Literature, 1900–1950.* Durham: Duke Univ. Press, 1954, 59.

COTTLE, ELDER JABEZ

WOODRESS, JAMES, et al. *American Literary Scholarship: An Annual.* Durham: Duke Univ. Press, (1965), 149–153.

COX, WILLIAM

LEARY, LEWIS. *Articles on American Literature, 1900–1950.* Durham: Duke Univ. Press, 1954, 60.

TAFT, KENDALL B., ed. *Minor Knickerbockers: Representative Selections,* with introduction, bibliography and notes. New York: American Book Co., 1947, cxxxi.

TRENT, WILLIAM PETERFIELD, et al. *Cambridge History of American Literature,* 4 Vols. New York: G. P. Putnam's Sons, 1917–1921, II, 504.

COZZENS, FREDERIC SWARTOUT

BLANCK, JACOB. *Bibliography of American Literature,* 5 Vols. New Haven: Yale Univ. Press, 1955–1969, II, 316–319.

TRENT, WILLIAM PETERFIELD, et al. *Cambridge History of American Literature,* 4 Vols. New York: G. P. Putnam's Sons, 1917–1921, II, 504–505.

CRADDOCK, CHARLES EGBERT, (see MURFREE)

CRAFTS, WILLIAM

HUBBELL, JAY B. *The South in American Literature, 1607–1900.* Durham: Duke Univ. Press, 1954, 929.

CRANCH, CHRISTOPHER PEARSE

BLANCK, JACOB. *Bibliography of American Literature,* 5 Vols. New Haven: Yale Univ. Press, 1955–1969, II, 320–328.

LEARY, LEWIS. *Articles on American Literature, 1900–1950.* Durham: Duke Univ. Press, 1954, 60.

CRANE, STEPHEN

AHNEBRINK, LARS. *The Beginnings of Naturalism in American Fiction: A Study of the Works of Hamlin Garland, Stephen Crane, and Frank Norris, with Special Reference to Some European Influences, 1891–1903.* New York: Russell and Russell, 1961, 468–484.

BASSAN, MAURICE, ed. *Stephen Crane: A Collection of Critical Essays.* Englewood Cliffs, New Jersey: Prentice Hall, 1967, 181–184.

BEEBE, MAURICE, and THOMAS A. GULLASON. "Criticism of Stephen Crane: A Selected Checklist with an Index to Studies of Separate Works." *MFS,* V (Autumn 1959), 282–291.

BERRYMAN, JOHN. *Stephen Crane.* New York: Sloane, 1950, 326–331.

BLANCK, JACOB. *Bibliography of American Literature,* 5 Vols. New Haven: Yale Univ. Press, 1955–1969, II, 329–338.

——————, ed. *Merle Johnson's American First Editions,* 4th edition, revised and enlarged. Waltham, Massachusetts: Mark Press, 1965, 128–130.

COLUMBIA UNIVERSITY, LIBRARIES. *Stephen Crane (1871–1900): An Exhibition of His Writings Held in the Columbia University Libraries September 17–November 30, 1956.* New York: Columbia Univ. Press, 1956, 61 pp.

CRANE, STEPHEN. *Stephen Crane: An Omnibus,* edited by Robert Wooster Stallman. New York: Knopf, 1952, 697–703.

DARTMOUTH COLLEGE, LIBRARY. *A Stephen Crane Collection.* Hanover, New Hampshire: Dartmouth College Library, 1948, 43 pp.

350 copies printed.

GERSTENBERGER, DONNA, and GEORGE HENDRICK. *The American Novel, 1789–1959: A Checklist of Twentieth Century Criticism.* Denver: Alan Swallow, 1961, 49–53.

HALLAM, GEORGE W. "Some New Stephen Crane Items." *SB,* XX (1967), 263–266.

JONES, C. E. "Stephen Crane: A Bibliography of His Short Stories and Essays." *BB,* XV (September–December 1935), 149–150; (January–April 1936), 170.

KATZ, JOSEPH. "Toward a Descriptive Bibliography of Stephen Crane's *The Black Riders.*" *PBSA,* LIX (2nd Quart. 1965), 150–157.

LEARY, LEWIS. *Articles on American Literature, 1900–1950.* Durham: Duke Univ. Press, 1954, 61–63.

SPILLER, ROBERT ERNEST, et al. *Literary History of the United States,* 2 Vols. New York: Macmillan, 1962, 458–461. Supplement, 100–102.

STALLMAN, ROBERT WOOSTER. "Stephen Crane: Some New Stories." *BNYPL,* LX (September 1956), 455–462; (October 1956), 477–486; LXI (January 1957), 36–46.

——————. "Stephen Crane's Letters to Ripley Hitchcock." *BNYPL,* LX (July 1956), 319–322.

STARRETT, VINCENT, comp. *Stephen Crane: A Bibliography.* Philadelphia: The Centaur Bookshop, 1923, 46 pp.

STOLPER, BENJAMIN JOHN REEMAN, comp. *Stephen Crane: A List of His Writings and Articles about Him.* Newark: Stephen Crane Association, 1930, 30 pp.

TAYLOR, WALTER FULLER. *A History of American Letters,* with bibliographies by Harry Hartwick. Boston: American Book Co., 1936, 563–564.

Subsequent editions entitled: *The Story of American Letters.*

WILLIAMS, AMES WILLIAM. "A Stephen Crane Collection." *Antiquarian Bookman,* I (May 1948), 717–718.

WILLIAMS, AMES WILLIAM, and VINCENT STARRETT. *Stephen Crane: A Bibliography.* Glendale, California: John Valentine, 1948, 172 pp.

WOODRESS, JAMES, et al. *American Literary Scholarship: An Annual.* Durham: Duke Univ. Press, (1963), 112–117; (1964), 117–119; (1965), 137–140; (1966), 124–127.

CRAWFORD, FRANCIS MARION

BLANCK, JACOB. *Bibliography of American Literature,* 5 Vols. New Haven: Yale Univ. Press, 1955– 1969, II, 341–363.

BROOKS, VAN WYCK. *The Dream of Arcadia: American Writers and Artists in Italy, 1760–1915.* New York: Dutton, 1958, bibliographical footnotes.

GERSTENBERGER, DONNA, and GEORGE HENDRICK. *The American Novel, 1789–1959: A Checklist of Twentieth Century Criticism.* Denver: Alan Swallow, 1961, 53–54.

LEARY, LEWIS. *Articles on American Literature, 1900–1950.* Durham: Duke Univ. Press, 1954, 63–64.

CROCKETT, DAVID

HUBBELL, JAY B. *The South in American Literature, 1607–1900.* Durham: Duke Univ. Press, 1954, 929–930.

LEARY, LEWIS. *Articles on American Literature, 1900–1950.* Durham: Duke Univ. Press, 1954, 64–65.

PAINE, GREGORY LANSING, ed. *Southern Prose Writers: Representative Selections,* with introduction, bibliography and notes. New York: American Book Co., 1947, cxxx–cxxxi.

TRENT, WILLIAM PETERFIELD, et al. *Cambridge History of American Literature,* 4 Vols. New York: G. P. Putnam's Sons, 1917–1921, II, 505.

CUMINGS, HENRY

ALLEN, WILKES. *A Sermon Preached at Billeria, September 8, 1823, at the Interment of the Rev. Henry Cumings, D.D. . . . .* Boston: Wells and Lilly, 1824, 24 pp.

CUMMINS, MARIA SUSANNA

BLANCK, JACOB. *Bibliography of American Literature,* 5 Vols. New Haven: Yale Univ. Press, 1955– 1969, II, 364–366.

CURRY, JABEZ LAMAR MONROE

TRENT, WILLIAM PETERFIELD, et al. *Cambridge History of American Literature,* 4 Vols. New York: G. P. Putnam's Sons, 1917–1921, II, 589–593.

CURTIS, GEORGE WILLIAM

BLANCK, JACOB. *Bibliography of American Literature,* 5 Vols. New Haven: Yale Univ. Press, 1955–1969, II, 367–393.

——————, ed. *Merle Johnson's American First Editions,* 4th edition, revised and enlarged. Waltham, Massachusetts: Mark Press, 1965, 133–134.

LEARY, LEWIS. *Articles on American Literature, 1900–1950.* Durham: Duke Univ. Press, 1954, 66.

CUSHMAN, CHARLOTTE

LEARY, LEWIS. *Articles on American Literature, 1900–1950.* Durham: Duke Univ. Press, 1954, 66.

CUSHMAN, ROBERT

DEANE, CHARLES. *A Sermon Preached at Plimmouth, in New England,* with a bibliography of the sermons of Robert Cushman. Boston: n.p., 1870, xiii.

DABNEY, RICHARD

HUBBELL, JAY B. *The South in American Literature, 1607–1900.* Durham: Duke Univ. Press, 1954, 930.

LEARY, LEWIS. *Articles on American Literature, 1900–1950.* Durham: Duke Univ. Press, 1954, 66.

DALY, AUGUSTIN

LEARY, LEWIS. *Articles on American Literature, 1900–1950.* Durham: Duke Univ. Press, 1954, 66.

DANA, RICHARD HENRY, SR.

BLANCK, JACOB. *Bibliography of American Literature,* 5 Vols. New Haven: Yale Univ. Press, 1955–1969, II, 394–399.

LEARY, LEWIS. *Articles on American Literature, 1900–1950.* Durham: Duke Univ. Press, 1954, 66.

TRENT, WILLIAM PETERFIELD, et al. *Cambridge History of American Literature,* 4 Vols. New York: G. P. Putnam's Sons, 1917–1921, I, 521.

DANA, RICHARD HENRY, JR.

BLANCK, JACOB. *Bibliography of American Literature,* 5 Vols. New Haven: Yale Univ. Press, 1955–1969, II, 400–410.

——————, ed. *Merle Johnson's American First Editions,* 4th edition, revised and enlarged. Waltham, Massachusetts: Mark Press, 1965, 135–136.

GERSTENBERGER, DONNA, and GEORGE HENDRICK. *The American Novel, 1789–1959: A Checklist of Twentieth Century Criticism.* Denver: Alan Swallow, 1961, 54.

HART, JAMES D. "The Other Writings of Richard Henry Dana, Jr." *The Colophon,* Part 19 (1934), no pagination.

LEARY, LEWIS. *Articles on American Literature, 1900–1950.* Durham: Duke Univ. Press, 1954, 66.

DAVIS, CHARLES AUGUSTUS

BLANCK, JACOB. *Bibliography of American Literature,* 5 Vols. New Haven: Yale Univ. Press, 1955–1969, II, 411–414.

TRENT, WILLIAM PETERFIELD, et al. *Cambridge History of American Literature,* 4 Vols. New York:

G. P. Putnam's Sons, 1917–1921, II, 505.

DAVIS, JOHN

HUBBELL, JAY B. *The South in American Literature, 1607–1900.* Durham: Duke Univ. Press, 1954, 931.

LEARY, LEWIS. *Articles on American Literature, 1900–1950.* Durham: Duke Univ. Press, 1954, 67.

DAVIS, REBECCA HARDING

GERSTENBERGER, DONNA, and GEORGE HENDRICK. *The American Novel, 1789–1959: A Checklist of Twentieth Century Criticism.* Denver: Alan Swallow, 1961, 55.

STEMPLE, RUTH M. "Rebecca Harding Davis: A Check List." *BB,* XXII (September–December 1957), 83–85.

DAVIS, RICHARD HARDING

BLANCK, JACOB. *Bibliography of American Literature,* 5 Vols. New Haven: Yale Univ. Press, 1955–1969, II, 415–427.

⸻, ed. *Merle Johnson's American First Editions,* 4th edition, revised and enlarged. Waltham, Massachusetts: Mark Press, 1965, 137–140.

GERSTENBERGER, DONNA, and GEORGE HENDRICK. *The American Novel, 1789–1959: A Checklist of Twentieth Century Criticism.* Denver: Alan Swallow, 1961, 55.

LEARY, LEWIS. *Articles on American Literature, 1900–1950.* Durham: Duke Univ. Press, 1954, 67.

QUINBY, HENRY COLE. *Richard Harding Davis: A Bibliography.* New York: E. P. Putnam and Co., 1924, 315 pp.

TRENT, WILLIAM PETERFIELD, et al. *Cambridge History of American Literature,* 4 Vols. New York: G. P. Putnam's Sons, 1917–1921, II, 620.

DAWES, RUFUS

BLANCK, JACOB. *Bibliography of American Literature,* 5 Vols. New Haven: Yale Univ. Press, 1955–1969, II, 428–431.

DEANE, JAMES

BOWDITCH, HENRY INGERSOLL. *An Address on the Life and Character of James Deane, M.D., of Greenfield, Mass. . . .* Greenfield, Connecticut: H. D. Mirick and Co., printers, 1858, 43–45.

DE BOW, JAMES DUNWOODY BROWNSON

LEARY, LEWIS. *Articles on American Literature, 1900–1950.* Durham: Duke Univ. Press, 1954, 67.

DeFOREST, JOHN WILLIAM

BLANCK, JACOB. *Bibliography of American Literature,* 5 Vols. New Haven: Yale Univ. Press, 1955–1969, II, 432–437.

GERSTENBERGER, DONNA, and GEORGE HENDRICK. *The American Novel, 1789–1959: A Checklist of Twentieth Century Criticism.* Denver: Alan Swallow, 1961, 55–56.

HAGEMANN, E. R. "A Checklist of the Writings of John William DeForest (1826–1906)." *SB,* VIII (1956), 185–194.

⸻. "John William DeForest and *The Galaxy:* Some

Letters, 1867–1872." *BNYPL*, LIX (April 1955), 175–194.

Contains a checklist of his contributions to *The Galaxy*.

LEARY, LEWIS. *Articles on American Literature, 1900–1950.* Durham: Duke Univ. Press, 1954, 67.

SPILLER, ROBERT ERNEST, et al. *Literary History of the United States*, 2 Vols. New York: Macmillan, 1962, 463–464. Supplement, 103.

DERBY, GEORGE HORATIO

BLANCK, JACOB. *Bibliography of American Literature*, 5 Vols. New Haven: Yale Univ. Press, 1955–1969, II, 443–445.

LEARY, LEWIS. *Articles on American Literature, 1900–1950.* Durham: Duke Univ. Press, 1954, 68.

STEWART, GEORGE RIPPEY. *John Phoenix, Esq., the Veritable Squibob: A Life of Captain George H. Derby, U.S.A.* New York: Henry Holt and Co., 1937, 209–217.

TRENT, WILLIAM PETERFIELD, et al. *Cambridge History of American Literature*, 4 Vols. New York: G. P. Putnam's Sons, 1917–1921, II, 505.

DICKINS, ASBURY

LEARY, LEWIS. *Articles on American Literature, 1900–1950.* Durham: Duke Univ. Press, 1954, 68.

DICKINSON, EMILY

BINGHAM, MILLICENT TODD. "Early Reviews of Books by Emily Dickinson, 1890–1896," in *Ancestors' Brocades: The Literary Debut of Emily Dickinson.* New

York and London: Harper and Brothers, 1945, 406–415.

From the preface: "Books by Emily Dickinson, a partial list of editions brought out by Mabel Loomis Todd and Thomas Wentworth Higginson," 412–415.

BIRSS, JOHN HOWARD. "Emily Dickinson: A Bibliographical Note." *N&Q*, CLXIV (June 1933), 421; CLXV (July 1933), 29.

BLANCK, JACOB. *Bibliography of American Literature*, 5 Vols. New Haven: Yale Univ. Press, 1955–1969, II, 446–454.

_____, ed. *Merle Johnson's American First Editions*, 4th edition, revised and enlarged. Waltham, Massachusetts: Mark Press, 1965, 144–145.

CECCHI, EMILIO, and GUIDITTA CECCHI. . . . *Emily Dickinson.* [Brescia] : Morcelliana, 1930, 143–152.

CLARK, HARRY HAYDEN, ed. *Major American Poets.* New York: American Book Co., 1936, 489–497.

GLENDENNING, SHEILA T. *Emily Dickinson: A Bibliography, 1850–1966.* Kent, Ohio: Kent State Univ. Press, 1968, 145 pp.

Intended to supersede the bibliographies of the Jones Library, Inc., and Alfred Lette Hampson, both published in 1930.

HAMPSON, ALFRED LETTE, comp. *Emily Dickinson: A Bibliography.* Northampton, Massachusetts: The Hampshire Bookshop, 1930, 36 pp.

JOHNSON, THOMAS H. "Establishing a Text: The Emily Dickinson Papers." *SB*, V (1952–1953), 21–32.

JONES LIBRARY, INC. *Emily Dickinson, December 10, 1830– May 15, 1886: A Bibliography,* with a foreward by George F. Whicher, 2nd edition. Amherst: Jones Library, Inc., 1931, 63 pp.

LEARY, LEWIS. *Articles on American Literature, 1900–1950.* Durham: Duke Univ. Press, 1954, 68–71.

PICKARD, JOHN B. *Emily Dickinson: An Introduction and Interpretation.* New York, 1967, 127–130.

Part of the *American Authors and Critics Series,* begun in 1961, and purchased by Holt, Rinehart and Winston from Barnes and Noble. The nine original and three new volumes were issued under the Holt imprint in January 1967.

SEWALL, RICHARD BENSON. *Emily Dickinson: A Collection of Critical Essays.* Englewood Cliffs, New Jersey: Prentice Hall, 1963, 183.

SMITH, RUSSELL ST. CLAIR. "Emily Dickinson: A Bibliographical Note." *N&Q,* CXCIII (May 1, 1948), 188–189.

SPILLER, ROBERT ERNEST, et al. *Literary History of the United States,* 2 Vols. New York: Macmillan, 1962, 467–470. Supplement, 105–107.

STARKE, AUBREY HARRISON. "Emily Dickinson as a Great Unknown." *ABC,* V (August-September 1934), 245–250.

TAYLOR, WALTER FULLER. *A History of American Letters,* with bibliographies by Harry Hartwick. Boston: American Book Co., 1936, 553–555.

Subsequent editions entitled: *The Story of American Letters.*

TRENT, WILLIAM PETERFIELD, et al. *Cambridge History of American Literature,* 4 Vols. New York: G. P. Putnam's Sons, 1917–1921, IV, 647.

WHICHER, GEORGE FRISBIE. *This Was a Poet: A Critical Biography of Emily Dickinson.* London and New York: C. Scribner's Sons, 1938, 311–329.

WHITE, WILLIAM. "Two Unlisted Emily Dickinson Poems." *CLQ,* III (February 1948), 69–70.

WHITE, WILLIAM, and C. R. GREEN. "Homage to Emily Dickinson." *BB,* XX (May–August 1951), 112–115.

A bibliography of poets, musicians, dramatists and choreographers who have paid tribute in their art to Emily Dickinson.

WOODRESS, JAMES, et al. *American Literary Scholarship: An Annual.* Durham: Duke Univ. Press, (1963), 126–128; (1964), 130–136; (1965), 153–159; (1966), 139–144.

DODGE, MARY ABIGAIL

BLANCK, JACOB. *Bibliography of American Literature,* 5 Vols. New Haven: Yale Univ. Press, 1955–1969, II, 455–463.

DODGE, MARY ELIZABETH MAPES

BLANCK, JACOB. *Bibliography of American Literature,* 5 Vols. New Haven: Yale Univ. Press, 1955–1969, II, 464–473.

_____, ed. *Merle Johnson's American First Editions,* 4th edition, revised and enlarged. Waltham, Massachusetts: Mark Press, 1965, 146.

DONNELLY, IGNATIUS LOYOLA

BLANCK, JACOB. *Bibliography of American Literature,* 5 Vols. New Haven: Yale Univ. Press, 1955–1969, II, 474–479.

DOUGLASS, FREDERICK

HOLLAND, FREDERIC MAY. *Frederick Douglass: The Colored Orator.* New York: Funk and Wagnalls, 1891, 402–407.

TRENT, WILLIAM PETERFIELD, et al. *Cambridge History of American Literature,* 4 Vols. New York: G. P. Putnam's Sons, 1917–1921, II, 614.

DRAKE, JOSEPH RODMAN

BLANCK, JACOB. *Bibliography of American Literature,* 5 Vols. New Haven: Yale Univ. Press, 1955–1969, II, 480–484.

——————, ed. *Merle Johnson's American First Editions,* 4th edition, revised and enlarged. Waltham, Massachusetts: Mark Press, 1965, 150.

LEARY, LEWIS. *Articles on American Literature, 1900–1950.* Durham: Duke Univ. Press, 1954, 73.

PALTSITS, VICTOR HUGO, ed. *Joseph Rodman Drake Memorial Celebration, May 29, 1915, and a Bibliography of Drake.* New York: The Bronx Society of Arts and Sciences, 1919, 93–117.

TAFT, KENDALL B., ed. *Minor Knickerbockers: Representative Selections,* with introduction, bibliography and notes. New York: American Book Co., 1947, cxxxi.

TRENT, WILLIAM PETERFIELD, et al. *Cambridge History of American Literature,* 4 Vols. New York: G. P. Putnam's Sons, 1917–1921, I, 521–522.

DRAPER, JOHN WILLIAM

BARKER, GEORGE FREDERICK. "Memoir of John William Draper." *National Academy of Science: Biographical Memoirs,* II (1883), 351–388.

DUGANNE, AUGUSTINE JOSEPH HICKEY

BLANCK, JACOB. *Bibliography of American Literature,* 5 Vols. New Haven: Yale Univ. Press, 1955–1969, II, 485–497.

DUNBAR, PAUL LAURENCE

BLANCK, JACOB. *Bibliography of American Literature,* 5 Vols. New Haven: Yale Univ. Press, 1955–1969, II, 498–505.

——————, ed. *Merle Johnson's American First Editions,* 4th edition, revised and enlarged. Waltham, Massachusetts: Mark Press, 1965, 156–157.

BRAWLEY, BENJAMIN GRIFFITH. *Paul Laurence Dunbar: Poet of His People.* Chapel Hill: Univ. of North Carolina Press, 1936, 141–151.

BURRIS, ANDREW M. "Bibliography of Works by Paul Laurence Dunbar." *AC,* V (November 1927), 69–73.

LEARY, LEWIS. *Articles on American Literature, 1900–1950.* Durham: Duke Univ. Press, 1954, 75–76.

LOGGINS, VERNON. *The Negro Author: His Development in*

America. New York: Columbia Univ. Press, 1931, 408–457.

SPILLER, ROBERT ERNEST, et al. *Literary History of the United States,* 2 Vols. New York: Macmillan, 1962, 477–478. Supplement, 110.

TRENT, WILLIAM PETERFIELD, et al. *Cambridge History of American Literature,* 4 Vols. New York: G. P. Putnam's Sons, 1917–1921, II, 614–615.

DURANT, CHARLES S.

LEARY, LEWIS. *Articles on American Literature, 1900–1950.* Durham: Duke Univ. Press, 1954, 76.

DUYCKINCK, GEORGE

LEARY, LEWIS. *Articles on American Literature, 1900–1950.* Durham: Duke Univ. Press, 1954, 76.

DWIGHT, JOHN SULLIVAN

LEARY, LEWIS. *Articles on American Literature, 1900–1950.* Durham: Duke Univ. Press, 1954, 76.

EARLE, ALICE MORSE

LEARY, LEWIS. *Articles on American Literature, 1900–1950.* Durham: Duke Univ. Press, 1954, 77.

EGGLESTON, EDWARD

BLANCK, JACOB. *Bibliography of American Literature,* 5 Vols. New Haven: Yale Univ. Press, 1955–1969, III, 1–15.

——————, ed. *Merle Johnson's American First Editions,* 4th edition, revised and enlarged. Waltham, Massachusetts: Mark Press, 1965, 161–162.

GERSTENBERGER, DONNA, and GEORGE HENDRICK. *The American Novel, 1789–1959: A Checklist of Twentieth Century Criticism.* Denver: Alan Swallow, 1961, 67.

LEARY, LEWIS. *Articles on American Literature, 1900–1950.* Durham: Duke Univ. Press, 1954, 79.

RANDEL, WILLIAM PIERCE. *Edward Eggleston: Author of "The Hoosier School-Master."* New York: King's Crown Press, 1946, 263–313.

SPILLER, ROBERT ERNEST, et al. *Literary History of the United States,* 2 Vols. New York: Macmillan, 1962, 485–486. Supplement, 111.

ELLIOTT, WILLIAM

HUBBELL, JAY B. *The South in American Literature, 1607–1900.* Durham: Duke Univ. Press, 1954, 931–932.

EMBURY, EMMA CATHERINE

LEARY, LEWIS. *Articles on American Literature, 1900–1950.* Durham: Duke Univ. Press, 1954, 86.

EMERSON, RALPH WALDO

AMERICAN ACADEMY OF ARTS AND LETTERS. *The Great Decade in American Writing, 1850–1860. . . .* New York: American Academy of Arts and Letters, 1954, 6–8.

Catalog of an exhibition of manuscripts, books and paintings displayed Dec. 3–30, 1954.

ANDERSON, PAUL RUSSELL, and MAX HAROLD FISCH, eds. *Philosophy in America from the Puritans to James, with Representative Selections.* New York: D. Appleton Century Co., Inc., 1939, 335–336.

ARNOLD, W. H. *First Editions of Bryant, Emerson, Hawthorne, Holmes, Longfellow, Lowell, Thoreau, Whittier.* Jamaica, New York: Marion Press, 1901, varying pagination.

BLANCK, JACOB. *Bibliography of American Literature,* 5 Vols. New Haven: Yale Univ. Press, 1955–1969, III, 16–70.

_____, ed. *Merle Johnson's American First Editions,* 4th edition, revised and enlarged. Waltham, Massachusetts: Mark Press, 1965, 163–167.

BOOTH, R. A., and ROLAND STROMBERG. "A Bibliography of Ralph Waldo Emerson, 1908– 1920." *BB,* XIX (September– December 1948), 180–183.

CAMERON, KENNETH WALTER, ed. *Nature.* New York: Scholars' Facsimiles and Reprints, 1940, 69 pp.

_____. *Ralph Waldo Emerson's Reading.* Raleigh: The Thistle Press, 1941, 144 pp.

_____. "Recent Emerson Bibliography." *ESQ* (1st Quart. 1959), 96–99.

_____. "Some Collections of Emerson Manuscripts." *ESQ* (2nd Quart. 1956), 1–3; (4th Quart. 1956), 20–21.

CARPENTER, FREDERIC IVES. *Emerson Handbook.* New York: Hendricks House, 1953, 282 pp.

_____, ed. *Ralph Waldo Emerson: Representative Selections,* with introduction, bibliography and notes. New York: American Book Co., 1934, xlix–lvi.

CHARVAT, WILLIAM. "A Chronological List of Emerson's American Lecture Engagements." *BNYPL,* LXIV (December 1960), 657–663.

CLARK, HARRY HAYDEN, ed. *Major American Poets.* New York: American Book Co., 1936, 817–-823.

CONCORD FREE PUBLIC LIBRARY. *Ralph Waldo Emerson: An Exhibition.* Concord, Massachusetts: Concord Free Public Library, 1953, 17 pp.

COOKE, GEORGE WILLIS, comp. *A Bibliography of Ralph Waldo Emerson.* Boston and New York: Houghton Mifflin, 1908, 349 pp.

FAIRCHILD, SALOME CUTTER. "Best Editions of Ralph Waldo Emerson." *BB,* III (January 1903), 58–59.

GORDON, JOHN D. "Ralph Waldo Emerson, 1803–1882: Catalogue of an Exhibition from the Berg Collection." *BNYPL,* LVII (July 1953), 392–408; (September 1953), 433–460.

HARDING, WALTER. *Emerson's Library.* Charlottesville: Univ. of Virginia Press, 1967, 338 pp.

HUBBELL, GEORGE SHELTON. *A Concordance to the Poems of Ralph Waldo Emerson.* New York: H. W. Wilson Co., 1932, 488 pp.

HUBBELL, JAY B. *The South in American Literature, 1607–1900.* Durham: Duke Univ. Press, 1954, 932.

Index to Early American Periodical Literature, 1728–1870: Part 4, Ralph Waldo Emerson, 1803–1882. New York: Pamphlet Distributing Co., 1942, 39 pp.

JONES, HOWARD MUMFORD, ed. *Emerson on Education: Selections.* New York: Columbia Univ. Press, 1966, 24.

KRONMAN, JEANNE. "Three Unpublished Lectures of Ralph Waldo Emerson." *NEQ,* XIX (March 1946), 98–110.

LEARY, LEWIS. *Articles on American Literature, 1900–1950.* Durham: Duke Univ. Press, 1954, 86–95.

POCHMANN, HENRY A. "The Emerson Canon." *Univ. of Toronto Quarterly,* XII (July 1943), 476–484.

POMMER, HENRY FRANCIS. *Emerson's First Marriage.* Carbondale: Southern Illinois Univ. Press, 1967, 107–122.

SCUDDER, TOWNSEND, III. "A Chronological List of Emerson's Lectures on His British Lecture Tour of 1847–1848." *PMLA,* LI (March 1936), 243–248.

SPILLER, ROBERT ERNEST, et al. *Literary History of the United States,* 2 Vols. New York: Macmillan, 1962, 492–501. Supplement, 115–118.

STEEVES, HARRISON ROSS. "Bibliographical Notes on Emerson." *MLN,* XXXII (November 1917), 431–434.

STOVALL, FLOYD, et al. *Eight American Authors: A Review of Research and Criticism.* New York: W. W. Norton and Co., 1963, 47–99, 424–428.

TAYLOR, WALTER FULLER. *A History of American Letters,* with bibliographies by Harry Hartwick. Boston: American Book Co., 1936, 509–513.

Subsequent editions entitled: *The Story of American Letters.*

TRENT, WILLIAM PETERFIELD, et al. *Cambridge History of American Literature,* 4 Vols. New York: G. P. Putnam's Sons, 1917–1921, I, 551–566.

WAKEMAN, STEPHEN H. *The Stephen H. Wakeman Collection of Books of Nineteenth Century American Writers: The Property of Mrs. Alice L. Wakeman, First Editions, Inscribed Presentation and Personal Copies, Original Manuscripts and Letters of Nine American Authors.* New York: American Art Association, 1924, Items 156–260.

WILSON, CARROLL ATWOOD. *Thirteen Author Collections of the Nineteenth Century and Five Centuries of Familiar Quotations,* edited by Jean C. S. Wilson and David A. Randall, 2 Vols. New York: privately printed for Scribner, 1950, I, 17–37.

WOODRESS, JAMES, et al. *American Literary Scholarship: An Annual.* Durham: Duke Univ. Press, (1963), 3–4; (1964), 3–11; (1965), 3–6; (1966), 3–11.

YOHANNAN, J. D. "Emerson's Translations of Persian Poetry from German Sources." *AL,* XIV (January 1943), 407–420.

ZINK, HARRIET R. "Emerson's Use of the Bible." *Univ. of Nebraska Studies in Language, Literature, and Criticism,* XIV (1935), 1–75.

EMMETT, DANIEL DECATUR

HUBBELL, JAY B. *The South in American Literature, 1607–1900.* Durham: Duke Univ. Press, 1954, 932.

LEARY, LEWIS. *Articles on American Literature, 1900–1950.* Durham: Duke Univ. Press, 1954, 95.

ENGLISH, THOMAS DUNN

BLANCK, JACOB. *Bibliography of American Literature,* 5 Vols. New Haven: Yale Univ. Press, 1955–1969, III, 71–81.

LEARY, LEWIS. *Articles on American Literature, 1900–1950.* Durham: Duke Univ. Press, 1954, 95.

EVANS, AUGUSTA JANE

GERSTENBERGER, DONNA, and GEORGE HENDRICK. *The American Novel, 1789–1959: A Checklist of Twentieth Century Criticism.* Denver: Alan Swallow, 1961, 68.

LEARY, LEWIS. *Articles on American Literature, 1900–1950.* Durham: Duke Univ. Press, 1954, 95.

EVERETT, ALEXANDER HILL

SOMKIN, FRED. "The Writings of Alexander Hill Everett (1790–1847): A Partial Checklist." *BB,* XXIII (January–April 1963), 238–239.

EVERETT, EDWARD

LEARY, LEWIS. *Articles on American Literature, 1900–1950.* Durham: Duke Univ. Press, 1954, 96.

TRENT, WILLIAM PETERFIELD, et al. *Cambridge History of American Literature,* 4 Vols. New York: G. P. Putnam's Sons, 1917–1921, II, 471–472.

FAIRFIELD, SUMNER LINCOLN

BLANCK, JACOB. *Bibliography of American Literature,* 5 Vols. New Haven: Yale Univ. Press, 1955–1969, III, 82–85.

FAWCETT, EDGAR

BLANCK, JACOB. *Bibliography of American Literature,* 5 Vols. New Haven: Yale Univ. Press, 1955–1969, III, 86–102.

FAY, THEODORE SEDGWICK

BLANCK, JACOB. *Bibliography of American Literature,* 5 Vols. New Haven: Yale Univ. Press, 1955–1969, III, 103–110.

TAFT, KENDALL B., ed. *Minor Knickerbockers: Representative Selections,* with introduction, bibliography and notes. New York: American Book Co., 1947, cxxxi–cxxxii.

FERN, FANNY (MRS. SARA PAYSON WILLIS PARTON)

GERSTENBERGER, DONNA, and GEORGE HENDRICK. *The American Novel, 1789–1959: A Checklist of Twentieth Century Criticism.* Denver: Alan Swallow, 1961, 89.

FESSENDEN, THOMAS GREEN

LEARY, LEWIS. *Articles on American Literature, 1900–1950.* Durham: Duke Univ. Press, 1954, 100.

FIELD, EUGENE

BLANCK, JACOB. *Bibliography of American Literature,* 5 Vols. New Haven: Yale Univ. Press, 1955–1969, III, 111–141.

_____, ed. *Merle Johnson's American First Editions,* 4th edition, revised and enlarged. Waltham,

Massachusetts: Mark Press, 1965, 176–179.

COLLECTORS CLUB. *First Editions, Manuscripts, Letters, etc., of Eugene Field.* New York: Collectors Club, 1915, 30 pp.

COMSTOCK, W. O. *Ida Comstock Below, Eugene Field in His Home.* New York: Dutton, 1898, 107–111.

HARPER, HENRY HOWARD, ed. *Verse and Prose by Eugene Field.* Boston: printed exclusively for the members of the Bibliophile Society, 1917, 47–60.

LEARY, LEWIS. *Articles on American Literature, 1900–1950.* Durham: Duke Univ. Press, 1954, 101.

TRENT, WILLIAM PETERFIELD, et al. *Cambridge History of American Literature,* 4 Vols. New York: G. P. Putnam's Sons, 1917–1921, II, 543–544, IV, 641.

FIELD, ROSWELL MARTIN

LEARY, LEWIS. *Articles on American Literature, 1900–1950.* Durham: Duke Univ. Press, 1954, 101.

FIELDS, JAMES THOMAS

BLANCK, JACOB. *Bibliography of American Literature,* 5 Vols. New Haven: Yale Univ. Press, 1955–1969, III, 142–158.

LEARY, LEWIS. *Articles on American Literature, 1900–1950.* Durham: Duke Univ. Press, 1954, 101.

FISHER, HENRY LEE

LEARY, LEWIS. *Articles on American Literature, 1900–1950.* Durham: Duke Univ. Press, 1954, 101.

FISKE, JOHN

BLANCK, JACOB. *Bibliography of American Literature,* 5 Vols. New Haven: Yale Univ. Press, 1955–1969, III, 159–179.

GREEN, SAMUEL S. "Reminiscences of John Fiske." *PAAS,* ns XIV (October 1901), 421–428.

LEARY, LEWIS. *Articles on American Literature, 1900–1950.* Durham: Duke Univ. Press, 1954, 102.

PERRY, THOMAS SERGEANT. *John Fiske.* Boston: Small, Maynard and Co., 1906, 103–105.

POWELL, LAWRENCE CLARK. "John Fiske–Bookman." *PBSA,* XXXV (4th Quart. 1941), 221–254.

SPILLER, ROBERT ERNEST, et al. *Literary History of the United States,* 2 Vols. New York: Macmillan, 1962, 503–505.

TRENT, WILLIAM PETERFIELD, et al. *Cambridge History of American Literature,* 4 Vols. New York: G. P. Putnam's Sons, 1917–1921, IV, 753.

FISKE, MINNIE MADERN

LIBRARY OF CONGRESS, MANUSCRIPT DIVISION. *Minnie Madern Fiske: A Register of His Papers in the Library of Congress.* Washington, 1962, 16 pp.

FITCH, WILLIAM CLYDE

BLANCK, JACOB. *Bibliography of American Literature,* 5 Vols. New Haven: Yale Univ. Press, 1955–1969, III, 180–186.

LEARY, LEWIS. *Articles on American Literature, 1900–1950.* Durham: Duke Univ. Press, 1954, 102.

LOWE, JOHN ADAMS. "Reading List on William Clyde Fitch." *BB,* VII (July 1912), 30–31.

FITZHUGH, GEORGE

HUBBELL, JAY B. *The South in American Literature, 1607–1900.* Durham: Duke Univ. Press, 1954, 932.

WISH, HARVEY. *George Fitzhugh: Propagandist of the Old South.* Baton Rouge: Louisiana State Univ. Press, 1943, 341–351.

FLINT, TIMOTHY

BLANCK, JACOB. *Bibliography of American Literature,* 5 Vols. New Haven: Yale Univ. Press, 1955–1969, III, 187–193.

GERSTENBERGER, DONNA, and GEORGE HENDRICK. *The American Novel, 1789–1959: A Checklist of Twentieth Century Criticism.* Denver: Alan Swallow, 1961, 96–97.

KIRKPATRICK, JOHN ERVIN. *Timothy Flint: Pioneer, Missionary, Author, Editor, 1780–1840.* Cleveland: The Arthur K. Clark Co., 1911, 305–318.

LEARY, LEWIS. *Articles on American Literature, 1900–1950.* Durham: Duke Univ. Press, 1954, 104.

TRENT, WILLIAM PETERFIELD, et al. *Cambridge History of American Literature,* 4 Vols. New York: G. P. Putnam's Sons, 1917–1921, I, 534.

FORCE, PETER

McGIRR, NEWMAN F. *Bio-Bibliography of Peter Force, 1790–1868.* Hattiesburg, Mississippi: The Book Farm, 1941, 30 pp.

FORD, PAUL LEICESTER

BLANCK, JACOB. *Bibliography of American Literature,* 5 Vols. New Haven: Yale Univ. Press, 1955–1969, III, 194–210.

_____, ed. *Merle Johnson's American First Editions,* 4th edition, revised and enlarged. Waltham, Massachusetts: Mark Press, 1965, 182–184.

LEARY, LEWIS. *Articles on American Literature, 1900–1950.* Durham: Duke Univ. Press, 1954, 104.

FOSS, SAM WALTER

LEARY, LEWIS. *Articles on American Literature, 1900–1950.* Durham: Duke Univ. Press, 1954, 104.

FOSTER, STEPHEN COLLINS

ADKINS, N. F. "A Note on the Bibliography of Stephen C. Foster." *N&Q,* CLXIII (Nov. 5, 1932), 331–332.

LEARY, LEWIS. *Articles on American Literature, 1900–1950.* Durham: Duke Univ. Press, 1954, 104.

FOX, JOHN WILLIAM, JR.

BLANCK, JACOB. *Bibliography of American Literature,* 5 Vols. New Haven: Yale Univ. Press, 1955–1969, III, 212–216.

_____, ed. *Merle Johnson's American First Editions,* 4th edition, revised and enlarged. Waltham, Massachusetts: Mark Press, 1965, 185–186.

LEARY, LEWIS. *Articles on American Literature, 1900–1950.* Durham: Duke Univ. Press, 1954, 105.

FREDERIC, HAROLD

BLANCK, JACOB. *Bibliography of American Literature,* 5 Vols. New Haven: Yale Univ. Press, 1955–1969, III, 217–223.

——————, ed. *Merle Johnson's American First Editions,* 4th edition, revised and enlarged. Waltham, Massachusetts: Mark Press, 1965, 187–188.

GARNER, STANTON B. "A Harold Frederic First." *SB,* XV (1962), 268–269.

GERSTENBERGER, DONNA, and GEORGE HENDRICK. *The American Novel, 1789–1959: A Checklist of Twentieth Century Criticism.* Denver: Alan Swallow, 1961, 98.

LEARY, LEWIS. *Articles on American Literature, 1900–1950.* Durham: Duke Univ. Press, 1954, 111.

SPILLER, ROBERT ERNEST, et al. *Literary History of the United States,* 2 Vols. New York: Macmillan, 1962, 515–516.

WOODWARD, ROBERT H. "Harold Frederic: A Bibliography." *SB,* XIII (1960), 247–257.

FREEMAN, MARY ELEANOR WILKINS

BLANCK, JACOB. *Bibliography of American Literature,* 5 Vols. New Haven: Yale Univ. Press, 1955–1969, III, 224–243.

——————, ed. *Merle Johnson's American First Editions,* 4th edition, revised and enlarged. Waltham, Massachusetts: Mark Press, 1965, 189–191.

FOSTER, EDWARD. *Mary E. Wilkins.* New York: Hendricks House, 1956, 210–222.

GERSTENBERGER, DONNA, and GEORGE HENDRICK. *The American Novel, 1789–1959: A Checklist of Twentieth Century Criticism.* Denver: Alan Swallow, 1961, 98–99.

LEARY, LEWIS. *Articles on American Literature, 1900–1950.* Durham: Duke Univ. Press, 1954, 111.

SPILLER, ROBERT ERNEST, et al. *Literary History of the United States,* 2 Vols. New York: Macmillan, 1962, 516–517. Supplement, 126.

TRENT, WILLIAM PETERFIELD, et al. *Cambridge History of American Literature,* 4 Vols. New York: G. P. Putnam's Sons, 1917–1921, II, 620–621.

FRENCH, ALICE (OCTAVE THANET)

LEARY, LEWIS. *Articles on American Literature, 1900–1950.* Durham: Duke Univ. Press, 1954, 111.

TRENT, WILLIAM PETERFIELD, et al. *Cambridge History of American Literature,* 4 Vols. New York: G. P. Putnam's Sons, 1917–1921, II, 621.

FULLER, HENRY BLAKE

BLANCK, JACOB. *Bibliography of American Literature,* 5 Vols. New Haven: Yale Univ. Press, 1955–1969, III, 257–261.

——————, ed. *Merle Johnson's American First Editions,* 4th edition, revised and enlarged. Waltham, Massachusetts: Mark Press, 1965, 198–199.

GERSTENBERGER, DONNA, and GEORGE HENDRICK. *The American Novel, 1789–1959: A Checklist*

of *Twentieth Century Criticism.*
Denver: Alan Swallow, 1961, 99.

GRIFFIN, CONSTANCE MAGEE.
*Henry Blake Fuller: A Critical
Biography.* Philadelphia: Univ. of
Pennsylvania Press, 1939, 92–113.

Also: London: Oxford Univ. Press.

LEARY, LEWIS. *Articles on American Literature, 1900–1950.* Durham:
Duke Univ. Press, 1954, 116–117.

SWAN, BRADFORD FULLER.
*A Bibliography of Henry Blake
Fuller.* New Haven: The Profile
Press, 1930.

Printed wrapper. 15 numbered
copies only.

FULLER, (SARAH) MARGARET

ANTHONY, KATHARINE SUSAN.
*Margaret Fuller: A Psychological
Biography.* New York: Harcourt,
Brace and Howe, 1920, 215–220.

BLANCK, JACOB. *Bibliography of
American Literature,* 5 Vols. New
Haven: Yale Univ. Press, 1955–1969,
III, 262–269.

BRAUN, FREDERICK AUGUSTUS.
Margaret Fuller and Goethe. New
York: H. Holt and Co., 1910,
259–261.

BROOKS, VAN WYCK. *The Dream
of Arcadia: American Writers and
Artists in Italy, 1760–1915.* New
York: Dutton, 1958, bibliographical
footnotes.

HIGGINSON, THOMAS WENT-
WORTH. *Margaret Fuller Ossoli.*
Boston and New York: Houghton
Mifflin, 1884, 315–318.

LEARY, LEWIS. *Articles on American Literature, 1900–1950.* Durham:
Duke Univ. Press, 1954, 117–118.

SPILLER, ROBERT ERNEST, et al.
*Literary History of the United
States,* 2 Vols. New York: Macmillan, 1962, 522–525. Supplement, 128–129.

STERN, MADELINE B. *The Life of
Margaret Fuller.* New York: E. P.
Dutton and Co., 1942, 493–523.

TRENT, WILLIAM PETERFIELD,
et al. *Cambridge History of American Literature,* 4 Vols. New York:
G. P. Putnam's Sons, 1917–1921,
I, 548–594.

WADE, MASON. *Margaret Fuller:
Whetstone of Genius.* New York:
The Viking Press, 1940, 294–297.

——————, ed. *The Writings of
Margaret Fuller.* New York: The
Viking Press, 1941, 595–600.

GALES, WINFRED AND JOSEPH

LEARY, LEWIS. *Articles on American Literature, 1900–1950.* Durham:
Duke Univ. Press, 1954, 118.

GALLAGHER, WILLIAM DAVIS

BLANCK, JACOB. *Bibliography of
American Literature,* 5 Vols. New
Haven: Yale Univ. Press, 1955–1969,
III, 270–274.

GALLATIN, ALBERT

TRENT, WILLIAM PETERFIELD,
et al. *Cambridge History of
American Literature,* 4 Vols. New
York: G. P. Putnam's Sons, 1917–
1921, II, 472.

GARRISON, WILLIAM LLOYD

LEARY, LEWIS. *Articles on American Literature, 1900–1950.* Durham:
Duke Univ. Press, 1954, 118–119.

TRENT, WILLIAM PETERFIELD, et al. *Cammbridge History of American Literature*, 4 Vols. New York: G. P. Putnam's Sons, 1917–1921, II, 522.

GAYARRE, CHARLES ÉTIENNE ARTHUR

ANDERSON, CHARLES R. "Charles Gayarre and Paul Hayne: The Last Literary Cavaliers," in *American Studies in Honor of William Kenneth Boyd.* Durham: Duke Univ. Press, 1940, 221–281.

GAYARRE, CHARLES. *History of Louisiana,* with city and topographical maps of the state, ancient and modern, 4 Vols. New Orleans: F. F. Hansell and Brothers, Ltd., 1903, I, xxx–lii.

Bibliography by William Beer.

HUBBELL, JAY B. *The South in American Literature, 1607–1900.* Durham: Duke Univ. Press, 1954, 932–933.

LEARY, LEWIS. *Articles on American Literature, 1900–1950.* Durham: Duke Univ. Press, 1954, 119.

SPILLER, ROBERT ERNEST, et al. *Literary History of the United States,* 2 Vols. New York: Macmillan, 1962, 529–530. Supplement, 130.

TINKER, EDWARD L. "Charles Gayarré, 1805–95." *PBSA,* XXVII (1933), 54–64.

GEORGE, HENRY

LEARY, LEWIS. *Articles on American Literature, 1900–1950.* Durham: Duke Univ. Press, 1954, 119.

POST, LOUIS FREELAND. *The Prophet of San Francisco . . . :*

Personal Memoirs and Interpretations of Henry George. New York: The Vanguard Press, 1930, 49–61.

From the Prefatory Note: "The first presentation of the substance of this volume was made by the author for the Literary Club of Chicago to which he read it as an essay at the regular meeting, November 16, 1902. The essay was published in 1903."

SPILLER, ROBERT ERNEST, et al. *Literary History of the United States,* 2 Vols. New York: Macmillan, 1962, 530–532. Supplement, 130.

GILDER, RICHARD WATSON

BLANCK, JACOB. *Bibliography of American Literature,* 5 Vols. New Haven: Yale Univ. Press, 1955–1969, III, 275–288.

LEARY, LEWIS. *Articles on American Literature, 1900–1950.* Durham: Duke Univ. Press, 1954, 119.

TRENT, WILLIAM PETERFIELD, et al. *Cambridge History of American Literature,* 4 Vols. New York: G. P. Putnam's Sons, 1917–1921, IV, 647–548.

GILDERSLEEVE, BASIL LANNEAU

LEARY, LEWIS. *Articles on American Literature, 1900–1950.* Durham: Duke Univ. Press, 1954, 119.

GILLETTE, WILLIAM

COOK, DORIS E. "The Library of William Gillette: A Partial Checklist." *BB,* XXII (September – December 1957), 88–93; (January–April 1958), 116–120; (May–August 1958), 137–142.

LEARY, LEWIS. *Articles on American Literature, 1900–1950.* Durham: Duke Univ. Press, 1954, 119.

GILMAN, MRS. SUSAN

LEARY, LEWIS. *Articles on American Literature, 1900–1950.* Durham: Duke Univ. Press, 1954, 119.

GILMER, FRANCIS WALKER

DAVIS, RICHARD BEALE. *Francis Walker Gilmer: Life and Learning in Jefferson's Virginia.* Richmond, Virginia: Dietz Press, 1939, 389–398.

HUBBELL, JAY B. *The South in American Literature, 1607–1900.* Durham: Duke Univ. Press, 1954, 933.

LEARY, LEWIS. *Articles on American Literature, 1900–1950.* Durham: Duke Univ. Press, 1954, 120.

GODKIN, EDWIN LAWRENCE

LEARY, LEWIS. *Articles on American Literature, 1900–1950.* Durham: Duke Univ. Press, 1954, 121.

GOODRICH, SAMUEL GRISWOLD

LEARY, LEWIS. *Articles on American Literature, 1900–1950.* Durham: Duke Univ. Press, 1954, 121.

TRENT, WILLIAM PETERFIELD, et al. *Cambridge History of American Literature,* 4 Vols. New York: G. P. Putnam's Sons, 1917–1921, II, 505.

GORDON, JOHN BROWN

TRENT, WILLIAM PETERFIELD, et al. *Cambridge History of American Literature,* 4 Vols. New York: G. P. Putnam's Sons, 1917–1921, II, 593.

GRADY, HENRY WOODFIN

LEARY, LEWIS. *Articles on American Literature, 1900–1950.* Durham: Duke Univ. Press, 1954, 121.

TRENT, WILLIAM PETERFIELD, et al. *Cambridge History of American Literature,* 4 Vols. New York: G. P. Putnam's Sons, 1917–1921, II, 593.

GRAYSON, WILLIAM JOHN

HUBBELL, JAY B. *The South in American Literature, 1607–1900.* Durham: Duke Univ. Press, 1954, 933–934.

LEARY, LEWIS. *Articles on American Literature, 1900–1950.* Durham: Duke Univ. Press, 1954, 121.

GREELEY, HORACE

LEARY, LEWIS. *Articles on American Literature, 1900–1950.* Durham: Duke Univ. Press, 1954, 121–122.

TRENT, WILLIAM PETERFIELD, et al. *Cambridge History of American Literature,* 4 Vols. New York: G. P. Putnam's Sons, 1917–1921, II, 522–523.

GREEN, DUFF

LEARY, LEWIS. *Articles on American Literature, 1900–1950.* Durham: Duke Univ. Press, 1954, 122.

GREENE, ASA

TRENT, WILLIAM PETERFIELD, et al. *Cambridge History of American Literature,* 4 Vols. New York: G. P. Putnam's Sons, 1917–1921, II, 505.

GREENHOW, ROBERT

LEARY, LEWIS. *Articles on Ameri-*

can Literature, 1900–1950. Durham: Duke Univ. Press, 1954, 123.

GRIERSON, FRANCIS

SIMONSON, HAROLD P. "Francis Grierson–A Biographical Sketch and Bibliography." Journal of the Illinois State Historical Society, LVI (Summer 1961), 198–203.

GRIFFITH, MARY

LEARY, LEWIS. Articles on American Literature, 1900–1950. Durham: Duke Univ. Press, 1954, 123.

GRISWOLD, RUFUS WILMOT

BLANCK, JACOB. Bibliography of American Literature, 5 Vols. New Haven: Yale Univ. Press, 1955–1969, III, 289–304.

LEARY, LEWIS. Articles on American Literature, 1900–1950. Durham: Duke Univ. Press, 1954, 123.

McCUSKER, HONOR. "The Correspondence of R. W. Griswold." More Books, 6th Series, XVI (March 1941), 105–116; (April 1941), 152–156; (May 1941), 190–196; (June 1941), 286–289; XVIII (February 1943), 57–68; (September 1943), 323–333.

GUNTER, A.C.

LOWRY, THOMAS C. F. "A Parallel-Text Edition of Two Nights in Rome by A. C. Gunter, with a Biography and Check List of Gunter's Plays." Unpublished docotral dissertation, Univ. of Chicago, 1956.

HALE, EDWARD EVERETT

HOLLOWAY, JEAN. "A Checklist of the Writings of Edward Everett Hale." BB, XXI (May–August 1954), 89–92; (September–December 1954),

114–120; (January–May 1955), 140–143.

LEARY, LEWIS. Articles on American Literature, 1900–1950. Durham: Duke Univ. Press, 1954, 123–124.

TRENT, WILLIAM PETERFIELD, et al. Cambridge History of American Literature, 4 Vols. New York: G. P. Putnam's Sons, 1917–1921, II, 621–622.

HALE, SARAH JOSEPHA BUELL

BLANCK, JACOB. Bibliography of American Literature, 5 Vols. New Haven: Yale Univ. Press, 1955–1969, III, 319–340.

LEARY, LEWIS. Articles on American Literature, 1900–1950. Durham: Duke Univ. Press, 1954, 124.

HALL, BAYNARD RUSH

BLANCK, JACOB. Bibliography of American Literature, 5 Vols. New Haven: Yale Univ. Press, 1955–1969, III, 341–343.

HALL, JAMES

BLANCK, JACOB. Bibliography of American Literature, 5 Vols. New Haven: Yale Univ. Press, 1955–1969, III, 344–355.

FLANAGAN, JOHN T. James Hall: Literary Pioneer of the Ohio Valley. Minneapolis: Univ. of Minnesota Press, 1941, 207–211.

LEARY, LEWIS. Articles on American Literature, 1900–1950. Durham: Duke Univ. Press, 1954, 124.

SPILLER, ROBERT ERNEST, et al. Literary History of the United States, 2 Vols. New York: Macmillan, 1962, 534–535. Supplement, 131.

THOMSON, PETER GIBSON. *A Bibliography of the State of Ohio.* Cincinnati: the author, 1880, 140–145.

HALL, SAMUEL STONE

DYKES, J. C. "A Bibliographical Check List of the Writing of Samuel Stone Hall." *ABC,* X (March 1960), 15–18.

HALLECK, FITZ-GREENE

ADKINS, NELSON FREDERICK. *Fitz-Greene Halleck: An Early Knickerbocker Wit and Poet.* New Haven: Yale Univ. Press, 1930, 376–387.

BLANCK, JACOB. *Bibliography of American Literature,* 5 Vols. New Haven: Yale Univ. Press, 1955–1969, III, 356–365.

—————————, ed. *Merle Johnson's American First Editions,* 4th edition, revised and enlarged. Waltham, Massachusetts: Mark Press, 1965, 210–211.

LEARY, LEWIS. *Articles on American Literature, 1900–1950.* Durham: Duke Univ. Press, 1954, 124.

SPILLER, ROBERT ERNEST, et al. *Literary History of the United States,* 2 Vols. New York: Macmillan, 1962, 535–536.

TAFT, KENDALL B., ed. *Minor Knickerbockers: Representative Selections,* with introduction, bibliography and notes. New York: American Book Co., 1947, cxxxii–cxxxiii.

TRENT, WILLIAM PETERFIELD, et al. *Cambridge History of American Literature,* 4 Vols. New York: G. P. Putnam's Sons, 1917–1921, I, 522.

HALLIBURTON, THOMAS CHANDLER

LEARY, LEWIS. *Articles on American Literature, 1900–1950.* Durham: Duke Univ. Press, 1954, 124.

HALPINE, CHARLES GRAHAM

BLANCK, JACOB. *Bibliography of American Literature,* 5 Vols. New Haven: Yale Univ. Press, 1955–1969, III, 366–371.

TRENT, WILLIAM PETERFIELD, et al. *Cambridge History of American Literature,* 4 Vols. New York: G. P. Putnam's Sons, 1917–1921, II, 506.

HAMMETT, SAMUEL A.

TRENT, WILLIAM PETERFIELD, et al. *Cambridge History of American Literature,* 4 Vols. New York: G. P. Putnam's Sons, 1917–1921, II, 506.

HARBAUGH, HENRY

LEARY, LEWIS. *Articles on American Literature, 1900–1950.* Durham: Duke Univ. Press, 1954, 124.

HARBEN, WILLIAM NATHANIEL

LEARY, LEWIS. *Articles on American Literature, 1900–1950.* Durham: Duke Univ. Press, 1954, 125.

HARDING, REBECCA

LEARY, LEWIS. *Articles on American Literature, 1900–1950.* Durham: Duke Univ. Press, 1954, 125.

HARDY, ARTHUR SHERBURNE

BLANCK, JACOB. *Bibliography of American Literature,* 5 Vols. New Haven: Yale Univ. Press, 1955–1969, III, 372–376.

HARLAND, HENRY

BLANCK, JACOB. *Bibliography of American Literature*, 5 Vols. New Haven: Yale Univ. Press, 1955–1969, III, 377–383.

LEARY, LEWIS. *Articles on American Literature, 1900–1950.* Durham: Duke Univ. Press, 1954, 125.

HARRIS, FRANK

TOBIN, A. I., and ELMER GERTZ. *Frank Harris: A Study in Black and White.* Chicago: Madeline Mendelsohn, 1931, 357–379.

1,000 copies printed.

HARRIS, GEORGE WASHINGTON

BLANCK, JACOB. *Bibliography of American Literature*, 5 Vols. New Haven: Yale Univ. Press, 1955–1969, III, 384–386.

DAY, DONALD. "The Life of George Washington Harris." *THQ,* VI (March 1947), 3–38.

HUBBELL, JAY B. *The South in American Literature, 1607–1900.* Durham: Duke Univ. Press, 1954, 934.

INGE, M. THOMAS, ed. *High Times and Hard Times: Sketches and Tales by George Washington Harris.* Nashville: Vanderbilt Univ. Press, 1967, 323–327.

LEARY, LEWIS. *Articles on American Literature, 1900–1950.* Durham: Duke Univ. Press, 1954, 125.

TRENT, WILLIAM PETERFIELD, et al. *Cambridge History of American Literature*, 4 Vols. New York: G. P. Putnam's Sons, 1917–1921, II, 506.

WOODRESS, JAMES, et al. *American Literary Scholarship: An Annual.* Durham: Duke Univ. Press, (1964), 136–138.

HARRIS, JOEL CHANDLER

BLANCK, JACOB. *Bibliography of American Literature*, 5 Vols. New Haven: Yale Univ. Press, 1955–1969, III, 387–401.

——————, ed. *Merle Johnson's American First Editions*, 4th edition, revised and enlarged. Waltham, Massachusetts: Mark Press, 1965, 212–215.

HARRIS, JULIA COLLIER. *The Life and Letters of Joel Chandler Harris.* Boston and New York: Houghton Mifflin Co., 1918, 603–610.

——————. "Uncle Remus at Home and Abroad." *SLM,* II (February 1940), 84–86.

HUBBELL, JAY B. *The South in American Literature, 1607–1900.* Durham: Duke Univ. Press, 1954, 934–935.

LEARY, LEWIS. *Articles on American Literature, 1900–1950.* Durham: Duke Univ. Press, 1954, 125–126.

MILLER, H. P. "Bibliography of Joel Chandler Harris." *Emory Alumnus,* V (March 1929), 13–14, 22.

PAINE, GREGORY LANSING, ed. *Southern Prose Writers: Representative Selections,* with introduction, bibliography and notes. New York: American Book Co., 1947, cxxxi–cxxxii.

SPILLER, ROBERT ERNEST, et al. *Literary History of the United States,* 2 Vols. New York: Macmillan, 1962, 540–542. Supplement, 132–133.

TRENT, WILLIAM PETERFIELD, et al. *Cambridge History of American Literature,* 4 Vols. New York: G. P. Putnam's Sons, 1917–1921, II, 611–614.

WIGGINS, ROBERT LEMUEL. *The Life of Joel Chandler Harris from Obscurity to Boyhood to Fame in Early Manhood.* Nashville: Publishing House, Methodist Episcopal Church, South, Smith and Lamar, agents, 1918, 429–444.

HARRIS, WILLIAM TORREY

LEARY, LEWIS. *Articles on American Literature, 1900–1950.* Durham: Duke Univ. Press, 1954, 126.

TRENT, WILLIAM PETERFIELD, et al. *Cambridge History of American Literature,* 4 Vols. New York: G. P. Putnam's Sons, 1917–1921, IV, 754.

HARRISON, CONSTANCE CARY

BLANCK, JACOB. *Bibliography of American Literature,* 5 Vols. New Haven: Yale Univ. Press, 1955–1969, III, 402–411.

HARRISSE, HENRY

ADAMS, RANDOLPH GREENFIELD. *Three Americanists: Henry Harrisse, Bibliographer; George Brinley, Book Collector; Thomas Jefferson, Librarian.* Philadelphia: Univ. of Pennsylvania Press, 1939, 101 pp.

VIGNAUD, HENRY. *Henry Harrisse: Etude biographique et morale avec la bibliographie critique de ses écrits.* Paris: C. Chadenat, 1912, 83 pp.

HART, ALBAN J. X.

LEARY, LEWIS. *Articles on American Literature, 1900–1950.* Durham: Duke Univ. Press, 1954, 126.

HART, JOEL TANNER

LEARY, LEWIS. *Articles on American Literature, 1900–1950.* Durham: Duke Univ. Press, 1954, 126.

HARTE, BRET

BLANCK, JACOB. *Bibliography of American Literature,* 5 Vols. New Haven: Yale Univ. Press, 1955–1969, III, 412–478.

_____, ed. *Merle Johnson's American First Editions,* 4th edition, revised and enlarged. Waltham, Massachusetts: Mark Press, 1965, 216–221.

DE PAUW UNIVERSITY, LIBRARY. *The Bret Harte Library of First Editions.* Greencastle, Indiana: De Pauw Univ., 1958, 19 pp.

GERSTENBERGER, DONNA, and GEORGE HENDRICK. *The American Novel, 1789–1959: A Checklist of Twentieth Century Criticism.* Denver: Alan Swallow, 1961, 105.

GOHDES, CLARENCE. "A Check-List of Bret Harte's Works in Book Form Published in the British Isles." *BB,* XVIII (May–August 1943), 19; (September–December 1943), 36–39.

HARRISON, JOSEPH B., ed. *Bret Harte: Representative Selections,* with introduction, bibliography and notes. New York: American Book Co., 1941, cxiii–cxxv.

HARTE, BRET. *Concerning "Condensed Novels,"* with introduction and bibliographical notes by Nathan

Van Patten. Palo Alto: Stanford Univ. Press, 1929, xxi pp.

_____ . *The Heathen Chinee: Plain Language from Truthful James,* with an introduction by Ina Coolbrith and a bibliography by Robert Ernest Cowan. San Francisco: John Henry Nash, 1934, xxxv—xli.

HISTORICAL RECORDS SURVEY, CALIFORNIA. *Calendar of the Francis Bret Harte Letters in the William Andrews Clark Memorial Library (University of California at Los Angeles).* Los Angeles: Southern California Historical Records Survey, 1942, 36 leaves.

LEARY, LEWIS. *Articles on American Literature, 1900—1950.* Durham: Duke Univ. Press, 1954, 126—128.

PENNSYLVANIA, UNIVERSITY, LIBRARY. *The Bret Harte Collection, University of Pennsylvania Library.* Philadelphia: Pennsylvania Univ. Library, 1954, 6 leaves.

SPILLER, ROBERT ERNEST, et al. *Literary History of the United States,* 2 Vols. New York: Macmillan, 1962, 542—544. Supplement, 133.

STEWART, GEORGE RIPPEY. "A Bibliography of the Writings of Bret Harte in the Magazines and Newspapers of California, 1857—1871." *Univ. of California Publications in English,* III (1931), 119—170.

_____ . *Bret Harte: Argonaut and Exile.* Boston and New York: Houghton Mifflin Co., 1931, 335—365.

TAYLOR, WALTER FULLER. *A History of American Letters,* with bibliographies by Harry Hartwick.

Boston: American Book Co., 1936, 541—543.

Subsequent editions entitled: *The Story of American Letters.*

TRENT, WILLIAM PETERFIELD, et al. *Cambridge History of American Literature,* 4 Vols. New York: G. P. Putnam's Sons, 1917—1921, II, 622—625.

VIRGINIA, UNIVERSITY, LIBRARY. *The Barrett Library Bret Hartes: A Checklist of Printed and Manuscript Works . . . ,* compiled by Lucy Trimble Clark. Charlottesville: Univ. of Virginia Press, 1957, 64 pp.

HAWTHORNE, JULIAN

LEARY, LEWIS. *Articles on American Literature, 1900—1950.* Durham: Duke Univ. Press, 1954, 128.

HAWTHORNE, NATHANIEL

ADERMAN, R. M. "Nathaniel Hawthorne's English Reputation to 1904." Unpublished doctoral dissertation, Univ. of Wisconsin, 1952.

AMERICAN ACADEMY OF ARTS AND LETTERS. *The Great Decade in American Writing, 1850—1860 . . .* New York: American Academy of Arts and Letters, 1954, 9—11.

The catalog of an exhibition of manuscripts, books, and painting displayed December 3—30, 1954.

ARNOLD, W. H. *First Editions of Bryant, Emerson, Hawthorne, Holmes, Longfellow, Lowell, Thoreau, Whittier.* Jamaica, New York: Marion Press, 1901, varying pagination.

BLANCK, JACOB. *Bibliography of American Literature,* 5 Vols. New

Haven: Yale Univ. Press, 1955–1969, IV, 1–36.

———————, ed. *Merle Johnson's American First Editions,* 4th edition, revised and enlarged. Waltham, Massachusetts: Mark Press, 1965, 222–226.

BROOKS, VAN WYCK. *The Dream of Arcadia: American Writers and Artists in Italy, 1760–1915.* New York: Dutton, 1958, bibliographical footnotes.

BROWNE, NINA ELIZA. "Best Editions of Nathaniel Hawthorne." *BB,* II (October 1901), 138–139.

———————. *A Bibliography of Nathaniel Hawthorne.* Boston and New York: Houghton Mifflin Co., 1905, 138 leaves and 75 pp.

The numbered leaves are printed on one side only. 550 copies printed.

BUFFALO, UNIVERSITY, LIBRARY. *A Catalogue of an Exhibition of First Editions, Association Books, Autograph Letters, and Manuscripts of Nathaniel Hawthorne.* Buffalo: Buffalo Univ. Library, 1937, 19 pp.

CATHCART, WALLACE HUGH. *Bibliography of the Works of Nathaniel Hawthorne.* Cleveland: The Rowfant Club, 1905, 217 pp.

CHAMBERLAIN, JACOB CHESTER. *First Editions of the Works of Nathaniel Hawthorne, together with Some Manuscripts, Letters, and Portraits Exhibited at the Grolier Club from December 24, 1904.* New York: Grolier Club, 1904, 88 pp.

FAUST, BERTHA. *Hawthorne's Contemporaneous Reputation: A Study of Literary Opinion in America and England, 1828–1864.* Philadelphia: Univ. of Pennsylvania Press, 1939, 158–163.

GERSTENBERGER, DONNA, and GEORGE HENDRICK. *The American Novel, 1789–1959: A Checklist of Twentieth Century Criticism.* Denver: Alan Swallow, 1961, 105–118.

GORDAN, JOHN DOZIER. *Nathaniel Hawthorne: The Years of Fulfillment, 1804–1853: An Exhibition from the Berg Collection First Editions, Manuscripts, Autograph Letters.* New York: New York Public Library, 1954, 50 pp.

Also: *BNYPL,* LIX (March 1955), 154–165; (April 1955), 182–217; (May 1955), 259–269; (June 1955), 316–321.

JONES, BUFORD. *A Checklist of Hawthorne Criticism, 1951–1966.* Hartford: Transcendental Books, 1967, 91 pp.

JUST, WALTER. *Die romantische Bewegung in der amerikanischen Literatur: Brown, Poe, Hawthorne: ein Beitrag zur Geschichte der Romantik.* Berlin: Mayer and Muller, 1910, 91–93.

KAWL, A. N. *Hawthorne: A Collection of Critical Essays.* Englewood Cliffs, New Jersey: Prentice Hall, 1966, 180–182.

LEARY, LEWIS. *Articles on American Literature, 1900–1950.* Durham: Duke Univ. Press, 1954, 128–134.

MOORE, HELEN-JEAN. "The American Criticism of Hawthorne, 1938–1948." Unpublished doctoral dissertation, Univ. of Pittsburgh, 1952.

O'CONNOR, EVANGELINE .
MARIA. *An Analytical Index to the
Works of Nathaniel Hawthorne,
with a Sketch of His Life.* Boston:
Houghton Mifflin Co., 1882, 294 pp.

PALTSITS, VICTOR HUGO. "List
of Books, etc, by and Relating to
Nathaniel Hawthorne, Prepared as an
Exhibition to Commemorate the
Centenary of His Birth." *BNYPL,*
VIII (July 1904), 312–322.

PHILLIPS, ROBERT S. *"The
Scarlet Letter:* A Selected Checklist
of Criticism, 1850–1962." *BB,*
(September–December 1962),
213–216.

PHILLIPS, ROBERT S., JACK
KLIGERMAN, ROBERT LONG
and ROBERT HASTINGS.
"Nathaniel Hawthorne: Criticism of
the Four Major Romances: A Selected Bibliography." *Thoth,* III
(Winter 1962), 39–50.

PICKARD, SAMUEL THOMAS.
*Hawthorne's First Diary, with an
Account of Its Discovery and Loss.*
Boston and New York: Houghton
Mifflin Co., 1897, 121 pp.

RANDALL, DAVID A., and
JOHN T. WINTERICH. "Collation
of First and Second Editions of
The Scarlet Letter." *PW* (Mar. 16,
1940), 1,181–1,182.

REID, WILLIAM. "A History of
Hawthorne Criticism, 1879–1932."
Unpublished Master's Thesis,
Univ. of Colorado, 1932.

SPILLER, ROBERT ERNEST, et al.
Literary History of the United States,
2 Vols. New York: Macmillan,
1962, 544–553. Supplement,
133–136.

STEWART, RANDALL. "Letters to
Sophia." *HLQ,* VII (August 1944),
387–395.

—————————. *Nathaniel
Hawthorne: A Biography.* New
Haven: Yale Univ. Press, 1949,
266–268.

STOVALL, FLOYD, et al. *Eight
American Authors: A Review of
Research and Criticism.* New York:
W. W. Norton and Co., 1963,
100–152, 428–434.

TAYLOR, WALTER FULLER. *A
History of American Letters,* with
bibliographies by Harry Hartwick.
Boston: American Book Co., 1936,
515–519.

Subsequent editions entitled: *The
Story of American Letters.*

TRENT, WILLIAM PETERFIELD,
et al. *Cambridge History of
American Literature,* 4 Vols. New
York: G. P. Putnam's Sons,
1917–1921, II, 415–424.

WAKEMAN, STEPHEN H. *The
Stephen H. Wakeman Collection of
Books of Nineteenth Century Ameri-
can Writers: The Property of Mrs.
Alice L. Wakeman, First Editions,
Inscribed Presentation and Personal
Copies, Original Manuscripts and
Letters of Nine American Authors.*
New York: American Art Associa-
tion, 1924, Items 261–439.

WARREN, AUSTIN, ed. *Nathaniel
Hawthorne: Representative Selections,* with introduction, bibliography
and notes. New York: American
Book Co., 1934, lxxv–lxxxiv.

WILSON, CARROLL ATWOOD.
*Thirteen Author Collections of the
Nineteenth Century and Five Cen-
turies of Familiar Quotations,*
edited by Jean C. S. Wilson and
David A. Randall, 2 Vols. New
York: privately printed for Scribner,
1950, I, 119–154.

WOODRESS, JAMES, et al. *American Literary Scholarship: An Annual.* Durham: Duke Univ. Press, (1963), 17–28; (1964), 16–31; (1965), 14–27; (1966), 12–24.

HAY, JOHN MILTON

BLANCK, JACOB. *Bibliography of American Literature,* 5 Vols. New Haven: Yale Univ. Press, 1955–1969, IV, 37–63.

_____, ed. *Merle Johnson's American First Editions,* 4th edition, revised and enlarged. Waltham, Massachusetts: Mark Press, 1965, 227–228.

DENNETT, TYLER. *John Hay: From Poetry to Politics.* New York: Dodd, Mead and Co., 1933, 445–449.

Appendix: "A Short List of His Writings," compiled by William E. Louttit Jr., 451–456.

LEARY, LEWIS. *Articles on American Literature, 1900–1950.* Durham: Duke Univ. Press, 1954, 134–135.

SPILLER, ROBERT ERNEST, et al. *Literary History of the United States,* 2 Vols. New York: Macmillan, 1962, 553–554.

WARD, SISTER SAINT IGNATIUS. *The Poetry of John Hay.* Washington: The Catholic Univ. of America Press, 1930, 71–78.

HAYNE, PAUL HAMILTON

BLANCK, JACOB. *Bibliography of American Literature,* 5 Vols. New Haven: Yale Univ. Press, 1955–1969, IV, 64–74.

HUBBELL, JAY B. *The South in American Literature, 1607–1900.*

Durham: Duke Univ. Press, 1954, 935–937.

LEARY, LEWIS. *Articles on American Literature, 1900–1950.* Durham: Duke Univ. Press, 1954, 135.

SPILLER, ROBERT ERNEST, et al. *Literary History of the United States,* 2 Vols. New York: Macmillan, 1962, 554–556. Supplement, 136.

WOODRESS, JAMES, et al. *American Literary Scholarship: An Annual.* Durham: Duke Univ. Press, (1964), 136–138; (1965), 159–160; (1966), 145–146.

HAYNE, ROBERT YOUNG

TRENT, WILLIAM PETERFIELD, et al. *Cambridge History of American Literature,* 4 Vols. New York: G. P. Putnam's Sons, 1917–1921, II, 473.

HEARN, LAFCADIO

ALABAMA, UNIVERSITY, LIBRARY. *A Bibliography of the Wallace Bruce Smith Collection of Lafcadio Hearn in the University of Alabama Library,* compiled by Mary Sue McGarity. University: Univ. of Alabama Press, 1958, 20 pp.

BLANCK, JACOB. *Bibliography of American Literature,* 5 Vols. New Haven: Yale Univ. Press, 1955–1969, IV, 75–106.

_____, ed. *Merle Johnson's American First Editions,* 4th edition, revised and enlarged. Waltham, Massachusetts: Mark Press, 1965, 229–234.

GERSTENBERGER, DONNA, AND GEORGE HENDRICK. *The American Novel, 1789–1959: A Checklist of Twentieth Century Criticism.*

Denver: Alan Swallow, 1961, 118—119.

GOULD, GEORGE MILBRY. *Concerning Lafcadio Hearn,* with a bibliography by Laura Stedman. Philadelphia: G. W. Jacobs and Co., 1908, 84—86, 336—416.

HARVARD UNIVERSITY, LIBRARY. "The Frances Blacker Kennedy Memorial Collection of Lafcadio Hearn." *Harvard University Library Notes,* IV (1914), 38—45.

JOHNSON, MERLE DE VORE. *Catalogue of First and Other Editions of the Writings of Mark Twain, Samuel Langhorne Clemens, and of Lafcadio Hearn.* New York: American Art Association, 1914, no pagination.

LEARY, LEWIS. *Articles on American Literature, 1900—1950.* Durham: Duke Univ. Press, 1954, 135—137.

McWILLIAMS, VERA S. *Lafcadio Hearn.* Boston: Houghton Mifflin Co., 1946, 447—453.

PERKINS, PERCIVAL DENSMORE, and IONE PERKINS. *Lafcadio Hearn: A Bibliography of His Writings,* with an introduction by Sanki Ichikawa. Tokyo: published for the Lafcadio Hearn Memorial Committee by the Hokuseido Press, 1934, 461 pp.

SISSON, MARTHA HOWARD, comp. "A Bibliography of Lafcadio Hearn." *BB,* XV (May-August 1933), 6—7; (September-December 1933), 32—34; (January-April 1934), 55—56; (May-August 1934), 73—75.

Also: *Bulletin of Bibliography Pamphlet,* No. 29.

Also: Boston: F. W. Faxon Co., 1933, 30 pp.

SPILLER, ROBERT ERNEST, et al. *Literary History of the United States,* 2 Vols. New York: Macmillan, 1962, 556—559. Supplement, 137.

TARG, WILLIAM. *Lafcadio Hearn: First Editions and Values: A Checklist for Collectors.* Chicago: The Black Archer Press, 1935, 51 pp.

500 copies printed.

HELPER, HINTON ROWAN

HUBBELL, JAY B. *The South in American Literature, 1607—1900.* Durham: Duke Univ. Press, 1954, 937.

LEARY, LEWIS. *Articles on American Literature, 1900—1950.* Durham: Duke Univ. Press, 1954, 137.

HEMANS, MRS. FELICIA DOROTHEA (BROWNE)

LEDDERBOGEN, W. *Felicia Dorothea Heman's Lyrik: Eine Stilkritik.* Heidelberger: C. Winter, 1913, v—viii.

HENNEMAN, JOHN BELL

TRENT, WILLIAM PETERFIELD, et al. *Cambridge History of American Literature,* 4 Vols. New York: G. P. Putnam's Sons, 1917—1921, II, 594—595.

HENTZ, CAROLINE LEE WHITING

GERSTENBERGER, DONNA, and GEORGE HENDRICK. *The American Novel, 1789—1959: A Checklist of Twentieth Century Criticism.* Denver: Alan Swallow, 1961, 128.

LEARY, LEWIS. *Articles on American Literature, 1900—1950.* Durham: Duke Univ. Press, 1954, 139.

HERBERT, HENRY WILLIAM (FRANK FORESTER)

BLANCK, JACOB. *Bibliography of American Literature*, 5 Vols. New Haven: Yale Univ. Press, 1955–1969, IV, 107–138.

——————, ed. *Merle Johnson's American First Editions*, 4th edition, revised and enlarged. Waltham, Massachusetts: Mark Press, 1965, 238–242.

LEARY, LEWIS. *Articles on American Literature, 1900–1950.* Durham: Duke Univ. Press, 1954, 139.

RANDALL, D. A. "A 'Frank Forester' Check List." *PW*, CXII (Sept. 24, 1932), 1276.

SEYBOLT, PAUL SPENCER, comp. *The First Editions of Henry William Herbert, "Frank Forester," 1807–1858: A Checklist.* Boston: privately printed, 1932, 16 pp.

VAN WINKLE, WILLIAM MITCHELL, comp. *Henry William Herbert (Frank Forester): A Bibliography of His Writings, 1832–1858,* with the bibliographical assistance of David A. Randall. Portland, Maine: Anthoensen Press, 1936, 207 pp.

HERNE, JAMES A.

LEARY, LEWIS. *Articles on American Literature, 1900–1950.* Durham: Duke Univ. Press, 1954, 140.

HEWITT, JOHN HILL

LEARY, LEWIS. *Articles on American Literature, 1900–1950.* Durham: Duke Univ. Press, 1954, 141.

HICKS, ELIAS

LEARY, LEWIS. *Articles on American Literature, 1900–1950.* Durham: Duke Univ. Press, 1954, 141.

HIGGINSON, THOMAS WENTWORTH STORROW

BLANCK, JACOB. *Bibliography of American Literature*, 5 Vols. New Haven: Yale Univ. Press, 1955–1969, IV, 139–184.

CAMBRIDGE PUBLIC LIBRARY (MASSACHUSETTS). *A Bibliography of Thomas Wentworth Higginson*, compiled by Winifred (Holt) Mather and Eva G. Moore. Cambridge: Cambridge Public Library, 1906, 47 pp.

HIGGINSON, MARY THACHER. *Thomas Wentworth Higginson: The Story of His Life.* Boston: Houghton Mifflin Co., 1914, 403–428.

LEARY, LEWIS. *Articles on American Literature, 1900–1950.* Durham: Duke Univ. Press, 1954, 141–142.

WOODRESS, JAMES, et al. *American Literary Scholarship: An Annual.* Durham: Duke Univ. Press, (1963), 129–130; (1965), 149–153.

HILDRETH, RICHARD

GERSTENBERGER, DONNA, and GEORGE HENDRICK. *The American Novel, 1789–1959: A Checklist of Twentieth Century Criticism.* Denver: Alan Swallow, 1961, 131.

HILL, BENJAMIN HARVEY

TRENT, WILLIAM PETERFIELD, et al. *Cambridge History of American Literature,* 4 Vols. New York: G. P. Putnam's Sons, 1917–1921, II, 595.

HILLHOUSE, JAMES ABRAHAM

BLANCK, JACOB. *Bibliography of American Literature*, 5 Vols. New Haven: Yale Univ. Press, 1955–1969, IV, 185–189.

HODGE, ARCHIBALD ALEXANDER

TRENT, WILLIAM PETERFIELD, et al. *Cambridge History of American Literature,* 4 Vols. New York: G. P. Putnam's Sons, 1917–1921, II, 534.

HODGE, CHARLES

TRENT, WILLIAM PETERFIELD, et al. *Cambridge History of American Literature,* 4 Vols. New York: G. P. Putnam's Sons, 1917–1921, II, 534.

HOFFMAN, CHARLES FENNO

BARNES, HOMER FRANCIS. *Charles Fenno Hoffman.* New York: Columbia Univ. Press, 1930, 317–333.

BLANCK, JACOB. *Bibliography of American Literature,* 5 Vols. New Haven: Yale Univ. Press, 1955–1969, IV, 190–203.

_____, ed. *Merle Johnson's American First Editions,* 4th edition, revised and enlarged. Waltham, Massachusetts: Mark Press, 1965, 252.

LEARY, LEWIS. *Articles on American Literature, 1900–1950.* Durham: Duke Univ. Press, 1954, 142.

SPILLER, ROBERT ERNEST, et al. *Literary History of the United States,* 2 Vols. New York: Macmillan, 1962, 563–564.

TAFT, KENDALL B., ed. *Minor Knickerbockers: Representative Selections,* with introduction, bibliography and notes. New York: American Book Co., 1947, cxxxiii–cxxxiv.

TRENT, WILLIAM PETERFIELD, et al. *Cambridge History of American Literature,* 4 Vols. New York: G. P. Putnam's Sons, 1917–1921, I, 522–523, 535.

HOLLAND, JOSIAH GILBERT

BLANCK, JACOB. *Bibliography of American Literature,* 5 Vols. New Haven: Yale Univ. Press, 1955–1969, IV, 204–218.

LEARY, LEWIS. *Articles on American Literature, 1900–1950.* Durham: Duke Univ. Press, 1954, 142.

PECKHAM, HARRY HOUSTON. *Josiah Gilbert Holland in Relation to His Times.* Philadelphia: Univ. of Pennsylvania Press, 1940, 208–214.

HOLLEY, MARIETTA

LEARY, LEWIS. *Articles on American Literature, 1900–1950.* Durham: Duke Univ. Press, 1954, 142.

HOLMES, GEORGE FREDERICK

LEARY, LEWIS. *Articles on American Literature, 1900–1950.* Durham: Duke Univ. Press, 1954, 142.

HOLMES, MARY JANE HAWES

BLANCK, JACOB. *Bibliography of American Literature,* 5 Vols. New Haven: Yale Univ. Press, 1955–1969, IV, 219–232.

HOLMES, OLIVER WENDELL

ARNOLD, W. H. *First Editions of Bryant, Emerson, Hawthorne, Holmes, Longfellow, Lowell, Thoreau, Whittier,* Jamaica, New York: Marion Press, 1901, varying pagination.

BLANCK, JACOB. *Bibliography of American Literature,* 5 Vols. New Haven: Yale Univ. Press, 1955–1969, IV, 233–339.

_____, ed. *Merle Johnson's American First Editions,* 4th edition, revised and enlarged. Waltham, Massachusetts: Mark Press, 1965, 253–262.

BROOKLYN PUBLIC LIBRARY. *Oliver Wendell Holmes, 1809–1894: A List of Books with References to Periodicals in the Brooklyn Public Library.* Brooklyn: Brooklyn Public Library, 1909, 15 pp.

BROWN, EMMA ELIZABETH. *Life of Oliver Wendell Holmes.* Boston: D. Lothrop and Co., 1884, 302–304.

Also: 1894, 333–336.

CLARK, HARRY HAYDEN, ed. *Major American Poets.* New York: American Book Co., 1936, 882–886.

CURRIER, THOMAS FRANKLIN. *"The Autocrat of the Breakfast Table:* A Bibliographical Study." *PBSA,* XXXVIII (3rd Quart. 1944), 284–311.

———————. *A Bibliography of Oliver Wendell Holmes,* edited by Eleanor M. Tilton for the Bibliographical Society of America. New York: New York Univ. Press, 1953, 720 pp.

GERSTENBERGER, DONNA, and GEORGE HENDRICK. *The American Novel, 1789–1959: A Checklist of Twentieth Century Criticism.* Denver: Alan Swallow, 1961, 131–132.

HAYAKAWA, S. I., and HOWARD MUMFORD JONES, eds. *Oliver Wendell Holmes: Representative Selections,* with introduction, bibliography and notes. New York: American Book Co., 1939, cxvii–cxxix.

IVES, GEORGE BURNHAM. *A Bibliography of Oliver Wendell Holmes.* Boston and New York: Houghton Mifflin Co., 1907, 348 pp.

KENNEDY, WILLIAM SLOANE. *Oliver Wendell Holmes: Poet, Litterateur, Scientist.* Boston: Cassino, 1883, 334–350.

LEARY, LEWIS. *Articles on American Literature, 1900–1950.* Durham: Duke Univ. Press, 1954, 142–144.

SCUDDER, HORACE E., ed. *The Complete Poetical Works of Oliver Wendell Holmes.* Boston: Houghton Mifflin Co., 1895, 341–344.

SPILLER, ROBERT ERNEST, et al. *Literary History of the United States,* 2 Vols. New York: Macmillan, 1962, 564–568. Supplement, 139–140.

TAYLOR, WALTER FULLER. *A History of American Letters,* with bibliographies by Harry Hartwick. Boston: American Book Co., 1936, 530–533.

Subsequent editions entitled: *The Story of American Letters.*

TRENT, WILLIAM PETERFIELD, et al. *Cambridge History of American Literature,* 4 Vols. New York: G. P. Putnam's Sons, 1917–1921, II, 540–543.

VIRGINIA, UNIVERSITY, LIBRARY. *The Barrett Library: Oliver Wendell Holmes: A Checklist of Printed and Manuscript Works . . . ,* compiled by Anita Rutman and Lucy Clark, the manuscripts by Marjorie Carver. Charlottesville: Univ. of Virginia Press, 1960, 109 pp.

WAKEMAN, STEPHEN H. *The Stephen H. Wakeman Collection of Books of Nineteenth Century American Writers: The Property of Mrs. Alice L. Wakeman, First Editions, Inscribed Presentation and Personal Copies, Original Manuscripts and Letters of Nine American Authors.* New York: American Art Association, 1924, Items 440–621.

WILSON, CARROLL ATWOOD. *Thirteen Author Collections of the Nineteenth Century and Five Centuries of Familiar Quotations,* edited by Jean C. S. Wilson and David A. Randall, 2 Vols. New York: privately printed for Scribner, 1950, II, 451–656.

WOODRESS, JAMES, et al. *American Literary Scholarship: An Annual.* Durham: Duke Univ. Press, (1963), 124–126; (1964), 126–130; (1965), 149–153; (1966), 136–139.

HOOPER, JOHNSON JONES

HOOLE, WILLIAM STANLEY. *Alias Simon Suggs: The Life and Times of Johnson Jones Hooper.* University: Univ. of Alabama Press, 1952, 252–271.

HUBBELL, JAY B. *The South in American Literature, 1607–1900.* Durham: Duke Univ. Press, 1954, 938.

TRENT, WILLIAM PETERFIELD, et al. *Cambridge History of American Literature,* 4 Vols. New York: G. P. Putnam's Sons, 1917–1921, II, 506.

HOPKINS, MARK

TRENT, WILLIAM PETERFIELD, et al. *Cambridge History of American Literature,* 4 Vols. New York: G. P. Putnam's Sons, 1917–1921, II, 534–535.

HOPKINSON, JOSEPH

LEARY, LEWIS. *Articles on American Literature, 1900–1950.* Durham: Duke Univ. Press, 1954, 144.

HORTON, GEORGE MOSES

WOODRESS, JAMES, et al. *American Library Scholarship: An Annual.* Durham: Duke Univ. Press, (1966), 145–146.

HOSMER, WILLIAM HOWE CUYLER

BLANCK, JACOB. *Bibliography of American Literature,* 5 Vols. New Haven: Yale Univ. Press, 1955–1969, IV, 340–344.

HOVEY, RICHARD

BLANCK, JACOB. *Bibliography of American Literature,* 5 Vols. New Haven: Yale Univ. Press, 1955–1969, IV, 356–362.

──────────, ed. *Merle Johnson's American First Editions,* 4th edition, revised and enlarged. Waltham, Massachusetts: Mark Press, 1965, 266–267.

LEARY, LEWIS. *Articles on American Literature, 1900–1950.* Durham: Duke Univ. Press, 1954, 145.

MacDONALD, ALLAN HOUSTON. *Richard Hovey: Man and Craftsman.* Durham: Duke Univ. Press, 1957, 229–250.

A bibliography of the first editions of books by Richard Hovey based on the collections of Hovey's works in the Dartmouth College Library, by Edward Connery Latham.

TRENT, WILLIAM PETERFIELD, et al. *Cambridge History of American Literature,* 4 Vols. New York: G. P. Putnam's Sons, 1917–1921, IV, 648–649.

HOWARD, BRONSON

AMERICAN DRAMATISTS CLUB. "Bronson Howard's Plays with Original Casts," in *In Memoriam: Bronson Howard, 1842–1908.* New York: Marion Press, 1910, 119–130.

LEARY, LEWIS. *Articles on American Literature, 1900–1950*. Durham: Duke Univ. Press, 1954, 145.

HOWARTH, E.C.

LEARY, LEWIS. *Articles on American Literature, 1900–1950*. Durham: Duke Univ. Press, 1954, 145.

HOWE, EDGAR WATSON

GERSTENBERGER, DONNA, and GEORGE HENDRICK. *The American Novel, 1789–1959: A Checklist of Twentieth Century Criticism.* Denver: Alan Swallow, 1961, 132.

HOWE, JOSEPH

LEARY, LEWIS. *Articles on American Literature, 1900–1950*. Durham: Duke Univ. Press, 1954, 145.

HOWE, JULIA WARD

BLANCK, JACOB. *Bibliography of American Literature,* 5 Vols. New Haven: Yale Univ. Press, 1955–1969, IV, 363–383.

LEARY, LEWIS. *Articles on American Literature, 1900–1950*. Durham: Duke Univ. Press, 1954, 145.

HOWE, SAMUEL GRIDLEY

LEARY, LEWIS. *Articles on American Literature, 1900–1950*. Durham: Duke Univ. Press, 1954, 146.

HOWELLS, WILLIAM DEAN

ARMS, GEORGE, and WILLIAM MERRIAM GIBSON, "A Bibliography of William Dean Howells." *BNYPL,* L (September 1946), 675–698; (November 1946), 857–868; (December 1946), 909–928; LI (January 1947), 49–65; (February 1947), 91–105; (April 1947), 213–248; (May 1947), 341–345; (June 1947), 384–388; (July 1947), 431–457; (August 1947), 486–512.

Also: New York: New York Public Library, 1948, 182 pp.

BAATZ, WILLIAM H. "William Dean Howells' Letters." *URLB,* VI (Winter 1951), 25–30.

BLANCK, JACOB. *Bibliography of American Literature,* 5 Vols. New Haven: Yale Univ. Press, 1955–1969, IV, 384–448.

————————, ed. *Merle Johnson's American First Editions,* 4th edition, revised and enlarged. Waltham, Massachusetts: Mark Press, 1965, 268–273.

BROOKS, VAN WYCK. *The Dream of Arcadia: American Writers and Artists in Italy, 1760–1915.* New York: Dutton, 1958, bibliographical footnotes.

CADY, EDWIN H. "Howells Bibliography: A 'Find' and a Clarification." *SB,* XII (1959), 230–234.

————————. "William Dean Howells in Italy: Some Bibliographical Notes." *Symposium,* VII (May 1953), 147–153.

COOKE, DELMAR GROSS. *William Dean Howells: A Critical Study.* New York: E. P. Dutton and Co., 1922, 257–272.

FIRKINS, OSCAR W. *William Dean Howells: A Study.* Cambridge: Harvard Univ. Press, 1924, 339–346.

GERSTENBERGER, DONNA, and GEORGE HENDRICK. *The American Novel, 1789–1959: A Checklist of Twentieth Century Criticism.* Denver: Alan Swallow, 1961, 133–139.

GRAHAM, PHILIP. "American First Editions at TxU: XI. William Dean Howells (1837–1920)." *LCUT,* VI (Spring 1958), 17–21.

HAMLIN, ARTHUR T. "The Howells Collection." *Harvard Library Notes,* III (1938), 147–153.

HOWELLS, MILDRED, ed. *Life and Letters of William Dean Howells,* 2 Vols. New York: Doubleday, Doran and Co., Inc., 1928, II, 403–409.

KIRK, CLARA MARBURG, and RUDOLF KIRK. "The Howells Sentinel," mimeographed bulletin for the Howells Group of the Modern Language Association. New Brunswick, Mar. 8, 1951.

Includes addenda to George Arms' and William Merriam Gibson's "A Bibliography of William Dean Howells," 1946–1947.

——————, eds. *William Dean Howells: Representative Selections,* with introduction, bibliography and notes. New York: American Book Co., 1962, clxviii–cxcix.

LEARY, LEWIS. *Articles on American Literature, 1900–1950.* Durham: Duke Univ. Press, 1954, 146–150.

MONTEIRO, GEORGE. "A Speech by W. D. Howells." *SB,* XX (1967), 262–263.

REEVES, JOHN K. "The Literary Manuscripts of W. D. Howells: A Descriptive Finding List." *BNYPL,* LXII (June 1958), 267–278; (July 1958), 350–363.

SMITH, HENRY NASH, and WILLIAM McGIBSON, eds. *Mark Twain – Howells' Letters: The Correspondence of Samuel L. Clemens and William D. Howells, 1872–1910,* 2 Vols.

Cambridge: Harvard Univ. Press, 1960, I, xxi–xxv.

SPILLER, ROBERT ERNEST, et al. *Literary History of the United States,* 2 Vols. New York: Macmillan, 1962, 571–576. Supplement, 140–142.

STAFFORD, WILLIAM T. "The Two Henry Jameses and Howells: A Bibliographical Mix-up." *BB,* XXI (January-April 1955), 135.

Corrects errors in standard bibliographies, which list Austin Warren's article "James and His Secrets," *SRL,* VIII (May 28, 1932), 959, as dealing with James Jr.

TAYLOR, WALTER FULLER. *A History of American Letters,* with bibliographies by Harry Hartwick. Boston: American Book Co., 1936, 559–562.

Subsequent editions entitled: *The Story of American Letters.*

TRENT, WILLIAM PETERFIELD, et al. *Cambridge History of American Literature,* 4 Vols. New York: G. P. Putnam's Sons, 1917–1921, IV, 663–666.

VIRGINIA, UNIVERSITY, LIBRARY. *The Barrett Library: W. D. Howells: A Checklist of Printed and Manuscript Works . . . ,* compiled by Fannie Mae Elliott and Lucy Clark. Charlottesville: Univ. of Virginia Press, 1959, 68 pp.

WOODRESS, JAMES. *Howells and Italy.* Durham: Duke Univ. Press, 1952, 202–213.

WOODRESS, JAMES, et al. *American Literary Scholarship: An Annual.* Durham: Duke Univ. Press, (1963), 112–117; (1964), 115–117; (1965), 135–137; (1966), 122–124.

HOYT, CHARLES HALE

LEARY, LEWIS. *Articles on American Literature, 1900–1950.* Durham: Duke Univ. Press, 1954, 150.

HUBBARD, ELBERT

LEARY, LEWIS. *Articles on American Literature, 1900–1950.* Durham: Duke Univ. Press, 1954, 150.

VAIL, ROBERT WILLIAM GLEN-ROIE. " 'A Message to Garcia': A Bibliographic Puzzle." *BNYPL,* XXXIV (February 1930), 71–78.

INGALLS, JOHN

LEARY, LEWIS. *Articles on American Literature, 1900–1950.* Durham: Duke Univ. Press, 1954, 151.

INGERSOLL, ROBERT

LEARY, LEWIS. *Articles on American Literature, 1900–1950.* Durham: Duke Univ. Press, 1954, 151.

INGRAHAM, JOSEPH HOLT

BLANCK, JACOB. *Bibliography of American Literature,* 5 Vols. New Haven: Yale Univ. Press, 1955–1969, IV, 459–491.

GERSTENBERG, DONNA, and GEORGE HENDRICK. *The American Novel, 1789–1959: A Checklist of Twentieth Century Criticism.* Denver: Alan Swallow, 1961, 140.

HUBBELL, JAY B. *The South in American Literature, 1607–1900.* Durham: Duke Univ. Press, 1954, 938.

LEARY, LEWIS. *Articles on American Literature, 1900–1950.*

Durham: Duke Univ. Press, 1954, 151.

IRVING, PETER

LEARY, LEWIS. *Articles on American Literature, 1900–1950.* Durham: Duke Univ. Press, 1954, 151.

IRVING, WASHINGTON

ADKINS, NELSON F. "Irving's 'Wolfert's Roost': A Bibliographical Note." *N&Q,* CLXIV (January 1933), 42.

BARNES, DANIEL R. "Washington Irving: An Unrecorded Periodical Publication." *SB,* XX (1967), 260–261.

BLANCK, JACOB. *Bibliography of American Literature,* 5 Vols. New Haven: Yale Univ. Press, 1955–1969, V, 1–96.

————, ed. *Merle Johnson's American First Editions,* 4th edition, revised and enlarged. Waltham, Massachusetts: Mark Press, 1965, 276–279.

————. "Salmagundi and Its Publisher: A Bibliographical Examination, with Notes on Its Publisher, David Longworth." *PBSA,* XLI (1st Quart. 1947), 1–32.

BOWDEN, EDWIN T. "American First Editions at the University of Texas: Washington Irving (1783–1859)." *LCUT,* VI (Spring 1959), 20–23.

BROOKS, VAN WYCK. *The Dream of Arcadia: American Writers and Artists in Italy, 1760–1915.* New York: Dutton, 1958, bibliographical footnotes.

EATON, VINCENT L. "The Leonard Kebler Gift of Washington Irving First

Editions." *LCQJ,* V (February 1948), 9–13.

HISPANIC SOCIETY OF AMERICA. *Washington Irving Diary, Spain, 1828–1829, edited from the Manuscript in the Library of the Society by Clara Louisa Penney.* New York: Hispanic Society of America, 1926, 142 pp.

HUBBELL, JAY B. *The South in American Literature, 1607–1900.* Durham: Duke Univ. Press, 1954, 938–939.

LANGFELD, WILLIAM ROBERT. "Washington Irving: A Bibliography." *BNYPL,* XXXVI (June 1932), 415–422; (July 1932), 487–494; (August 1932), 561–571; (September 1932), 627–636; (October 1932), 683–689; (November 1932), 755–778; (December 1932), 828–841.

Also: New York: New York Public Library, 1933, 97 pp.

LEARY, LEWIS. *Articles on American Literature, 1900–1950.* Durham: Duke Univ. Press, 1954, 151–154.

MORRIS, G. D. "Washington Irving's Fiction in the Light of French Criticism." *Indiana Univ. Studies,* III (May 1916), 1–27.

Bibliography of French reviews.

NEW YORK PUBLIC LIBRARY. "Catalogue of the Seligman Collection of Irvingiana: List of Manuscripts and Other Materials by or about Washington Irving Given by Mrs. Isaac N. Seligman and Mr. George S. Hellman." *BNYPL,* XXX (February 1926), 83–109.

PENNEY, CLARA LOUISA, ed. "Washington Irving in Spain: Unpublished Letters Chiefly to Mrs. Henry

O'Shea, 1844–1854." *BNYPL,* LXII (December 1958), 615–631; LXIII (January 1959), 23–39.

POCHMANN, HENRY A., ed. *Washington Irving: Representative Selections,* with introduction, bibliography and notes. New York: American Book Co., 1934, xciii–cx.

PRADES, JUANA DE JOSE. "Cuentos de la Alhambra' y Otros Temas Hispánicos de W. Irving." *Libro Español,* II (August–September 1959), 509–514.

Includes bibliography of Spanish translations of Irving.

REICHART, WALTER A. "The Earliest German Translation of Washington Irving's Writings: A Bibliography." *BNYPL,* LXI (October 1957), 491–498.

SPILLER, ROBERT ERNEST, et al. *Literary History of the United States,* 2 Vols. New York: Macmillan, 1962, 578–583. Supplement, 143–144.

TAYLOR, WALTER FULLER. *A History of American Letters,* with bibliographies by Harry Hartwick. Boston: American Book Co., 1936, 492–495.

Subsequent editions entitled: *The Story of American Letters.*

TRENT, WILLIAM PETERFIELD, et al. *Cambridge History of American Literature,* 4 Vols. New York: G. P. Putnam's Sons, 1917–1921, I, 510–517.

VAIL, ROBERT WILLIAM GLENROIE. "Catalogue of the Hellman Collection of Irvingiana: List of Manuscripts and Other Material by or about Washington Irving Given by Mr. George S.

Hellman." *BNYPL*, XXXIII (April 1929), 209–219.

WILLIAMS, STANLEY THOMAS, and MARY ALLEN EDGE, comps. *A Bibliography of the Writings of Washington Irving: A Check List.* New York: Oxford Univ. Press, 1936, 219 pp.

WILSON, CARROLL ATWOOD. *Thirteen Author Collections of the Nineteenth Century and Five Centuries of Familiar Quotations,* edited by Jean C.S. Wilson and David A. Randall, 2 Vols. New York: privately printed for Scribner, 1950, I, 155–171.

WOODRESS, JAMES, et al. *American Literary Scholarship: An Annual.* Durham: Duke Univ. Press, (1963), 110–112; (1964), 111–113; (1965), 129–133; (1966), 115–118.

IRVING, WILLIAM

TAFT, KENDALL B., ed. *Minor Knickerbockers: Representative Selections,* with introduction, bibliography and notes. New York: American Book Co., 1947, cxxxiv.

JACKSON, HELEN HUNT

BLANCK, JACOB. *Bibliography of American Literature,* 5 Vols. New Haven: Yale Univ. Press, 1955–1969, V, 97–116.

—————, ed, *Merle Johnson's American First Editions,* 4th edition, revised and enlarged. Waltham, Massachusetts: Mark Press, 1965, 280–281.

GERSTENBERGER, DONNA, and GEORGE HENDRICK. *The American Novel, 1789–1959: A Checklist of Twentieth Century Criticism.* Denver: Alan Swallow, 1961, 140–141.

LEARY, LEWIS. *Articles on American Literature, 1900–1950.* Durham: Duke Univ. Press, 1954, 154–155.

ODELL, RUTH. *Helen Hunt Jackson (H. H.).* New York and London: D. Appleton-Century Co., 1939, 249–314.

TRENT, WILLIAM PETERFIELD, et al. *Cambridge History of American Literature,* 4 Vols. New York: G. P. Putnam's Sons, 1917–1921, II, 626.

JAMES, HENRY, SR.

GRATTIN, C. HARTLEY. *The Three Jameses: A Family of Minds: Henry James, Sr., William James, Henry James.* New York: Longmans, Green and Co., 1932, 369–373.

JAMES, WILLIAM. *The Literary Remains of the Late Henry James.* Boston: Osgood, 1885, 469–471.

STAFFORD, WILLIAM T. "The Two Henry Jameses and Howells: A Bibliographical Mix-up." *BB*, XXI (January–April 1955), 135.

Corrects errors in standard bibliographies, which list Austin Warren's article, "James and His Secrets." *SRL*, VIII (May 28, 1932), 959, as dealing with James Jr.

JAMES, HENRY

BEACH, JOSEPH WARREN. *The Method of Henry James.* Philadelphia: A. Saifer, 1954, 272–276, 281–283.

BEEBE, MAURICE, and W. T. STAFFORD. "Criticism of Henry James: A Selected Check List with an Index to Studies of Separate Works." *MFS*, III (Spring 1957), 73–96.

BLANCK, JACOB. *Bibliography of American Literature,* 5 Vols. New Haven: Yale Univ. Press, 1955–1969, V, 117–181.

_____, ed. *Merle Johnson's American First Editions,* 4th edition, revised and enlarged. Waltham, Massachusetts: Mark Press, 1965, 282–286.

BOWDEN, EDWIN T. "Henry James and the Struggle for International Copyright: An Unnoticed Item in the James Bibliography." *AL,* XXIV (January 1953), 537–539.

_____. "In Defense of a Henry James Collection." *LCUT,* VI (Winter 1960), 7–12.

BROOKS, VAN WYCK. *The Dream of Arcadia: American Writers and Artists in Italy, 1760–1915.* New York: Dutton, 1958, bibliographical footnotes.

CARY, ELIZABETH LUTHER. *The Novels of Henry James: A Study,* with a bibliography by Frederick A. King. New York: G. P. Putnam's Sons, 1905, 189–215.

DUNBAR, VIOLA R. "Addenda to 'Biographical and Critical Studies of Henry James, 1941–1948,' *American Literature,* XX, 424–435 (January 1949)." *AL,* XXII (March 1950), 56–61.

DUPEE, FREDERICK WILCOX, ed. *The Question of Henry James.* New York: H. Holt and Co., 1945, 281–297.

EDEL, LEON. *Henry James.* Philadelphia: Lippincott, 1953, 337–344.

Also: London: Hart-Davis, 345–351.

_____. *Henry James: A Collection of Critical Essays.* Englewood Cliffs, New Jersey: Prentice Hall, 1965, 184–186.

_____. *Henry James: Les Années Dramatiques.* Paris: Jouve and Co., 1931, 245–252.

EDEL, LEON, and DAN H. LAURENCE, eds. *A Bibliography of Henry James,* 2nd edition, revised. London: R. Hart-Davis, 1961, 427 pp.

EDEL, LEON, and LYALL H. POWERS. "Henry James and the *Bazar* Letters." *BNYPL,* LXII (February 1958), 75–103.

FERGUSON, ALFRED R. "Some Bibliographical Notes on the Short Stories of Henry James." *AL,* XII (November 1949), 292–297.

FOLEY, RICHARD NICHOLAS. *Criticism in American Periodicals of the Works of Henry James from 1866 to 1916.* Washington: Catholic Univ. of America Press, 1944, 175 pp.

GALE, ROBERT L. *The Caught Image: Figurative Language in the Fiction of Henry James.* Chapel Hill: Univ. of North Carolina Press, 1964, bibliographical footnotes.

GERSTENBERGER, DONNA, and GEORGE HENDRICK. *The American Novel, 1789–1959: A Checklist of Twentieth Century Criticism.* Denver: Alan Swallow, 1961, 141–164.

GRATTAN, C. HARTLEY. *The Three Jameses: A Family of Minds: Henry James, Sr., William James, Henry James.* New York: Longmans, Green and Co., 1932, 369–373.

HAMILTON, EUNICE C. "Biographical and Critical Studies of Henry James, 1941–1948." *AL,* XX (January 1949), 424–435.

HOFFMAN, CHARLES G. *The Short Novels of Henry James.* New

York: Bookman Associates, 1957, 133–139.

JAMES, HENRY. *Selected Fiction,* edited with an introduction and notes by Leon Edel. New York: Dutton, 1953, xxi–xxiv.

KELLEY, CORNELIA PULSIFER. *The Early Development of Henry James.* Urbana: Univ. of Illinois Press, 1965, 301–314.

KENTON, EDNA. "Some Bibliographical Notes on Henry James." *Hound and Horn,* VII (April–June 1934), 535–540.

KRAFT, JAMES. "An Unpublished Review by Henry James." *SB,* XX (1967), 267–273.

LEARY, LEWIS. *Articles on American Literature, 1900–1950.* Durham: Duke Univ. Press, 1954, 155–163.

LE CLAIR, ROBERT CHARLES. *Three American Travellers in England: James Russell Lowell, Henry Adams, Henry James.* Philadelphia: Univ. of Pennsylvania Press, 1945, 216–219.

——————. *Young Henry James, 1843–1870.* New York: Bookman Associates, 1955, 455–462.

McELDERRY, B. R., JR. "The Published Letters of Henry James: A Survey." *BB,* XX (January–April 1952), 165–171; (May–August 1952), 187.

——————. "The Uncollected Stories of Henry James." *AL,* XXI (November 1949), 279–291.

MATTHIESSEN, FRANCIS OTTO, and KENNETH BALLARD MURDOCK, eds. *The Notebooks of Henry James.* New York: Oxford Univ. Press, 1947, 453 pp.

NOWELL-SMITH, SIMON. *The Legend of the Master.* New York: C. Scribner's Sons, 1947, 172–176.

PHILLIPS, LE ROY. *Bibliography of the Writings of Henry James.* Boston and New York: Houghton Mifflin Co., 1906, 196 pp.

Also: 1930.

RICHARDSON, LYON N., ed. *Henry James: Representative Selections,* with introduction, bibliography and notes. New York: American Book Co., 1941, xci–cxi.

ROBERTS, MORRIS. *Henry James's Criticism.* Cambridge: Harvard Univ. Press, 1929, 121–125.

RUSSELL, J. R. "The Henry James Collection." *URLB,* XI (Spring 1956), 50–52.

SPILLER, ROBERT ERNEST, et al. *Literary History of the United States,* 2 Vols. New York: Macmillan, 1962, 584–590. Supplement, 144–148.

STAFFORD, WILLIAM T. "The Two Henry Jameses and Howells: A Bibliographical Mix-up." *BB,* XXI (January–April 1955), 135.

Corrects error in standard bibliographies, which list Austin Warren's article, "James and His Secret," *SRL,* VIII (May 28, 1932), 959, as dealing with James Jr.

STALLMAN, ROBERT WOOSTER. *The Houses that James Built and Other Literary Studies.* East Lansing: Michigan State Univ. Press, 1961, bibliographical references.

STEVENSON, ELIZABETH. *The Crooked Corridor.* New York: Macmillan, 1949, 164–166.

STOVALL, FLOYD, et al. *Eight American Authors: A Review of Research and Criticism.* New York: W. W. Norton and Co., 1963, 364–418, 458–466.

SWAN, MICHAEL. *Henry James: A Select Bibliography.* London and New York: published for the British Council and the National Book League by Longmans, Green, 1950, 43 pp.

TAYLOR, WALTER FULLER. *A History of American Letters,* with bibliographies by Harry Hartwick. Boston: American Book Co., 1936, 556–559.

Subsequent editions entitled: *The Story of American Letters.*

TRENT, WILLIAM PETERFIELD, et al. *Cambridge History of American Literature,* 4 Vols. New York: G. P. Putnam's Sons, 1917–1921, IV, 671–675.

VALLETTE, JACQUES. "Petite Bibliographie de Henry James depuis la Guerre." *Mercure de France,* CCXV (July 1952), 528–531.

WARD, JOSEPH ANTHONY. *The Search for Form: Studies in the Structure of James's Fiction.* Chapel Hill: Univ. of North Carolina Press, 1967, bibliographical footnotes.

WEST, REBECCA. *Henry James.* New York: H. Holt and Co., 1916, 119–126.

WOODRESS, JAMES, et al. *American Literary Scholarship: An Annual.* Durham: Duke Univ. Press, (1963), 64–71; (1964), 62–72; (1965), 69–81; (1966), 65–78.

JAMES, WILLIAM

ALLEN, GAY WILSON. *William James: A Biography.* New York: Viking Press, 1967, 523–545.

ANDERSON, PAUL RUSSELL, and MAX HAROLD FISCH, eds. *Philosophy in America from the Puritans to James, with Representative Selections.* New York: D. Appleton Century Co., Inc., 1939, 524–526.

GRATTIN, C. HARTLEY. *The Three Jameses: A Family of Minds: Henry James, Sr., William James, Henry James.* New York: Longmans, Green and Co., 1932, 369–373.

LEARY, LEWIS. *Articles on American Literature, 1900–1950.* Durham: Duke Univ. Press, 1954, 163–165.

PERRY, RALPH BARTON. *Annotated Bibliography of the Writings of William James.* New York: Longmans, Green and Co., 1921, 69 pp.

SPILLER, ROBERT ERNEST, et al. *Literary History of the United States,* 2 Vols. New York: Macmillan, 1962, 590–593. Supplement, 148–149.

TRENT, WILLIAM PETERFIELD, et al. *Cambridge History of American Literature,* 4 Vols. New York: G. P. Putnam's Sons, 1917–1921, IV, 755–756.

JEMISON, MARY

LEARY, LEWIS. *Articles on American Literature, 1900–1950.* Durham: Duke Univ. Press, 1954, 170.

JEWETT, SARAH ORNE

BLANCK, JACOB. *Bibliography of American Literature,* 5 Vols. New Haven: Yale Univ. Press, 1955–1969, V, 189–205.

_____, ed. *Merle Johnson's American First Editions,* 4th edition, revised and enlarged. Waltham, Massachusetts: Mark Press, 1965, 294–295.

FROST, JOHN ELDRIDGE. "The Letters of Sarah Orne Jewett." *CLQ,* V (September 1959), 38–44.

_____. "Sarah Orne Jewett Bibliography: 1949–1963." *CLQ,* VI (June 1964), 405–417.

GERSTENBERGER, DONNA, and GEORGE HENDRICK. *The American Novel, 1789–1959: A Checklist of Twentieth Century Criticism.* Denver: Alan Swallow, 1961, 164–165.

LEARY, LEWIS. *Articles on American Literature, 1900–1950.* Durham: Duke Univ. Press, 1954, 170.

MARRINER, ERNEST C. "Sarah Orne Jewett Letters." *CLQ,* 4th Series, VIII (November 1956), 148–150.

MATTHIESSEN, FRANCIS OTTO. *Sarah Orne Jewett.* Boston: Houghton Mifflin Co., 1929, 153–155.

SPILLER, ROBERT ERNEST, et al. *Literary History of the United States,* 2 Vols. New York: Macmillan, 1962, 602–604. Supplement, 152–153.

TAYLOR, WALTER FULLER. *A History of American Letters,* with bibliographies by Harry Hartwick. Boston: American Book Co., 1936, 544–545.

Subsequent editions entitled: *The Story of American Letters.*

TRENT, WILLIAM PETERFIELD, et al. *Cambridge History of*

American Literature, 4 Vols. New York: G. P. Putnam's Sons, 1917–1921, II, 626.

WALTON, CLARENCE E. "The Jewett Collection." *HAB,* XXXV (1933), 474–476.

WEBER, CLARA CARTER, and CARL J. WEBER. *A Bibliography of the Published Writings of Sarah Orne Jewett.* Waterville, Maine: Colby College Press, 1949, 116 pp.

JOHNSON, WALTER ROGERS

LEARY, LEWIS. *Articles on American Literature, 1900–1950.* Durham: Duke Univ. Press, 1954, 171.

JOHNSTON, RICHARD MALCOLM

BLANCK, JACOB. *Bibliography of American Literature,* 5 Vols. New Haven: Yale Univ. Press, 1955–1969, V, 206–213.

HUBBELL, JAY B. *The South in American Literature, 1607–1900.* Durham: Duke Univ. Press, 1954, 940–941.

LEARY, LEWIS. *Articles on American Literature, 1900–1950.* Durham: Duke Univ. Press, 1954, 171.

STEDMAN, EDMUND C., and STEPHEN B. WEEKS. "Literary Estimate and Bibliography of Richard Malcolm Johnston." *Publications of the Southern Historical Association,* II (October 1898), 315–327.

TRENT, WILLIAM PETERFIELD, et al. *Cambridge History of American Literature,* 4 Vols, New York: G. P. Putnam's Sons, 1917–1921, II, 626.

JONES, CHARLES COLCOCK, JR.

LEARY, LEWIS. *Articles on American Literature, 1900−1950.* Durham: Duke Univ. Press, 1954, 171.

TRENT, WILLIAM PETERFIELD, et al. *Cambridge History of American Literature,* 4 Vols. New York: G. P. Putnam's Sons, 1917−1921, II, 596−599.

JONES, JOHN BEAUCHAMP

BLANCK, JACOB. *Bibliography of American Literature,* 5 Vols. New Haven: Yale Univ. Press, 1955−1969, V, 214−220.

JONES, WILLIAM A.

LEARY, LEWIS. *Articles on American Literature, 1900−1950.* Durham: Duke Univ. Press, 1954, 171.

JUDAH, SAMUEL

BLANCK, JACOB. *Bibliography of American Literature,* 5 Vols. New Haven: Yale Univ. Press, 1955−1969, V, 221−223.

LEARY, LEWIS. *Articles on American Literature, 1900−1950.* Durham: Duke Univ. Press, 1954, 171.

JUDD, SYLVESTER

BLANCK, JACOB. *Bibliography of American Literature,* 5 Vols. New Haven: Yale Univ. Press, 1955−1969, V, 224−227.

GERSTENBERGER, DONNA, and GEORGE HENDRICK. *The American Novel, 1789−1959: A Checklist of Twentieth Century Criticism.* Denver: Alan Swallow, 1961, 166.

LEARY, LEWIS. *Articles on American Literature, 1900−1950.* Durham: Duke Univ. Press, 1954, 171.

TRENT, WILLIAM PETERFIELD, et al. *Cambridge History of American Literature,* 4 Vols. New York: G. P. Putnam's Sons, 1917−1921, I, 535.

JUDSON, EDWARD ZANE CARROL

LEARY, LEWIS. *Articles on American Literature, 1900−1950.* Durham: Duke Univ. Press, 1954, 171.

KEENAN, HENRY FRANCIS

LEARY, LEWIS. *Articles on American Literature, 1900−1950.* Durham: Duke Univ. Press, 1954, 172.

KELLOG, ELIJAH

LEARY, LEWIS. *Articles on American Literature, 1900−1950.* Durham: Duke Univ. Press, 1954, 172.

KENNEDY, JOHN PENDLETON

BLANCK, JACOB. *Bibliography of American Literature,* 5 Vols. New Haven: Yale Univ. Press, 1955−1969, V, 228−242.

──────────, ed. *Merle Johnson's American First Editions,* 4th edition, revised and enlarged. Waltham, Massachusetts: Mark Press, 1965, 298−299.

GERSTENBERGER, DONNA, and GEORGE HENDRICK. *The American Novel, 1789−1959: A Checklist of Twentieth Century Criticism.* Denver: Alan Swallow, 1961, 166.

HUBBELL, JAY B. *The South in American Literature, 1607–1900.* Durham: Duke Univ. Press, 1954, 941–942.

LEARY, LEWIS. *Articles on American Literature, 1900–1950.* Durham: Dûke Univ. Press, 1954, 172.

LEISY, ERNEST E., ed. *Horse-Shoe Robinson,* with introduction, chronology and bibliography. New York: American Book Co., 1937, xxix–xxxii.

PAINE, GREGORY LANSING, ed. *Southern Prose Writers: Representative Selections,* with introduction, bibliography and notes. New York: American Book Co., 1947, cxxxiii–cxxxiv.

SPILLER, ROBERT ERNEST, et al. *Literary History of the United States,* 2 Vols. New York: Macmillan, 1962, 604–605. Supplement, 153.

TRENT, WILLIAM PETERFIELD, et al. *Cambridge History of American Literature,* 4 Vols. New York: G. P. Putnam's Sons, 1917–1921, I, 535–636; II, 506.

KENT, JAMES

TRENT, WILLIAM PETERFIELD, et al. *Cambridge History of American Literature,* 4 Vols. New York: G. P. Putnam's Sons, 1917–1921, II, 473–474.

KETTELL, SAMUEL

LEARY, LEWIS. *Articles on American Literature, 1900–1950.* Durham: Duke Univ. Press, 1954, 172.

KEY, FRANCIS SCOTT

BLANCK, JACOB. *Bibliography of American Literature,* 5 Vols. New Haven: Yale Univ. Press, 1955–1969, V, 243–251.

HUBBELL, JAY B. *The South in American Literature, 1607–1900.* Durham: Duke Univ. Press, 1954, 942.

LEARY, LEWIS. *Articles on American Literature, 1900–1950.* Durham: Duke Univ. Press, 1954, 172–173.

KIRKLAND, CAROLINE, MATILDA STANSBURY

BLANCK, JACOB. *Bibliography of American Literature,* 5 Vols. New Haven: Yale Univ. Press, 1955–1969, V, 260–269.

TRENT, WILLIAM PETERFIELD, et al. *Cambridge History of American Literature,* 4 Vols. New York: G. P. Putnam's Sons, 1917–1921, I, 536.

KIRKLAND, JOSEPH

BLANCK, JACOB. *Bibliography of American Literature,* 5 Vols. New Haven: Yale Univ. Press, 1955–1969, V, 270–273.

GERSTENBERGER, DONNA, and GEORGE HENDRICK. *The American Novel, 1789–1959: A Checklist of Twentieth Century Criticism.* Denver: Alan Swallow, 1961, 167.

LEARY, LEWIS. *Articles on American Literature, 1900–1950.* Durham: Duke Univ. Press, 1954, 173.

KNORTZ, KARL

LEARY, LEWIS. *Articles on
American Literature, 1900–1950.*
Durham: Duke Univ. Press,
1954, 173.

KNOWLES, FREDERIC LAWRENCE

LEARY, LEWIS. *Articles on
American Literature, 1900–1950.*
Durham: Duke Univ. Press,
1954, 173.

*LAMAR, LUCIUS QUINTUS,
CINCINNATUS*

TRENT, WILLIAM PETERFIELD,
et al. *Cambridge History of
American Literature,* 4 Vols.
New York: G. P. Putnam's Sons,
1917–1921, II, 600.

LAMAR, MIRABEAU BONAPARTE

GRAHAM, PHILIP. *The Life and
Poems of Mirabeau B. Lamar.*
Chapel Hill: Univ. of North
Carolina Press, 1938, 317–321.

HUBBELL, JAY B. *The South in
American Literature, 1607–1900.*
Durham: Duke Univ. Press,
1954, 943.

LEARY, LEWIS. *Articles on
American Literature, 1900–1950.*
Durham: Duke Univ. Press,
1954, 174.

LANDON, MELVILLE De LANCEY

BLANCK, JACOB. *Bibliography of
American Literature,* 5 Vols.
New Haven: Yale Univ. Press,
1955–1969, V, 274–279.

LANIER, SIDNEY

ANDERSON, CHARLES R., et al.,
eds. *The Centennial Edition of the
Works of Sidney Lanier,* 10 Vols.

Baltimore: Johns Hopkins Press,
1945, VI, 377–412.

Bibliography by Philip Graham and
Frieda C. Thies.

BLANCK, JACOB. *Bibliography of
American Literature,* 5 Vols.
New Haven: Yale Univ. Press,
1955–1969, V, 280–298.

_____, ed. *Merle
Johnson's American First Editions,*
4th edition, revised and enlarged.
Waltham, Massachusetts: Mark
Press, 1965, 306–308.

CALLOWAY, MORGAN, JR., ed.
Selected Poems of Sidney Lanier.
New York: C. Scribner's Sons,
1895, 152 pp.

Introduction includes 11 pp. bibliographical section.

CLARK, HARRY HAYDEN, ed.
Major American Poets. New York:
American Book Co., 1936, 903–907.

GERSTENBERGER, DONNA, and
GEORGE HENDRICK. *The American
Novel, 1789–1959: A Checklist of
Twentieth Century Criticism.*
Denver: Alan Swallow, 1961, 168.

GRAHAM, PHILIP, and JOSEPH
JONES, comps. *A Concordance of
the Poems of Sidney Lanier.*
Austin: Univ. of Texas Press, 1939,
447 pp.

HUBBELL, JAY B. *The South in
American Literature, 1607–1900.*
Durham: Duke Univ. Press,
1954, 943.

LEARY, LEWIS. *Articles on
American Literature, 1900–1950.*
Durham: Duke Univ. Press,
1954, 174–177.

MAYFIELD, JOHN S. "Lanier in
the Florae; or, 'What Would You

Have Done?' " *ABC*, X (February 1960), 7–10.

Bibliographical material on *Tiger-Lilies.*

PAINE, GREGORY LANSING, ed. *Southern Prose Writers: Representative Selections*, with introduction, bibliography and notes. New York: American Book Co., 1947, cxxxv–cxxxvi.

SPILLER, ROBERT ERNEST, et al. *Literary History of the United States*, 2 Vols. New York: Macmillan, 1962, 605–608. Supplement, 153–154.

STARKE, AUBREY HARRISON. *Sidney Lanier: A Biographical and Critical Study.* Chapel Hill: Univ. of North Carolina Press, 1933, 455–473.

TAYLOR, WALTER FULLER. *A History of American Letters,* with bibliographies by Henry Hartwick. Boston: American Book Co., 1936, 550–553.

Subsequent editions entitled: *The Story of American Letters.*

TRENT, WILLIAM PETERFIELD, et al. *Cambridge History of American Literature*, 4 Vols. New York: G. P. Putnam's Sons, 1917–1921, II, 600–603.

WOODRESS, JAMES, et al. *American Literary Scholarship: An Annual.* Durham: Duke Univ. Press, (1964), 136–138; (1965), 159–160; (1966), 145–146.

LARCOM, LUCY

BLANCK, JACOB. *Bibliography of American Literature*, 5 Vols. New Haven: Yale Univ. Press, 1955–1969, V, 299–325.

LATHROP, GEORGE PARSONS

BLANCK, JACOB. *Bibliography of American Literature*, 5 Vols. New Haven: Yale Univ. Press, 1955–1969, V, 326–339.

LAZARUS, EMMA

BLANCK, JACOB. *Bibliography of American Literature*, 5 Vols. New Haven: Yale Univ. Press, 1955–1969, V, 340–346.

LEARY, LEWIS. *Articles on American Literature, 1900–1950.* Durham: Duke Univ. Press, 1954, 178.

LEA, HENRY CHARLES

LEARY, LEWIS. *Articles on American Literature, 1900–1950.* Durham: Duke Univ. Press, 1954, 178.

LEE, RICHARD HENRY

HUBBELL, JAY B. *The South in American Literature, 1607–1900.* Durham: Duke Univ. Press, 1954, 944.

LEGARÉ, HUGH SWINTON

HUBBELL, JAY B. *The South in American Literature, 1607–1900.* Durham: Duke Univ. Press, 1954, 945–946.

LEARY, LEWIS. *Articles on American Literature, 1900–1950.* Durham: Duke Univ. Press, 1954, 178.

PAINE, GREGORY LANSING, ed. *Southern Prose Writers: Representative Selections*, with introduction, bibliography and notes. New York: American Book Co., 1947, cxxxvi–cxxxvii.

RHEA, LINDA. *Hugh Swinton Legaré: A Charleston Intellectual.* Chapel Hill: Univ. of North Carolina Press, 1934, 253–265.

LEGARE, JAMES MATHEWES

HUBBELL, JAY B. *The South in American Literature, 1607–1900.* Durham: Duke Univ. Press, 1954, 946–947.

LEARY, LEWIS. *Articles on American Literature, 1900–1950.* Durham: Duke Univ. Press, 1954, 178.

LEGGETT, WILLIAM

LEARY, LEWIS. *Articles on American Literature, 1900–1950.* Durham: Duke Univ. Press, 1954, 178–179.

TAFT, KENDALL B., ed. *Minor Knickerbockers: Representative Selections,* with introduction, bibliography and notes. New York: American Book Co., 1947, cxxxiv.

LEIGH, FRANCIS BUTLER

TRENT, WILLIAM PETERFIELD, et al. *Cambridge History of American Literature,* 4 Vols. New York: G. P. Putnam's Sons, 1917–1921, II, 603.

LELAND, CHARLES GODFREY (HANS BREITMANN)

BLANCK, JACOB. *Bibliography of American Literature,* 5 Vols. New Haven: Yale Univ. Press, 1955–1969, V, 347–398.

JACKSON, JOSEPH. "A Bibliography of the Works of Charles Godfrey Leland." *PMHB,* XLIX (No. 3, 1925), 261–288; (No. 4, 1925), 329–348; L (No. 1, 1926), 38–63; (No. 2, 1926), 149–162; (No. 3, 1926), 254–266; (No. 4, 1926), 367–374; LI (No. 1, 1927), 79–91.

LEARY, LEWIS. *Articles on American Literature, 1900–1950.* Durham: Duke Univ. Press, 1954, 179.

TRENT, WILLIAM PETERFIELD, et al. *Cambridge History of American Literature,* 4 Vols. New York: G. P. Putnam's Sons, 1917–1921, IV, 642.

LESLIE, ELIZA

LEARY, LEWIS. *Articles on American Literature, 1900–1950.* Durham: Duke Univ. Press, 1954, 179.

LE VERT, OCTAVIA

LEARY, LEWIS. *Articles on American Literature, 1900–1950.* Durham: Duke Univ. Press, 1954, 179.

LEWIS, ALFRED HENRY

BLANCK, JACOB. *Bibliography of American Literature,* 5 Vols. New Haven: Yale Univ. Press, 1955–1969, V, 399–404.

LEYPOLDT, FREDERICK

LEARY, LEWIS. *Articles on American Literature, 1900–1950.* Durham: Duke Univ. Press, 1954, 182.

LIEBER, FRANCIS

LEARY, LEWIS. *Articles on American Literature, 1900–1950.* Durham: Duke Univ. Press, 1954, 182.

LINCOLN, ABRAHAM

ANGLE, PAUL McCLELLAND.
*A Shelf of Lincoln Books: A
Critical, Selective Bibliography
of Lincolniana.* New Brunswick:
Rutgers Univ. Press, 1946,
131–136.

BARTLETT, JOHN RUSSELL.
*The Literature of the Rebellion:
A Catalogue of Books and Pamphlets Relating to the Civil War
in the United States. . . .* Boston:
Draper and Halliday, 1866,
486 pp.

Describes 300 eulogies, sermons
and poems on Lincoln's death.

BOOKER, RICHARD, comp.
*Check List of Lincolniana in the
Journals and Publications of the
Illinois State Historical Society,
1899–1938.* Chicago: The
Home of Books, Inc., 1939, 17 pp.

BOYD, ANDREW. *A Memorial
Lincoln Bibliography: Being an
Account of Books, Eulogies,
Sermons, Portraits, Engravings,
Medals, etc., Published upon
Abraham Lincoln, Sixteenth
President of the United States,
Assassinated Good Friday, April 14,
1865.* Albany: A. Boyd, 1870,
183 pp.

DENVER PUBLIC LIBRARY.
*Abraham Lincoln: A List of
Books and Magazine Articles on
Abraham Lincoln in the Library.*
Denver: Denver Public Library,
1909, 10 pp.

FISH, DANIEL. *Lincoln Bibliog-
raphy: A List of Books and
Pamphlets Relating to Abraham
Lincoln.* New York: F.D. Tandy
Co., 1906, 137–380.

——————. "Lincoln
Collections and Lincoln Bibliog-

raphy." *PBSA,* III (1908),
49–64.

——————. *Lincoln Litera-
ture: A Bibliographical Account
of Books and Pamphlets Relating
to Abraham Lincoln.* Minneapolis:
Minneapolis Public Library Board,
1900, 142 pp.

HEARTMAN, BOOKSELLERS,
NEW YORK. *Two Hundred and
Fifty-four Sermons, Orations,
Eulogies, and Other Pamphlets
Relating to Abraham Lincoln to
Be Sold at Unrestricted Auction
Sale . . . February 11, 1914, at
Heartman's Bookstore. . .
New York City. . . .* Lancaster,
Pennsylvania: Lancaster Printing
Co. Press, 1914, 30 pp.

From the preface: "The items
offered in the sale are from
the Lambert Collection."

LAMBERT, WILLIAM HARRI-
SON. *Abraham Lincoln, 1809–
1909: Lincoln Literature.*
Philadelphia: n.p., 1909, 16 pp.

LEARY, LEWIS. *Articles on
American Literature, 1900–1950.*
Durham: Duke Univ. Press,
1954, 183–184.

MONOGHAN, JAY, comp.
*Lincoln Bibliography, 1839–
1939,* 2 Vols. Springfield:
Illinois State Historical Society,
1943–1945.

*Collections of the Illinois State
Historical Library,* Nos. 31 and
32.

NEWMAN, RALPH G. "Basic
Lincolniana." *Civil War History,*
III (June 1957), 199–208.

NICOLAY, JOHN G., and
JOHN HAY, eds. *Complete*

Works of Abraham Lincoln,
with a bibliography by Daniel
Fish, 12 Vols. New York:
F. D. Tandy Co., 1905, XI,
135–380.

Gettysburg edition.

OAKLEAF, JOSEPH BENJAMIN.
Lincoln Bibliography. Cedar
Rapids, Iowa: Torch Press,
1925, 424 pp.

RANDALL, JAMES GARFIELD.
Lincoln the President, 2 Vols.
New York: Dodd, Mead and Co.,
1945, II, 343–400.

SMITH, WILLIAM HAWLEY, JR.
A Priced Lincoln Bibliography.
New York: privately printed,
1906, 70 pp.

SPILLER, ROBERT ERNEST,
et al. *Literary History of the
United States,* 2 Vols. New York:
Macmillan, 1962, 613–616.
Supplement, 156–158.

TRENT, WILLIAM PETERFIELD,
et al. *Cambridge History of
American Literature,* 4 Vols.
New York: G.P. Putnam's
Sons, 1917–1921, IV, 784–794.

WESSEN, ERNEST J. "Debates
of Lincoln and Douglas: A
Bibliographical Discussion."
PBSA, XL (2nd Quart. 1946),
91–106.

—————————. "Lincoln Bibliog-
raphy–Its Present Status and
Needs." *PBSA,* XXXIV (4th
Quart. 1940), 327–348.

LIPPARD, GEORGE

BLANCK, JACOB. *Bibliography
of American Literature,* 5 Vols.
New Haven: Yale Univ. Press,
1955–1969, V, 405–418.

GERSTENBERGER, DONNA,
and GEORGE HENDRICK. *The
American Novel, 1789–1959:
A Checklist of Twentieth Century
Criticism.* Denver: Alan Swallow,
1961, 174.

JACKSON, JOSEPH. "Bibliography of the Works of George
Lippard." *PMHB,* LIV (April
1930), 131–154.

LEARY, LEWIS. *Articles on
American Literature, 1900–1950.*
Durham: Duke Univ. Press,
1954, 186.

LOCKE, DAVID ROSS

BLANCK, JACOB. *Bibliography
of American Literature,* 5 Vols.
New Haven: Yale Univ. Press,
1955–1969, V, 419–430.

GERSTENBERGER, DONNA,
and GEORGE HENDRICK. *The
American Novel, 1789–1959:
A Checklist of Twentieth Century
Criticism.* Denver: Alan Swallow,
1961, 174.

LEARY, LEWIS. *Articles on
American Literature, 1900–1950.*
Durham: Duke Univ. Press,
1954, 186.

TRENT, WILLIAM PETERFIELD,
et al. *Cambridge History of
American Literature,* 4 Vols.
New York: G. P. Putnam's Sons,
1917–1921, II, 506.

LODGE, HENRY CABOT

LEARY, LEWIS. *Articles on
American Literature, 1900–1950.*
Durham: Duke Univ. Press,
1954, 186.

LONGFELLOW, HENRY WADSWORTH

ARNOLD, W. H. *First Editions of Bryant, Emerson, Hawthorne, Holmes, Longfellow, Lowell, Thoreau, Whittier.* Jamaica, New York: Marion Press, 1901, varying pagination.

AUSTIN, GEORGE LOWELL. *Henry Wadsworth Longfellow: His Life, His Works, His Friendships.* Boston: Lee and Shepard, 1883, 405–410.

BLANCK, JACOB. *Bibliography of American Literature,* 5 Vols. New Haven: Yale Univ. Press, 1955–1969, V, 468–640.

——————, ed. *Merle Johnson's American First Editions,* 4th edition, revised and enlarged. Waltham, Massachusetts: Mark Press, 1965, 323–329.

BROOKS, VAN WYCK. *The Dream of Arcadia: American Writers and Artists in Italy, 1760–1915.* New York: Dutton, 1958, bibliographical footnotes.

CARPENTER, GEORGE RICE. *Henry Wadsworth Longfellow.* Boston: Small, Maynard and Co., 1901, 147–150.

CHEW, BEVERLY. *The Longfellow Collectors' Hand-Book: A Bibliography of First Editions.* New York: W.E. Benjamin, 1885, 56 pp.

250 copies printed.

CLARK, HARRY HAYDEN, ed. *Major American Poets.* New York: American Book Co., 1936, 847–850.

GERSTENBERGER, DONNA, and GEORGE HENDRICK. *The American Novel, 1789–1959: A Checklist of Twentieth Century Criticism.* Denver: Alan Swallow, 1961, 177.

GOHDES, CLARENCE, comp. "A Check-List of Volumes by Longfellow Published in the British Isles during the Nineteenth Century." *BB,* XVII (September– December 1940), 46; (January– April 1941), 67–69; (May– August 1941), 93–96.

HIGGINSON, THOMAS WENT- WORTH. *Henry Wadsworth Long- fellow.* Boston and New York: Houghton Mifflin Co., 1914, 303–316.

KENNEDY, WILLIAM SLOANE. *Henry W. Longfellow: Biography, Anecdote, Letters, Criticism.* Cambridge, Massachusetts: M. King, 1882, 353–362.

KRAMER, SIDNEY. " 'There Was a Little Girl': Its First Printing, Its Author, Its Variants." *PBSA,* XL (4th Quart. 1946), 287–310.

LEARY, LEWIS. *Articles on American Literature, 1900–1950.* Durham: Duke Univ. Press, 1954, 188–192.

LIVINGSTON, LUTHER SAMUEL. *A Bibliography of the First Editions in Book Forms of the Writings of Henry Wadsworth Longfellow,* compiled largely from the collection formed by the late Jacob Chester Chamberlain with assistance from his notes and memoranda. New York: privately printed, 1908, 147 pp.

LONGFELLOW, HENRY WADS- WORTH. *The Complete Poetical Works of Henry Wadsworth Long-*

fellow. Boston: Houghton, 1902, 676–679.

"List of Mr. Longfellow's Poems."

LONGFELLOW, SAMUEL. *Final Memorials of Henry Wadsworth Longfellow.* Boston: Ticknor, 1887, 421–435.

_____. *Life of Henry Wadsworth Longfellow,* 2 Vols. Boston: Ticknor and Co., 1886.

Also: 3 Vols. Boston and New York: Houghton, Mifflin and Co., 1891, III, 427–437.

MORIN, PAUL. *Les Sources de l'OEuvre de Henry Wadsworth Longfellow.* Paris: E. Larose, 1913, i–xxxvii.

ROBERTSON, ERIC SUTHER-LAND. *Life of Henry Wadsworth Longfellow.* London: W. Scott, 1887, I–xii.

SHEPARD, ODELL, ed. *Henry Wadsworth Longfellow: Representative Selections,* with introduction, bibliography and notes. New York: American Book Co., 1934, lvii–lxii.

SPILLER, ROBERT ERNEST, et al. *Literary History of the United States,* 2 Vols. New York: Macmillan, 1962, 622–626. Supplement, 160.

TAYLOR, WALTER FULLER. *A History of American Letters,* with bibliographies by Harry Hartwick. Boston: American Book Co., 1936, 523–526.

Subsequent editions entitled: *The Story of American Letters.*

THOMPSON, LAWRENCE R. "Longfellow's Projected Sketch

Book of New England." *The Colophon,* Part 15 (1933), no pagination.

THOMPSON, RALPH. "Additions to Longfellow Bibliography Including a New Prose Tale." *AL,* III (November 1931), 303–308.

TRENT, WILLIAM PETERFIELD, et al. *Cambridge History of American Literature,* 4 Vols. New York: G. P. Putnam's Sons, 1917–1921, II, 425–436.

UNDERWOOD, FRANCIS HENRY. *Henry Wadsworth Longfellow: A Biographical Sketch.* Boston: J. R. Osgood and Co., 1882, 344–354.

WAKEMAN, STEPHEN H. *The Stephen H. Wakeman Collection of Books of Nineteenth Century American Writers: The Property of Mrs. Alice L. Wakeman, First Editions, Inscribed Presentation and Personal Copies, Original Manuscripts and Letters of Nine American Authors.* New York: American Art Association, 1924, Items 622–800.

WILLIAMSON, JOSEPH. *A Bibliography of the State of Maine from the Earliest Period to 1891,* 2 Vols. Portland, Maine: Thurston, 1896, I, 717–722.

WILSON, CARROLL ATWOOD. *Thirteen Author Collections of the Nineteenth Century and Five Centuries of Familiar Quotations,* edited by Jean C.S. Wilson and David A. Randall, 2 Vols. New York: privately printed for Scribner, 1950, I, 173–292.

WOODRESS, JAMES, et al. *American Literary Scholarship: An Annual.* Durham: Duke Univ. Press, (1963), 124–126; (1964),

126–130; (1965), 149–153;
(1966), 136–139.

LONGSTREET, AUGUSTUS BALDWIN

HUBBELL, JAY B. *The South in American Literature, 1607–1900.* Durham: Duke Univ. Press, 1954, 947–948.

LEARY, LEWIS. *Articles on American Literature, 1900–1950.* Durham: Duke Univ. Press, 1954, 192.

PAINE, GREGORY LANSING, ed. *Southern Prose Writers: Representative Selections,* with introduction, bibliography and notes. New York: American Book Co., 1947, cxxxvii–cxxxviii.

TAYLOR, WALTER FULLER. *A History of American Letters,* with bibliographies by Harry Hartwick. Boston: American Book Co., 1936, 535–536.

Subsequent editions entitled: *The Story of American Letters.*

TRENT, WILLIAM PETERFIELD, et al. *Cambridge History of American Literature,* 4 Vols. New York: G.P. Putnam's Sons, 1917–1921, II, 507.

WADE, JOHN DONALD. *Augustus Baldwin Longstreet: A Study of the Development of Culture in the South.* New York: Macmillan, 1924, 373–383.

LORD, WILLIAM WILBERFORCE

LEARY, LEWIS. *Articles on American Literature, 1900–1950.* Durham: Duke Univ. Press, 1954, 192.

LOVEJOY, ELIJAH PARISH

LEARY, LEWIS. *Articles on American Literature, 1900–1950.* Durham: Duke Univ. Press, 1954, 192.

LOW, JOHN

LEARY, LEWIS. *Articles on American Literature, 1900–1950.* Durham: Duke Univ. Press, 1954, 192.

LOWELL, JAMES RUSSELL

ARNOLD, W. H. *First Editions of Bryant, Emerson, Hawthorne, Holmes, Longfellow, Lowell, Thoreau, Whittier.* Jamaica, New York: Marion Press, 1901, varying pagination.

BEATTY, RICHMOND CROOM. *James Russell Lowell.* Nashville: Vanderbilt Univ. Press, 1942, 298–311.

BLANCK, JACOB, ed. *Merle Johnson's American First Editions,* 4th edition, revised and enlarged. Waltham, Massachusetts: Mark Press, 1965, 332–336.

CAMPBELL, KILLIS. "Bibliographical Notes on Lowell." *Univ. of Texas Studies in England,* IV (1924), 115–119.

CHAMBERLAIN, JACOB CHESTER, and LUTHER SAMUEL LIVINGSTON, comps. *A Bibliography of the First Editions in Book Forms of the Writings of James Russell Lowell,* compiled largely from the collection formed by the late Jacob Chester Chamberlain, with assistance from his notes and memoranda, by Luther S. Livingston. New York: privately printed, 1914, 153 pp.

CLARK, HARRY HAYDEN,
and NORMAN FOERSTER, eds.
*James Russell Lowell: Repre-
sentative Selections,* with introduction, bibliography and notes.
New York: American Book Co.,
1947, cxliii–clxvi.

COOKE, GEORGE WILLIS.
*A Bibliography of James Russell
Lowell.* Boston: Houghton Mifflin
Co., 1906, 208 pp.

530 copies printed.

HUBBELL, JAY B. *The South in
American Literature, 1607–1900.*
Durham: Duke Univ. Press,
1954, 948.

JOYCE, H.E. "A Bibliographical
Note on James Russell Lowell."
MLN, XXXV (April 1920),
249–250.

LEARY, LEWIS. *Articles on
American Literature, 1900–1950.*
Durham: Duke Univ. Press,
1954, 194–197.

LE CLAIR, ROBERT CHARLES.
*Three American Travellers in
England: James Russell Lowell,
Henry Adams, Henry James.*
Philadelphia: Univ. of Pennsyl-
vania Press, 1945, 216–219.

McELDERRY, B. R. "J. R.
Lowell and 'Richard III'–A
Bibliographical Error." *N&Q,*
CCIII (April 1958), 179–180.

McGLINCHEE, CLAIRE. *James
Russell Lowell.* New York:
Twayne, 1967, 135–139.

MILLER, F. DE WOLFE.
"Twenty-eight Additions to the
Canon of Lowell's Criticism."
SB, IV (1951), 205–210.

POTTER, ALFRED C. "James
Russell Lowell's Library."
Harvard Library Notes, III
(1935), 57–60.

SCUDDER, HORACE ELISHA.
*James Russell Lowell: A Bio-
graphy.* 2 Vols. Boston: Houghton
Mifflin Co., 1901, II, 421–427.

SPILLER, ROBERT E., et al.
*Literary History of the United
States,* 2 Vols. New York:
Macmillan, 1962, 628–634.
Supplement, 161–162.

TAYLOR, WALTER FULLER.
A History of American Letters,
with bibliographies by Harry
Hartwick. Boston: American
Book Co., 1936, 526–530.

Subsequent editions entitled:
The Story of American Letters.

TRENT, WILLIAM PETERFIELD,
et al. *Cambridge History of
American Literature,* 4 Vols.
New York: G. P. Putnam's Sons,
1917–1921, II, 544–550.

WAKEMAN, STEPHEN H. *The
Stephen H. Wakeman Collection
of Books of Nineteenth Century
American Writers: The Property
of Mrs. Alice L. Wakeman, First
Editions, Inscribed Presentation
and Personal Copies, Original
Manuscripts and Letters of Nine
American Authors.* New York:
American Art Association, 1924,
Items 801–930.

WHEELER, MARTHA THORNE.
"Best Editions of James Russell
Lowell." *BB,* III (October 1902),
42–43.

WILSON, CARROLL ATWOOD.
*Thirteen Author Collections
of the Nineteenth Century and
Five Centuries of Familiar*

Quotations, edited by Jean C. S. Wilson and David A. Randall, 2 Vols. New York: privately printed for Scribner, 1950, I, 293–304.

WOODRESS, JAMES L. "A Note on Lowell Bibliography: The Review of Howells' *Venetian Life.*" *SB,* IV (1951), 210–211.

WOODRESS, JAMES, et al. *American Literary Scholarship: An Annual.* Durham: Duke Univ. Press, (1963), 124–126; (1964), 126–130; (1965), 149–153; (1966), 136–139.

LOWELL, ROBERT TRAILL SPENCE

LEARY, LEWIS. *Articles on American Literature, 1900–1950.* Durham: Duke Univ. Press, 1954, 197.

LOWRY, ROBERT

LEARY, LEWIS. *Articles on American Literature, 1900–1950.* Durham: Duke Univ. Press, 1954, 197.

LUMMIS, CHARLES FLETCHER

LEARY, LEWIS. *Articles on American Literature, 1900–1950.* Durham: Duke Univ. Press, 1954, 197.

MacDOWELL, KATHERINE SHERWOOD (BONNER)

PAINE, GREGORY LANSING, ed. *Southern Prose Writers: Representative Selections,* with introduction, bibliography and notes. New York: American Book Co., 1947, cxxv–cxxvi.

MacKAYE, PERCY

GROVER, EDWIN OSGOOD, ed. *Annals of an Era: Percy Mackaye and the Mackaye Family, 1826–1932.* Washington: Pioneer Press, 1932, 534 pp.

LEARY, LEWIS. *Articles on American Literature, 1900–1950.* Durham: Duke Univ. Press, 1954, 197–198.

MacKAYE, STEELE

LEARY, LEWIS. *Articles on American Literature, 1900–1950.* Durham: Duke Univ. Press, 1954, 198.

MAHAN, ALFRED THAYER

LIVEZEY, WILLIAM EDMUND. *Mahan on Sea Power.* Norman: Univ. of Oklahoma Press, 1947, 312–326.

MANN, HORACE

KING, CLYDE S. *Horace Mann, 1796–1859: A Bibliography.* Dobbs Ferry, New York: Oceana Publications, 1966, 453 pp.

LEARY, LEWIS. *Articles on American Literature, 1900–1950.* Durham: Duke Univ. Press, 1954, 199.

MARSH, GEORGE PERKINS

LEARY, LEWIS. *Articles on American Literature, 1900–1950.* Durham: Duke Univ. Press, 1954, 201.

MARSH, JAMES

LEARY, LEWIS. *Articles on American Literature, 1900–1950.* Durham: Duke Univ. Press, 1954, 201.

MARSHALL, HUMPHREY

LEARY, LEWIS. *Articles on American Literature, 1900–1950.* Durham: Duke Univ. Press, 1954, 201.

MARSHALL, JOHN

HUBBELL, JAY B. *The South in American Literature, 1607–1900.* Durham: Duke Univ. Press, 1954, 949.

SERVIES, JAMES ALBERT. *A Bibliography of John Marshall.* Washington, 1956, 192 pp.

TRENT, WILLIAM PETERFIELD, et al. *Cambridge History of American Literature,* 4 Vols. New York: G. P. Putnam's Sons, 1917–1921, II, 474–475.

MARTINEAU, HARRIET

RIVLIN, JOSEPH B. "Harriet Martineau: A Bibliography of Her Separately Printed Books." *BNYPL,* L (May 1946), 387–408; (June 1946), 476–498; (July 1946), 550–572; (October 1946), 789–808; (November 1946), 838–856; (December 1946), 888–908; LI (January 1947), 26–48.

MATHEWS, CORNELIUS

GERSTENBERGER, DONNA, and GEORGE HENDRICK. *The American Novel, 1789–1959: A Checklist of Twentieth Century Criticism.* Denver: Alan Swallow, 1961, 180.

SPILLER, ROBERT ERNEST, et al. *Literary History of the United States,* 2 Vols. New York: Macmillan, 1962, 646–647.

TAFT, KENDALL B., ed. *Minor Knickerbockers: Repre-sentative Selections,* with introduction, bibliography and notes. New York: American Book Co., 1947, cxxxv.

TRENT, WILLIAM PETERFIELD, et al. *Cambridge History of American Literature,* 4 Vols. New York: G. P. Putnam's Sons, 1917–1921, II, 507–508.

MAURY, MATTHEW F.

LEARY, LEWIS. *Articles on American Literature, 1900–1950.* Durham: Duke Univ. Press, 1954, 204.

MAYO, WILLIAM STARBUCK

TRENT, WILLIAM PETERFIELD, et al. *Cambridge History of American Literature,* 4 Vols. New York: G.P. Putnam's Sons, 1917–1921, I, 536.

McCLELLAND, MARY GREENWAY

LEARY, LEWIS. *Articles on American Literature, 1900–1950.* Durham: Duke Univ. Press, 1954, 197.

McCONNEL, JOHN LUDLUM

TRENT, WILLIAM PETERFIELD, et al. *Cambridge History of American Literature,* 4 Vols. New York: G. P. Putnam's Sons, 1917–1921, II, 507.

McCOSH, JAMES

DULLES, JOSEPH HEATLY. *McCosh Bibliography.* Princeton: n.p., 1895, 9 leaves.

Appeared originally in the March 1895 issue of *Princeton College Bulletin.*

SLOANE, WILLIAM MILLIGAN, ed. *Life of James McCosh.*

New York: C. Scribner's Sons, 1896, 269—282.

TRENT, WILLIAM PETERFIELD, et al. *Cambridge History of American Literature,* 4 Vols. New York: G.P. Putnam's Sons, 1917—1921, II, 537.

McDOUGALL, FRANCES H. (WHIPPLE)

RIDER, SIDNEY SMITH. *Bibliographical Memoirs of Three Rhode Island Authors: Joseph K. Angell, Frances H. (Whipple) McDougall, Catharine R. Williams.* Providence: S.S. Rider, 1880, 92 pp.

Rhode Island Historical Tracts, No. 11.

McHENRY, JAMES

LEARY, LEWIS. *Articles on American Literature, 1900—1950.* Durham: Duke Univ. Press, 1954, 197.

McJILTON, JOHN NELSON

LEARY, LEWIS. *Articles on American Literature, 1900—1950.* Durham: Duke Univ. Press, 1954, 197.

MEEK, ALEXANDER BEAUFORT

HUBBELL, JAY B. *The South in American Literature, 1607—1900.* Durham: Duke Univ. Press, 1954, 950.

LEARY, LEWIS. *Articles on American Literature, 1900—1950.* Durham: Duke Univ. Press, 1954, 204.

MALLEN, GRENVILLE

TAFT, KENDALL B., ed. *Minor Knickerbockers: Repre-* *sentative Selections,* with introduction, bibliography and notes. New York: American Book Co., 1947, cxxxvi.

MELVILLE, HERMAN

AMENT, W. S. "Bowdler and the Whale." *AL,* IV (March 1932), 39—46.

AMERICAN ACADEMY OF ARTS AND LETTERS. *The Great Decade in American Writing, 1850—1860. . . .* New York: American Academy of Arts and Letters, 1954, 12—15.

The catalog of an exhibition of manuscripts, books and paintings displayed Dec. 3—30, 1954.

ANDERSON, CHARLES ROBERTS. *Melville in the South Seas.* New York: Columbia Univ. Press, 1940, 497—505.

BEEBE, MAURICE, HARRISON HAYFORD and GORDON ROPER. "Criticism of Herman Melville: A Selected Checklist." *MFS,* VIII (Autumn 1962), 211—346.

BLANCK, JACOB, ed. *Merle Johnson's American First Editions,* 4th edition, revised and enlarged. Waltham, Massachusetts: Mark Press, 1965, 355—357.

——————. "News from the Rare Book Sellers." *PW,* CLII (Aug. 23, 1947), B122.

Bibliographical details on the three issues of the first edition of *Moby Dick.*

BRODTKORB, PAUL, JR. *Ishmael's White World: A Phenomenological Reading of* Moby Dick. New Haven: Yale Univ. Press, 1965, 149—150.

CAHOON, HERBERT. "Herman Melville: A Check List of Books and Manuscripts in the Collections of the New York Public Library." *BNYPL*, LV (June 1951), 263–275; (July 1951), 325–338.

GERSTENBERGER, DONNA, and GEORGE HENDRICK. *The American Novel, 1789–1959: A Checklist of Twentieth Century Criticism.* Denver: Alan Swallow, 1961, 181–202.

HETHERINGTON, HUGH W. *Melville's Reviewers, British and American, 1846–1891.* Chapel Hill: Univ. of North Carolina Press, 1961, 314 pp.

HILLWAY, TYRUS. *Herman Melville.* New Haven: Yale Univ. Press, 1963, 162–170.

_____. *Melville and the Whale.* Stonington, Connecticut: Stonington Publishing Co., 1950, 11–12.

_____. "Some Recent Articles Relating to Melville (January 1947 to September 1948)." *Melville Society News Letter,* IV (No. 3, 1948), no pagination.

HILLWAY, TYRUS, and HERSHEL PARKER, comps. *A Directory of Melville Dissertations,* compiled for the Melville Society. Evanston, Illinois: n.p., 1962, 63 pp.

From the title page: "A revision and expansion of Tyrus Hillway's *Doctoral Dissertations on Herman Melville* (1953)."

HOWARD, LEON. *Herman Melville.* Minneapolis: Univ. of Minnesota Press, 1961, 48 pp.

Univ. of Minnesota Pamphlets on American Writers, No. 13.

LEARY, LEWIS. *Articles on American Literature, 1900–1950.* Durham: Duke Univ. Press, 1954, 204–211.

LEYDA, JAY. *The Melville Log: A Documentary Life of Herman Melville, 1819–1891,* 2 Vols. New York: Harcourt, Brace, 1951.

MELVILLE, HERMAN. *The Encantadas: or, Enchanted Isles,* with an introduction, critical epilogue and bibliographical notes by Victor Wolfgang Von Hagen. Burlingame, California: W.P. Wreden, 1940, 115–119.

"The Melville Room in the Berkshire Athenaeum." *Bay State Librarian,* XLVII (Winter 1957), 9.

MILLER, JAMES EDWIN, JR. *A Reader's Guide to Herman Melville.* New York: Farrar, Straus and Cudahy, 1962, 266 pp.

MILLS, GORDON H. "American First Editions at Texas University: Herman Melville (1819–1891)." *LCUT,* IV (Summer 1951), 89–92.

MINNIGERODE, MEADE, ed. *Some Personal Letters of Herman Melville.* New York: The Brick Row Book Shop, Inc., 1922, 101–195.

MUMFORD, LEWIS. *Herman Melville.* New York: Harcourt, Brace and Co., 1929, 369.

PRINCETON UNIVERSITY, LIBRARY. Moby Dick *by Herman Melville: A Century of an American Classic, 1851–1951: An Exhibition, Princeton University Library.* Princeton: Princeton Univ. Library, 1951, 4 pp.

_____. *"Moby Dick* by Herman Melville: A Century of an American Classic, 1851–1951: Catalogue of an Exhibition." *PULC,* XIII (Winter 1952), 63–118.

ROPER, GORDON. "Bibliography and Works by and on Herman Melville." Mimeographed sheets, privately issued.

The author teaches at Trinity College, Univ. of Toronto.

SADLIER, MICHAEL. *Excursions in Victorian Bibliography.* London: Chaundy and Co., 1922, 222–234.

SEALTS, MERTON M., JR. "Melville and the Shakers." *SB,* II (1949–1950), 105–114.

_____. "Melville's Reading: A Check-List of Books Owned and Borrowed." *HLB,* II (Spring 1948), 141–163; (Autumn 1948), 378–392; III (Winter 1949), 119–130; (Spring 1949), 268–277; (Autumn 1949), 407–421; IV (Winter 1950), 98–109.

_____. *Melville's Reading: A Check-List of Books Owned and Borrowed.* Madison: Univ. of Wisconsin Press, 1966, 134 pp.

_____. "Melville's Reading: A Supplement List of Books Owned and Borrowed." *HLB,* VI (Spring 1952), 239–247.

_____. "The Publication of Melville's *Piazza Tales." MLN,* LIX (January 1944), 56–59.

From the incomplete correspondence between Melville and his publishers, a portion of the bibliographical history of *Piazza Tales* (1856) is reconstructed.

SIMON, JEAN. *Herman Melville: Marin, métaphysicien et poète.* Paris: Boivin et Cie., 1939, 587–602.

_____. "Travaux recents sur Herman Melville." *EA,* VI (February 1953), 40–49.

SPILLER, ROBERT ERNEST, et al. *Literary History of the United States,* 2 Vols. New York: Macmillan, 1962, 647–654. Supplement, 164–168.

STERN, MILTON R. *The Fine Hammered Steel of Herman Melville.* Urbana: Univ. of Illinois Press, 1957, 251–291.

STOVALL, FLOYD, et al. *Eight American Authors: A Review of Research and Criticism.* New York: W. W. Norton and Co., 1963, 207–270, 438–445.

TAYLOR, WALTER FULLER. *A History of American Letters,* with bibliographies by Harry Hartwick. Boston: American Book Co., 1936, 506–509.

Subsequent editions entitled: *The Story of American Letters.*

THORP, WILLARD, ed. *Herman Melville: Representative Selections,* with introduction, bibliography and notes. New York: American Book Co., 1938, cxxxiii–clxi.

TRENT, WILLIAM PETERFIELD, et al. *Cambridge History of American Literature,* 4 Vols. New York: G.P. Putnam's Sons, 1917–1921, I, 536–538.

WEAVER, RAYMOND MEL-BOURNE. *Herman Melville: Mariner and Mystic.* New York: George H. Doran Co., 1931, 385–388.

WILLIAMS, M. L. "Some Notices and Reviews of Melville's Novels in American Religious Periodicals, 1846–1849." *AL,* XXII (May 1950), 121–127.

WILSON, CARROLL ATWOOD, *Thirteen Author Collections of the Nineteenth Century and Five Centuries of Familiar Quotations,* edited by Jean C.S. Wilson and David A. Randall, 2 Vols. New York: privately printed for Scribner, 1950, I, 305–316.

WOODRESS, JAMES, et al. *American Literary Scholarship: An Annual.* Durham: Duke Univ. Press, (1963), 29–40; (1964), 32–42; (1965), 28–44; (1966), 25–39.

MILES, GEORGE HENRY

LEARY, LEWIS. *Articles on American Literature, 1900–1950.* Durham: Duke Univ. Press, 1954, 213.

MILLER, JOAQUIN

BLANCK, JACOB, ed. *Merle Johnson's American First Editions,* 4th edition, revised and enlarged. Waltham, Massachusetts: Mark Press, 1965, 365–368.

FROST, ORCUTT WILLIAM. *Joaquin Miller.* New York: Twayne, 1967, 129–134.

HALLINE, ALLAN GATES. *American Plays.* New York: American Book Co., 1935, 758.

LEARY, LEWIS. *Articles on American Literature, 1900–1950.* Durham: Duke Univ. Press, 1954, 215.

PETERSON, MARTIN SEVERIN. *Joaquin Miller: Literary Frontiers-*

man. Palo Alto: Stanford Univ. Press, 1937, 179–191.

SPILLER, ROBERT ERNEST, et al. *Literary History of the United States,* 2 Vols. New York: Macmillan, 1962, 658–660. Supplement, 170.

TAYLOR, WALTER FULLER. *A History of American Letters,* with bibliographies by Harry Hartwick. Boston: American Book Co., 1936, 549–550.

Subsequent editions entitled: *The Story of American Letters.*

TRENT, WILLIAM PETERFIELD, et al. *Cambridge History of American Literature,* 4 Vols. New York: G. P. Putnam's Sons, 1917–1921, IV, 649–650.

WOODRESS, JAMES, et al. *American Literary Scholarship: An Annual.* Durham: Duke Univ. Press, (1963), 129–130; (1965), 159–160.

MILLER, SAMUEL

LEARY, LEWIS. *Articles on American Literature, 1900–1950.* Durham: Duke Univ. Press, 1954, 215.

PRINCETON UNIVERSITY, LIBRARY. *A Landmark in American Intellectual History: Samuel Miller's "A Brief Retrospect of the 18th Century," 1803: An Exhibition Commemorating the 150th Anniversary of Its Publication: Catalogue of the Exhibition.* Princeton: Princeton Univ. Library, 1953, 35 leaves.

MITCHELL, DONALD GRANT

BLANCK, JACOB, ed. *Merle Johnson's American First Editions,*

4th edition, revised and enlarged. Waltham, Massachusetts: Mark Press, 1965, 369—371.

LEARY, LEWIS. *Articles on American Literature, 1900—1950.* Durham: Duke Univ. Press, 1954, 216.

MITCHELL, SILAS WEIR

BLANCK, JACOB, ed. *Merle Johnson's American First Editions,* 4th edition, revised and enlarged. Waltham, Massachusetts: Mark Press, 1965, 372—375.

GERSTENBERGER, DONNA, and GEORGE HENDRICK. *The American Novel, 1789—1959: A Checklist of Twentieth Century Criticism.* Denver: Alan Swallow, 1961, 204.

LEARY, LEWIS. *Articles on American Literature, 1900—1950.* Durham: Duke Univ. Press, 1954, 216.

MITCHILL, SAMUEL LATHAM

TAFT, KENDALL B., ed. *Minor Knickerbockers: Representative Selections,* with introduction, bibliography and notes. New York: American Book Co., 1947, cxxxvi—cxxxvii.

MONK, MARIA

LEARY, LEWIS. *Articles on American Literature, 1900—1950.* Durham: Duke Univ. Press, 1954, 216.

MONROE, JAMES

GILMAN, DANIEL COIT. *James Monroe in His Relations to the Public Service during Half a Century, 1776—1826.* Boston: Houghton Mifflin Co., 1892, 253—280.

LIBRARY OF CONGRESS, DIVISION OF MANUSCRIPTS. *Papers of James Monroe, Listed in Chronological Form from the Original Manuscripts in the Library of Congress,* compiled by Worthington Chauncey Ford. Washington, 1904, 114 pp.

TRENT, WILLIAM PETERFIELD, et al. *Cambridge History of American Literature,* 4 Vols. New York: G. P. Putnam's Sons, 1917—1921, II, 475.

MOORE, CHARLES LEONARD

LEARY, LEWIS. *Articles on American Literature, 1900—1950.* Durham: Duke Univ. Press, 1954, 217.

MOORE, CLEMENT CLARKE

LEARY, LEWIS. *Articles on American Literature, 1900—1950.* Durham: Duke Univ. Press, 1954, 217.

TAFT, KENDALL B., ed. *Minor Knickerbockers: Representative Selections,* with introduction, bibliography and notes. New York: American Book Co., 1947, cxxxvii—cxxxviii.

MOORE, JULIA A.

GREENLY, ALBERT H. "The Sweet Singer of Michigan Bibliographically Considered." *PBSA,* XXXIX (2nd Quart. 1945), 91—118.

MORRIS, GEORGE POPE

LEARY, LEWIS. *Articles on American Literature, 1900—1950.* Durham: Duke Univ. Press, 1954, 219.

TAFT, KENDALL B., ed. *Minor Knickerbockers: Representa-*

tive Selections, with introduction, bibliography and notes. New York: American Book Co., 1947, cxxxviii–cxxxix.

TRENT, WILLIAM PETERFIELD, et al. *Cambridge History of American Literature,* 4 Vols. New York: G. P. Putnam's Sons, 1917–1921, I, 523; II, 508.

MORSE, JEDEDIAH

LEARY, LEWIS. *Articles on American Literature, 1900–1950.* Durham: Duke Univ. Press, 1954, 219.

MOTLEY, JOHN LOTHROP

HIGBY, CHESTER PENN, and B. T. SCHANTZ, eds. *John Lothrop Motley: Representative Selections,* with introduction, bibliography and notes. New York: American Book Co., 1939, cxxxv–clxi.

LEARY, LEWIS. *Articles on American Literature, 1900–1950.* Durham: Duke Univ. Press, 1954, 220.

SPILLER, ROBERT ERNEST, et al. *Literary History of the United States,* 2 Vols. New York: Macmillan, 1962, 664–666.

TRENT, WILLIAM PETERFIELD, et al. *Cambridge History of American Literature,* 4 Vols. New York: G.P. Putnam's Sons, 1917–1921, II, 501–503.

MOULTON, LOUISE CHANDLER

LEARY, LEWIS. *Articles on American Literature, 1900–1950.* Durham: Duke Univ. Press, 1954, 220.

VAIL, ROBERT WILLIAM GLENROIE. "Report of the Librarian: A Check List of the Writings of Louise Chandler Moulton." *PAAS,* ns XLIII (October 1933), 234–236.

MUNFORD, WILLIAM

HUBBELL, JAY B. *The South in American Literature, 1607–1900.* Durham: Duke Univ. Press, 1954, 951.

LEARY, LEWIS. *Articles on American Literature, 1900–1950.* Durham: Duke Univ. Press, 1954, 220.

MUNSEY, FRANK ANDREW

LEARY, LEWIS. *Articles on American Literature, 1900–1950.* Durham: Duke Univ. Press, 1954, 220.

MURFREE, MARY NOAILLES (CHARLES EGBERT CRADDOCK)

GERSTENBERGER, DONNA, and GEORGE HENDRICK. *The American Novel, 1789–1959: A Checklist of Twentieth Century Criticism.* Denver: Alan Swallow, 1961, 205.

LEARY, LEWIS. *Articles on American Literature, 1900–1950.* Durham: Duke Univ. Press, 1954, 220–221.

PAINE, GREGORY LANSING, ed. *Southern Prose Writers: Representative Selections,* with introduction, bibliography and notes. New York: American Book Co., 1947, cxxxviii.

PARKS, EDD WINFIELD. *Charles Egbert Craddock (Mary Noailles Murfree).* Chapel Hill: Univ. of North Carolina Press,

1941, 237—249, bibliographical footnotes.

SPILLER, ROBERT ERNEST, et al. *Literary History of the United States,* 2 Vols. New York: Macmillan, 1962, 667—668.

TRENT, WILLIAM PETERFIELD, et al. *Cambridge History of American Literature,* 4 Vols. New York: G.P. Putnam's Sons, 1917—1921, II, 627.

NEAL, JOHN

LEARY, LEWIS. *Articles on American Literature, 1900—1950.* Durham: Duke Univ. Press, 1954, 221.

TRENT, WILLIAM PETERFIELD, et al. *Cambridge History of American Literature,* 4 Vols. New York: G. P. Putnam's Sons, 1917—1921, I, 538.

NEAL, JOSEPH CLAY

TRENT, WILLIAM PETERFIELD, et al. *Cambridge History of American Literature,* 4 Vols. New York: G. P. Putnam's Sons, 1917—1921, II, 508.

NEAL, ROBERT

GERSTENBERGER, DONNA, and GEORGE HENDRICK. *The American Novel, 1789—1959: A Checklist of Twentieth Century Criticism.* Denver: Alan Swallow, 1961, 206.

NEVILLE, MORGAN

LEARY, LEWIS. *Articles on American Literature, 1900—1950.* Durham: Duke Univ. Press, 1954, 222.

NEWELL, ROBERT HENRY

LEARY, LEWIS. *Articles on American Literature, 1900—1950.* Durham: Duke Univ. Press, 1954, 222.

TRENT, WILLIAM PETERFIELD, et al. *Cambridge History of American Literature,* 4 Vols. New York: G. P. Putnam's Sons, 1917—1921, II, 508.

NILES, HEZIKIAH

LEARY, LEWIS. *Articles on American Literature, 1900—1950.* Durham: Duke Univ. Press, 1954, 222.

NOBLE, LOUIS LEGRAND

LEARY, LEWIS. *Articles on American Literature, 1900—1950.* Durham: Duke Univ. Press, 1954, 222.

NORTON, ANDREWS

LEARY, LEWIS. *Articles on American Literature, 1900—1950.* Durham: Duke Univ. Press, 1954, 223.

TRENT, WILLIAM PETERFIELD, et al. *Cambridge History of American Literature,* 4 Vols. New York: G.P. Putnam's Sons, 1917—1921, II, 538—539.

NORTON, CHARLES ELIOT

LEARY, LEWIS. *Articles on American Literature, 1900—1950.* Durham: Duke Univ. Press, 1954, 223.

NORTON, CHARLES ELIOT. *Letters of Charles Eliot Norton,* with biographical comments by Sara Norton and Mark Anthony De Wolfe Howe, 2 Vols.

Boston and New York: Houghton Mifflin Co., 1913.

WINSHIP, GEORGE P. "The Norton Collection in the Library." *HAB*, XXIII (1921), 706–707.

NOTT, HENRY JUNIUS

TRENT, WILLIAM PETERFIELD, et al. *Cambridge History of American Literature*, 4 Vols. New York: G.P. Putnam's Sons, 1917–1921, II, 508.

NYE, EDGAR WATSON

LEARY, LEWIS. *Articles on American Literature, 1900–1950.* Durham: Duke Univ. Press, 1954, 223.

O'BRIEN, FITZ-JAMES

LEARY, LEWIS. *Articles on American Literature, 1900–1950.* Durham: Duke Univ. Press, 1954, 223–224.

TRENT, WILLIAM PETERFIELD, et al. *Cambridge History of American Literature*, 4 Vols. New York: G.P. Putnam's Sons, 1917–1921, II, 628.

ODIORNE, THOMAS

LEARY, LEWIS. *Articles on American Literature, 1900–1950.* Durham: Duke Univ. Press, 1954, 224.

OGILVIE, JAMES

LEARY, LEWIS. *Articles on American Literature, 1900–1950.* Durham: Duke Univ. Press, 1954, 224.

O'HARA, THEODORE

HUBBELL, JAY B. *The South in*

American Literature, 1607–1900. Durham: Duke Univ. Press, 1954, 951–952.

LEARY, LEWIS. *Articles on American Literature, 1900–1950.* Durham: Duke Univ. Press, 1954, 224.

OLMSTED, FREDERICK LAW

LIBRARY OF CONGRESS, MANUSCRIPT DIVISION. *Frederick Law Olmsted: A Register of His Papers in the Library of Congress.* Washington, 1963, 13 leaves.

O'REILLY, JOHN BOYLE

LEARY, LEWIS. *Articles on American Literature, 1900–1950.* Durham: Duke Univ. Press, 1954, 228.

OWEN, ROBERT DALE

LEARY, LEWIS. *Articles on American Literature, 1900–1950.* Durham: Duke Univ. Press, 1954, 228.

PAGE, THOMAS NELSON

BLANCK, JACOB, ed. *Merle Johnson's American First Editions,* 4th edition, revised and enlarged. Waltham, Massachusetts: Mark Press, 1965, 404–407.

GERSTENBERGER, DONNA, and GEORGE HENDRICK. *The American Novel, 1789–1959: A Checklist of Twentieth Century Criticism.* Denver: Alan Swallow, 1961, 210.

HUBBELL, JAY B. *The South in American Literature, 1607–1900.* Durham: Duke Univ. Press, 1954, 952.

LEARY, LEWIS. *Articles on American Literature, 1900–1950.* Durham: Duke Univ. Press, 1954, 228.

PAINE, GREGORY LANSING, ed. *Southern Prose Writers: Representative Selections,* with introduction, bibliography and notes. New York: American Book Co., 1947, cxxxix–cxl.

ROBERSON, JOHN R. "The Manuscript of Page's 'Marse Chan.' " *SB,* IX (1957), 259–262.

SPILLER, ROBERT ERNEST, et al. *Literary History of the United States,* 2 Vols. New York: Macmillan, 1962, 673–674. Supplement, 174–175.

TRENT, WILLIAM PETERFIELD, et al. *Cambridge History of American Literature,* 4 Vols. New York: G.P. Putnam's Sons, 1917–1921, II, 628.

PAGE, WALTER HINES

LEARY, LEWIS. *Articles on American Literature, 1900–1950.* Durham: Duke Univ. Press, 1954, 228.

PAINE, GREGORY LANSING, ed. *Southern Prose Writers: Representative Selections,* with introduction, bibliography and notes. New York: American Book Co., 1947, cxxxviii–cxxxix.

PAINE, ROBERT TREAT, JR.

LEARY, LEWIS. *Articles on American Literature, 1900–1950.* Durham: Duke Univ. Press, 1954, 228.

PALMER, JOHN WILLIAMSON

HUBBELL, JAY B. *The South in*

American Literature, 1607–1900. Durham: Duke Univ. Press, 1954, 952–953.

PARKER, THEODORE

CHADWICK, JOHN WHITE. *Theodore Parker: Preacher and Reformer.* Boston: Houghton Mifflin Co., 1900, xi–xx.

COMMAGER, HENRY STEELE. *Theodore Parker.* Boston: Little, Brown and Co., 1936, 311–331.

LEARY, LEWIS. *Articles on American Literature, 1900–1950.* Durham: Duke Univ. Press, 1954, 230.

PARKER, THEODORE. *The Works of Theodore Parker,* with a bibliography by Charles W. Wendte, 15 Vols. Boston: American Unitarian Association, 1907–1913, XV, 11–50.

Centenary edition.

SPILLER, ROBERT ERNEST, et al. *Literary History of the United States,* 2 Vols. New York: Macmillan, 1962, 678–680. Supplement, 176.

TRENT, WILLIAM PETERFIELD, et al. *Cambridge History of American Literature,* 4 Vols. New York: G.P. Putnam's Sons, 1917–1921, I, 549.

PARKMAN, FRANCIS

BLANCK, JACOB, ed. *Merle Johnson's American First Editions,* 4th edition, revised and enlarged. Waltham, Massachusetts: Mark Press, 1965, 409–410.

FARNHAM, CHARLES HAIGHT. *A Life of Francis Parkman.* Boston: Little, Brown and Co., 1900, xii–xiii, 359–364.

GERSTENBERGER, DONNA, and GEORGE HENDRICK. *The American Novel, 1789–1959: A Checklist of Twentieth Century Criticism.* Denver: Alan Swallow, 1961, 210.

LEARY, LEWIS. *Articles on American Literature, 1900–1950.* Durham: Duke Univ. Press, 1954, 230–231.

SCHRAMM, WILBUR L., ed. *Francis Parkman: Representative Selections,* with introduction, bibliography and notes. New York: American Book Co., 1938, cxxi–cxliv.

SEITZ, DON CARLOS, ed. *Letters from Francis Parkman to E. G. Squier.* Cedar Rapids, Iowa: The Torch Press, 1911, 47–58.

SPILLER, ROBERT ERNEST, et al. *Literary History of the United States,* 2 Vols. New York: Macmillan, 1962, 680–682, Supplement, 176.

WADE, MASON. *Francis Parkman: Heroic Historian.* New York: The Viking Press, 1942, 453–456.

WALSH, JAMES E. "The California and Oregon Trail: A Bibliographical Study." *The New Colophon,* III (1950), 279–285.

PARSONS, THOMAS WILLIAM

LEARY, LEWIS. *Articles on American Literature, 1900–1950.* Durham: Duke Univ. Press, 1954, 231.

PARTON, SARA PAYSON (WILLIS)

LEARY, LEWIS. *Articles on American Literature, 1900–1950.* Durham: Duke Univ. Press, 1954, 231.

PAULDING, JAMES KIRKE

ADERMAN, RALPH M. "James Kirke Paulding's Contributions to American Magazines." *SB,* XVII (1964), 141–151.

ADKINS, NELSON F. "A Study of James K. Paulding's 'Westward Ho!' " *AC,* III (March 1927), 221–229.

BLANCK, JACOB, ed. *Merle Johnson's American First Editions,* 4th edition, revised and enlarged. Waltham, Massachusetts: Mark Press, 1965, 411–413.

GERSTENBERGER, DONNA, and GEORGE HENDRICK. *The American Novel, 1789–1959: A Checklist of Twentieth Century Criticism.* Denver: Alan Swallow, 1961, 210–211.

HALLINE, ALLAN GATES. *American Plays.* New York: American Book Co., 1935, 753.

HEROLD, AMOS LEE. *James Kirke Paulding: Versatile American.* New York: Columbia Univ. Press, 1926, 148–160.

LEARY, LEWIS. *Articles on American Literature, 1900–1950.* Durham: Duke Univ. Press, 1954, 232.

ROBBINS, J. ALBERT. "Some Unrecorded Poems of James Kirke Paulding: An Annotated Check-List." *SB,* III (1950–1951), 229–240.

SPILLER, ROBERT ERNEST, et al. *Literary History of the United States,* 2 Vols. New York: Macmillan, 1962, 684–686. Supplement, 177.

TAFT, KENDALL B., ed. *Minor Knickerbockers: Representative*

Selections, with introduction, bibliography and notes. New York: American Book Co., 1947, cxxxix—cxl.

TRENT, WILLIAM PETERFIELD, et al. *Cambridge History of American Literature,* 4 Vols, New York: G.P. Putnam's Sons, 1917—1921, I, 523, 538—539.

WEGELIN, OSCAR. "A Bibliography of the Separate Publications of James Kirke Paulding: Poet, Novelist, Humorist, Statesman, 1779—1860." *PBSA,* XII (January—April 1918), 34—40.

PAYNE, JOHN HOWARD

LEARY, LEWIS. *Articles on American Literature, 1900—1950.* Durham: Duke Univ. Press, 1954, 232—233.

SPILLER, ROBERT ERNEST, et al. *Literary History of the United States,* 2 Vols. New York: Macmillan, 1962, 686—687. Supplement, 177.

TAFT, KENDALL B., ed. *Minor Knickerbockers: Representative Selections,* with introduction, bibliography and notes. New York: . American Book Co., 1947, cxl—cxlii.

TRENT, WILLIAM PETERFIELD, et al. *Cambridge History of American Literature,* 4 Vols. New York: G.P. Putnam's Sons, 1917—1921, I, 502—504.

PEABODY, ELIZABETH PALMER

LEARY, LEWIS. *Articles on American Literature, 1900—1950.* Durham: Duke Univ. Press, 1954, 233.

PEIRCE, CHARLES SANDERS

LEARY, LEWIS. *Articles on American Literature, 1900—1950.* Durham: Duke Univ. Press, 1954, 233.

TRENT, WILLIAM PETERFIELD, et al. *Cambridge History of American Literature,* 4 Vols. New York: G.P. Putnam's Sons, 1917—1921, IV, 754—755.

PERCIVAL, JAMES GATES

LEARY, LEWIS. *Articles on American Literature, 1900—1950.* Durham: Duke Univ. Press, 1954, 234.

LEGLER, HENRY EDWARD. *James Gates Percival: An Anecdotal Sketch and Bibliography.* Milwaukee: The Mequon Club, 1901, 61 pp.

TRENT, WILLIAM PETERFIELD, et al. *Cambridge History of American Literature,* 4 Vols. New York: G.P. Putnam's Sons, 1917—1921, I, 523—524.

WILSON, ALTHEA G. "The James Gates Percival Papers." *YULG,* XXVIII (October 1953), 77—81.

PERRY, NORA

LEARY, LEWIS. *Articles on American Literature, 1900—1950.* Durham: Duke Univ. Press, 1954, 234.

PERRY, THOMAS SERGEANT

LEARY, LEWIS. *Articles on American Literature, 1900—1950.* Durham: Duke Univ. Press, 1954, 234.

PHELPS, ELIZABETH STUART

LEARY, LEWIS. *Articles on American Literature, 1900–1950.* Durham: Duke Univ. Press, 1954, 234.

PHILLIPS, WENDELL

LEARY, LEWIS. *Articles on American Literature, 1900–1950.* Durham: Duke Univ. Press, 1954, 235.

LIBRARY OF CONGRESS, DIVISION OF BIBLIOGRAPHY. *Wendell Phillips (1811–1884): A Bibliographical List.* Washington, 1931, 11 leaves.

PIATT, JOHN JAMES

DOWLER, CLARE. "John James Piatt, Representative Figure of a Momentous Period." *Ohio Archeological and Historical Quarterly,* XLV (1936), 1–26,

LEARY, LEWIS. *Articles on American Literature, 1900–1950.* Durham: Duke Univ. Press, 1954, 235.

PIERPONT, JOHN

LEARY, LEWIS. *Articles on American Literature, 1900–1950.* Durham: Duke Univ. Press, 1954, 235.

PIKE, ALBERT

HUBBELL, JAY B. *The South in American Literature, 1607–1900.* Durham: Duke Univ. Press, 1954, 953–954.

LEARY, LEWIS. *Articles on American Literature, 1900–1950.* Durham: Duke Univ. Press, 1954, 235.

TRENT, WILLIAM PETERFIELD, et al. *Cambridge History of American Literature,* 4 Vols. New York: G.P. Putnam's Sons, 1917–1921, I, 539.

PINCKNEY, SUSANNA SHULRICK HAYNE

LEARY, LEWIS. *Articles on American Literature, 1900–1950.* Durham: Duke Univ. Press, 1954, 235.

PINKERTON, ALLAN

BLANCK, JACOB, ed. *Merle Johnson's American First Editions,* 4th edition, revised and enlarged. Waltham, Massachusetts: Mark Press, 1965, 414–415.

LEARY, LEWIS. *Articles on American Literature, 1900–1950.* Durham: Duke Univ. Press, 1954, 235.

PINKNEY, EDWARD COOTE

HUBBELL, JAY B. *The South in American Literature, 1607–1900.* Durham: Duke Univ. Press, 1954, 954–955.

LEARY, LEWIS. *Articles on American Literature, 1900–1950.* Durham: Duke Univ. Press, 1954, 235.

POE, EDGAR ALLAN

ALTERTON, MARGARET, and HARDIN CRAIG, eds. *Edgar Allan Poe: Representative Selections,* with introduction, bibliography and notes. New York: American Book Co., 1935, cxix–cxxxiii.

BANGS AND COMPANY. *Catalogue of an Exceedingly Interesting and Valuable Private*

Library, Comprising the Largest and Most Complete Collection of the Original Editions of the Works of Edgar Allan Poe and of "Poeana." New York: D. Taylor and Co., 1895, 87 pp.

BLANCK, JACOB, ed. *Merle Johnson's American First Editions,* 4th edition, revised and enlarged. Waltham, Massachusetts: Mark Press, 1965, 416–418.

BOOTH, BRADFORD ALLEN, and CLAUDE E. JONES. *A Concordance of the Poetical Works of Edgar Allan Poe.* Baltimore: Johns Hopkins Press, 1941, 225 pp.

BRADDY, HALDEN, *Glorious Incense: The Fulfillment of Edgar Allan Poe.* Washington: Scarecrow Press, 1953, 208–234.

BRIGHAM, CLARENCE SAUNDERS. "Edgar Allan Poe's Contributions to *Alexander's Weekly Messenger." PAAS,* ns LII (April 1942), 45–125.

CAMPBELL, KILLIS. "Bibliographical Notes on Poe." *The Nation,* LXXXIX (Dec. 23, 1909), 623–624; (Dec. 30, 1909), 647–648; XCIII (Oct. 19, 1911), 362–363.

——————. "Gleanings in the Bibliography of Poe." *MLN,* XXXII (May 1917), 267–272.

——————. *The Mind of Poe and Other Studies.* Cambridge: Harvard Univ. Press, 1933, bibliographical footnotes.

——————. "Poe Documents in the Library of Congress." *MLN,* XXV (April 1910), 127–128.

——————. "Recent Books about Poe." *SP,* XXIV (July 1927), 474–479.

——————. "Some Unpublished Documents Relating to Poe's Early Years." *SR,* XX (April 1912), 201–212.

CARLSON, ERIC W. *Introduction to Poe: A Thematic Reader.* Glenview, Illinois: Scott, Foresman, 1967, xxxvi–xxxix.

CAUTHEN, I. B., JR. "Poe's *Alone:* Its Background, Source, and Manuscript." *SB,* III (1950–1951), 284–291.

CHAMBERLAIN, JACOB CHESTER. *First Editions of Ten American Authors,* 2 Parts. New York: Anderson Auction Co., 1909, Part 1, 126–132; Part 2, 67.

CLARK, HARRY HAYDEN. *Major American Poets.* New York: American Book Co., 1936, 834–839.

COLUMBIA UNIVERSITY, LIBRARY. *Material by and about Edgar Allan Poe to be Found in the Library of Columbia University,* prepared by Clara W. Bragg. New York: Columbia Univ. Library, 1909, 18 pp.

DAMERON, JOHN LASLEY. "Poe in the Twentieth Century: Poe's Literary Reputation, 1928–1960, and a Bibliography of Poe Criticism, 1942–1960." Unpublished doctoral dissertation, Univ. of Tennessee, 1962.

DEDMOND, FRANCIS B. "A Checklist of Edgar Allen Poe's Works in Book Form Published in the British Isles." *BB,* XXI (May–August 1953), 16–20.

──────────. "Poe in Drama, Fiction, and Poetry: A Bibliography." *BB*, XXI (September–December 1954), 107–114.

EATON, VINCENT L. "Two Poe Rarities." *LCQJ*, XII (May 1955), 103–104.

ENGEL, CLAIRE-ELIANE. "L'État des travaux sur Poe en France." *MP*, XXIX (May 1932), 482–488.

ENGLEKIRK, JOHN EUGENE. *Edgar Allan Poe in Hispanic Literature.* New York: Instituto de las Españas en los Estados Unidos, 1934, 478–504.

──────────. " 'My Nightmare': The Last Tale of Poe." *PMLA*, LII (June 1937), 511–527.

Appendices contain a "Bibliography of Mexican Versions of Poe" and a "Bibliography of Mexican Criticism of Poe."

ENOCH PRATT FREE LIBRARY. *Edgar Allan Poe: Letters and Documents in the Enoch Pratt Free Library,* by Arthur H. Quinn and Richard H. Hart. New York: Scholars' Facsimiles and Reprints, 1941, 84 pp.

Reprints 41 important items from the Amelia F. Poe Collection of 298 items.

EVANS, MAY GARRETTSON. *Music and Edgar Allan Poe: A Bibliographical Study.* Baltimore: Johns Hopkins Press, 1939, 97 pp.

GERSTENBERGER, DONNA, and GEORGE HENDRICK. *The American Novel, 1789–1959: A Checklist of Twentieth Century*

Criticism. Denver: Alan Swallow, 1961, 212–213.

GIACCARI, ADA. "La fortuna di E. A. Poe in Italia: Nota bibliografica." *SA*, V (1959), 91–118.

GIMBEL, RICHARD. "'Quoth the Raven': A Catalogue of the Exhibition." *YULG*, XXXIII (April 1959), 139–189.

GORDON, JOHN D. "Edgar Allan Poe: An Exhibition on the Centenary of His Death, October 7, 1849: A Catalogue of the First Editions, Manuscripts, Autograph Letters from the Berg Collection." *BNYPL*, LIII (October 1949), 471–491.

GROLIG, MORIZ. *Edgar Allan Poe: Bibliographie.* Minden: J. C. C. Bruns, hof-buchhandlung, 1907, 181–236.

HEARTMAN, CHARLES FREDERICK, and JAMES R. CANNY. *Bibliography of First Printings of the Writings of Edgar Allan Poe.* Hattiesburg, Mississippi: Book Farm, 1940, 264 pp.

Revised edition: 1943, 294 pp.

HEARTMAN, CHARLES FREDERICK, and KENNETH REDE. *A Census of First Editions and Source Materials by Edgar Allan Poe in American Collections,* 2 Vols. Metuchen, New Jersey: printed for the editor of *American Book Collector,* 1932.

240 copies printed.

HUBBELL, JAY B. *The South in American Literature, 1607–1900.* Durham: Duke Univ. Press, 1954, 955–956.

Index to Early American Periodical Literature, 1728–1870: Part 2, Edgar Allan Poe. New York: Pamphlet Distributing Co., 1941, 19 pp.

JUST, WALTER. *Die romantische Bewegung in der amerikanischen Literatur: Brown, Poe, Hawthorne: ein Beitrag zur Geschichte der Romantik.* Berlin: Mayer and Muller, 1910, 91–93.

LAUVRIERE, EMILE. *Edgar Poe, sa vie et son oeuvre: Étude de psychologie pathologique.* Paris: Alcan, 1904, 721–730.

LEARY, LEWIS. *Articles on American Literature, 1900–1950.* Durham: Duke Univ. Press, 1954, 236–249.

MABBOTT, THOMAS. "Additions to 'A List of Poe's Tales.' " *N&Q,* CLXXXII (Sept. 12, 1942), 163–164.

—————. "A List of Books from Poe's Library." *N&Q,* ns II (May 1955), 222–223.

MARKHAM, EDWIN. *Edgar Allan Poe: Works,* 10 Vols. New York: Funk and Wagnalls, 1904, I, v–xxv.

McCUSKER, HONOR. "The Correspondence of R. W. Griswold." *More Books,* XVI (March 1941), 105–116; (April 1941), 152–156; (May 1941), 190–196; (June 1941), 286–289.

McELDERRY, B. R., JR. "The Edgar Allan Poe Collection." *Univ. of Southern California Library Bulletin,* IV (January 1948), 4–6.

OSTROM, JOHN WARD. *Check List of Letters to and from Poe.*

Charlottesville: Aldeman Library, 1941, 57 pp.

Univ. of Virginia Bibliographical Series, No. 4. 250 copies mimeographed.

—————, ed. *The Letters of Edgar A. Poe,* 2 Vols. Cambridge: Harvard Univ. Press, 1948.

—————. "Supplement to *The Letters of Poe.*" *AL,* XXIV (November 1952), 358–366.

POE, EDGAR ALLAN. *The Complete Poems and Stories of Edgar Allan Poe,* with selections from his critical writings, an introduction and explanatory notes by Arthur Hobson Quinn and texts established with bibliographical notes by Edward Hayes O'Neill, 2 Vols. New York: A. A. Knopf, 1946, II, 1,089–1,092.

QUINN, ARTHUR HOBSON. *Edgar Allan Poe: A Critical Biography.* New York: Appleton-Century-Crofts, 1963, 763–770.

RANDALL, DAVID. *The J.K. Lilly Collection of Edgar Allan Poe: An Account of Its Formation.* Bloomington: Lilly Library, Indiana Univ. Press, 1964, 62 pp.

—————. "Robertson's Poe Bibliography." *PW,* CXXV (April 21, 1934), 1,540–1,543.

REDE, KENNETH, and CHARLES FREDERICK HEARTMAN. "A Census of First Editions and Source Materials by or Relating to Edgar Allan Poe in American Public and Private Collections." *ABC,* I (January 1932), 45–49; (February 1932), 80–84;

(March 1932), 143–147; (April 1932), 207–211; (May 1932), 274–277; (June 1932), 339–343; II (July 1932), 28–32; (August–September 1932), 141–153; (October 1932), 232–234; (November 1932), 290–292; (December 1932), 334–338.

REGAN, ROBERT. *Poe: A Collection of Critical Essays.* Englewood Cliffs, New Jersey: Prentice Hall, 1967, bibliographical references.

ROBERTSON, JOHN WOOSTER. *A Bibliography of the Writings of Edgar A. Poe,* 2 Vols. San Francisco: Grabhorn Press, 1934.

SPARKS, A. "Edgar Allan Poe: Bibliography." *N&Q,* CLIX (Dec. 27, 1930), 465.

SPILLER, ROBERT ERNEST, et al. *Literary History of the United States,* 2 Vols. New York: Macmillan, 1962, 689–696. Supplement, 178–180.

STOVALL, FLOYD, et al. *Eight American Authors: A Review of Research and Criticism.* New York: W. W. Norton and Co., 1963, 1–46, 421–424.

TANSELLE, G. THOMAS. "An Unknown Early Appearance of 'The Raven.' " *SB,* XVI (1963), 220–223.

TAYLOR, WALTER FULLER. *A History of American Letters,* with bibliographies by Harry Hartwick. Boston: American Book Co., 1936, 501–506.

Subsequent editions entitled: *The Story of American Letters.*

THOMPSON, JOHN REUBEN. *The Genius and Character of Edgar Allan Poe,* edited and arranged by James H. Whitty and James H. Rindfleisch. Richmond, Virginia: privately printed, 1929, 71 pp.

TRENT, WILLIAM PETERFIELD, et al. *Cambridge History of American Literature,* 4 Vols. New York: G.P. Putnam's Sons, 1917–1921, II, 452–468.

WAKEMAN, STEPHEN H. *The Stephen H. Wakeman Collection of Books of Nineteenth Century American Writers: The Property of Mrs. Alice L. Wakeman, First Editions, Inscribed Presentation and Personal Copies, Original Manuscripts and Letters of Nine American Authors.* New York: American Art Association, 1924, Items 931–971.

WILSON, CARROLL ATWOOD. *Thirteen Author Collections of the Nineteenth Century and Five Centuries of Familiar Quotations,* edited by Jean C.S. Wilson and David A. Randall, 2 Vols. New York: privately printed for Scribner, 1950, I, 317–329.

WOODBERRY, GEORGE EDWARD. "The Poe-Chivers Papers." *Century Magazine,* LXV (January 1903), 435–447; (February 1903), 545–558.

_____. *Poe's Works,* 10 Vols. Chicago: Stone and Kimball, 1894–1895, X, 267–281.

WOODRESS, JAMES, et al. *American Literary Scholarship: An Annual.* Durham: Duke Univ. Press, (1963), 118–123; (1964), 120–126; (1965), 142–149; (1966), 129–136.

PORTER, WILLIAM T.

LEARY, LEWIS. *Articles on
American Literature, 1900–1950.*
Durham: Duke Univ. Press,
1954, 252.

POST, CHARLES CYREL

LEARY, LEWIS. *Articles on
American Literature, 1900–1950.*
Durham: Duke Univ. Press,
1954, 252.

PRENTICE, GEORGE DENISON

TRENT, WILLIAM PETERFIELD,
et al. *Cambridge History of
American Literature,* 4 Vols.
New York: G.P. Putnam's Sons,
1917–1921, II, 508.

PRESCOTT, WILLIAM HICKLING

CHARVAT, WILLIAM, and
MICHAEL KRAUS, eds. *William
Hickling Prescott: Representative
Selections,* with introduction,
bibliography and notes. New York:
American Book Co., 1943,
cxxxi–cxlii.

FERGUSON, JOHN DeLANCEY.
American Literature in Spain.
New York: Columbia Univ. Press,
1916, 203–260.

GARDINER, CLINTON HARVEY,
ed. *The Papers of William
Hickling Prescott.* Urbana: Univ.
of Illinois Press, 1964, 441 pp.

LEARY, LEWIS. *Articles on
American Literature, 1900–1950.*
Durham: Duke Univ. Press,
1954, 254.

PATTERSON, JERRY E. "A
Checklist of Prescott Manuscripts."
HAHR, XXXIX (February 1959),
116–128.

SPILLER, ROBERT ERNEST,
et al. *Literary History of the
United States,* 2 Vols. New York:
Macmillan, 1962, 700–702.
Supplement, 184.

TICKNOR, GEORGE. *Life of
William Hickling Prescott.*
Boston: J. B. Lippincott, 1864,
501 pp.

TRENT, WILLIAM PETERFIELD,
et al. *Cambridge History of
American Literature,* 4 Vols.
New York: G.P. Putnam's Sons,
1917–1921, II, 500–501.

PRESTON, MARGARET JUNKIN

HUBBELL, JAY B. *The South in
American Literature, 1607–1900.*
Durham: Duke Univ. Press,
1954, 956.

PULITZER, JOSEPH

LEARY, LEWIS. *Articles on
American Literature, 1900–1950.*
Durham: Duke Univ. Press,
1954, 254.

PYLE, HOWARD

BLANCK, JACOB, ed. *Merle
Johnson's American First Editions,*
4th edition, revised and enlarged.
Waltham, Massachusetts: Mark
Press, 1965, 423–425.

MORSE, WILLARD SAMUEL,
and GERTRUDE BRINCKLE,
comps. *Howard Pyle.* Wilmington,
Delaware: The Wilmington
Society of Fine Arts, 1921, 242 pp.

QUIMBY, PHINEAS PARKHURST

LEARY, LEWIS. *Articles on
American Literature, 1900–1950.*
Durham: Duke Univ. Press,
1954, 255.

QUINCY, ELIZA SUSAN

LEARY, LEWIS. *Articles on American Literature, 1900–1950.* Durham: Duke Univ. Press, 1954, 255.

RANDALL, JAMES RYDER

HUBBELL, JAY B. *The South in American Literature, 1607–1900.* Durham: Duke Univ. Press, 1954, 956.

LEARY, LEWIS. *Articles on American Literature, 1900–1950.* Durham: Duke Univ. Press, 1954, 255.

RANDOLPH, INNES

HUBBELL, JAY B. *The South in American Literature, 1607–1900.* Durham: Duke Univ. Press, 1954, 957.

RANDOLPH, JOHN

HUBBELL, JAY B. *The South in American Literature, 1607–1900.* Durham: Duke Univ. Press, 1954, 957.

LEARY, LEWIS. *Articles on American Literature, 1900–1950.* Durham: Duke Univ. Press, 1954, 255.

TRENT, WILLIAM PETERFIELD, et al. *Cambridge History of American Literature, 4 Vols.* New York: G.P. Putnam's Sons, 1917–1921, II, 476.

RAWLE, WILLIAM

TRENT, WILLIAM PETERFIELD, et al. *Cambridge History of American Literature, 4 Vols.* New York: G.P. Putnam's Sons, 1917–1921, II, 476.

RAYMOND, HENRY JARVIS

TRENT, WILLIAM PETERFIELD, et al. *Cambridge History of American Literature, 4 Vols.* New York: G.P. Putnam's Sons, 1917–1921, II, 523.

READ, THOMAS BUCHANAN

LEARY, LEWIS. *Articles on American Literature, 1900–1950.* Durham: Duke Univ. Press, 1954, 256.

WOODRESS, JAMES, et al. *American Literary Scholarship: An Annual.* Durham: Duke Univ. Press, (1965), 149–153.

REALF, RICHARD

LEARY, LEWIS. *Articles on American Literature, 1900–1950.* Durham: Duke Univ. Press, 1954, 256.

REMINGTON, FREDERICK

ALLEN, E. DOUGLAS, comp. "Frederick Remington—Author and Illustrator." *BNYPL*, LI (December 1945), 895–912.

A list of Remington's illustrations and articles published in periodicals, 1886–1913.

BLANCK, JACOB, ed. *Merle Johnson's American First Editions,* 4th editions, revised and enlarged, Waltham, Massachusetts: Mark Press, 1965, 426–427.

LEARY, LEWIS. *Articles on American Literature, 1900–1950.* Durham: Duke Univ. Press, 1954, 256.

REID, CHRISTIAN (see *TIERNAN*)

REID, WHITELAW

LIBRARY OF CONGRESS, MANUSCRIPT DIVISION. *Whitelaw Reid: A Register of His Papers in the Library of Congress.* Washington, 1958, 62 pp.

REYNOLDS, JEREMIAH N.

LEARY, LEWIS. *Articles on American Literature, 1900–1950.* Durham: Duke Univ. Press, 1954, 256.

RICH, OBADIAH

KNEPPER, ADRIAN W. "Obadiah Rich: Bibliophile." *PBSA*, XLIX (2nd Quart. 1955), 112–130.

RICHARDSON, ABBY SAGE

LEARY, LEWIS. *Articles on American Literature, 1900–1950.* Durham: Duke Univ. Press, 1954, 257.

RILEY, JAMES WHITCOMB

BLANCK, JACOB, ed. *Merle Johnson's American First Editions,* 4th edition, revised and enlarged. Waltham, Massachusetts: Mark Press, 1965, 430–433.

LEARY, LEWIS. *Articles on American Literature, 1900–1950.* Durham: Duke Univ. Press, 1954, 257–258.

NOLAN, JEANETTE COVERT. *James Whitcomb Riley: Hoosier Poet.* New York: J. Messner, Inc., 1941, 257–260.

RUSSO, ANTHONY J., and DOROTHY R. RUSSO. *A Bibliography of James Whitcomb Riley.* Indianapolis: privately

printed for the Indiana Historical Society, 1944, 372 pp.

SPILLER, ROBERT ERNEST, et al. *Literary History of the United States,* 2 Vols. New York: Macmillan, 1962, 703–705. Supplement, 184.

TRENT, WILLIAM PETERFIELD, et al. *Cambridge History of American Literature,* 4 Vols. New York: G.P. Putnam's Sons, 1917–1921, IV, 651–653.

WOODRESS, JAMES, et al. *American Literary Scholarship: An Annual.* Durham: Duke Univ. Press, (1965), 159–160.

RIPLEY, GEORGE

LEARY, LEWIS. *Articles on American Literature, 1900–1950.* Durham: Duke Univ. Press, 1954, 258.

TRENT, WILLIAM PETERFIELD, et al. *Cambridge History of American Literature,* 4 Vols. New York: G.P. Putnam's Sons, 1917–1921, I, 550.

RITCHIE, THOMAS

TRENT, WILLIAM PETERFIELD, et al. *Cambridge History of American Literature,* 4 Vols. New York: G.P. Putnam's Sons, 1917–1921, II, 523.

ROBINSON, MARIUS RACINE

LEARY, LEWIS. *Articles on American Literature, 1900–1950.* Durham: Duke Univ. Press, 1954, 263.

ROBINSON, ROWLAND EVANS

BLANCK, JACOB, ed. *Merle Johnson's American First Editions,*

4th edition, revised and enlarged. Waltham, Massachusetts: Mark Press, 1965, 443.

LEARY, LEWIS. *Articles on American Literature, 1900–1950.* Durham: Duke Univ. Press, 1954, 263.

ROE, E. P.

LEARY, LEWIS. *Articles on American Literature, 1900–1950.* Durham: Duke Univ. Press, 1954, 263.

ROGERS, NATHANIEL PEABODY

LEARY, LEWIS. *Articles on American Literature, 1900–1950.* Durham: Duke Univ. Press, 1954, 263.

ROMBERG, JOHANNES CHRISTLIEB NATHANIEL

LEARY, LEWIS. *Articles on American Literature, 1900–1950.* Durham: Duke Univ. Press, 1954, 264.

ROYALL, ANNE NEWPORT

LEARY, LEWIS. *Articles on American Literature, 1900–1950.* Durham: Duke Univ. Press, 1954, 265.

ROYCE, JOSIAH

LEARY, LEWIS. *Articles on American Literature, 1900–1950.* Durham: Duke Univ. Press, 1954, 265.

RAND, BENJAMIN. "A Bibliography of the Writings of Josiah Royce," in *Papers in Honor of Josiah Royce on His Sixtieth Birthday.* New York: Longmans Green and Co., 1916, 287–294.

TRENT, WILLIAM PETERFIELD, et al. *Cambridge History of American Literature,* 4 Vols. New York: G.P. Putnam's Sons, 1917–1921, IV, 755.

RUFFNER, HENRY

LEARY, LEWIS. *Articles on American Literature, 1900–1950.* Durham: Duke Univ. Press, 1954, 265.

RUPPIUS, OTTO

LEARY, LEWIS. *Articles on American Literature, 1900–1950.* Durham: Duke Univ. Press, 1954, 265.

RUSH, JAMES

LEARY, LEWIS. *Articles on American Literature, 1900–1950.* Durham: Duke Univ. Press, 1954, 265.

RUSSELL, IRWIN

HARRELL, L. D. S. "A Bibliography of Irwin Russell." *Journal of Mississippi History,* VIII (January 1946), 3–23.

LEARY, LEWIS. *Articles on American Literature, 1900–1950.* Durham: Duke Univ. Press, 1954, 265.

TRENT, WILLIAM PETERFIELD, et al. *Cambridge History of American Literature,* 4 Vols. New York: G.P. Putnam's Sons, 1917–1921, II, 615.

RUTHERFORD, MARK (see *WHITE*)

RUXTON, GEORGE FREDERICK

LEARY, LEWIS. *Articles on American Literature, 1900–1950.* Durham: Duke Univ. Press, 1954, 266.

RYAN, ABRAM JOSEPH

HUBBELL, JAY B. *The South in American Literature, 1607–1900.* Durham: Duke Univ. Press, 1954, 958.

LEARY, LEWIS. *Articles on American Literature, 1900–1950.* Durham: Duke Univ. Press, 1954, 266.

SANBORN, FRANKLIN BENJAMIN

LEARY, LEWIS. *Articles on American Literature, 1900–1950.* Durham: Duke Univ. Press, 1954, 266.

SANDERSON, JOHN

TRENT, WILLIAM PETERFIELD, et al. *Cambridge History of American Literature,* 4 Vols. New York: G.P. Putnam's Sons, 1917–1921, II, 508.

SANDS, ROBERT CHARLES

TAFT, KENDALL B., ed. *Minor Knickerbockers: Representative Selections,* with introduction, bibliography and notes. New York: American Book Co., 1947, cxlii.

TRENT, WILLIAM PETERFIELD, et al. *Cambridge History of American Literature,* 4 Vols. New York: G.P. Putnam's Sons, 1917–1921, I, 524.

SAXE, JOHN GODFREY

TRENT, WILLIAM PETERFIELD, et al. *Cambridge History of American Literature,* 4 Vols. New York: G.P. Putnam's Sons, 1917–1921, II, 543.

SCHINDLER, SOLOMON

LEARY, LEWIS. *Articles on American Literature, 1900–1950.* Durham: Duke Univ. Press, 1954, 270.

SCHOOLCRAFT, HENRY ROWE

FREEMAN, JOHN F. "Pirated Editions of Schoolcraft's *Oneota." PBSA,* LIII (3rd Quart. 1959), 252–261.

LEARY, LEWIS. *Articles on American Literature, 1900–1950.* Durham: Duke Univ. Press, 1954, 270.

STREETER, FLOYD B. "Henry Rowe Schoolcraft." *AC,* V (October 1927), 2–8.

SCOTT, WINFIELD

LEARY, LEWIS. *Articles on American Literature, 1900–1950.* Durham: Duke Univ. Press, 1954, 270.

SCUDDER, HORACE ELISHA

LEARY, LEWIS. *Articles on American Literature, 1900–1950.* Durham: Duke Univ. Press, 1954, 270.

SEALSFIELD, CHARLES

HELLER, OTTO, and THEODORE H. LEON. *Charles Sealsfield: Bibliography of His Writings, together with a Classified and Annotated Catalogue of Literature Relating to His Works and His Life.* St. Louis: n.p., 1939, 98 pp.

Washington Univ. Studies, New Series, Language and Literature, No. 8.

LEARY, LEWIS. *Articles on American Literature, 1900–1950.*

Durham: Duke Univ. Press, 1954, 270–271.

SPILLER, ROBERT ERNEST, et al. *Literary History of the United States,* 2 Vols. New York: Macmillan, 1962, 715–717. Supplement, 189.

SEDGWICK, CATHERINE MARIA

GERSTENBERGER, DONNA, and GEORGE HENDRICK. *The American Novel, 1789–1959: A Checklist of Twentieth Century Criticism.* Denver: Alan Swallow, 1961, 218.

LEARY, LEWIS. *Articles on American Literature, 1900–1950.* Durham: Duke Univ. Press, 1954, 271.

TRENT, WILLIAM PETERFIELD, et al. *Cambridge History of American Literature,* 4 Vols. New York: G.P. Putnam's Sons, 1917–1921, I, 540.

SHAW, HENRY WHEELER

LEARY, LEWIS. *Articles on American Literature, 1900–1950.* Durham: Duke Univ. Press, 1954, 272.

TRENT, WILLIAM PETERFIELD, et al. *Cambridge History of American Literature,* 4 Vols. New York: G.P. Putnam's Sons, 1917–1921, II, 509.

SHEA, JOHN GILMARY

SPILLANE, EDWARD. "Bibliography of John Gilmary Shea." *United States Historical Society Records and Studies,* VI (No. 2, 1913), 249–274.

SHELDON, CHARLES M.

GERSTENBERGER, DONNA,

and GEORGE HENDRICK. *The American Novel, 1789–1959: A Checklist of Twentieth Century Criticism.* Denver: Alan Swallow, 1961, 219.

SHELTON, FREDERICK WILLIAM

TRENT, WILLIAM PETERFIELD, et al. *Cambridge History of American Literature,* 4 Vols. New York: G.P. Putnam's Sons, 1917–1921, H, 509.

SHERIDAN, PHILIP HENRY

LIBRARY OF CONGRESS, MANUSCRIPT DIVISION. *Philip H. Sheridan: A Register of His Papers in the Library of Congress.* Washington, 1962, 18 leaves.

SHILLABER, BENJAMIN PENHALLOW

LEARY, LEWIS. *Articles on American Literature, 1900–1950.* Durham: Duke Univ. Press, 1954, 273.

TRENT, WILLIAM PETERFIELD, et al. *Cambridge History of American Literature,* 4 Vols. New York: G.P. Putnam's Sons, 1917–1921, II, 509.

SIGOURNEY, LYDIA HUNTLEY

LEARY, LEWIS. *Articles on American Literature, 1900–1950.* Durham: Duke Univ. Press, 1954, 273.

SILL, EDWARD ROWLAND

LEARY, LEWIS. *Articles on American Literature, 1900–1950.* Durham: Duke Univ. Press, 1954, 273.

SIMITIÈRE, PIERRE EUGENE DU

LEARY, LEWIS. *Articles on American Literature, 1900–1950.* Durham; Duke Univ. Press, 1954, 273.

SIMMS, WILLIAM GILMORE

BLANCK, JACOB, ed. *Merle Johnson's American First Editions,* 4th edition, revised and enlarged. Waltham, Massachusetts: Mark Press, 1965, 464–468.

GERSTENBERGER, DONNA, and GEORGE HENDRICK. *The American Novel, 1789–1959: A Checklist of Twentieth Century Criticism.* Denver: Alan Swallow, 1961, 219–220.

GUILDS, JOHN C., JR. "Simms's First Magazine: *The Album.*" *SB,* VIII (1956), 169–183.

——————. "William Gilmore Simms and the *Southern Literary Gazette.*" *SB,* XXI (1968), 59–92.

HUBBELL, JAY B. *The South in American Literature, 1607–1900.* Durham: Duke Univ. Press, 1954, 958–961.

LEARY, LEWIS. *Articles on American Literature, 1900–1950.* Durham: Duke Univ. Press, 1954, 273–274.

MORRIS, J. ALLEN. "The Stories of William Gilmore Simms." *AL,* XIV (March 1942), 20–35.

PAINE, GREGORY LANSING, ed. *Southern Prose Writers: Representative Selections,* with introduction, bibliography and notes. New York: American Book Co., 1947, cxli–cxlii.

SALLEY, A.S., JR. "A Bibliography of William Gilmore Simms." *Publications of the Southern Historical Association,* XI (September 1907), 343–344.

SPILLER, ROBERT ERNEST, et al. *Literary History of the United States,* 2 Vols. New York: Macmillan, 1962, 720–723. Supplement, 189–190.

TAYLOR, WALTER FULLER. *A History of American Letters,* with bibliographies by Harry Hartwick. Boston: American Book Co., 1936, 533–534.

Subsequent editions entitled: *The Story of American Letters.*

TRENT, WILLIAM PETERFIELD. *William Gilmore Simms.* Boston: Houghton Mifflin Co., 1892, 333–342.

TRENT, WILLIAM PETERFIELD, et al. *Cambridge History of American Literature,* 4 Vols. New York: G.P. Putnam's Sons, 1917–1921, I, 540–544.

WEGELIN, OSCAR, comp. *A List of the Separate Writings of William Gilmore Simms of South Carolina, 1806–1870.* New York: published by the compiler, 1906, 31 pp.

110 copies printed.

——————. "Simms's First Publication." *NYHSQ,* XXV (January 1941), 26–27.

——————. "William Gilmore Simms: A Short Sketch, with a Bibliography of His Separate Writings." *ABC,* III (February 1933), 113–116; (March 1933), 149–151; (April 1933), 216–218; (May–June 1933), 284–286.

SMEDES, SUSAN DABNEY

TRENT, WILLIAM PETERFIELD, et al. *Cambridge History of American Literature,* 4 Vols. New York: G.P. Putnam's Sons, 1917–1921, II, 604.

SMITH, CHARLES HENRY (BILL ARP)

HUBBELL, JAY B. *The South in American Literature, 1607–1900.* Durham: Duke Univ. Press, 1954, 961.

LEARY, LEWIS. *Articles on American Literature, 1900–1950.* Durham: Duke Univ. Press, 1954, 275.

TRENT, WILLIAM PETERFIELD, et al. *Cambridge History of American Literature,* 4 Vols. New York: G.P. Putnam's Sons, 1917–1921, II, 509–510.

SMITH, FRANCIS HOPKINSON

BLANCK, JACOB, ed. *Merle Johnson's American First Editions,* 4th edition, revised and enlarged. Waltham, Massachusetts: Mark Press, 1965, 469–471.

GERSTENBERGER, DONNA, and GEORGE HENDRICK. *The American Novel, 1789–1959: A Checklist of Twentieth Century Criticism.* Denver: Alan Swallow, 1961, 222.

LEARY, LEWIS. *Articles on American Literature, 1900–1950.* Durham: Duke Univ. Press, 1954, 275.

TRENT, WILLIAM PETERFIELD, et al. *Cambridge History of American Literature,* 4 Vols. New York: G.P. Putnam's Sons, 1917–1921, II, 628.

SMITH, MARGARET CAMERON

LEARY, LEWIS. *Articles on American Literature, 1900–1950.* Durham: Duke Univ. Press, 1954, 276.

SMITH, RICHARD PENN

LEARY, LEWIS. *Articles on American Literature, 1900–1950.* Durham: Duke Univ. Press, 1954, 276.

TRENT, WILLIAM PETERFIELD, et al. *Cambridge History of American Literature,* 4 Vols. New York: G.P. Putnam's Sons, 1917–1921, I, 504–505.

SMITH, SEBA

TRENT, WILLIAM PETERFIELD, et al. *Cambridge History of American Literature,* 4 Vols. New York: G.P. Putnam's Sons, 1917–1921, II, 510.

SNELLING, WILLIAM JOSEPH

LEARY, LEWIS. *Articles on American Literature, 1900–1950.* Durham: Duke Univ. Press, 1954, 276.

SOUTHWORTH, EMMA DOROTHY ELIZA NEVILLE

GERSTENBERGER, DONNA, and GEORGE HENDRICK. *The American Novel, 1789–1959: A Checklist of Twentieth Century Criticism.* Denver: Alan Swallow, 1961, 222–223.

SPAFFORD, HORATIO GATES

LEARY, LEWIS. *Articles on American Literature, 1900–1950.* Durham: Duke Univ. Press, 1954, 276.

SPARKS, JARED

ADAMS, HERBERT BAXTER.
*The Life and Writings of Jared
Sparks,* 2 Vols. Boston: Houghton
Mifflin Co., 1893.

LEARY, LEWIS. *Articles on
American Literature, 1900–1950.*
Durham: Duke Univ. Press,
1954, 276.

SPOFFORD, HARRIET PRESCOTT

TRENT, WILLIAM PETERFIELD,
et al. *Cambridge History of
American Literature,* 4 Vols.
New York: G.P. Putnam's Sons,
1917–1921, II, 628–629.

SPOONER, LYSANDER

LEARY, LEWIS. *Articles on
American Literature, 1900–1950.*
Durham: Duke Univ. Press,
1954, 276.

SPRAGUE, ACHSA W.

LEARY, LEWIS. *Articles on
American Literature, 1900–1950.*
Durham: Duke Univ. Press,
1954, 276.

STARNES, EBENEZER

LEARY, LEWIS. *Articles on
American Literature, 1900–1950.*
Durham: Duke Univ. Press,
1954, 276.

STEDMAN, EDMUND CLARENCE

LEARY, LEWIS. *Articles on
American Literature, 1900–1950.*
Durham: Duke Univ. Press,
1954, 267–277.

SPILLER, ROBERT ERNEST,
et al. *Literary History of the
United States,* 2 Vols. New York:
Macmillan, 1962, 727–728.
Supplement, 191.

STEDMAN, LAURA, and
GEORGE MILBRY GOULD.
*Life and Letters of Edmund
Clarence Stedman,* with a bibliog-
raphy by Alice Marsland, 2 Vols.
New York: Moffat, Yard and
Co., 1910, II, 613–654.

TRENT, WILLIAM PETERFIELD,
et al. *Cambridge History of
American Literature,* 4 Vols.
New York: G.P. Putnam's Sons,
1917–1921, IV, 653–654.

STOCKTON, FRANK RICHARD

BLANCK, JACOB, ed. *Merle
Johnson's American First Editions,*
4th edition, revised and enlarged.
Waltham, Massachusetts: Mark
Press, 1965, 477–480.

GERSTENBERGER, DONNA,
and GEORGE HENDRICK. *The
American Novel, 1789–1959:
A Checklist of Twentieth Century
Criticism.* Denver: Alan Swallow,
1961, 230.

GRIFFIN, MARTIN IGNATIUS
JOSEPH. *Frank R. Stockton:
A Critical Biography.* Philadelphia:
Univ. of Pennsylvania Press,
1939, 149–173.

LEARY, LEWIS. *Articles on
American Literature, 1900–1950.*
Durham: Duke Univ. Press,
1954, 281.

STOCKTON, FRANK RICHARD.
A Bicycle of Cathay, with a
memorial sketch of Stockton and
a bibliography of his works. New
York: C. Scribner's Sons, 1904,
209–216.

_____. *The Captain's Toll-
gate,* with a memorial sketch by
Mrs. Stockton and a bibliography....
New York: D. Appleton and Co.,
1903, 353–359.

TRENT, WILLIAM PETERFIELD, et al. *Cambridge History of American Literature,* 4 Vols. New York: G.P. Putnam's Sons, 1917–1921, II, 629–630.

STODDARD, CHARLES WARREN

LEARY, LEWIS. *Articles on American Literature, 1900–1950.* Durham: Duke Univ. Press, 1954, 281.

SPILLER, ROBERT ERNEST, et al. *Literary History of the United States,* 2 Vols. New York: Macmillan, 1962, 734–735.

STODDARD, RICHARD HENRY

LEARY, LEWIS. *Articles on American Literature, 1900–1950.* Durham: Duke Univ. Press, 1954, 281–282.

SPILLER, ROBERT ERNEST, et al. *Literary History of the United States,* 2 Vols. New York: Macmillan, 1962, 735–736.

TRENT, WILLIAM PETERFIELD, et al. *Cambridge History of American Literature,* 4 Vols. New York: G.P. Putnam's Sons, 1917–1921, IV, 654–655.

STORY, JOSEPH

TRENT, WILLIAM PETERFIELD, et al. *Cambridge History of American Literature,* 4 Vols. New York: G.P. Putnam's Sons, 1917–1921, II, 476–478.

STOWE, HARRIET BEECHER

ANDERSON, JOHN PARKER. *Mrs. Kate Brannon Knight: History of the Work of Connecticut Women at the World's Columbian Exposition, Chicago, 1893.* Hartford: Case, Lockwood and Brainard Co., 1898, 107–123.

BLANCK, JACOB, ed. *Merle Johnson's American First Editions,* 4th edition, revised and enlarged. Waltham, Massachusetts: Mark Press, 1965, 481–484.

CHICAGO HISTORICAL SOCIETY. *"Uncle Tom's Cabin* 100th Anniversary Exhibit." *Chicago History,* II (Summer 1951), 353–364.

DETROIT PUBLIC LIBRARY. Uncle Tom's Cabin *as Book and Legend: A Guide to an Exhibition.* Detroit: Friends of the Detroit Public Library, 1952, 51 pp.

GERSTENBERGER, DONNA, and GEORGE HENDRICK. *The American Novel, 1789–1959: A Checklist of Twentieth Century Criticism.* Denver: Alan Swallow, 1961, 231–232.

HUBBELL, JAY B. *The South in American Literature, 1607–1900.* Durham: Duke Univ. Press, 1954, 962.

LEARY, LEWIS. *Articles on American Literature, 1900–1950.* Durham: Duke Univ. Press, 1954, 282–283.

MACLEAN, GRACE EDITH. Uncle Tom's Cabin *in Germany.* New York: D. Appleton and Co., 1910, 96–101.

MAY, HENRY FARNHAM, ed. *Old Folks.* Cambridge: Harvard Univ. Press, 1966, bibliographical footnotes.

RANDALL, DAVID A., and JOHN T. WINTERICH. "One Hundred Good Novels: Stowe, Harriet Beecher: *Uncle Tom's Cabin." PW,* CXXXVII (May 8, 1940). 1931–1932.

SPILLER, ROBERT ERNEST, et al. *Literary History of the United States,* 2 Vols. New York: Macmillan, 1962, 736–738. Supplement, 195–196.

STOWE, HARRIET BEECHER. *Uncle Tom's Cabin; or, Life among the Lowly,* with a bibliography of the work by George Bullen, new edition. Boston: Houghton, Osgood and Co., 1879, xxxix–lviii.

TALBOT, WILLIAM. *"Uncle Tom's Cabin:* First English Editions." *ABC,* III (May–June 1933), 292–297.

TAYLOR, WALTER FULLER. *A History of American Letters,* with bibliographies by Harry Hartwick. Boston: American Book Co., 1936, 521–523.

Subsequent editions entitled: *The Story of American Letters.*

"Uncle Tom's Cabin." *TLS,* July 8, 1926, 468.

WILSON, ROBERT FORREST. *Crusader in Crinoline: The Life of Harriet Beecher Stowe.* Philadelphia: J.B. Lippincott Co., 1941, 643–657.

WOODRESS, JAMES, et al. *American Literary Scholarship: An Annual.* Durham: Duke Univ. Press, (1963), 107–109.

STRANGE, ROBERT

LEARY, LEWIS. *Articles on American Literature, 1900–1950.* Durham: Duke Univ. Press, 1954, 283.

STREET, ALFRED BILLINGS

TAFT, KENDALL B., ed. *Minor Knickerbockers: Representative Selections,* with introduction, bibliography and notes. New York: American Book Co., 1947, cxlii–cxliii.

STUART, GILBERT

PARK, LAWRENCE. *Gilbert Stuart: An Illustrated Descriptive List of His Works,* 4 Vols. New York: W.E. Rudge, 1926.

SYMONDS, JOHN ADDINGTON

BABINGTON, PERCY LANCELOT. *Bibliography of the Writings of John Addington Symonds.* London: J. Castle, 1925, 255 pp.

500 copies printed.

TABB, JOHN BANNISTER

BLANCK, JACOB, ed. *Merle Johnson's American First Editions,* 4th edition, revised and enlarged. Waltham, Massachusetts: Mark Press, 1965, 487–488.

LEARY, LEWIS. *Articles on American Literature, 1900–1950.* Durham: Duke Univ. Press, 1954, 283–284.

STARKE, AUBREY. "Father John B. Tabb: A Checklist." *ABC,* VI (March 1935), 101–104.

TRENT, WILLIAM PETERFIELD, et al. *Cambridge History of American Literature,* 4 Vols. New York: G.P. Putnam's Sons, 1917–1921, II, 604.

TANNEHILL, WILKINS

HUBBELL, JAY B. *The South in*

American Literature, 1607–1900.
Durham: Duke Univ. Press,
1954, 963.

TAYLOR, BAYARD

BEATTY, RICHMOND CROOM.
*Bayard Taylor: Laureate of the
Gilded Age.* Norman: Univ. of
Oklahoma Press, 1936, 363–374.

GERSTENBERGER, DONNA,
and GEORGE HENDRICK. *The
American Novel, 1789–1959:
A Checklist of Twentieth Century
Criticism.* Denver: Alan Swallow,
1961, 235.

LEARY, LEWIS. *Articles on
American Literature, 1900–1950.*
Durham: Duke Univ. Press,
1954, 285–286.

SMYTH, ALBERT H. *Bayard
Taylor.* Boston: Houghton
Mifflin Co., 1896, 299–307.

SPILLER, ROBERT ERNEST,
et al. *Literary History of the
United States,* 2 Vols. New York:
Macmillan, 1962, 738–740.
Supplement, 196.

TRENT, WILLIAM PETERFIELD,
et al. *Cambridge History of
American Literature,* 4 Vols.
New York: G.P. Putnam's Sons,
1917–1921, IV, 655–656.

TAYLOR, EDWARD ROBESON

LEARY, LEWIS. *Articles on
American Literature, 1900–1950.*
Durham: Duke Univ. Press,
1954, 286.

TAYLOR, JOHN

PAINE, GREGORY LANSING,
ed. *Southern Prose Writers:
Representative Selections,* with
introduction, bibliography and

notes. New York: American
Book Co., 1947, cxlii–cxliii.

THAXTER, CELIA

LEARY, LEWIS. *Articles on
American Literature, 1900–1950.*
Durham: Duke Univ. Press,
1954, 287.

THOMPSON, DANIEL PIERCE

BLANCK, JACOB, ed. *Merle
Johnson's American First Editions,*
4th edition, revised and enlarged.
Waltham, Massachusetts: Mark
Press, 1965, 498.

FLITCROFT, JOHN EHRET,
*The Novelist of Vermont: A
Biographical and Critical Study
of Daniel Pierce Thompson.*
Cambridge: Harvard Univ. Press,
1929, 321–324.

GERSTENBERGER, DONNA,
and GEORGE HENDRICK. *The
American Novel, 1789–1959:
A Checklist of Twentieth Century
Criticism.* Denver: Alan Swallow,
1961, 235.

TRENT, WILLIAM PETERFIELD,
et al. *Cambridge History of
American Literature,* 4 Vols.
New York: G.P. Putnam's Sons,
1917–1921, I, 544–545.

THOMPSON, JAMES MAURICE

RUSSO, DOROTHY RITTER,
and THELMA LOIS SULLIVAN.
*Bibliographical Studies of Seven
Authors of Crawfordsville,
Indiana: Lew and Susan Wallace,
Maurice and Will Thompson,
Mary Hannah and Caroline
Virginia Krout, and Meredith
Nicholson.* Indianapolis:
Indiana Historical Society,
1952, 173–282.

THOMPSON, JOHN R.

HUBBELL, JAY B. *The South in American Literature, 1607–1900.* Durham: Duke Univ. Press, 1954, 964.

LEARY, LEWIS. *Articles on American Literature, 1900–1950.* Durham: Duke Univ. Press, 1954, 287.

THOMPSON, MAURICE

BLANCK, JACOB, ed. *Merle Johnson's American First Editions,* 4th edition, revised and enlarged. Waltham, Massachusetts: Mark Press, 1965, 499–500.

LEARY, LEWIS. *Articles on American Literature, 1900–1950.* Durham: Duke Univ. Press, 1954, 287.

THOMPSON, WILL HENRY

RUSSO, DOROTHY RITTER, and THELMA LOIS SULLIVAN. *Bibliographical Studies of Seven Authors of Crawfordsville, Indiana: Lew and Susan Wallace, Maurice and Will Thompson, Mary Hannah and Caroline Virginia Krout, and Meredith Nicholson.* Indianapolis: Indiana Historical Society, 1952, 285–303.

THOMPSON, WILLIAM TAPPAN

HUBBELL, JAY B. *The South in American Literature, 1607–1900.* Durham: Duke Univ. Press, 1954, 964.

LEARY, LEWIS. *Articles on American Literature, 1900–1950.* Durham: Duke Univ. Press, 1954, 287.

TRENT, WILLIAM PETERFIELD, et al. *Cambridge History of American Literature,* 4 Vols. New York: G.P. Putnam's Sons, 1917–1921, II, 510.

THOMSON, MORTIMER NEAL

LEARY, LEWIS. *Articles on American Literature, 1900–1950.* Durham: Duke Univ. Press, 1954, 287.

TRENT, WILLIAM PETERFIELD, et al. *Cambridge History of American Literature,* 4 Vols. New York: G.P. Putnam's Sons, 1917–1921, II, 510.

THOREAU, HENRY DAVID

ADAMS, RAYMOND. "The Bibliographical History of Thoreau's *A Week on the Concord and Merrimack Rivers." PBSA,* XLII (1st Quart. 1949), 39–47.

——————. "A Bibliographical Note on *Walden." AL,* II (May 1930), 166–168.

——————. *The Thoreau Library of Raymond Adams: A Catalogue.* Chapel Hill: n.p., 1936, 80 leaves.

ALLEN, FRANCIS HENRY. *A Bibliography of Henry David Thoreau.* Boston: Houghton Mifflin Co., 1928, 219 pp.

530 copies printed.

AMERICAN ACADEMY OF ARTS AND LETTERS. *The Great Decade in American Writing, 1850–1860. . . .* New York: American Academy of Arts and Letters, 1954, 3–5.

The catalog of an exhibition of manuscripts, books and paintings displayed Dec. 3–30, 1954.

ARNOLD, W. H. *First Editions of Bryant, Emerson, Hawthorne, Holmes, Longfellow, Lowell, Thoreau, Whittier.* Jamaica, New York: Marion Press, 1901, varying pagination.

BLANCK, JACOB, ed. *Merle Johnson's American First Editions,* 4th edition, revised and enlarged. Waltham, Massachusetts: Mark Press, 1965, 501–504.

BURNHAM, P. E., and CARVEL COLLINS. "Contribution to a Bibliography of Thoreau, 1938–1945," *BB,* XIX (September–December 1946), 16–18; (January–April 1947), 37–39.

COOK, REGINALD LANSING. *The Concord Saunterer,* including a discussion of the nature mysticism of Thoreau by Reginald Lansing Cook, original letters by Thoreau and a checklist of Thoreau items in the Abernethy Library of Middlebury College compiled by Viola C. White. Middlebury, Vermont: Middlebury College Press, 1940, 71–91.

CRAWFORD, BARTHOLOW V., ed. *Henry David Thoreau: Representative Selections,* with introduction, bibliography and notes. New York: American Book Co., 1934, lix–lxix.

DEDMOND, FRANCIS B. "A Check List of Manuscripts Relating to Thoreau in the Huntington Library, the Houghton Library of Harvard University, and the Berg Collection of the New York Public Library." *TSB,* XLIII (Spring 1953), 2–4.

GORDAN, JOHN D. "A Thoreau Handbill." *BNYPL,* LIX (May 1955), 253–258.

HARDING, WALTER. "A Bibliography of Thoreau in Poetry, Fiction, and Drama." *BB,* XVIII (May–August 1943), 15–18.

_____. *A Centennial Check List of the Editors of Henry David Thoreau's* Walden. Charlottesville: Univ. of Virginia Press for the Bibliographical Society of the Univ. of Virginia, 1954, 32 pp.

_____. "A Check List of Thoreau's Lectures." *BNYPL,* LII (February 1948), 78–87.

_____. "The Francis H. Allen Papers: A Catalog." *TSB,* XXXIV (January 1951), 4.

Additions to the Thoreau Society Archives in the Concord Free Public Library.

_____. "The Thoreau Collection of the Pierpont Morgan Library of New York City." *TSB,* XIX (April 1947), 2.

_____. *Thoreau's Library.* Charlottesville: Univ. of Virginia Press, 1957, 102 pp.

HARDING, WALTER, and CARL BODE. "Henry David Thoreau: A Check List of His Correspondence." *BNYPL,* LIX (May 1955), 227–252.

JONES, JOSEPH JAY, comp. *Index to Walden, with Notes, Map, and Vocabulary Lists.* Austin: Univ. of Texas Press, 1955, 66 pp.

JONES, SAMUEL ARTHUR. *Bibliography of Henry David Thoreau, with an Outline of His Life.* New York: printed for the

Rowfant Club of Cleveland by the DeVinne Press, 1894, 80 pp.

90 copies printed.

KENT, H. W. "A Catalog of the Thoreau Collection in the Concord Antiquarian Society." *TSB*, XLVII (Spring 1954), 1–4.

KERN, ALEXANDER. "Thoreau Manuscripts at Harvard." *TSB*, No. 53 (Fall 1955), 1–2.

LEARY, LEWIS. *Articles on American Literature, 1900–1950.* Durham: Duke Univ. Press, 1954, 287–293.

MORRISON, HELEN B. "Thoreau and the New York Tribune: A Checklist." *TSB*, No. 77 (Fall 1961), 1–2.

PAUL, SHERMAN, ed. *Henry David Thoreau: A Collection of Critical Essays.* Englewood Cliffs, New Jersey: Prentice Hall, 1962, 188 pp.

SALT, HENRY STEPHENS. *Life of Henry David Thoreau.* London: R. Bentley and Son, 1890, 300–307.

Also: W. Scott, Ltd., 1896, i–x.

SHANLEY, JAMES LYNDON. *The Making of Walden, with the Text of the First Version.* Chicago: Univ. of Chicago Press, 1957, 208 pp.

SPILLER, ROBERT ERNEST, et al. *Literary History of the United States,* 2 Vols. New York: Macmillan, 1962, 742–747. Supplement, 197–199.

STOVALL, FLOYD, et al. *Eight American Authors: A Review of Research and Criticism.*

New York: W. W. Norton and Co., 1963, 153–206, 434–438.

SWANSON, EVADENE B. "The Manuscript Journal of Thoreau's Last Journey." *Minnesota History,* XX (June 1931), 169–173.

TAYLOR, WALTER FULLER. *A History of American Letters,* with bibliographies by Harry Hartwick. Boston: American Book Co., 1936, 513–515.

Subsequent editions entitled: *The Story of American Letters.*

TRENT, WILLIAM PETERFIELD, et al. *Cambridge History of American Literature,* 4 Vols. New York: G.P. Putnam's Sons, 1917–1921, II, 411–415.

WADE, JOSEPH SANFORD. "A Contribution to a Bibliography from 1900–1936 of Henry David Thoreau." *Journal of the New York Entomological Society,* XLVII (June 1939), 163–203.

WAKEMAN, STEPHEN H. *The Stephen H. Wakeman Collection of Books of Nineteenth Century American Writers: The Property of Mrs. Alice L. Wakeman, First Editions, Inscribed Presentation and Personal Copies, Original Manuscripts and Letters of Nine American Authors.* New York: American Art Association, 1924, Items 972–1,075.

WHITE, WILLIAM. "Henry David Thoreau Bibliography, 1908–1937." *BB,* XVI (January–April 1938), 90–92; (May–August 1938), 111–113; (September–December 1938), 131–132; (January–April 1939), 163; (May–August 1939), 181–

182; (September–December 1939), 199–202.

Also: *Bulletin of Bibliography Pamphlet,* No. 35.

Also: Boston: F.W. Faxon, 1939, 51 pp.

WILSON, CARROLL ATWOOD. *Thirteen Author Collections of the Nineteenth Century and Five Centuries of Familiar Quotations,* edited by Jean C. S. Wilson and David A. Randall, 2 Vols. New York: privately printed for Scribner, 1950, I, 331–338.

WOODRESS, JAMES, et al. *American Literary Scholarship: An Annual.* Durham: Duke Univ. Press, (1963), 9–15; (1964), 11–15; (1965), 6–10; (1966), 3–11.

THORPE, THOMAS BANGS

LEARY, LEWIS. *Articles on American Literature, 1900–1950.* Durham: Duke Univ. Press, 1954, 293.

RICKELS, MILTON. "A Bibliography of the Writings of Thomas Bangs Thorpe." *AL,* XXIX (May 1957), 171–179.

TRENT, WILLIAM PETERFIELD, et al. *Cambridge History of American Literature,* 4 Vols. New York: G.P. Putnam's Sons, 1917–1921, II, 510.

THWAITES, REUBEN GOLD

TURNER, FREDERICK JACKSON. *Reuben Gold Thwaites: A Memorial Address.* Madison: State Historical Society of Wisconsin, 1914, 61–94.

TICKNOR, FRANCIS ORRAY

HUBBELL, JAY B. *The South in American Literature, 1607–1900.* Durham: Duke Univ. Press, 1954, 965.

TICKNOR, GEORGE

LEARY, LEWIS. *Articles on American Literature, 1900–1950.* Durham: Duke Univ. Press, 1954, 293–294.

TIERNAN, FRANCES CHRISTINE (CHRISTIAN REID)

LEARY, LEWIS. *Articles on American Literature, 1900–1950.* Durham: Duke Univ. Press, 1954, 256.

TIMROD, HENRY

CARDWELL, GUY A., JR., ed. *The Uncollected Poems of Henry Timrod.* Athens: Univ. of Georgia Press, 1942, 111–114.

HUBBELL, JAY B. *The South in American Literature, 1607–1900.* Durham: Duke Univ. Press, 1954, 965–966.

LEARY, LEWIS. *Articles on American Literature, 1900–1950.* Durham: Duke Univ. Press, 1954, 294.

PARKS, EDD WINFIELD. *Henry Timrod.* New York: Twayne Publishers, 1964, 146–149.

SHEPHERD, HENRY E. "Henry Timrod: Literary Estimate and Bibliography," compiled by A. S. Salley Jr. *Publications of the Southern Historical Association,* III (1899), 267–280.

SPILLER, ROBERT ERNEST, et al. *Literary History of the United States*, 2 Vols. New York: Macmillan, 1962, 747–748. Supplement, 200.

TAYLOR, WALTER FULLER. *A History of American Letters*, with bibliographies by Harry Hartwick. Boston: American Book Co., 1936, 534–535.

Subsequent editions entitled: *The Story of American Letters.*

WOODRESS, JAMES, et al. *American Literary Scholarship: An Annual.* Durham: Duke Univ. Press, (1964), 136–138; (1965), 159–160.

TORREY, BRADFORD

LEARY, LEWIS. *Articles on American Literature, 1900–1950.* Durham: Duke Univ. Press, 1954, 294.

TOURGÉE, ALBION W.

DIBBLE, ROY FLOYD. *Albion W. Tourgée.* New York: Lemeke and Buechner, 1921, 149–153.

GERSTENBERGER, DONNA, and GEORGE HENDRICK. *The American Novel, 1789–1959: A Checklist of Twentieth Century Criticism.* Denver: Alan Swallow, 1961, 235–236.

KELLER, DEAN H. "A Checklist of the Writings of Albion W. Tourgée." *SB*, XVIII (1965), 269–279.

LEARY, LEWIS. *Articles on American Literature, 1900–1950.* Durham: Duke Univ. Press, 1954, 294.

WOODRESS, JAMES, et al. *American Literary Scholarship: An Annual.* Durham: Duke Univ. Press, (1963), 107–109.

TROWBRIDGE, JOHN T.

BLANCK, JACOB, ed. *Merle Johnson's American First Editions*, 4th edition, revised and enlarged. Waltham, Massachusetts: Mark Press, 1965, 505–508.

LEARY, LEWIS. *Articles on American Literature, 1900–1950.* Durham: Duke Univ. Press, 1954, 295.

TUCKER, GEORGE

HUBBELL, JAY B. *The South in American Literature, 1607–1900.* Durham: Duke Univ. Press, 1954, 967–968.

LEARY, LEWIS. *Articles on American Literature, 1900–1950.* Durham: Duke Univ. Press, 1954, 295.

TRENT, WILLIAM PETERFIELD, et al. *Cambridge History of American Literature*, 4 Vols. New York: G.P. Putnam's Sons, 1917–1921, I, 545.

TUCKER, NATHANIEL BEVERLEY

HUBBELL, JAY B. *The South in American Literature, 1607–1900.* Durham: Duke Univ. Press, 1954, 966–967.

LEARY, LEWIS. *Articles on American Literature, 1900–1950.* Durham: Duke Univ. Press, 1954, 295.

TRENT, WILLIAM PETERFIELD, et al. *Cambridge History of American Literature*, 4 Vols. New York: G.P. Putnam's Sons, 1917–1921, I, 545.

TUCKERMAN, FREDERICK GODDARD

LEARY, LEWIS. *Articles on American Literature, 1900–1950.* Durham: Duke Univ. Press, 1954, 296.

WOODRESS, JAMES, et al. *American Literary Scholarship: An Annual.* Durham: Duke Univ. Press, (1965), 149–153; (1966), 136–139.

TURNER, JOSEPH ADDISON

LEARY, LEWIS. *Articles on American Literature, 1900–1950.* Durham: Duke Univ. Press, 1954, 296.

TWAIN, MARK (see CLEMENS)

TYLER, MOSES COIT

JONES, HOWARD MUMFORD. *The Life of Moses Coit Tyler.* Ann Arbor: Univ. of Michigan Press, 1933, 277–288.

LEARY, LEWIS. *Articles on American Literature, 1900–1950.* Durham: Duke Univ. Press, 1954, 296.

UNDERWOOD, FRANCIS HENRY

LEARY, LEWIS. *Articles on American Literature, 1900–1950.* Durham: Duke Univ. Press, 1954, 296.

VANCE, ZEBULON BAIRD

TRENT, WILLIAM PETERFIELD, et al. *Cambridge History of American Literature,* 4 Vols. New York: G. P. Putnam's Sons, 1917–1921, II, 604–605.

VERPLANCK, GULIAN CROMMELIN

HARVEY, SARA KING. "A Bibli-ography of the Miscellaneous Prose of Gulian Crommelin Verplanck." *AL,* VIII (May 1936), 199–203.

LEARY, LEWIS. *Articles on American Literature, 1900–1950.* Durham: Duke Univ. Press, 1954, 297.

TAFT, KENDALL B., ed. *Minor Knickerbockers: Representative Selections,* with introduction, bibliography and notes. New York: American Book Co., 1947, cxliii-cxliv.

VERY, JONES

BARTLETT, WILLIAM IRVING. *Jones Very: Emerson's "Brave Saint."* Durham: Duke Univ. Press, 1942, 209–227.

LEARY, LEWIS. *Articles on American Literature, 1900–1950.* Durham: Duke Univ. Press, 1954, 297.

SPILLER, ROBERT ERNEST, et al. *Literary History of the United States,* 2 Vols. New York: Macmillan, 1962, 750–751. Supplement, 200.

WAITE, MORRISON REMICK

LIBRARY OF CONGRESS, MANU-SCRIPT DIVISION. *Morrison R. Waite: A Register of His Papers in the Library of Congress.* Washington, 1959, 8 leaves.

WALLACE, LEWIS

BLANCK, JACOB, ed. *Merle Johnson's American First Editions,* 4th edition, revised and enlarged. Waltham, Massachusetts: Mark Press, 1965, 512–513.

LEARY, LEWIS. *Articles on American Literature, 1900–1950.* Durham: Duke Univ. Press, 1954, 298.

RUSSO, DOROTHY RITTER, and THELMA LOIS SULLIVAN. *Bibliographical Studies of Seven Authors of Crawfordsville, Indiana: Lew and Susan Wallace, Maurice and Will Thompson, Mary Hannah and Caroline Virginia Krout, and Meredith Nicholson.* Indianapolis: Indiana Historical Society, 1952, 305–416.

WALLACE, SUSAN ARNOLD ELSTON (MRS. LEW WALLACE)

RUSSO, DOROTHY RITTER, and THELMA LOIS SULLIVAN. *Bibliographical Studies of Seven Authors of Crawfordsville, Indiana: Lew and Susan Wallace, Maurice and Will Thompson, Mary Hannah and Caroline Virginia Krout, and Meredith Nicholson.* Indianapolis: Indiana Historical Society, 1952, 417–446.

WALLIS, SEVERN TEACKLE

LEARY, LEWIS. *Articles on American Literature, 1900–1950.* Durham: Duke Univ. Press, 1954, 298.

WARD, ELIZABETH STUART PHELPS

GERSTENBERGER, DONNA, and GEORGE HENDRICK. *The American Novel, 1789–1959: A Checklist of Twentieth Century Criticism.* Denver: Alan Swallow, 1961, 251.

WARE, WILLIAM

GERSTENBERGER, DONNA, and GEORGE HENDRICK. *The American Novel, 1789–1959: A Checklist of Twentieth Century Criticism.* Denver: Alan Swallow, 1961, 251.

TRENT, WILLIAM PETERFIELD, et al. *Cambridge History of American Literature,* 4 Vols. New York: G. P. Putnam's Sons, 1917–1921, I, 545–546.

WARNER, CHARLES DUDLEY

GERSTENBERGER, DONNA, and GEORGE HENDRICK. *The American Novel, 1789–1959: A Checklist of Twentieth Century Criticism.* Denver: Alan Swallow, 1961, 251.

LEARY, LEWIS. *Articles on American Literature, 1900–1950.* Durham: Duke Univ. Press, 1954, 298.

WARNER, SUSAN

GERSTENBERGER, DONNA, and GEORGE HENDRICK. *The American Novel, 1789–1959: A Checklist of Twentieth Century Criticism.* Denver: Alan Swallow, 1961, 251.

WASHINGTON, BOOKER T.

LIBRARY OF CONGRESS, MANUSCRIPT DIVISION. *Booker T. Washington: A Register of His Papers in the Library of Congress.* Washington, 1958, 105 pp.

TRENT, WILLIAM PETERFIELD, et al. *Cambridge History of American Literature,* 4 Vols. New York: G. P. Putnam's Sons, 1917–1921, II, 605–611.

WATTERSON, HENRY

LEARY, LEWIS. *Articles on American Literature, 1900–1950.* Durham: Duke Univ. Press, 1954, 300.

WEBB, JOHN

LEARY, LEWIS. *Articles on American Literature, 1900–1950.* Durham: Duke Univ. Press, 1954, 300.

WEBSTER, DANIEL

CLAPP, C. B. "The Speeches of Daniel Webster: A Bibliographical Review." *PBSA,* XIII (1919), 3—63.

FUESS, CLAUDE MOORE. *Daniel Webster,* 2 Vols. Boston: Little, Brown and Co., 1930, II, 419—430.

HART, CHARLES HENRY. *Bibliographia Websteriana: A List of the Publications Occasioned by the Death of Daniel Webster.* Philadelphia: n.p., 1883, 4 pp.

LCN: "Extracted from the *Bulletin of the Mercantile Library,* 1883."

LEARY, LEWIS. *Articles on American Literature, 1900—1950.* Durham: Duke Univ. Press, 1954, 300.

SPILLER, ROBERT ERNEST, et al. *Literary History of the United States,* 2 Vols. New York: Macmillan, 1962, 755—757. Supplement, 202.

TRENT, WILLIAM PETERFIELD, et al. *Cambridge History of American Literature,* 4 Vols. New York: G. P. Putnam's Sons, 1917—1921, II, 480—488.

WEBSTER, DANIEL. *The Writings and Speeches of Daniel Webster . . . ,* national edition, 18 Vols. Boston: Little, Brown and Co., 1903, XVIII, 579—619.

WEBSTER, NOAH

FORD, MRS. EMILY ELLSWORTH (FOWLER). *Notes on the Life of Noah Webster,* 2 Vols. New York: privately printed, 1912, II, 523—544.

LEARY, LEWIS. *Articles on American Literature, 1900—1950.* Durham: Duke Univ. Press, 1954, 300.

SKEEL, EMILY ELLSWORTH (FORD). *A Bibliography of the Writings of Noah Webster,* edited by Edwin H. Carpenter Jr. New York: New York Public Library, 1958, 694 pp.

500 copies printed.

WEEDEN, HOWARD

WOODRESS, JAMES, et al. *American Literary Scholarship: An Annual.* Durham: Duke Univ. Press, (1964). 136—138.

WEEMS, MASON LOCKE

HUBBELL, JAY B. *The South in American Literature, 1607—1900.* Durham: Duke Univ. Press, 1954, 969—970.

LEARY, LEWIS. *Articles on American Literature, 1900—1950.* Durham: Duke Univ. Press, 1954, 300—301.

SKEEL, EMILY ELLSWORTH (FORD), ed. *Mason Locke Weems: His Works and Ways,* 3 Vols. New York: Plimton Press, 1929.

I contains an unfinished bibliography by Paul Leicester Ford. 200 copies printed.

WEISSELBERG, MARIE ANNA

LEARY, LEWIS. *Articles on American Literature, 1900—1950.* Durham: Duke Univ. Press, 1954, 301.

WENDELL, BARRETT

LEARY, LEWIS. *Articles on American Literature, 1900—1950.* Durham: Duke Univ. Press, 1954, 301.

WESTCOTT, EDWARD NOYES

BLANCK, JACOB, ed. *Merle Johnson's American First Editions,* 4th edition, revised and enlarged. Waltham, Massachusetts: Mark Press, 1965, 516.

WETMORE, PROSPER MONTGOMERY

TAFT, KENDALL B., ed. *Minor Knickerbockers: Representative Selections,* with introduction, bibliography, and notes. New York: American Book Co., 1947, cxliv-cxlv.

WHIPPLE, EDWIN PERCY

LEARY, LEWIS. *Articles on American Literature, 1900–1950.* Durham: Duke Univ. Press, 1954, 303.

WHISTLER, JAMES A. McNEILL

BLANCK, JACOB, ed. *Merle Johnson's American First Editions,* 4th edition, revised and enlarged. Waltham, Massachusetts: Mark Press, 1965, 521–522.

WHITCHER, FRANCES MIRIAM BERRY

TRENT, WILLIAM PETERFIELD, et al. *Cambridge History of American Literature,* 4 Vols. New York: G. P. Putnam's Sons, 1917–1921, II, 511.

WHITE, JOHN BLAKE

LEARY, LEWIS. *Articles on American Literature, 1900–1950.* Durham: Duke Univ. Press, 1954, 303.

WHITE, RICHARD GRANT

LEARY, LEWIS. *Articles on American Literature, 1900–1950.* Durham: Duke Univ. Press, 1954, 303.

WHITE, THOMAS WILLIS

LEARY, LEWIS. *Articles on American Literature, 1900–1950.* Durham: Duke Univ. Press, 1954, 303.

WHITE, WILLIAM HALE (MARK RUTHERFORD)

GERSTENBERGER, DONNA, and GEORGE HENDRICK. *The American Novel, 1789–1959: A Checklist of Twentieth Century Criticism.* Denver: Alan Swallow, 1961, 260.

STONE, WILFRED. *Religion and Art of William Hale White (Mark Rutherford).* Palo Alto: Standford Univ. Press, 1954, 215–232.

WHITECOTTON, MOSES

LEARY, LEWIS. *Articles on American Literature, 1900–1950.* Durham: Duke Univ. Press, 1954, 303.

WHITMAN, WALT

AIZEN DE MOSHINSKY, ELENA. *"Walt Whitman" y la America Latina.* Mexico: n.p., 1950, 98–99.

ALEGRÍA, FERNANDO. *Walt Whitman en Hispanoamérica.* México: n.p., 1954, 411–419.

Colleción Studium, No. 5.

ALLEN, EVIE ALLISON, and GAY WILSON ALLEN. "Walt Whitman Bibliography, 1944–1954." *Walt Whitman Foundation Bulletin,* VIII (April 1955), 10–34.

ALLEN, GAY WILSON. "Biblical Echoes in Whitman's Works." *AL,* VI (November 1934), 302–315.

_____. *Twenty-five Years of Walt Whitman Bibliography, 1918–1942.* Boston: F. W. Faxon Co., 1943, 57 pp.

Bulletin of Bibliography Pamphlet, No. 38.

_____. Walt Whitman as Man, Poet, and Legend, with a checklist of Whitman publications, 1945–1960, by Evie Allison Allen. Carbondale: Southern Illinois Univ. Press, 1961, 179–224.

_____. "Walt Whitman Bibliography, 1918–1934." BB, XV (September–December 1934), 84–88; (January–April 1935), 106–109.

Also: Bulletin of Bibliography Pamphlet, No. 30.

_____. "Walt Whitman Bibliography: 1935–1942." BB, XVII (January–April 1943), 209–210; XVIII (May–August 1943), 9–10.

AMERICAN ACADEMY OF ARTS AND LETTERS. The Great Decade in American Writing, 1850–1860. . . . New York: American Academy of Arts and Letters, 1954, 16–18.

The catalog of an exhibition of manuscripts, books and paintings displayed Dec. 3–30, 1954.

AMERICAN LIBRARY IN LONDON. Walt Whitman: Catalogue of an Exhibition Held at the American Library, London, March–April 1954. London: U.S. Information Service, 1954, 32 pp.

ARVIN, NEWTON. Whitman. New York: Macmillan, 1938, 297–312.

ASSELINEAU, ROGER. "Etat présent des études Whitmaniennes." EA, XI (January–March 1958), 31–40.

_____. L'Evolution de Walt Whitman après la première édition des Feuilles d'Herbe. Paris: Didier, 1954, 528–545.

BARRUS, CLARA. Whitman and Burroughs, Comrades. Boston: Houghton Mifflin Co., 1931, 375–379.

BAZALGETTE, LEON. Walt Whitman: The Man and His Work, translated from the French by Ellen Fitz-Gerald. Garden City: Doubleday, Page and Co., 1920, bibliographical footnotes.

BEAVER, JOSEPH. Walt Whitman: Poet of Science. New York: King's Crown Press, 1951, 171–174.

BLANCK, JACOB, ed. Merle Johnson's American First Editions, 4th edition, revised and enlarged. Waltham, Massachusetts: Mark Press, 1965, 528–532.

BLODGETT, HAROLD W. "Bibliographical Description as a Key to Whitman." Walt Whitman Newsletter, II (March–June 1956), 8–9.

_____. "Walt Whitman in England." Cornell Studies in English, XXIV (1934), 223–234.

BOLTON PUBLIC LIBRARIES (LANCASHIRE, ENGLAND). A Catalogue of Works by and Relating to Walt Whitman. Bolton: Bolton Public Libraries, 1955, 52 pp.

BOWEN, DOROTHY, and PHILIP DURHAM. "Walt Whitman Materials in the Huntington Library." HLQ, XIX (November 1955), 81–96.

BOWERS, FREDSON. "The Earliest Manuscript of Whitman's 'Passage to India' and Its Notebook." BNYPL, LXI (July 1957), 319–352.

_____. "The Manuscripts of Whitman's 'Song of the Redwoodtree.'" PBSA, L (1st Quart. 1956), 53–85.

_____. "Whitman's Manuscripts for the Original 'Calamus' Poems." *SB,* VI (1954), 257−265.

BUCKE, RICHARD M. *Catalogue of Important Letters, Manuscripts and Books by or Relating to Walt Whitman.* London: printed by Kitchen and Barratt, Ltd., 1935, 31 pp.

From the title page: "The property of his intimate friend, biographer and literary executor, the late Richard Maurice Bucke, of London, Ontario, [sold by order of H. L. Bucke, esq.] which will be sold by auction by Messrs. Sotheby and Co. . . . the 13th of May, 1935."

_____. *Manuscripts, Autograph Letters, First Editions and Portraits of Walt Whitman.* New York: American Art Association, 1936, 127 pp.

From the title page: "Formerly the property of the late Dr. Richard Maurice Bucke . . . purchased at public sale in London, England, by the Ulysses Bookshop, Ltd., or by private treaty by Dr. Jacob Schwartz." . . . to be dispersed at public sale April 15 and 16 . . . by order of Dr. Jacob Schwartz"

CANBY, HENRY SEIDEL. *Walt Whitman, an American: A Study in Biography.* Boston: Houghton Mifflin Co., 1943, 371−375.

CATEL, JEAN. *Rythme et langage dans la Ire Edition des* Leaves of Grass *(1855).* Paris: Rieder, 1930, 188−195.

_____. *Walt Whitman: La Naissance du poète.* Paris: Rieder, 1929, 471−479.

CHUKOVSKIÍ, KORNEI I. *Uot Uitmén i Ego "List ia Travy."* Izd. 6., dop. Moskva, Gos, izd-vo, 1923, 5−9.

CLARK, HARRY HAYDEN, ed. *Major American Poets.,* New York: American Book Co., 1936, 914−919.

COOKE, ALICE L. "American First Editions at Texas University: Walt Whitman." *LCUT,* II (June 1946), 95−105.

DETROIT PUBLIC LIBRARY. *An Exhibition of the Works of Walt Whitman,* including books, manuscripts, letters, portraits, association items, sponsored by Friends of the Detroit Public Library, Inc. Detroit: n.p., 1945, 40 pp.

DEUTSCH, BABETTE. *Walt Whitman: Builder for America,* illustrated by Rafaello Busoni. New York: J. Messner, Inc., 1941, 269−274.

DUKE UNIVERSITY, LIBRARY. *Catalogue of the Whitman Collection in the Duke University Library,* compiled by Ellen Frances Frey. Durham: Duke Univ. Library, 1945, 148 pp.

_____. *The Trent Collection in the Rare Book Room of the Duke University Library, in Honor of Mary Duke Trent, Sarah Elizabeth Trent, Rebecca Grey Trent.* Durham: Duke Univ. Library, 1943, 7 pp.

Described more fully in Duke University Library's *Catalogue of the Whitman Collection,* 1945.

_____. *Walt Whitman: A Checklist of an Exhibition of Manuscripts and Books from the Trent Collection,* compiled by Thomas M. Simkins. Durham: Friends of Duke Univ. Library, 1955, 8 pp.

THE EDITORS. "A Bibliography of Walt Whitman." *Bookman* (New York), VI (September 1897), 81−82.

ENGLEKIRK, JOHN EUGENE. *Bibliografia de Obras Norte-americanas en Traducción Española.* Mexico: n.p., 1944, 72–73.

_____. *A Literature Norteamericana do Brasil.* México: n.p., 1950, 132–135.

FANER, ROBERT D. *Walt Whitman and Opera.* Philadelphia: Univ. of Pennsylvania Press, 1951, 237–244.

FAUSSET, HUGH I'ANSON. *Walt Whitman: Poet of Democracy.* New Haven: Yale Univ. Press, 1942, 309–310.

FEINBERG, CHARLES E., comp. *Walt Whitman: A Selection of the Manuscripts, Books, and Association Items Gathered by Charles E. Feinberg.* Detroit: Detroit Public Library, 1955, 140 pp.

FREY, ELLEN. "The Trent Collection." *Antiquarian Bookman,* VI (Oct. 14, 1950), 917–918.

GERSTENBERGER, DONNA, and GEORGE HENDRICK. *The American Novel, 1789–1959: A Checklist of Twentieth Century Criticism.* Denver: Alan Swallow, 1961, 261.

GRANT, RENA. "The Livezey-Whitman Manuscripts." *WWR* VII (March 1961), 3–14.

GREBANIER, MRS. FRANCES (VINCIGUERRA). *American Giant: Walt Whitman and His Times.* New York: Harper and Brothers, 1941, 322–331.

Spanish edition: Buenos Aires: Editorial Sudamericana, 1944, 381–390.

HARDING, WALTER. "A Sheaf of Whitman Letters." *SB,* V (1952–1953), 203–210.

Index to Early American Periodical Literature, 1728–1870: No. 3, Walt

Whitman, 1819–1892. New York: Pamphlet Distributing Co., 1941, 19 pp.

JOHNSON, MAURICE O. "Walt Whitman as a Critic of Literature." *Univ. of Nebraska Studies in Language, Literature, and Criticism,* XVI (1938), 70–73.

JONES, JOSEPH. "Rare Book Collections: I, Walt Whitman; II, T. S. Eliot." *LCUT,* VI (Spring 1958), 44–46.

JONES, P. M. "Whitman in France: A List of Translations from, and Studies, etc., on Whitman Published in France before 1909." *MLR,* X (January 1915), 25–27.

KENNEDY, WILLIAM SLOANE. *The Fight of a Book for the World.* West Yarmouth, Massachusetts: The Stonecraft Press, 1926, 237–286.

LANDAUER, BELLA CLARA. *Leaves of Music by Walt Whitman,* from the Collection of Bella C. Landauer. New York: privately printed, 1937, 84 pp.

LEARY, LEWIS. *Articles on American Literature, 1900–1950.* Durham: Duke Univ. Press, 1954, 303–316.

LIBRARY OF CONGRESS, REF–ERENCE DEPARTMENT. *Walt Whitman: A Catalog Based upon the Collections of the Library of Congress.* Washington, 1955, 155 pp.

"Notes on Whitman Collections and Collectors" by Charles E. Feinberg.

McCAIN, REA. "Walt Whitman in Italy: A Bibliography." *BB,* XVII (January–April 1941), 66–67; (May–August 1941), 92–93.

McCUSKER, HONOR. *"Leaves of Grass:* First Editions and Manu-

scripts in the Whitman Collection."
More Books, XII (May 1938),
179—192.

MELIADO, MARIOLINA. "La
fortuna di Walt Whitman in Italia."
SA, VII (1961), 43—76.

Introduction and bibliography of
translations, articles and books.

MICHEL, PIERRE. "Whitman Re-
visited." *Revue des Langues
Vivantes,* XXIX (January—February
1963), 79—83.

MILLER, EDWIN HAVILAND.
"Walt Whitman's Correspondence
with Whitelaw Reid, Editor of the
New York *Tribune." SB,* VIII
(1956), 242—249.

MILLER, EDWIN HAVILAND, and
ROSALIND S. MILLER. *Walt Whitman's Correspondence: A Checklist.*
New York: New York Public Library,
1957, 171 pp.

MONTOLÍU Y DE TOGORES,
CIPRIANO, MARQUÉS DE. *Walt
Whitman: l'Home is sa Tasca.* Bar-
celona: Societat Catalána d'edictións,
1913, 197—203.

NEILSON, KENNETH P. *The World
of Walt Whitman Music: A Bibliographical Study.* New York: N.p. 1963,
144 pp.

NEW YORK PUBLIC LIBRARY.
*Walt Whitman's Blue Book: The
1860—61* Leaves of Grass *Containing
His Manuscript Additions and Re-
visions,* 2 Vols. New York: New
York Public Library, 1968.

———————. *Walt Whitman's*
Leaves of Grass: *A Centenary Exhibition from the Lion Whitman
Collection and the Berg Collection of
the New York Public Library,* compiled by Lewis M. Stark and John D.

Gordan. New York: New York
Public Library, 1955, 46 pp.

NORTH, ERNEST DRESSEL. "A
Check List of Walt Whitman." *Book
Buyer,* XVIII (April 1899), 48.

PENNSYLVANIA, UNIVERSITY.
Whitman Manuscript Collection, including letters, memoranda, notes,
post cards, photographs, clippings
and lecture programs. Philadelphia:
Univ. of Pennsylvania, 1948.

On microfilm.

PLATT, ISAAC HULL. *Walt Whitman.* Boston: Small, Maynard and
Co., 1904, 141—147.

RESNICK, NATHAN. *Walt Whitman
and the Authorship of the Good
Gray Poet.* Brooklyn: Long Island
Univ. Press, 1948, bibliographical
footnotes.

SAUNDERS, HENRY SCHOLEY,
comp. *Whitman in Fiction: A List.*
Toronto: Henry Scholey Saunders,
1950, 9 leaves.

8 mimeographed copies.

———————. *Whitman Music List,*
including items from *Leaves of Music
by Walt Whitman,* by Bella C.
Landauer, 1937, with index, 9th
edition. Toronto: Henry Scholey
Saunders, 1950, 24 pp.

8 mimeographed copies.

SCHYBERG, FREDERIK. *Walt
Whitman,* translated from the
Danish by Evie Allison Allen, with
an introduction by Gay Wilson Allen.
New York: Columbia Univ. Press,
1951, 361—365.

SHAY, FRANK. *The Bibliography
of Walt Whitman.* New York:
Friedman's, 1920, 46 pp.

SPILLER, ROBERT ERNEST, et al. *Literary History of the United States,* 2 Vols. New York: Macmillan, 1962, 759–768. Supplement, 203–207.

STARK, LEWIS M., et al. "Walt Whitman: The Oscar Lion Collection." *BNYPL,* LVIII (May 1954), 213–229; (June 1954), 305–308; (July 1954), 348–359; (August 1954), 397–410; (September 1954), 455–461; (October 1954), 497–514.

STOVALL, FLOYD, ed. *Walt Whitman: Representative Selections,* with introduction, bibliography and notes. New York: American Book Co., 1939, liii-lxiii.

STOVALL, FLOYD, et al. *Eight American Authors: A Review of Research and Criticism.* New York: W. W. Norton and Co., 1963, 271–318, 445–451.

TANNER, JAMES T. F. *Walt-Whitman: A Supplementary Bibliography.* Kent, Ohio: Kent State Univ. Press, 1968, 59 pp.

Supplements the Evie Allison Allen bibliography in Gay Wilson Allen's *Walt Whitman as Man, Poet, and Legend,* 1961. The Allen work covers 1945–1960, the Tanner 1960–1968.

TAYLOR, WALTER FULLER. *A History of American Letters,* with bibliographies by Harry Hartwick. Boston: American Book Co., 1936, 536–541.

Subsequent editions entitled: *The Story of American Letters.*

TRENT, WILLIAM PETERFIELD, et al. *Cambridge History of American Literature,* 4 Vols. New York: G. P. Putnam's Sons, 1917–1921, II, 551–581.

TRIGGS, OSCAR LOVELL. *The Complete Writings of Walt Whitman,* 10 Vols. New York: G.P. Putnam's Sons, 1902, X, 135–233.

_____. *Selections from the Prose and Poetry of Walt Whitman.* Boston: Small, Maynard and Co., 1898, 251–257.

TRIMBLE, WILLIAM HEYWOOD. *Catalogue of a Collection of Walt Whitman Literature Compiled and Published by the Owner.* Dunedin, New Zealand: Budget, Ltd., 1912, 36 pp.

_____. *Walt Whitman and Leaves of Grass: An Introduction.* London: Watts and Co., 1905, 92–100.

TULSA BIBLIOPHILES. *A List of Whitman Items,* gathered by the Tulsa Bibliophiles from its February 1947 inception to February 1949, and presented to members at the second anniversary meeting. Tulsa: n.p., 1949, 46 leaves.

"Walt Whitman: The Oscar Lion Collection." *BNYPL,* LVIII (May 1954), 213–229; (June 1954), 305–308; (July 1954), 348–359; (August 1954), 397–410; (September 1954), 455–461; (October 1954), 497–514.

WHITE, WILLIAM. "Addenda to Whitman's Short Stories." *PBSA,* LVII (2nd Quart 1963), 221–222.

WELLS, CAROLYN, and ALFRED F. GOLDSMITH. *A Concise Bibliography of the Works of Walt Whitman, with a Supplement of Fifty Books about Whitman.* Boston and New York: Houghton Mifflin Co., 1922, 114 pp.

Limited edition.

_____. "Bibliography." *Walt Whitman Newsletter,* II (September 1956), 29; III (March 1957), 13—14.

—————. "Walt Whitman's Short Stories: Some Comments and a Bibliography." *PBSA*, LII (4th Quart. 1958), 300—306.

—————. "Whitman: A Current Bibliography." *WWR*, XI (March 1965), 21—23.

—————. "Whitman in Paperback." *ABC*, XI (May 1961), 28—30.

—————. "Whitman's *Leaves of Grass:* Notes on the Pocketbook (1889) Edition." *SB*, XVIII (1965), 280—281.

"The Whitman Collection: Some New Manuscripts." *LCUP*, XIV (April 1957), 29—31.

WILLARD, C. B. "The Saunders Collection of Whitmaniana in the Brown University Library." *BBr*, XVIII (May 1965), 14—22.

WILLIAMS, STANLEY T. "The Adrian Van Sinderen Collection of Walt Whitman." *YULG*, XV (January 1941), 49—53.

WILLIAMSON, GEORGE MILLAR. *Catalogue of a Collection of Books, Letters, and Manuscripts Written by Walt Whitman, in the Library of George M. Williamson.* New York: Dodd, Mead and Co., 1903, 52 pp.

WOODRESS, JAMES, et al. *American Literary Scholarship: An Annual.* Durham: Duke Univ. Press, (1963), 41—52; (1964), 43—49; (1965), 45—56; (1955), 40—47.

WHITTIER, JOHN GREENLEAF

ARNOLD, W. H. *First Editions of Bryant, Emerson, Hawthorne,* *Holmes, Longfellow, Lowell, Thoreau, Whittier.* Jamaica, New York: Marion Press, 1901, varying pagination.

BENNETT, WHITMAN. *Whittier: Bard of Freedom.* Chapel Hill: Univ. of North Carolina Press, 1941, 335—340.

BIERSTADT, E. H. "A Bibliography of the Original Editions of the Works of John Greenleaf Whittier." *The Book Buyer,* XII (May 1895), 216—221; (June 1895), 268—274; (July 1895), 324—330; (August 1895), 382—388; (September 1895), 432—436; (October 1895), 498—499.

BLANCK, JACOB, ed. *Merle Johnson's American First Editions,* 4th edition, revised and enlarged. Waltham, Massachusetts: Mark Press, 1965, 533—540.

BURTON, RICHARD. *John Greenleaf Whittier.* Boston: Small, Maynard and Co., 1901, 131—134.

CARPENTER, GEORGE RICE. *John Greenleaf Whittier.* Boston: Houghton Mifflin Co., 1903, 304—307.

CARTER, G. F. "Some Little Known Whittierana." *Literary Collector,* VII (April 1904), 169—172.

CLARK, HARRY HAYDEN, ed. *Major American Poets.* New York: American Book Co., 1936, 798—802.

CURRIER, THOMAS FRANKLIN, comp. *A Bibliography of John Greenleaf Whittier.* Cambridge: Harvard Univ. Press, 1937, 705 pp.

ESSEX INSTITUTE. "The John Greenleaf Whittier Centenary Exhibition at the Essex Institute, December 17, 1907, to January 31, 1908."

Essex Institute Historical Collections, XLIV (April 1908), 123–146.

LEARY, LEWIS. *Articles on American Literature, 1900–1950.* Durham: Duke Univ. Press, 1954, 316–319.

LINTON, WILLIAM JAMES. *Life of John Greenleaf Whittier.* London: W. Scott, Ltd., 1893, i-viii.

MORDELL, ALBERT. *Quaker Militant: John Greenleaf Whittier.* Boston: Houghton Mifflin Co., 1933, 333–343.

PICKARD, JOHN B. *John Greenleaf Whittier: An Introduction and Interpretation.* New York, 1967, 135–137.

Part of the *American Authors and Critics Series,* begun in 1961, and purchased by Holt, Rinehart and Winston from Barnes and Noble. The nine original and three new volumes were issued under the Holt imprint in January 1967.

SPILLER, ROBERT ERNEST, et al. *Literary History of the United States.* 2 Vols. New York: Macmillan, 1962, 769–772. Supplement, 207–208.

TAYLOR, WALTER FULLER. *A History of American Letters,* with bibliographies by Harry Hartwick. Boston: American Book Co., 1936, 519–521.

Subsequent editions entitled: *The Story of American Letters.*

TRENT, WILLIAM PETERFIELD, et al. *Cambridge History of American Literature,* 4 Vols. New York: G. P. Putnam's Sons, 1917–1921, II, 436–451.

WAGENKNECHT, EDWARD CHARLES. *John Greenleaf Whittier: A Portrait in Paradox.* New York: Oxford Univ. Press, 1967, 241–249.

WAKEMAN, STEPHEN H. *The Stephen H. Wakeman Collection of Books of Nineteenth Century American Writers: The Property of Mrs. Alice L. Wakeman, First Editions, Inscribed Presentation and Personal Copies, Original Manuscripts and Letters of Nine American Authors.* New York: American Art Association, 1924, Items 1,076–1,279.

WILSON, CARROLL ATWOOD. *Thirteen Author Collections of the Nineteenth Century and Five Centuries of Familiar Quotations,* edited by Jean C.S. Wilson and David A. Randall, 2 Vols. New York: privately printed for Scribner, 1950, II, 705–889.

WOODMAN, MRS. ABBY JOHNSON. "List of the First Editions, Portraits, Engravings, Manuscripts, and Personal Relics of John Greenleaf Whittier, Exhibited at the Essex Institute December 17, 1907, to January 31, 1908," in *Reminiscences of John Greenleaf Whittier's Life at Oak Knoll, Danvers, Massachusetts.* Salem: Essex Institute, 1908, 52 pp.

200 copies printed.

WOODRESS, JAMES, et al. *American Literary Scholarship: An Annual.* Durham: Duke Univ. Press, (1963), 129–130; (1964), 126–130; (1965), 149–153; (1966), 136–139.

WHITTIER, MATTHEW FRANKLIN

LEARY, LEWIS. *Articles on American Literature, 1900–1950.* Durham: Duke Univ. Press, 1954, 319.

WIDENER, HARRY ELKINS

LEARY, LEWIS. *Articles on American Literature, 1900–1950.* Durham: Duke Univ. Press, 1954, 319.

WIGGIN, KATE DOUGLAS

LEARY, LEWIS. *Articles on American Literature, 1900–1950.* Durham: Duke Univ. Press, 1954, 319.

WILCOX, ELLA WHEELER

LEARY, LEWIS. *Articles on American Literature, 1900–1950.* Durham: Duke Univ. Press, 1954, 320.

WILDE, RICHARD HENRY

HUBBELL, JAY B. *The South in American Literature, 1607–1900.* Durham: Duke Univ. Press, 1954, 970–972.

LEARY, LEWIS. *Articles on American Literature, 1900–1950.* Durham: Duke Univ. Press, 1954, 320.

WOODRESS, JAMES, et al. *American Literary Scholarship: An Annual.* Durham: Duke Univ. Press, (1966), 145–146.

WILLARD, FRANCES E.

LEARY, LEWIS. *Articles on American Literature, 1900–1950.* Durham: Duke Univ. Press, 1954, 321.

WILLIAMS, CATHARINE R.

RIDER, SIDNEY SMITH. *Bibliographical Memoirs of Three Rhode Island Authors: Joseph K. Angell, Frances H. (Whipple) McDougall, Catharine R. Williams.* Providence: S.S. Rider, 1880, 92 pp.

Rhode Island Historical Tracts, No. 11.

WILLIS, NATHANIEL PARKER

BEERS, HENRY AUGUSTIN. *Nathaniel Parker Willis.* Boston: Houghton Mifflin Co., 1913, 353–356.

GERSTENBERGER, DONNA, and GEORGE HENDRICK. *The American Novel, 1789–1959: A Checklist of Twentieth Century Criticism.* Denver: Alan Swallow, 1961, 262.

HALLINE, ALLAN GATES. *American Plays.* New York: American Book Co., 1935, 755–756.

LEARY, LEWIS. *Articles on American Literature, 1900–1950.* Durham: Duke Univ. Press, 1954, 322.

SPILLER, ROBERT ERNEST, et al. *Literary History of the United States,* 2 Vols. New York: Macmillan, 1962, 777–779.

TAFT, KENDALL B., ed. *Minor Knickerbockers: Representative Selections,* with introduction, bibliography and notes. New York: American Book Co., 1947, cxlv-cxlvii.

TRENT, WILLIAM PETERFIELD, et al. *Cambridge History of American Literature,* 4 Vols. New York: G. P. Putnam's Sons, 1917–1921, I, 524.

WILLIS, SARAH PAYSON

LEARY, LEWIS. *Articles on American Literature, 1900–1950.* Durham: Duke Univ. Press, 1954, 322.

WILSON, ALEXANDER

LEARY, LEWIS. *Articles on American Literature, 1900–1950.* Durham: Duke Univ. Press, 1954, 322.

WILSON, AUGUSTA JANE EVANS

HUBBELL, JAY B. *The South in American Literature, 1607–1900.* Durham: Duke Univ. Press, 1954, 972.

LEARY, LEWIS. *Articles on American Literature, 1900–1950.* Durham: Duke Univ. Press, 1954, 322.

WILSON, ROBERT BURNS

TRENT, WILLIAM PETERFIELD, et al. *Cambridge History of American Literature,* 4 Vols. New York: G. P. Putnam's Sons, 1917–1921, II, 611.

WINTER, WILLIAM

LEARY, LEWIS. *Articles on American Literature, 1900–1950.* Durham: Duke Univ. Press, 1954, 324.

WINTHROP, THEODORE

COLBY, ELBRIDGE. "Bibliographical Notes on Theodore Winthrop." *BNYPL,* XXI (January 1917), 3–13.

LEARY, LEWIS. *Articles on American Literature, 1900–1950.* Durham: Duke Univ. Press, 1954, 324–325.

MARTIN, WILLIARD E., JR. "The Life and Works of Theodore Winthrop." Unpublished doctoral dissertation, Duke Univ., 1944.

WIRT, WILLIAM

HUBBELL, JAY B. *The South in American Literature, 1607–1900.* Durham: Duke Univ. Press, 1954, 972–974.

LEARY, LEWIS. *Articles on American Literature, 1900–1950.* Durham: Duke Univ. Press, 1954, 325.

PAINE, GREGORY LANSING, ed. *Southern Prose Writers: Representative Selections,* with introduction, bibliography and notes. New York: American Book Co., 1947, cxliv-cxlv.

WELLFORD, B. RANDOLPH. "Checklist of Editions of William

Wirt's *The Letters of the British Spy.*" *Bibliographical Society of the University of Virginia, Secretary's News Sheet,* No. 31 (October 1954), 10–16.

WISE, HENRY AUGUSTUS

TRENT, WILLIAM PETERFIELD, et al. *Cambridge History of American Literature,* 4 Vols. New York: G. P. Putnam's Sons, 1917–1921, II, 511.

WISE, JOHN SARGENT

DAVIS, CURTIS. "Wise Words from Virginia: The Published Writings of John S. Wise of the Eastern Shore and New York City." *PBSA,* LIV (4th Quart. 1960), 273–285.

WOLFF, ALBERT

LEARY, LEWIS. *Articles on American Literature, 1900–1950.* Durham: Duke Univ. Press, 1954, 327.

WOODWARD, HENRY W.

LEARY, LEWIS. *Articles on American Literature, 1900–1950.* Durham: Duke Univ. Press, 1954, 328.

WOODWORTH, SAMUEL

LEARY, LEWIS. *Articles on American Literature, 1900–1950.* Durham: Duke Univ. Press, 1954, 328.

TAFT, KENDALL B., ed. *Minor Knickerbockers: Representative Selections,* with introduction, bibliography and notes. New York: American Book Co., 1947, cxlvii-cxlviii.

TRENT, WILLIAM PETERFIELD, et al. *Cambridge History of American Literature,* 4 Vols. New York: G. P. Putnam's Sons, 1917–1921, I, 524–525, 546.

WOOLSON, CONSTANCE FENIMORE

BROOKS, VAN WYCK. *The Dream of Arcadia: American Writers and Artists in Italy, 1760–1915.* New York: Dutton, 1958, bibliographical footnotes.

GERSTENBERGER, DONNA, and GEORGE HENDRICK. *The American Novel, 1789–1959: A Checklist of Twentieth Century Criticism.* Denver: Alan Swallow, 1961, 268–269.

HUBBELL, JAY B. *The South in American Literature, 1607–1900.* Durham: Duke Univ. Press, 1954, 974.

KERN, JOHN DWIGHT. *Constance Fenimore Woolson: Literary Pioneer.* Philadelphia: Univ. of Pennsylvania Press, 1934, 180–194.

LEARY, LEWIS. *Articles on American Literature, 1900–1950.* Durham: Duke Univ. Press, 1954, 328.

TRENT, WILLIAM PETERFIELD, et al. *Cambridge History of American Literature,* 4 Vols. New York: G. P. Putnam's Sons, 1917-1921, II, 630–631.

WRIGHT, CHAUNCEY

LEARY, LEWIS. *Articles on American Literature, 1900–1950.* Durham: Duke Univ. Press, 1954, 328.

TRENT, WILLIAM PETERFIELD, et al. *Cambridge History of American Literature,* 4 Vols. New York: G. P. Putnam's Sons, 1917–1921, IV, 753–754.

WRIGHT, WILLIAM

LEARY, LEWIS. *Articles on American Literature, 1900–1950.* Durham: Duke Univ. Press, 1954, 329.

WYETH, JOHN ALLAN

LEARY, LEWIS. *Articles on American Literature, 1900–1950.* Durham: Duke Univ. Press, 1954, 329.

4. 20TH CENTURY

ADAMIC, LOUIS

LEARY, LEWIS. *Articles on American Literature, 1900–1950.* Durham: Duke Univ. Press, 1954, 3.

ADAMS, ANDY

LEARY, LEWIS. *Articles on American Literature, 1900–1950.* Durham: Duke Univ. Press, 1954, 3.

ADAMS, BROOKS

LEARY, LEWIS. *Articles on American Literature, 1900–1950.* Durham: Duke Univ. Press, 1954, 3.

ADAMS, FRANKLIN PIERCE

LEARY, LEWIS. *Articles on American Literature, 1900–1950.* Durham: Duke Univ. Press, 1954, 3.

ADAMS, JAMES TRUSLOW

McCRACKEN, MARY JANE. "Author Biography of James Truslow Adams." *BB,* XV (May–August 1934), 65–67.

ADAMS, LÉONIE FULLER

LEARY, LEWIS. *Articles on American Literature, 1900–1950.* Durham: Duke Univ. Press, 1954, 7.

LIBRARY OF CONGRESS, GENERAL REFERENCE AND BIBLIOGRAPHY DIVISION. *Sixty American Poets, 1896–1944,* selected, with a preface and critical notes by Allen Tate and a preliminary checklist by Francis Cheney. Washington, 1945, 1.

Revised edition: 1954, 1.

ADE, GEORGE

BLANCK, JACOB, ed. *Merle Johnson's American First Editions,* 4th edition, revised and enlarged. Waltham, Massachusetts: Mark Press, 1965, 6–8.

LEARY, LEWIS. *Articles on American Literature, 1900–1950.* Durham: Duke Univ. Press, 1954, 7.

RUSSO, DOROTHY RITTER. *A Bibliography of George Ade.* Indianapolis: Indiana Historical Society, 1947, 329 pp.

SPILLER, ROBERT ERNEST, et al. *Literary History of the United States,* 2 Vols. New York: Macmillan, 1962, 380. Supplement, 74.

AGEE, JAMES

GERSTENBERGER, DONNA, and GEORGE HENDRICK. *The American Novel, 1789–1959: A Checklist of Twentieth Century Criticism.* Denver: Alan Swallow, 1961, 8.

LIBRARY OF CONGRESS, GENERAL REFERENCE AND BIBLIOGRAPHY DIVISION. *Sixty American Poets, 1896–1944,* selected, with a preface and critical notes by Allen Tate and a preliminary checklist by Francis Cheney. Washington, 1945, 2.

Revised edition: 1954, 1.

AIKEN, CONRAD (POTTER)

BLANCK, JACOB, ed. *Merle Johnson's American First Editions,* 4th edition, revised and enlarged. Waltham, Massachusetts: Mark Press, 1965, 9–11.

GERSTENBERGER, DONNA, and GEORGE HENDRICK. *The American Novel, 1789–1959: A Checklist of Twentieth Century Criticism.* Denver: Alan Swallow, 1961, 8.

LEARY, LEWIS. *Articles on American Literature, 1900–1950.* Durham: Duke Univ. Press, 1954, 7–8.

LIBRARY OF CONGRESS, GENERAL REFERENCE AND BIBLIOGRAPHY DIVISION. *Sixty American Poets, 1896–1944,* selected, with a preface and critical notes by Allen Tate and a preliminary checklist by Francis Cheney. Washington, 1945, 3–6.

Revised edition: 1954, 2–5.

MILLETT, FRED BENJAMIN. *Contemporary American Authors: A Critical Survey and 219 Bio-bibliographies.* New York: Harcourt, Brace and World, 1940, 213–216.

SPILLER, ROBERT ERNEST, et al. *Literary History of the United States,* 2 Vols. New York: Macmillan, 1962, 380–381. Supplement, 74–75.

STALLMAN, ROBERT WOOSTER. "Annotated Checklist on Conrad Aiken: A Critical Study." *Wake,* XI (1952), 114–121.

WOODRESS, JAMES, et al. *American Literary Scholarship: An Annual.* Durham: Duke Univ. Press, (1964), 190–191; (1965), 217–219; (1966), 201–203.

ALBEE, EDWARD

WOODRESS, JAMES, et al. *American Literary Scholarship: An Annual.* Durham: Duke Univ. Press, (1965), 244–246; (1966), 228–230.

ALDRICH, BESS STREETER

GERSTENBERGER, DONNA, and GEORGE HENDRICK. *The American Novel, 1789–1959: A Checklist of Twentieth Century Criticism.* Denver: Alan Swallow, 1961, 9.

ALGREN, NELSON

GERSTENBERGER, DONNA, and GEORGE HENDRICK. *The American Novel, 1789–1959: A Checklist of Twentieth Century Criticism.* Denver: Alan Swallow, 1961, 10.

ALLEN, FREDERICK LEWIS

LIBRARY OF CONGRESS, MANUSCRIPT DIVISION. *Frederick Lewis Allen: A Register of His Papers in the Library of Congress.* Washington, 1958, 7 leaves.

ALLEN, HENRY TUREMAN

LIBRARY OF CONGRESS, MANUSCRIPT DIVISION. *Henry T. Allen: A Register of His Papers in the Library of Congress.* Washington, 1958, 10 leaves.

ALLEN, HERVEY

BLANCK, JACOB, ed. *Merle Johnson's American First Editions,* 4th edition, revised and enlarged. Waltham, Massachusetts: Mark Press, 1965, 20–22.

COHEN, LOUIS HENRY, comp. "American First Editions: Hervey Allen, 1889–   ." *PW,* CXXIV (Sept. 16, 1933), 914–915.

GARLOCH, LORENA A. "The Hervey Allen Collection." *Pennsylvania Library Association Bulletin,* XIII (Winter 1958), 1–3.

——————. "The Hervey Allen Collection, University of Pittsburgh Library." *Pitt,* LXI (Autumn 1957), 53.

GERSTENBERGER, DONNA, and GEORGE HENDRICK. *The American Novel, 1789–1959: A Checklist of Twentieth Century Criticism.* Denver: Alan Swallow, 1961, 10.

LEARY, LEWIS. *Articles on American Literature, 1900–1950.* Durham: Duke Univ. Press, 1954, 10.

STARRETT, AGNUS L. "A Biography in Search of an Author." *Pitt,* LVIII (Autumn 1956), 19–26.

ANDERSON, MAXWELL

GILBERT, VEDDER M. "The Career of Maxwell Anderson: A Check List of Books and Articles." *MD,* II (February 1960), 386–394.

LEARY, LEWIS. *Articles on American Literature, 1900–1950.* Durham: Duke Univ. Press, 1954, 11.

MILLETT, FRED BENJAMIN. *Contemporary American Authors: A Critical Survey and 219 Bio-bibliographies.* New York: Harcourt, Brace and World, 1940, 219–221.

MOSES, MONTROSE JONAS. *Dramas of Modernism and Their Forerunners.* Boston: Little, Brown and Co., 1931, 703–733.

Also: 1941, 898–935.

SPILLER, ROBERT ERNEST, et al. *Literary History of the United States,* 2 Vols. New York: Macmillan, 1962, 386–388. Supplement, 76.

ANDERSON, SHERWOOD

ANDERSON, DAVID. *Sherwood Anderson: An Introduction and Interpretation.* New York, 1967, 174–177.

Part of the *American Authors and Critics Series,* begun in 1961, and purchased by Holt, Rinehart and Winston from Barnes and Noble. The nine original and three new volumes were issued under the Holt imprint in January 1967.

ASSELINEAU, ROGER. "Sélection bibliographique des études consacrées à Sherwood Anderson." *Revue des Lettres Modernes,* X (No. 4, 1963), 137–157.

BLANCK, JACOB, ed. *Merle Johnson's American First Editions,* 4th edition, revised and enlarged. Waltham, Massachusetts: Mark Press, 1965, 25–27.

GERSTENBERGER, DONNA, and GEORGE HENDRICK. *The American Novel, 1789–1959: A Checklist of Twentieth Century Criticism.* Denver: Alan Swallow, 1961, 11–15.

GOZZI, R. D. "A Bibliography of Sherwood Anderson's Contributions to Periodicals." *NLB,* II (December 1948), 71–82.

LEARY, LEWIS. *Articles on American Literature, 1900–1950.* Durham: Duke Univ. Press, 1954, 11–13.

MILLETT, FRED BENJAMIN. *Contemporary American Authors: A Critical Survey and 219 Bio-bibliographies.* New York: Harcourt, Brace and World, 1940, 221–225.

NEWBERRY LIBRARY. "The Anderson Papers." *NLB,* 2nd Series, II (December 1948), 64–70.

PHILLIPS, WILLIAM L. "The First Printing of Sherwood Anderson's *Winesburg, Ohio.*" *SB,* IV (1951–1952), 211–213.

SHEEHY, EUGENE PAUL, and KENNETH A. LOHF, comps. *Sherwood Anderson: A Bibliography.* Los Gatos, California: Talisman Press, 1960, 125 pp.

SPILLER, ROBERT ERNEST, et al. *Literary History of the United States,* 2 Vols. New York: Macmillan, 1962, 388–389. Supplement, 77–78.

TANSELLE, G. THOMAS. "Additional Reviews of Sherwood Anderson's Work." *PBSA,* LVI (3rd Quart. 1962), 358–365).

Supplements Eugene Paul Sheehy and Kenneth A. Lohf's *Sherwood Anderson: A Bibliography,* 1960.

TAYLOR, WALTER FULLER. *A History of American Letters,* with bibliographies by Harry Hartwick. Boston: American Book Co., 1936, 576–577.

Subsequent editions entitled: *The Story of American Letters.*

WHITE, RAY LEWIS, ed. *Return to Winesburg: Selections from Four Years of Writing for a Country Newspaper.* Chapel Hill: Univ. of North Carolina Press, 1967, 217–223.

WOODRESS, JAMES, et al. *American Literary Scholarship: An Annual.* Durham: Duke Univ. Press, (1965), 174–176; (1966), 158–161.

ANGELL, JOSEPH K.

RIDER, SIDNEY SMITH. *Bibliographical Memoirs of Three Rhode Island Authors: Joseph K. Angell, Frances H. (Whipple) McDougall, Catharine R. Williams.* Providence: S.S. Rider, 1880, 92 pp.

Rhode Island Historical Tracts,
No. 11.

ASCH, SHOLEM

LEARY, LEWIS. *Articles on American Literature, 1900–1950.* Durham: Duke Univ. Press, 1954, 13.

SPILLER, ROBERT ERNEST, et al. *Literary History of the United States.* 2 Vols. New York: Macmillan, 1962, 389–390. Supplement, 78.

YALE UNIVERSITY, LIBRARY, ASCH-RABINOWITZ COLLECTION. *Catalogue of Hebrew and Yiddish Manuscripts and Books from the Library of Sholem Asch, Presented to Yale University by Louis M. Rabinowitz,* compiled by Leon Nemoy, with an introductory essay by Sholem Asch. New Haven: Yale Univ. Press, 1945, 69 pp.

ATHERTON, GERTRUDE

BLANCK, JACOB, ed. *Merle Johnson's American First Editions,* 4th edition, revised and enlarged. Waltham, Massachusetts: Mark Press, 1965, 28–30.

GERSTENBERGER, DONNA, and GEORGE HENDRICK. *The American Novel, 1789–1959: A Checklist of Twentieth Century Criticism.* Denver: Alan Swallow, 1961, 15.

LEARY, LEWIS. *Articles on American Literature, 1900–1950.* Durham: Duke Univ. Press, 1954, 13–14.

ATKINSON, BROOKS

LEARY, LEWIS. *Articles on American Literature, 1900–1950,* Durham: Duke Univ. Press, 1954, 14.

AUDEN, W.H.

BLOOMFIELD, BARRY CAMBRAY.

W. H. Auden, A Bibliography: The Early Years through 1955, with a foreword by W. H. Auden. Charlottesville: published for the Bibliographical Society of the Univ. of Virginia by the Univ. of Virginia Press, 1964, 174 pp.

LEARY, LEWIS. *Articles on American Literature, 1900–1950.* Durham: Duke Univ. Press, 1954, 14.

AUSTIN, MARY

BLANCK, JACOB, ed. *Merle Johnson's American First Editions,* 4th edition, revised and enlarged. Waltham, Massachusetts: Mark Press, 1965, 35–36.

GERSTENBERGER, DONNA, and GEORGE HENDRICK. *The American Novel, 1789–1959: A Checklist of Twentieth Century Criticism.* Denver: Alan Swallow, 1961, 15–16.

LEARY, LEWIS. *Articles on American Literature, 1900–1950.* Durham: Duke Univ. Press, 1954, 15.

BABBITT, IRVING

LEARY, LEWIS. *Articles on American Literature, 1900–1950.* Durham: Duke Univ. Press, 1954, 15–16.

MANCHESTER, FREDERICK ALEXANDER, et al. *Spanish Character.* Boston: Houghton Mifflin Co., 1940, 249–259.

MILLETT, FRED BENJAMIN. *Contemporary American Authors: A Critical Survey and 219 Bio-bibliographies.* New York: Harcourt, Brace and World, 1940, 231–234.

SPILLER, ROBERT ERNEST, et al. *Literary History of the United States,* 2 Vols. New York: Macmillan, 1962, 392–393. Supplement, 79.

TAYLOR, WALTER FULLER. *A History of American Letters,* with bibliographies by Harry Hartwick. Boston: American Book Co., 1936, 595–596.

Subsequent editions entitled: *The Story of American Letters.*

BACHELLER, IRVING

BLANCK, JACOB, ed. *Merle Johnson's American First Editions,* 4th edition, revised and enlarged. Waltham, Massachusetts: Mark Press, 1965, 37–38.

HANNA, A. J. "A Bibliography of the Writings of Irving Bacheller." *Rollins College Bulletin,* XXV (September 1939), 15–45.

LEARY, LEWIS. *Articles on American Literature, 1900–1950.* Durham: Duke Univ. Press, 1954, 16.

WATKINS, EDNA W. "The Irving Bacheller Collection." *NYHSQ,* XXVI (July 1942), 64.

BAKER, GEORGE PIERCE

KINNE, WISNER PAYNE. *George Pierce Baker and the American Theatre.* Cambridge: Harvard Unvi. Press, 1954, 295–332.

BAKER, HOWARD

LIBRARY OF CONGRESS, GENERAL REFERENCE AND BIBLIOGRAPHY DIVISION. *Sixty American Poets, 1896–1944,* selected, with a preface and critical notes by Allen Tate and a preliminary checklist by Francis Cheney. Washington, 1945, 10.

Revised edtion: 1954, 7.

BAKER, RAY STANNARD

LEARY, LEWIS. *Articles on Ameri-can Literature, 1900–1950.* Durham: Duke Univ. Press, 1954, 16.

BALDWIN, JAMES

HARPER, HOWARD M., JR. *Desperate Faith: A Study of Bellow, Salinger, Mailer, Baldwin, and Updike.* Chapel Hill: Univ. of North Carolina Press, 1967, bibliographical footnotes.

WOODRESS, JAMES, et al. *American Literary Scholarship: An Annual.* Durham: Duke Univ. Press, (1963), 150–152; (1964), 159–150; (1965), 186–187; (1966), 171–172.

BARING, MAURICE

CHAUNDY, LESLIE. *A Bibliography of the First Editions of the Works of Maurice Baring,* with poems by Marice Baring and an introductory note on Baring by Desmond McCarthy. London: Dulau, 1925, 48 pp.

BARNEY, DANFORD

BANGS, FRANCIS H. "Danford Barney: Poet." *YULG,* XXVII (April 1953), 131–150.

BARRY, PHILIP

LEARY, LEWIS. *Articles on American Literature, 1900–1950.* Durham: Duke Univ. Press, 1954, 18.

MILLETT, FRED BENJAMIN. *Contemporary American Authors: A Critical Survey and 219 Bio-bibliographies.* New York: Harcourt, Brace and World, 1940, 235–236.

SPILLER, ROBERT ERNEST, et al. *Literary History of the United States,* 2 Vols. New York: Macmillan, 1962, 398. Supplement, 80.

WOODRESS, JAMES, et al. *American Literary Scholarship: An Annual.*

Durham: Duke Univ. Press, (1965), 235–236.

BARTH, JOHN

BRYER, JACKSON R. "Two Bibliographies." *Critique,* VI (Autumn 1963), 86–94.

BURNS, MILDRED BLAIR. "Books by John Barth." *HC,* III (December 1966), 7.

WOODRESS, JAMES, et al. *American Literary Scholarship: An Annual.* Durham: Duke Univ. Press, (1963), 155–156; (1966), 172–173.

BASSO, HAMILTON

GERSTENBERGER, DONNA, and GEORGE HENDRICK. *The American Novel, 1789–1959: A Checklist of Twentieth Century Criticism.* Denver: Alan Swallow, 1961, 16.

BATES, ERNEST SUTHERLAND

LEARY, LEWIS. *Articles on American Literature, 1900–1950.* Durham: Duke Univ. Press, 1954, 18.

BATES, KATHARINE LEE

LEARY, LEWIS. *Articles on American Literature, 1900–1950.* Durham: Duke Univ. Press, 1954, 18.

BEACH, REX

LEARY, LEWIS. *Articles on American Literature, 1900–1950.* Durham: Duke Univ. Press, 1954, 18.

BEAGLE, PETER S.

COSTIGAN, CHRISTINE R. "Books by Peter S. Beagle." *HC,* V (April 1968), 7.

BEEBE, WILLIAM

BLANCK, JACOB, ed. *Merle Johnson's American First Editions,* 4th edition, revised and enlarged. Waltham, Massachusetts: Mark Press, 1965, 43–44.

LEARY, LEWIS. *Articles on American Literature, 1900–1950.* Durham: Duke Univ. Press, 1954, 19.

BEER, THOMAS

GERSTENBERGER, DONNA, and GEORGE HENDRICK. *The American Novel, 1789–1959: A Checklist of Twentieth Century Criticism.* Denver: Alan Swallow, 1961, 16.

LEARY, LEWIS. *Articles on American Literature, 1900–1950.* Durham: Duke Univ. Press, 1954, 19.

BEHRMAN, SAMUEL NATHANIEL

LEARY, LEWIS. *Articles on American Literature, 1900–1950.* Durham: Duke Univ. Press, 1954, 19.

MILLETT, FRED BENJAMIN. *Contemporary American Authors: A Critical Survey and 219 Bio-bibliographies.* New York: Harcourt, Brace and World, 1940, 244–245.

SPILLER, ROBERT ERNEST, et al. *Literary History of the United States,* 2 Vols. New York: Macmillan, 1962, 401. Supplement 81.

BELASCO, DAVID

LEARY, LEWIS. *Articles on American Literature, 1900–1950.* Durham: Duke Univ. Press, 1954, 19.

BELLOW, SAUL

GERSTENBERGER, DONNA, and GEORGE HENDRICK. *The American Novel, 1789–1959: A Checklist*

of Twentieth Century Criticism.
Denver: Alan Swallow, 1961, 17–18.

HARPER, HOWARD M., JR.
Desperate Faith: A Study of Bellow,
Salinger, Mailer, Baldwin, and Updike.
Chapel Hill: Univ. of North Carolina
Press, 1967, bibliographical footnotes.

MALIN, IRVING, ed. Saul Bellow and
the Critics. New York: New York Univ.
Press, 1967, bibliographical footnotes.

SCHNEIDER, HAROLD W. "Two
Bibliographies: Saul Bellow, William
Styron." Critique, III (Summer
1960), 71–86.

WOODRESS, JAMES, et al. American Literary Scholarship: An Annual.
Durham: Duke Univ. Press, (1963),
156–157; (1964), 160–162; (1965),
187–189; (1966), 173–174.

BENCHLEY, ROBERT

LEARY, LEWIS. Articles on American Literature, 1900–1950. Durham:
Duke Univ. Press, 1954, 20.

BENÉT, STEPHEN VINCENT

BENÉT, WILLIAM ROSE, and JOHN
FARRAR. Stephen Vincent Benét.
New York: The Saturday Review of
Literature and Farrar and Rinehart,
Inc., 1943, 37–39.

BLANCK, JACOB, ed. Merle Johnson's American First Editions, 4th
edition, revised and enlarged.
Waltham, Massachusetts: Mark Press,
1965, 46–49.

LEARY, LEWIS. Articles on American Literature, 1900–1950. Durham:
Duke Univ. Press, 1954, 20.

LEWIS, MARY D. "S. V. Benét: His
Major Work, His Preparation for It,
and a Bibliography of His Writings."
Unpublished doctoral dissertation,
Univ. of Illinois, 1953.

LIBRARY OF CONGRESS,
GENERAL REFERENCE AND
BIBLIOGRAPHY DIVISION. Sixty
American Poets, 1896–1944,
selected, with a preface and critical
notes by Allen Tate and a preliminary
checklist by Francis Cheney. Washington, 1945, 11–16.

Revised edition: 1954, 7–13.

MADDOCKS, GLADYS LOUISE.
"Stephen Vincent Benet: A Bibliography." BB, XX (September–December 1951), 142–146; (January–April
1952), 158–160.

MILLETT, FRED BENJAMIN. Contemporary American Authors: A
Critical Survey and 219 Bio-bibliographies. New York: Harcourt, Brace
and World, 1940, 246–249.

SPILLER, ROBERT ERNEST, et al.
Literary History of the United States,
2 Vols. New York: Macmillan, 1962,
403–404. Supplement, 82.

BENÉT, WILLIAM ROSE

BLANCK, JACOB, ed. Merle Johnson's American First Editions, 4th
edition, revised and enlarged.
Waltham, Massachusetts: Mark Press,
1965, 50–52.

LEARY, LEWIS. Articles on American Literature, 1900–1950. Durham:
Duke Univ. Press, 1954, 21.

BENSON, STELLA

LEARY, LEWIS. Articles on American Literature, 1900–1950. Durham:
Duke Univ. Press, 1954, 21.

BERGE, WENDELL

LIBRARY OF CONGRESS, MANU-
SCRIPT DIVISION. Wendell Berge:
A Register of His Papers in the

Library of Congress. Washington, 1958, 12 pp.

BERRYMAN, JOHN

LEARY, LEWIS. *Articles on American Literature, 1900–1950.* Durham: Duke Univ. Press, 1954, 21.

BINYON, LAURENCE

LEARY, LEWIS. *Articles on American Literature, 1900–1950.* Durham: Duke Univ. Press, 1954, 22.

BISHOP, JOHN PEALE

LEARY, LEWIS. *Articles on American Literature, 1900–1950.* Durham: Duke Univ. Press, 1954, 22.

LIBRARY OF CONGRESS, GENERAL REFERENCE AND BIBLIOGRAPHY DIVISION. *Sixty American Poets, 1896–1944,* selected, with a preface and critical notes by Allen Tate and a preliminary checklist by Francis Cheney. Washington, 1945, 17–18.

Revised edition: 1954, 13–14.

MILLETT, FRED BENJAMIN. *Contemporary American Authors: A Critical Survey and 219 Bio-bibliographies.* New York: Harcourt, Brace and World, 1940, 252–253.

PATRICK, J.M., and ROBERT WOOSTER STALLMAN. "John Peale Bishop: A Checklist." *PULC,* VII (February 1946), 62–79.

WOODRESS, JAMES, et al. *American Literary Scholarship: An Annual.* Durham: Duke Univ. Press, (1964), 192–194; (1966), 203–204.

BLACKMUR, RICHARD PALMER

BAKER, CARLOS. "R. P. Blackmur:

A Checklist." *PULC,* III (April 1942), 99–106.

LEARY, LEWIS. *Articles on American Literature, 1900–1950.* Durham: Duke Univ. Press, 1954, 22–23.

LIBRARY OF CONGRESS, GENERAL REFERENCE AND BIBLIOGRAPHY DIVISION. *Sixty American Poets, 1896–1944,* selected, with a preface and critical notes by Allen Tate and a preliminary checklist by Francis Cheney. Washington, 1945, 19–20.

Revised edition: 1954, 15–16.

BLAND, H. M.

LEARY, LEWIS. *Articles on American Literature, 1900–1950.* Durham: Duke Univ. Press, 1954, 23.

BODENHEIM, MAXWELL.

LEARY, LEWIS. *Articles on American Literature, 1900–1950.* Durham: Duke Univ. Press, 1954, 23.

BOGAN, LOUISE

LEARY, LEWIS. *Articles on American Literature, 1900–1950.* Durham: Duke Univ. Press, 1954, 23.

LIBRARY OF CONGRESS, GENERAL REFERENCE AND BIBLIOGRAPHY DIVISION. *Sixty American Poets, 1896–1944,* selected, with a preface and critical notes by Allen Tate and a preliminary checklist by Francis Cheney. Washington, 1945, 21.

Revised edition: 1954, 16.

BONNER, AMY

BAUER, ROBERT VAN AKIN, ed. *Amy Bonner, Poet and Friend of*

Poets: A Selection from the Amy Bonner Collection at the Pattee Library. University Park: Pennsylvania State Univ. Library, 1958, 96 pp.

BOURJAILY, VANCE

GERSTENBERGER, DONNA, and GEORGE HENDRICK. *The American Novel, 1789–1959: A Checklist of Twentieth Century Criticism.* Denver: Alan Swallow, 1961, 19.

BOURNE, RANDOLPH

FILLER, LOUIS. *Randolph Bourne.* Washington: American Council on Public Affairs, 1945, 152–155.

LEARY, LEWIS. *Articles on American Literature, 1900–1950.* Durham: Duke Univ. Press, 1954, 24.

SPILLER, ROBERT ERNEST, et al. *Literary History of the United States,* 2 Vols. New York: Macmillan, 1962, 409–410. Supplement, 83.

BOWLES, PAUL

GERSTENBERGER, DONNA, and GEORGE HENDRICK. *The American Novel, 1789–1959: A Checklist of Twentieth Century Criticism.* Denver: Alan Swallow, 1961, 19.

BOYD, JAMES

BLANCK, JACOB, ed. *Merle Johnson's American First Editions,* 4th edition, revised and enlarged. Waltham, Massachusetts: Mark Press, 1965, 57.

GERSTENBERGER, DONNA, and GEORGE HENDRICK. *The American Novel, 1789–1959: A Checklist of Twentieth Century Criticism.* Denver: Alan Swallow, 1961, 19.

LEARY, LEWIS. *Articles on American Literature, 1900–1950.* Durham: Duke Univ. Press, 1954, 24.

McLAURY, HELEN, and MALCOLM YOUNG. "James Boyd: A Checklist," *PULC,* VI (February 1945), 77–81.

BOYLE, KAY

GERSTENBERGER, DONNA, and GEORGE HENDRICK. *The American Novel, 1789–1950: A Checklist of Twentieth Century Criticism.* Denver: Alan Swallow, 1961, 20.

LEARY, LEWIS. *Articles on American Literature, 1900–1950.* Durham: Duke Univ. Press, 1954, 24.

BRACE, GERALD WARNER

GERSTENBERGER, DONNA, and GEORGE HENDRICK. *The American Novel, 1789–1959: A Checklist of Twentieth Century Criticism.* Denver: Alan Swallow, 1961, 20.

BRADFORD, GAMALIEL

BLANCK, JACOB, ed. *Merle Johnson's American First Editions,* 4th edition, revised and enlarged. Waltham, Massachusetts. Mark Press, 1965, 60–62.

LEARY, LEWIS. *Articles on American Literature, 1900–1950.* Durham: Duke Univ. Press, 1954, 25.

BRADFORD, ROARK

BLANCK, JACOB, ed. *Merle Johnson's American First Editions,* 4th edition, revised and enlarged. Waltham, Massachusetts: Mark Press, 1965, 63.

BRAITHWAITE, WILLIAM STANLEY

LEARY, LEWIS. *Articles on Ameri-*

can Literature, 1900–1950. Durham: Duke Univ. Press, 1954, 26.

BRENT, CHARLES HENRY

LIBRARY OF CONGRESS, MANU-SCRIPT DIVISION. *Bishop Charles Henry Brent: A Register of His Papers in the Library of Congress.* Washington, 1959, 10 leaves.

BRIDGES, ROBERT

SMITH, NOWELL SIMON. "Check List of the Works of Robert Bridges." *Book-Collector's Quarterly,* XVI (October 1934), 30–40.

BRINNIN, JOHN MALCOLM

LEARY, LEWIS. *Articles on American Literature, 1900–1950.* Durham: Duke Univ. Press, 1954, 26.

BRISBANE, ARTHUR

LEARY, LEWIS. *Articles on American Literature, 1900–1950.* Durham: Duke Univ. Press, 1954, 26.

BROMFIELD, LOUIS

BLANCK, JACOB, ed. *Merle Johnson's American First Editions,* 4th edition, revised and enlarged. Waltham, Massachusetts: Mark Press, 1965, 64–65.

DERRENBACHER, MERLE, comp. "Louis Bromfield: A Bibliography." *BB,* XVII (September–December 1941), 112; (January–April 1942), 141–145.

GERSTENBERGER, DONNA, and GEORGE HENDRICK. *The American Novel, 1789–1959: A Checklist of Twentieth Century Criticism.* Denver: Alan Swallow, 1961, 21.

LEARY, LEWIS. *Articles on American Literature, 1900–1950.* Durham: Duke Univ. Press, 1954, 26.

BROOKHOUSER, FRANK

LEARY, LEWIS. *Articles on American Literature, 1900–1950.* Durham: Duke Univ. Press, 1954, 26.

BROOKS, CLEANTH

BRADBURY, JOHN M. *The Fugitives: A Critical Account.* Chapel Hill: Univ. of North Carolina Press, 1958, 287–290.

LEARY, LEWIS. *Articles on American Literature, 1900–1950.* Durham: Duke Univ. Press, 1954, 27.

STALLMAN, ROBERT WOOSTER. "Cleanth Brooks: A Checklist of His Critical Writings." *UKCR,* XIV (Summer 1948), 317–324.

BROOKS, VAN WYCK

LEARY, LEWIS. *Articles on American Literature, 1900–1950.* Durham: Duke Univ. Press, 1954, 27.

MILLETT, FRED BENJAMIN. *Contemporary American Authors: A Critical Survey and 219 Bio-bibliographies.* New York: Harcourt, Brace and World, 1940, 262–264.

SPILLER, ROBERT ERNEST, et al. *Literary History of the United States,* 2 Vols. New York: Macmillan, 1962, 415–417. Supplement, 84–85.

BROTHER ANTONINUS

KHERDIAN, DAVID. *Six Poets of the San Francisco Renaissance.* Fresno, California: The Giligia Press, 1965, 115–129.

BROUN, HEYWOOD

LEARY, LEWIS. *Articles on American Literature, 1900–1950.* Durham: Duke Univ. Press, 1954, 28.

BROWN, HARRIET CONNOR

LEARY, LEWIS. *Articles on American Literature, 1900–1950.* Durham: Duke Univ. Press, 1954, 29.

BROWN, MARGARET WISE

LEARY, LEWIS. *Articles on American Literature, 1900–1950.* Durham: Duke Univ. Press, 1954, 29.

BROWN, WILLIAM GARROTT

LEARY, LEWIS. *Articles on American Literature, 1900–1950.* Durham: Duke Univ. Press, 1954, 29.

BUCK, PEARL

BLANCK, JACOB, ed. *Merle Johnson's American First Editions,* 4th edition, revised and enlarged. Waltham, Massachusetts: Mark Press, 1965, 71–72.

BRENNI, VITO J. "Pearl Buck: A Selected Bibliography." *BB,* XXII (May–August 1957), 65–69; (September–December 1957), 94–96.

GERSTENBERGER, DONNA, and GEORGE HENDRICK. *The American Novel, 1789–1959: A Checklist of Twentieth Century Criticism.* Denver: Alan Swallow, 1961, 24–25.

LEARY, LEWIS. *Articles on American Literature, 1900–1950.* Durham: Duke Univ. Press, 1954, 32.

BUECHNER, FREDERICK

GERSTENBERGER, DONNA, and GEORGE HENDRICK. *The American Novel, 1789–1959: A Checklist of Twentieth Century Criticism.* Denver: Alan Swallow, 1961, 25.

BURGESS, GELETT

BLANCK, JACOB, ed. *Merle Johnson's American First Editions,* 4th edition, revised and enlarged. Waltham, Massachusetts: Mark Press, 1965, 76–78.

LEARY, LEWIS. *Articles on American Literature, 1900–1950.* Durham: Duke Univ. Press, 1954, 32.

BURKE, KENNETH

LEARY, LEWIS. *Articles on American Literature, 1900–1950.* Durham: Duke Univ. Press, 1954, 33.

MILLETT, FRED BENJAMIN. *Contemporary American Authors: A Critical Survey and 219 Bio-bibliographies.* New York: Harcourt, Brace and World, 1940, 268–269.

BURNETT, FRANCIS ELIZA HODGSON TOWNESEND)

BLANCK, JACOB. *Bibliography of American Literature,* 5 Vols. New Haven: Yale Univ. Press, 1955–1969, I, 413–432.

LEARY, LEWIS. *Articles on American Literature, 1900–1950.* Durham: Duke Univ. Press, 1954, 33.

BURROUGHS, EDGAR RICE

DAY, BRADFORD M. *Edgar Rice Burroughs: A Bibliography.* Woodhaven, New York: Science-Fiction and Fantasy Publications, 1962, 7–45.

BURT, MAXWELL STRUTHERS

LEARY, LEWIS. *Articles on American Literature, 1900–1950.* Durham: Duke Univ. Press, 1954, 34.

BYNNER, EDWIN LASSETTER

BLANCK, JACOB. *Bibliography of American Literature.* 5 Vols. New Haven: Yale Univ. Press, 1955–1969, I, 460–462.

BYNNER, HAROLD WITTER

BLANCK, JACOB, ed. *Merle Johnson's American First Editions,* 4th edition, revised and enlarged. Waltham, Massachusetts: Mark Press, 1965, 82–83.

LEARY, LEWIS. *Articles on American Literature, 1900–1950.* Durham: Duke Univ. Press, 1954, 34.

LINDSAY, ROBERT O. *Witter Bynner: A Bibliography.* Albuquerque: Univ. of New Mexico Press, 1967, 120 pp.

Also: *Univ. of New Mexico Publications, Library Series,* No. 2.

MILLETT, FRED BENJAMIN. *Contemporary American Authors: A Critical Survey and 219 Bio-bibliographies.* New York: Harcourt, Brace and World, 1940, 274–276.

SPILLER, ROBERT ERNEST, et al. *Literary History of the United States,* 2 Vols. New York: Macmillan, 1962, 428–429. Supplement, 88.

BYRNE, DONN (BRIAN OSWALD)

BLANCK, JACOB. *Bibliography of American Literature,* 5 Vols. New Haven: Yale Univ. Press, 1955–1969, I, 463–470.

—————————, ed. *Merle Johnson's American First Editions,* 4th edition, revised and enlarged. Waltham Massachusetts: Mark Press, 1965, 84–86.

WETHERBEE, WINTHROP, JR. "(Brian Oswald) Donn Byrne: A Bibliography." *BB,* XVI (September–December 1937), 66–67; (January–April 1938), 96; (May–August 1938), 117–118; (January–April 1939), 160–161; (May–August 1939), 179–180.

Also: *Bulletin of Bibliography Pamphlets,* No. 34.

—————————. *Donn Byrne: A Bibliography.* New York: New York Public Library, 1949, 89 pp.

CABELL, JAMES BRANCH

BLANCK, JACOB, ed. *Merle Johnson's American First Editions,* 4th edition, revised and enlarged. Waltham, Massachusetts: Mark Press, 1965, 87–91.

BREWER, FRANCES JOAN. *James Branch Cabell: A Bibliography of His Writings, Biography and Criticism,* 2 Vols. Charlottesville: Univ. of Virginia Press, 1957.

BRUSSEL, ISIDORE ROSENBAUM. *A Bibliography of the Writings of James Branch Cabell: A Revised Bibliography.* Philadelphia: The Centaur Book Shop, 1932, 126 pp.

A revision of Guy Holt's *A Bibliography of the Writings of James Branch Cabell,* 1924.

GERSTENBERGER, DONNA, and GEORGE HENDRICK. *The American Novel, 1789–1959: A Checklist of Twentieth Century Criticism.* Denver: Alan Swallow, 1961, 25–28.

HOLT, GUY. *A Bibliography of the Writings of James Branch Cabell.* Philadelphia: The Centaur Book Shop, 1924, 81 pp.

JOHNSON, M. *A Bibliographic Check-List of the Works of James Branch Cabell, 1904–1921.* New York: Frank Shay, 1921, 27 pp.

200 copies printed.

LEARY, LEWIS. *Articles on American Literature, 1900–1950.* Durham; Duke Univ. Press, 1954, 35–36.

MILLETT, FRED BENJAMIN. *Contemporary American Authors: A Critical Survey and 219 Bio-bibliographies.* New York: Harcourt, Brace and World, 1940, 276–280.

SPILLER, ROBERT ERNEST, et al. *Literary History of the United States,* 2 Vols. New York: Macmillan, 1962, 431–433. Supplement, 88–89.

TAYLOR, WALTER FULLER. *A History of American Letters,* with bibliographies by Harry Hartwick. Boston: American Book Co., 1936, 589–591.

Subsequent editions entitled: *The Story of American Letters.*

CAHAN, ABRAHAM

LEARY, LEWIS. *Articles on American Literature, 1900–1950.* Durham: Duke Univ. Press, 1954, 37.

CAIN, JAMES M.

GERSTENBERGER, DONNA, and GEORGE HENDRICK. *The American Novel, 1789–1959: A Checklist of Twentieth Century Criticism.* Denver: Alan Swallow, 1961, 29–30.

HAGEMANN, E. R., and PHILIP C. DURHAM. "James M. Cain, 1922–1958: A Selected Checklist." *BB,* XXIII (September–December 1960), 57–60.

LEARY, LEWIS. *Articles on American Literature, 1900–1950.* Durham: Duke Univ. Press, 1954, 37.

CALDWELL, ERSKINE

BLANCK, JACOB, ed. *Merle John-son's American First Editions,* 4th edition, revised and enlarged. Waltham, Massachusetts: Mark Press, 1965, 94–95.

GERSTENBERGER, DONNA, and GEORGE HENDRICK. *The American Novel, 1789–1959: A Checklist of Twentieth Century Criticism.* Denver: Alan Swallow, 1961, 30.

LEARY, LEWIS. *Articles on American Literature, 1900–1950.* Durham: Duke Univ. Press, 1954, 37–38.

MILLETT, FRED BENJAMIN. *Contemporary American Authors: A Critical Survey and 219 Bio-bibliographies.* New York: Harcourt, Brace and World, 1940, 281–282.

SPILLER, ROBERT ERNEST, et al. *Literary History of the United States,* 2 Vols. New York: Macmillan, 1962, 434–435. Supplement, 90.

CALLAWAY, MORGAN

CALLAWAY, MRS. MORGAN, JR. "A Bibliography of the Writings of Morgan Callaway, Jr." *Univ. of Texas Studies in English,* XVI (July 1936), 8–16.

CALVERTON, VICTOR FRANCIS

LEARY, LEWIS. *Articles on American Literature, 1900–1950.* Durham: Duke Univ. Press, 1954, 38.

CAMPBELL, KILLIS

CAMPBELL, MARY, and HAWES CAMPBELL. "A Bibliography of the Writings of Killis Campbell, Found in *Killis Campbell, 1872–1937* by Robert A. Law." *Univ. of Texas Studies in English,* XVII (July 1937), 7–14.

LEARY, LEWIS. *Articles on American Literature, 1900–1950.* Durham: Duke Univ. Press, 1954, 38.

CANBY, HENRY SEIDEL

LEARY, LEWIS. *Articles on American Literature, 1900–1950.* Durham: Duke Univ. Press, 1954, 38.

CAPOTE, TRUMAN

THE EDITORS. "Books by Truman Capote." *HC,* III (February 1966), 6–7.

GERSTENBERGER, DONNA, and GEORGE HENDRICK. *The American Novel, 1789–1959: A Checklist of Twentieth Century Criticism.* Denver: Alan Swallow, 1961, 31.

CARMER, CARL

LEARY, LEWIS. *Articles on American Literature, 1900–1950.* Durham: Duke Univ. Press, 1954, 39.

CARVER, GEORGE WASHINGTON

GUZMAN, JESSIE PARKHURST. "George Washington Carver: A Classified Bibliography." *BB,* XXI (August 1953), 13–16; (December 1953), 34–38.

CATHER, WILLA

ADAMS, FREDERICK B., JR. "Willa Cather, Early Years: Trial and Error." *The Colophon,* ns IV (No. 1, 1939), 89–100.

——————. "Willa Cather, Middle Years: The Right Road Taken." *The Colophon,* ns IV (No. 1, 1939), 103–108.

BLANCK, JACOB, ed. *Merle Johnson's American First Editions,* 4th edition, revised and enlarged. Waltham, Massachusetts: Mark Press, 1965, 103–105.

BROWN, EDWARD KILLORAN. *Willa Cather: A Critical Biography,*

completed by Leon Edel. New York: A. A. Knopf, 1953, 346–351.

——————. "Willa Cather: The Benjamin D. Hitz Collection." *NLB,* V (December 1950), 158–160.

DU BOSE, LA ROCQUE. "American First Editions at the University of Texas: Willa Cather (1876–1947)." *LCUT,* V (Spring 1955), 44–47.

GERSTENBERGER, DONNA, and GEORGE HENDRICK. *The American Novel, 1789–1959: A Checklist of Twentieth Century Criticism.* Denver: Alan Swallow, 1961, 31–36.

HINTZ, J. P. "Willa Cather in Pittsburgh." *The New Colophon,* III (1950), 198–207.

Includes checklist of Cather's contributions to Pittsburgh periodicals and newspapers, 1896–1902.

HUTCHINSON, PHYLLIS MARTIN. "The Writings of Willa Cather: A List of Works by and about Her." *BNYPL,* LX (June 1956), 267–287; (July 1956), 338–356; (August 1956), 378–400.

JESSUP, JOSEPHINE LURIE. *The Faith of Our Feminists: A Study of the Novels of Edith Wharton, Ellen Glasgow, Willa Cather.* New York: R. R. Smith, 1950, 126–128.

JESSUP, MARY E. "A Bibliography of the Writings of Willa Cather." *AC,* VI (May–June 1928), 67.

KNOPF, ALFRED A., INC. *Willa Cather: A Biographical Sketch, an English Opinion, an American Opinion, Reviews and Articles, and an Abridged Bibliography.* New York: Alfred A. Knopf, Inc., 1927, 15–16.

LEARY, LEWIS. *Articles on American Literature, 1900–1950.* Durham: Duke Univ. Press, 1954, 39–40.

MILLETT, FRED BENJAMIN. *Contemporary American Authors: A Critical Survey and 219 Bio-bibliographies.* New York: Harcourt, Brace and World, 1940, 289–292.

SPILLER, ROBERT ERNEST, et al. *Literary History of the United States,* 2 Vols. New York: Macmillan, 1962, 436–438. Supplement, 91–92.

TAYLOR, WALTER FULLER. *A History of American Letters,* with bibliographies by Harry Hartwick. Boston: American Book Co., 1956, 573–574.

Subsequent editions entitled: *The Story of American Letters.*

WOODRESS, JAMES, et al. *American Literary Scholarship: An Annual.* Durham: Duke Univ. Press, (1965), 167–160; (1966), 151–155.

CATTELL, JAMES McKEEN

LIBRARY OF CONGRESS, MANUSCRIPT DIVISION. *James McKeen Cattell: A Register of His Papers in the Library of Congress.* Washington, 1962, 24 pp.

CHANDLER, RAYMOND

DURHAM, PHILIP. *Down These Mean Streets a Man Must Go: Raymond Chandler's Knight.* Chapel Hill: Univ. of North Carolina Press, 1963, 149–168.

GERSTENBERGER, DONNA, and GEORGE HENDRICK. *The American Novel, 1789–1959: A Checklist of Twentieth Century Criticism.* Denver: Alan Swallow, 1961, 37.

CHAPMAN, JOHN JAY

LEARY, LEWIS. *Articles on American Literature, 1900–1950.* Durham: Duke Univ. Press, 1954, 42.

STOCKING, D. M. "John Jay Chapman: A Checklist." *BB,* XX (September–December 1951), 6; (January–April 1952), 7.

CHASE, MARY ELLEN

CARY, RICHARD. "A Bibliography of the Published Writings of Mary Ellen Chase." *CLQ,* VI (March 1962), 34–45.

GERSTENBERGER, DONNA, and GEORGE HENDRICK. *The American Novel, 1789–1959: A Checklist of the Twentieth Century Criticism.* Denver: Alan Swallow, 1961, 37.

LEARY, LEWIS. *Articles on American Literature, 1900–1950.* Durham: Duke Univ. Press, 1954, 42.

CHEEVER, JOHN

WHITTET, CORNELIA MAGILL. "Books." *HC,* I (April 1964), 5.

CHESNUTT, CHARLES WADDELL

BLANCK, JACOB, ed. *Merle Johnson's American First Editions,* 4th edition, revised and enlarged. Waltham, Massachusetts: Mark Press, 1965, 106.

BONTEMPS, ARNA. "Chesnutt Papers Go to Fisk." *LJ,* LXXVII (August 1952), 1,288–1,289.

FISK UNIVERSITY, LIBRARY. *A List of Manuscripts, Published Works, and Related Items in the Charles Waddell Chesnutt Collection of the Erastus Milo Cravath Memorial Library,* prepared by Mildred Freeney

and Mary T. Henry. Nashville: Fisk
Univ. Library, 1954, 32 pp.

LEARY, LEWIS. *Articles on American Literature, 1900–1950.* Durham:
Duke Univ. Press, 1954, 42.

SPILLER, ROBERT ERNEST, et al.
Literary History of the United States,
2 Vols. New York: Macmillan, 1962,
440. Supplement, 93.

CHURCHILL, WINSTON

BLANCK, JACOB, ed. *Merle Johnson's American First Editions,* 4th
edition, revised and enlarged.
Waltham, Massachusetts: Mark Press,
1965, 108–109.

COOPER, FREDERIC TABER.
Some American Story Tellers, 2nd
edition. New York: H. Holt and
Co., 1912, 361–362.

GERSTENBERGER, DONNA, and
GEORGE HENDRICK. *The American Novel, 1789–1959: A Checklist
of Twentieth Century Criticism.*
Denver: Alan Swallow, 1961, 37–38.

LEARY, LEWIS. *Articles on American Literature, 1900–1950.* Durham:
Duke Univ. Press, 1954, 43.

CIARDI, JOHN

LEARY, LEWIS. *Articles on American Literature, 1900–1950.* Durham:
Duke Univ. Press, 1954, 43.

WHITE, WILLIAM. *John Ciardi: A
Bibliography,* with a note by John
Ciardi. Detroit: Wayne State Univ.
Press, 1959, 65 pp.

CLARK, WALTER VAN TILBURG

GERSTENBERGER, DONNA, and
GEORGE HENDRICK. *The American Novel, 1789–1959: A Checklist
of Twentieth Century Criticism.*
Denver: Alan Swallow, 1961, 38–39.

KUEHL, JOHN R. "Walter Van
Tilburg Clark: A Bibliography." *BB,*
XXII (September–December 1956),
18–20.

WILNER, HERBERT. "Walter Van
Tilburg Clark." *WR,* XX (Winter
1956), 103–122.

COBB, FRANK IRVING

LEARY, LEWIS. *Articles on American Literature, 1900–1950.* Durham:
Duke Univ. Press, 1954, 55.

COBB, IRVIN S.

BLANCK, JACOB, ed. *Merle Johnson's American First Editions,* 4th
edition, revised and enlarged.
Waltham, Massachusetts: Mark Press,
1965, 116–120.

LEARY, LEWIS. *Articles on American Literature, 1900–1950.* Durham:
Duke Univ. Press, 1954, 55.

COFFIN, ROBERT P. TRISTRAM

LEARY, LEWIS. *Articles on American Literature, 1900–1950.* Durham:
Duke Univ. Press, 1954, 55.

COLBY, FRANK MOORE

LEARY, LEWIS. *Articles on American Literature, 1900–1950.* Durham:
Duke Univ. Press, 1954, 55.

CONKLING, HILDA

LEARY, LEWIS. *Articles on American Literature, 1900–1950.* Durham:
Duke Univ. Press, 1954, 56.

CONNALLY, THOMAS TERRY

LIBRARY OF CONGRESS, MANU-
SCRIPT DIVISION. *Tom Connally:
A Register of His Papers in the
Library of Congress.* Washington,
1958, 31 pp.

CONNELLY, MARC

LEARY, LEWIS. *Articles on American Literature, 1900–1950.* Durham: Duke Univ. Press, 1954, 56.

COREY, HERBERT

LIBRARY OF CONGRESS, MANUSCRIPT DIVISION. *Herbert Corey: A Register of His Papers in the Library of Congress.* Washington, 1959, 7 leaves.

COSTAIN, THOMAS B.

GERSTENBERGER, DONNA, and GEORGE HENDRICK. *The American Novel, 1789–1959: A Checklist of Twentieth Century Criticism.* Denver: Alan Swallow, 1961, 47.

COWLEY, MALCOLM

LIBRARY OF CONGRESS, GENERAL REFERENCE AND BIBLIOGRAPHY DIVISION. *Sixty American Poets, 1896–1944,* selected, with a preface and critical notes by Allen Tate and a preliminary checklist by Francis Cheney. Washington, 1945, 22–23.

Revised edition: 1954, 16–18.

COZZENS, JAMES GOULD

GERSTENBERGER, DONNA, and GEORGE HENDRICK. *The American Novel, 1789–1959: A Checklist of Twentieth Century Criticism.* Denver: Alan Swallow, 1961, 47–49.

LEARY, LEWIS. *Articles on American Literature, 1900–1950.* Durham: Duke Univ. Press, 1954, 60.

LUDWIG, RICHARD M. "James Gould Cozzens: A Review of Research and Criticism." *TSLL,* I (Spring 1959), 123–136.

_____. "A Reading of the James Gould Cozzens Manuscripts." *PULC,* XIX (Autumn 1957), 1–14.

MERIWETHER, JAMES B. "The English Editions of James Gould Cozzens." *SB,* XV (1962), 207–217.

_____. "A James Gould Cozzens Check List." *Critique,* I (Winter 1958), 57–63.

CRAIG, EDWARD GORDON

FLETCHER, IFAN KYRLE. "Edward Gordon Craig: A Check List." *Theatre Arts Monthly,* XIX (April 1935), 293–304.

CRANE, HART

BIRSS, J. H. "American First Editions: Hart Crane (1899–1932)." *PW,* CXXV (June 16, 1934), 2,223.

BLOOMINGDALE, JUDITH. "Three Decades in Periodical Criticism of Hart Crane's 'The Bridge.'" *PBSA,* LVII (3rd Quart. 1963), 360–371.

LEARY, LEWIS. *Articles on American Literature, 1900–1950.* Durham: Duke Univ. Press, 1954, 60–61.

LEWIS, RICHARD WARRINGTON BALDWIN. *The Poetry of Hart Crane: A Critical Study.* Princeton: Princeton Univ. Library, 1967, bibliographical footnotes.

LIBRARY OF CONGRESS, GENERAL REFERENCE AND BIBLIOGRAPHY DIVISION. *Sixty American Poets, 1896–1944,* selected, with a preface and critical notes by Allen Tate and a preliminary checklist by Francis Cheney. Washington, 1945, 24.

Revised edition: 1954, 18–19.

LOHF, KENNETH A. *The Literary Manuscripts of Hart Crane.* Columbus: Ohio State Univ. Press, 1966, 235 pp.

MILLETT, FRED BENJAMIN. *Contemporary American Authors: A Critical Survey and 219 Bio-bibliographies.* New York: Harcourt, Brace and World, 1940, 305–306.

ROBINSON, JETHRO. "The Hart Crane Collection." *CLC,* IV (February 1955), 3–7.

ROWE, HERSHEL D. "Hart Crane: A Bibliography." *TCL,* I (July 1955), 94–113.

Also: Denver: Alan Swallow, 1955, 30 pp.

SPILLER, ROBERT ERNEST, et al. *Literary History of the United States,* 2 Vols. New York: Macmillan, 1962, 457–458. Supplement, 97–100.

WEBER, BROM. *Hart Crane: A Biographical and Critical Study.* New York: Bodley Press, 1948, 441–443.

WOODRESS, JAMES, et al. *American Literary Scholarship: An Annual.* Durham: Duke Univ. Press, (1963), 177–180; (1964), 189–190; (1965), 210–213; (1966), 201–203.

CRAPSEY, ADELAIDE

BLANCK, JACOB. *Bibliography of American Literature,* 5 Vols. New Haven: Yale Univ. Press, 1955–1969, II, 339–340.

LEARY, LEWIS. *Articles on American Literature, 1900–1950.* Durham: Duke Univ. Press, 1954, 63.

CROTHERS, RACHEL

LEARY, LEWIS. *Articles on Ameri-*

can Literature, 1900–1950. Durham: Duke Univ. Press, 1954, 65.

CROTHERS, SAMUEL McCHORD

LEARY, LEWIS. *Articles on American Literature, 1900–1950.* Durham: Duke Univ. Press, 1954, 65.

CULBERTSON, WILLIAM SMITH

LIBRARY OF CONGRESS, MANUSCRIPT DIVISION. *William S. Culbertson: A Register of His Papers in the Library of Congress.* Washington, 1963, 12 leaves.

CULLEN, COUNTEE

LEARY, LEWIS. *Articles on American Literature, 1900–1950.* Durham: Duke Univ. Press, 1954, 65.

WOODRESS, JAMES, et al. *American Literary Scholarship: An Annual.* Durham: Duke Univ. Press, (1966), 203–204.

CUMMINGS, E. E.

BLANCK, JACOB, ed. *Merle Johnson's American First Editions,* 4th edition, revised and enlarged. Waltham, Massachusetts: Mark Press, 1965, 131–132.

FIRMAGE, GEORGE. *E. E. Cummings: A Bibliography.* Middletown, Connecticut: Wesleyan Univ. Press, 1960, 129 pp.

LAUTER, PAUL, comp. *E. E. Cummings: Index to First Lines and Bibliography of Works by and about the Poet.* Denver: Alan Swallow, 1955, 44 leaves.

LEARY, LEWIS. *Articles on American Literature, 1900–1950.* Durham: Duke Univ. Press, 1954, 65–66.

LIBRARY OF CONGRESS, GENERAL REFERENCE AND BIBLIOGRAPHY DIVISION. *Sixty American Poets, 1896–1944,* selected, with a preface and critical notes by Allen Tate and a preliminary checklist by Francis Cheney. Washington, 1945, 25–27.

Revised edition: 1954, 19–21.

MILLETT, FRED BENJAMIN. *Contemporary American Authors: A Critical Survey and 219 Bio-bibliographies.* New York: Harcourt, Brace and World, 1940, 310–311.

SPILLER, ROBERT ERNEST, et al. *Literary History of the United States,* 2 Vols. New York: Macmillan, 1962, 462–463. Supplement, 102–103.

WOODRESS, JAMES, et al. *American Literary Scholarship: An Annual.* Durham: Duke Univ. Press, (1963), 172; (1964), 186–189; (1965), 215–217; (1966), 200–201.

CURRY, WALTER CLYDE

BRADBURY, JOHN M. *The Fugitives: A Critical Account.* Chapel Hill: Univ. of North Carolina Press, 1958, 294.

DARGAN, OLIVE TILFORD

LEARY, LEWIS. *Articles on American Literature, 1900–1950.* Durham: Duke Univ. Press, 1954, 67.

DAVIDSON, DONALD

BRADBURY, JOHN M. *The Fugitives: A Critical Account.* Chapel Hill: Univ. of North Carolina Press, 1958, 290–291.

LEARY, LEWIS. *Articles on American Literature, 1900–1950.* Durham: Duke Univ. Press, 1954, 67.

LIBRARY OF CONGRESS, GENERAL REFERENCE AND BIBLIOGRAPHY DIVISION. *Sixty American Poets, 1896–1944,* selected, with a preface and critical notes by Allen Tate and a preliminary checklist by Francis Cheney. Washington, 1945, 28–29.

Revised edition: 1954, 21–22.

WOODRESS, JAMES, et al. *American Literary Scholarship: An Annual.* Durham: Duke Univ. Press, (1965), 217–219.

DAVIES, W. H.

LOOKER, SAMUEL J. "W. H. Davies: His Later Bibliography, 1922–1928." *Bookman's Journal,* XVII (1929), 122–127.

DAVIS, HAROLD LENOIR

GERSTENBERGER, DONNA, and GEORGE HENDRICK. *The American Novel, 1789–1959: A Checklist of Twentieth Century Criticism.* Denver: Alan Swallow, 1961, 55.

DAVIS, JAMES JOHN

LIBRARY OF CONGRESS, MANUSCRIPT DIVISION. *James J. Davis: A Register of His Papers in the Library of Congress.* Washington, 1958, 9 leaves.

DAVIS, OWEN

LEARY, LEWIS. *Articles on American Literature, 1900–1950.* Durham: Duke Univ. Press, 1954, 67.

DAVIS, WILLIAM STEARNS

LEARY, LEWIS. *Articles on American Literature, 1900–1950.* Durham: Duke Univ. Press, 1954, 67.

DE CASSERES, BENJAMIN

LEARY, LEWIS. *Articles on American Literature, 1900–1950.* Durham: Duke Univ. Press, 1954, 67.

DELAND, MARGARET

BLANCK, JACOB, ed. *Merle Johnson's American First Editions,* 4th edition, revised and enlarged. Waltham, Massachusetts: Mark Press, 1965, 141–143.

HUMPHRY, JAMES, III. "The Works of Margaret Deland, together with a Check-List of Eighty of Her Works Now in the Colby College Library." *CLQ,* 2nd Series, VIII (November 1948), 134–140.

LEARY, LEWIS. *Articles on American Literature, 1900–1950.* Durham: Duke Univ. Press, 1954, 67–68.

TRENT, WILLIAM PETERFIELD, et al. *Cambridge History of American Literature,* 4 Vols. New York: G. P. Putnam's Sons, 1917–1921, II, 620.

DELL, FLOYD

GERSTENBERGER, DONNA, and GEORGE HENDRICK. *The American Novel, 1789–1959: A Checklist of Twentieth Century Criticism.* Denver: Alan Swallow, 1961, 56.

LEARY, LEWIS. *Articles on American Literature, 1900–1950.* Durham: Duke Univ. Press, 1954, 68.

DE VOTO, BERNARD

LEARY, LEWIS. *Articles on American Literature, 1900–1950.* Durham: Duke Univ. Press, 1954, 68.

LEE, ROBERT E. "The Easy Chair of Bernard De Voto: A Finding List." *BB,* XXIII (September–December 1960), 64–69.

——————. "The Work of Bernard De Voto: Introduction and Annotated Check List." Unpublished doctoral dissertation, Univ. of Iowa, 1957.

STANFORD UNIVERSITY, LIBRARY. *The Papers of Bernard De Voto: A Description and a Checklist of His Works: Exhibition in the Albert M. Bender Room,* compiled by Julius P. Barclay. Palo Alto: Stanford Univ. Library, 1960, 62 pp.

De Voto's personal papers, consisting of more than 40,000 items and a 5,000-volume library.

DEWEY, JOHN

MILLETT, FRED BENJAMIN. *Contemporary American Authors: A Critical Survey and 219 Bio-bibliographies.* New York: Harcourt, Brace and World, 1940, 318–327.

SCHILPP, PAUL ARTHUR. *The Philosophy of John Dewey.* Evanston: North-western Univ. Press, 1939, 609–676.

SPILLER, ROBERT ERNEST, et al. *Literary History of the United States,* 2 Vols. New York: Macmillan, 1962, 465–467. Supplement, 104–105.

THOMAS, MILTON HALSEY, and H. W. SCHNEIDER. *A Bibliography of John Dewey.* New York: Columbia Univ. Press, 1929, 173 pp.

Revised edition: 1939, 262 pp.

TRENT, WILLIAM PETERFIELD, et al. *Cambridge History of American Literature,* 4 Vols. New York: G. P. Putnam's Sons, 1917–1921, IV, 756.

DILLON, GEORGE

LEARY, LEWIS. *Articles on Ameri-*

can Literature, 1900–1950. Durham: Duke Univ. Press, 1954, 71.

DOBIE, J. FRANK

McVICKER, MARY LOUISE. *The Writings of J. Frank Dobie: A Bibliography.* Lawton, Oklahoma: Museum of the Great Plains, 1968, 258 pp.

DONLEAVY, J. P.

THE EDITORS. "Books." *HC,* I (February 1964), 5.

DOOLITTLE, HILDA (ALDINGTON) "H. D."

LEARY, LEWIS. *Articles on American Literature, 1900–1950.* Durham: Duke Univ. Press, 1954, 71–72.

LIBRARY OF CONGRESS, GENERAL REFERENCE AND BIBLIOGRAPHY DIVISION. *Sixty American Poets, 1896–1944,* selected, with a preface and critical notes by Allen Tate and a preliminary checklist by Francis Cheney. Washington, 1945, 7–9.

Revised edition: 1954, 5–7.

MILLETT, FRED BENJAMIN. *Contemporary American Authors: A Critical Survey and 219 Bio-bibliographies.* New York: Harcourt, Brace and World, 1940, 328–329.

SPILLER, ROBERT ERNEST, et al. *Literary History of the United States,* 2 Vols. New York: Macmillan, 1962, 472–473. Supplement, 107.

TAYLOR, WALTER FULLER. *A History of American Letters,* with bibliographies by Harry Hartwick. Boston: American Book Co., 1936, 581–582.

Subsequent editions entitled: *The Story of American Letters.*

DOS PASSOS, JOHN

BLANCK, JACOB, ed. *Merle Johnson's American First Editions,* 4th edition, revised and enlarged. Waltham, Massachusetts: Mark Press, 1965, 147–149.

GERSTENBERGER, DONNA, and GEORGE HENDRICK. *The American Novel, 1789–1959: A Checklist of Twentieth Century Criticism.* Denver: Alan Swallow, 1961, 57–60.

GIBSON, WILLIAM. "A Dos Passos Checklist." *Book Collector's Journal,* I (May 1936), 6–9.

KALLICH, MARTIN. "Bibliography of John Dos Passos." *BB,* XIX (May–August 1949), 231–235.

LEARY, LEWIS. *Articles on American Literature, 1900–1950.* Durham: Duke Univ. Press, 1954, 72–73.

MILLETT, FRED BENJAMIN. *Contemporary American Authors: A Critical Survey and 219 Bio-bibliographies.* New York: Harcourt, Brace and World, 1940, 329–332.

POTTER, JACK. *A Bibliography of John Dos Passos.* Chicago: Normandie House, 1950, 94 pp.

SPILLER, ROBERT ERNEST, et al. *Literary History of the United States,* 2 Vols. New York: Macmillan, 1962, 473–474. Supplement, 107–108.

WHITE, WILLIAM. "More Dos Passos: Bibliographical Addenda." *PBSA,* XLV (2nd Quart. 1951), 156–158.

Supplements Martin Kallich's "Bibliography of John Dos Passos," 1949, and Jack Potter's *A Bibliography of John Dos Passos,* 1950.

WOODRESS, JAMES, et al. *American Literary Scholarship: An Annual.* Durham: Duke Univ. Press, (1965), 169–172.

WRENN, JOHN H. *John Dos Passos.* New York: Twayne, 1961, 198–205.

DOUGLAS, LLOYD C.

GERSTENBERGER, DONNA, and GEORGE HENDRICK. *The American Novel, 1789–1959: A Checklist of Twentieth Century Criticism.* Denver: Alan Swallow, 1961, 60.

LEARY, LEWIS. *Articles on American Literature, 1900–1950.* Durham: Duke Univ. Press, 1954, 73.

DOUGLAS NORMAN

McDONALD, EDWARD DAVID. *A Bibliography of the Writings of Norman Douglas,* with notes by Norman Douglas. Philadelphia: The Centaur Book Shop, 1927, 165 pp.

DREISER, THEODORE

BIRSS, J. H. "A Bibliographical Note on Theodore Dreiser." *N&Q,* CLXV (September 1933), 266.

BLANCK, JACOB, ed. *Merle Johnson's American First Editions,* 4th edition, revised and enlarged. Waltham, Massachusetts: Mark Press, 1965, 151–155.

ELIAS, ROBERT H. "The Library's Dreiser Collection." *LCUP,* XVII (Fall 1950), 78–80.

GERSTENBERGER, DONNA, and GEORGE HENDRICK. *The American Novel, 1789–1959: A Checklist of Twentieth Century Criticism.* Denver: Alan Swallow, 1961, 60–66.

KAZIN, ALFRED, and CHARLES SHAPIRO. *The Stature of Theodore Dreiser.* Bloomington: Univ. of Indiana Press, 1955, 271–303.

LEARY, LEWIS. *Articles on American Literature, 1900–1950.* Durham: Duke Univ. Press, 1954, 73–75.

McDONALD, EDWARD DAVID. *A Bibliography of the Writings of Theodore Dreiser,* with a foreword by Theodore Dreiser. Philadelphia: The Centaur Book Shop, 1928, 144 pp.

MILLER, RALPH N. *A Preliminary Checklist of Books and Articles on Theodore Dreiser.* Kalamazoo: Western Michigan College Library, 1947, 11 leaves.

MILLETT, FRED BENJAMIN. *Contemporary American Authors: A Critical Survey and 219 Bio-bibliographies.* New York: Harcourt, Brace and World, 1940, 332–337.

ORTON, VREST. *Dreiserana: A Book about His Books.* New York: printed at the Stratford Press, 1929, 93 pp.

Chocorua bibliography.

SPILLER, ROBERT E., et al. *Literary History of the United States,* 2 Vols. New York: Macmillan, 1962, 474–475. Supplement, 108–109.

TAYLOR, WALTER FULLER. *A History of American Letters,* with bibliographies by Harry Hartwick. Boston: American Book Co., 1936, 574–575.

Subsequent editions entitled: *The Story of American Letters.*

WESTLAKE, NEDA M. "The Theodore Dreiser Collection at the University of Pennsylvania." *Pennsylvania Library Association Bulletin,* XIV (Fall 1958), 11–12.

WOODRESS, JAMES, et al. *American Literary Scholarship:An Annual.* Durham: Duke Univ. Press, (1965), 167–169; (1966), 155–158.

DRESBACH, GLENN WARD

WOODRESS, JAMES, et al. *American Literary Scholarship: An Annual.* Durham: Duke Univ. Press, (1965), 217–219.

DU BOIS, WILLIAM EDWARD BURGHARDT

LEARY, LEWIS. *Articles on American Literature, 1900–1950.* Durham: Duke Univ. Press, 1954, 75.

TRENT, WILLIAM PETERFIELD, et al. *Cambridge History of American Literature,* 4 Vols. New York: G. P. Putnam's Sons, 1917–1921, II, 614.

DUNNE, FINLEY PETER

BLANCK, JACOB, ed. *Merle Johnson's American First Editions,* 4th edition, revised and enlarged. Waltham, Massachusetts: Mark Press, 1965, 158.

LEARY, LEWIS, *Articles on American Literature, 1900–1950.* Durham: Duke Univ. Press, 1954, 76.

DURRELL, LAWRENCE

CALIFORNIA, UNIVERSITY, LOS ANGELES, LIBRARY. *Lawrence Durrell: A Checklist.* Los Angeles: Univ. of California at Los Angeles Library, 1961, 50 pp.

EAKINS, THOMAS

GOODRICH, LLOYD. *Thomas Eakins: His Life and Work.* New York: Whitney Museum of American Art, 1933, 217–220.

EAMES, WILBERFORCE

Bibliographical Essays: A Tribute to Wilberforce Eames. Cambridge: Harvard Univ. Press, 1924, 440 pp.

LEARY, LEWIS. *Articles on American Literature, 1900–1950.* Durham: Duke Univ. Press, 1954, 77.

PALTSITS, VICTOR HUGO. "Wilberforce Eames, American Bibliographer." *BNYPL,* LIX (October 1955), 505–514.

STARK, LEWIS M. "The Writings of Wilberforce Eames." *BNYPL,* LIX (October 1955), 515–519.

EASTMAN, MAX

LEARY, LEWIS. *Articles on American Literature, 1900–1950.* Durham: Duke Univ. Press, 1954, 77.

EBERHART, LOWELL

WOODRESS, JAMES, et al. *American Literary Scholarship: An Annual.* Durham: Duke Univ. Press, (1964), 211–212.

EBERHART, RICHARD

THE EDITORS. "Books by Richard Eberhart." *HC,* I (October 1964), 7.

LEARY, LEWIS. *Articles on American Literature, 1900–1950.* Durham: Duke Univ. Press, 1954, 77.

LIBRARY OF CONGRESS, GENERAL REFERENCE AND BIBLIOGRAPHY DIVISION. *Sixty American Poets, 1896–1944,* selected, with a preface and critical notes by Allen Tate and a preliminary checklist by Francis Cheney. Washington, 1945, 30.

Revised edition: 1954, 22–24.

EDMONDS, WALTER DUMAUX

BLANCK, JACOB, ed. *Merle Johnson's American First Editions,* 4th edition, revised and enlarged. Waltham, Massachusetts: Mark Press, 1965, 159–160.

GERSTENBERGER, DONNA, and GEORGE HENDRICK. *The American Novel, 1789–1959: A Checklist of Twentieth Century Criticism.* Denver: Alan Swallow, 1961, 67.

LEARY, LEWIS. *Articles on American Literature, 1900–1950.* Durham: Duke Univ. Press, 1954, 77.

ELIOT, THOMAS STEARNS

BEARE, ROBERT L. "Notes on the Text of T. S. Eliot: Variants from Russell Square." *SB,* IX (1957), 21–49.

FRY, VARIAN. "A Bibliography of the Writings of Thomas Stearns Eliot." *Hound and Horn,* I (March 1928), 214–218; (June 1928), 320–324.

GALLUP, DONALD CLIFFORD. *A Catalogue of English and American First Editions of Writings of T. S. Eliot.* New Haven: Yale Univ. Press, 1937, 42 pp.

—————————. *T. S. Eliot: A Bibliography.* London: Faber and Faber, 1952, 188 pp.

JONES, JOSEPH. "Rare Book Collections: I, Walt Whitman; II, T. S. Eliot." LCUT, VI (Spring 1958), 46–50.

LEARY, LEWIS. *Articles on American Literature, 1900–1950.* Durham: Duke Univ. Press, 1954, 79–86.

LIBRARY OF CONGRESS, GENERAL REFERENCE AND BIBLIOGRAPHY DIVISION. *Sixty*

American Poets, 1896–1944, selected, with a preface and critical notes by Allen Tate and a preliminary checklist by Francis Cheney. Washington, 1945, 31–42.

Revised edition: 1954, 24–39.

MARSHALL, WILLIAM H. "The Text of T. S. Eliot's 'Gerontion.' " *SB,* IV (1951–1952), 213–216.

NICHOLLS, NORAH. "A Preliminary Check-List of T. S. Eliot." *ABC,* III (February 1933), 105–106.

SKINNER, AUBREY E. "Rare Book Collections: I, Walt Whitman; II, T. S. Eliot." *LCUT,* VI (Spring 1958), 46–50.

SPILLER, ROBERT ERNEST, et al. *Literary History of the United States,* 2 Vols. New York: Macmillan, 1962, 488–492. Supplement, 111–115.

TAYLOR, WALTER FULLER. *A History of American Letters,* with bibliographies by Harry Hartwick. Boston: American Book Co., 1936, 593–595.

Subsequent editions entitled: *The Story of American Letters.*

ELLIOTT, GEORGE P.

EMERSON, CORNELIA. "Books by George P. Elliott." *HC,* V (December 1968), 7.

ELLISON, RALPH

GERSTENBERGER, DONNA, and GEORGE HENDRICK. *The American Novel, 1789–1959: A Checklist of Twentieth Century Criticism.* Denver: Alan Swallow, 1961, 67–68.

ENGLE, PAUL

LEARY, LEWIS. *Articles on Ameri-*

can Literature, 1900–1950. Durham: Duke Univ. Press, 1954, 95.

LIBRARY OF CONGRESS, GENERAL REFERENCE AND BIBLIOGRAPHY DIVISION. *Sixty American Poets, 1896–1944,* selected, with a preface and critical notes by Allen Tate and a preliminary checklist by Francis Cheney. Washington, 1945, 43–45.

Revised edition: 1954, 39–41.

ERSKINE, JOHN

LEARY, LEWIS. *Articles on American Literature, 1900–1950.* Durham: Duke Univ. Press, 1954, 95.

EVANS, CHARLES

HOLLEY, EDWARD G. *Charles Evans: American Bibliographer.* Urbana: Univ. of Illinois Press, 1963, 323–330.

EVANS, CHARLES N. B.

LEARY, LEWIS. *Articles on American Literature, 1900–1950.* Durham: Duke Univ. Press, 1954, 96.

EVANS, DONALD

LEARY, LEWIS. *Articles on American Literature, 1900–1950.* Durham: Duke Univ. Press, 1954, 96.

FARRELL, JAMES THOMAS

BLANCK, JACOB, ed. *Merle Johnson's American First Editions,* 4th edition, revised and enlarged. Waltham, Massachusetts: Mark Press, 1965, 168–169.

BRANCH, EDGAR MARQUESS. *A Bibliography of James T. Farrell's Writings, 1921–1957.* Philadelphia: Univ. of Pennsylvania Press, 1959, 161 pp.

GERSTENBERGER, DONNA, and GEORGE HENDRICK. *The American Novel, 1789–1959: A Checklist of Twentieth Century Criticism.* Denver: Alan Swallow, 1961, 68–70.

LEARY, LEWIS. *Articles on American Literature, 1900–1950.* Durham: Duke Univ. Press, 1954, 96.

MILLETT, FRED BENJAMIN. *Contemporary American Authors: A Critical Survey and 219 Bio-bibliographies.* New York: Harcourt, Brace and World, 1940, 345–346.

SPILLER, ROBERT ERNEST, et al. *Literary History of the United States,* 2 Vols. New York: Macmillan, 1962, 501–502. Supplement, 118–119.

FAST, HOWARD

GERSTENBERGER, DONNA, and GEORGE HENDRICK. *The American Novel, 1789–1959: A Checklist of Twentieth Century Criticism.* Denver: Alan Swallow, 1961, 71.

LEARY, LEWIS. *Articles on American Literature, 1900–1950.* Durham: Duke Univ. Press, 1954, 96.

FAULKNER, WILLIAM

BEEBE, MAURICE. "Criticism of William Faulkner: A Selected Checklist with an Index to Studies of Separate Works." *MFS,* II (Autumn 1956), 150–164.

"Bibliography." *Faulkner Studies,* I (Spring 1952), 12–16; (Summer 1952), 29–32; (Autumn 1952), 47–48; (Winter 1953), 62–66; II (Spring 1953), 15–16; (Autumn 1953), 44–48; (Winter 1954), 65–67; III (Summer–Autumn 1954), 44–45.

BLANCK, JACOB, ed. *Merle Johnson's American First Editions,* 4th revised and enlarged. Waltham,

Massachusetts: Mark Press, 1965, 170–172.

DANIEL, ROBERT WOODHAM. *A Catalogue of the Writings of William Faulkner.* New Haven: Yale Univ. Press, 1942, 32 pp.

GERSTENBERGER, DONNA, and GEORGE HENDRICK. *The American Novel, 1789–1959: A Checklist of Twentieth Century Criticism.* Denver: Alan Swallow, 1961, 71–89.

HOFFMAN, FREDERICK JOHN, and OLGA W. VICKERY, eds. *William Faulkner: Three Decades of Criticism.* East Lansing: Michigan State Univ. Press, 1961, 393–428.

——————, eds. *William Faulkner: Two Decades of Criticism.* East Lansing: Michigan State Univ. Press, 1951, 269–280.

KIRK, ROBERT W. "An Index and Encyclopedia of the Characters in the Fictional Works of William Faulkner." Unpublished doctoral dissertation, Univ. of Southern California, 1959.

LEARY, LEWIS. *Articles on American Literature, 1900–1950.* Durham: Duke Univ. Press, 1954, 97–100.

LONGLEY, JOHN L. JR. and ROBERT DANIEL. "Faulkner's Critics: A Selective Bibliography." *Perspective,* III (Autumn 1950), 202–208.

MASSEY, LINTON. "Notes on the Unrevised Galleys of Faulkner's *Sanctuary.*" *SB,* VIII (1956), 195–208.

MERIWETHER, JAMES B. "The Literary Career of William Faulkner: Catalogue of an Exhibition in the Princeton University Library." *PULC,* XXI (Spring 1960), 111–164.

——————. "William Faulkner: A Check List." *PULC,* XVII (Spring 1957), 136–158.

MILLETT, FRED BENJAMIN. *Contemporary American Authors: A Critical Survey and 219 Bio-bibliographies.* New York: Harcourt, Brace and World, 1940, 346–348.

MILLGATE, MICHAEL. "Faulkner Criticism: An Annotated Bibliography." *Venture,* II (June 1961), 128–134.

O'CONNOR, WILLIAM VAN. *William Faulkner.* Minneapolis: Univ. of Minnesota Press, 1959, 41–43.

——————. "William Faulkner: in *Tres escritores norteamericanos.* Madrid: Editorial Gredos, 1961, 148–152.

OREGON, UNIVERSITY, LIBRARY, HUMANITIES DIVISION. *William Faulkner: Biography and Criticism, 1951–1954.* Eugene: Univ. of Oregon Library, 1955, 11 pp.

PERRY, BRADLEY T. "Faulkner Critics: A Bibliographic Breakdown." *Faulkner Studies,* II (Spring 1953), 11–14; (Summer 1953), 30–32; (Winter 1954), 60–64.

——————. "A Selected Bibliography of Critical Works on William Faulkner." *UKCR,* XVIII (Winter 1951), 159–164.

RUNYAN, HARRY. "Faulkner's Non-Fiction Prose: An Annotated Checklist." *Faulkner Studies,* III (Winter 1954), 67–69.

SLEETH, IRENE LYNN. "William Faulkner: A Bibliography of Criticism." *TCL,* VIII (April 1962), 18–43.

Also: Denver: Alan Swallow, 1962, 28 pp.

SPILLER, ROBERT ERNEST, et al. *Literary History of the United States,* 2 Vols. New York: Macmillan, 1962, 502–503. Supplement, 119–121.

STARKE, AUBREY. "An American Comedy: An Introduction to a Bibliography of William Faulkner." *The Colophon,* Part 19 (1934), no pagination.

TAYLOR, WALTER FULLER. *A History of American Letters,* with bibliographies by Harry Hartwick. Boston: American Book Co., 1936, 598.

Subsequent editions entitled: *The Story of American Letters.*

TEXAS, UNIVERSITY, HUMANITIES RESEARCH CENTER. *William Faulkner: An Exhibition of Manuscripts,* prepared by James B. Meriwether. Austin: Humanities Research Center, 1959, 16 pp.

THOMPSON, LAWRANCE ROGER. *William Faulkner: An Introduction and Interpretation.* New York, 1967, 177–179.

Part of the *American Authors and Critics Series,* begun in 1961, and purchased by Holt, Rinehart and Winston from Barnes and Noble. The nine original and three new volumes were issued under the Holt imprint in January 1967.

VIRGINIA, UNIVERSITY, LIBRARY. *William Faulkner: Man Working, 1919–1959.* Charlottesville: Univ. of Virginia Library, 1959, 4 pp.

WARREN, ROBERT PENN. *Faulkner: A Collection of Critical Essays.* Englewood Cliffs: Prentice Hall, 1966, 310–311.

WOODRESS, JAMES, et al. *American Literary Scholarship: An Annual.* Durham: Duke Univ. Press, (1963), 72–80; (1964), 73–81; (1965), 82–89; (1966), 79–84.

WOODWORTH, STANLEY D. "Sélection bibliographique d'ouvrages ou d'articles sur William Faulkner en France (1931–1952)." *La Revue des Lettres Modernes,* (2e Trim. 1957), 191–196.

FEARING, KENNETH

LEARY, LEWIS. *Articles on American Literature, 1900–1950.* Durham: Duke Univ. Press, 1954, 100.

LIBRARY OF CONGRESS, GENERAL REFERENCE AND BIBLIOGRAPHY DIVISION. *Sixty American Poets, 1896–1944,* selected, with a preface and critical notes by Allen Tate and a preliminary checklist by Francis Cheney. Washington, 1945, 46–47.

Revised edition: 1954, 41–42.

FEIKEMA, FEIKE (see *MANFRED*)

FERBER, EDNA

BLANCK, JACOB, ed. *Merle Johnson's American First Editions,* 4th edition, revised and enlarged. Waltham, Massachusetts: Mark Press, 1965, 173–175.

BRENNI, VITO J., and BETTY LEE SPENCER. "Edna Ferber: A Selected Bibliography." *BB,* XXII (September–December 1958), 152–156.

GERSTENBERGER, DONNA, and GEORGE HENDRICK. *The American Novel, 1789–1959: A Checklist of Twentieth Century Criticism.* Denver: Alan Swallow, 1961, 89.

LEARY, LEWIS. *Articles on American Literature, 1900–1950.* Durham: Duke Univ. Press, 1954, 100.

FERLINGHETTI, LAWRENCE

KHERDIAN, DAVID. *Six Poets of the San Francisco Renaissance.* Fresno, California: The Giligia Press, 1965, 9–44.

FERRIL, THOMAS HORNSBY

LEARY, LEWIS. *Articles on American Literature, 1900–1950.* Durham: Duke Univ. Press, 1954, 100.

FICKE, ARTHUR DAVISON

LEARY, LEWIS. *Articles on American Literature, 1900–1950.* Durham: Duke Univ. Press, 1954, 100.

FINDLATER, JANE

LEARY, LEWIS. *Articles on American Literature, 1900–1950.* Durham: Duke Univ. Press, 1954, 101.

FINDLATER, MARY

LEARY, LEWIS. *Articles on American Literature, 1900–1950.* Durham: Duke Univ. Press, 1954, 101.

FIRKINS, OSCAR W.

LEARY, LEWIS. *Articles on American Literature, 1900–1950.* Durham: Duke Univ. Press, 1954, 101.

FISHER, DOROTHY CANFIELD

GERSTENBERGER, DONNA, and GEORGE HENDRICK. *The American Novel, 1789–1959: A Checklist of Twentieth Century Criticism.* Denver: Alan Swallow, 1961, 89–90.

LEARY, LEWIS. *Articles on American Literature, 1900–1950.* Durham: Duke Univ. Press, 1954, 101.

FISHER, VARDIS

BLANCK, JACOB, ed. *Merle Johnson's American First Editions,* 4th edition, revised and enlarged. Waltham, Massachusetts: Mark Press, 1965, 180–181.

GERSTENBERGER, DONNA, and GEORGE HENDRICK. *The American Novel, 1789–1959: A Checklist of Twentieth Century Criticism.* Denver: Alan Swallow, 1961, 90.

KELLOGG, GEORGE. *Vardis Fisher: A Bibliography.* Moscow, Idaho: Univ. of Idaho Library, 1961, 19 leaves.

LEARY, LEWIS. *Articles on American Literature, 1900–1950.* Durham: Duke Univ. Press, 1954, 101.

FISHER, WALTER LOWRIE

LIBRARY OF CONGRESS, MANUSCRIPT DIVISION. *Walter L. Fisher: A Register of His Papers in the Library of Congress.* Washington, 1960, 9 leaves.

FITZGERALD, F. SCOTT

BEEBE, MAURICE, and JACKSON R. BRYER. "Criticism of F. Scott Fitzgerald: A Selected Checklist." *MFS,* VII (Spring 1961), 82–94.

BRUCCOLI, MATTHEW J. "Bibliographical Notes on F. Scott Fitzgerald's *The Beautiful and Damned.*" *SB,* XIII (1960), 258–261.

—————. "A Collation of F. Scott Fitzgerald's *This Side of Paradise.*" *SB,* IX (1957), 263–265.

—————. comp. *F. Scott Fitzgerald: Collector's Handlist.* Columbus, Ohio: the compiler, 113 East Lane Ave., 1964, 11 pp.

——————. "Material for a Centenary Edition of *Tender Is the Night.*" *SB*, XVII (1964), 177–193.

BRYER, JACKSON B. *The Critical Reputation of F. Scott Fitzgerald: A Bibliographical Study.* Hamden, Connecticut: The Shoe String Press, 1967, 451 pp.

——————. "F. Scott Fitzgerald: A Review of Research and Scholarship." *TSLL*, V (Spring 1963), 147–163.

GERSTENBERGER, DONNA, and GEORGE HENDRICK. *The American Novel, 1789–1959: A Checklist of Twentieth Century Criticism.* Denver: Alan Swallow, 1961, 90–96.

HOFFMAN, FREDERICK JOHN, ed. *The Great Gatsby: A Study.* New York: Scribner, 1962, 335–338.

LEARY, LEWIS. *Articles on American Literature, 1900–1950.* Durham: Duke Univ. Press, 1954, 102–103.

MILLER, JAMES EDWIN. *F. Scott Fitzgerald: His Art and Technique.* New York: New York Univ. Press, 1964, 163–165.

MILLETT, FRED BENJAMIN. *Contemporary American Authors: A Critical Survey and 219 Bio-bibliographies.* New York: Hartcourt, Brace and World, 1940, 354–356.

MIZENER, ARTHUR. *F. Scott Fitzgerald: A Collection of Critical Essays.* Englewood Cliffs, New Jersey: Prentice Hall, 1963, 173–174.

——————. "The F. Scott Fitzgerald Papers." *PULC*, XII (Summer 1951), 190–195.

PIPER, HENRY DAN. "F. Scott Fitzgerald: A Check List." *PULC*, XII (Summer 1951), 196–208.

PORTER, BERNARD H. "The First Publications of F. Scott Fitzgerald." *TCL*, V (January 1960), 176–182.

SKLAR, ROBERT. *F. Scott Fitzgerald: The Last Laocoön.* New York: Oxford Univ. Press, 1967, 347–369.

SPILLER, ROBERT ERNEST, et al. *Literary History of the United States,* 2 Vols. New York: Macmillan, 1962, 505–506. Supplement, 121–122.

WOODRESS, JAMES, et al. *American Literary Scholarship: An Annual.* Durham: Duke Univ. Press, (1963), 81–91; (1964), 81–88; (1965), 90–103; (1966), 85–94.

FITZGERALD, ZELDA SAYRE

PIPER, HENRY DAN. "Zelda Sayre Fitzgerald: A Check List." *PULC*, XII (Summer 1951), 209–210.

FLACCUS, KIMBALL

LIBRARY OF CONGRESS, GENERAL REFERENCE AND BIBLIOGRAPHY DIVISION. *Sixty American Poets, 1896–1944,* selected, with a preface and critical notes by Allen Tate and a preliminary checklist by Francis Cheney. Washington, 1945, 48.

Revised edition: 1954, 42–43.

FLEMING, WALTER L.

LEARY, LEWIS. *Articles on American Literature, 1900–1950.* Durham: Duke Univ. Press, 1954, 103.

FLETCHER, JOHN GOULD

ARKANSAS, UNIVERSITY, LIB-

RARY. "University of Arkansas Library Gets John Gould Fletcher Library." *Arkansas Alumnus,* VI (December 1952), 10.

LEARY, LEWIS. *Articles on American Literature, 1900–1950.* Durham: Duke Univ. Press, 1954, 103–104.

LIBRARY OF CONGRESS, GENERAL REFERENCE AND BIBLIOGRAPHY DIVISION. *Sixty American Poets, 1896–1944,* selected, with a preface and critical notes by Allen Tate and a preliminary checklist by Francis Cheney. Washington, 1945, 49–51.

Revised edition: 1954, 43–45.

MILLETT, FRED BENJAMIN. *Contemporary American Authors: A Critical Survey and 219 Bio-bibliographies.* New York: Harcourt, Brace and World, 1940, 356–358.

SPILLER, ROBERT ERNEST, et al. *Literary History of the United States,* 2 Vols. New York: Macmillan, 1962, 506–507. Supplement, 123.

STEPHENS, EDNA B. *John Gould Fletcher.* New York: Twayne, 1967, 154–156.

TAYLOR, WALTER FULLER. *A History of American Letters,* with bibliographies by Harry Hartwick. Boston: American Book Co., 1936, 582.

Subsequent editions entitled: *The Story of American Letters.*

WOODRESS, JAMES, et al. *American Literary Scholarship: An Annual.* Durham: Duke Univ. Press, (1965), 217–219; (1966), 201–203.

FLOWER, BENJAMIN ORANGE

LEARY, LEWIS. *Articles on Ameri-*

can Literature, 1900–1950. Durham: Duke Univ. Press, 1954, 104.

FOOTE, MARY HALLOCK

LEARY, LEWIS. *Articles on American Literature, 1900–1950.* Durham: Duke Univ. Press, 1954, 104.

FRANK, WALDO

GERSTENBERGER, DONNA, and GEORGE HENDRICK. *The American Novel, 1789–1959: A Checklist of Twentieth Century Criticism.* Denver: Alan Swallow, 1961, 97–98.

LEARY, LEWIS. *Articles on American Literature, 1900–1950.* Durham: Duke Univ. Press, 1954, 105.

MUNSON, GORHAM BERT. *Waldo Frank: A Study.* New York: Boni and Liveright, 1923, 70–72.

FREEMAN, DOUGLAS SOUTHALL

LIBRARY OF CONGRESS, MANUSCRIPT DIVISION. *Douglas Southall Freeman: A Register of His Papers in the Library of Congress.* Washington, 1960, 14 leaves.

FRIERSON, WILLIAM C.

BRADBURY, JOHN M. *The Fugitives: A Critical Account.* Chapel Hill: Univ. of North Carolina Press, 1958, 294.

FROST, ROBERT

BLANCK, JACOB, ed. *Merle Johnson's American First Editions,* 4th edition, revised and enlarged. Waltham, Massachusetts: Mark Press, 1965, 194–197.

BOUTELL, H. S., comp. "A Bibliography of Robert Frost." *The Colophon,* Part 2 (May 1930), no pagination.

CLYMER, WILLIAM BRANFORD SHUBRICK, and CHARLES R. GREEN, comps. *Robert Frost: A Bibliography.* Amherst, Massachusetts: Jones Library, Inc., 1937, 158 pp.

COX, JAMES MELVILLE. *Robert Frost: A Collection of Critical Essays.* Englewood Cliffs, New Jersey: Prentice Hall, 1962, 205.

LEARY, LEWIS. *Articles on American Literature, 1900–1950.* Durham: Duke Univ. Press, 1954, 113–116.

LIBRARY OF CONGRESS, GENERAL REFERENCE AND BIBLIOGRAPHY DIVISION. *Sixty American Poets, 1896–1944,* selected with a preface and critical notes by Allen Tate and a preliminary checklist by Francis Cheney. Washington, 1945, 53–58.

Revised edition: 1954, 45–50.

LONG, W. S. "Robert Frost, Teacher and Educator: An Annotated Bibliography." *Journal of Higher Education,* VII (June 1936), 342–344.

MELCHER, FREDERIC G. "Robert Frost and His Books." *The Colophon,* Part 2 (May 1930), no pagination.

MERTINS, MARSHALL LOUIS, and ESTHER MERTINS. *The Intervals of Robert Frost: A Critical Bibliography,* with an introduction by Fulmer Mood. Berkeley: Univ. of California Press, 1947, 91 pp.

MILLETT, FRED BENJAMIN. *Contemporary American Authors: A Critical Survey and 219 Bio-bibliographies.* New York: Harcourt, Brace and World, 1940, 362–366.

NEWDICK, ROBERT S. "Bibliographies and Exhibits of the Work of Robert Frost." *Amherst Graduates'*

Quarterly, XXVI (November 1936), 79–80.

——————. "Three Poems by Robert Frost." *AL,* VII (November 1935), 329.

"Robert Frost: A Check-list Bibliography." *Reading & Collecting,* September 1937, 15.

SPILLER, ROBERT ERNEST, et al. *Literary History of the United States,* 2 Vols. New York: Macmillan, 1962, 520–522. Supplement, 127–128.

TAYLOR, WALTER FULLER. *A History of American Letters,* with bibliographies by Harry Hartwick. Boston: American Book Co., 1936, 570–571.

Subsequent editions entitled: *The Story of American Letters.*

THOMPSON, LAWRANCE. "Robert Frost," in *Tres escritores norteamericanos.* Madrid: Editorial Gredos, 1961, 152–153.

WESLEYAN UNIVERSITY, LIBRARY. *Robert Frost: A Chronological Survey.* Middletown, Connecticut: Wesleyan Univ. Library, 1936, 58 pp.

WOODRESS, JAMES, et al. *American Literary Scholarship: An Annual.* Durham: Duke Univ. Press, (1963), 165–170; (1964), 179–183; (1965), 213–215; (1966), 189–193.

GALE, ZONA

GERSTENBERGER, DONNA, and GEORGE HENDRICK. *The American Novel, 1789–1959: A Checklist of Twentieth Century Criticism.* Denver: Alan Swallow, 1961, 99.

LEARY, LEWIS. *Articles on American Literature, 1900–1950.* Durham: Duke Univ. Press, 1954, 118.

MILLETT, FRED BENJAMIN. *Contemporary American Authors: A Critical Survey and 219 Bio-bibliographies.* New York: Harcourt, Brace and World, 1940, 366–368.

SPILLER, ROBERT ERNEST, et al. *Literary History of the United States,* 2 Vols. New York: Macmillan, 1962, 525–526.

GARLAND, HAMLIN

AHNEBRINK, LARS. *The Beginnings of Naturalism in American Fiction: A Study of the Works of Hamlin Garland, Stephen Crane, and Frank Norris, with Special Reference to Some European Influences, 1891–1903.* New York: Russell and Russell, 1961, 468–484.

BLANCK, JACOB, ed. *Merle Johnson's American First Editions,* 4th edition, revised and enlarged. Waltham, Massachusetts: Mark Press, 1965, 200–203.

GERSTENBERGER, DONNA, and GEORGE HENDRICK. *The American Novel, 1789–1959: A Checklist of Twentieth Century Criticism.* Denver: Alan Swallow, 1961, 100–101.

LEARY, LEWIS. *Articles on American Literature, 1900–1950.* Durham: Duke Univ. Press, 1954, 118.

MILLETT, FRED BENJAMIN. *Contemporary American Authors: A Critical Survey and 219 Bio-bibliographies.* New York: Harcourt, Brace and World, 1940, 368–372.

PIZER, DONALD. "Hamlin Garland: A Bibliography of Newspaper and Periodical Publications (1885–1895)." *BB,* XXII (January-April 1957), 41–44.

SPILLER, ROBERT ERNEST, et al. *Literary History of the United States,*

2 Vols. New York: Macmillan, 1962, 526–528. Supplement, 129.

TAYLOR, WALTER FULLER. *A History of American Letters,* with bibliographies by Harry Hartwick. Boston: American Book Co., 1936, 562–536.

Subsequent editions entitled: *The Story of American Letters.*

TRENT, WILLIAM PETERFIELD, et al. *Cambridge History of American Literature,* 4 Vols. New York: G. P. Putnam's Sons, 1917–1921, II, 621.

GEROULD, KATHERINE FULLERTON

LEARY, LEWIS. *Articles on American Literature, 1900–1950.* Durham: Duke Univ. Press, 1954, 119.

GHISELIN, BREWSTER

LEARY, LEWIS. *Articles on American Literature, 1900–1950.* Durham: Duke Univ. Press, 1954, 119.

GLASGOW, ELLEN ANDERSON GHOLSON

BLANCK, JACOB, ed. *Merle Johnson's American First Editions,* 4th edition, revised and enlarged. Waltham, Massachusetts: Mark Press, 1965, 204–205.

COLVERT, JAMES B. "Agent and Author: Ellen Glasgow's Letters to Paul Revere Reynolds." *SB,* XIV (1961), 177–196.

COOPER, FREDERIC TABER. *Some American Story Tellers,* 2nd edition. New York: H. Holt and Co., 1912, 367–368.

EGLY, WILLIAM H. "A Bibliography of Ellen Anderson Gholson

Glasgow." *BB,* XVII (September-December 1940), 47–50.

GERSTENBERGER, DONNA, and GEORGE HENDRICK. *The American Novel, 1789–1959: A Checklist of Twentieth Century Criticism.* Denver: Alan Swallow, 1961, 101–104.

GLASGOW, ELLEN ANDERSON GHOLSON. *A Certain Measure: An Interpretation of Prose Fiction.* New York: Harcourt Brace and Co., 1943, 265–272.

JESSUP, JOSEPHINE LURIE. *The Faith of Our Feminists: A Study of the Novels of Edith Wharton, Ellen Glasgow, Willa Cather.* New York: R. R. Smith, 1950, 122–125.

LEARY, LEWIS. *Articles on American Literature, 1900–1950.* Durham: Duke Univ. Press, 1954, 120.

MILLETT, FRED BENJAMIN. *Contemporary American Authors: A Critical Survey and 219 Bio-bibliographies.* New York: Harcourt, Brace and World, 1940, 374–376.

QUENSENBERY, W. D., JR. "Ellen Glasgow: A Critical Bibliography." *BB,* XXII (May-August 1959), 201–206; (September-December 1959), 230–236.

SPILLER, ROBERT ERNEST, et al. *Literary History of the United States,* 2 Vols. New York: Macmillan, 1962, 532–533. Supplement, 130–131.

STEELE, OLIVER L. "Early Impressions of Ellen Glasgow's *The Miller of Old Church,* 1911." *The Library,* 5th Series, XVI (March 1961), 50–52.

STONE, GRACE. "Ellen Glasgow's Novels." *SR,* L (July-September 1942), 289–300.

WOODRESS, JAMES, et al. *American Literary Scholarship: An Annual.* Durham: Duke Univ. Press, (1965), 165–167; (1966), 151–155.

GLASPELL, SUSAN

LEARY, LEWIS. *Articles on American Literature, 1900–1950.* Durham: Duke Univ. Press, 1954, 120–121.

GOLD, HERBERT

GERSTENBERGER, DONNA, and GEORGE HENDRICK. *The American Novel, 1789–1959: A Checklist of Twentieth Century Criticism.* Denver: Alan Swallow, 1961, 104.

GORDON, CAROLINE

GERSTENBERGER, DONNA, and GEORGE HENDRICK. *The American Novel, 1789–1959: A Checklist of Twentieth Century Criticism.* Denver: Alan Swallow, 1961, 104.

GIRSCOM, JOAN. "Bibliography of Caroline Gordon." *Critique,* I (Winter 1956), 74–78.

LEARY, LEWIS. *Articles on American Literature, 1900–1950.* Durham: Duke Univ. Press, 1954, 121.

GRANVILLE-BARKER, HARLEY

DAVID, MARY LOUISE. "Reading List on Harley Granville Barker." *BB,* VII (July 1913), 130–132.

GREEN, ANNA KATHARINE

BLANCK, JACOB, ed. *Merle Johnson's American First Editions,* 4th edition, revised and enlarged. Waltham, Massachusetts: Mark Press, 1965, 206–207.

LEARY, LEWIS. *Articles on American Literature, 1900–1950.* Durham: Duke Univ. Press, 1954, 122.

GREEN, JULIAN

LEARY, LEWIS. *Articles on American Literature, 1900–1950*. Durham: Duke Univ. Press, 1954, 122.

GREEN, PAUL

LEARY, LEWIS. *Articles on American Literature, 1900–1950*. Durham: Duke Univ. Press, 1954, 122.

GREG, WALTER WILSON

FRANCIS, F. C. "A List of Dr. Greg's Writings." *The Library*, 4th Series, XXVI (June 1945), 72–97.

GREGORY, HORACE

LEARY, LEWIS. *Articles on American Literature, 1900–1950*. Durham: Duke Univ. Press, 1954, 123.

LIBRARY OF CONGRESS, GENERAL REFERENCE AND BIBLIOGRAPHY DIVISION. *Sixty American Poets, 1896–1944*, selected, with a preface and critical notes by Allen Tate and a preliminary checklist by Francis Cheney. Washington, 1945, 59–60.

Revised edition: 1954, 50–52.

GRIFFIN, JOHN HOWARD

GERSTENBERGER, DONNA, and GEORGE HENDRICK. *The American Novel, 1789–1959: A Checklist of Twentieth Century Criticism*. Denver: Alan Swallow, 1961, 105.

GRIGGS, SUTTON E.

LEARY, LEWIS. *Articles on American Literature, 1900–1950*. Durham: Duke Univ. Press, 1954, 123.

GUEST, EDGAR A.

LEARY, LEWIS. *Articles on Ameri-*

can Literature, 1900–1950. Durham: Duke Univ. Press, 1954, 123.

GUINEY, LOUISE IMOGEN

BLANCK, JACOB. *Bibliography of American Literature*, 5 Vols. New Haven: Yale Univ. Press, 1955–1969, III, 305–318.

_____, ed. *Merle Johnson's American First Editions*, 4th edition, revised and enlarged. Waltham, Massachusetts: Mark Press, 1965, 208–209.

LEARY, LEWIS. *Articles on American Literature, 1900–1950*. Durham: Duke Univ. Press, 1954, 123.

TENISON, EVA MABEL. "A Bibliography of Louise Imogen Guiney, 1861–1920." *Bookman Journal and Print Collector*, ns VII (December 1922), 86–87; (January 1923), 123–124; (March 1923), 181–182.

Also: *Louise Imogen Guiney: Her Life and Works*. London: Macmillan and Co., 1923, 299–325.

GUNTHER, JOHN

LEARY, LEWIS. *Articles on American Literature, 1900–1950*. Durham: Duke Univ. Press, 1954, 123.

GUTHRIE, ALFRED BERTRAM, JR.

GERSTENBERGER, DONNA, and GEORGE HENDRICK. *The American Novel, 1789–1959: A Checklist of Twentieth Century Criticism*. Denver: Alan Swallow, 1961, 105.

LEARY, LEWIS. *Articles on American Literature, 1900–1950*. Durham: Duke Univ. Press, 1954, 123.

GUTHRIE, WILLIAM NORMAN

LEARY, LEWIS. *Articles on Ameri-*

can Literature, 1900–1950. Durham: Duke Univ. Press, 1954, 123.

HALDEMAN-JULIUS, EMANUEL

LEARY, LEWIS. *Articles on American Literature, 1900–1950.* Durham: Duke Univ. Press, 1954, 123.

HALL, HAZEL

LEARY, LEWIS. *Articles on American Literature, 1900–1950.* Durham: Duke Univ. Press, 1954, 124.

SAUL, GEORGE BRANDON. "Hazel Hall: A Chronological List of Acknowledged Verses in the Periodicals." *TCL,* I (April 1955), 34–36.

HAMILTON, GEORGE L.

THE EDITORS. "George L. Hamilton (1874–1940): A Bibliography." *RR,* XXXII (February 1941), 79–81.

HAMMETT, DASHIEL

LEARY, LEWIS. *Articles on American Literature, 1900–1950.* Durham: Duke Univ. Press, 1954, 124.

HARRIMAN, FLORENCE JAFFRAY

LIBRARY OF CONGRESS, MANUSCRIPT DIVISION. *Florence Jaffray Harriman: A Register of His Papers in the Library of Congress.* Washington, 1958, 10 leaves.

HARRIS, CORRA

LEARY, LEWIS. *Articles on American Literature, 1900–1950.* Durham: Duke Univ. Press, 1954, 125.

HART, MOSS

LEARY, LEWIS. *Articles on American Literature, 1900–1950.* Durham: Duke Univ. Press, 1954, 126.

HAWKES, JOHN

BRYER, JACKSON R. "Two Bibliographies." *Critique,* VI (Fall 1963), 86–94.

WOODRESS, JAMES, et al. *American Literary Scholarship: An Annual.* Durham: Duke Univ. Press, (1963), 155–156.

HAYCOX, ERNEST

GERSTENBERGER, DONNA, and GEORGE HENDRICK. *The American Novel, 1789–1959: A Checklist of Twentieth Century Criticism.* Denver: Alan Swallow, 1961, 118.

HECHT, BEN

GERSTENBERGER, DONNA, and GEORGE HENDRICK. *The American Novel, 1789–1959: A Checklist of Twentieth Century Criticism.* Denver: Alan Swallow, 1961, 119.

HEGGEN, THOMAS O.

LEARY, LEWIS. *Articles on American Literature, 1900–1950.* Durham: Duke Univ. Press, 1954, 137.

HELLMAN, LILLIAN

LEARY, LEWIS. *Articles on American Literature, 1900–1950.* Durham: Duke Univ. Press, 1954, 137.

TRISCH, MANFRED. *The Lillian Hellman Collection at the University of Texas.* Austin: Univ. of Texas Press, 1967, 167 pp.

HEMINGWAY, ERNEST

BAKER, SHERIDAN WARNER. *Ernest Hemingway: An Introduction and Interpretation.* New York, 1967, 137–142.

Part of the *American Authors and Critics Series,* begun in 1961, and purchased by Holt, Rinehart and Winston from Barnes and Noble. The nine original and three new volumes were issued under the Holt imprint in January 1967.

BEEBE, MARIUS. "Criticism of Ernest Hemingway: A Selected Check List with an Index to Studies of Separate Works." *MFS,* I (August 1955), 36–45.

BLANCK, JACOB, ed. *Merle Johnson's American First Editions.* 4th edition, revised and enlarged. Waltham, Massachusetts: Mark Press, 1965, 235-237.

COHN, LOUIS HENRY. *A Bibliography of the Works of Ernest Hemingway.* New York: Random House, 1931, 116 pp.

GERSTENBERGER, DONNA, and GEORGE HENDRICK. *The American Novel, 1789–1959: A Checklist of Twentieth Century Criticism.* Denver: Alan Swallow, 1961, 119–128.

LEARY, LEWIS. *Articles on American Literature, 1900–1950.* Durham: Duke Univ. Press, 1954, 137–139.

MILLETT, FRED BENJAMIN. *Contemporary American Authors: A Critical Survey and 219 Bio-bibliographies.* New York: Harcourt, Brace and World, 1940, 385–388.

ORTON, VREST. "Some Notes Bibliographical and Otherwise on the Books of Ernest Hemingway." *PW,* CXVII (February 15, 1930), 884–886.

SAMUELS, LEE. *A Hemingway Check List.* New York: Scribner, 1951, 63 pp.

SPILLER, ROBERT ERNEST, et al. *Literary History of the United States,*

2 Vols. New York: Macmillan, 1962, 559–561. Supplement, 137–139.

TAYLOR, WALTER FULLER. *A History of American Letters,* with bibliographies by Harry Hartwick. Boston: American Book Co., 1936, 596–597.

Subsequent editions entitled: *The Story of American Letters.*

WEEKS, ROBERT PERCY. *Hemingway: A Collection of Critical Essays.* Englewood Cliffs, New Jersey: Prentice Hall, 1963, 179–180.

WOODRESS, JAMES, et al. *American Literary Scholarship: An Annual.* Durham: Duke Univ. Press, (1963), 81–91; (1964), 81–88; (1965), 90–103; (1966), 85–94.

YOUNG, PHILIP. "Ernest Hemingway," in *Tres escritores norteamericanos.* Madrid: Editorial Gredos, 1961, 147–148.

Also: Minneapolis: Univ. of Minnesota Press, 1959, 42–44.

HENDERSON, ARCHIBALD

LEARY, LEWIS. *Articles on American Literature, 1900–1950.* Durham:

HENRY, O. (see *PORTER)* Duke Univ. Press, 1954, 139.

HERFORD, OLIVER

BLANCK, JACOB, ed. *Merle Johnson's American First Editions.* 4th edition, revised and enlarged. Waltham, Massachusetts: Mark Press, 1965, 243–246.

HERGESHEIMER, JOSEPH

BLANK, JACOB, ed. *Merle Johnson's American First Editions.* 4th edition, revised and enlarged. Waltham, Massachusetts: Mark Press, 1965, 247–249.

GERSTENBERGER, DONNA, and GEORGE HENDRICK. *The American Novel, 1789–1959: A Checklist of Twentieth Century Criticism.* Denver: Alan Swallow, 1961, 128–129.

HERGESHEIMER, JOSEPH. "Biography and Bibliographies." *The Colophon,* Part 8 (1931), no pagination.

LEARY, LEWIS. *Articles on American Literature, 1900–1950.* Durham: Duke Univ. Press, 1954, 139–140.

MILLETT, FRED BENJAMIN. *Contemporary American Authors: A Critical Survey and 219 Bio-bibliographies.* New York: Harcourt, Brace and World, 1940, 390–392.

SPILLER, ROBERT ERNEST, et al. *Literary History of the United States,* 2 Vols. New York: Macmillan, 1962, 561–563.

SWIRE, HERBERT L. R. *A Bibliography of the Works of Joseph Hergesheimer.* Philadelphia: The Centaur Book Shop, 1923, 39 pp.

TAYLOR, WALTER FULLER. *A History of American Letters,* with bibliographies by Harry Hartwick. Boston: American Book Co., 1936, 591–593.

Subsequent editions entitled: *The Story of American Letters.*

HERRICK, ROBERT

COOPER, FREDERIC TABER. *Some American Story Tellers,* 2nd edition. New York: H. Holt and Co., 1912, 369–370.

GERSTENBERGER, DONNA, and GEORGE HENDRICK. *The American Novel, 1789–1959: A Checklist of Twentieth Century Criticism.*

Denver: Alan Swallow, 1961, 129–130.

LEARY, LEWIS. *Articles on American Literature, 1900–1950.* Durham: Duke Univ. Press, 1954, 140–141.

HERSEY, JOHN

GERSTENBERGER, DONNA, and GEORGE HENDRICK. *The American Novel, 1789–1959: A Checklist of Twentieth Century Criticism.* Denver: Alan Swallow, 1961, 130.

LEARY, LEWIS. *Articles on American Literature, 1900–1950.* Durham: Duke Univ. Press, 1954, 141.

HEWLETT, MAURICE HENRY

SUTHERLAND, BRUCE. "A Bibliography of Maurice Henry Hewlett." *BB,* XV (May–August 1935), 126–129.

HEYWARD, DuBOSE

BLANCK, JACOB, ed. *Merle Johnson's American First Editions.* 4th edition, revised and enlarged. Waltham, Massachusetts: Mark Press, 1965, 250–251.

GERSTENBERGER, DONNA, and GEORGE HENDRICK. *The American Novel, 1789–1959: A Checklist of Twentieth Century Criticism.* Denver: Alan Swallow, 1961, 130–131.

LEARY, LEWIS. *Articles on American Literature, 1900–1950.* Durham: Duke Univ. Press, 1954, 141.

HICKS, GRANVILLE

LEARY, LEWIS. *Articles on American Literature, 1900–1950.* Durham: Duke Univ. Press, 1954, 141.

HILLYER, ROBERT

GERSTENBERGER, DONNA, and GEORGE HENDRICK. *The American Novel, 1789–1959: A Checklist of Twentieth Century Criticism.* Denver: Alan Swallow, 1961, 131.

LEARY, LEWIS. *Articles on American Literature, 1900–1950.* Durham: Duke Univ. Press, 1954, 142.

HORGAN, PAUL

LEARY, LEWIS. *Articles on American Literature, 1900–1950.* Durham: Duke Univ. Press, 1954, 144.

HOUGH, EMERSON

BLANCK, JACOB. *Bibliography of American Literature,* 5 Vols. New Haven: Yale Univ. Press, 1955–1969, IV, 345–355.

_____, ed. *Merle Johnson's American First Editions,* 4th edition, revised and enlarged. Waltham, Massachusetts: Mark Press, 1965, 263–265.

LEARY, LEWIS. *Articles on American Literature, 1900–1950.* Durham: Duke Univ. Press, 1954, 144.

HOWARD, SIDNEY

LEARY, LEWIS. *Articles on American Literature, 1900–1950.* Durham: Duke Univ. Press, 1954, 145.

HOWE, EDGAR WATSON

LEARY, LEWIS. *Articles on American Literature, 1900–1950.* Durham: Duke Univ. Press, 1954, 145.

HOWE, MARK ANTHONY De WOLFE

LEARY, LEWIS. *Articles on American*
can Literature, 1900–1950.* Durham: Duke Univ. Press, 1954, 145.

HUBBARD, FRANK McKINNEY

LEARY, LEWIS. *Articles on American Literature, 1900–1950.* Durham: Duke Univ. Press, 1954. 150.

HUDSON, WILLIAM HENRY

HILL, JAMES J., JR., and O. M. BRACK JR. "First Editions of William Henry Hudson." *LCUT,* VIII (Spring 1965), 45–46.

HUGHES, HATCHER

LEARY, LEWIS. *Articles on American Literature, 1900–1950.* Durham: Duke Univ. Press, 1954, 150.

HUGHES, LANGSTON

KAISER, ERNEST. "Selected Bibliography of the Published Writings of Langston Hughes." *Freedomways,* VIII (Spring 1968), 185–191.

LEARY, LEWIS. *Articles on American Literature, 1900–1950.* Durham: Duke Univ. Press, 1954, 150.

LIBRARY OF CONGRESS. GENERAL REFERENCE AND BIBLIOGRAPHY DIVISION. *Sixty American Poets, 1896–1944,* selected, with a preface and critical notes by Allen Tate and a preliminary checklist by Francis Cheney. Washington, 1945, 61–62.

Revised edition: 1954, 52–54.

MILLETT, FRED BENJAMIN. *Contemporary American Authors: A Critical Survey and 219 Bio-bibliographies.* New York: Harcourt, Brace and World, 1940. 403–404.

SPILLER, ROBERT ERNEST, et al. *Literary History of the United States,*

2 Vols. New York: Macmillan, 1962. 576–577. Supplement, 142.

HUNEKER, JAMES GIBBONS

BLANCK, JACOB. *Bibliography of American Literature*, 5 Vols. New Haven: Yale Univ. Press, 1955–1969, IV, 449–458.

_____, ed. *Merle Johnson's American First Editions*, 4th edition, revised and enlarged. Waltham, Massachusetts: Mark Press, 1965, 274–275.

DE CASSERES, BENJAMIN. *James Gibbons Huneker.* New York: Joseph Lawren, 1925, 41–62.

"James Gibbons Huneker: A Bibliography," by Joseph Lawren.

GERSTENBERGER, DONNA, and GEORGE HENDRICK. *The American Novel, 1789–1959: A Checklist of Twentieth Century Criticism.* Denver: Alan Swallow, 1961, 140.

LEARY, LEWIS. *Articles on American Literature, 1900–1950.* Durham: Duke Univ. Press, 1954, 150.

SPILLER, ROBERT ERNEST, et al. *Literary History of the United States,* 2 Vols. New York: Macmillan, 1962, 577–578. Supplement, 143.

HURST, FANNIE

GERSTENBERGER, DONNA and GEORGE HENDRICK. *The American Novel, 1789–1959: A Checklist of Twentieth Century Criticism.* Denver: Alan Swallow, 1961, 140.

LEARY, LEWIS. *Articles on American Literature, 1900–1950.* Durham: Duke Univ. Press, 1954, 150–151.

HURSTON, ZORA NEALE

LEARY, LEWIS. *Articles on American Literature, 1900–1950.* Durham: Duke Univ. Press, 1954, 151.

IDELL, ALBERT EDWARD

LEARY, LEWIS. *Articles on American Literature, 1900–1950.* Durham: Duke Univ. Press, 1954, 151.

INGE, WILLIAM

WOODRESS, JAMES, et al. *American Literary Scholarship: An Annual.* Durham: Duke Univ. Press, (1965), 243–244.

JACKSON, SHIRLEY

PHILLIPS, ROBERT S. "Shirley Jackson: A Checklist." *PBSA,* LVI (1st Quart. 1962), 110–113.

PHILLIPS, ROBERT S. "Shirley Jackson: A Chronology and a Supplementary Checklist." *PBSA,* LX (2nd Quart. 1966), 203–213.

JAMES, WILL

AMARAL, ANTHONY A. *Will James, the Gilt Edged Cowboy.* Los Angeles: Westernlore Press, 1967, 189–201.

BLANCK, JACOB, ed. *Merle Johnson's American First Editions,* 4th edition, revised and enlarged. Waltham, Massachusetts: Mark Press, 1965, 287–288.

JANVIER, THOMAS ALLIBONE

BLANCK, JACOB. *Bibliography of American Literature,* 5 Vols. New Haven: Yale Univ. Press, 1955–1969, V, 182–188.

_____, ed. *Merle Johnson's American First Editions,* 4th edition, revised and enlarged. Waltham, Massachusetts: Mark Press, 1965, 289–290.

LEARY, LEWIS. *Articles on American Literature, 1900–1950.* Durham: Duke Univ. Press, 1954, 165.

JARRELL, RANDALL

ADAMS, CHARLES MARSHALL. *Randall Jarrell: A Bibliography.* Chapel Hill: Univ. of North Carolina Press, 1958, 72 pp.

_____. "A Supplement to *Randall Jarrell: A Bibliography.*" *Analects,* I (Spring 1961), 49–56.

LEARY, LEWIS. *Articles on American Literature, 1900–1950.* Durham: Duke Univ. Press, 1954, 165.

LIBRARY OF CONGRESS, GENERAL REFERENCE AND BIBLIOGRAPHY DIVISION. *Sixty American Poets, 1896–1944,* selected, with a preface and critical notes by Allen Tate and a preliminary checklist by Francis Cheney. Washington, 1945, 63.

Revised edition: 1954, 55.

JEFFERS, ROBINSON

ALABAMA, UNIVERSITY, LIBRARY. *The Robinson Jeffers Collection in the Rare Book Room, University of Alabama Library,* complied by Mrs. Sarah A Verner and Mrs. Catherine T. Jones. University: Univ. of Alabama Press, 1961, no pagination.

ALBERTS, SYDNEY SEYMOUR, comp. *Bibliography of the Works of Robinson Jeffers.* New York: Random House, 1933, 264 pp.

BLANCK, JACOB, ed. *Merle Johnson's American First Editions.* 4th edition, revised and enlarged. Waltham, Massachusetts: Mark Press, 1965, 291–293.

LEARY, LEWIS. *Articles on American Literature, 1900–1950.* Durham: Duke Univ. Press, 1954, 165–167.

LIBRARY OF CONGRESS, GENERAL REFERENCE AND BIBLIOGRAPHY DIVISION. *Sixty American Poets, 1896–1944,* selected, with a preface and critical notes by Allen Tate and a preliminary checklist by Francis Cheney. Washington, 1945, 64–68.

Revised edition: 1954, 55–59.

MILLETT, FRED BENJAMIN. *Contemporary American Authors: A Critical Survey and 219 Bio-bibliographies.* New York: Harcourt, Brace and World, 1940, 406–409.

OCCIDENTAL COLLEGE LIBRARY. *Robinson Jeffers at Occidental College: A Checklist of the Jeffers Collection in the Mary Norton Clapp Library,* prepared by Alice Gay. Los Angeles: Ward Ritchie Press, 1955, 23 pp.

SPILLER, ROBERT ERNEST, et al. *Literary History of the United States,* 2 Vols. New York: Macmillan, 1962, 593–595. Supplement, 149.

TAYLOR, WALTER FULLER. *A History of American Letters,* with bibliographies by Harry Hartwick. Boston: American Book Co., 1936, 598–599.

Subsequent editions entitled: *The Story of American Letters.*

VIRGINIA, UNIVERSITY, LI-
BRARY. *The Barrett Library:
Robinson Jeffers: A Checklist of
Printed and Manuscript Works . . .*,
compiled by Anita Rutman and Lucy
Clark, the manuscripts by Marjorie
Carver. Charlottesville: Univ. of
Virginia Press, 1960, 41 pp.

WHITE, WILLIAM. "Bibliographical
Notes: Robinson Jeffers." *PBSA*,
XXXIV (1940), 362–363.

WOODRESS, JAMES, et al. *American Literary Scholarship: An Annual.* Durham: Duke Univ. Press,
(1966), 196–198.

JOHNSON, JAMES WELDON

LEARY, LEWIS. *Articles on American Literature, 1900–1950.* Durham:
Duke Univ. Press, 1954, 170.

LIBRARY OF CONGRESS, GEN-
ERAL REFERENCE AND BIBLIOG-
RAPHY DIVISION. *Sixty American
Poets, 1896–1944,* selected, with a
preface and critical notes by Allen
Tate and a preliminary checklist by
Francis Cheney. Washington, 1945,
69–71.

Revised edition: 1954, 59–61.

JOHNSON, OWEN

LEARY, LEWIS. *Articles on American Literature, 1900–1950.* Durham:
Duke Univ. Press, 1954, 171.

JOHNSON, STANLEY

BRADBURY, JOHN M. *The Fugitives: A Critical Account.* Chapel
Hill: Univ. of North Carolina Press,
1958, 294.

JOHNSTON, MARY

BLANCK, JACOB, ed. *Merle Johnson's American First Editions,* 4th

revised and enlarged. Waltham, Massachusetts: Mark Press, 1965, 296–
297.

GERSTENBERGER, DONNA, and
GEORGE HENDRICK. *The American Novel, 1789–1959: A Checklist
of Twentieth Century Criticism.*
Denver: Alan Swallow, 1961, 165.

LEARY, LEWIS. *Articles on American Literature, 1900–1950.* Durham:
Duke Univ. Press, 1954, 171.

JONES, JAMES

GERSTENBERGER, DONNA and
GEORGE HENDRICK. *The American Novel, 1789–1959: A Checklist
of Twentieth Century Criticism.*
Denver: Alan Swallow, 1961, 165.

JONES, ROBERT EDMOND

LEARY, LEWIS. *Articles on American Literature, 1900–1950.* Durham:
Duke Univ. Press, 1954, 171.

JORDAN, DAVID STARR

LEARY, LEWIS. *Articles on American Literature, 1900–1950.* Durham:
Duke Univ. Press, 1954, 171.

KANTOR, MACKINLAY

GERSTENBERGER, DONNA, and
GEORGE HENDRICK. *The American Novel, 1789–1959: A Checklist
of Twentieth Century Criticism.*
Denver: Alan Swallow, 1961, 166.

LEARY, LEWIS. *Articles on American Literature, 1900–1950.* Durham:
Duke Univ. Press, 1954, 171.

KAUFMAN, GEORGE S.

LEARY, LEWIS. *Articles on American Literature, 1900–1950.* Durham:
Duke Univ. Press, 1954, 172.

KAZIN, ALFRED

LEARY, LEWIS. *Articles on American Literature, 1900–1950.* Durham: Duke Univ. Press, 1954, 172.

KELLY, GEORGE

LEARY, LEWIS. *Articles on American Literature, 1900–1950.* Durham: Duke Univ. Press, 1954, 172.

KENT, ROCKWELL

BLANCK, JACOB, ed. *Merle Johnson's American First Editions,* 4th edition, revised and enlarged. Waltham, Massachusetts: Mark Press, 1965, 300–303.

KEROUAC, JACK (JEAN LOUIS LEBRIS DE KEROUAC)

CHARTERS, ANN. *A Bibliography of Works by Jack Kerouac (Jean Louis Lebris De Kerouac) 1939– 1967.* New York: Phoenix Book Shop, 1967, 99 pp.

GERSTENBERGER, DONNA, and GEORGE HENDRICK. *The American Novel, 1789–1959: A Checklist of Twentieth Century Criticism.* Denver: Alan Swallow, 1961, 166–167.

KEYES, FRANCES PARKINSON

LEARY, LEWIS. *Articles on American Literature, 1900–1950.* Durham: Duke Univ. Press, 1954, 173.

KILMER, JOYCE

BLANCK, JACOB. *Bibliography of American Literature,* 5 Vols. New Haven: Yale Univ. Press, 1955–1969, V, 252–259.

––––––––––––, ed. *Merle Johnson's American First Editions.* 4th edition, revised and enlarged. Waltham, Mas-

sachusetts: Mark Press, 1965, 304–305.

LEARY, LEWIS. *Articles on American Literature, 1900–1950.* Durham: Duke Univ. Press, 1954, 173.

KING, GRACE ELIZABETH

BEER, WILLIAM. "List of Writings of Grace King." *Louisiana Historical Quarterly,* VI (July 1923), 378–379.

LEARY, LEWIS. *Articles on American Literature, 1900–1950.* Durham: Duke Univ. Press, 1954, 173.

PAINE, GREGORY LANSING, ed. *Southern Prose Writers: Representative Selections,* with introduction, bibliography and notes. New York: American Book Co., 1947, cxxxiv– cxxxv.

TRENT, WILLIAM PETERFIELD, et al. *Cambridge History of American Literature,* 4 Vols. New York: G. P. Putnam's Sons, 1917–1921, II, 627.

VAUGHAN, BESS. "A Bio-Bibliography of Grace Elizabeth King." *Louisiana Historical Quarterly,* XVII (October 1934), 725–770.

KING, JUDSON

LIBRARY OF CONGRESS, MANUSCRIPT DIVISION. *Judson King: A Register of His Papers in the Library of Congress.* Washington, 1960, 10 leaves.

KINSELLA, THOMAS

"Books by Thomas Kinsella." *HC,* V (October 1968), 8–9.

KIRKLAND, JACK

LEARY, LEWIS. *Articles on American Literature, 1900–1950.* Durham: Duke Univ. Press, 1954, 173.

KLAEBER, FREDERICK

EINARSSON, STEFAN. "A Bibliography of the Works of Frederick Klaeber," in *Studies in English Philology: A Miscellany in Honor of Frederick Klaeber*. Minneapolis: Univ. of Minnesota Press, 1929, 477–485.

KRAPP, GEORGE PHILIP

DOBBIE, ELLIOTT V. K. "Addenda to the Bibliography of the Writings of George Philip Krapp." *AS*, X (April 1935), 106.

—————. "Bibliography of the Writings of George Philip Krapp." *AS*, IX (December 1934), 252–254.

KREYMBORG, ALFRED

LEARY, LEWIS. *Articles on American Literature, 1900–1950*. Durham: Duke Univ. Press, 1954, 173.

LIBRARY OF CONGRESS, GENERAL REFERENCE AND BIBLIOGRAPHY DIVISION. *Sixty American Poets, 1896–1944*, selected, with a preface and critical notes by Allen Tate and a preliminary checklist by Francis Cheney. Washington, 1945, 72–76.

Revised edition: 1954, 61–64.

KROUT, CAROLINE VIRGINIA

RUSSO, DOROTHY RITTER, and THELMA LOIS SULLIVAN. *Bibliographical Studies of Seven Authors of Crawfordsville, Indiana: Lew and Susan Wallace, Maurice and Will Thompson, Mary Hannah and Caroline Virginia Krout, and Meredith Nicholson*. Indianapolis: Indiana Historical Society, 1952, 1–12.

KROUT, MARY HANNAH

RUSSO, DOROTHY RITTER, and

THELMA LOIS SULLIVAN. *Bibliographical Studies of Seven Authors of Crawfordsville, Indiana: Lew and Susan Wallace, Maurice and Will Thompson, Mary Hannah and Caroline Virginia Krout, and Meredith Nicholson*. Indianapolis: Indiana Historical Society, 1952, 13–68.

KRUTCH, JOSEPH WOOD

LEARY, LEWIS. *Articles on American Literature, 1900–1950*. Durham: Duke Univ. Press, 1954, 173–174.

KYNE, PETER B.

GERSTENBERGER, DONNA, and GEORGE HENDRICK. *The American Novel, 1789–1959: A Checklist of Twentieth Century Criticism*. Denver: Alan Swallow, 1961, 168.

LEARY, LEWIS. *Articles on American Literature, 1900–1950*. Durham: Duke Univ. Press, 1954, 174.

LA FARGE, OLIVER

GERSTENBERGER, DONNA, and GEORGE HENDRICK. *The American Novel, 1789–1959: A Checklist of Twentieth Century Criticism*. Denver: Alan Swallow, 1961, 168.

LEARY, LEWIS. *Articles on American Literature, 1900–1950*. Durham: Duke Univ. Press, 1954, 174.

LAMB, HAROLD

LEARY, LEWIS. *Articles on American Literature, 1900–1950*. Durham: Duke Univ. Press, 1954, 174.

LAND, EMORY SCOTT

LIBRARY OF CONGRESS, MANUSCRIPT DIVISION. *Emory Scott Land: A Register of His Papers in the Library of Congress*. Washington, 1958, 7 leaves.

LANGLEY, ADRIA LOCKE

GERSTENBERGER, DONNA, and
GEORGE HENDRICK. *The American Novel, 1789–1959: A Checklist
of Twentieth Century Criticism.*
Denver: Alan Swallow, 1961, 168.

LANGMUIR, IRVING

LIBRARY OF CONGRESS, MANU-
SCRIPT DIVISION. *Irving Langmuir:
A Register of His Papers in the Library of Congress.* Washington,
1962, 9 leaves.

LARDNER, RING

BLANCK, JACOB, ed. *Merle Johnson's American First Editions,* 4th
edition, revised and enlarged. Waltham, Massachusetts: Mark Press,
1965, 309–310.

GOLDSMITH, ROBERT H. "Ring
W. Lardner: A Checklist of His Published Work." *BB,* XXI (December
1954), 104–106.

LEARY, LEWIS. *Articles on American Literature, 1900–1950.* Durham:
Duke Univ. Press, 1954, 177–178.

MILLETT, FRED BENJAMIN. *Contemporary American Authors: A Critical Survey and 219 Bio-bibliographies.* New York: Harcourt, Brace
and World, 1940, 429–431.

SPILLER, ROBERT ERNEST, et al.
Literary History of the United States,
2 Vols. New York: Macmillan, 1962,
608–609. Supplement, 154.

LAWRENCE, JOSEPHINE

LEARY, LEWIS. *Articles on American Literature, 1900–1950.* Durham:
Duke Univ. Press, 1954, 178.

LAWSON, JOHN HOWARD

BRUNING, BERNHARD. "Eine
erste Bibliographie der bisher
erschienenen Werke John Howard
Lawson." *ZAA,* IV (November 17,
1956), 125–130.

HUBBELL, JAY B. *The South in
American Literature, 1607–1900.*
Durham: Duke Univ. Press, 1954,
944.

LEA, TOM

GERSTENBERGER, DONNA, and
GEORGE HENDRICK. *The American Novel, 1789–1959: A Checklist
of Twentieth Century Criticism.*
Denver: Alan Swallow, 1961, 168.

LEONARD, WILLIAM ELLERY

LEARY, LEWIS, *Articles on American Literature, 1900–1950.* Durham:
Duke Univ. Press, 1954, 179.

LIBRARY OF CONGRESS, GEN-
ERAL REFERENCE AND BIBLIOG-
RAPHY DIVISION. *Sixty American
Poets, 1896–1944,* selected, with a
preface and critical notes by Allen
Tate and a preliminary checklist by
Francis Cheney. Washington, 1945,
77–80.

Revised edition: 1954, 64–67.

LERNER, ALAN JAY

LEARY, LEWIS. *Articles on American Literature, 1900–1950.* Durham:
Duke Univ. Press, 1954, 179.

LEWIS, JAMES FRANKLIN

LEARY, LEWIS. *Articles on American Literature, 1900–1950.* Durham:
Duke Univ. Press, 1954, 179.

LEWIS, JANET

GERSTENBERGER, DONNA, and

GEORGE HENDRICK. *The American Novel, 1789–1959: A Checklist of Twentieth Century Criticism.* Denver: Alan Swallow, 1961, 168.

LEWIS, SINCLAIR

ANDERSON, CARL L. *The Swedish Acceptance of American Literature.* Philadelphia: Univ. of Pennsylvania Press, 1957, 103–152.

BLANCK, JACOB, ed. *Merle Johnson's American First Editions,* 4th edition, revised and enlarged. Waltham, Massachusetts: Mark Press, 1965, 311–314.

GERSTENBERGER, DONNA, and GEORGE HENDRICK. *The American Novel, 1789–1959: A Checklist of Twentieth Century Criticism.* Denver: Alan Swallow, 1961, 169–173.

GOFF, FREDERICK R. "The Hersholt Gift of Works of Hugh Walpole and Sinclair Lewis." *LCQJ,* XI (August 1954), 195–198.

LEARY, LEWIS. *Articles on American Literature, 1900–1950.* Durham: Duke Univ. Press, 1954, 180–182.

MILLETT, FRED BENJAMIN. *Contemporary American Authors: A Critical Survey and 219 Bio-bibliographies.* New York: Harcourt, Brace and World, 1940, 436–441.

SCHORER, MARK, ed. *Sinclair Lewis: A Collection of Critical Essays.* Englewood Cliffs, New Jersey: Prentice Hall, 1962, 173–174.

SPAYD, BARBARA GRACE, ed. *Arrowsmith.* New York: Harcourt, Brace and Co., 1946, 465–466, 484–486.

SPILLER, ROBERT ERNEST, et al. *Literary History of the United States,*

2 Vols. New York: Macmillan, 1962, 609–611. Supplement, 154–155.

TAYLOR, WALTER FULLER. *A History of American Letters,* with bibliographies by Harry Hartwick. Boston: American Book Co., 1936, 578–580.

Subsequent editions entitled: *The Story of American Letters.*

TEXAS, UNIVERSITY, HUMANITIES RESEARCH CENTER. *Sinclair Lewis: An Exhibition from the Grace Hegger Lewis-Sinclair Lewis Collection,* prepared by F. W. Roberts. Austin: Humanities Research Center, 1960, 28 pp.

VAN DOREN, CARL. *Sinclair Lewis: A Biographical Sketch,* with a bibliography by Harvey Taylor. Garden City: Doubleday, Doran and Co., 1933, 77–187.

WOODRESS, JAMES, et al. *American Literary Scholarship: An Annual.* Durham: Duke Univ. Press, (1965), 169–172; (1966), 158–161.

LEWISOHN, LUDWIG

GERSTENBERGER, DONNA, and GEORGE HENDRICK. *The American Novel, 1789–1959: A Checklist of Twentieth Century Criticism.* Denver: Alan Swallow, 1961, 173–174.

LEARY, LEWIS. *Articles on American Literature, 1900–1950.* Durham: Duke Univ. Press, 1954, 182.

MILLETT, FRED BENJAMIN. *Contemporary American Authors: A Critical Survey and 219 Bio-bibliographies.* New York: Hartcourt, Brace and World, 1940, 441–444.

SPILLER, ROBERT ERNEST, et al. *Literary History of the United States,*

2 Vols. New York: Macmillan, 1962, 612—613. Supplement, 156.

LIBBEY, LAURA JEAN

LEARY, LEWIS. *Articles on American Literature, 1900—1950.* Durham: Duke Univ. Press, 1954, 182.

LIDDELL, MARK H.

LEARY, LEWIS. *Articles on American Literature, 1900—1950.* Durham: Duke Univ. Press, 1954, 182.

LINDERMAN, FRANK BIRD

LEARY, LEWIS. *Articles on American Literature, 1900—1950.* Durham: Duke Univ. Press, 1954, 184.

LINDSAY, HOWARD

LEARY, LEWIS. *Articles on American Literature, 1900—1950.* Durham: Duke Univ. Press, 1954, 184.

LINDSAY, VACHEL

BLANCK, JACOB, ed. *Merle Johnson's American First Editions,* 4th edition, revised and enlarged. Waltham, Massachusetts: Mark Press, 1965, 315—317.

BYRD, CECIL K. "Check List of the Melcher Lindsay Collection." *IUB,* V (December 1960), 64—106.

CLARK, HARRY HAYDEN, ed. *Major American Poets.* New York: American Book Co., 1936, 929—931.

DARTMOUTH COLLEGE LIBRARY. *The George Matthew Adams—Vachel Lindsay Collection: A Note and Descriptive List,* by Herbert F. West. Hanover, New Hampshire: Dartmouth College Library, 1945, 11 pp.

LEARY, LEWIS. *Articles on American Literature, 1900—1950.* Durham: Duke Univ. Press, 1954, 184—186.

LIBRARY OF CONGRESS, GENERAL REFERENCE AND BIBLIOGRAPHY DIVISION. *Sixty American Poets, 1896—1944,* selected, with a preface and critical notes by Allen Tate and a preliminary checklist by Francis Cheney. Washington, 1945, 81—84.

Revised edition: 1954, 67—70.

MILLETT, FRED BENJAMIN. *Contemporary American Authors: A Critical Survey and 219 Bio-bibliographies.* New York: Harcourt, Brace and World, 1940, 445—449.

REED, DORIS M. "Letters of Vachel Lindsay in the Lilly Library at Indiana University." *IUB,* V (December 1960), 21—63.

SPILLER, ROBERT ERNEST, et al. *Literary History of the United States,* 2 Vols. New York: Macmillan, 1962, 616—618. Supplement, 159.

TAYLOR, WALTER FULLER. *A History of American Letters,* with bibliographies by Harry Hartwick. Boston: American Book Co., 1936, 583—584.

Subsequent editions entitled: *The Story of American Letters.*

WOODRESS, JAMES, et al. *American Literary Scholarship: An Annual.* Durham: Duke Univ. Press, (1963), 180—182.

LOCKRIDGE, ROSS, JR.

GERSTENBERGER, DONNA, and GEORGE HENDRICK. *The American Novel, 1789—1959: A Checklist of Twentieth Century Criticism.* Denver: Alan Swallow, 1961, 174.

LOENING, GROVER CLEVELAND

LIBRARY OF CONGRESS, MANU-SCRIPT DIVISION. *Grover C. Loening: A Register of His Papers in the Library of Congress.* Washington, 1959, 9 leaves.

LOMAX, JOHN

LEARY, LEWIS. *Articles on American Literature, 1900–1950.* Durham: Duke Univ. Press, 1954, 186.

LONDON, JACK

ANDERSON, CARL L. *The Swedish Acceptance of American Literature.* Philadelphia: Univ. of Pennsylvania Press, 1957, 103–152.

BLANCK, JACOB. *Bibliography of American Literature,* 5 Vols. New Haven: Yale Univ. Press, 1955–1969, V, 431–467.

——————, ed *Merle Johnson's American First Editions,* 4th edition, revised and enlarged. Waltham, Massachusetts: Mark Press, 1965, 318–322.

CHOMET, OTTO. "Jack London: Works, Reviews, and Criticism Published in German." *BB,* XIX (January–April 1949), 211–215; (May–August 1949), 239–240.

FONER, PHILIP SHELDON, ed. *Jack London, American Rebel: A Collection of His Social Writings together with an Extensive Study of the Man and His Times.* New York: Citadel Press, 1947, 531–533.

GAER, JOSEPH, ed. *Jack London: Bibliography and Biographical Data.* N.p., 1934, 37 leaves.

California Literary Research Project Monograph, No. 1

GERSTENBERGER, DONNA, and GEORGE HENDRICK. *The American Novel, 1789–1959: A Checklist of Twentieth Century Criticism.* Denver: Alan Swallow, 1961, 174–176.

HYDOCK, JAMES. "Jack London: A Bibliography of Criticism." *BB,* XXIII (May–August 1960), 42–46.

LEARY, LEWIS. *Articles on American Literature, 1900–1950.* Durham: Duke Univ. Press, 1954, 186–188.

LONDON, CHARMIAN. *The Book of Jack London,* 2 Vols. New York: Century Co., 1921, II, 397–414.

MILLS, GORDON H. "American First Editions at TxU: Jack London (1876–1916)." *LCUT,* IV (Fall 1952), 189–192.

MURPHY, CELESTE G. "Library Collected by Jack London." *Overland Monthly,* XC (May 1932), 111–112.

ROMM, CHARLES. "Jack London: A Bibliographical Checklist, 1876–1916." *PW,* CII (February 4, 1923), 1,021.

SPILLER, ROBERT ERNEST, et al. *Literary History of the United States,* 2 Vols. New York: Macmillan, 1962, 619–622. Supplement, 159–160.

TAYLOR, WALTER FULLER. *A History of American Letters,* with bibliographies by Harry Hartwick. Boston: American Book Co., 1936, 565–567.

Subsequent editions entitled: *The Story of American Letters.*

TRENT, WILLIAM PETERFIELD, et al. *Cambridge History of American Literature,* 4 Vols. New York: G. P. Putnam's Sons, 1917–1921, II, 627.

WOODBRIDGE, HENSLEY CHARLES, JOHN LONDON and GEORGE H. TWENEY. *Jack London: A Bibliography.* Georgetown, California: Talisman Press, 1966, 422 pp.

WOODRESS, JAMES, et al. *American Literary Scholarship: An Annual.* Durham: Duke Univ. Press, (1965), 174–176; (1966), 155-158.

LOOMIS, EDWARD

GERSTENBERGER, DONNA, and GEORGE HENDRICK. *The American Novel, 1789–1959: A Checklist of Twentieth Century Criticism.* Denver: Alan Swallow, 1961, 177.

LOWELL, AMY

BLANCK, JACOB, ed. *Merle Johnson's American First Editions,* 4th edition, revised and enlarged. Waltham, Massachusetts: Mark Press, 1965, 330–331.

DAMON, SAMUEL FOSTER. *Amy Lowell: A Chronicle, with Extracts from Her Correspondence.* Boston: Houghton Mifflin Co., 1935, 729–742.

KEMP, FRANCES, comp. "Bibliography of Amy Lowell." *BB,* XV (May–August 1933), 8–9; (September–December 1933), 25–26; (January–April 1934), 50–53.

LEARY, LEWIS. *Articles on American Literature, 1900–1950.* Durham: Duke Univ. Press, 1954, 192–194.

LIBRARY OF CONGRESS, GENERAL REFERENCE AND BIBLIOGRAPHY DIVISION. *Sixty American Poets, 1896–1944,* selected, with a preface and critical notes by Allen Tate and a preliminary checklist by Francis Cheney. Washington, 1945, 85–88.

Revised edition: 1954, 71–73.

MILLETT, FRED BENJAMIN. *Contemporary American Authors: A Critical Survey and 219 Bio-bibliographies.* New York: Harcourt, Brace and World, 1940, 452–457.

SPILLER, ROBERT ERNEST, et al. *Literary History of the United States,* New York: Macmillan, 1962, 626–628. Supplement, 161.

TAYLOR, WALTER FULLER. *A History of American Letters,* with bibliographies by Harry Hartwick. Boston: American Book Co., 1936, 580–581.

Subsequent editions entitled: *The Story of American Letters.*

LOWELL, ROBERT

BURNS, MILDRED BLAIR. "Books by Robert Lowell." *HC,* IV (February 1967), 8–9.

LEARY, LEWIS, *Articles on American Literature, 1900–1950.* Durham: Duke Univ. Press, 1954, 197.

WOODRESS, JAMES, et al. *American Literary Scholarship: An Annual.* Durham: Duke Univ. Press, (1963), 196–197; (1964), 211–212.

LYTLE, ANDREW NELSON

BRADBURY, JOHN M. *The Fugitives: A Critical Account.* Chapel Hill: Univ. of North Carolina Press, 1958, 293.

DEBELLIS, JACK, comp. "An Andrew Nelson Lytle Check List." *Bibliographical Society of the University of Virginia, Secretary's News Sheet No. 46 (June 1960), 3–15.*

GERSTENBERGER, DONNA, and GEORGE HENDRICK. *The Ameri-*

can Novel, 1789–1959: A Checklist of Twentieth Century Criticism. Denver: Alan Swallow, 1961, 177.

MABIE, HAMILTON WRIGHT

LEARY, LEWIS. Articles on American Literature, 1900–1950. Durham: Duke Univ. Press, 1954, 197.

McADOO, WILLIAM GIBBS

LIBRARY OF CONGRESS, MANU-SCRIPT DIVISION. William Gibbs McAdoo: A Register of His Papers in the Library of Congress. Washington, 1959, 35 p.p.

MACAULEY, ROBIE

GERSTENBERGER, DONNA, and GEORGE HENDRICK. The American Novel, 1789–1959: A Checklist of Twentieth Century Criticism. Denver: Alan Swallow, 1961, 177.

McCARTHY, MARY

GERSTENBERGER, DONNA, and GEORGE HENDRICK. The American Novel, 1789–1959: A Checklist of Twentieth Century Criticism. Denver: Alan Swallow, 1961, 180–181.

McCLURE, MICHAEL

KHERDIAN, DAVID. Six Poets of the San Francisco Renaissance. Fresno, California: The Giligia Press, 1965, 115-129.

McCLURE, S. S.

LYON, PETER. Success Story: The Life and Times of S. S. McClure. New New York: Scribner, 1963, 413–422.

McCULLERS, CARSON

LEARY, LEWIS. Articles on Ameri-

can Literature, 1900–1950. Durham: Duke Univ. Press, 1954, 197.

STEWART, STANLEY. "Carson Mc-Cullers, 1940–1956: A Selected Checklist." BB, XXII (January–April 1959), 182–185.

WOODRESS, JAMES, et al. American Literary Scholarship: An Annual. Durham: Duke Univ. Press, (1965), 190; (1966), 175–176.

McCUTCHEON, GEORGE BARR

BLANCK, JACOB, ed. Merle Johnson's American First Editions, 4th edition, revised and enlarged. Waltham, Massachusetts: Mark Press, 1965, 337–339.

McFEE, WILLIAM

BABB, JAMES TINKHAM. A Bibliography of the Writings of William McFee. New York: Doubleday, Doran and Co., 1931, 141 pp.

360 copies printed.

BLANCK, JACOB, ed. Merle Johnson's American First Edition, 4th edition, revised and enlarged. Waltham, Massachusetts: Mark Press, 1965, 340–343.

LEARY, LEWIS. Articles on American Literature, 1900–1950. Durham: Duke Univ. Press, 1954, 197.

McGIRT, JAMES EPHRAIM

PARKER, J. W. "James Ephraim McGirt: Poet of 'Hope Deferred.'" NCHR, XXXI (July 1954), 321–335.

McKAY, CLAUDE

LEARY, LEWIS. Articles on American Literature, 1900–1950. Durham: Duke Univ. Press, 1954, 197.

McKINLEY, CARLYLE

TRENT, WILLIAM PETERFIELD, et al. *Cambridge History of American Literature,* 4 Vols. New York: G. P. Putnam's Sons, 1917–1921, II 603.

MacLEISH, ARCHIBALD

BLANCK, JACOB, ed. *Merle Johnson's American First Editions,* 4th edition, revised and enlarged. Watham, Massachusetts: Mark Press, 1965, 344–346.

LEARY, LEWIS. *Articles on American Literature, 1900–1950.* Durham: Duke Univ. Press, 1954, 198–199.

LIBRARY OF CONGRESS, DIVISION OF BIBLIOGRAPHY. *Writings of Archibald MacLeish (Supplementing "A Catalogue of the First Editions of Archibald MacLeish," by Arthur Mizener, 1938),* complied by Florence S. Hellman. Washington, 1942, 19 leaves.

Supplementary List: 1944, 11 leaves.

LIBRARY OF CONGRESS, GENERAL REFERENCE AND BIBLIOGRAPHY DIVISION. *Archibald MacLeish: Writings in Anthologies.* Washington, 1944, 10 leaves.

——————. *Sixty American Poets, 1896–1944,* selected, with a preface and critical notes by Allen Tate and a preliminary checklist by Francis Cheney. Washington, 1945, 89–97.

Revised edition: 1954, 73–80.

MELCHER, F. G. "Check List of Archibald MacLeish." *PW,* CXXIV (July 15, 1933), 180.

MIZENER, ARTHUR. *Catalogue of the First Editions of Archibald Mac-*

Leish. New Haven: Yale Univ. Library, 1938, 30 pp.

SPILLER, ROBERT ERNEST, et al. *Literary History of the United States,* 2 Vols. New York: Macmillan, 1962, 634–636. Supplement, 162–163.

THURBER, GERRISH. "MacLeish Published Books." *LJ,* LXIV (November 1, 1939), 864–866.

WOODRESS, JAMES, et al. *American Literary Scholarship: An Annual.* Durham: Duke Univ. Press, (1963), 180–183; (1965), 217–219; (1966), 203–204.

MacLEOD, NORMAN

LIBRARY OF CONGRESS, GENERAL REFERENCE AND BIBLIOGRAPHY DIVISION. *Sixty American Poets, 1896–1944,* selected, with a preface and critical notes by Allen Tate and a preliminary checklist by Francis Cheney. Washington, 1945, 98.

Revised edition: 1954, 80–81.

McMASTER, JOHN BACH

LEARY, LEWIS. *Articles on American Literature, 1900–1950.* Durham: Duke Univ. Press, 1954, 199.

MacNEICE, LOUIS

LEARY, LEWIS. *Articles on American Literature, 1900–1950.* Durham: Duke Univ. Press, 1954, 199.

MAILER, NORMAN

THE EDITORS. "Books by Norman Mailer." *HC,* II (June 1965), 7.

GERSTENBERGER, DONNA, and GEORGE HENDRICK. *The American Novel, 1789–1959: A Checklist of Twentieth Century Criticism.*

Denver: Alan Swallow, 1961, 177–178.

HARPER, HOWARD M., JR. *Desperate Faith: A Study of Bellow, Salinger, Mailer, Baldwin, and Updike.* Chapel Hill: Univ. of North Carolina Press, 1967, bibliographical footnotes.

LEARY, LEWIS. *Articles on American Literature, 1900–1950.* Durham: Duke Univ. Press, 1954, 199.

MAJOR, CHARLES

HEPBURN, WILLIAM MURRAY. "The Charles Major Manuscripts in the Purdue University Libraries." *Indiana Quarterly for Bookmen,* II (July 1946), 71–81.

LEARY, LEWIS. *Articles on American Literature, 1900–1950.* Durham: Duke Univ. Press, 1954, 199.

MALAMUD, BERNARD

WOODRESS, JAMES, et al. *American Literary Scholarship: An Annual.* Durham: Duke Univ. Press, (1964), 162–163; (1965), 189–190; (1966), 174–175.

MANFRED, FREDERICK, (FEIKE FEIKEMA)

GERSTENBERGER, DONNA, and GEORGE HENDRICK. *The American Novel, 1789–1959: A Checklist of Twentieth Century Criticism.* Denver: Alan Swallow, 1961, 178.

KELLOGG, GEORGE ALEXIS. "Frederick Manfred: A Bibliography." *TCL,* XI (April 1965), 30–35.

MARCH, WILLIAM

GERSTENBERGER, DONNA, and GEORGE HENDRICK. *The Ameri-*

can Novel, 1789–1959: A Checklist of Twentieth Century Criticism. Denver: Alan Swallow, 1961, 178.

LEARY, LEWIS. *Articles on American Literature, 1900–1950.* Durham: Duke Univ. Press, 1954, 199.

MARKHAM, EDWIN

BLANCK, JACOB, ed. *Merle Johnson's American First Editions,* 4th edition, revised and enlarged. Waltham, Massachusetts: Mark Press, 1965, 347–348.

LEARY, LEWIS. *Articles on American Literature, 1900–1950.* Durham: Duke Univ. Press, 1954, 199–200.

WOODRESS, JAMES, et al. *American Literary Scholarship: An Annual.* Durham: Duke Univ. Press, (1963), 180–182; (1966), 196–198.

MARQUAND, JOHN P.

GERSTENBERGER, DONNA, and GEORGE HENDRICK. *The American Novel, 1789–1959: A Checklist of Twentieth Century Criticism.* Denver: Alan Swallow, 1961, 178–180.

LEARY, LEWIS. *Articles on American Literature, 1900–1950.* Durham: Duke Univ. Press, 1954, 200.

WHITE, WILLIAM. "John P. Marquand: A Preliminary Checklist." *BB,* XIX (September–December 1949), 268–271.

——————— . "John P. Marquand since 1950." *BB,* XXI (May–August 1956), 230–234.

——————— . "Marquandiana." *BB,* XX (January–April 1950), 8–12.

MARQUIS, DON

BLANCK, JACOB, ed. *Merle Johnson's American First Editions,* 4th edition, revised and enlarged. Waltham, Massachusetts: Mark Press, 1965, 349–351.

LEARY, LEWIS. *Articles on American Literature, 1900–1950.* Durham: Duke Univ. Press, 1954, 201.

MASTERS, EDGAR LEE

BLANCK, JACOB, ed. *Merle Johnson's American First Editions,* 4th edition, revised and enlarged. Waltham, Massachusetts: Mark Press, 1965, 352–354.

GERSTENBERGER, DONNA, and GEORGE HENDRICK. *The American Novel, 1789–1959: A Checklist of Twentieth Century Cirticism.* Denver: Alan Swallow, 1961, 180.

LEARY, LEWIS. *Articles on American Literature, 1900–1950.* Durham: Duke Univ. Press, 1954, 201–202.

LIBRARY OF CONGRESS, GENERAL REFERENCE AND BIBLIOGRAPHY DIVISION. *Sixty American Poets, 1896–1944,* selected, with a preface and critical notes by Allen Tate and a preliminary checklist by Francis Cheney. Washington, 1945, 99–103.

Revised edition: 1954, 81–85.

MILLETT, FRED BENJAMIN. *Contemproary American Authors: A Critical Survey and 219 Bio-bibliographies.* New York: Harcourt, Brace and World, 1940, 476–480.

SPILLER, ROBERT ERNEST, et al. *Literary History of the United States,* 2 Vols. New York: Macmillan, 1962, 638–640. Supplement, 163.

TAYLOR, WALTER FULLER. *A History of American Letters,* with bibliographies by Harry Hartwick. Boston: American Book Co., 1936, 584–585.

Subsequent editions entitled: *The Story of American Letters.*

WOODRESS, JAMES, et al. *American Literary Scholarship: An Annual.* Durham: Duke Univ. Press, (1963), 180–182; (1964), 192–194; (1965), 217–219; (1966), 196–199.

MATTHEWS, BRANDER

HOWSON, ROGER, comp. *The Bookshelf of Brander Matthews.* New York: Columbia Univ. Press, 1931, 131. pp.

MATTHIESSEN, F. O.

LEARY, LEWIS. *Articles on American Literature, 1900–1950.* Durham: Duke Univ. Press, 1954, 204.

LEARY, LEWIS. *Articles on American Literature, 1900–1950.* Durham: Duke Univ. Press, 1954, 204.

"Preliminary Bibliography." *Monthly Review,* II (November 1950), 316–322.

"A Supplementary Bibliography of F. O. Matthiessen." *Monthly Review,* IV (September 1952), 174–175.

MELTZER, DAVID

KHERDIAN, DAVID. *Six Poets of the San Francisco Renaissance.* Fresno, California: The Giligia Press, 1965, 99–106.

MENCKEN, HENRY LOUIS

ADLER, BETTY. "Bibliographic Check List." *Menckeniana,* I

(Spring 1962), 5–8; II (Summer 1962), 8–11; III (Fall 1962), 5–9; IV (Winter 1962), 7–10.

BLANCK, JACOB, ed. *Merle Johnson's American First Editions*, 4th edition, revised and enlarged. Waltham, Massachusetts: Mark Press, 1965, 358–361.

FREY, CARROLL. *A Bibliography of the Writings of H. L. Mencken.* Philadelphia: The Centaur Bookshop, 1924, 70 pp.

LEARY, LEWIS. *Articles on American Literature, 1900–1950.* Durham: Duke Univ. Press, 1954, 211–213.

MILLETT, FRED BENJAMIN. *Contemporary American Authors: A Critical Survey and 219 Bio-bibliographies.* New York: Harcourt, Brace and World, 1940, 480–486.

SPILLER, ROBERT ERNEST, et al. *Literary History of the United States,* 2 Vols. New York: Macmillan, 1962, 654–656. Supplement, 168–169.

SWAN, BRADFORD F. "Making a Mencken Collection." *YULG,* XXIV (January 1950), 101–113.

TAYLOR, WALTER FULLER. *A History of American Letters,* with bibliographies by Harry Hartwick. Boston: American Book Co., 1936, 577–578.

Subsequent editions entitled: *The Story of American Letters.*

MERRILL, STUART

LEARY, LEWIS. *Articles on American Literature, 1900–1950.* Durham: Duke Univ. Press, 1954, 213.

MERTON, THOMAS

DELL'ISOLLA, FRANK, comp. "A Bibliography of Thomas Merton." *Thought,* XXIX (Winter 1954–1955), 574–596.

LEARY, LEWIS. *Articles on American Literature, 1900–1950.* Durham: Duke Univ. Press, 1954, 213.

MERWIN, WILLIAM S.

"Books by William S. Merwin." *HC,* V (June 1968), 6–7.

MICHENER, JAMES

GERSTENBERGER, DONNA, and GEORGE HENDRICK. *The American Novel, 1789–1959: A Checklist of Twentieth Century Criticism.* Denver: Alan Swallow, 1961, 202.

MIDDLETON, GEORGE

LEARY, LEWIS. *Articles on American Literature, 1900–1950.* Durham: Duke Univ. Press, 1954, 213.

MILLAY, EDNA ST. VINCENT

BLANCK, JACOB, ed. *Merle Johnson's American First Editions,* 4th edition, revised and enlarged. Waltham, Massachusetts: Mark Press, 1965, 362–364.

BRITTIN, NORMAN A. *Edna St. Vincent Millay.* New York: Twayne, 1967, 180–187.

KOHN, JOHN S. VAN E. "Some Undergraduate Printings of Edna St. Vincent Millay. *PW,* CXXXVII (November 30, 1940), 2026–2029.

LEARY, LEWIS. *Articles on American Literature, 1900–1950.* Durham: Duke Univ. Press, 1954, 213–214.

LIBRARY OF CONGRESS, GENERAL REFERENCE AND BIBLIOGRAPHY DIVISION. *Sixty American Poets, 1896–1944,* selected, with a preface and critical notes by Allen Tate and a preliminary checklist by Francis Cheney. Washington, 1945, 104–109.

Revised edition: 1954, 85–89.

MESERVE, WALTER J. "Edna St. Vincent Millay." *Books and Libraries,* I (November 1955), 2–4.

MILLETT, FRED BENJAMIN. *Contemporary American Authors: A Critical Survey and 219 Bio-bibliographies.* New York: Harcourt, Brace and World, 1940, 487–491.

SPILLER, ROBERT ERNEST, et al. *Literary History of the Unites States,* 2 Vols. New York: Macmillan, 1962, 656–568. Supplement, 169–170.

TAYLOR, WALTER FULLER. *A History of American Letters,* with bibliographies by Harry Hartwick. Boston: American Book Co., 1936, 589.

Subsequent editions entitled: *The Story of American Letters.*

WOODRESS, JAMES, et al. *American Literary Scholarship: An Annual.* Durham: Duke Univ. Press, (1964), 192–194.

YOST, KARL. *A Bibliography of the Works of Edna St. Vincent Millay.* New York: Harper and Brothers, 1936, 255 pp.

MILLER, ARTHUR

EISSENSTAT, MARTHA T. "Arthur Miller: A Bibliography." *MD,* V (May 1962), 93–106.

LEARY, LEWIS. *Articles on American Literature, 1900–1950.* Durham: Duke Univ. Press, 1954, 214.

WIEGAND, WILLIAM. "Arthur Miller and the Man Who Knows." *WR,* XXI (Winter 1957), 85–103.

WOODRESS, JAMES, et al. *American Literary Scholarship: An Annual.* Durham: Duke Univ. Press, (1965), 243–244; (1966), 227.

MILLER, HENRY

GERSTENBERGER, DONNA, and GEORGE HENDRICK. *The American Novel, 1789–1959: A Checklist of Twentieth Century Criticism.* Denver: Alan Swallow, 1961, 202–204.

LEARY, LEWIS. *Articles on American Literature, 1900–1950.* Durham: Duke Univ. Press, 1954, 214–215.

MOORE, THOMAS HAMILTON, comp. *Bibliography: Henry Miller.* Minneapolis: Henry Miller Literary Society, 1961, 32 pp.

RENKEN, MAXINE. "Bibliography of Henry Miller, 1945–1961." *TCL,* VII (January 1962), 180–190.

Also: Denver: Alan Swallow, 1962, 13 pp.

RILEY, ESTA LOU. *Henry Miller: An Informal Bibliography, 1924–1960.* Hays: Fort Hays Kansas State College, 1961, 52 pp.

Fort Hays Studies, ns, Bibliography Series, No. 1.

WOODRESS, JAMES, et al. *American Literary Scholarship: An Annual.* Durham: Duke Univ. Press, (1965), 185–186; (1966), 176.

MILTON, GEORGE FORT

LIBRARY OF CONGRESS, MANUSCRIPT DIVISION. *George Fort Milton: A Register of His Papers in* the Library of Congress. Washington, 1958, 7 leaves.

MITCHELL, MARGARET

GERSTENBERGER, DONNA, and GEORGE HENDRICK. *The American Novel, 1789–1959: A Checklist of Twentieth Century Criticism.* Denver: Alan Swallow, 1961, 204.

LEARY, LEWIS. *Articles on American Literature, 1900–1950.* Durham: Duke Univ. Press, 1954, 216.

MONROE, HARRIET

LEARY, LEWIS. *Articles on American Literature, 1900–1950.* Durham: Duke Univ. Press, 1954, 216.

MONTAGUE, MARGARET P.

STEMPLE, RUTH M. "Margaret Prescott Montague, 1878–1955: A Check List." *BB,* XXII (May-August 1957), 62–64.

MOODY, WILLIAM VAUGHN

BLANCK, JACOB, ed. *Merle Johnson's American First Editions,* 4th edition, revised and enlarged. Waltham, Massachusetts: Mark Press, 1965, 376.

HENRY, DAVID D. *William Vaughn Moody: A Study.* Boston: B. Humphries, Inc., 1934, 263–272.

LEARY, LEWIS. *Articles on American Literature, 1900–1950.* Durham: Duke Univ. Press, 1954, 217.

MacKAYE, PERCY, ed. *Letters to Harriet.* Boston: Houghton Mifflin Co., 1935, 439–443.

SPILLER, ROBERT ERNEST, et al. *Literary History of the United States,* 2 Vols. New York: Macmillan, 1962, 660–662. Supplement, 170.

TAYLOR, WALTER FULLER. *A History of American Letters,* with bibliographies by Harry Hartwick. Boston: American Book Co., 1936. 555.

Subsequent editions entitled: *The Story of American Letters.*

TRENT, WILLIAM PETERFIELD, et al. *Cambridge History of American Literature,* 4 Vols. New York: G. P. Putnam's Sons, 1917–1921, IV, 650–651.

WOODRESS, JAMES, et al. *American Literary Scholarship: An Annual.* Durham: Duke Univ. Press, (1964), 192–194.

MOORE, JOHN TROTWOOD

LEARY, LEWIS. *Articles on American Literature, 1900–1950.* Durham: Duke Univ. Press, 1954, 217.

MOORE, MARIANNE

LEARY, LEWIS. *Articles on American Literature, 1900–1950.* Durham: Duke Univ. Press, 1954, 217–218.

LIBRARY OF CONGRESS, GENERAL REFERENCE AND BIBLIOGRAPHY DIVISION. *Sixty American Poets, 1896–1944,* selected, with a preface and critical notes by Allen Tate and a preliminary checklist by Francis Cheney. Washington, 1945, 110–111.

Revised edition: 1954, 89–91.

MILLETT, FRED BENJAMIN. *Contemporary American Authors: A Critical Survey and 219 Bio-bibliographies.* New York: Harcourt, Brace and World, 1940, 491–492.

SHEEHY, EUGENE P., and KENNETH A. LOHF, comps. "The Achievement of Marianne Moore: A

Bibliography." *BNYPL*, LXII (March 1958), 132–149; (April 1958), 183–190; (May 1958), 249–259.

SPILLER, ROBERT ERNEST, et al. *Literary History of the United States,* 2 Vols. New York: Macmillan, 1962. 662–663. Supplement, 170.

WOODRESS, JAMES, et al. *American Literary Scholarship: An Annual.* Durham: Duke Univ. Press, (1963), 193–194; (1964), 207–208.

MOORE, MERRILL

BRADBURY, JOHN M. *The Fugitives: A Critical Account.* Chapel Hill: Univ. of North Carolina Press, 1958, 291–292.

LEARY, LEWIS. *Articles on American Literature, 1900–1950.* Durham: Duke Univ. Press, 1954, 218.

LIBRARY OF CONGRESS, GENERAL REFERENCE AND BIBLIOGRAPHY DIVISION. *Sixty American Poets, 1896–1944,* selected, with a preface and critical notes by Allen Tate and a preliminary checklist by Francis Cheney. Washington, 1945, 112–113.

Revised edition: 1954, 91–92.

MORE, PAUL ELMER

LEARY, LEWIS. *Articles on American Literature, 1900–1950.* Durham: Duke Univ. Press, 1954, 218–219.

SPILLER, ROBERT ERNEST, et al. *Literary History of the United States,* 2 Vols. New York: Macmillan, 1962, 663–664. Supplement, 171.

TAYLOR, WALTER FULLER. *A History of American Letters,* with bibliographies by Harry Hartwick. Boston: American Book Co., 1936, 596.

Subsequent editions entitled: *The Story of American Letters.*

YOUNG, MALCOLM. *Paul Elmer More: A Bibliography.* Princeton: Princeton Univ. Press, 1941, 40 pp.

MORLEY, CHRISTOPHER

BLANCK, JACOB, ed. *Merle Johnson's American First Editions,* 4th edition, revised and enlarged. Waltham, Massachusetts: Mark Press, 1965, 377–385.

GERSTENBERGER, DONNA, and GEORGE HENDRICK. *The American Novel, 1789–1959: A Checklist of Twentieth Century Criticism.* Denver: Alan Swallow, 1961, 204–205.

LEARY, LEWIS. *Articles on American Literature, 1900–1950.* Durham: Duke Univ. Press, 1954, 219.

SARGENT, RALPH M. "Dear Chris." *Haverford Review,* III (Winter 1944), 22–25.

MORRIS, WRIGHT

LINDEN, STANTON J., and DAVID MADDEN. "A Wright Morris Bibliography." *Critique,* IV (Winter 1961–1962), 77–87.

MOORE, JOHN REES. "Books by Wright Morris." *HC,* IV (June 1967), 6–7.

WOODRESS, JAMES, et al. *American Literary Scholarship: An Annual.* Durham: Duke Univ. Press, (1965), 191.

MORTON, DAVID

KILEY, MARK. "David Morton: A Bibliography." *BB,* XIII (September–December 1929), 202; XIV (May–August 1930), 25–28.

MOTLEY, WILLARD

LEARY, LEWIS. *Articles on American Literature, 1900–1950.* Durham: Duke Univ. Press, 1954, 220.

MUIR, JOHN

BLANCK, JACOB, ed. *Merle Johnson's American First Editions,* 4th edition, revised and enlarged. Waltham, Massachusetts: Mark Press, 1965, 386–387.

LEARY, LEWIS. *Articles on American Literature, 1900–1950.* Durham: Duke Univ. Press, 1954, 220.

SPILLER, ROBERT ERNEST, et al. *Literary History of the United States,* 2 Vols. New York: Macmillan, 1962, 666–667. Supplement, 172.

WOLFE, LINNIE MARSH. *Son of the the Wilderness: The Life of John Muir.* New York: A. A. Knopf, 1945, 349–350.

MUMFORD, LEWIS

LEARY, LEWIS. *Articles on American Literature, 1900–1950.* Durham: Duke Univ. Press, 1954, 220.

NABOKOV, VLADIMIR

BURNS, MILDRED BLAIR. "Books by Vladimir Nabokov." *HC,* III (June 1966), 6–7.

WOODRESS, JAMES, et al. *American Literary Scholarship: An Annual.* Durham: Duke Univ. Press, (1964), 163–164; (1966), 177–178.

NATHAN, GEORGE JEAN

BLANCK, JACOB, ed. *Merle Johnson's American First Editions,* 4th edition, revised and enlarged. Waltham, Massachusetts: Mark Press, 1965, 388–390.

LEARY, LEWIS. *Articles on American Literature, 1900–1950.* Durham: Duke Univ. Press, 1954, 221.

NATHAN, ROBERT

BLANCK, JACOB, ed. *Merle Johnson's American First Editions,* 4th edition, revised and enlarged. Waltham, Massachusetts: Mark Press, 1965, 391–393.

GERSTENBERGER, DONNA, and GEORGE HENDRICK. *The American Novel, 1789–1959: A Checklist of Twentieth Century Criticism.* Denver: Alan Swallow, 1961, 205–206.

LEARY, LEWIS. *Articles on American Literature, 1900–1950.* Durham: Duke Univ. Press, 1954, 221.

NEIHARDT, JOHN G.

BLANCK, JACOB, ed. *Merle Johnson's American First Editions,* 4th edition, revised and enlarged. Waltham, Massachusetts: Mark Press, 1965, 394–395.

LEARY, LEWIS. *Articles on American Literature, 1900–1950.* Durham: Duke Univ. Press, 1954, 221–222.

NEWTON, ALFRED EDWARD

BLANCK, JACOB, ed. *Merle Johnson's American First Editions.* 4th edition, revised and enlarged. Waltham, Massachusetts: Mark Press, 1965, 396–398.

LEARY, LEWIS. *Articles on American Literature, 1900–1950.* Durham: Duke Univ. Press, 1954, 222.

NICHOLSON, SIR FRANCIS

LEARY, LEWIS. *Articles on American Literature, 1900–1950.* Durham: Duke Univ. Press, 1954, 222.

NICHOLSON, MEREDITH

RUSSO, DOROTHY RITTER, and THELMA LOIS SULLIVAN. *Bibliographical Studies of Seven Authors of Crawfordsville, Indiana: Lew and Susan Wallace, Maurice and Will Thompson, Mary Hannah and Caroline Virginia Krout, and Meredith Nicholson*. Indianapolis: Indiana Historical Society, 1952, 69–172.

NIMS, JOHN FREDERICK

LEARY, LEWIS. *Articles on American Literature, 1900–1950*. Durham: Duke Univ. Press, 1954, 222.

NORRIS, FRANK

AHNEBRINK, LARS. *The Beginnings of Naturalism in American Fiction: A Study of the Works of Hamlin Garland, Stephen Crane, and Frank Norris, with Special Reference to Some European Influences, 1891–1903*. New York: Russell and Russell, 1961, 468–484.

_____. *The Influence of Emile Zola on Frank Norris*. Cambridge: Harvard Univ. Press, 1947, 67–68.

BIENCOURT, MARIUS. *Une Influence du Naturalisme francais en Amérique: Frank Norris*. Paris: Marcel Giard, 1933, 233–244.

BLANCK, JACOB, ed. *Merle Johnson's American First Editions*, 4th edition, revised and enlarged. Waltham, Massachusetts: Mark Press, 1965, 399–400.

COOPER, FREDERIC TABER. *Some American Story Tellers*, 2nd edition. New York: H. Holt and Co., 1912, 370–372.

GERSTENBERGER, DONNA, and GEORGE HENDRICK. *The American Novel, 1789–1959: A Checklist of Twentieth Century Criticism*. Denver: Alan Swallow, 1961, 206–209.

LEARY, LEWIS. *Articles on American Literature, 1900–1950*. Durham: Duke Univ. Press, 1954, 222–223.

LOHF, KENNETH A., and EUGENE P. SHEEHY. *Frank Norris*. Los Gatos, California: The Talisman Press, 1959, 123 pp.

MARCHAND, ERNEST. *Frank Norris: A Study*. Palo Alto: Stanford Univ. Press, 1942, 241–249.

NORRIS, FRANK. *The Responsibilities of the Novelist*. New York: Doubleday, Page and Co., 1903, 305–311.

SPILLER, ROBERT ERNEST, et al. *Literary History of the United States*, 2 Vols. New York: Macmillan, 1962, 668–669. Supplement, 172.

TAYLOR, WALTER FULLER. *A History of American Letters*, with bibliographies by Harry Hartwick. Boston: American Book Co., 1936, 564–565.

Subsequent editions entitled: *The Story of American Letters*.

WALKER, F. "Frank Norris at the University of California." *Univ. of California Chronicle*, XXXIII (July 1931), 320–349.

WHITE, WILLIAM. "Frank Norris: Bibliographical Addenda." *BB*, XXII (September-December 1959), 227–228.

NORRIS, KATHLEEN

GERSTENBERGER, DONNA, and GEORGE HENDRICK. *The American Novel, 1789–1959: A Checklist*

of Twentieth Century Criticism.
Denver: Alan Swallow, 1961, 209.

NUTT, HOWARD

LIBRARY OF CONGRESS,
GENERAL REFERENCE AND
BIBLIOGRAPHY DIVISION. *Sixty
American Poets, 1896–1944,*
selected, with a preface and critical
notes by Allen Tate and a preliminary
checklist by Francis Cheney. Washington, 1945, 114.

Revised edition: 1954, 92–93.

O'CONNOR, FLANNERY

THE EDITORS. "Books by Flannery
O'Connor." *HC,* II (September 1965),
7.

GERSTENBERGER, DONNA, and
GEORGE HENDRICK. *The American Novel, 1789–1959: A Checklist
of Twentieth Century Criticism.*
Denver: Alan Swallow, 1961, 209.

WEDGE, GEORGE F. "Two Bibliographies: Flannery O'Connor – J.
F. Powers." *Critique,* II (Fall 1958),
59–63.

WOODRESS, JAMES, et al. *American
Literary Scholarship: An Annual.*
Durham: Duke Univ. Press, (1963),
154–155; (1964), 164; (1965), 191–
193; (1966), 178–180.

ODETS, CLIFFORD

LEARY, LEWIS. *Articles on American Literature, 1900–1950.* Durham:
Duke Univ. Press, 1954, 224.

MILLETT, FRED BENJAMIN. *Contemporary American Authors: A
Critical Survey and 219 Bio-bibliographies.* New York: Harcourt, Brace
and World, 1940, 512–514.

SPILLER, ROBERT ERNEST, et al.
Literary History of the United States,

2 Vols. New York: Macmillan, 1962,
670. Supplement, 173.

O'HARA, JOHN

GERSTENBERGER, DONNA and
GEORGE HENDRICK. *The American Novel, 1789–1959: A Checklist
of Twentieth Century Criticism.*
Denver: Alan Swallow, 1961, 209–
210.

LEARY, LEWIS. *Articles on American Literature, 1900–1950.* Durham:
Duke Univ. Press, 1954, 224.

MILLETT, FRED BENJAMIN. *Contemporary American Authors: A
Critical Survey and 219 Bio-bibliographies.* New York: Harcourt, Brace
and World, 1940, 514.

O'NEILL, EUGENE

BLANCK, JACOB, ed. *Merle Johnson's American First Editions,* 4th
edition, revised and enlarged.
Waltham, Massachusetts: Mark Press,
1965, 401–403.

BRYER, JACKSON R. "Forty
Years of O'Neill Criticism: A Selected
Bibliography." *MD,* IV (September
1961), 196–216.

CLARK, BARRETT HARPER.
*Eugene O'Neill: The Man and His
Plays,* revised edition. New York: R.
M. McBride and Co., 1929, 201–218.

FRENZ, HORST. "List of Foreign
Editions and Translations of Eugene
O'Neill's Dramas." *BB,* XVIII
(September-December 1943), 33–34.

GASSNER, JOHN, ed. *O'Neill: A
Collection of Critical Essays.* Englewood Cliffs, New Jersey: Prentice
Hall, 1964, 177–180.

HALLINE, ALLAN GATES. *American Plays.* New York: American
Book Co., 1935, 763–766.

LEARY, LEWIS. *Articles on American Literature, 1900–1950.* Durham: Duke Univ. Press, 1954, 224–228.

LIBRARY OF CONGRESS, DIVISION OF BIBLIOGRAPHY. *Eugene O'Neill: A List of Recent References.* Washington, 1940, 15 leaves.

MACKALL, L. L. "Notes for Bibliophiles: Eugene O'Neill's Bibliography." *NYHTB,* LCI (Aug. 9, 1931), 15.

McANENY, MARGUERITE L. "Eleven Manuscripts of Eugene O'Neill." *PULC,* IV (February-April 1943), 86–89.

MILLER, JORDAN Y. "A Critical Bibliography of Eugene O'Neill." Unpublished doctoral dissertation, Columbia Univ., 1957.

NICHOLLS, NORAH. "Checklist of Eugene O'Neill." *Bookman* (London), LXXXIV (September 1933), 300.

SANBORN, RALPH, and BARRETT H. CLARK, eds. *A Bibliography of the Works of Eugene O'Neill.* New York: Random House, 1931, 185 pp.

Also: New York: Benjamin Blom, 1965.

SPILLER, ROBERT ERNEST, et al. *Literary History of the United States,* 2 Vols. New York: Macmillan, 1962, 670–672. Supplement, 173–174.

TAYLOR, WALTER FULLER. *A History of American Letters,* with bibliographies by Harry Hartwick. Boston: American Book Co., 1936, 586–588.

Subsequent editions entitled: *The Story of American Letters.*

WOODRESS, JAMES, et al. *American Literary Scholarship: An Annual.* Durham: Duke Univ. Press, (1965), 237–239; (1966), 223–225..

OSTENSO, MARTHA

LEARY, LEWIS. *Articles on American Literature, 1900–1950.* Durham: Duke Univ. Press, 1954, 228.

O'SULLIVAN, VINCENT

LEARY, LEWIS. *Articles on American Literature, 1900–1950.* Durham: Duke Univ. Press, 1954, 228.

SIMS, GEORGE. "Some Uncollected Authors XV: Vincent O'Sullivan." *BC,* VI (Winter 1957), 395–402.

OSWALD, BRIAN (see BYRNE)

PALMER, THEODORE SHERMAN

LIBRARY OF CONGRESS, MANUSCRIPT DIVISION. *Theodore Sherman Palmer: A Register of His Papers in the Library of Congress.* Washington, 1958, 8 leaves.

PARKER, CARLETON H.

LEARY, LEWIS. *Articles on American Literature, 1900–1950.* Durham: Duke Univ. Press, 1954, 230.

PARKER, DOROTHY

BLANCK, JACOB, ed. *Merle Johnson's American First Editions,* 4th edition, revised and enlarged. Waltham, Massachusetts: Mark Press, 1965, 408.

LEARY, LEWIS. *Articles on American Literature, 1900–1950.* Durham: Duke Univ. Press, 1954, 230.

PARRINGTON, VERNON LOUIS

LEARY, LEWIS. *Articles on American Literature, 1900–1950.* Durham: Duke Univ. Press, 1954, 231.

PARRISH, ANNE

LEARY, LEWIS. *Articles on American Literature, 1900–1950.* Durham: Duke Univ. Press, 1954, 231.

PATCHEN, KENNETH

LEARY, LEWIS. *Articles on American Literature, 1900–1950.* Durham: Duke Univ. Press, 1954, 231–232.

SEE, CAROLYN. "Kenneth Patchen, 1934–1958: A Partial Bibliography." *BB,* XXIII (January-April 1961), 81–84.

PATTEE, FRED LEWIS

LEARY, LEWIS. *Articles on American Literature, 1900–1950.* Durham: Duke Univ. Press, 1954, 232.

WERNER, WILLIAM L. "The Writing Career of Fred Lewis Pattee." *Headlight on Books at Penn State,* ns III (May 1956), 5–32.

PAUL, ELLIOT

LEARY, LEWIS. *Articles on American Literature, 1900–1950.* Durham: Duke Univ. Press, 1954, 232.

PEABODY, JOSEPHINE PRESTON

LEARY, LEWIS. *Articles on American Literature, 1900–1950.* Durham: Duke Univ. Press, 1954, 233.

PEATTIE, DONALD CULROSS

LEARY, LEWIS. *Articles on American Literature, 1900–1950.* Durham: Duke Univ. Press, 1954, 233.

PECK, BRADFORD

LEARY, LEWIS. *Articles on American Literature, 1900–1950.* Durham: Duke Univ. Press, 1954, 233.

PETERKIN, JULIA

GERSTENBERGER, DONNA, and GEORGE HENDRICK. *The American Novel, 1789–1959: A Checklist of Twentieth Century Criticism.* Denver: Alan Swallow, 1961, 211.

LEARY, LEWIS. *Articles on American Literature, 1900–1950.* Durham: Duke Univ. Press, 1954, 234.

PETRY, ANN

GERSTENBERGER, DONNA, and GEORGE HENDRICK. *The American Novel, 1789–1959: A Checklist of Twentieth Century Criticism.* Denver: Alan Swallow, 1961, 211.

LEARY, LEWIS. *Articles on American Literature, 1900–1950.* Durham: Duke Univ. Press, 1954, 234.

PHELPS, WILLIAM LYON

LEARY, LEWIS. *Articles on American Literature, 1900–1950.* Durham: Duke Univ. Press, 1954, 234.

PHILLIPS, DAVID GRAHAM

FELDMAN, ABRAHAM. "David Graham Phillips: His Works and His Critics." *BB,* XIX (May-August 1948), 144–146; (September-December 1948), 177–179.

GERSTENBERGER, DONNA, and GEORGE HENDRICK. *The American Novel, 1789–1959: A Checklist of Twentieth Century Criticism.* Denver: Alan Swallow, 1961, 211–212.

LEARY, LEWIS. *Articles on American Literature, 1900–1950.* Durham: Duke Univ. Press, 1954, 234–235.

PHILLPOTTS, EDEN

HINTON, PERCIVAL. *Eden Phillpotts: A Bibliography of First*

Editions. Birmingham, England: G. Worthington, 1931, 180 pp.

PODHORETZ, NORMAN

COSTIGAN, CHRISTINE R. "Books by Norman Podhoretz." *HC,* V (February 1968), 7.

POLLARD, PERCIVAL

LEARY, LEWIS. *Articles on American Literature, 1900–1950.* Durham: Duke Univ. Press, 1954, 249.

POOLE, ERNEST

LEARY, LEWIS. *Articles on American Literature, 1900–1950.* Durham: Duke Univ. Press, 1954, 249.

PORTER, ELEANOR HODGMAN (ELEANOR STEWART)

LEARY, LEWIS. *Articles on American Literature, 1900–1950.* Durham: Duke Univ. Press, 1954, 249.

PORTER, KATHERINE ANNE

BLANCK, JACOB, ed. *Merle Johnson's American First Editions,* 4th edition, revised and enlarged. Waltham, Massachusetts: Mark Press, 1965, 419.

LEARY, LEWIS. *Articles on American Literature, 1900–1950.* Durham: Duke Univ. Press, 1954, 249.

NANCE, WILLIAM L. *Katherine Anne Porter and the Art of Rejection.* Chapel Hill: Univ. of North Carolina Press, 1964, 251–253.

SYLVESTER, WILLIAM A. "Selected and Critical Bibliography of the Uncollected Works of Katherine Anne Porter." *BB,* XIX (January-April 1947), 36.

WOODRESS, JAMES, et al. *American Literary Scholarship: An Annual.* Durham: Duke Univ. Press, (1963), 149–150; (1965), 174–176; (1966), 162–164.

PORTER, WILLIAM SYDNEY (O. HENRY)

BLANCK, JACOB, ed. *Merle Johnson's American First Editions,* 4th edition, revised and enlarged. Waltham, Massachusetts: Mark Press, 1965, 420–422.

CLARKSON, PAUL STEPHEN, comp. *A Bibliography of William Sydney Porter (O. Henry).* Caldwell, Idaho: Caxton, 1938, 161 pp.

COOPER, FREDERIC TABER. *Some American Story Tellers,* 2nd edition. New York: H. Holt and Co., 1912, 368–369.

HENRY, O. *Waifs and Strays: Twelve Stories.* Garden City, New York: Doubleday, Page and Co., 1917, 281–305.

LEARY, LEWIS. *Articles on American Literature, 1900–1950.* Durham: Duke Univ. Press, 1954, 250–251.

PAINE, GREGORY LANSING, ed. *Southern Prose Writers: Representative Selections,* with introduction, bibliography and notes. New York: American Book Co., 1947, cxl–cxli.

ROLLINS, HYDER E. "Book Reviews." *AL,* XI (March 1909), 107–109.

SPILLER, ROBERT ERNEST, et al. *Literary History of the United States,* 2 Vols. New York: Macmillan, 1962, 696–698. Supplement, 180.

TRENT, WILLIAM PETERFIELD, et al. *Cambridge History of American Literature,* 4 Vols. New York: G. P. Putnam's Sons, 1917–1921, II, 625.

POUND, EZRA

AMDUR, ALICE STEINER. *The Poetry of Ezra Pound.* Cambridge: Harvard Univ. Press, 1936, 191–106.

300 copies printed.

EDWARDS, JOHN HAMILTON. *A Preliminary Checklist of the Writings of Ezra Pound, Especially His Contributions to Periodicals.* New Haven: Yale Univ. Press, 1953, 81 pp.

GALLUP, DONALD CLIFFORD. *A Bibliography of Ezra Pound.* London: Hart-Davis, 1964, 454 pp.

LEARY, LEWIS. *Articles on American Literature, 1900–1950.* Durham: Duke Univ. Press, 1954, 252–254.

LIBRARY OF CONGRESS, GENERAL REFERENCE AND BIBLIOGRAPHY DIVISION. *Sixty American Poets, 1896–1944,* selected, with a preface and critical notes by Allen Tate and a preliminary checklist by Francis Cheney. Washington, 1945, 115–122.

Revised edition: 1954, 93–101.

MILLETT, FRED BENJAMIN. *Contemporary American Authors: A Critical Survey and 219 Bio-bibligraphies.* New York: Harcourt, Brace and World, 1940, 529–533.

SLATIN, MYLES. "More by Ezra Pound." *YULG,* XXX (October 1955), 74–80.

SPILLER, ROBERT ERNEST, et al. *Literary History of the United States,* 2 Vols. New York: Macmillan, 1962, 699–700. Supplement, 181–183.

SUTTON, WALTER, ed. *Ezra Pound: A Collection of Critical Essays.* Englewood Cliffs, New Jersey: Prentice Hall, 1963, 183–184.

VASSE, WILLIAM. "Bibliography." *The Pound Newsletter.*

A continuing bibliography is found in each of the 10 issues, January 1954–April 1956.

——————. "A Checklist of Explications: I: The Pre-Canto Poetry." *The Pound Newsletter,* V (January 1955), 20–21.

——————. "A Checklist of Explications: II: The Cantos." *The Pound Newsletter,* VI (April 1955), 16–19.

WOODRESS, JAMES, et al. *American Literary Scholarship: An Annual.* Durham: Duke Univ. Press, (1963), 173–177; (1964), 184–186; (1965), 204–208; (1966), 193–196.

YALE UNIVERSITY, LIBRARY. "The Ezra Pound Exhibition." *YULG,* XXX (January 1956), 126–127.

POWERS, J. F.

HAGOPIAN, JOHN V. *J. F. Powers.* New York: Twayne, 1968, 174.

WEDGE, GEORGE F. "Two Bibliographies: Flannery O'Connor – J. F. Powers." *Critique,* II (Fall 1958), 63–70.

PROKOSCH, FREDERIC

LEARY, LEWIS. *Articles on American Literature, 1900–1950.* Durham: Duke Univ. Press, 1954, 254.

LIBRARY OF CONGRESS, GENERAL REFERENCE AND BIBLIOGRAPHY DIVISION. *Sixty American Poets, 1896–1944,* selected, with a preface and critical notes by Allen Tate and a preliminary checklist by Francis Cheney. Washington, 1945, 123–124.

Revised edition: 1954, 101–102.

PUTNAM, HOWARD PHELPS

LEARY, LEWIS. *Articles on American Literature, 1900–1950.* Durham: Duke Univ. Press, 1954, 254–255.

LIBRARY OF CONGRESS, GENERAL REFERENCE AND BIBLIOGRAPHY DIVISION. *Sixty American Poets, 1896–1944,* selected, with a preface and critical notes by Allen Tate and a preliminary checklist by Francis Cheney. Washington, 1945, 125.

Revised edition: 1954, 102–103.

QUEEN, ELLERY

TEXAS, UNIVERSITY, HUMANITIES RESEARCH CENTER. *An Exhibition on the Occasion of the Opening of the Ellery Queen Collection.* Austin: Humanities Research Center, 1959, 27 pp.

RAND, AYN

GERSTENBERGER, DONNA, and GEORGE HENDRICK. *The American Novel, 1789–1959: A Checklist of Twentieth Century Criticism.* Denver: Alan Swallow, 1961, 213.

RANSOM, JOHN CROWE

BRADBURY, JOHN M. *The Fugitives: A Critical Account.* Chapel Hill: Univ. of North Carolina Press, 1958, 277–279.

LEARY, LEWIS. *Articles on American Literature, 1900–1950.* Durham: Duke Univ. Press, 1954, 255.

LIBRARY OF CONGRESS, GENERAL REFERENCE AND BIBLIOGRAPHY DIVISION. *Sixty American Poets, 1896–1944,* selected, with a preface and critical notes by Allen

Tate and a preliminary checklist by Francis Cheney. Washington, 1945, 126–127.

Revised edition: 1954, 103–104.

MILLETT, FRED BENJAMIN. *Contemporary American Authors: A Critical Survey and 219 Bio-bibliographies.* New York: Harcourt, Brace and World, 1940, 535–636.

STALLMAN, ROBERT WOOSTER. "John Crowe Ransom: A Checklist." *SR,* LVI (July-September 1948), 442–476.

WOODRESS, JAMES, et al. *American Literary Scholarship: An Annual.* Durham: Duke Univ. Press, (1963), 194–196; (1964), 208–209.

RAWLINGS, MARJORIE KINNAN

GERSTENBERGER, DONNA, and GEORGE HENDRICK. *The American Novel, 1789–1959: A Checklist of Twentieth Century Criticism.* Denver: Alan Swallow, 1961, 213.

LEARY, LEWIS. *Articles on American Literature, 1900–1950.* Durham: Duke Univ. Press, 1954, 255.

READ, OPIE

LEARY, LEWIS. *Articles on American Literature, 1900–1950.* Durham: Duke Univ. Press, 1954, 255.

READ, WILLIAM A.

CAFFEE, NATHANIEL MONTIER, THOMAS A. KIRBY et al., eds. *Studies for William A. Read: A Miscellany Presented by Some of His Colleagues and Friends.* Baton Rouge: Louisiana State Univ. Press, 1940, vi–viii.

REED, JOHN

LEARY, LEWIS. *Articles on Ameri-*

can Literature, 1900–1950. Durham:
Duke Univ. Press, 1954, 256.

REEDY, WILLIAM MARION

LEARY, LEWIS. *Articles on American Literature, 1900–1950.* Durham:
Duke Univ. Press, 1954, 256.

REESE, LIZETTE WOODWORTH

LEARY, LEWIS. *Articles on American Literature, 1900–1950.* Durham:
Duke Univ. Press, 1954, 256.

REPPLIER, AGNES

BLANCK, JACOB, ed. *Merle Johnson's American First Editions,* 4th
edition, revised and enlarged.
Waltham, Massachusetts: Mark
Press, 1965, 428–429.

LEARY, LEWIS. *Articles on American Literature, 1900–1950.* Durham:
Duke Univ. Press, 1954, 256.

REYNOLDS, GEORGE FULLMER

SELLECK, ELIZABETH F., comp.
"Bibliography of the Writings of
George Fullmer Reynolds, 1905–
1945," in *Elizabethan Studies and
Other Essays in Honor of George F.
Reynolds.* Boulder, Colorado: n.p.,
1945, 1–4.

*Univ. of Colorado Studies in the
Humanities,* II, No. 4.

RHODES, EUGENE MANLOVE

LEARY, LEWIS. *Articles on American Literature, 1900–1950.* Durham:
Duke Univ. Press, 1954, 256.

RICE, CALE YOUNG

LEARY, LEWIS. *Articles on American Literature, 1900–1950.* Durham:
Duke Univ. Press, 1954, 256.

RICE, ELMER

LEARY, LEWIS. *Articles on American Literature, 1900–1950.* Durham:
Duke Univ. Press, 1954, 256–257.

MILLETT, FRED BENJAMIN. *Contemporary American Authors: A
Critical Survey and 219 Bio-bibliographies.* New York: Harcourt, Brace
and World, 1940, 539–541.

SPILLER, ROBERT ERNEST, et al.
Literary History of the United States,
2 Vols. New York: Macmillan, 1962,
702–703. Supplement, 184.

WOODRESS, JAMES, et al. *American
Literary Scholarship: An Annual.*
Durham: Duke Univ. Press, (1965),
235–236.

RICHARDSON, DOROTHY M.

GLIKIN, GLORIA. "A Checklist of
Writings of Dorothy M. Richardson."
ELT, VIII (No. 1, 1965), 1–11.

_____. "Dorothy M.
Richardson: An Annotated Bibliography of Writings about Her." *ELT,*
VIII (No. 1, 1965), 12–35.

RICHTER, CONRAD

GERSTENBERGER, DONNA, and
GEORGE HENDRICK. *The American Novel, 1789–1959: A Checklist
of Twentieth Century Criticism.*
Denver: Alan Swallow, 1961, 213.

LEARY, LEWIS. *Articles on American Literature, 1900–1950.* Durham:
Duke Univ. Press, 1954, 257.

RIDGE, LOLA

LEARY, LEWIS. *Articles on American Literature, 1900–1950.* Durham:
Duke Univ. Press, 1954, 257.

RIDING, LAURA

LEARY, LEWIS. *Articles on American Literature, 1900–1950*. Durham: Duke Univ. Press, 1954, 257.

LIBRARY OF CONGRESS, GENERAL REFERENCE AND BIBLIOGRAPHY DIVISION. *Sixty American Poets, 1896–1944*, selected, with a preface and critical notes by Allen Tate and a preliminary checklist by Francis Cheney. Washington, 1945, 128–131.

Revised edition: 1954, 104–106.

RIGGS, LYNN

LEARY, LEWIS. *Articles on American Literature, 1900–1950*. Durham: Duke Univ. Press, 1954, 257.

RINEHART, MARY ROBERTS

GERSTENBERGER, DONNA, and GEORGE HENDRICK. *The American Novel, 1789–1959: A Checklist of Twentieth Century Criticism*. Denver: Alan Swallow, 1961, 213.

LEARY, LEWIS. *Articles on American Literature, 1900–1950*. Durham: Duke Univ. Press, 1954, 258.

ROBERTS, ELIZABETH MADOX

BLANCK, JACOB, ed. *Merle Johnson's American First Editions*. 4th edition, revised and enlarged. Waltham, Massachusetts: Mark Press, 1965, 434.

GERSTENBERGER, DONNA, and GEORGE HENDRICK. *The American Novel, 1789–1959: A Checklist of Twentieth Century Criticism*. Denver: Alan Swallow, 1961, 214.

LEARY, LEWIS. *Articles on American Literature, 1900–1950*. Durham: Duke Univ. Press, 1954, 258.

TATE, ALLEN. "The Elizabeth Maddox Roberts Papers." *LCQJ*, I (October-December 1943), 29–31.

ROBERTS, KENNETH LEWIS

ALBERT, GEORGE. "Bibliography of Kenneth Lewis Roberts." *BB*, XVII (September-December 1942), 191–192; (January-April 1943), 218–219; XVIII (May-August 1943), 13–15; (September-December 1943), 34–36.

BLANCK, JACOB, ed. *Merle Johnson's American First Editions*, 4th edition, revised and enlarged. Waltham, Massachusetts: Mark Press, 1965, 435–436.

ELLIS, MARJORIE M. "Supplementary Bibliography of Kenneth Roberts." *CLQ*, VI (September 1962), 99–105.

GERSTENBERGER, DONNA, and GEORGE HENDRICK. *The American Novel, 1789–1959: A Checklist of Twentieth Century Criticism*. Denver: Alan Swallow, 1961, 215.

LEARY, LEWIS. *Articles on American Literature, 1900–1950*. Durham: Duke Univ. Press, 1954, 258.

STEMPLE, RUTH. "Kenneth Roberts: A Supplementary Checklist." *BB*, XXII (September 1959), 228–301.

ROBINSON, EDWIN ARLINGTON

ADAMS, LEONIE. "The Ledoux Collection of Edwin Arlington Robinson." *LCQJ*, VII (November 1949), 9–13.

ANDERSON, WALLACE LUDWIG. *Edwin Arlington Robinson*. Boston: Houghton Mifflin Co., 1967, 155–165.

BEEBE, LUCIUS MORRIS. *Aspects of the Poetry of Edwin Arlington Robinson,* with a bibliography by Bradley Fisk. Cambridge: privately printed for sale by the Dunster House Bookshop, 1928, 69–107.

BEEBE, LUCIUS MORRIS, and ROBERT J. BULKLEY JR., comps. *A Bibliography of the Writings of Edwin Arlington Robinson.* Cambridge: Harvard Univ. Press, 1931, 59 pp.

BLANCK, JACOB, ed. *Merle Johnson's First Editions,* 4th edition, revised and enlarged. Waltham, Massachusetts: Mark Press, 1965, 438–442.

BURNS, WINIFRED. "Edwin Arlington Robinson in the Hands of the Reviewers." *Poet Lore,* XLVIII (Summer 1942), 164–175.

CLARK, HARRY HAYDEN, ed. *Major American Poets.* New York: American Book Co., 1936, 938–940.

COLBY COLLEGE LIBRARY. *Edwin Arlington Robinson at Colby College.* Waterville, Maine: Colby College Library, 1944, 4 pp.

_____. *The Library of Edwin Arlington Robinson: A Descriptive Catalogue,* by James Humphry, III. Waterville, Maine: Colby College Press, 1950, 52 pp.

HILL, ROBERT W. "More Light on a Shadowy Figure: A. H. Louis, the Original of E. A. Robinson's 'Captain Craig.'" *BNYPL,* LX (August 1956), 373–377.

HOGAN, CHARLES BEECHER, comp. *A Bibliography of Edwin Arlington Robinson.* New Haven: Yale Univ. Press, 1938, 234 pp.

_____. "Edwin Arlington Robinson: New Bibliographical Notes." *PBSA,* XXXV (2nd Quart. 1941), 115–144.

ISAACS, EDITH J. R. "Edwin Arlington Robinson: A Descriptive List of the Lewis M. Isaacs Collection of Robinsoniana." *BNYPL,* LII (May 1948), 211–233.

KAPLAN, ESTELLE. *Philosophy in the Poetry of Edwin Arlington Robinson.* New York: Columbia Univ. Press, 1940, 145–153.

LEARY, LEWIS. *Articles on American Literature, 1900–1950.* Durham: Duke Univ. Press, 1954, 258–263.

LIBRARY OF CONGRESS, GENERAL REFERENCE AND BIBLIOGRAPHY DIVISION. *Sixty American Poets, 1896–1944,* selected, with a preface and critical notes by Allen Tate and a preliminary checklist by Francis Cheney. Washington, 1945, 132–140.

Revised edition: 1954, 107–113.

LIPPINCOTT, LILLIAN, comp. *A Bibliography of the Writings and Criticisms of Edwin Arlington Robinson.* Boston: F. W. Faxon Co., 1937, 86 pp.

MORRIS, LLOYD R. *The Poetry of Edwin Arlington Robinson: An Essay in Appreciation,* with a bibliography by W. Van R. Whitall. New York: George H. Doran Co., 1923, 81–112.

PAYNE, LEONIDAS W., JR. "The First Edition of E. A. Robinson's *The Peterborough Idea.*" *Univ. of Texas Bulletin,* No. 3,926 (1939), 210–231.

ROBINSON, WILLIAM RONALD. *Edwin Arlington Robinson: A Poetry of the Act.* Cleveland: Western Reserve Univ. Press, 1967, 167–177.

SPILLER, ROBERT ERNEST, et al. *Literary History of the United States,* 2 Vols. New York: Macmillan, 1962, 705–708. Supplement, 184–185.

TAYLOR, WALTER FULLER. *A History of American Letters,* with bibliographies by Harry Hartwick. Boston: American Book Co., 1936, 569–570.

Subsequent editions entitled: *The Story of American Letters.*

WOODRESS, JAMES, et al. *American Literary Scholarship: An Annual.* Durham: Duke Univ. Press, (1963), 170–172; (1964), 192–194; (1965), 208–210; (1966), 198–200.

ROETHKE, THEODORE

WOODRESS, JAMES, et al. *American Literary Scholarship: An Annual.* Durham: Duke Univ. Press, (1964), 212–213.

ROGERS, WILL

LEARY, LEWIS. *Articles on American Literature, 1900–1950.* Durham: Duke Univ. Press, 1954, 264.

RÖLVAAG, OLE EDVART

GERSTENBERGER, DONNA, and GEORGE HENDRICK. *The American Novel, 1789–1959: A Checklist of Twentieth Century Criticism.* Denver: Alan Swallow, 1961, 215.

LEARY, LEWIS. *Articles on American Literature, 1900–1950.* Durham: Duke Univ. Press, 1954, 264.

MILLETT, FRED BENJAMIN. *Contemporary American Authors: A Critical Survey and 219 Bio-bibliogra-*

phies. New York: Harcourt, Brace and World, 1940, 554–556.

Includes list of untranslated Norwegian writings.

PARRINGTON, VERNON LOUIS, ed. *Giants in the Earth.* New York: Harper and Brothers, 1929, 467–468.

SOLUM, NORA O. "The Sources of the Rölvaag Biography." *Norwegian-American Studies and Records,* XI (1940), 150–159.

SPILLER, ROBERT ERNEST, et al. *Literary History of the United States,* 2 Vols. New York: Macmillan, 1962, 708–709.

ROOSEVELT, FRANKLIN DELANO

LEARY, LEWIS. *Articles on American Literature, 1900–1950.* Durham: Duke Univ. Press, 1954, 264.

ROOSEVELT, THEODORE

BLANCK, JACOB, ed. *Merle Johnson's American First Editions,* 4th edition, revised and enlarged. Waltham, Massachusetts: Mark Press, 1965, 444–448.

LEARY, LEWIS. *Articles on American Literature, 1900–1950.* Durham: Duke Univ. Press, 1954, 264.

ROSENFELD, PAUL

LEARY, LEWIS. *Articles on American Literature, 1900–1950.* Durham: Duke Univ. Press, 1954, 264.

ROSS, HAROLD

LEARY, LEWIS. *Articles on American Literature, 1900–1950.* Durham: Duke Univ. Press, 1954, 264.

ROURKE, CONSTANCE

LEARY, LEWIS. *Articles on American Literature, 1900–1950.* Durham: Duke Univ. Press, 1954, 264–265.

RUKEYSER, MURIEL

LEARY, LEWIS. *Articles on American Literature, 1900–1950.* Durham: Duke Univ. Press, 1954, 265.

LIBRARY OF CONGRESS, GENERAL REFERENCE AND BIBLIOGRAPHY DIVISION. *Sixty American Poets, 1896–1944,* selected, with a preface and critical notes by Allen Tate and a preliminary checklist by Francis Cheney. Washington, 1945, 141–142.

Revised edition: 1954, 113–114.

RUSSELL, JOHN

LEARY, LEWIS. *Articles on American Literature, 1900–1950.* Durham: Duke Univ. Press, 1954, 265.

RUTLEDGE, ARCHIBALD

LEARY, LEWIS. *Articles on American Literature, 1900–1950.* Durham: Duke Univ. Press, 1954, 266.

SALINGER, HERMAN

LEARY, LEWIS. *Articles on American Literature, 1900–1950.* Durham: Duke Univ. Press, 1954, 266.

SALINGER, J. D.

GERSTENBERGER, DONNA, and GEORGE HENDRICK. *The American Novel, 1789–1959: A Checklist of Twentieth Century Criticism.* Denver: Alan Swallow, 1961, 215–216.

GWYNN, FREDERICK LANDIS, and JOSEPH L. BLOTNER. *The Fiction of J. D. Salinger.* Pittsburgh: Univ. of Pittsburgh Press, 1958, 57–59.

HARPER, HOWARD M., JR. *Desperate Faith: A Study of Bellow, Salinger, Mailer, Baldwin, and Updike.* Chapel Hill: Univ. of North Carolina Press, 1967, bibliographical footnotes.

HASSAN, IHAB H. "Rare Quixotic Gesture: The Fiction of J. D. Salinger." *WR,* XXI (Summer 1957), 261–280.

WOODRESS, JAMES, et al. *American Literary Scholarship: An Annual.* Durham: Duke Univ. Press, (1963), 146–149; (1964), 165–166; (1965), 193–195; (1966), 180–181.

SALTUS, EDGAR

BLANCK, JACOB, ed. *Merle Johnson's American First Editions,* 4th edition, revised and enlarged. Waltham, Massachusetts: Mark Press, 1965, 451–454.

GERSTENBERGER, DONNA, and GEORGE HENDRICK. *The American Novel, 1789–1959: A Checklist of Twentieth Century Criticism.* Denver: Alan Swallow, 1961, 216.

LEARY, LEWIS. *Articles on American Literature, 1900–1950.* Durham: Duke Univ. Press, 1954, 266.

SPILLER, ROBERT ERNEST, et al. *Literary History of the United States,* 2 Vols. New York: Macmillan, 1962, 709–710. Supplement, 186.

SANDBURG, CARL

BLANCK, JACOB, ed. *Merle Johnson's American First Editions,* 4th edition, revised and enlarged. Waltham, Massachusetts: Mark Press, 1965, 455–457.

HAAS, JOSEPH. *Carl Sandburg: A Pictorial Biography.* New York: G. P. Putnam's Sons, 1967, 211–212.

ILLINOIS, UNIVERSITY, LIBRARY. *The Sandburg Range: An Exhibition of Materials from Carl Sandburg's Library.* Urbana: Illinois Univ. Library, 1958, 47 pp.

LEARY, LEWIS. *Articles on American Literature, 1900–1950.* Durham: Duke Univ. Press, 1954, 266–267.

LIBRARY OF CONGRESS, GENERAL REFERENCE AND BIBLIOGRAPHY DIVISION. *Carl Sandburg: A Bibliography,* compiled by Thomas Shuler Shaw. Washington, 1948, 62 leaves.

——————. *Sixty American Poets, 1896–1944,* selected, with a preface and critical notes by Allen Tate and a preliminary checklist by Francis Cheney. Washington, 1945, 143–147.

Revised edition: 1954, 114–119.

MILLETT, FRED BENJAMIN. *Contemporary American Authors: A Critical Survey and 219 Bio-bibliographies.* New York: Harcourt, Brace and World, 1940, 557–561.

NEWMAN, RALPH G. "A Selective Checklist of Sandburg's Writings." *Journal of the Illinois State Historical Society,* XLV (Winter 1952), 402–406.

SCHENK, WILLIAM P., comp. "Carl Sandburg: A Bibliography." *BB,* XVI (September-December 1936), 4–7.

SPILLER, ROBERT ERNEST, et al. *Literary History of the United States,* 2 Vols. New York: Macmillan, 1962, 711–712. Supplement, 186–187.

TAYLOR, WALTER FULLER. *A History of American Letters,* with bibliographies by Harry Hartwick. Boston: American Book Co., 1936, 585–586.

Subsequent editions entitled: *The Story of American Letters.*

WOODRESS, JAMES, et al. *American Literary Scholarship: An Annual.* Durham: Duke Univ. Press, (1964), 191–192; (1966), 196–198.

SANTAYANA, GEORGE

BLANCK, JACOB, ed. *Merle Johnson's American First Editions,* 4th edition, revised and enlarged. Waltham, Massachusetts: Mark Press, 1965, 458–460.

CORY, DANIEL. "The 'George Santayana Collection.'" *CLC,* V (February 1956), 23–25.

GERSTENBERGER, DONNA, and GEORGE HENDRICK. *The American Novel, 1789–1959: A Checklist of Twentieth Century Criticism.* Denver: Alan Swallow, 1961, 216–217.

HOWGATE, GEORGE WASHBURNE. *George Santayana.* Philadelphia: Univ. of Pennsylvania Press, 1938, 349–352.

LEARY, LEWIS. *Articles on American Literature, 1900–1950.* Durham: Duke Univ. Press, 1954, 268–269.

MILLETT, FRED BENJAMIN. *Contemporary American Authors: A Critical Survey and 219 Bio-bibliographies.* New York: Harcourt, Brace and World, 1940, 561–565.

SCHILPP, PAUL A. *The Philosophy of George Santayana.* Chicago: Northwestern Univ. Press, 1940, 607–668.

Bibliography by Shohig Terzian.

SPILLER, ROBERT ERNEST, et al. *Literary History of the United States,* 2 Vols. New York: Macmillan, 1962, 712–714. Supplement, 187–188.

TRENT, WILLIAM PETERFIELD, et al. *Cambridge History of American Literature,* 4 Vols. New York: G. P. Putnam's Sons, 1917–1921, IV, 757.

SARETT, LEW

LEARY, LEWIS. *Articles on American Literature, 1900–1950.* Durham: Duke Univ. Press, 1954, 269.

SAROYAN, WILLIAM

GERSTENBERGER, DONNA, and GEORGE HENDRICK. *The American Novel, 1789–1959: A Checklist of Twentieth Century Criticism.* Denver: Alan Swallow, 1961, 217.

LEARY, LEWIS. *Articles on American Literature, 1900–1950.* Durham: Duke Univ. Press, 1954, 269–270.

MILLETT, FRED BENJAMIN. *Contemporary American Authors: A Critical Survey and 219 Bio-bibliographies.* New York: Harcourt, Brace and World, 1940, 567–569.

SPILLER, ROBERT ERNEST, et al. *Literary History of the United States,* 2 Vols. New York: Macmillan, 1962, 714–715. Supplement, 188–189.

SAXON, LYLE

LEARY, LEWIS. *Articles on American Literature, 1900–1950.* Durham: Duke Univ. Press, 1954, 270.

SAYERS, DOROTHY L.

SANDOE, JAMES. "Contribution toward a Bibliography of Dorothy L. Sayers." *BB,* XVIII (May-August 1944), 76–81.

SCHAEFER, JACK

GERSTENBERGER, DONNA, and GEORGE HENDRICK. *The American Novel, 1789–1959: A Checklist of Twentieth Century Criticism.* Denver: Alan Swallow, 1961, 217.

SCHULBERG, BUDD

GERSTENBERGER, DONNA, and GEORGE HENDRICK. *The American Novel, 1789–1959: A Checklist of Twentieth Century Criticism.* Denver: Alan Swallow, 1961, 217–218.

SCHUTZE, MARTIN

LEARY, LEWIS. *Articles on American Literature, 1900–1950.* Durham: Duke Univ. Press, 1954, 270.

SCHWARTZ, DELMORE

LIBRARY OF CONGRESS, GENERAL REFERENCE AND BIBLIOGRAPHY DIVISION. *Sixty American Poets, 1896–1944,* selected, with a preface and critical notes by Allen Tate and a preliminary checklist by Francis Cheney. Washington, 1945, 148–149.

Revised edition: 1954, 119–120.

SCOTT, EVELYN

GERSTENBERGER, DONNA, and GEORGE HENDRICK. *The American Novel, 1789–1959: A Checklist of Twentieth Century Criticism.* Denver: Alan Swallow, 1961, 218.

LEARY, LEWIS. *Articles on American Literature, 1900–1950.* Durham: Duke Univ. Press, 1954, 270.

SCOTT, FRED NEWTON

THROPE, CLARENCE DE WITT, and CHARLES E. WHITMORE, eds.

Fred Newton Scott Anniversary Papers. Chicago: Univ. of Chicago Press, 1929, 313–319.

SEAGER, ALLAN

HANNA, ALLAN. "An Allan Seager Bibliography." *Critique,* V (Winter 1962–1963), 75–90.

SEDGWICK, ANNE DOUGLAS

GERSTENBERGER, DONNA, and GEORGE HENDRICK. *The American Novel, 1789–1959: A Checklist of Twentieth Century Criticism.* Denver: Alan Swallow, 1961, 218.

LEARY, LEWIS. *Articles on American Literature, 1900–1950.* Durham: Duke Univ. Press, 1954, 271.

SEEGER, ALAN

LEARY, LEWIS. *Articles on American Literature, 1900–1950.* Durham: Duke Univ. Press, 1954, 271.

SETON, ERNEST THOMPSON

BLANCK, JACOB, ed. *Merle Johnson's American First Editions,* 4th edition, revised and enlarged. Waltham, Massachusetts: Mark Press, 1965, 461–463.

LEARY, LEWIS. *Articles on American Literature, 1900–1950.* Durham: Duke Univ. Press, 1954, 271.

SHAPIRO, KARL JAY

THE EDITORS. "Books by Karl Shapiro." *HC,* I (December 1964), 7.

ENOCH PRATT FREE LIBRARY. *Bibliography of the Work of Karl Jay Shapiro,* by Louise Quesnel and William Webster, revised edition. Baltimore: Enoch Pratt Free Library, 1950, 13 pp.

Complete listing of Shapiro's published prose and verse.

LEARY, LEWIS. *Articles on American Literature, 1900–1950.* Durham: Duke Univ. Press, 1954, 271–272.

LIBRARY OF CONGRESS, GENERAL REFERENCE AND BIBLIOGRAPHY DIVISION. *Sixty American Poets, 1896–1944,* selected, with a preface and critical notes by Allen Tate and a preliminary checklist by Francis Cheney. Washington, 1945, 149.

Revised edition: 1954, 120–121.

WOODRESS, JAMES, et al. *American Literary Scholarship: An Annual.* Durham: Duke Univ. Press, (1964), 209–211.

SHAW, IRWIN

GERSTENBERGER, DONNA, and GEORGE HENDRICK. *The American Novel, 1789–1959: A Checklist of Twentieth Century Criticism.* Denver: Alan Swallow, 1961, 218–219.

SHEEAN, VINCENT

LEARY, LEWIS. *Articles on American Literature, 1900–1950.* Durham: Duke Univ. Press, 1954, 272.

SHERMAN, FRANCIS

LEARY, LEWIS. *Articles on American Literature, 1900–1950.* Durham: Duke Univ. Press, 1954, 272.

SHERMAN, STUART PRATT

LEARY, LEWIS. *Articles on American Literature, 1900–1950.* Durham: Duke Univ. Press, 1954, 272.

MILLETT, FRED BENJAMIN. *Contemporary American Authors: A*

Critical Survey and 219 Bio-bibliographies. New York: Harcourt, Brace and World, 1940, 575–578.

SPILLER, ROBERT ERNEST, et al. *Literary History of the United States,* 2 Vols. New York: Macmillan, 1962, 719–720.

ZEITLIN, JACOB, and HOMER WOODBRIDGE. *Life and Letters of Stuart P. Sherman,* 2 Vols. New York: Farrar and Rinehart, 1929, II, 801–860.

SHERWOOD, ROBERT E.

LEARY, LEWIS. *Articles on American Literature, 1900–1950.* Durham: Duke Univ. Press, 1954, 273.

MILLETT, FRED BENJAMIN. *Contemporary American Authors: A Critical Survey and 219 Bio-bibliographies.* New York: Harcourt, Brace and World, 1940, 578–579.

WOODRESS, JAMES, et al. *American Literary Scholarship: An Annual.* Durham: Duke Univ. Press, (1965), 235–236.

SHOREY, PAUL

LEARY, LEWIS. *Articles on American Literature, 1900–1950.* Durham: Duke Univ. Press, 1954, 273.

SINCLAIR, UPTON

ANDERSON, CARL L. *The Swedish Acceptance of American Literature.* Philadelphia: Univ. of Pennsylvania Press, 1957, 103–152.

BANTZ, ELIZABETH. "Upton Sinclair: Book Reviews and Criticisms Published in German and French Periodicals and Newspapers." *BB,* XVIII (January–April 1946), 204–206.

GAER, JOSEPH, ed. *Upton Sinclair: Bibliography and Biographical Data.* N.p., 1935, 54 leaves.

California Literary Research Project Monograph, No. 6

GERSTENBERGER, DONNA, and GEORGE HENDRICK. *The American Novel, 1789–1959: A Checklist of Twentieth Century Criticism.* Denver: Alan Swallow, 1961, 220–222.

INDIANA, UNIVERSITY, LIBBY LIBRARY. *A Catalogue of Books, Manuscripts, and Other Materials from the Upton Sinclair Archives.* Bloomington: Univ. of Indiana Press, 1963, 56 pp.

LEARY, LEWIS. *Articles on American Literature, 1900–1950.* Durham: Duke Univ. Press, 1954, 274–275.

MILLETT, FRED BENJAMIN. *Contemporary American Authors: A Critical Survey and 219 Bio-bibliographies.* New York: Harcourt, Brace and World, 1940, 579–586.

SINCLAIR, UPTON. *Books of Upton Sinclair in Translations and Foreign Editions: A Bibliography of 525 Titles in 34 Countries.* Pasadena, California: privately printed by the author, 1930, 34 pp.

Also: 1938, 48 pp.

SPILLER, ROBERT ERNEST, et al. *Literary History of the United States,* 2 Vols. New York: Macmillan, 1962, 723–725. Supplement, 190.

SINGMASTER, ELSIE

LEARY, LEWIS. *Articles on American Literature, 1900–1950.* Durham: Duke Univ. Press, 1954, 275.

SMITH, BETTY

GERSTENBERGER, DONNA, and GEORGE HENDRICK. *The American Novel, 1789–1959: A Checklist of Twentieth Century Criticism.* Denver: Alan Swallow, 1961, 222.

SMITH, LILLIAN

GERSTENBERGER, DONNA, and GEORGE HENDRICK. *The American Novel, 1789–1959: A Checklist of Twentieth Century Criticism.* Denver: Alan Swallow, 1961, 222.

LEARY, LEWIS. *Articles on American Literature, 1900–1950.* Durham: Duke Univ. Press, 1954, 275.

SMITH, LOGAN PEARSALL

LEARY, LEWIS. *Articles on American Literature, 1900–1950.* Durham: Duke Univ. Press, 1954, 276.

SMITH, THORNE

LEARY, LEWIS. *Articles on American Literature, 1900–1950.* Durham: Duke Univ. Press, 1954, 276.

SNYDER, GARY

KHERDIAN, DAVID. *Six Poets of the San Francisco Renaissance.* Fresno, California: The Giligia Press, 1965, 55–70.

SPENCER, THEODORE

LEARY, LEWIS. *Articles on American Literature, 1900–1950.* Durham: Duke Univ. Press, 1954, 276.

SPEYER, LEONORA

LEARY, LEWIS. *Articles on American Literature, 1900–1950.* Durham: Duke Univ. Press, 1954, 276.

SPILLANE, MICKEY

GERSTENBERGER, DONNA, and GEORGE HENDRICK. *The American Novel, 1789–1959: A Checklist of Twentieth Century Criticism.* Denver: Alan Swallow, 1961, 223.

SPINGARN, J. E.

LEARY, LEWIS. *Articles on American Literature, 1900–1950.* Durham: Duke Univ. Press, 1954, 276.

SPRINGS, ELLIOTT WHITE

GERSTENBERGER, DONNA, and GEORGE HENDRICK. *The American Novel, 1789–1959: A Checklist of Twentieth Century Criticism.* Denver: Alan Swallow, 1961, 223.

STAFFORD, JEAN

GERSTENBERGER, DONNA, and GEORGE HENDRICK. *The American Novel, 1789–1959: A Checklist of Twentieth Century Criticism.* Denver: Alan Swallow, 1961, 223.

STEELE, WILBUR DANIEL

LEARY, LEWIS. *Articles on American Literature, 1900–1950.* Durham: Duke Univ. Press, 1954, 277.

STEFFENS, LINCOLN

LEARY, LEWIS. *Articles on American Literature, 1900–1950.* Durham: Duke Univ. Press, 1954, 277.

STEIN, GERTRUDE

FIRMAGE, GEORGE JAMES. *A Checklist of the Published Writings of Gertrude Stein.* Amherst: Univ. of Massachusetts Press, 1954, 8 pp.

GALLUP, D. C. "The Gertrude Stein Collection." *YULG,* XXII (October 1947), 22–32.

GERSTENBERGER, DONNA, and GEORGE HENDRICK. *The American Novel, 1789–1959: A Checklist of Twentieth Century Criticism.* Denver: Alan Swallow, 1961, 223–224.

LEARY, LEWIS. *Articles on American Literature, 1900–1950.* Durham: Duke Univ. Press, 1954, 277–278.

LIBRARY OF CONGRESS, GENERAL REFERENCE AND BIBLIOGRAPHY DIVISION. *Sixty American Poets, 1896–1944,* selected, with a preface and critical notes by Allen Tate and a preliminary checklist by Francis Cheney. Washington, 1945, 150–155.

Revised edition: 1954, 121–126.

MILLER, ROSALIND S. *Gertrude Stein: Form and Intelligibility.* New York: Exposition Press, 1949, 157–160.

PEARSON, N. H. "The Gertrude Stein Collection." *YULG,* XVI (January 1942), 45–47.

REID, BENJAMIN LAWRENCE. *Art by Subtraction: A Dissenting Opinion of Gertrude Stein.* Norman: Univ. of Oklahoma Press, 1958, 209–216.

SAWYER, JULIAN. *Gertrude Stein: A Bibliography.* New York: Arrow Editions, 1941, 33–153.

_____. "Gertrude Stein: A Bibliography, 1941–1948." *BB,* XIX (May–August 1948), 152–156; (September–December 1948), 183–187.

_____. "Gertrude Stein (1874–   ): A Checklist Comprising Critical and Miscellaneous Writings about Her Work, Life and Personality from 1913–1942." *BB,*

XVII (January–April 1943), 211–212; XVIII (May–August 1943), 11–13; XIX (January–April 1948), 128–131.

TITLE VARIES.

SPILLER, ROBERT ERNEST, et al. *Literary History of the United States,* 2 Vols. New York: Macmillan, 1962, 729–730. Supplement, 191–192.

STEIN, GERTRUDE. "Bibliography." *Transition,* III (February 1929), 47–55.

STEWART, ALLEGRA. *Gertrude Stein and the Present.* Cambridge: Harvard Univ. Press, 1967, bibliographical footnotes.

WOODRESS, JAMES, et al. *American Literary Scholarship: An Annual.* Durham: Duke Univ. Press, (1964), 192–194; (1966), 161–162.

YALE UNIVERSITY, LIBRARY. *A Catalogue of the Published and Unpublished Writings of Gertrude Stein Exhibited in the Yale University Library, 22 February to 29 March 1941,* compiled by Robert Bartlett Hass and Donald Clifford Gallup. New Haven: Yale Univ. Library, 1941, 64 pp.

Most of this material now in Yale Univ. Library.

STEINBECK, JOHN

BEEBE, MAURICE, and JACKSON R. BRYER. "Criticism of John Steinbeck: A Selected Checklist." *MFS,* XI (Spring 1965), 90–103.

BLANCK, JACOB, ed. *Merle Johnson's American First Editions,* 4th edition, revised and enlarged. Waltham, Massachusetts: Mark Press, 1965, 472–473.

FONTENROSE, JOSEPH EDDY.
*John Steinbeck: An Introduction and
Interpretation.* New York, 1967,
142–146.

Part of the *American Authors and
Critics Series,* begun in 1961, and
purchased by Holt, Rinehart and
Winston from Barnes and Noble.
The nine original and three new
volumes were issued under the Holt
imprint in January 1967.

GERSTENBERGER, DONNA, and
GEORGE HENDRICK. *The American Novel, 1789–1959: A Checklist
of Twentieth Century Criticism.*
Denver: Alan Swallow, 1961,
225–230.

LEARY, LEWIS. *Articles on American Literature, 1900–1950.* Durham:
Duke Univ. Press, 1954, 278–279.

MILLETT, FRED BENJAMIN. *Contemporary American Authors: A
Critical Survey and 219 Bio-bibliographies.* New York: Harcourt, Brace
and World, 1940, 596–597.

POWELL, LAWRENCE CLARK.
"Toward a Bibliography of John
Steinbeck." *The Colophon,* ns III
(Autumn 1938), 558–568.

REMORDS, GEORGES. "John
Steinbeck – note bibliographique."
*Bulletin de la Faculté des Lettres de
Strasbourg,* XXVIII (April 1950),
301–305.

SPILLER, ROBERT ERNEST, et al.
Literary History of the United States,
2 Vols. New York: Macmillan, 1962,
730–731. Supplement, 192–193.

WOODRESS, JAMES, et al. *American Literary Scholarship: An Annual.*
Durham: Duke Univ. Press, (1965),
172–174; (1966), 162–164.

STERLING, GEORGE

BLANCK, JACOB, ed. *Merle Johnson's American First Editions,* 4th
edition, revised and enlarged.
Waltham, Massachusetts: Mark Press,
1965, 474–476.

JOHNSON, CECIL, comp. *A Bib-
liography of the Writings of George
Sterling.* San Francisco: Windsor
Press, 1931, 66 pp.

LEARY, LEWIS. *Articles on American Literature, 1900–1950.* Durham:
Duke Univ. Press, 1954, 279–280.

SPILLER, ROBERT ERNEST, et al.
Literary History of the United States,
2 Vols. New York: Macmillan, 1962,
731–732.

STEVENS, WALLACE

BORROFF, MARIE, ed. *Wallace
Stevens: A Collection of Critical
Essays.* Englewood Cliffs, New
Jersey: Prentice Hall, 1963, 181.

BRYER, JACKSON R., and JOSEPH
N. RIDDEL. "A Checklist of Stevens
Criticism." *TCL,* VIII (October
1962–January 1963), 124–142.

DARTMOUTH COLLEGE,
LIBRARY. "A Supplementing List
of Items in the Wallace Stevens Collection at Dartmouth College." *Dartmouth College Library Bulletin,* ns
IV (December 1961), 67–71.

Supplements Samuel French Morse's
*Wallace Stevens: A Preliminary Check-
list of His Published Writings, 1898–
1954,* 1954.

LEARY, LEWIS. *Articles on American Literature, 1900–1950.* Durham:
Duke Univ. Press, 1954, 280–281.

LIBRARY OF CONGRESS,
GENERAL REFERENCE AND

BIBLIOGRAPHY DIVISION. *Sixty American Poets, 1896–1944,* selected, with a preface and critical notes by Allen Tate and a preliminary checklist by Francis Cheney. Washington, 1945, 156–157.

Revised edition: 1954, 127–129.

MILLETT, FRED BENJAMIN. *Contemporary American Authors: A Critical Survey and 219 Bio-bibliographies.* New York: Harcourt, Brace and World, 1940, 597–598.

MITCHELL, ROGER S. "Wallace Stevens: A Checklist of Criticism." *BB,* XXIII (September–December 1962), 208–210.

MORSE, SAMUEL FRENCH. *Wallace Stevens: A Preliminary Checklist of His Published Writings, 1898–1954.* New Haven: Yale Univ. Library, 1954, 66 pp.

MORSE, SAMUEL FRENCH, JACKSON R. BRYER and JOSEPH N. RIDDEL. *Wallace Stevens Checklist and Bibliography of Stevens Criticism.* Denver: Alan Swallow, 1963, 98 pp.

Supersedes Samuel French Morse's *Wallace Stevens: A Preliminary Checklist of His Published Writings, 1898–1954,* 1954, and Jackson R. Bryer and Joseph N. Riddel's "A Checklist of Stevens Criticism," 1963.

O'CONNOR, WILLIAM VAN. *The Shaping Spirit: A Study of Wallace Stevens.* Chicago: Regnery, 1950, 141–146.

SPILLER, ROBERT ERNEST, et al. *Literary History of the United States,* 2 Vols. New York: Macmillan, 1962, 732–734. Supplement, 193–195.

WOODRESS, JAMES, et al. *American Literary Scholarship: An Annual.* Durham: Duke Univ. Press, (1963), 189–192; (1964), 204–206.

STEWART, CHARLES DAVID

JONES, JOSEPH J. "American First Editions at TxU: Charles David Stewart (b. 1868)." *LCUT,* V (Spring 1956), 34–37.

STICKNEY, TRUMBULL

LEARY, LEWIS. *Articles on American Literature, 1900–1950.* Durham: Duke Univ. Press, 1954, 281.

STILL, JAMES

GERSTENBERGER, DONNA, and GEORGE HENDRICK. *The American Novel, 1789–1959: A Checklist of Twentieth Century Criticism.* Denver: Alan Swallow, 1961, 230.

LEARY, LEWIS. *Articles on American Literature, 1900–1950.* Durham: Duke Univ. Press, 1954, 281.

STREET, JAMES

GERSTENBERGER, DONNA, and GEORGE HENDRICK. *The American Novel, 1789–1959: A Checklist of Twentieth Century Criticism.* Denver: Alan Swallow, 1961, 233.

LEARY, LEWIS. *Articles on American Literature, 1900–1950.* Durham: Duke Univ. Press, 1954, 283.

STRIBLING, T. S.

BLANCK, JACOB, ed. *Merle Johnson's American First Editions,* 4th edition, revised and enlarged. Waltham, Massachusetts: Mark Press, 1965, 485–486.

GERSTENBERGER, DONNA, and GEORGE HENDRICK. *The American Novel, 1789–1959: A Checklist of Twentieth Century Criticism.* Denver: Alan Swallow, 1961, 233.

LEARY, LEWIS. *Articles on American Literature, 1900–1950.* Durham: Duke Univ. Press, 1954, 283.

STONE, FRANK. "American First Editions: T. S. Stribling, 1881–   ." *PW,* CXXXII (August 21, 1937), 592.

STUART, JESSE

BLAIR, EVERETTA LOVE. *Jesse Stuart: His Life and Works.* Columbia: Univ. of South Carolina Press, 1967, 267–279.

GERSTENBERGER, DONNA, and GEORGE HENDRICK. *The American Novel, 1789–1959: A Checklist of Twentieth Century Criticism.* Denver: Alan Swallow, 1961, 233.

HAGEMANN, E. R., and JAMES E. MARSH. "Contributions to *Esquire,* 1933–1941." *BB,* XXII (May–August 1957), 71.

LEARY, LEWIS. *Articles on American Literature, 1900–1950.* Durham: Duke Univ. Press, 1954, 283.

LIBRARY OF CONGRESS, GENERAL REFERENCE AND BIBLIOGRAPHY DIVISION. *Sixty American Poets, 1896–1944,* selected, with a preface and critical notes by Allen Tate and a preliminary checklist by Francis Cheney. Washington, 1945, 158–159.

Revised edition: 1954, 129–130.

WOODBRIDGE, HENSLEY C. "Articles by Jesse Stuart: A Bibliography." *Bulletin of the Kentucky Library Association,* XXIII (July 1959), 89–91.

_____. "Jesse Stuart: A Bibliographical Note." *ABC,* IX (September 1958), 8–22.

_____. "Jesse Stuart's Contributions to Newspapers." *Bulletin of the Kentucky Library Association,* XXIII (April 1959), 45–47.

_____. "Supplement to a Jesse Stuart Bibliography." *Bulletin of the Kentucky Library Association,* XXIII (January 1959), 9.

WOODBRIDGE, HENSLEY C., et al., comps. *Jesse Stuart: A Bibliography.* Harrogate, Tennessee: Lincoln Memorial Univ. Press, 1960, 74 pp.

STURGIS, HOWARD OVERING

LEARY, LEWIS. *Articles on American Literature, 1900–1950.* Durham: Duke Univ. Press, 1954, 283.

STYRON, WILLIAM

THE EDITORS. "Books by William Styron." *HC,* IV (December 1967), 7.

GERSTENBERGER, DONNA, and GEORGE HENDRICK. *The American Novel, 1789–1959: A Checklist of Twentieth Century Criticism.* Denver: Alan Swallow, 1961, 233.

SCHNEIDER, HAROLD W. "Two Bibliographies: Saul Bellow, William Styron." *Critique,* III (Summer 1960), 86–91.

WOODRESS, JAMES, et al. *American Literary Scholarship: An Annual.* Durham: Duke Univ. Press, (1965), 195; (1966), 181.

SUCKOW, RUTH

GERSTENBERGER, DONNA, and GEORGE HENDRICK. *The American Novel, 1789–1959: A Checklist of Twentieth Century Criticism.* Denver: Alan Swallow, 1961, 233.

LEARY, LEWIS. *Articles on American Literature, 1900–1950.* Durham: Duke Univ. Press, 1954, 283.

SUMMERALL, CHARLES PELOT

LIBRARY OF CONGRESS, MANU-SCRIPT DIVISION. *Charles Pelot Summerall: A Register of His Papers in the Library of Congress.* Washington, 1958, 9 leaves.

TAGGARD, GENEVIEVE

DARTMOUTH COLLEGE, LIBRARY. "Taggard Collection." *Dartmouth College Library Bulletin,* IV (February 1947), 87–91.

LEARY, LEWIS. *Articles on American Literature, 1900–1950.* Durham: Duke Univ. Press, 1954, 284.

LIBRARY OF CONGRESS, GENERAL REFERENCE AND BIBLIOGRAPHY DIVISION. *Sixty American Poets, 1896–1944,* selected, with a preface and critical notes by Allen Tate and a preliminary checklist by Francis Cheney. Washington, 1945, 160–161.

Revised edition: 1954, 130–131.

TARKINGTON, BOOTH

"Additions to the Tarkington Bibliography." *PULC,* XVI (Winter 1955), 89–94.

BLANCK, JACOB, ed. *Merle Johnson's American First Editions,* 4th edition, revised and enlarged. Waltham, Massachusetts: Mark Press, 1965, 489–495.

CURRIE, BARTON WOOD. *Booth Tarkington: A Bibliography.* New York: Doubleday, Doran and Co., 1932, 161 pp.

GERSTENBERGER, DONNA, and GEORGE HENDRICK. *The American Novel, 1789–1959: A Checklist of Twentieth Century Criticism.* Denver: Alan Swallow, 1961, 234.

LEARY, LEWIS. *Articles on American Literature, 1900–1950.* Durham: Duke Univ. Press, 1954, 284–285.

MILLETT, FRED BENJAMIN. *Contemporary American Authors: A Critical Survey and 219 Bio-bibliographies.* New York: Harcourt, Brace and World, 1940, 604–609.

PRINCETON UNIVERSITY, LIBRARY. *An Exhibition of Booth Tarkington's Works in the Treasure Room, March–April, 1946.* Princeton: Princeton Univ. Library, 1946, 11 pp.

RUSSO, DOROTHY RITTER, and THELMA L. SULLIVAN. *A Bibliography of Booth Tarkington, 1869–1946.* Indianapolis: Indiana Historical Society, 1949, 322 pp.

TATE, ALLEN

BRADBURY, JOHN M. *The Fugitives: A Critical Account.* Chapel Hill: Univ. of North Carolina Press, 1958, 280–283.

GERSTENBERGER, DONNA, and GEORGE HENDRICK. *The American Novel, 1789–1959: A Checklist of Twentieth Century Criticism.* Denver: Alan Swallow, 1961, 235.

LEARY, LEWIS. *Articles on American Literature, 1900–1950.* Durham: Duke Univ. Press, 1954, 285.

LIBRARY OF CONGRESS, GENERAL REFERENCE AND BIBLIOGRAPHY DIVISION. *Sixty American Poets, 1896–1944,* selected, with a preface and critical notes by Allen Tate and a preliminary checklist by Francis Cheney. Washington, 1945, 162–164.

Revised edition: 1954, 131–134.

MILLETT, FRED BENJAMIN. *Contemporary American Authors: A*

Critical Survey and 219 Bio-bibliographies. New York: Harcourt, Brace and World, 1940, 609–610.

THORP, WILLARD. "Allen Tate: A Checklist." *PULC,* III (April 1942), 85–98.

WOODRESS, JAMES, et al. *American Literary Scholarship: An Annual.* Durham: Duke Univ. Press, (1963), 196; (1964), 209–211.

TEASDALE, SARA

BLANCK, JACOB, ed. *Merle Johnson's American First Editions,* 4th edition, revised and enlarged. Waltham, Massachusetts: Mark Press, 1965, 496–497.

LEARY, LEWIS. *Articles on American Literature, 1900–1950.* Durham: Duke Univ. Press, 1954, 286–287.

LIBRARY OF CONGRESS, GENERAL REFERENCE AND BIBLIOGRAPHY DIVISION. *Sixty American Poets, 1896–1944,* selected, with a preface and critical notes by Allen Tate and a preliminary checklist by Francis Cheney. Washington, 1945, 165–167.

Revised edition: 1954, 134–136.

MILLETT, FRED BENJAMIN. *Contemporary American Authors: A Critical Survey and 219 Bio-bibliographies.* New York: Harcourt, Brace and World, 1940, 610–613.

SPILLER, ROBERT ERNEST, et al. *Literary History of the United States,* 2 Vols. New York: Macmillan, 1962, 741–742.

THIELEN, BENEDICT

GERSTENBERGER, DONNA, and GEORGE HENDRICK. *The American Novel, 1789–1959: A Checklist*

of Twentieth Century Criticism. Denver: Alan Swallow, 1961, 235.

THOMAS, AUGUSTUS

LEARY, LEWIS. *Articles on American Literature, 1900–1950.* Durham: Duke Univ. Press, 1954, 287.

THOMASON, JOHN W.

LEARY, LEWIS. *Articles on American Literature, 1900–1950.* Durham: Duke Univ. Press, 1954, 287.

THOMPSON, DOROTHY

LEARY, LEWIS. *Articles on American Literature, 1900–1950.* Durham: Duke Univ. Press, 1954, 287.

THURBER, JAMES

LEARY, LEWIS. *Articles on American Literature, 1900–1950.* Durham: Duke Univ. Press, 1954, 293.

TIETJENS, EUNICE

LEARY, LEWIS. *Articles on American Literature, 1900–1950.* Durham: Duke Univ. Press, 1954, 294.

TIPPMANN, HUGO KARL

LEARY, LEWIS. *Articles on American Literature, 1900–1950.* Durham: Duke Univ. Press, 1954, 294.

TORRENCE, RIDGELY

LEARY, LEWIS. *Articles on American Literature, 1900–1950.* Durham: Duke Univ. Press, 1954, 294.

TRENT, WILLIAM PETERFIELD

LEARY, LEWIS. *Articles on American Literature, 1900–1950.* Durham: Duke Univ. Press, 1954, 294.

TRILLING, LIONEL

GERSTENBERGER, DONNA, and GEORGE HENDRICK. *The American Novel, 1789–1959: A Checklist of Twentieth Century Criticism.* Denver: Alan Swallow, 1961, 236.

LEARY, LEWIS. *Articles on American Literature, 1900–1950.* Durham: Duke Univ. Press, 1954, 294.

TRINE, RALPH WALDO

LEARY, LEWIS. *Articles on American Literature, 1900–1950.* Durham: Duke Univ. Press, 1954, 295.

TUCKER, BENJAMIN R.

LEARY, LEWIS. *Articles on American Literature, 1900–1950.* Durham: Duke Univ. Press, 1954, 295.

TULLY, JIM

LEARY, LEWIS. *Articles on American Literature, 1900–1950.* Durham: Duke Univ. Press, 1954, 296.

TURNER, FREDERICK JACKSON

LEARY, LEWIS. *Articles on American Literature, 1900–1950.* Durham: Duke Univ. Press, 1954, 296.

ULLMAN, JAMES RAMSEY

GERSTENBERGER, DONNA, and GEORGE HENDRICK. *The American Novel, 1789–1959: A Checklist of Twentieth Century Criticism.* Denver: Alan Swallow, 1961, 250.

UNTERMEYER, LOUIS

LEARY, LEWIS. *Articles on American Literature, 1900–1950.* Durham: Duke Univ. Press, 1954, 296.

UPDIKE, DANIEL BERKELEY

LEARY, LEWIS. *Articles on American*

can Literature, 1900–1950. Durham: Duke Univ. Press, 1954, 296.

UPDIKE, JOHN

HARPER, HOWARD M., JR. *Desperate Faith: A Study of Bellow, Salinger, Mailer, Baldwin, and Updike.* Chapel Hill: Univ. of North Carolina Press, 1967, bibliographical footnotes.

TAYLOR, C. CLARKE. *John Updike: A Bibliography.* Kent, Ohio: Kent State Univ. Press, 1968, 82 pp.

390 references to original works and 349 to critical essays.

WOODRESS, JAMES, et al. *American Literary Scholarship: An Annual.* Durham: Duke Univ. Press, (1964), 166–167; (1966), 181–182.

UPSON, ARTHUR

LEARY, LEWIS. *Articles on American Literature, 1900–1950.* Durham: Duke Univ. Press, 1954, 296.

URIS, LEON

GERSTENBERGER, DONNA, and GEORGE HENDRICK. *The American Novel, 1789–1959: A Checklist of Twentieth Century Criticism.* Denver: Alan Swallow, 1961, 250.

VAN DOREN, CARL

LEARY, LEWIS. *Articles on American Literature, 1900–1950.* Durham: Duke Univ. Press, 1954, 297.

VAN DOREN, MARK

LEARY, LEWIS. *Articles on American Literature, 1900–1950.* Durham: Duke Univ. Press, 1954, 297.

LIBRARY OF CONGRESS, GENERAL REFERENCE AND BIBLIOGRAPHY DIVISION. *Sixty*

American Poets, 1896–1944,
selected, with a preface and critical
notes by Allen Tate and a preliminary
checklist by Francis Cheney.
Washington, 1945, 168–172.

Revised edition: 1954, 136–140.

VAN DYKE, HENRY

LEARY, LEWIS. *Articles on American Literature, 1900–1950.* Durham:
Duke Univ. Press, 1954, 297.

VAN DYKE, TERTIUS. *Henry Van Dyke: A Biography.* New York and
London: Harper and Brothers, 1935,
427–433.

VAN LOON, HENDRIK WILLEM

BLANCK, JACOB, ed. *Merle Johnson's American First Editions,* 4th
edition, revised and enlarged.
Waltham, Massachusetts: Mark Press,
1965, 509–511.

VAN VECHTEN, CARL

CUNNINGHAM, SCOTT. *A Bibliography of the Writings of Carl Van
Vechten.* Philadelphia: The Centaur
Book Shop, 1924, 62 pp.

GERSTENBERGER, DONNA, and
GEORGE HENDRICK. *The American Novel, 1789–1959: A Checklist
of Twentieth Century Criticism.*
Denver: Alan Swallow, 1961, 250–251.

GORDAN, JOHN D. "Carl Van
Vechten: Notes for an Exhibition in
Honor of His Seventy-fifth Birthday."
BNYPL, LIX (July 1955), 331–366.

JONAS, KLAUS W. "Additions to
the Bibliography of Carl Van
Vechten." *PBSA,* LV (1st Quart.
1961), 42–45.

——————. *Carl Van Vechten:
A Bibliography.* New York: Knopf,
1955, 94 pp.

LEARY, LEWIS. *Articles on American Literature, 1900–1950.* Durham:
Duke Univ. Press, 1954, 297.

MILLETT, FRED BENJAMIN. *Contemporary American Authors: A
Critical Survey and 219 Bio-bibliographies.* New York: Harcourt, Brace
and World, 1940, 626–628.

VEBLEN, THORSTEIN

DORFMAN, JOSEPH. *Thorstein
Veblen and His America.* New York:
Viking Press, 1934, 519–524.

INNES, HAROLD W. "A Bibliography of Thorstein Veblen." *Southwestern Political and Social Science
Quarterly,* X (March 1929–1930),
56–58.

Title of journal varies.

LEARY, LEWIS. *Articles on American Literature, 1900–1950.* Durham:
Duke Univ. Press, 1954, 297.

VIDAL, GORE

GERSTENBERGER, DONNA, and
GEORGE HENDRICK. *The American Novel, 1789–1959: A Checklist
of Twentieth Century Criticism.*
Denver: Alan Swallow, 1961, 251.

VIERECK, PETER

LEARY, LEWIS. *Articles on American Literature, 1900–1950.* Durham:
Duke Univ. Press, 1954, 297.

VILLARD, OSWALD GARRISON

LEARY, LEWIS. *Articles on American Literature, 1900–1950.* Durham:
Duke Univ. Press, 1954, 297.

WALKER, MARGARET

LEARY, LEWIS. *Articles on American Literature, 1900–1950.* Durham: Duke Univ. Press, 1954, 298.

WARREN, ROBERT PENN

BEEBE, MAURICE, and ERIN MARCUS. "Criticism of Robert Penn Warren: A Selected Checklist." *MFS,* VI (Spring 1960), 83–88.

BRADBURY, JOHN M. *The Fugitives: A Critical Account.* Chapel Hill: Univ. of North Carolina Press, 1958, 283–287.

GERSTENBERGER, DONNA, and GEORGE HENDRICK. *The American Novel, 1789–1959: A Checklist of Twentieth Century Criticism.* Denver: Alan Swallow, 1961, 252–254.

LEARY, LEWIS. *Articles on American Literature, 1900–1950.* Durham: Duke Univ. Press, 1954, 298–299.

LIBRARY OF CONGRESS, GENERAL REFERENCE AND BIBLIOGRAPHY DIVISION. *Sixty American Poets, 1896–1944,* selected, with a preface and critical notes by Allen Tate and a preliminary checklist by Francis Cheney. Washington, 1945, 173–174.

Revised edition: 1954, 140–142.

LONGLEY, JOHN LEWIS, JR., ed. *Robert Penn Warren: A Collection of Critical Essays.* New York: New York Univ. Press, 1965, 247–257.

McDOWELL, FREDERICK P. W. "Robert Penn Warren's Criticism." *Accent,* XV (Summer 1955), 173–196.

MILLETT, FRED BENJAMIN. *Contemporary American Authors: A Critical Survey and 219 Bio-bibliogra-* phies. New York: Harcourt, Brace and World, 1940, 628–629.

STALLMAN, ROBERT WOOSTER. "Robert Penn Warren: A Checklist of His Critical Writings." *UKCR,* XIV (Autumn 1947), 78–83.

WOODRESS, JAMES, et al. *American Literary Scholarship: An Annual.* Durham: Duke Univ. Press, (1963), 152–153; (1964), 167–168; (1965), 195–196.

WASSON, GEORGE SAVARY

LEARY, LEWIS. *Articles on American Literature, 1900–1950.* Durham: Duke Univ. Press, 1954, 299.

WATERS, FRANK

GERSTENBERGER, DONNA, and GEORGE HENDRICK. *The American Novel, 1789–1959: A Checklist of Twentieth Century Criticism.* Denver: Alan Swallow, 1961, 254.

WELLER, GEORGE

GERSTENBERGER, DONNA, and GEORGE HENDRICK. *The American Novel, 1789–1959: A Checklist of Twentieth Century Criticism.* Denver: Alan Swallow, 1961, 255.

LEARY, LEWIS. *Articles on American Literature, 1900–1950.* Durham: Duke Univ. Press, 1954, 301.

WELTY, EUDORA

APPEL, ALFRED, JR. *A Season of Dreams: The Fiction of Eudora Welty.* Baton Rouge: Louisiana State Univ. Press, 1965, 265–267.

COLE, McKELVA. "Book Reviews by Eudora Welty: A Checklist." *BB,* XXIII (January-April 1963), 240.

GERSTENBERGER, DONNA, and
GEORGE HENDRICK. *The American Novel, 1789—1959: A Checklist
of Twentieth Century Criticism.*
Denver: Alan Swallow, 1961, 255.

GROSS, SEYMOUR L., comp.
"Eudora Welty: A Bibliography of
Criticism and Comment." *Bibliogra-
phical Society of the University of
Virginia, Secretary's News Sheet,*
No. 45 (April 1960), 1—32.

LEARY, LEWIS. *Articles on American Literature, 1900—1950.* Durham:
Duke Univ. Press, 1954, 301.

SMYTHE, KATHERINE H. "Eudora
Welty: A Checklist." *BB,* XXI
(January-April 1965), 207—208.

WOODRESS, JAMES, et al. *American Literary Scholarship: An Annual.*
Durham: Duke Univ. Press, (1963),
153—154; (1964), 168—169; (1965),
196—197.

WESCOTT, GLENWAY

BLANCK, JACOB, ed. *Merle Johnson's American First Editions,* 4th
edition, revised and enlarged. Waltham,
Massachusetts: Mark Press, 1965,
514—515.

GERSTENBERGER, DONNA, and
GEORGE HENDRICK. *The American Novel, 1789—1959: A Checklist
of Twentieth Century Criticism.*
Denver: Alan Swallow, 1961, 255.

LEARY, LEWIS. *Articles on American Literature, 1900—1950.* Durham:
Duke Univ. Press, 1954, 301.

KAHN, SY M. "Glenway Wescott: A
Bibliography." *BB,* XXII (September-December 1958), 155—160.

WEST, JESSAMYN

GERSTENBERGER, DONNA, and

GEORGE HENDRICK. *The American Novel, 1789—1959: A Checklist
of Twentieth Century Criticism.*
Denver: Alan Swallow, 1961, 255.

WEST, NATHANIEL

GERSTENBERGER, DONNA, and
GEORGE HENDRICK. *The American Novel, 1789—1959: A Checklist
of Twentieth Century Criticism.*
Denver: Alan Swallow, 1961, 256.

LEARY, LEWIS. *Articles on American Literature, 1900—1950.* Durham:
Duke Univ. Press, 1954, 301.

REID, RANDALL. *The Fiction of
Nathanael West.* Chicago: Univ. of
Chicago Press, 1967, 165—169.

WHITE, WILLIAM. "How Forgotten
Was Nathanael West?" *ABC,* VIII
(December 1957), 13—17.

_____. "Nathanäel West: A
Bibliography." *SB,* XI (1958), 207—
224.

WHALEN, PHILIP

KHERDIAN, DAVID. *Six Poets of
the San Francisco Renaissance.*
Fresno, California: The Giligia Press,
1965, 77—92.

WHALER, JAMES

LIBRARY OF CONGRESS, GEN-
ERAL REFERENCE AND BIBLIOG-
RAPHY DIVISION. *Sixty American
Poets, 1896—1944,* selected, with a
preface and critical notes by Allen
Tate and a preliminary checklist by
Francis Cheney. Washington, 1945,
175.

Revised edition: 1954, 142—143.

WHARTON, EDITH

BLANCK, JACOB, ed. *Merle Johnson's *American First Editions,* 4th edition, revised and enlarged. Waltham, Massachusetts: Mark Press, 1965, 517–520.

BROOKS, VAN WYCK. *The Dream of Arcadia: American Writers and Artists in Italy, 1760–1915.* New York: Dutton, 1958, bibliographical footnotes.

BROWN, EDWARD KILLORAN. *Edith Wharton: Etude critique.* Paris: E. Droz, 1935, 331–340.

DAVIS, MRS. LAVINIA (RIKER), comp. *A Bibliography of the Writings of Edith Wharton.* Portland, Maine: The Southworth Press, 1933, 72 pp.

GERSTENBERGER, DONNA, and GEORGE HENDRICK. *The American Novel, 1789–1959: A Checklist of Twentieth Century Criticism.* Denver: Alan Swallow, 1961, 257–260.

HOWE, IRVING, ed. *Edith Wharton: A Collection of Critical Essays.* Englewood Cliffs, New Jersey: Prentice Hall, 1962, 179–180.

JESSUP, JOSEPHINE LURIE. *The Faith of Our Feminists: A Study of the Novels of Edith Wharton, Ellen Glasgow, Willa Cather.* New York: R. R. Smith, 1950, 119–121.

LEARY, LEWIS. *Articles on American Literature, 1900–1950.* Durham: Duke Univ. Press, 1954, 301–302.

MELISH, LAWSON McCLUNG. *A Bibliography of the Collected Writings of Edith Wharton.* New York: The Brick Row Book Shop, Inc., 1927, 98 pp.

MILLETT, FRED BENJAMIN. *Contemporary American Authors: A Critical Survey and 219 Bio-bibliographies.* New York: Harcourt, Brace and World, 1940, 633–639.

NEVIUS, BLAKE. *Edith Wharton: A Study of Her Fiction.* Berkeley: Univ. of California Press, 1953, 260-265.

——————. "Pussie Jones's Verses: A Bibliographical Note on Edith Wharton." *AL,* XXIII (January 1952), 494–497.

SPILLER, ROBERT ERNEST, et al. *Literary History of the United States,* 2 Vols. New York: Macmillan, 1962, 757–759. Supplement, 202–203.

TAYLOR, WALTER FULLER. *A History of American Letters,* with bibliographies by Harry Hartwick. Boston: American Book Co., 1936, 571–572.

Subsequent editions entitled: *The Story of American Letters.*

WOODRESS, JAMES, et al. *American Literary Scholarship: An Annual.* Durham: Duke Univ. Press, (1965), 165–167; (1966), 151–155.

WHEELER, EDWARD L.

LEARY, LEWIS. *Articles on American Literature, 1900–1950.* Durham: Duke Univ. Press, 1954, 302.

WHEELOCK, JOHN HALL

LEARY, LEWIS. *Articles on American Literature, 1900–1950.* Durham: Duke Univ. Press, 1954, 302–303.

WHITE, E.B.

LEARY, LEWIS. *Articles on American Literature, 1900–1950.* Durham: Duke Univ. Press, 1954, 303.

WHITE, STEWART EDWARD

BLANCK, JACOB, ed. *Merle Johnson's American First Editions,* 4th edition, revised and enlarged.

Waltham, Massachusetts: Mark Press, 1965, 523—525.

GERSTENBERGER, DONNA, and GEORGE HENDRICK. *The American Novel, 1789—1959: A Checklist of Twentieth Century Criticism.* Denver: Alan Swallow, 1961, 260.

LEARY, LEWIS. *Articles on American Literature, 1900—1950.* Durham: Duke Univ. Press, 1954, 303.

WHITE, WALLACE HUMPHREY

LIBRARY OF CONGRESS, MANUSCRIPT DIVISION. *Wallace H. White: A Register of His Papers in the Library of Congress.* Washington, 1959, 23 pp.

WHITE, WILLIAM ALLEN

BLANCK, JACOB, ed. *Merle Johnson's American First Editions,* 4th edition, revised and enlarged. Waltham, Massachusetts: Mark Press, 1965, 526—527.

GERSTENBERGER, DONNA, and GEORGE HENDRICK. *The American Novel, 1789—1959: A Checklist of Twentieth Century Criticism.* Denver: Alan Swallow, 1961, 260.

LEARY, LEWIS. *Articles on American Literature, 1900—1950.* Durham: Duke Univ. Press, 1954, 303.

RICH, EVERETT. *William Allen White: A Man from Emporia.* New York: Farrar and Rinehart, Inc., 1941, 347—361.

WHITLOCK, BRAND

GERSTENBERGER, DONNA, and GEORGE HENDRICK. *The American Novel, 1789—1959: A Checklist of Twentieth Century Criticism.* Denver: Alan Swallow, 1961, 261.

WILBUR, RICHARD

HILL, DONALD LOUIS. *Richard Wilbur.* New York: Twayne, 1967, 183—186.

WILDER, THORNTON

BLANCK, JACOB, ed. *Merle Johnson's American First Editions,* 4th edition, revised and enlarged. Waltham, Massachusetts: Mark Press, 1965, 541—542.

BRYER, JACKSON R. "Thornton Wilder and the Reviewers." *PBSA,* LVIII (1st Quart. 1964), 35—49.

EDELSTEIN, JEROME MELVIN, comp. *A Bibliographical Check List of the Writings of Thornton Wilder.* New Haven: Yale Univ. Library, 1959, 62 pp.

GERSTENBERGER, DONNA, and GEORGE HENDRICK. *The American Novel, 1789—1959: A Checklist of Twentieth Century Criticism.* Denver: Alan Swallow, 1961, 261—262.

KOSOK, HEINZ. "Thornton Wilder: A Bibliography of Criticism." *TCL,* IX (July 1963), 93—100.

LEARY, LEWIS. *Articles on American Literature, 1900—1950.* Durham: Duke Univ. Press, 1954, 320—321.

MILLETT, FRED BENJAMIN. *Contemporary American Authors: A Critical Survey and 219 Bio-bibliographies.* New York: Harcourt, Brace and World, 1940, 643—645.

WILLIAMS, BEN AMES

LEARY, LEWIS. *Articles on American Literature, 1900—1950.* Durham: Duke Univ. Press, 1954, 321.

WILLIAMS, OSCAR

LEARY, LEWIS. *Articles on American Literature, 1900–1950.* Durham: Duke Univ. Press, 1954, 321.

WILLIAMS, TENNESSEE

ASSELINEAU, ROGER. "Tennessee Williams on la Nostalgie de la Pureté." *EA,* X (October-December 1957), 431–443.

CARPENTER, CHARLES A., JR., and ELIZABETH COOK. "Addenda to 'Tennessee Williams: A Selected Bibliography.'" *MD,* II (December 1959), 220–223.

DONY, NADINE. "Tennessee Williams: A Selected Bibliography." *MD,* I (December 1958), 181–191.

GERSTENBERGER, DONNA, and GEORGE HENDRICK. *The American Novel, 1789–1959: A Checklist of Twentieth Century Criticism.* Denver: Alan Swallow, 1961, 262.

WOODRESS, JAMES, et al. *American Literary Scholarship: An Annual.* Durham: Duke Univ. Press, (1965), 241–243; (1966), 227–228.

WILLIAMS, THOMAS LANIER

LEARY, LEWIS. *Articles on American Literature, 1900–1950.* Durham: Duke Univ. Press, 1954, 321–322.

WILLIAMS, WILLIAM CARLOS

GERSTENBERGER, DONNA, and GEORGE HENDRICK. *The American Novel, 1789–1959: A Checklist of Twentieth Century Criticism.* Denver: Alan Swallow, 1961, 262.

HEAL, EDITH, ed. *I Wanted to Write a Poem: The Autobiography of the Works of a Poet.* Boston: Beacon Press, 1958, 99 pp.

LEARY, LEWIS. *Articles on American Literature, 1900–1950.* Durham: Duke Univ. Press, 1954, 322.

LIBRARY OF CONGRESS, GENERAL REFERENCE AND BIBLIOGRAPHY DIVISION. *Sixty American Poets, 1896–1944,* selected, with a preface and critical notes by Allen Tate and a preliminary checklist by Francis Cheney. Washington, 1945, 177–179.

Revised Edition: 1954, 143–146.

MILLETT, FRED BENJAMIN. *Contemporary American Authors: A Critical Survey and 219 Bio-bibliographies.* New York: Harcourt, Brace and World, 1940, 646–647.

SPILLER, ROBERT ERNEST, et al. *Literary History of the United States,* 2 Vols. New York: Macmillan, 1962, 776–777. Supplement, 209–210.

WAGNER, LINDA WELSHIMER. "A Decade of Discovery, 1953–1963: Checklist of Criticism: William Carlos Williams' Poetry." *TCL,* X (January 1965), 166–169.

WOODRESS, JAMES, et al. *American Literary Scholarship: An Annual.* Durham: Duke Univ. Press, (1963), 192–193; (1964), 206–207; (1966), 203–204.

WILLKIE, WENDELL

LEARY, LEWIS. *Articles on American Literature, 1900–1950.* Durham: Duke Univ. Press, 1954, 322.

WILLS, RIDLEY

BRADBURY, JOHN M. *The Fugitives: A Critical Account.* Chapel Hill: Univ. of North Carolina Press, 1958, 293.

WILSON, EDMUND

GERSTENBERGER, DONNA, and GEORGE HENDRICK. *The American Novel, 1789–1959: A Checklist of Twentieth Century Criticism.* Denver: Alan Swallow, 1961, 263.

LEARY, LEWIS. *Articles on American Literature, 1900–1950.* Durham: Duke Univ. Press, 1954, 323.

MILLETT, FRED BENJAMIN. *Contemporary American Authors: A Critical Survey and 219 Bio-bibliographies.* New York: Harcourt, Brace and World, 1940, 649–651.

MIZENER, ARTHUR. "Edmund Wilson: A Checklist." *PULC,* V (February 1944), 62–78.

WILSON, HARRY LEON

BLANCK, JACOB, ed. *Merle Johnson's American First Editions,* 4th edition, revised and enlarged. Waltham, Massachusetts: Mark Press, 1965, 543–544.

WILSON, LOUIS ROUND

THORNTON, MARY LINDSAY. "Bibliography of Louis Round Wilson." *LQ,* XII (July 1942), 339–352.

WILSON, WOODROW

BLANCK, JACOB, ed. *Merle Johnson's American First Editions,* 4th edition, revised and enlarged. Waltham, Massachusetts: Mark Press, 1965, 545–546.

BRAND, KATHERINE E. "Woodrow Wilson in His Own Time." *LCQJ,* XIII (February 1956), 61–72.

BROWN, GEORGE DOBBIN. *An Essay Towards a Bibliography of the Published Writings and Addresses of Woodrow Wilson.* Princeton: Princeton Univ. Library, 1917, 52 pp.

Continuation of the bibliography of Harry Clemens, 1913. Continued by the bibliography of Howard Seavoy Leach, 1922.

"Catalog of the Woodrow Wilson Centennial Exhibit." *LCQJ,* XIII (February 1956), 73–105.

CLEMONS, HARRY. *An Essay Towards a Bibliography of the Published Writings and Addresses of Woodrow Wilson, 1875–1910.* Princeton: Princeton Univ. Library, 1913, 26 pp.

Continued by the bibliographies of George Dobbin Brown, 1917, and Howard Seavoy Leach, 1922.

LEACH, HOWARD SEAVOY. *An Essay Towards a Bibliography of the Published Writings and Addresses of Woodrow Wilson, March 1917 to March 1921.* Princeton: Princeton Univ. Library, 1922, 73 pp.

Continuation of the bibliographies of Harry Clemens, 1913, and George Dobbin Brown, 1917.

LEARY, LEWIS. *Articles on American Literature, 1900–1950.* Durham: Duke Univ. Press, 1954, 323–324.

LINK, ARTHUR S. *Woodrow Wilson and the Progressive Era, 1910–1917.* New York: Harper, 1954, 283–313, bibliographical footnotes.

PAINE, GREGORY LANSING, ed. *Southern Prose Writers: Representative Selections,* with introduction, bibliography and notes. New York: American Book Co., 1947, cxliii–cxliv.

SPILLER, ROBERT ERNEST, et al. *Literary History of the United States,* 2 Vols. New York: Macmillan, 1962, 779–781. Supplement, 210–212.

TURNBULL, LAURA SHEARER. *Woodrow Wilson: A Selected Bibliography of His Published Writings, Addresses, and Public Papers.* Princeton: Princeton Univ. Press, 1948, 179 pp.

WINSOR, KATHLEEN

LEARY, LEWIS. *Articles on American Literature, 1900–1950.* Durham: Duke Univ. Press, 1954, 324.

WINTERS, YVOR

LEARY, LEWIS. *Articles on American Literature, 1900–1950.* Durham: Duke Univ. Press, 1954, 324.

LIBRARY OF CONGRESS, GENERAL REFERENCE AND BIBLIOGRAPHY DIVISION. *Sixty American Poets, 1896–1944,* selected, with a preface and critical notes by Allen Tate and a preliminary checklist by Francis Cheney. Washington, 1945, 180–181.

Revised edition: 1954, 146–148.

LOHF, KENNETH A., and EUGENE P. SHEEHY, comps. *Yvor Winters: A Bibliography.* Denver: Alan Swallow, 1959, 35 pp.

WINTER, SOPHUS

LEARY, LEWIS. *Articles on American Literature, 1900–1950.* Durham: Duke Univ. Press, 1954, 324.

WISTER, OWEN

BLANCK, JACOB, ed. *Merle Johnson's American First Editions,* 4th edition, revised and enlarged. Waltham, Massachusetts: Mark Press, 1965, 547–548.

GERSTENBERGER, DONNA, and GEORGE HENDRICK. *The American Novel, 1789–1959: A Checklist of Twentieth Century Criticism.* Denver: Alan Swallow, 1961, 263.

HORNBERGER, THEODORE. "American First Editions at Texas University: Owen Wister." *LCUT,* I (Fall 1945), 33–34.

LEARY, LEWIS. *Articles on American Literature, 1900–1950.* Durham: Duke Univ. Press, 1954, 325.

PENNSYLVANIA HISTORICAL JUNTO. "The Owen Wister Papers in the Library of Congress: with a Supplementary Note on Owen Wister and His Heritage." *Pennsylvanian,* X (August 1952), 1–3.

WOLFE, THOMAS

BEEBE, MAURICE, and LESLIE A. FIELD. "Criticism of Thomas Wolfe: A Selected Checklist." *MFS,* XI (Autumn 1965), 315–328.

BLANCK, JACOB, ed. *Merle Johnson's American First Editions,* 4th edition, revised and enlarged. Waltham, Massachusetts: Mark Press, 1965, 549–550.

GERSTENBERGER, DONNA, and GEORGE HENDRICK. *The American Novel, 1789–1959: A Checklist of Twentieth Century Criticism.* Denver: Alan Swallow, 1961, 263–268.

GIBBS, ROBERT COLEMAN. "Thomas Wolfe's Hour Years at Chapel Hill: A Study of Biographical Source Material." Unpublished master's thesis, Univ. of North Carolina, 1958.

HOLMAN, C. HUGH. "Thomas Wolfe: A Bibliographical Study." *TSLL,* I (Autumn 1959), 427–445.

JOHNSON, ELMER D. *Of Time and Thomas Wolfe: A Bibliography with a Character Index of Works.* New York: Scarecrow Press, 1959, 226 pp.

KAUFFMAN, BERNICE, comp. "Bibliography of Periodical Articles on Thomas Wolfe." *BB,* XVII (May–August 1942), 162–165.

KENNEDY, RICHARD S. *The Window of Memory: The Literary Career of Thomas Wolfe.* Chapel Hill: Univ. of North Carolina Press, 1962, 339–349.

LEARY, LEWIS. *Articles on American Literature, 1900–1950.* Durham: Duke Univ. Press, 1954, 325–327.

LITTLE, THOMAS. "The Thomas Wolfe Collection of William B. Wisdom (at Harvard College Library)." *HLB,* I (1947), 280–287.

POLLOCK, THOMAS CLARK, and OSCAR CARGILL. *Thomas Wolfe at Washington Square.* New York: New York Univ. Press, 1954, 153–163.

PRESTON, GEORGE RILEY, JR. *Thomas Wolfe: A Bibliography.* New York: C. S. Boesen, 1943, 127 pp.

SPILLER, ROBERT ERNEST, et al. *Literary History of the United States,* 2 Vols. New York: Mac-

millan, 1962, 784–786. Supplement, 213–215.

TURNBULL, ANDREW. *Thomas Wolfe.* New York: Scribner's, 1967, 325–347.

WAISER, RICHARD GAITHER. *Thomas Wolfe: An Introduction and Interpretation.* New York, 1967, 145–148.

Part of the *American Authors and Critics Series,* begun in 1961, and purchased by Holt, Rinehart and Winston from Barnes and Noble. The nine original and three new volumes were issued under the Holt imprint in January 1967.

WILKINSON, BILLY RAYFORD. "The Thomas Wolfe Collection of the University of North Carolina Library." Unpublished master's thesis, Univ. of North Carolina, 1960.

WOODRESS, JAMES, et al. *American Literary Scholarship: An Annual.* Durham: Duke Univ. Press, (1965), 169–172; (1966), 162–164.

WOLFERT, IRA

GERSTENBERGER, DONNA, and GEORGE HENDRICK. *The American Novel, 1789–1959: A Checklist of Twentieth Century Criticism.* Denver: Alan Swallow, 1961, 268.

WOODBERRY, GEORGE EDWARD

DOYLE, JOSEPH. "A Finding List of Manuscript Materials Relating to George Edward Woodberry." *PBSA,* XLVI (2nd Quart. 1952), 165–168.

_____. "George Edward Woodberry: A Bibliography." *BB,* XXI (January–April 1955), 136–139; (May–August 1955), 163–168;

(September—December 1955), 176—181; (January—April 1956), 209—214.

HAWKINS, R. R. "A List of Writings by and about George Edward Woodberry." *BNYPL*, XXXIV (May 1930), 279—296.

LEARY, LEWIS. *Articles on American Literature, 1900—1950.* Durham: Duke Univ. Press, 1954, 327—328.

LEDOUX, LOUIS VERNON. *George Edward Woodberry: A Study of His Poetry.* Cambridge, Massachusetts: The Poetry Review Co., 1917, 57—72.

_____. *The Poetry of George Edward Woodberry: A Critical Study.* New York: Dodd, Mead and Co., 1918, 57—72.

SPILLER, ROBERT ERNEST, et al. *Literary History of the United States,* 2 Vols. New York: Macmillan, 1962, 786—787. Supplement, 215.

WOOLEY, ROBERT WICKLIFFE

LIBRARY OF CONGRESS, MANUSCRIPT DIVISION. *Robert W. Wooley: A Register of His Papers in the Library of Congress.* Washington, 1960, 21 leaves.

WOOLLCOTT, ALEXANDER

LEARY, LEWIS. *Articles on American Literature, 1900—1950.* Durham: Duke Univ. Press, 1954, 328.

WOUK, HERMAN

GERSTENBERGER, DONNA, and GEORGE HENDRICK. *The American Novel, 1789—1959: A Checklist of Twentieth Century Criticism.* Denver: Alan Swallow, 1961, 269—270.

WRIGHT, HAROLD BELL

GERSTENBERGER, DONNA, and GEORGE HENDRICK. *The American Novel, 1789—1959: A Checklist of Twentieth Century Criticism.* Denver: Alan Swallow, 1961, 270.

LEARY, LEWIS. *Articles on American Literature, 1900—1950.* Durham: Duke Univ. Press, 1954, 328—329.

WRIGHT, RICHARD

BRYER, JACKSON R. "Richard Wright: A Selected Check List of Criticism." *WSCL*, I (Fall 1960), 22—23.

GERSTENBERGER, DONNA, and GEORGE HENDRICK. *The American Novel, 1789—1959: A Checklist of Twentieth Century Criticism.* Denver: Alan Swallow, 1961, 270—271.

LEARY, LEWIS. *Articles on American Literature, 1900—1950.* Durham: Duke Univ. Press, 1954, 329.

SPILLER, ROBERT ERNEST, et al. *Literary History of the United States,* 2 Vols. New York: Macmillan, 1962, 789. Supplement, 216.

SPRAGUE, M. D. "Richard Wright: A Bibliography." *BB*, XXI (September—December 1953), 39.

WEBB, CONSTANCE. *Richard Wright: A Biography.* New York: Putnam, 1968, 423—429.

WRIGHT, WILLARD HUNTINGTON

LEARY, LEWIS. *Articles on American Literature, 1900—1950.* Durham: Duke Univ. Press, 1954, 329.

WYLIE, ELINOR

BLANCK, JACOB, ed. *Merle Johnson's American First Editions,* 4th edition, revised and enlarged. Waltham, Massachusetts: Mark Press, 1965, 551–553.

GERSTENBERGER, DONNA, and GEORGE HENDRICK. *The American Novel, 1789–1959: A Checklist of Twentieth Century Criticism.* Denver: Alan Swallow, 1961, 271.

LEARY, LEWIS. *Articles on American Literature, 1900–1950.* Durham: Duke Univ. Press, 1954, 329–330.

LIBRARY OF CONGRESS, GENERAL REFERENCE AND BIBLIOGRAPHY DIVISION. *Sixty American Poets, 1896–1944,* selected, with a preface and critical notes by Allen Tate and a preliminary checklist by Francis Cheney. Washington, 1945, 182–184.

Revised edition: 1954, 148–150.

MILLETT, FRED BENJAMIN. *Contemporary American Authors: A Critical Survey and 219 Bio-bibliographies.* New York: Harcourt, Brace and World, 1940, 661–663.

SPILLER, ROBERT ERNEST, et al. *Literary History of the United States,* 2 Vols. New York: Macmillan, 1962, 789–790.

WOODRESS, JAMES, et al. *American Literary Scholarship: An Annual.* Durham: Duke Univ. Press, (1966), 203–204.

WRIGHT, ELIZABETH V. "A Bibliographic Study of Elinor Wylie." Unpublished doctoral dissertation, Loyola Univ. (Chicago), 1954.

YOUNG, STARK

GERSTENBERGER, DONNA, and GEORGE HENDRICK. *The American Novel, 1789–1959: A Checklist of Twentieth Century Criticism.* Denver: Alan Swallow, 1961, 271.

LEARY, LEWIS. *Articles on American Literature, 1900–1950.* Durham: Duke Univ. Press, 1954, 330.

THURMAN, BEDFORD. "Stark Young: A Bibliography of His Writings with a Selective Index to His Criticism of the Arts." Unpublished doctoral dissertation, Cornell Univ., 1954.

ZATURENSKA, MARYA

LIBRARY OF CONGRESS, GENERAL REFERENCE AND BIBLIOGRAPHY DIVISION. *Sixty American Poets, 1896–1944,* selected, with a preface and critical notes by Allen Tate and a preliminary checklist by Francis Cheney. Washington, 1945, 185.

Revised edition: 1954, 150.

III

GENRE

1. LITERARY HISTORY AND CRITICISM

ADELMAN, IRVING, and RITA DIVORKIN. *Modern Drama: A Checklist of Critical Literature on Twentieth Century Plays.* Metuchen, New Jersey: The Scarecrow Press, 1967, 343–370.

ALDRIDGE, JOHN W., ed. *Critiques and Essays on Modern Fiction, 1920–1951, Representing the Achievement of Modern American and British Critics.* New York: Ronald Press Co., 1952, 553–610.

"A Selected Bibliography of Criticism of Modern Fiction," by Robert Wooster Stallman.

ARMS, GEORGE WARREN, and JOSEPH MARSHALL KUNTZ. *Poetry Explication: A Checklist of Interpretations since 1925 of British and American Poems Past and Present.* New York: Swallow Press and Morrow, 1950, 187 pp.

An expansion of *A Check List of Poetry Explications, 1925–1947.* Albuquerque: prepared for private circulation, 1948, 48 pp.

Revised edition: Denver: Alan Swallow, 1962, 331 pp.

BAKER, BLANCH (MERRITT). *Dramatic Bibliography: An Annotated List of Books on the History and Criticism of the Drama and Stage and on the Allied Arts of the Theatre.* New York: H. W. Wilson Co., 1933, 336 pp.

––––––––––––. *Theatre and Allied Arts: A Guide to Books Dealing with the History, Criticism, and Technic of the Drama and Theatre and Related Arts and Crafts.* New York: H. W. Wilson Co., 1952, 163–190.

BAKER, GEORGE H., ed. *List of Books Chiefly on the Drama and Literary Criticism.* New York: privately printed for Columbia Univ., 1897, 64 pp.

BALDENSPERGER, FERNAND, and WERNER P. FRIEDERICH. *Bibliography of Comparative Literature.* New York: Russell and Russell, 1960, 729 pp.

BEACH, JOSEPH WARREN. *The Twentieth Century Novel: Studies in Technique.* New York: Century Co., 1932, 555–557.

Also: Appleton-Century-Crofts, 1960.

BELL, INGLIS FREEMAN, and DONALD BAIRD. *The English Novel, 1578–1956: A Checklist of Twentieth Century Criticisms.* Denver: Alan Swallow, 1959, 181 pp.

BOGAN, LOUISE. *Achievement in American Poetry, 1900–1950.* Chicago: H. Regnery Co., 1951, 147–150.

BOYS, RICHARD C. "The English Poetical Miscellany in Colonial America." *SP,* XLII (January 1945), 114–130.

BRADBURY, JOHN M. *The Fugitives: A Critical Account.* Chapel Hill: Univ. of North Carolina Press, 1958, 274–294.

BROOKS, VAN WYCK. *The Confident Years: 1885–1915.* New York: Dutton, 1952, bibliographical footnotes.

_____. *The Dream of Arcadia: American Writers and Artists in Italy, 1760–1915.* New York: Dutton, 1958, bibliographical footnotes.

BROWNE, RAY BROADUS, and MARTIN LIGHT, eds. *Critical Approaches to American Literature,* 2 Vols. New York: Crowell, 1965, I, 340–351; II, 331–344.

BURKE, WILLIAM JEREMIAH, and WILL D. HOWE, comps. *American Authors and Books, 1640 to the Present Day.* New York: Crown Publishers, 1962, 834 pp.

CAIRNS, WILLIAM B. *British Criticism of American Writings, 1815–1833: A Contribution to the Study of Anglo-American Literary Relationships.* Madison: Univ. of Wisconsin Press, 1922, 319 pp.

Wisconsin Studies in Language and Literature, No. 14.

_____. *On the Development of American Literature from 1815 to 1833, with Special Reference to Periodicals.* Madison: Univ. of Wisconsin Press, 1898, 87 pp.

Lists of periodicals in appendices.

CAMPBELL, KILLIS. "Recent Additions to American Literary History." *SP,* XXXIII (July 1936), 534–543.

CARDWELL, GUY A. "On Scholarship and Southern Literature." *SAQ,* XL (January 1941), 60–72.

CONWAY, ADALINE MAY. *The Essay in American Literature.* New York: Faculty of the Graduate School, New York Univ., 1914, 85–127.

COOKE, G. W. *"The Dial:* An Historical and Biographical Introduction, with a List of the Contributors." *Journal of Speculative Philosophy,* XIX (July 1885), 225–265.

COPE, JACKSON, OTIS B. DAVIS, SAMUEL HENDERSON, ELIZABETH A. LARSEN and JOSEPH SMEALE. "Addenda to *Articles on American Literature Appearing in Current Periodicals, 1920–1945."* *AL,* XXII (March 1950), 61–74.

COWAN, LOUISE (SHILLINGBURG). *The Fugitive Group: A Literary History.* Baton Rouge: Louisiana State Univ. Press, 1959, bibliographical footnotes.

CUNLIFFE, MARCUS. *The Literature of the United States,* 3rd edition. Baltimore: Penguin Books, 1967, 375–386.

"Current Literature: I. Fiction, Drama, and Poetry. II. Criticism and Biography." *English Studies,* 1919–

A bibliographical essay in two parts, originally entitled, "Bibliography."

DONOVAN, FRANK PIERCE. *The Railroad in Literature.* Boston: Railway and Locomotive Historical Society, Baker Library, Harvard Business School, 1940, 138 pp.

DUFFEY, BERNARD I. *The Chicago Renaissance in American Letters: A Critical History.* East Lansing: Michigan State Univ. Press, 1954, bibliographical references.

DUYCKINCK, EVERT AUGUSTUS, and GEORGE LONG DUYCKINCK, eds. *Cyclopaedia of American Literature. . . ,* 2 Vols. New York: C. Scribner, 1855.

2nd edition: 1856.

3rd edition: 1866, 162 pp. One-volume edition.

4th edition: Philadelphia: T. E. Zell, 1875.

5th edition: Detroit: Bale Research Co., 1965.

FLANAGAN, HALLIE. *Arena: The History of the Federal Theatre.* New York: B. Blom, 1965, 439–447.

FOERSTER, NORMAN, ed. *Humanism and America: Essays on the Outlook of Modern Civilization.* New York: Farrar and Rinehart, 1930, 291–294.

FOLEY, PATRICK KEVIN. *American Authors, 1795–1895: A Bibliography.* Boston: The Publishers' Printing Co., 1897, 350 pp.

75 copies printed for subscribers.

FOSTER, MARGARET E. *Handbook of American Literature: Historical, Biographical, and Critical.* Philadelphia: Lippincott, 1850, 333 pp.

FRAHNE, KARL HEINRICH. *Von Franklin bis Hemingway: eine Einfuhrung in die Literatur Nordamerikas.* Hamburg: J. P. Toth, 1949, bibliographical notes.

FRIEDMAN, ALAN. *The Turn of the Novel: Studies in the Transition to Modern Fiction.* New York: Oxford Univ. Press, 1967, 189–207.

FRIEDMAN, MELVIN J. *Stream of Consciousness: A Study in Literary Method.* New Haven: Yale Univ. Press, 1955, 263–268.

FULLERTON, BRADFORD MORTON. *Selective Bibliography of American Literature, 1775–1900: A Brief Estimate of the More Important American Authors and a Description of Their Representative Works.* New York: Dial Press, 1936, 339 pp.

GERSTENBERGER, DONNA, and GEORGE HENDRICK. *The American Novel, 1789–1959: A Checklist of Twentieth Century Criticism.* Denver: Alan Swallow, 1961, 333 pp.

GODDARD, HAROLD CLARKE. *Studies in New England Transcendentalism.* New York: Columbia Univ. Press, 1908, 207–212.

GOHDES, CLARENCE. *American Literature in Nineteenth-Century England.* New York: Columbia Univ. Press, 1944, 151–180.

Representative articles on American literature appearing in British periodicals, 1833–1901.

GRATTAN, C. HARTLEY. "The Present Situation in American Literary Criticism." *SR,* XL (January 1932), 11–23.

GURKO, LEO. *The Angry Decade.* New York: Dodd, Mead, 1947, 287–294.

HARLOW, VICTOR EMMANUEL. *Bibliography and Genetic Study of American Realism.* Oklahoma City: Harlow Publishing Co., 1931, 110 pp.

HEFLING, HELEN, and EVA RICHARDS. *Index to Contemporary Biography and Criticism,* 1st edition. Boston: F. W. Faxon, 1929, 124 pp.

Also: *Hefling and Richards' Index. . .,* revised by Hefling, Richards and Jessie W. Dyde., 1934, 220 pp.

HELLMAN, HUGO E. "The Greatest American Oratory." *QJS,* XXIV (February 1938), 36–39.

HICKS, GRANVILLE. *The Great Tradition: An Interpretation of American Literature since the Civil War.* New York: Macmillan, 1933, 307–312.

HOFFMAN, FREDERICK JOHN. *The Twenties: American Writing in the Post-War Decade.* New York: Viking Press, 1955, 431–434, bibliographical footnotes.

2nd edition: Collier Books, 1962, bibliographical footnotes.

3rd edition: Macmillan, 1965, bibliographical footnotes.

HOFFMAN, FREDERICK JOHN, CHARLES ALLEN and CAROLYN F. ULRICH. *The Little Magazine: A History and Bibliography.* Princeton: Princeton Univ. Press, 1946, 233–403.

HUBBELL, JAY B. *The South in American Literature, 1607–1900.* Durham: Duke Univ. Press, 1954, 881–914.

Covers Southern authors and others who deal with the region.

Supersedes all preceding studies in thoroughness, especially for the pre-Civil War period.

JOHNSON, ALBERT E., and W. H. CRAIN JR. "Dictionary of American Drama Critics, 1850–1910." *Theatre Annual,* XIII (1955), 65–89.

JOHNSON, MERLE DE VORE. *High Spots of American Literature: A Practical Bibliography and Brief Literary Estimate of Outstanding American Books.* New York: Bennett Book Studios, 1929, 111 pp.

JOHNSON, THOMAS HERBERT, and PERRY MILLER. *The Puritans.* New York: American Book Co., 1938, 785–834.

Revised edition: 2 Vols. Harper and Row, 1963.

JONES, HOWARD MUMFORD. *Guide to American Literature and Its Backgrounds since 1890.* Cambridge: Harvard Univ. Press, 1953, 151 pp.

Omits drama. Is both bibliography and attempt to order the literature and its backgrounds.

2nd edition: 1959, 152 pp.

——————. *Humane Traditions in America: A List of Suggested Readings.* Cambridge: Harvard Univ. Press, 1961, 80 pp.

——————. *Ideas in America.* New York: Russell and Russell, 1965, 237–304.

KERMODE, FRANK. *The Sense of an Ending: Studies in the Theory of Fiction.* New York: Oxford Univ. Press, 1967, 181–187.

KINDILIEN, CARLIN T. *American Poetry in the Eighteen Nineties: A Study of American Verse, 1890– 1899 . . . .* Providence: Brown Univ. Press, 1956, 209–214.

KITZHABER, ALBERT RAYMOND. *A Bibliography of Rhetoric in American Colleges, 1850–1900.* Denver: Denver Public Library, 1954, 5 pp., 21 leaves.

KNIGHT, GRANT COCHRAN. *American Literature and Culture.* New York: R. Long and R. R. Smith, 1932.

"Selected Bibliography" at the end of each part.

——————. *The Strenuous Age in American Literature, 1900–1910.* Chapel Hill: Univ. of North Carolina Press, 1954, 231–253.

KRIEGER, MURRAY. *The New Apologists for Poetry.* Minneapolis: Univ. of Minnesota Press, 1956, 205–220.

KUNTZ, JOSEPH MARSHALL. *Poetry Explication: A Checklist of Interpretation since 1925 of British and American Poems Past and Present,* revised edition. Denver: Alan Swallow, 1962, 331 pp.

LA DRIERE, CRAIG, comp. "Annotated Bibliography of Recent Publications to Literary Theory and Criticism." *American Bookman,* I (No. 1, 1944), 100–126; (No. 2, 1944), 74–121.

LEARY, LEWIS. *Articles on American Literature, 1900–1950.* Durham: Duke Univ. Press, 1954, 437 pp.

——————. *Articles on American Literature, 1900–1950.* Durham: Duke Univ. Press, 1954, 331–335.

"American Literature, Aims and Methods."

——————. *Articles on American Literature, 1900–1950.* Durham: Duke Univ. Press, 1954, 372–379.

"Literary Criticism."

——————. *Articles on American Literature, 1900–1950.* Durham: Duke Univ. Press, 1954, 379–384.

"Literary History."

——————. *Articles on American Literature, 1900–1950.* Durham: Duke Univ. Press, 1954, 412–413.

"Prose."

——————. "Bibliographical and Textual Studies and American Literary History." *TQ,* III (Summer 1960), 160–166.

LEISY, ERNEST ERWIN. *American Literature: An Interpretative Survey.* New York: Thomas Y. Crowell Co., 1929, 273–287.

LEMAY, J. A. LEO. "Seventeenth Century American Poetry: A Bibliography of the Scholarship, 1943 to 1966." *EALN,* I (Winter 1966), 9–18.

LIBRARY ASSOCIATION, COUNTY LIBRARIES SECTION (ENGLAND). *Modern Drama, 1900–1938: A Selected List of Plays. . . and Other Works on Dramatic Theory and Other Related Subjects.* London: The Library Association, County Libraries Section, 1939, 77 pp.

LIBRARY OF CONGRESS. *A Guide to the Study of the United States of America: Representative Books Reflecting the Development of American Life and Thought.* Washington, 1960, 1,193 pp.

_____. *Recent American Poetry and Poetic Criticism: A Selected List of References,* compiled by Allen Tate. Washington, 1943, 13 leaves.

LIBRARY OF CONGRESS, DIVISION OF BIBLIOGRAPHY. *List of References on the Development of American Literature.* Washington, 1914, 10 leaves.

_____. *A List of Some Books on Current American Literature.* Washington, 1930, 6 leaves.

LOGGINS, VERNON. *I Hear America: Literature in the United States since 1900.* New York: Thomas Y. Crowell Co., 1937, 349–357.

LYNN, KENNETH SCHUYLER. *The Dream of Success: A Study of the Modern American Imagination.* Boston: Little, Brown, 1955, 269 pp.

MARTIN, JAY. *Harvests of Change: American Literature, 1865–1914.* Englewood Cliffs, New Jersey: Prentice Hall, 1967, bibliographical footnotes.

MAY, HENRY FARNHAM. *The End of American Innocence: A Study of the First Years of Our Own Time, 1912–1917.* New York: Knopf, 1959, bibliographical footnotes.

MILLER, JAMES EDWIN, JR., ed. *Myth and Method: Modern Theories of Fiction.* Lincoln: Univ. of Nebraska Press, 1960, 163–164.

MILLETT, FRED BENJAMIN. *Contemporary American Authors: A Critical Survey and 219 Biobibliographies.* New York: Harcourt, Brace and World, 1940, 729 pp.

MORRIS, LLOYD R. *Postscript to Yesterday: America, The Last Fifty Years.* New York: Random House, 1947, 451–465.

MOULTON, C. W. *The Library of Literary Criticism of English and American Authors,* 8 Vols. Buffalo: Moulton Publishing Co., 1901–1904.

MUNSON, GORHAM BERT. *Destinations: A Canvass of American Literature since 1900.* New York: J. H. Sears and Co., Inc., 1928, 211–212.

NYREN, DOROTHY, ed. *A Library of Literary Criticism.* New York: F. Unger Publishing Co., 1960, 552 pp.

PAINE, GREGORY LANSING, ed. *Southern Prose Writers: Representative Selections,* with introduction, bibliography and notes. New York: American Book Co., 1947, cxix-cxlv.

PALTSITS, VICTOR HUGO. "An Account of the Bay Psalm Book during the Seventeenth Century." *Literary Collector,* III (December 1901), 69–72.

PARRINGTON, VERNON LOUIS. *Main Currents in American Thought: An Interpretation of American Literature from the Beginning to 1920,* 3 Vols. New York: Harcourt, Brace and Co., 1927–1930.

Bibliography at the end of each volume.

PERAGALLO, OLGA. *Italian-American Authors and Their Contribution to American Literature,* edited by Anita Peragallo. New York: S. F. Vanni, 1949, 254 pp.

PIERCE, WILLIAM. "A Select Bibliography of the Pilgrim Fathers of New England." *Congregational Historical Society Transactions,* VIII

(February 1920), 16–23; (August 1920), 59–68.

POHLE, HELEN L. "New Literary Forms for a New Age: A Contribution to Bibliography." *BB*, XV (September–December 1934), 92–95; (January–April 1935), 114–116; (May–August 1935), 133–135; (September–December 1935), 153–154.

QUINN, ARTHUR HOBSON. *American Fiction: An Historical and Critical Survey.* New York: D. Appleton-Century Co., 1936, 725–772.

——————. *A History of the American Drama from the Beginning to the Civil War,* 2nd edition. New York: Appleton-Century-Crofts, 1951, 393–421.

——————. *A History of the American Drama from the Civil War to the Present Day,* revised edition. New York: Appleton-Century-Crofts, 1964, 303–404.

——————. *Literature of the American People: An Historical and Critical Survey.* New York: Appleton-Century-Crofts, 1951, 985–1,107.

RANSOM, JOHN CROWE, ed. *The Kenyon Critics: Studies in Modern Literature from the Kenyon Review.* New York and Cleveland: World Publishing Co., 1951, 341–342.

REGIER, CORNELIUS C. *The Era of the Muckrakers.* Chapel Hill: Univ. of North Carolina Press, 1932, 217–241.

SIMONINI, RINALDO C. *Southern Writers: Appraisals in Our Time.* Charlottesville: Univ. Press of Virginia, 1964, bibliographical footnotes.

SMITH, HENRY NASH. *Popular Culture and Industrialism, 1865–1890.* Garden City: Anchor Books, 1967, 521–522.

SPILLER, ROBERT ERNEST, and HAROLD BLODGETT. *The Roots of National Culture: American Literature to 1830, revised edition.* New York: Macmillan, 1949, 893–992.

SPILLER, ROBERT ERNEST, et al. *Literary History of the United States,* 3 Vols. New York: Macmillan, 1948.

Revised edition: 2 Vols. 1953. I: History. II: Bibliography.

Supplement: 1959. A bibliographical supplement.

Also: 1962. A bibliographical edition combining II, 1953, with bibliographical supplement, 1959.

STANTON, THEODORE, ed. *A Manual of American Literature.* Leipzig: Tauchnitz, 1909, 505–522.

STEVENSON, ELIZABETH. *Babbitts and Bohemians: The American 1920's.* New York: Macmillan, 1967, 264–284.

STOVALL, FLOYD, ed. *The Development of American Literary Criticism.* Chapel Hill: Univ. of North Carolina Press, 1955, 247–253.

STOVALL, FLOYD, et al. *Eight American Authors: A Review of Research and Criticism.* New York: W. W. Norton and Co., 1963, 466 pp.

"Bibliographical Supplement: A Selected Checklist, 1955–1962," by J. Chesley Mathews.

SUTCLIFFE, DENHAM. "New Light on the 'Chicago Writers.' "

NLB, 2nd Series, No. 5 (December 1950), 146–157.

SWIFT, LINDSAY. *Brook Farm: Its Members, Scholars and Visitors.* New York: Macmillan, 1900, 283–292.

"List of Books and Magazine Articles" on Brook Farm.

TAFT, KENDALL B., ed. *Minor Knickerbockers: Representative Selections,* with introduction, bibliography and notes. New York: American Book Co., 1947, cxxviii–cxlviii.

TAYLOR, WALTER FULLER. *A History of American Letters,* with bibliographies by Harry Hartwick. Boston: American Book Co., 1936, 447–664.

Subsequent editions entitled *The Story of American Letters.*

THORP, WILLARD. *American Writing in the Twentieth Century.* Cambridge: Harvard Univ. Press, 1960, 325–332.

THURSTON, JARVIS, O. B. EMERSON, CARL HARTMAN and ELIZABETH V. WRIGHT. *Short Fiction Criticism: A Checklist of Interpretation since 1925 of Stories and Novelettes (American, British, Continental), 1800–1958.* Denver: Alan Swallow, 1960, 265 pp.

TRAUB, HAMILTON, ed. *The American Literary Yearbook: A Biographical and Bibliographical Dictionary of Living Authors,* Vol. I. Henning, Minnesota: P. Traub, 1919.

No further volumes published.

TRENT, WILLIAM PETERFIELD. *A History of American Literature,* *1607–1865.* New York: D. Appleton and Co., 1903, 581–593.

TRENT, WILLIAM PETERFIELD, et al. *Cambridge History of American Literature,* 4 Vols. New York: G. P. Putnam's Sons, 1917–1921.

Also: 1927.

Also: Macmillan, 1931.

Also: 3 Vols. 1933 (without bibliographies).

_____. "The Early Essayists," in *Cambridge History of American Literature,* 4 Vols. New York: G. P. Putnam's Sons, 1917–1921, I, 507–510.

_____. "Later Essayists," in *Cambridge History of American Literature,* 4 Vols. New York: G. P. Putnam's Sons, 1917–1921, IV, 675–681.

_____. "Publicists and Orators, 1800–1850," in *Cambridge History of American Literature,* 4 Vols. New York: G. P. Putnam's Sons, 1917–1921, II, 468–480.

TRILLING, LIONEL. *The Liberal Imagination: Essays on Literature and Society.* Garden City: Doubleday, 1953, xv–xvi.

TYLER, MOSES COIT. *The Literary History of the American Revolution, 1763–1783,* 2 Vols. New York: Putnam, 1897, II, 429–483.

VAN DOREN, CARL CLINTON, ed. *Modern American Prose.* New York: Literary Guild, 1934, 925–939.

WARD, ALFRED CHARLES. *American Literature, 1880–1930.* New York: L. MacVeagh, Dial Press, 1932, 261–268.

WATSON, MELVIN RAY. *Magazine Serials and the Essay Tradition, 1746–1820.* Baton Rouge: Louisiana State Univ. Press, 1956, 107–155.

Louisiana State Univ. Studies, Humanities Series, No. 6.

WEIRICK, BRUCE. *From Whitman to Sandburg in American Poetry: A Critical Survey.* New York: Macmillan, 1924, 223–240.

WHEELER, HAROLD L. *Contemporary Novels and Novelists: A List of References to Biographical and Critical Material.* Rolla: Univ. of Missouri, School of Mines and Metallurgy, 1921, 140 pp.

WHIPPLE, THOMAS KING. *Spokesmen: Modern Writers and American Life.* New York: Appleton, 1928.

Bibliography at end of all chapters except the first.

WHITCOMB, SELDON LINCOLN. *Chronological Outlines of American Literature,* with an introduction by Brander Matthews. New York: Macmillan Co., 1914, 286 pp.

WILSON, JAMES GRANT. "The Knickerbocker Authors," in *Memorial History of the City of New York,* 4 Vols. New York: New York History Co., 1893, IV, 54–77.

WOODRESS, JAMES, et al. *American Literary Scholarship: An Annual.* Durham: Duke Univ. Press, 1963–

To date four volumes issued.

WRIGHT, ELIZABETH V. "A Supplementary Checklist: American Short Fiction Explications." *CE,* XVIII (December 1956), 161–164.

ZABEL, MORTON DAUWEN. *Literary Opinion in America,* 3rd edition, 2 Vols. New York: Harper and Row, 1962, II, 793–891.

2. DRAMA

ADELMAN, IRVING, and RITA DIVORKIN. *Modern Drama: A Checklist of Critical Literature on Twentieth Century Plays.* Metuchen, New Jersey: The Scarecrow Press, 1967, 343–370.

AMERICAN DRAMATISTS CLUB. *The American Dramatists Club List: A Standard of Reference for the Protection of Dramatic Property.* New York: published for the American Dramatists Club, 1895–

Issued annually.

AMERICAN EDUCATIONAL THEATRE ASSOCIATION. *A Bibliography of Theatre Arts*

Publications in English, 1963. Lansing, Michigan: American Educational Theatre Association, 1965, 82 pp.

Continuation of the Association's *Theatre Arts Publications Available in the United States,* 1964.

—————— . *Theatre Arts Publications Available in the United States, 1953–1957: A Five Year Bibliography.* Evanston, Illinois: American Educational Theatre Association, 1964, 188 pp.

Continuation of William W. Melnitz's *Theatre Arts Publications in the United States,* 1959.

ANDERSON, JOHN, JR.
*Catalogue of the late Frank R.
Burbank's Collection of Books,
Autographs, and Playbills (mainly
relating to the drama).* New York:
John Anderson Jr., 1902, 78 pp.

ATKINSON, FRED WASHING-
TON. "American Drama in the
Atkinson Collection: Part 1,
1756—1830, March 1, 1918," a col-
lection in the Univ. of Chicago
Library. 134 typed leaves.

BAKER, BLANCH (MERRITT).
*Dramatic Bibliography: An
Annotated List of Books on the
History and Criticism of the Drama
and Stage and on the Allied Arts of
the Theatre.* New York: H. W.
Wilson Co., 1933, 336 pp.

Bibliography of bibliographies
(indexes, lists, catalogs), 246—263.

_____. *Theatre and Allied
Arts: A Guide to Books Dealing with
the History, Criticism, and Technic
of the Drama and Theatre and Related Arts and Crafts.* New York:
H. W. Wilson Co., 1952.

Treats United States, Canada, 163—
190. Includes regional studies,
works on individual actors, playwrights. Entries annotated.

BAKER, GEORGE H., ed. *List of
Books Chiefly on the Drama and
Literary Criticism.* New York:
privately printed for Columbia Univ.,
1897, 64 pp.

BARLOW, ROBERT. "A University
Approach to the American Musical
Theater." *Notes,* XIII (December
1955), 25—32.

_____. "Yale and the
American Musical Theater." *YULG,*
XXVIII (April 1954), 144—149.

"Becks Collection of Prompt Books
in the New York Public Library."
BNYPL, X (February 1906), 100—
148.

BEMAN, LAMAR T., comp.
*Selected Articles on Censorship of
the Theater and Moving Pictures.*
New York: H. W. Wilson Co., 1931.

Bibliographical notes accompany
each article.

BERGQUIST, G. WILLIAM, ed.
*Three Centuries of English and
American Plays: A Checklist:
England, 1500—1800; United States,
1714—1830.* New York: Hafner
Publishing Co., 1963, 281 pp.

BERNHEIM, ALFRED. *The Business of the Theatre: An Economic
History of the American Theatre,
1750—1932.* New York: B. Blom,
1932, bibliographical footnotes.

BIEBER, ALBERT ALOYSIUS.
*The Albert Bieber Collection of
American Plays, Poetry and
Songsters . . . .* New York: Cooper
Square Publishers, 1963, 103 pp.

BLUM, DANIEL C. *Great Stars of
the American Stage: A Pictorial
Record.* New York: Greenberg,
1952, no pagination.

BROCKETT, O. G. "The Theatre of
the Southern United States from the
Beginnings through 1865: A Bibliographical Essay." *Theatre Research,*
II (No. 3, 1960), 163—174.

BROWN, THOMAS ALLSTON.
*History of the American Stage, Con-
taining Biographical Sketches of
Nearly Every Member of the Pro-
fession That Has Appeared on the
American Stage from 1733 to 1870.*
New York: Dick and Fitzgerald,
1870, 421 pp.

——————. *A History of the New York Stage: From the First Performance in 1732 to 1901,* 3 Vols. New York: Dodd, Mead and Co., 1903.

BROWNE, WALTER, and E. DE ROY KOCH, eds. *Who's Who on the Stage, 1908.* New York: B. W. Dodge and Co., 1908, 467 pp.

BULLOCH, J. M. "American Stage History." *N&Q,* CLXVII (Sept. 29, 1934), 219.

An inventory of the "Chief Books which Have Been Done on the American Stage."

CARSON, WILLIAM GLASCOW BRUCE. *Managers in Distress: The St. Louis Stage, 1840–1844.* St. Louis: St. Louis Historical Documents Foundation, 1949.

Record of performances of individual plays, 299–305; bibliography, 311–313.

——————. *The Theatre on the Frontier: The Early Years of the St. Louis Stage.* New York: B. Blom, 1965, 331–335.

CHAPMAN, JOHN, and GARRISON P. SHERWOOD, eds. *The Best Plays.* New York: Dodd, Mead and Co., 1894–

Biannual, 1919 to date. Issued over longer periods earlier: 1894–1899, 1899–1909, 1909–1919. Title varies slightly.

Index: 1950. Covers 1899–1950.

CINCINNATI PUBLIC LIBRARY. *Catalogue of the Dramas and Dramatic Poems Contained in the Public Library of Cincinnati.* Cincinnati: the Board of Managers, 1879, 192 pp.

CLAPP, JOHN BOUVE, and EDWIN FRANCIS EDGETT. *Plays of the Present.* New York: Dunlap Society, 1902, 334 pp.

COHEN, HELEN LOUISE. *Longer Plays by Modern Authors (American).* New York: Harcourt, Brace and Co., 1922, 347–357.

COLBY, ELBRIDGE. "Early American Comedy." *BNYPL,* XXIII (July 1919), 427–435.

COLE, WENDELL. "Early Theatre in America West of the Rockies: A Bibliographical Essay." *Theatre Research,* IV (No. 1, 1962), 36–45.

COLEMAN, EDWARD DAVIDSON. *The Jew in English Drama: An Annotated Bibliography.* New York: New York Public Library, 1943, 257 pp.

Includes American plays to 1938.

"Current Literature: I. Fiction, Drama, and Poetry. II. Criticism and Biography." *English Studies,* 1919–

A bibliographical essay in two parts, originally entitled, "Bibliography."

DORMON, JAMES H., JR. *Theater in the Ante Bellum South, 1815–1861.* Chapel Hill: Univ. of North Carolina Press, 1967, 291–309.

Dramatic Index. Boston: F. W. Faxon Co., 1909–

Issued quarterly as part of the *Bulletin of Bibliography,* and listed as Part 2 of the *Annual Magazine Subject Index.* Also issued separately.

DRUMMOND, A. M. *Plays for the Country Theatre.* Ithaca: Cornell Univ. Press. 1922, 68 pp.

Cornell Univ. Extension Bulletin.
No. 53.

DRURY, FRANCIS KEESE
WYNKOOP. *Drury's Guide to
Best Plays.* Washington: Scarecrow
Press, 1953, 367 pp.

_____. *Viewpoint in
Modern Drama: An Arrangement of
Plays According to Their Essential
Interest.* Chicago: American Library Association, 1925, 119 pp.

DUNLAP, WILLIAM. "Catalogue of
American Plays and Their Authors,"
in *History of the American Theatre.*
New York: J. and J. Harper, 1832,
407–410.

Also: 2 Vols. London: R. Bentley,
1833, II, 381–387.

DUSENBURY, WINIFRED LOESCH.
*The Theme of Loneliness in
Modern American Drama.* Gainesville: Univ. of Florida Press, 1960,
219–223.

ELDREDGE, H. J., comp. *"The
Stage" Cyclopedia: A Bibliography
of Plays . . . .* London: "The
Stage," 1909, 503 pp.

Alphabetical list of nearly 50,000
English plays, covering more than
500 years. Includes descriptions,
authors' names, dates, places of
production and other useful
information.

ELLIOTT, EUGENE CLINTON.
*A History of Variety-Vaudeville in
Seattle from the Beginning to 1914.*
Seattle: Univ. of Washington Press,
1944, 81–83, bibliographical
footnotes.

FLANAGAN, HALLIE. *Arena: The
History of the Federal Theatre.*
New York: B. Blom, 1965, 439–447.

Includes an extensive production
record and financial statements,
377–436.

FORD, PAUL LEICESTER. *Some
Notes Towards an Essay on the
Beginnings of American Dramatic
Literature, 1606–1789.* Brooklyn:
Historical Printing Club, 1893, 29 pp.

In manuscript form.

FREEDLEY, GEORGE. "The 26
Principal Theatre Collections in
American Libraries and Museums."
BNYPL, LXII (July 1958), 319–329.

GAGEY, EDMOND McADOO.
Revolution in American Drama.
New York: Columbia Univ. Press,
1947, 323 pp.

GILDER, ROSAMOND. *A Theatre
Library: A Bibliography of One
Hundred Books Relating to the
Theatre.* New York: Theatre Arts,
Inc., for the National Theatre Conference, 1932, 88 pp.

GILDER, ROSAMOND, and
GEORGE FREEDLEY. *Theatre
Collections in Libraries and Museums:
An International Handbook.* New
York: Theatre Arts, Inc., 1936,
182 pp.

"Graduate Projects in Progress in
Theatre Arts." *Educational Theatre
Journal,* 1949–

Annually surveys graduate work in
progress, usually in the May issue.

HALLINE, ALLAN GATES.
*American Plays: Selected and
Edited with Critical Introductions
and Bibliographies.* New York:
American Book Co., 1935, 751–776.

HARRIS, CALEB FISKE. *Index to
American Poetry and Plays in the
Collection of C. Fiske Harris.*

Providence: printed for private distribution by Hammond, Angell and Co., 1874, 171 pp.

HARTNOLL, PHYLLIS, comp. *The Oxford Companion to the Theatre.* London: Oxford Univ. Press, 1957, 856—888.

2nd edition: 1967, 1,029—1,074.

HARWELL, RICHARD BARKS-DALE. *Confederate Belles-Lettres: A Bibliography and a Finding List of the Fiction, Poetry, Drama, Songsters, and Miscellaneous Literature Published in the Confederate States of America.* Hattiesburg: Book Farm, 1941, 79 pp.

199 copies printed.

HASKELL, DANIEL CARL. "List of American Dramas in the New York Public Library." *BNYPL,* XIX (October 1915), 739—786.

Also issued as a separate pamphlet.

HILL, FRANK PIERCE, comp. *American Plays Printed 1714—1830: A Bibliographical Record.* Palo Alto: Stanford Univ. Press, 1934, 163 pp.

HOBSON, HAROLD, ed. *International Theatre Annual.* 4 Vols. London: J. Calder, 1956—1961.

Also: New York: Citadel Press.

HODGE, FRANCIS. *Yankee Theatre: The Image of America on the Stage, 1825—1850.* Austin: Univ. of Texas Press, 1964, 273—296.

HOOLE, WILLIAM STANLEY. *The Ante-Bellum Charleston Theatre.* University: Univ. of Alabama Press, 1946, bibliographical footnotes.

HYAMS, FRANCES I. "A Brief History of the American Theatre, with Especial Reference to the Eighteenth Century, Supplemented by Collections toward a Bibliography before 1800." Unpublished doctoral dissertation, Radcliffe College, 1954.

IRELAND, JOSEPH NORTON. *Records of the New York Stage, 1750—1860,* 2 Vols. New York: T. H. Morrell, 1866—1867.

2nd edition: B. Blom, 1966.

IRELAND, NORMA, ed. *Index to Full Length Plays, 1944—1964.* Boston: F. W. Faxon Co., 1965, 328 pp.

Continues Ruth Gibbons Thompson's *Index to Full Length Plays,* 1946, 1956.

JOHNSON, ALBERT E., and W. H. CRAIN JR. "Dictionary of American Drama Critics, 1850—1910." *Theatre Annual,* XIII (1955), 65—89.

KERNAN, ALVIN B., ed. *The Modern American Theatre.* Englewood Cliffs, New Jersey: Prentice Hall, 1967, 181—183.

KOCH, FREDERICK HENRY. *American Folk Plays.* New York: D. Appleton-Century, 1939.

LCN: "The Carolina Playmakers: A Selected Bibliography, September, 1931, to September, 1938," 557—570. " 'For a selected bibliography of The Carolina Playmakers from 1918 to 1931 see Appendix I of the Second Series and Appendix I of the Third Series of *Carolina Folk Plays* (Henry Holt & Co.), and Appendix I of *Carolina Plays* (Samuel French).' "

KOSTER, DONALD NELSON. "The Theme of Divorce in American Drama, 1871–1939." Unpublished doctoral dissertation, Univ. of Pennsylvania, 1942.

LAWSON, HILDA J., comp. "The Negro in American Drama (Bibliography of Contemporary Negro Drama)." *BB*, XVII (January 1940), 7–8; (May 1940), 27–30.

LEARY, LEWIS. *Articles on American Literature, 1900–1950.* Durham: Duke Univ. Press, 1954, 428–437.

"Theater."

LELAND STANFORD JUNIOR UNIVERSITY, DRAMATISTS ALLIANCE. *Stanford Writers, 1891–1941.* Palo Alto: Dramatists Alliance, 1941, 141 pp.

Brief biographical notes and selected bibliographies.

LIBRARY ASSOCIATION, COUNTY LIBRARIES SECTION (ENGLAND). *Modern Drama, 1900–1938: A Selected List of Plays . . . and Other Works on Dramatic Theory and Other Related Subjects.* London: The Library Association, County Libraries Section, 1939, 77 pp.

_____. *Reader's Guide to Books on Stagecraft and the Theatre.* London: Library Association, 1952, 30 pp.

New Series, No. 15.

LIBRARY OF CONGRESS, DIVISION OF BIBLIOGRAPHY. *A Partial List of War Plays in the Library of Congress.* Washington, 1921, 4 leaves.

MARSHALL, THOMAS F. "Beyond New York: A Bibliography of the Nineteenth Century American Stage from the Atlantic to the Mississippi." *Theatre Research,* III (No. 3, 1961), 208–217.

MATHEWS, JANE DE HART. *The Federal Theatre, 1935–1939: Plays, Relief, and Politics.* Princeton: Princeton Univ. Press, 1967, 315–331.

MAYORGA, MARGARET (GARDNER). *A Short History of the American Drama: Commentaries on Plays prior to 1920.* New York: Dodd, Mead, 1943, 357–472.

McDOWELL, JOHN H., and CHARLES J. McGAW, et al., eds. "A Bibliography on Theatre and Drama in American Colleges and Universities, 1937–1947." *Speech Monographs,* XVI (November 1949), 1–124.

MELNITZ, WILLIAM W., ed. *Theatre Arts Publications in the United States, 1947–1952: A Five Year Bibliography.* Dubuque, Iowa: American Educational Theatre Association, 1959, 91 pp.

Monograph, No. 1.

Continued by the American Educational Theatre Association's *Theatre Arts Publications Available in the United States, 1953–1957,* 1959.

MICHIGAN, UNIVERSITY, WILLIAM L. CLEMENTS LIBRARY. *The Clements Library Presents an Exhibition of Early American Drama.* Ann Arbor: William L. Clements Library, 1947, 3 pp.

_____. *Early American Drama: A Guide to an Exhibition in the William L. Clements Library.*

Ann Arbor: William L. Clements Library, 1945, 18 pp.

MOODY, RICHARD. *Dramas from the American Theatre, 1762–1909.* Cleveland: World Publishing Co., 1966, 857–873.

MOSES, MONTROSE JONAS. *The American Dramatist.* Boston: B. Blom, 1911, 315–326.

2nd edition: 1917, 379–394.

Revised edition: 1925, 443–459.

Reissued: 1964.

——————, ed. *Dramas of Modernism and Their Forerunners.* Boston: Little, Brown and Co., 1931, 703–733.

Revised edition: 1941, 898–935.

——————. *The Fabulous Forrest: The Record of an American Actor.* Boston: Little, Brown and Co., 1929, 345–355.

——————. *Famous Actor-Families in America.* New York: Crowell, 1906, 309–341.

——————, ed. *Representative American Dramas, National and Local.* Boston: Little, Brown and Co., 1933, 1,013–1,041.

NAESETH, HENRIETTE. "Drama in Early Deadwood (1876–1879)." *AL,* X (November 1938), 289–312.

NANNES, CASPER H. *Politics in American Drama.* Washington: Catholic Univ. of America Press, 1960, 241–246.

NATHAN, GEORGE JEAN, ed. *The Theatre Book of the Year . . . .* New York: Alfred A. Knopf, 1942/1943–1950/1951.

NOLAN, PAUL T., and AMOS E. SIMPSON. "Arkansas Drama before World War I: An Unexplored Country." *AHQ,* XXII (Spring 1963), 61–75.

A checklist of Arkansas playwrights.

NORTON, CLARA (MULLIKEN), FRANK K. WALTER and FANNY ELSIE MARQUAND, comps. *Modern Drama and Opera: Reading Lists on the Works of Various Authors,* 2 Vols. Boston: Boston Book Co., 1911–1915.

ODELL, GEORGE CLINTON DENSMORE. *Annals of the New York Stage,* 15 Vols. New York: Columbia Univ. Press, 1927–1949.

Covers New York plays, operas up to 1894, including first performances, original casts, criticisms. Valuable also for theatrical history outside the New York area in cases of touring shows.

OTTEMILLER, JOHN HENRY, comp. *Index to Plays in Collections: An Author and Title Index to Plays Appearing in Collections Published 1900–1942.* New York: H. W. Wilson Co., 1943, 143 pp.

Revised edition: 1964, 370 pp. Covers 1900–1962.

PARKER, JOHN, ed. *Who Is Who in the Theatre: A Biographical Record of the Contemporary Stage,* 12th edition. London: Sir Isaac Pitman and Sons, Ltd., 1957, 1,722 pp.

1st edition: 1912. Irregularly issued since.

PENCE, JAMES HARRY, comp. *The Magazine and the Drama: An Index.* New York: Dunlap Society, 1896, 190 pp.

From the preface: "A guide to the mass of literature the magazines have published concerning the acted drama and the men and women directly connected with it." 250 copies printed.

PENNSYLVANIA, UNIVERSITY, LIBRARY. *Checklist of American Drama Published in the English Colonies of North America and the United States through 1865 in the Possession of the Library, University of Pennsylvania,* compiled by Albert Von Chorba Jr. Philadelphia: Univ. of Pennsylvania Press, 1951, 92 leaves.

PERRY, CLARENCE ARTHUR. *The Work of the Little Theatres.* New York: Russell Sage, 1933, 196–207.

POLLOCK, THOMAS CLARK. *The Philadelphia Theatre in the Eighteenth Century, together with the Day Book of the Same Period.* Philadelphia: Univ. of Pennsylvania Press, 1933, 71–439.

POULTNEY, GEORGE W. *An Index of Plays of the American Theatre in Manuscript Form,* from the collection of George W. Poultney, to accompany the exhibit for the Dramatists Alliance of Stanford University. Palo Alto: Stanford Univ. Press, 1939, 21 leaves.

QUINN, ARTHUR HOBSON. "American Drama at Pennsylvania." *LCUP,* XVIII (Winter 1951–52), 3–6.

Printed and manuscript plays in the Univ. of Pennsylvania Library.

—————. *A History of the American Drama from the Beginning to the Civil War,* 2nd edition. New York: Appleton-Century-Crofts, 1951, 393–421.

—————. *A History of the American Drama from the Civil War to the Present Day,* revised edition. New York: Appleton-Century-Crofts, 1964, 303–404.

REES, JAMES. *The Dramatic Authors of America.* Philadelphia: G. B. Zieber and Co., 1845, 144 pp.

RODEN, ROBERT F. *Later American Plays, 1831–1900: Being a Compilation of the Titles of Plays by American Authors Published and Performed in America Since 1831.* New York: Dunlap Society, 1900, 132 pp.

Dunlap Society Publications, ns XII.

Continuation of Oscar Wegelin's *Early American Plays, 1714–1830,* 1900. A very incomplete catalog. 265 copies printed.

SANTANIELL, A. E. *Theatre Books in Print.* New York: Drama Book Shop, 1963, 266 pp.

2nd edition: 1966, 509 pp.

SAYLER, OLIVER MARTIN. "Important Productions on the American Stage," in *Our American Theatre.* New York: Brentano's, 1923, 287–315.

SCHOBERLIN, MELVIN. *From Candles to Footlights: A Biography of the Pike's Peak Theatre, 1859–1876.* Denver: F. A. Rosenstock, Old West Publishing Co., 1941, 293–300.

Lists Colorado theaters, 1859–1876, 265–271.

SEILHAMER, GEORGE OVERCASH. *History of the American Theatre during the Revolution and After,* 3 Vols. Philadelphia: Globe, 1891.

The text incorporates numerous cast lists, play bills, seasonal records.

I: 1749—1774.

II: 1774—1792.

III: 1792—1797.

SHEDD, ROBERT G. "Modern Drama: A Selective Bibliography of Works Published in English in 1960 and 1961." *MD,* V (September 1962), 223—244.

SIEVERS, W. DAVID. *Freud on Broadway: A History of Psychoanalysis and the American Drama.* New York: Hermitage House, 1955, 455—461.

SMITHER, NELLE. *A History of the English Theatre at New Orleans, 1806—1842,* revised edition. New York: B. Blom, 1967, 193—194.

SOCIETY FOR THEATRE RE-SEARCH, LIBRARY. *Catalogue.* London: Society for Theatre Research, 1953, 37 pp.

SPER, FELIX. *From Native Roots: A Panorama of Our Regional Drama.* Caldwell, Idaho: Caxton Printers, 1948, 279—334.

STALLINGS, ROY, and PAUL MYERS. *A Guide to Theatre Reading.* New York: National Theatre Conference, 1949, 138 pp.

STODDARD, ROGER E. "C. Fiske Harris, Collector of American Poetry and Plays." *PBSA,* LVII (1st Quart. 1963), 14—32.

_____. "The Harris Collection of American Poetry and Plays: Report of Acquisitions for 1961—1962." *BBr,* XIX (1963), 161—175.

STRATMAN, CARL JOSEPH. *Bibliography of the American Theatre Excluding New York City.* Chicago: Loyola Univ. Press, 1965, 397 pp.

Books, periodical articles, theses arranged by state, city.

_____. "Unpublished Dissertations in the History and Theory of Tragedy, 1889—1957." *BB,* XXII (September—December 1958), 161—165; (January—April 1959), 190—192; (May—August 1959), 214—216; (September—December 1959), 237—240; XXIII (January—April 1960), 15—20.

_____. "Unpublished Dissertations in the History and Theory of Tragedy, 1889—1957—Addenda." *BB,* XXIII (January—April 1962), 162—165; (May—August 1962), 187—192.

THEATRE WORLD. New York: Greenberg, 1944/1945—

Volumes issued annually. Title, — editor vary.

THOMPSON, RUTH GIBBONS. *Index to Full Length Plays, 1895 to 1925.* Boston: F. W. Faxon Co., 1956, 172 pp.

Also: 1946, 306 pp. Covers 1926—1944.

TRENT, WILLIAM PETERFIELD, et al. "The Drama, 1860—1918," in *Cambridge History of American Literature,* 4 Vols. New York: G. P. Putnam's Sons, 1917—1921, IV, 760—774.

_____. "The Early Drama," in *Cambridge History of American Literature,* 4 Vols. New York: G. P. Putnam's Sons, 1917—1921, I, 490—507.

UNITED STATES, COPYRIGHT OFFICE. *Dramatic Compositions Copyrighted in the United States, 1870 to 1916*, 2 Vols. Washington, 1918.

VOWLES, RICHARD B. "Dramatic Theory: A Bibliography." *BNYPL*, LIX (August 1955), 412–428; (September 1955), 464–482; (October 1955), 525–534; (November 1955), 575–585.

_____. "Psychology and Drama: A Selected Checklist." *WSCL*, III (Winter 1962), 35–48.

WALBRIDGE, EARLE FRANCIS. *Drames à Clef: A List of Plays with Characters Based on Real People.* New York: New York Public Library, 1956, 25–38.

WARREN, KATHERINE. "American Plays." *Harvard Library Notes*, 1 (1920), 35–38.

WEGELIN, OSCAR. *Early American Plays, 1714–1830: Being a Compilation of the Titles of Plays by American Authors, Published and Performed in America Previous to 1830.* New York: Dunlap Society, 1900, 113 pp.

Continued by Robert F. Roden's *Later American Plays, 1831–1900*, 1900.

Revised edition: title varies slightly, 1905.

WILLSON, CLAIR EUGENE. *Mimes and Miners: A Historical Study of the Theatre in Tombstone.* Tucson: Univ. of Arizona Press, 1935, 206–207.

3. FICTION

ADLER, FREDERICK HENRY HERBERT, and IRMA TALMAGE. *American and British Novels of Our Day, 1890–1929.* Cleveland: Western Reserve Univ. Press, 1929, 51 pp.

ADLER, SIDNEY. "The Image of the Jew in the American Novel: A Selected Checklist." *BB*, XXIII (September–December 1962), 211–213.

Covers novels published 1930–1961.

ADMARI, RALPH. "Bibliography of Dime Novels." *ABC*, V (July 1934), 215–217.

AGATHA, SISTER M. *Texas Prose Writings: A Reader's Digest.* Dallas: B. Upshaw, 1936, xvii–xx.

AGNEW, JANET MARGARET. *A Southern Bibliography*, 4 Vols. University: Louisiana State Univ. and Agricultural and Mechanical College, 1939–1942.

I: Fiction.

II: Historical Fiction.

III: Poetry.

IV: Biography.

ALDRED, THOMAS. *A List of English and American Sequel Stories.* London: Association of Assistant Librarians, 1922, 74 pp.

_____. *Sequels, Incorporating Aldred & Parker's Sequel Stories*, 3rd edition. London: Association of Assistant Librarians, 1947, 133 pp.

ALDRIDGE, JOHN W., ed. *Critiques and Essays on Modern Fiction, 1920–1951, Representing the Achievement of Modern American and British Critics.* New York: Ronald Press Co., 1952, 553–610.

"A Selected Bibliography of Criticism of Modern Fiction" by Robert Wooster Stallman.

ANDERSON, ELEANOR COPEN-HAVER, comp. *A List of Novels and Stories about Workers.* New York: Woman's Press, 1938, 12 pp.

BAIL, HAMILTON VAUGHAN. "Harvard Fiction: Some Critical and Bibliographical Notes." *PAAS,* ns LXVIII (October 1958), 211–347.

Lists novels with Harvard backgrounds.

BAKER, ERNEST ALBERT. *A Descriptive Guide to the Best Fiction, British and American.* London: Sonnenschein, 1903, 610 pp.

——————. *A Guide to the Best Fiction in English.* London: G. Routledge and Sons, Ltd., 1913, 825 pp.

——————. *A Guide to Historical Fiction.* New York: Macmillan Co., 1914, 573 pp.

Also: London: G. Routledge and Sons, Ltd.

BAKER, ERNEST ALBERT, and JAMES PACKMAN. *A Guide to the Best Fiction, English and American, Including Translations from Foreign Languages.* New York: Macmillan Co., 1932, 642 pp.

BATTEAU, D. WAYNE. "Science Fiction, Prophet & Critic." *HAB,* LX (1957), 209–211, 223.

BAUMBACH, JONATHAN. *The Landscape of Nightmare: Studies in the Contemporary American Novel.* New York: New York Univ. Press, 1965, 171–173.

BEACH, JOSEPH WARREN. *The Twentieth Century Novel: Studies in Technique.* New York: Century Co., 1932, 555–557.

Also: Appleton-Century-Crofts, 1960.

"The Beadle Collection of Dime Novels." *BNYPL,* XXVI (January 1922), 555–628.

BEATTY, RICHMOND CROOM, and WILLIAM PERRY FIDLER, eds. *Contemporary Southern Prose.* Boston: D. C. Heath and Co., 1940, 313–320.

BELL, INGLIS FREEMAN, and DONALD BAIRD. *The English Novel, 1578–1956: A Checklist of Twentieth Century Criticisms.* Denver: Alan Swallow, 1959, 181 pp.

BERNARD, HARRY. *Le Roman Regionaliste aux Etats-Unis, 1913–1940.* Montreal: Fides, 1949, 357–364.

BERNBAUM, ERNEST. "Recent Works on Prose Fiction before 1800." *MLN,* XLVI (February 1931), 95–107.

BEWLEY, MARIUS. *The Eccentric Design: Form in the Classic American Novel.* New York: Columbia Univ. Press, 1959, 314–324.

BLACK, ALBERT GEORGE. *Michigan Novels: An Annotated Bibliography.* Ann Arbor: Michigan Council of Teachers of English, 1963, 64 pp.

BLEILER, EVERETT
FRANKLIN. *Checklist of Fantastic
Literature: A Bibliography of
Fantasy, Weird and Science Fiction
Books Published in the English
Language,* with a preface by Melvin
Korshak. Chicago: Shasta Pub-
lishers, 1948, 455 pp.

BLOTNER, JOSEPH. *The Modern
American Political Novel, 1900–
1960.* Austin: Univ. of Texas Press,
1966, 370–389.

BOGART, E. L. "Historical Novels
in American History." *History
Teachers' Magazine,* VIII (September
1917), 226–230.

BOSTON PUBLIC LIBRARY.
*A Chronological Index to His-
torical Fiction, Including Prose
Fiction, Plays and Poems,* 2nd
edition, revised and enlarged.
Boston: Boston Public Library,
1875, 25 pp.

BRAGIN, CHARLES. *Dime Novels:
Bibliography, 1860–1928.*
Brooklyn: C. Bragin, 1938, 34 pp.

BROWN, HERBERT ROSS. *The
Sentimental Novel in America,
1789–1860.* Durham: Duke Univ.
Press, 1940, 407 pp.

BROWN, STEPHEN JAMES
MEREDITH. *Novels and Tales by
Catholic Writers.* New York:
American Press, 1930, 125 pp.

CALIFORNIA STATE LIBRARY.
"Fiction in the State Library
Having a California Coloring."
News Notes of California Libraries,
IX (1914), 228–242; XIII (1918),
874–878.

──────────. "Fiction in the State
Library Having a California Coloring,
compiled by the California Department." *News Notes of California
Libraries,* XXI (1926), 101–127.

CARRIER, ESTHER JANE. *Fiction
in Public Libraries, 1876–1960.*
New York: The Scarecrow Press,
1965, 458 pp.

CHAPMAN, MARISTAN. "Is Our
Ink Well?: A Catalogue Comment
upon Southern Novelists from 1917
to 1934." *Westminster Magazine,*
XXIII (January–March 1935),
259–277.

CHASE, RICHARD VOLNEY.
*The American Novel and Its
Tradition.* Garden City, New York:
Doubleday, 1957, 247–248.

CHICAGO PUBLIC LIBRARY.
Historical Novels: A Bibliography,
compiled by Ruth Utter. Chicago:
Chicago Public Library, 1940, 43 pp.

CLARESON, THOMAS D. "An
Annotated Checklist of American
Science-Fiction: 1880–1915."
Extrapolation, I (No. 1, 1959), 5–23.

COAN, OTIS W., and RICHARD G.
LILLARD. *America in Fiction: An
Annotated List of Novels That
Interpret Aspects of Life in the
United States.* Palo Alto: Stanford
Univ. Press, 1956, 208 pp.

Also: Pacific Books, 1967, 240 pp.

COLLINS, CARVEL E., comp.
"Nineteenth Century Fiction of the
Southern Appalachians." *BB,*
XVII (September–December 1942),
186–190; (January–April 1942),
215–218.

COOPERMAN, STANLEY.
*World War I and the American
Novel.* Baltimore: Johns Hopkins
Press, 1967, 243–251.

COTTON, GERALD BROOKS, and ALAN GLENCROSS. *Fiction Index: A Guide to over 10,000 Works of Fiction, Including Short Story Collections, Anthologies, . . . Arranged under 2,000 Subject Headings.* London: Association of Assistant Librarians, 1953, 223 pp.

CUMMINGS, RALPH F. *The Ralph F. Cummings Standard Dime and Nickel Catalogue of Old Weeklies, Novels, and Story Papers of America, 1936–1937.* Grafton, Massachusetts: R. F. Cummings, 1936, 16 pp.

"Current Literature: I. Fiction, Drama, and Poetry. II. Criticism and Biography." *English Studies,* 1919–

"A bibliographical essay in two parts, originally entitled, "Bibliography."

DAVIDSON, DONALD. "The 43 Best Southern Novels for Readers and Collectors." *PW,* CXXVII (April 27, 1935), 1,675–1,676.

DAVIS, DAVID BRION. *Homicide in American Fiction, 1798–1860: A Study in Social Values.* Ithaca: Cornell Univ. Press, 1968, 315–340.

DICKINSON, ARTHUR TAYLOR. *American Historical Fiction.* New York: Scarecrow Press, 1958, 314 pp.

Lists 1,224 novels, published 1917–1956, classified according to historical events treated.

DIXSON, ZELLA ALLEN. *The Comprehensive Subject Index* to *Universal Prose Fiction.* New York: Dodd, Mead and Co., 1897, 421 pp.

DORNBUSCH, C. E. "The G.I. Stories." *BNYPL,* LIV (November 1950), 523–527.

DOUGHERTY, CHARLES T. "Novels of the Middle Border: A Critical Bibliography for Historians." *Historical Bulletin,* XXV (1947), 77–78, 85–88.

DU BREILL, ALICE JOUVEAU. *The Novel of Democracy in America.* Baltimore: J. H. Furst Co., 1923, 114 pp.

DUNLAP, GEORGE ARTHUR. *The City in the American Novel.* New York: Russell and Russell, 1965, 176–183.

DURHAM, PHILIP. "A General Classification of 1,531 Dime Novels." *HLQ,* XVII (May 1954), 287–291.

DYE, CHARITY. "References upon the Study of Fiction," in *The Story Teller's Art.* Boston: Ginn, 1898, 79–85.

EMCH, LUCILLE B. "Ohio in Short Stories, 1824–1839." *Ohio Archeological and Historical Quarterly,* LIII (July-September 1944), 209–250.

FLANAGAN, JOHN T., comp. "A Bibliography of Middle Western Farm Novels." *Minnesota History,* XXIII (June 1942), 156–158.

FLIPEL, LOUIS N. "The Fiction of 1920 – A Library Survey." *LJ,* XLVI (Sept. 15, 1921), 749–754.

FRIEDMAN, ALAN. *The Turn of the Novel: Studies in the Transition to Modern Fiction.* New York: Oxford Univ. Press, 1967, 189–207.

GELFANT, BLANCHE HOUSMAN. *The American City Novel.* Norman: Univ. of Oklahoma Press, 1954, 265–276.

GERSTENBERGER, DONNA, and GEORGE HENDRICK. *The Ameri-*

can Novel, 1789–1959: A Checklist of Twentieth Century Criticism. Denver: Alan Swallow, 1961, 333 pp.

GLASGOW, ELLEN ANDERSON GHOLSON. *A Certain Measure: An Interpretation of Prose Fiction.* New York: Harcourt, Brace and Co., 1943, 265–272.

GOODRICH, NATHANIEL L. "Prose Fiction: A Bibliography." *BB,* IV (July 1906), 118–121; (October 1906), 133–136; (January 1907), 153–155; V (April 1907), 11–13; (July 1907), 38–39; (October 1907), 54–55; (January 1908), 77–78.

GRAY, GORDON. "A Bibliography of American Regional Novels for the Use of Teachers." Unpublished doctoral dissertation, Teachers' College, Columbia Univ.

GRISWOLD, WILLIAM McCRILLIS. *Descriptive List of American, International, Romantic and British Novels.* Cambridge, Massachusetts: W. M. Griswold, 1891, 617 pp.

_____. *Descriptive List of Novels and Tales Dealing with American City Life.* Cambridge, Massachusetts: W. M. Griswold, 1891, 120 pp.

_____. *Descriptive List of Novels and Tales Dealing with American Country Life.* Cambridge, Massachusetts: W. M. Griswold, 1893, 51 pp.

_____. *Descriptive List of Novels and Tales Dealing with the History of North America.* Cambridge, Massachusetts: W. M. Griswold, 1895, 101–183.

HACKETT, ALICE PAYNE. *60 Years of Best Sellers, 1895–1955.* New York: R. R. Bowker Co., 1956, 223–229.

HANNIGAN, FRANCIS JAMES. *The Standard Index of Short Stories, 1900–1914.* Boston: Small, Maynard and Co., 1918, 334 pp.

Index of 24 magazines, 3,000 authors.

HARDING, WALTER. "American History in the Novel: The Period of Expansion, 1815–1861." *Midwest Journal,* VIII (Spring-Fall 1956), 393–398.

Contains annotated list of recommended books.

HARKNESS, BRUCE. "Bibliography and the Novelistic Fallacy." *SB,* XII (1958), 59–73.

Covers errors in texts of novels, including works of Melville and Fitzgerald, with particular attention to *The Great Gatsby.*

HARKNESS, DAVID J. "The Biographical Novel: A Bibliography with Notes." *Univ. of Tennessee News Letter,* XXIX (1950), 1–45.

HARRISON, JAMES G. "Nineteenth-Century American Novels on American Journalism." *JQ,* XXII (September 1945), 215–224; (December 1945), 335–345.

HART, JAMES D. *The Popular Book: A History of America's Literary Taste.* New York: Oxford Univ. Press, 1950, 289–300.

HARTIN, JOHN S. "The Southeastern United States in the Novel through 1950: A Bibliographic Review." Unpublished doctoral dissertation, Univ. of Michigan, 1957.

HARTWICK, HARRY HENTHORNE. *The Foreground of American Fiction.* New York: American Book Co., 1934, 410–430.

Also: Gordian Press, 1967.

HARWELL, RICHARD BARKSDALE. *Confederate Belles-Lettres: A Bibliography and a Finding List of the Fiction, Poetry, Drama, Songsters, and Miscellaneous Literature Published in the Confederate States of America.* Hattiesburg: Book Farm, 1941, 79 pp.

199 copies printed.

HATCHER, HARLAN. *Creating the Modern American Novel.* New York: Russell and Russell, 1965, 295.

HOFFMAN, FREDERICK JOHN. *The Art of Southern Fiction: A Study of Some Modern Novelists.* Carbondale: Southern Illinois Univ. Press, 1967, 170–192.

_____. *The Modern Novel in America, 1900–1950.* Chicago: Regnery, 1951, 205–208.

HURLEY, LEONARD B. "The American Novel, 1830–1850: Its Reflections of Contemporary Religious Conditions, with a Bibliography of Fiction." Unpublished doctoral dissertation, Univ. of North Carolina, 1932.

HUSTON, A. J. "A List of Maine Novels." *PW,* CXXVIII (July 6, 1935), 12–13.

JOHANNSEN, ALBERT. *The House of Beadle and Adams and Its Dime and Nickel Novels,* 2 Vols. Norman: Univ. of Oklahoma Press, 1950.

Contains list of authors and novels. The Beadle firm was a chief publisher of dime novels.

JOHNSON, JAMES GIBSON. *Southern Fiction Prior to 1860: An Attempt at a First-hand Bibliography.* Charlottestville: Michie Co., printers, 1909, 126 pp.

KAPLAN, CHARLES. "American History in the Novel: The Period of Development, 1861–1900." *Midwest Journal,* VIII (Spring-Fall 1956), 399–406.

Contains annotated list of recommended novels.

KAROLIDES, NICHOLAS J. *The Pioneer in the American Novel, 1900–1950.* Norman: Univ. of Oklahoma Press, 1967, 299–311.

KERMODE, FRANK. *The Sense of an Ending: Studies in the Theory of Fiction.* New York: Oxford Univ. Press, 1967, 181–187.

KERR, ELIZABETH MARGARET. *Bibliography of the sequence Novel.* Minneapolis: Univ. of Minnesota Press, 1950, 126 pp.

Lists 3,173 separate novels, 999 sequences.

KILPATRICK, CLAYTON E. "Mystery, Honor, Western and S/F Roundup No. 2." *LJ,* LXXXIII (Oct. 1, 1958), 2,628–2,630.

KRAUS, JOE W. "Missouri in Fiction: A Review and a Bibliography." *Missouri Historical Review,* XLII (April-July 1948), 209–225; 310–324.

LEARY, LEWIS. *Articles on American Literature, 1900–1950.* Durham: Duke Univ. Press, 1954, 342–353.

"Fiction."

LEISY, ERNEST ERWIN. *The American Historical Novel.* Norman: Univ. of Oklahoma Press, 1950, 219–259.

LEYPOLDT, FREDERICK. *A Reading Diary of Modern Fiction.* New York: Leypoldt, 1881, 150 pp.

LIBRARY OF CONGRESS, READ-
ING ROOM. *A List of Fiction in the
Library of Congress by American
Authors or Published in America,
1775–1800.* Washington, 1936, 22
leaves.

LIEBERMAN, ELIAS, ed. *The
American Short Story: A Study of
the Influence of Locality in Its
Development.* Ridgewood, New
Jersey: the editor, 1912, 169–175.

LIVELY, ROBERT A. *Fiction
Fights the Civil War: An Unfinished
Chapter in the Literary History of
the American People.* Chapel Hill:
Univ. of North Carolina Press, 1957,
197–224.

Lists some 500 Civil War novels.

LOSHE, LILLIE DENNING. *The
Early American Novel.* New York:
Columbia Univ. Press, 1907, 106–
124.

McRORY, MARY O. *Florida in
Fiction: A Bibliography.* Tallahassee: Florida State Library, 1958, 67
pp.

McVOY, LIZZIE CARTER, and
RUTH BATES CAMPBELL. *A Bibliography of Fiction by Louisianians
and on Louisiana Subjects.* Baton
Rouge: Louisiana State Univ. Press,
1935, 87 pp.

Also: *Louisiana State Univ. Studies,*
XVIII.

MEYER, ROY WILLARD. *The
Middle Western Farm Novel in the
Twentieth Century.* Lincoln: Univ.
of Nebraska Press, 1965, 243–252.

An annotated bibliography of
Middle Western farm fiction, 1891–
1962, 200–242. This special list
supplements the general bibliography
cited above.

MILLER, JAMES EDWIN, JR., ed.
*Myth and Method: Modern Theories
of Fiction.* Lincoln: Univ. of
Nebraska Press, 1960, 163–164.

MOTT, FRANK LUTHER. *Golden
Multitudes: The Story of Best
Sellers in the United States.* New
York: Macmillan, 1947, bibliogra-
phical footnotes.

MULLER, HERBERT JOSEPH.
Modern Fiction: A Study of Values.
New York and London: Funk and
Wagnalls, 1937, 436–437.

NEWBERRY LIBRARY. *American
Novels with an American Setting
Printed before 1880: A Checklist of
Books in the Library, August 1941.*
Chicago: Newberry Library, 1941,
36 leaves.

NEW YORK STATE LIBRARY.
"Contributions to a Bibliography of
Civil War Fiction."

Available only in manuscript.

NIELD, JONATHAN. *A Guide to
the Best Historical Novels and Tales.*
New York: G. P. Putnam's Sons,
1925, 518 pp.

NORELL, IRENE P., ed. "Prose
Writers of North Dakota: A Special
Issue." *NDQ,* XXVI (Winter 1958),
37.

O'BRIEN, EDWARD JOSEPH
HARRINGTON. *The Advance of
the American Short Story,* revised
edition. New York: Dodd, Mead
and Co., 1931, 286–314.

O'DONNELL, THOMAS F. "Notes
for a Bibliography of the Canals of
New York." *Bottoming Out* (Canal
Society Quarterly), II (January 1958),
5–7, 11–13.

Covers canals in fiction and other
literature.

ORIANS, G. HARRISON. "Lafitte: A Bibliographical Note." *AL*, IX (November 1937), 351—353.

Bibliographical information concerning an early nineteenth-century novel, *The Memoirs of Lafitte.*

PATTEE, FRED LEWIS. *The Development of the American Short Story.* New York: Harper, 1923, bibliographical footnotes.

PATTERSON, LEWIS. "Dime Novel Heroes Abound in University's Walter Library." *St. Paul* (Minn.) *Dispatch,* June 21, 1961.

Discusses the Univ. of Minnesota Library collection of 40,000 dime novels.

PEARSON, EDMUND. *Dime Novels: or, Following an Old Trail in Popular Literature.* Boston: Little, Brown and Co., 1929, 259—272.

PHILADELPHIA MERCANTILE LIBRARY COMPANY. *Alphabetical List (by Title) of the Class of Prose Fiction in the Mercantile Library of Philadelphia.* Philadelphia: printed for the Philadelphia Mercantile Library Co., by Woodruff and Van Horn, 1891, 166 pp.

——————. *Finding Lists for Novels in the Mercantile Library of Philadelphia.* Philadelphia: printed for the Philadelphia Mercantile Library Co., 1878, 187 pp.

PHILLIPS, WILLIAM. "American History in the Novel: The Colonial Period, 1585—1775." *Midwest Journal,* VIII (Spring-Fall 1956), 376—384.

Contains annotated list of recommended novels.

POWELL, LAWRENCE CLARK. *Heart of the Southwest: A Selected Bibliography of Novels, Stories and Tales Laid in Arizona and New Mexico and Adjacent Lands.* Los Angeles: Dawson's Book Shop, 1955, 42 pp.

Great Southwest Travel Series, No. 2.

POWELL, WILLIAM STEVENS, ed. *North Carolina Fiction, 1734—1957: An Annotated Bibliography.* Chapel Hill: Univ. of North Carolina Library, 1958, 207 pp.

PRESTRIDGE, VIRGINIA WILLIAMSON. *The Worker in American Fiction: An Annotated Bibliography.* Champaign: Institute of Labor and Industrial Relations, Univ. of Illinois, 1954, 27 leaves.

"Publications consulted," leaves 26—27.

PRINCETON UNIVERSITY, LIBRARY. "Shapers of the Modern Novel: A Catalogue of an Exhibition." *PULC,* XI (Spring 1950), 134—141.

QUEEN, ELLERY. *The Detective Short Story: A Bibliography.* Boston: Little, Brown and Co., 1942, 135 pp.

QUINN, ARTHUR HOBSON. *American Fiction: An Historical and Critical Survey.* New York: D. Appleton-Century Co., 1936, 725—772.

RADDIN, GEORGE GATES, JR. *An Early New York Library of Fiction, with a Checklist of the Fiction in H. Caritat's Circulating Library, No. 1 City Hotel, Broadway, 1804.* New York, H. W. Wilson Co., 1940, 113 pp.

RIDEOUT, WALTER BATES. *The Radical Novel in the United States,*

1900–1954: Some Interrelations of Literature and Society. Cambridge: Harvard Univ. Press, 1956, 301–325.

ROSE, LISLE A. "A Bibliographical Survey of Economic and Political Writings, 1865–1900." AL, XV (January 1944), 381–410.

A considerable amplification of the bibliography found in Walter Fuller Taylor's The Economic Novel in America, 1942.

_____. "A Descriptive Catalogue of Economic and Politico-Economic Fiction in the United States, 1902–1909." Unpublished doctoral dissertation, Univ. of Chicago, 1936.

ROUCEK, JOSEPH SLABEY. The Immigrant in Fiction and Biography. New York: Bureau for Intercultural Education, 1945, 32 pp.

RUBIN, LOUIS DECIMUS, and JOHN REES MOORE, eds. The Idea of an American Novel. New York: Crowell, 1961, 394 pp.

SADLEIR, MICHAEL. XIX Century Fiction: A Bibliographical Record Based on His Own Collection, 2 Vols. Berkeley: Univ. of California Press, 1951.

SCHNEIDER, REBECCA. Bibliography of Jewish Life in the Fiction of England and America. Albany: New York State Library School, 1916, 41 pp.

SCHOLL, RALPH. "Science Fiction: A Selected Check List." BB, XXII (January-April 1958), 114–115.

A list of critical articles and bibliographies from periodicals from Sept. 29, 1928–May 12, 1956.

SMITH, FRANK R. "Periodical Articles on the American Short Story: A Selected, Annotated Bibliography." BB, XXIII (January-April 1960), 9–13; (May-August 1960), 46–48; (September-December 1960), 69–72; (January-April 1961), 95–96.

SMITH, REBECCA W., comp. "Catalogue of the Chief Novels and Short Stories by American Authors Dealing with the Civil War and Its Effects, 1861–1899." BB, XV (September-December 1935), 193–194; XVII (January-April 1940), 10–12; (May-August 1940), 33–35; (September-December 1940), 53–55; (January-April 1941), 72–75.

_____. "The Civil War and Its Aftermath in American Fiction, 1861–1899." Unpublished doctoral dissertation, Univ. of Chicago, 1932.

SMITH, VELDREN M. "Small Town Life in American Fiction." BB, XIII (May-August 1928), 113–114; (September-December 1928), 130–131.

SYRACUSE PUBLIC LIBRARY (NEW YORK). Gold Star List of American Fiction, 1821–1940. Syracuse: Syracuse Public Library, 1940.

Issued at irregular intervals with slightly varying titles.

SYRACUSE UNIVERSITY, LIBRARY. Fictional Accounts of Trips to the Moon, 160–1901 (A.D.). Syracuse: Syracuse Univ. Library, 1959, 14 pp.

TAYLOR, WALTER FULLER. The Economic Novel in America. Chapel Hill: Univ. of North Carolina Press, 1942, 341–365.

Covers 1865–1900.

THIESSEN, N.J. *An Annotated Bibliography of American Fiction.* Emporia: Kansas State Teachers College, 1938, 65 pp.

Also: Kansas State Teachers College, Emporia, *Bulletin of Information,* XVIII, No. 5.

THOMPSON, LAWRENCE SIDNEY. "The Civil War in Fiction." *CWH,* II (1956), 83–95.

—————. "The War between the States in Kentucky Novel." *KSHSR,* L (January 1952), 26–34.

THOMPSON, LAWRENCE SIDNEY, and ALGERNON D. THOMPSON. *The Kentucky Novel.* Lexington: Univ. of Kentucky Press, 1953, 158–160.

THURSTON, JARVIS. "Analyses of Short Fiction: A Checklist." *Perspective,* VII (1953), 127–170.

THURSTON, JARVIS, O. B. EMERSON, CARL HARTMAN and ELIZABETH V. WRIGHT. *Short Fiction Criticism: A Checklist of Interpretation since 1925 of Stories and Novelettes (American, British, Continental), 1800–1958.* Denver: Alan Swallow, 1960, 265 pp.

TRENT, WILLIAM PETERFIELD, et al. "Fiction," in *Cambridge History of American Literature,* 4 Vols. New York: G. P. Putnam's Sons, 1917–1921, I, 525–546.

—————. "The Later Novel," in *Cambridge History of American Literature,* 4 Vols. New York; G. P. Putnam's Sons, 1917–1921, IV, 656–671.

—————. "The Short Story," in *Cambridge History of American Literature,* 4 Vols. New York: G. P. Putnam's Sons, 1917–1921, II, 616–631.

VAN DOREN, CARL CLINTON. *The American Novel, 1789–1939,* 2nd edition. New York: Macmillan, 1940, 367–382.

—————. *Contemporary American Novelists, 1900–1920.* New York: Macmillan, 1922, 176 pp.

VOLLMER, CLEMENT. *The American Novel in Germany, 1871–1913.* Philadelphia: International Printing Co., 1918, 52–94.

WAGENKNECHT, EDWARD. *Cavalcade of the American Novel.* New York: Holt, Rinehart and Winston, 1952, 497–555.

WARREN, ROBERT PENN, ed. *A Southern Harvest: Short Stories by Southern Writers.* Boston: Houghton Mifflin, 1937, 353–360.

WEEKS, EDWARD. "The Best Sellers since 1875." *PW,* CXXV (April 21, 1934), 1503–1507.

WEGELIN, OSCAR, comp. *Early American Fiction, 1774–1830: Being a Compilation of the Titles of American Novels, Written by Writers Born or Residing in America, and Published Previous to 1831.* Stamford, Connecticut: the compiler, 1902, 28 pp.

2nd edition: 1913, 37 pp.

3rd edition: New York: P. Smith, 1929, 37 pp.

WEST, RAY BENEDICT. *The Short Story in America, 1900–1950.* Chicago: H. Regnery Co., 1952, 131–137.

WHEELER, HAROLD L. *Contemporary Novels and Novelists: A List of References to Biographical and Critical Material.* Rolla: Univ. of Missouri, School of Mines and Metallurgy, 1921, 140 pp.

WHITEMAN, MAXWELL, ed. *A Century of Fiction by American Negroes, 1853–1952: A Descriptive Bibliography*. Philadelphia: n.p., 1955, 64 pp.

WIGMORE, JOHN HENRY. *A List of Legal Novels*. Chicago: Northwestern Univ. Press, 1908, 574–593.

Extract from *Illinois Law Review*, II (April 1908).

_____. "One Hundred Legal Novels." *LJ*, LII (February 15, 1927), 189–190.

WILLIAMS, BLANCHE COLTON. "Short Stories of 1921-First Quarter." *New York Evening Post Literary Review*, Apr. 9, 1921.

_____. "Short Stories of the Past Year." *New York Evening Post Literary Review*, Apr. 24, 1920.

WILSON, LOUIS ROUND. "Fiction with North Carolina Setting." *North Carolina Review*, June 2, 1912, p. 3.

WING, DONALD GODDARD. "Novels by Yale Men." *YULG*, XII (January 1938), 63–69.

WOODRESS, JAMES. "American History in the Novel: The Revolution and Early National Periods, 1775–1815." *Midwest Journal*, VIII (Spring-Fall 1956), 385–392.

Includes an annotated list of recommended novels.

WRIGHT, ELIZABETH V. "A Supplementary Checklist: American Short Fiction Explications." *CE*, XVIII (December 1956), 161–164.

WRIGHT, LYLE HENRY, comp. *American Fiction, 1774–1850: A Contribution toward a Bibliography*. San Marino, California: Huntington Library, 1948, 355 pp.

_____. *American Fiction, 1851–1875*. San Marino, California: Huntington Library, 1957, 433 pp.

_____. "Eighteenth Century American Fiction," in *Essays Honoring Lawrence C. Wroth*. Portland, Maine: Anthoensen Press, 1951, 457–473.

_____. "Propaganda in Early American Fiction." *PBSA*, XXXIII (1939), 98–106.

4. POETRY

AGNEW, JANET MARGARET. *A Southern Bibliography*, 4 Vols. University: Louisiana State Univ. and Agricultural and Mechanical College, 1939–1942.

I: Fiction.

II: Historical Fiction.

III: Poetry.

IV: Biography

ALDIN, JOHN. "American Catholic Poets." *Common-weal*, V (Jan. 19, 1927), 299–300.

ARMS, GEORGE WARREN, and JOSEPH MARSHALL KUNTZ. *Poetry Explication: A Checklist of Interpretation since 1925 of British and American Poems Past and Present.* New York: Swallow Press and Morrow, 1950, 187 pp.

An expansion of *A Check List of Poetry Explications, 1925–1947*. Albuquerque: prepared for private circulation, 1948, 48 pp.

Revised edition: Denver: Alan Swallow, 1962, 331 pp.

AUSLANDER, JOSEPH, and KENTON KILMER. "Citadel: Poetry in the National Library. *Sat R*, XXV (April 25, 1942), 34.

Description of the Library of Congress Poetry Collections.

BEACH, JOSEPH WARREN. *Obsessive Images: Symbolism in the Poetry of the 1930's and 1940's*, edited by William Van O'Connor. Minneapolis: Univ. of Minnesota Press, 1960, 379–382.

BIEBER, ALBERT ALOYSIUS. *The Albert Bieber Collection of American Plays, Poetry and Songsters . . . .*New York: Cooper Square Publishers, 1963, 103 pp.

BLACK, GEORGE FRASER. *A Gypsy Bibliography.* London: Quaritch, 1914, 220.

BOGAN, LOUISE. *Achievement in American Poetry, 1900–1950.* Chicago: H. Regnery Co., 1951, 147–150.

BOYS, RICHARD C. "The English Poetical Miscellany in Colonial America." *SP*, XLII (January 1945), 114–130.

BRADSHAW, SIDNEY ERNEST. *On Southern Poetry Prior to 1860.* Richmond: B. F. Johnson Publishing Co., 1900, 148–157.

BRAITHWAITE, WILLIAM STANLEY BEAUMONT, ed *Anthology of Magazine Verse and Yearbook of American Poetry.* New York: G. Sully and Co., Inc., 1913–1929.

Issued annually, 1913–1929. Publisher varies.

BREWTON, JOHN EDMOND, and SARA WESTBROOK BREWTON, comps. *Index to Children's Poetry.* New York: H. W. Wilson Co., 1942, 997 pp.

Supplement: 1954, 427 pp.

BROWN UNIVERSITY, LIBRARY. *The Anthony Memorial: A Catalogue of the C. Fiske Harris Collection of American Poetry and Plays,* with biographical and bibliographical notes by J.C. Stockbridge. Providence, Rhode Island: Providence Press Co., printers, 1886, 820 pp.

_____. *Colonial Poets, 1609–1760: A Selection from the C. Fiske Harris Collection of American Poetry and Plays,* with an introduction by S. Foster Damon. Providence: friends of the Library of Brown Univ., 1947, 32 pp.

_____. "Series of Old American Songs, Reproduced in Facsimile from Original or Early Editions" in the C. Fiske *Harris Collection of American Poetry and Plays,* with brief annotations by S. Foster Damon. Providence: Brown Univ. Library, 1936, 50 facsimiles.

CLARK, HARRY HAYDEN. *Major American Poets,* selected and edited with chronologies, bibliographies and notes. New York: American Book Co., 1936, 779–950.

COATES, WALTER J., comp. *A Bibliography of Vermont Poetry and Gazetteer of Vermont Poets.* Montpelier: Vermont Historical Society, 1942– .

Continuous project of Vermont Historical Society.

COFFIN, TRISTRAM P.
*The British Traditional Ballad
in North America.* Philadelphia:
American Folklore Society,
1950, 171–181.

COFFMAN, STANLEY K.
*Imagism: A Chapter for the
History of Modern Poetry.*
Norman: Univ. of Oklahoma
Press, 1951, bibliographical
footnotes.

"Current Literature: I. Fiction,
Drama, and Poetry. II. Criticism
and Biography." *English Studies,*
1919– .

A bibliographical essay in two
parts, originally entitled,
"Bibliography."

DEUTSCH, BABETTE. *This
Modern Poetry.* New York:
W. W. Norton and Co., Inc.,
1935, 295–302.

DREW, ELIZABETH A.
Discovering Poetry. New York:
W. W. Norton and Co., Inc., 1933,
211–216.

THE EDITORS. "Classified List
of Books and Current Magazine
Articles on Poets and Poetry."
The Poetry Journal, II (March
1913), 141–152.

ELLINGER, ESTHER PARKER.
*The Southern War Poetry of the
Civil War.* Philadelphia: The
Hershey Press, 1918, 49–55.

Index of Southern war poems,
58–192.

FORD, WORTHINGTON
CHAUNCEY. *Broadsides, Ballads,
etc., Printed in Massachusetts,
1639–1800.* Boston: Massachusetts Historical Society, 1922,
499 pp.

————————. "The Isaiah
Thomas Collection of Ballads."
PAAS, ns XXXIII (April 1923),
34–112.

FRANK, J. C. "Early American
Poetry to 1820: A List of Works
in the New York Public Library."
BNYPL, XXI (April 1917),
517–578.

GARDNER, MARTIN, comp.
*The Annotated Casey at the Bat:
A Collection of Ballads about
the Mighty Casey.* New York:
C. N. Potter, 1967, 195–198.

GRANGER, EDITH. *Index to
Poetry,* 4th edition, revised and
enlarged, indexing anthologies
published through Dec. 31. 1950,
edited by Raymond J. Dixon.
New York: Columbia Univ. Press,
1953, 1,869 pp.

Previous editions published under
the title, *Index to Poetry and
Recitations.*

Supplement: 1957, 474 pp.
Covers Jan. 1, 1951–Dec. 31,
1955.

Supplement: 1962, 2,162 pp.
Covers Jan. 1, 1956–June 30,
1960.

GREGORY, HORACE, and
MARYA ZATURENSKA. *A
History of American Poetry,
1900–1940.* New York: Harcourt,
Brace, 1946, 497–503.

HANDLEY-TAYLOR, GEOFFREY.
*The International Who's Who in
Poetry,* 2 Vols. London: Cranbrook
Tower Press, 1958.

HARPEL, OSCAR HENRY.
*Poets and Poetry of Printerdom:
A Collection of Original, Selected
and Fugitive Lyrics, Written by*

Persons Connected with Printing.
Cincinnati: privately printed,
1875, bibliographical notes.

HARRIS, CALEB FISKE.
*Index to American Poetry and
Plays in the Collection of C. Fiske
Harris.* Providence: printed for
private distribution by Hammond,
Angell and Co., 1874, 171 pp.

HARWELL, RICHARD BARKS-
DALE. *Confederate Belles-Lettres:
A Bibliography and a Finding List
of the Fiction, Poetry, Drama,
Songsters, and Miscellaneous
Literature Published in the Con-
federate States of America.*
Hattiesburg: Book Farm, 1941,
79 pp.

199 copies printed.

HUGHES, GLENN. *Imagism
and the Imagists: A Study in
Modern Poetry.* Palo Alto:
Stanford Univ. Press, 1931,
251–267.

HUNGERLAND, ISABEL
PAYSON (CREED). *Poetic
Discourse.* Berkeley: Univ. of
California Press, 1958, bibliographi-
cal footnotes.

IRISH, WYNOT R., comp. *The
Modern American Muse: A
Complete Bibliography of Ameri-
ca Verse, 1900–1925.* Syracuse:
Syracuse Univ. Press, 1950,
259 pp.

JANTZ, HAROLD S. "The
First Century of New England
Verse." *PAAS*, LIII (October
1943), 219–508.

Bibliographies of 164 pre-1701
writers.

JOHNSON, MERLE DE VORE.
You Know These Lines! A

*Bibliography of the Most Quoted
Verses in American Poetry,* with
a foreword by H. L. Mencken.
New York: G. A. Baker and Co.,
1935, 208 pp.

KINDILIEN, CARLIN T.
*American Poetry in the Eighteen
Nineties: A Study of American
Verse, 1890–1899 . . . .*Providence:
Brown Univ. Press, 1956,
209–214.

KRIEGER, MURRAY. *The New
Apologists for Poetry.* Minneapolis:
Univ. of Minnesota Press, 1956,
205–220.

LAWS, GEORGE MALCOLM.
*Native American Balladry: A
Descriptive Study and a Bibliog-
raphical Syllabus.* Philadelphia:
American Folklore Society,
1950, 267–270.

LEARY, LEWIS. *Articles on
American Literature, 1900–1950.*
Durham: Duke Univ. Press,
1954, 397–405.

"Poetry."

LEMAY, J. A. LEO. "Seven-
teenth Century American Poetry:
A Bibliography of the Scholarship, 1943 to 1966." *EALN,*
I (Winter 1966), 9–18.

LEMON, ROBERT, ed. *Catalogue
of a Collection of Printed Broadsides in the Possession of The
Society of Antiquaries of London.*
London: the Society of Antiquaries of London, 1866, no
pagination.

LIBRARY OF CONGRESS.
*Recent American Poetry and
Poetic Criticism: A Selected List
of References,* compiled by
Allen Tate. Washington, 1943,
13 leaves.

LIBRARY OF CONGRESS, DIVISION OF MUSIC. *Twentieth Century Poetry in English, Contemporary Recordings of the Poets Reading Their Own Poems, Catalog of Phonograph Records.* Washington, 1949, 12 pp.

LIBRARY OF CONGRESS, GENERAL REFERENCE AND BIBLIOGRAPHY DIVISION. *Archive of Recorded Poetry and Literature: A Checklist.* Washington, 1961, 132 pp.

LIBRARY OF CONGRESS, GENERAL REFERENCE AND BIBLIOGRAPHY DIVISION. *Sixty American Poets, 1896–1944,* selected, with a preface and critical notes by Allen Tate and a preliminary checklist by Francis Cheney. Washington, 1945, 188 pp.

Revised edition: 1945, 155 pp.

LOMAX, JOHN AVERY, and ALAN LOMAX, comps. *American Ballads and Folk Songs,* with a bibliography by Harold W. Thompson. New York: Macmillan Co., 1934, 613–621.

LOWELL, AMY. *Tendencies in Modern American Poetry.* Boston and New York: Houghton Mifflin Co., 1921, 345–349.

MALONE, TED. *A Listener's Aid to "Pilgrimage of Poetry": Ted Malone's Album of Poetic Shrines.* New York: Columbia Univ. Press for the National Broadcasting Co., 1939, 11 pp., unpaginated.

METCALF, FRANK JOHNSON, comp. *American Psalmody: or, Titles of Books Containing Tunes Printed in America from 1721–1820.* New York: C. F. Heartman, 1917, 54 pp.

Heartman's Historical Series, No. 27.

MILLER, JAMES EDWIN, JR., KARL SHAPIRO and BERNICE SLOTE. *Start With the Sun: Studies in Cosmic Poetry.* Lincoln: Univ. of Nebraska Press, 1960, 241–249.

MORRISON, HUGH ALEXANDER, ed. *Guide to the Poetry of the World War.* Washington, 1921, 376 leaves.

O'CONNOR, WILLIAM VAN. *Sense and Sensibility in Modern Poetry.* Chicago: Univ. of Chicago Press, 1948, 265–270.

OTIS, WILLIAM BRADLEY. *American Verse, 1625–1807: A History.* New York: Moffat, 1909, 277–293.

PARKS, EDD WINFIELD, ed. *Southern Poets: Representative Selections,* with introduction, bibliography and notes. New York: American Book Co., 1936, cxxxi–cxlviii.

PENNSYLVANIA, UNIVERSITY, LIBRARY. *Check List of Poetry by American Authors Published in the English Colonies of North America and the United States through 1865, in the Possession of the Rare Book Collection, University of Pennsylvania,* compiled by Albert von Chorba Jr. Philadelphia: Univ. of Pennsylvania Press, 1951, 63 leaves.

POETRY SOCIETY OF AMERICA. "Books by Twentieth Century American Poets." *LJ,* XLVI (Feb. 1, 1921), 111–112.

—————. "A List of Twentieth Century American Poetic Drama." *LJ,* XLV (May 1, 1920), 395–396.

PORTER, DOROTHY BURNETT.
North American Negro Poets:
A Bibliographical Checklist of
Their Writings, 1760–1944.
Hattiesburg: The Book Farm,
1945, 90 pp.

QUINN, KERKER, et al., comps.
"American Poetry, 1930–1940."
Accent, I (Summer 1941), 213–228.

RITTENHOUSE, JESSIE BELLE.
The Younger American Poets.
Boston: Little Brown, 1904, 366 pp.

RUDOLPH, EARLE LEIGHTON.
Confederate Broadside Verse: A
Bibliography and Finding List of
Confederate Broadside Ballads and
Songs. New Braunfels, Texas:
Book Farm, 1950, 118 pp.

Heartman's Historical Series,
No. 76.

SCHOMBURG, ARTHUR
ALFONSO. *A Bibliographical*
Checklist of American Negro
Poetry. New York: C. F.
Heartman, 1916, 57 pp.

SHAPIRO, KARL JAY.
A Bibliography of Modern
Prosody. Baltimore: Johns
Hopkins Press, 1948, 36 pp.

STARK, LOUIS M. "Gilder
Poetry Collection." *BNYPL,*
LII (July 1948), 341–354.

STODDARD, ROGER E.
"C. Fiske Harris, Collector of
American Poetry and Plays."
PBSA, LVII (1st Quart. 1963),
14–32.

_____. "The C. Fiske
Harris Collection of American
Poetry and Plays: Report of

Acquisitions for 1961–1962."
BBr, XIX (1963), 161–175.

TANSELLE, G. THOMAS.
"The Lyric Year: A Bibliographi-
cal Study." *PBSA,* LVI (4th
Quart. 1962), 454–471.

TRENT, WILLIAM PETERFIELD,
et al. "The Beginning of Verse,
1610–1808," in *Cambridge History*
of American Literature, 4 Vols.
New York: G.P. Putnam's
Sons, 1917–1921, I, 457–467.

_____. "Later Poets,"
in *Cambridge History of American*
Literature, 4 Vols. New York:
G. P. Putnam's Sons, 1917–1921,
IV, 644–656.

_____. "Poets of the
Civil War," in *Cambridge History*
of American Literature, 4 Vols.
New York: G. P. Putnam's Sons,
1917–1921, II, 582–588.

WEGELIN, OSCAR, comp.
Early American Poetry: A
Compilation of the Titles of
Volumes of Verse and Broadsides,
Written by Writers Born or
Residing in North America, and
Issued during the Seventeenth and
Eighteenth Centuries, 2 Vols.
New York: the compiler,
1903–1907.

2nd edition: P. Smith, 1930.

WEIRICK, BRUCE. *From*
Whitman to Sandburg in Ameri-
can Poetry: A Critical Survey.
New York: Macmillan, 1924,
223–240.

WINSLOW, OLA ELIZABETH.
American Broadside Verse from
Imprints of the Seventeenth and
Eighteenth Centuries. New Haven:
Yale Univ. Press, 1930, 250 pp.

IV

ANCILLARY

1. ALMANACS, ANNUALS, CHAP BOOKS, GIFT BOOKS

BATES, ALBERT CARLOS. "Checklist of Connecticut Almanacs, 1709–1805." *PAAS,* ns XXIV (April 1914), 93–215.

BOOTH, BRADFORD A. "A Note on an Index to the American Annuals and Gift Books." *AL,* X (November 1938), 349–350.

BOWMAN, J, R. "A Bibliography of *The First Book of the American Chronicles of the Times, 1774–1775.*" *AL,* I (March 1929), 69–73.

"Catalogue of Literary Annuals and Gift Books in the New York Public Library." *BNYPL,* VI (July 1902), 270–275.

CHAPIN, H. M. "Check List of Rhode Island Almanacs, 1643–1850." *PAAS,* XXXV (April 1915), 19–54.

"Check List of New York City Almanacs in the New York Public Library." *BNYPL,* V (May 1901), 186–189.

DRAKE, MILTON, comp. *Almanacs of the United States.* New York: Scarecrow Press, 1962, 1374–1397.

FAXON, FREDERICK WINTHROP. *Literary Annuals and Gift-Books: A Bibliography with a Descriptive Introduction.* Boston: Boston Book Co., 1912, 140 pp.

GOOLD, CLARISSA L. "Literary Annuals and Gift-Books: Their Value in Library Collections, with a List Supplementing F. W. Faxon's *Literary Annuals and Gift-Books.*" Unpublished master's thesis, Columbia Univ., 1925.

HARPER, EMILY F. "Seventeenth Century American Almanacs." *Literary Collector,* IX (January–February 1905), 41–48.

HEARTMAN, CHARLES FREDERICK. *Preliminary Check List of Almanacs Printed in New Jersey Prior to 1850.* Metuchen, New Jersey: privately printed, 1929, 39 pp.

LEARY, LEWIS. *Articles on American Literature, 1900–1950.* Durham: Duke Univ. Press, 1954, 330–331.

"Almanacs, Annuals, and Gift Books."

"Lists of Almanacks, Ephemerides, etc., and of Works Relating to the Calendar, in the New York Public Library." *BNYPL,* VII (July 1903), 246–267; (August 1903), 281–302.

LITTLEFIELD, G. E. "Notes on the Calendar and Almanac." *PAAS,* ns XXIV (April 1914), 11–64.

MORRISON, HUGH ALEX-ANDER, ed. *Preliminary Check List of American Almanacs, 1639–1800.* WASHINGTON, 1907, 160 pp.

NICHOLS, CHARLES LEMUEL. *Checklist of Maine, New Hampshire, and Vermont Almanacs.* Worcester, Massachusetts: American Antiquarian Society, 1929, 103 pp.

Also: *PAAS,* ns XXXVIII (April 1928), 63–163.

——————. "Notes on the Almanacs of Massachusetts." *PAAS,* ns XXII (April 1912), 15–134.

PAGE, A. B. "John Tulley's Almanacs, 1687–1702." *PCSM,* XIII (1912), 207–223.

SEVERANCE, F. H. "The Story of Phinney's Western Almanack, with Notes on Other Calendars

and Weather Forecasters of Buffalo." *Publications of the Buffalo Historical Society,* XXIV (1920), 343–358.

THOMPSON, RALPH. *American Library Annuals and Gift Books, 1825–1865.* New York: H. W. Wilson Co., 1936, 183 pp.

WALL, ALEXANDER J. "A List of New York Almanacs, 1649–1850." *BNYPL,* XXIV (May 1920), 287–296; (June 1920), 335–355; (July 1920), 389–413; (August 1920), 443–460; (September 1920), 508–519; (October 1920), 543–559; (November 1920), 620–641.

WEBBER, MABEL L. "South Carolina Almanacs to 1800." *South Carolina Historical and General Magazine,* XV (April 1914), 73–81.

WEISS, HARRY BISCHOFF. "American Chapbooks, 1722–1842," *BNYPL,* XLIX (July 1945), 491–498; (August 1945), 587–596.

——————. *A Book about Chapbooks: The People's Literature of Bygone Times.* Ann Arbor: Edwards Brothers, Inc., 1942, 145–149.

100 copies printed.

2. ARTS

Art and Archaeology Technical Abstracts, 1955-1957–   .

A biannual, originally issued as *IIC Abstracts,* International Institute for Conservation of Historic and Artistic Works, London. Intended for same use as R. J. Getten's *Abstracts of Technical*

Studies in Art and Archaeology, 1943–1952.

AVERY MEMORIAL LIBRARY. *Catalogue of the Avery Architectural Library: A Memorial Library of Architecture, Archaeology, and Decorative Art.* New York: Columbia Univ.,

Avery Memorial Architectural Library, 1895, 1,139 pp.

BEAUMONT, CYRIL WILLIAM, comp. *A Bibliography of Dancing.* New York: B. Blom, 1963, 239 pp.

BUSHNELL, CHARLES IRA. *Catalogue of the Library of Charles I. Bushnell, Esq.: Comprising His Extensive Collections of Rare and Curious Americana of Engravings, Autographs, Historical Relics, Woodblocks Engraved by Dr. Anderson,* compiled by Alexander Denham. New York, 1883, 283 pp.

Sold at auction by Messrs. Bangs and Co.

CRESSON, MARGARET. *Journey into Fame: The Life of Daniel Chester French.* Cambridge: Harvard Univ. Press, 1947, 315–316.

EDGELL, GEORGE HAROLD. *The American Architecture of Today.* New York and London: C. Scribner's Sons, 1928, 379–401.

HITCHCOCK, HENRY RUSSELL. *The Architecture of H. H. Richardson and His Times.* New York: Museum of Modern Art, 1936, 305–306.

IRWIN, THEODORE. *Catalogue of the Library and a Brief List of the Engravings and Etchings Belonging to Theodore Irwin, Oswego, New York.* New York: privately printed by the press of J. J. Little and Co., 1887, 534 pp.

100 copies printed.

ISHAM, SAMUEL. *The History of American Painting,* revised edition. New York: Macmillan Co., 1927, 593–600.

KIMBALL, SIDNEY FISKE. *American Architecture.* Indianapolis and New York: Bobbs-Merrill Co., 1928, 231–243.

KRIS, ERNST. *Psychoanalytic Explorations in Art.* New York: International Universities Press, 1952, 319–343, bibliographical footnotes.

LARKIN, OLIVER W. *Art and Life in America.* New York: Rinehart, 1949, 483–514.

McCAUSLAND, ELIZABETH. "A Selected Bibliography on American Painting and Sculpture from Colonial Times to the Present." *Magazine of Art,* XXXIX (November 1946), 329–349.

Reprinted in *Who's Who in American Art,* IV. Washington, 1947, 611–653.

MAGRIEL, PAUL DAVID. *A Bibliography of Dancing.* New York: H. W. Wilson Co., 1936, 230 pp.

Supplement: 1938, 41 pp. Covers 1936–1937.

Cumulative supplement: 1938, 62 pp. Covers 1936–1938.

MORRISON, HUGH SINCLAIR. *Louis Sullivan: Prophet of Modern Architecture.* New York: Museum of Modern Art and W. W. Norton and Co., Inc., 1935, bibliographical footnotes.

NEW YORK HISTORICAL SOCIETY. *Catalogue of American Portraits in the New York Historical Society.* New York: New York Historical Society, 1941, 374 pp.

REED, WALT, ed. *The Illustrator in America, 1900–1960's.*

New York: Reinhold Publishing Co., 1966, 271–272.

RICHARDSON, EDGAR PRESTON. *Painting in America: The Story of 450 Years.* New York: Crowell, 1956, 417–427.

TAFT, LORADO. *The History of American Sculpture,* new edition. New York: Macmillan Co., 1930, 539–542.

WOLFE, RICHARD J. *Secular Music in America, 1801–1825: A Bibliography,* 3 Vols. New York: New York Public Library, 1964.

WYCKOFF, ALEXANDER, EDWARD WARWICK and HENRY PITZ. *Early American Dress: The Colonial and Revolutionary Periods.* New York: B. Blom, 1965, bibliographical footnotes.

The second volume of a projected *History of American Dress.*

3. BIOGRAPHIES, DIARIES, GENEALOGIES

ADAMS, OSCAR FAY. *A Brief Handbook of American Authors.* Boston: Houghton, Mifflin and Co., 1884, 188 pp.

Also: 1885, 204 pp.

Also: 1897, 444 pp.

Also: 1901, 522 pp.

Also: 1905, 583 pp. Title changed to *A Dictionary of American Authors.*

AGNEW, JANET MARGARET. *A Southern Bibliography,* 4 Vols. University: Louisiana State Univ. and Agricultural and Mechanical College, 1939–1942.

I.   Fiction.

II. Historical Fiction.

III. Poetry.

IV: Biography.

ALLIBONE, SAMUEL AUSTIN. *A Critical Dictionary of English Literature and British and American Authors, Living and Deceased, from the Earliest Accounts to the Middle*

of the Nineteenth Century, 3 Vols. Philadelphia: J. B. Lippincott and Co., 1858–1871.

Contains 30,000 biographies and literary notices, with 40 indexes of subjects.

BACON, CORINNE. *Standard Catalog: Biography Section, One Thousand Titles of the Most Representative, Interesting and Useful Biographies.* New York: H. W. Wilson Co., 1919, 99 pp.

Biography Index: A Cumulative Index of Biographical Materials in Books and Magazines. New York: H. W. Wilson Co., 1946–   .

Cumulations cover three-year periods, with seven issued to date. Quarterly and yearly supplements issued regularly until they form a three-year cumulation.

BROWN, THOMAS ALLSTON. *History of the American Stage, Containing Biographical Sketches of Nearly Every Member of the Profession That Has Appeared on the American Stage from 1733 to 1870.* New York: Dick and Fitzgerald, 1870, 421 pp.

BROWNING, DAVID CLAYTON.
Everyman's Dictionary of Literary Biography, English and American.
London: Dent, 1958, 752 pp.

Supersedes *Biographical Dictionary of English Literature,* compiled by John William Cousin. London: Dent, 1946, 456 pp.

CAPPON, LESTER JESSE.
American Genealogical Periodicals: A Bibliography with a Chronological Finding List. New York: New York Public Library, 1962, 29 pp.

——————. "Preparing a Bibliography of American Genealogical Periodicals." *BNYPL,* LXVI (January 1962), 63—66.

CARLOCK, MARY S. "American Autobiographies, 1840—1870: A Bibliography." *BB,* XXIII (May—August 1961), 118—120.

CARNEGIE LIBRARY (PITTS-BURGH). *Contemporary Biography: References to Books and Magazine Articles on Prominent Men and Women of the Time,* compiled by Agnes M. Elliott. Pittsburgh: Carnegie Library, 1903, 171 pp.

"Current Literature: I. Fiction, Drama, and Poetry. II. Criticism and Biography." *English Studies,* 1919— .

A bibliographical essay in two parts, originally entitled, "Bibliography."

DURRIE, DANIEL STEELE.
Bibliographia Genealogica Americana: An Alphabetical Index to American Genealogies and Pedigrees Contained in State, County, and Town Histories, Printed Genealogies and Kindred Works.
Albany: J. Munsell, 1868, 296 pp.

2nd edition: 1878, 238 pp.

3rd edition: 1886, 245 pp.

FORBES, HARRIETTE (MERRIFIELD). *New England Diaries, 1602—1800: A Descriptive Catalogue of Diaries, Orderly Books and Sea Journals.* Topsfield, Massachusetts: privately printed, 1923, 440 pp.

HANDLEY-TAYLOR, GEOFFREY.
Dictionary of International Biography, 3 Vols, London: Dictionary of International Biography Co., 1963—1966.

A guide to 43 other reference works.

HARKNESS, DAVID J. "The Biographical Novel: A Bibliography with Notes." *Univ. of Tennessee News Letter,* XXIX (1950), 1—45.

HARVARD UNIVERSITY.
Quinquennial Catalogue of the Officers and Graduates of Harvard University, 1636—1915.
Cambridge: Harvard Univ. Press, 1915.

Issued triannually. Superseded by *Harvard Alumni Directory.*

HEFLING, HELEN, and EVA RICHARDS. *Index to Contemporary Biography and Criticism,* 1st edition. Boston: F. W. Faxon Co., 1929, 124 pp.

Also: *Hefling and Richards' Index . . . ,* revised by Hefling, Richards and Jessie W. Dyde. 1934, 220 pp.

HOEHN, MATHEW, ed.
Catholic Authors: Contemporary Biographical Sketches, 1930—1947, 2 Vols. Newark: St. Mary's Abbey, 1948—1952.

Also: 1957, 814 pp. One-volume edition.

—————, ed. *Catholic Authors: Contemporary Biographical Sketches, 1948–1952.* Newark: St. Mary's Abbey, 1952, 633 pp.

JOHNSON, ALLEN, and DUMAS MALONE, eds. *Dictionary of American Biography,* 20 Vols. New York: Scribners, 1928–1936.

JONES, CLAUDE E. "Collected Biographies to 1825." *BB,* XVII (1941), 90–92.

KAPLAN, LOUIS, JAMES TYLER COOK, CLINTON E. COLBY JR. and DANIEL C. HASKELL. *A Bibliography of American Autobiographies.* Madison: Univ. of Wisconsin Press, 1961, 384 pp.

Coverage ceases with 1945.

KUNITZ, STANLEY JASSPON, ed. *Authors Today and Yesterday.* New York: H. W. Wilson Co., 1934, 726 pp.

KUNITZ, STANLEY JASSPON, and HOWARD HAYCRAFT, eds. *American Authors, 1600–1900: A Biographical Dictionary of American Literature.* New York: H. W. Wilson Co., 1938, 846 pp.

—————, eds. *Twentieth Century Authors: A Biographical Dictionary of Modern Literature.* New York: H. W. Wilson Co., 1942, 1,577 pp.

Supplement: 1955, 1,123 pp.

LEARY, LEWIS. *Articles on American Literature, 1900–1950.* Durham: Duke Univ. Press, 1954, 340.

"Biography."

—————. *Articles on American Literature, 1900–1950.* Durham: Duke Univ. Press, 1954, 341–342.

"Diaries and Letters."

LIBRARY OF CONGRESS. *Biographical Sources for the United States.* Washington, 1961, 58 pp.

LILLARD, RICHARD GORDON. *American Life in Autobiography: A Descriptive Guide.* Palo Alto: Stanford Univ. Press, 1956, 140 pp.

MATTHEWS, WILLIAM. *American Diaries: An Annotated Bibliography of American Diaries Written prior to the Year 1861,* with the assistance of Roy Harvey Pearce. Berkeley: Univ. of California Press, 1945, 397 pp.

McTURNAN, LAWRENCE. *The Personal Equation.* New York: Moffat, Yard and Co., 1910, 221–247.

MERRILL, DANA KINSMAN. *American Biography: Its Theory and Practice.* Portland, Maine: Bowker, 1957.

Selective list of biographies, 1920–1955, 251–256.

NEW ENGLAND HISTORIC GENEALOGICAL SOCIETY, *New-England Historical and Genealogical Register.* Boston: S. G. Drake, 1847– .

Entitled *New-England Historical and Genealogical Register and Antiquarian Journal,* 1923–1927.

O'NEILL, EDWARD HAYES. *Biography by Americans, 1658–*

1936: A Subject Bibliography.
Philadelphia: Univ. of Pennsylvania Press, 1939, 475 pp.

A checklist of biographies written
by Americans. For famous men,
only the more important books
on them are recorded.

——————. *A History of*
American Biography, 1800–1935.
Philadelphia: Univ. of Pennsylvania
Press, 1935, 367–417.

PEARSON, THOMAS SCOTT.
Catalogue of the Graduates of
Middlebury College, Embracing
a Biographical Register and
Directory. . . .Windsor, Vermont:
printed at the Vermont
Chronicle Press, 1853, 144 pp.

PRESCOTT, WILLIAM
HICKLING. *Biographical and*
Critical Miscellanies. New York:
Harper and Brothers, 1845, 638 pp.

Also: 1851.

Also: Boston: Phillips, Sampson
and Co., 1859, 729 pp.

Also: Philadelphia: J. B. Lippincott
and Co., 1882, 682 pp.

Also: 1896.

Also: 1903.

RICHES, PHYLLIS M., comp.
An Analytical Bibliography of
Universal Collected Biography,
Comprising Books Published in
the English Tongue in Great Britain
and Ireland, America and the
British Dominions. London: The
Library Association, 1934, 718 pp.

ROUCEK, JOSEPH SLABEY.
The Immigrant in Fiction and
Biography. New York: Bureau
for Intercultural Education,
1945, 32 pp.

RUSCHENBERGER, W. R. S.
"Roll of Fellows of the College
of Physicians of Philadelphia,
Elected during the Century
Ending January, 1887," in
An Account of the Institution
and Progress of the College of
Physicians of Philadelphia. Phila-
delphia: W. J. Dorman, 1887,
107–304.

SIBLEY, JOHN LANGDON.
Biographical Sketches of
Graduates of Harvard University,
3 Vols. Cambridge: Harvard
Univ. Press, 1873–1885.

Continued as: SHIPTON, CLIF-
FORD K., ed. *Sibley's Harvard*
Graduates: Biographical Sketches
of Those Who Attended
Harvard College.

SMITH, ELSDON COLES.
"Books in English on Personal
Names." *Names,* I (September
1953), 197–202.

——————. "Literature on
Personal Names in English."
Names, III (June 1955), 117–122.

SMITH, RALPH CLIFTON.
A Biographical Index of
American Artists. Baltimore:
Williams and Wilkins, 1930, 102 pp.

SPARKS, JARED. *The Library*
of American Biography, 25 Vols.
London: R. J. Kennett, 1834–1848.

A reprint of 22 of the 26 lives
in the 1st Series is found in Sparks'
American Biography, 12 Vols.
New York and London: Harper
and Brothers, 1902.

STOKES, ANSON PHELPS.
Memorials of Eminent Yale
Men: A Biographical Study of
Student Life and University In-
fluences during the Eighteenth

and Nineteenth Centuries, 2 Vols.
New Haven and London: Yale
Univ. Press, 1914, II, 421–452.

THOMAS, WILLIAM S. "Ameri-
can Revolutionary Diaries: Also
Journals, Narratives, Autobiog-
raphies, Reminiscences and
Personal Memoirs, Catalogued and
Described with an Index to Places
and Events." *NYSQ,* VI (April
1922), 32–35; (July 1922), 61–71;
(October 1922), 101–107;
(January 1923), 143–147.

TRAUB, HAMILTON, ed.
*The American Literary Yearbook:
A Biographical and Bibliographical
Dictionary of Living Authors,*
I. Henning, Minnesota: P. Traub,
1919.

No further volumes published.

WALLACE, WILLIAM STEWART,
comp. *A Dictionary of North
American Authors Deceased before*

1950. Toronto: Ryerson Press,
1951, 525 pp.

WHITMORE, WILLIAM HENRY.
*American Genealogist: Being a
Catalogue of Family Histories and
Publications Containing Genealogi-
cal Information Issued in the United
States.* Albany: J. Munsell, 1868,
287 pp.

Title varies slightly.

Also: 1875, 346 pp.

Also: 1897.

Also: 1900.

*Who's Who among North American
Authors,* 7 Vols. Los Angeles:
Golden Syndicate Publishing Co.,
1921–1939.

I–V cover two-year periods,
beginning 1923; VI, VII cover
three-year periods, ending 1939.

4. CHILDREN'S LITERATURE

AMERICAN LIBRARY
ASSOCIATION. *Booklist and
Subscription Books Bulletin:
Books for Children, 1960–1965.*
Chicago: American Library
Association, 1966, 447 pp.

BAKER, FRANKLIN THOMAS,
and ALLAN ABOTT. *A Bibliography of Children's Reading.*
New York: Teachers College,
1908, 133 pp.

BINSSE, H. L. "Children's
Books–1946." *Commonweal,*
XLV (Nov. 15, 1946), 119–124.

A survey and a selected
bibliography.

BLANCK, JACOB. *Peter Parley
to Penrod: A Bibliographical*

*Description of the Best-loved
American Juvenile Books.*
New York: R. R. Bowker Co.,
1938, 159 pp.

BREWTON, JOHN EDMOND,
and SARA WESTBROOK
BREWTON, comps. *Index to
Children's Poetry.* New York:
H. W. Wilson Co., 1942, 997 pp.

Supplement: 1954, 427 pp.

ELLIS, ALEC. *How to Find Out
about Children's Literature.*
Oxford: Pergamon Press, 1966,
196 pp.

FIELD, WALTER TAYLOR.
*Fingerposts to Children's
Reading,* 8th edition. Chicago:

A.C. McClurg and Co., 1918, 42–46.

GRISWOLD, WILLIAM McCRILLIS. *Descriptive List of Books for the Young.* Cambridge: W. M. Griswold, 1895, 183 pp.

HALSEY, ROSALIE VRYLINA. *Forgotten Books of the American Nursery: A History of the Development of the American Story-Book.* Boston: C. E. Goodspeed and Co., 1911, 252 pp.

HARDY, GEORGE EDWARD PAUL. *Five Hundred Books for the Young: A Graded and Annotated List,* 2nd edition. New York: C. Scribner's Sons, 1892, 94 pp.

HARRINGTON, MILDRED PRISCILLA. *The Southwest in Children's Books: A Bibliography.* Baton Rouge: Louisiana State Univ. Press, 1952, 143 pp.

KENNERLY, SARAH L. "Confederate Juvenile Imprints: Children's Books and Periodicals Published in the Confederate States of America, 1861–1865." Unpublished doctoral dissertation, Univ. of Michigan, 1957.

LANDREY, KATHLEEN BENEDICTA. "A Bibliography of Books Written by Children of the Twentieth Century." *More Books,* XII (April 1937), 149–157.

Also: *A Bibliography of Books Written by Children of the Twentieth Century.* Boston: Boston Public Library, 1937, 13 pp.

LEARY, LEWIS. *Articles on American Literature, 1900–1950.*

Durham: Duke Univ. Press, 1954, 341.

"Children's Literature."

MILLER, BERTHA E. (MAHONEY). *Realms of Gold in Children's Books.* Boston: Doubleday, Doran and Co., 1929, 796 pp.

MILLER, BERTHA E. (MAHONEY), LOUISE PAYSON LATIMER and BEULAH FOLMSBEE, comps. *Illustrators of Children's Books, 1744–1945.* Boston: Horn Book, 1947, 543 pp.

Supplement: 1958, 299 pp. Covers 1946–1956.

PEARSON, EDWIN. *Banbury Chap-books and Nursery Toy Book Literature (of the Eighteenth and Early Nineteenth Centuries)* . . . .London: A. Reader, 1890, 116 pp.

PITZ, HENRY CLARENCE. *Illustrating Children's Books— History-Technique-Production.* New York: Watson-Guptill Publications, 1963, 207 pp.

ROSENBACH, A. S. W. *Early American Children's Books with Bibliographical Descriptions of the Books in His Private Collection.* Portland, Maine: The Southworth Press, 1933, 354 pp.

SHAFFER, ELLEN. "The Rosenbach Collection of Early American Children's Books in the Free Library of Philadelphia." *ABC,* VI (March 1956), 3–7.

SLOANE, WILLIAM. *Children's Books in England and America in the Seventeenth Century: A History and Checklist together*

with the Young Christian's, the
First Printed Catalogue of Books
for Children. New York: King's
Crown Press, Columbia Univ.,
1955, 251 pp.

——————. "English and
American Children's Books of the
Seventeenth Century: An Annotated
Check-list, together with the First
Printed Catalogue of Children's
Books." Unpublished doctoral
dissertation, Columbia Univ., 1953.

SMITH, ELVA SOPHRONIA.
*The History of Children's Literature:
A Syllabus with Selected Bibliog-
raphies.* Chicago: American
Library Association, 1937, 244 pp.

SOUTHERN CONNECTICUT
STATE COLLEGE, LIBRARY.
*The Carolyn Sherwin Bailey
Historical Collection of Children's
Books: A Catalogue,* compiled by
Dorothy R. Davis. New Haven:
Southern Connecticut State
College, 1966, 232 pp.

TRENT, WILLIAM PETERFIELD,
et al. "Books for Children," in
*Cambridge History of American
Literature,* 4 Vols. New York:
G. P. Putnam's Sons, 1917–
1921, II, 631–638.

WELCH, D'ALTE. "A Bibliog-
raphy of Children's Books
Printed Prior to 1821." *PAAS,*
LXXIII (April 1963), 121–324.

5. CINEMA

AR VIDSON, LINDA (see GRIFFITH)
BEMAN, LAMAR T., comp.
*Selected Articles on Censorship
of the Theater and Moving
Pictures.* New York: H. W. Wilson
Co., 1931, bibliographical notes.

ENSER, A. G. S. *Filmed Books
and Plays: A List of Books and
Plays from which Films Have Been
Made, 1928–1949.* London:
Grafton and Co., 1951, 218 pp.

Supplement: 1956, 69 pp.
Covers 1952–1954.

FELDMAN, JOSEPH, and HARRY
FELDMAN. *Dynamics of the
Film.* New York: Hermitage
House, 1952, 243–248.

FILM COUNCIL OF AMERICA,
EDITORIAL BOARD. *A Guide
to Film Services of National
Associations.* Evanston, Illinois:
Film Council of America, 1954,
146 pp.

Film Councilor Series, No. 2.

FOX FILM CORPORATION.
*Catalogue of the Stories and
Plays Owned by Fox Film Cor-
poration.* Los Angeles: *Times-
Mirror* Press, 1935, 326 pp.

GRIFFITH, MRS. D. W. (LINDA
ARVIDSON). *When the Movies
Were Young.* New York: E. P.
Dutton and Co., 1925, 256 pp.

Also: B. Blom, 1968.

HARLEY, JOHN EUGENE.
*World-wide Influences of the
Cinema: A Study of Official
Censorship and the International
Cultural Aspects of Motion Pic-
tures.* Los Angeles: Univ. of
Southern California Press, 1940,
169–291.

*Univ. of Southern California
Cinematography Series,* No. 2.

LIBRARY OF CONGRESS.
*The Civil War in Motion Pictures:
A Bibliography of Films Produced
in the United States since 1897.*
Washington, 1961, 109 pp.

LIBRARY OF CONGRESS,
DIVISION OF BIBLIOGRAPHY.
*Moving Pictures in the United
States and Foreign Countries: A
Selected List of Recent Writing.*
Washington, 1936, 72 leaves.

LIBRARY OF CONGRESS,
DIVISION OF BIBLIOGRAPHY.
*Select List of References on Motion
Pictures.* Washington, 1912, 7 leaves.

Supplement: 1914, 5 leaves.

WRIGLEY, MAURICE JACKSON,
and ERIC LEYLAND. *The Cinema,
Historical, Technical and Bibliographical: A Survey for Librarians
and Students.* London: Grafton
and Co., 1939, 109—185.

6. DISSERTATIONS

CANTRELL, CLYDE HULL,
and WALTON R. PATRICK.
*Southern Literary Culture: A
Bibliography of Masters' and
Doctors' Theses.* University:
Univ. of Alabama Press, 1955,
124 pp.

EELLS, WALTER C. "American
Doctoral Theses on Modern
Languages Written by Women in
the Nineteenth Century." *MLJ,*
XLI (May 1957), 209—211.

HENRY, EDWARD A. "Doctoral
Dissertations Accepted—Ten
Years of History." *CRL,* V
(September 1944), 309—314.

HEYL, LAWRENCE. "Sources
of Information Covering Research
in Progress and University
Dissertations." *School and Society,*
XXIX (June 1929), 808—810.

LEARY, LEWIS, comp.
"Doctoral Dissertations in
American Literature, 1933—1948."
AL, XX (1948), 169—230.

Also: Durham: Duke Univ. Press,
1948, 71 pp.

LEAVITT, S. E., and H. K.
RUSSELL. "Theses in English

and Modern Foreign Languages
Accepted in the Colleges of North
Carolina, South Carolina, Georgia,
Florida, and Alabama." *SAB,*
IV (April 1938), 1—15.

LEISY, ERNEST ERWIN.
"Materials for Investigation in
American Literature: A Bibliog-
raphy of Dissertations, Articles,
Research in Progress, and Collec-
tions of Americana . . . . " *SP,*
XXIII (1926), 90—115.

Additions and corrections: *SP,*
XXIV (1927), 480—483.

LEISY, ERNEST ERWIN, and
JAY B. HUBBELL, comps.
"Doctoral Dissertations in American Literature." *AL,* IV (January
1933), 419—465.

Also: Durham: Duke Univ.
Press, 1933, 46 pp.

LIBRARY OF CONGRESS.
*A List of American Doctoral
Dissertations,* 9 Vols. Washington,
1912, 1931—1938.

LIBRARY OF CONGRESS.
*A List of American Doctoral
Dissertations Printed in 1913 and
1914,* prepared by Alida M.

Stephens, 2 Vols. Washington, 1914–1915.

LIBRARY OF CONGRESS, CATALOGUE DIVISION. *List of American Doctoral Dissertations,* 27 Vols. Washington, 1912–1938.

Continued in National Research Council's and American Council of Learned Societies' *Doctoral Dissertations Accepted by American Universities,* 1933–1955.

LONDON, UNIVERSITY. *Theses and Dissertations Accepted for Higher Degrees.* London: n.p., 1937– .

Title varies. First volume covers 1937–1944. Issued annually thereafter.

NATIONAL RESEARCH COUNCIL and THE AMERICAN COUNCIL OF LEARNED SOCIETIES. *Doctoral Dissertations Accepted by American Universities,* 22 Vols. New York: H. W. Wilson Co., 1933–1955.

OXFORD, UNIVERSITY, COMMITTEE FOR ADVANCED STUDIES. *Abstracts of Dissertations for the Degree of Doctor of Philosophy.* Oxford: Clarendon Press, 1928– .

I covers 1925–1928. Subsequently issued annually.

PALFREY, THOMAS ROSSMAN, and HENRY E. COLEMAN. *Guide to Bibliographies of Theses, United States and Canada.* Chicago: American Library Association, 1936, 48 pp.

ROSENBERG, RALPH P. "Bibliographies of Theses in America." *BB,* XVIII (September–December 1945), 181–182.

WOODRESS, JAMES, comp. *Dissertations in American Literature, 1891–1955, with Supplement, 1956–1961.* Durham: Duke Univ. Press, 1962, 138 pp.

7. EDUCATION

BRIAN, SISTER MARY. "A Bibliography of Audio-Visual Aids for Courses in American Literature." *CE,* XV (1953), 159–171.

CUBBERLEY, ELLWOOD PATTERSON. *Public Education in the United States: A Study and Interpretation of American Educational History,* revised edition. Boston: Houghton Mifflin Co., 1934, 782 pp.

Bibliographies at end of each chapter.

DEXTER, FRANKLIN BOWDITCH. *Documentary History of Yale University, under the Original Charter of the Collegiate School of Connecticut, 1701–1745.* New Haven: Yale Univ. Press, 1916, 400 pp.

FORD, PAUL LEICESTER. *The New England Primer: A History of Its Origin and Development . . . .* New York: Dodd, Mead, 1897, 354 pp.

GRAY, GORDON. "A Bibliography of American Regional Novels for the Use of Teachers." Unpublished doctoral dissertation, Teachers College, Columbia Univ., 1952.

HEARTMAN, CHARLES
FREDERICK, comp. *The New
England Primer Issued prior to
1830: A Bibliographical Checklist for the More Easy Attaining
the True Knowledge of This
Book.* New York: printed for the
compiler, 1915, 190 pp.

110 copies printed.

Also: 1922. 265 copies printed.

Also: R. R. Bowker Co., 1934,
148 pp. 300 copies printed.

JENKINSON, EDWARD B.,
and PHILIP B. DAGHLIAN, eds.
*Books for Teachers of English:
An Annotated Bibliography.*
Bloomington: Indiana Univ.
Press, 1968, 173 pp.

LAWLER, THOMAS BONA-
VENTURE. *Seventy Years of
Text-book Publishing, 1867–1937.*
Boston: Ginn and Co., 1938,
304 pp.

LITTLEFIELD, GEORGE
EMERY. *Early Schools and School-
Books of New England.* Boston: The
Club of Odd Volumes, 1904,
354 pp.

167 copies printed.

MONROE, WALTER SCOTT,
and LOUIS SHORES, comps.
*Bibliographies and Summaries
in Education to July, 1935. . . .*
New York: H. W. Wilson Co.,
1936, 470 pp.

MONROE, WALTER SCOTT,
and OLLIE ASHER. *A Bibliography of Bibliographies.* Urbana:
Univ. of Illinois Press, 1927,
60 pp.

Univ. of Illinois College of
Education, *Bureau of Educational
Research Bulletin,* No. 36.

NASH, RAY. *American Writing
Masters and Copybooks: History
and Bibliography through
Colonial Times.* Boston: The
Colonial Society of Massachusetts,
1959, 78 pp.

THONSSEN, LESTER, and
ELIZABETH FATHERSON.
Bibliography of Speech Education.
New York: Wilson, 1939, 800 pp.

Supplement: 1950, 393 pp.
Covers 1939–1948.

TRENT, WILLIAM PETERFIELD,
et al. "Education," in *Cambridge
History of American Literature,*
4 Vols. New York: G. P. Putnam's
Sons, 1917–1921, IV, 794.

———————. "Scholars," in
*Cambridge History of American
Literature,* 4 Vols. New York:
G. P. Putnam's Sons, 1917–1921,
IV, 795–797.

YALE UNIVERSITY. *Bibliog-
raphies of the Present Officers of
Yale University.* New Haven:
Yale Univ. Press, 1893, 160 pp.

8. FOLKLORE, LEGEND, MYTH

Abstracts of Folklore Studies. Philadelphia: The American Folklore
Society, 1963–   .

ARLT, GUSTAVE O., et al. "Bibliography of California Folklore."

CFQ, II (January 1943), 63–70;
(April 1943), 169–175; (July 1943),
245–251; (October 1943), 347–352.

BROWN, WILLIAM EDGAR.
"Books on Legends and Traditions,"

in *Echoes of the Forest: American Indian Legends.* Boston: R. G. Badger, 1918, 261–264.

CHAMBERLAIN, ISABEL C. "Contributions Toward a Bibliography of Folklore Relating to Women." *JAF,* XII (January-March 1899), 32–37.

COLVILLE, DEREK. "A Rich Store of Southern Tall Tales." Univ. of Virginia Bibliographical Society, *Secretary's News Sheet,* XXXIII (June 1955).

COMBS, JOSIAH H. *Folk-Songs of the Southern United States* (Folk-Songs du Midi des Etats-Unis), edited by Donald Knight Wilgus. Austin: published for the American Folklore Society by the Univ. of Texas Press, 1967, 195–238.

DYKES, JEFFERSON CHENOWETH. *Billy the Kid: The Bibliography of a Legend.* Albuquerque: Univ. of New Mexico Press, 1952, 186 pp.

Univ. of New Mexico Publications in Language and Literature, No. 7.

FLANAGAN, JOHN T. "Humor and Folklore Galore." *Manuscripts,* IX (1957), 89–95, 128.

Describes Franklin J. Meirie Collection of Folklore in Univ. of Illinois Library.

GARDNER, MARTIN, comp. *The Annotated Casey at the Bat: A Collection of Ballads about the Mighty Casey.* New York: C. N. Potter, 1967, 195–198.

HANEY, GLADYS J. "Paul Bunyan Twenty-five Years After." *JAF,* LV (July-September 1942), 155–168.

HAYWOOD, CHARLES. *A Bibliography of North American Folklore and Folksong,* 2nd revised edition, 2

Vols. New York: Dover Publications, 1961.

JACKSON, BRUCE, ed. *The Negro and His Folklore in Nineteenth-Century Periodicals.* Austin: printed for the American Folklore Society by the Univ. of Texas Press, 1967, 353–367.

JOBES, GERTRUDE. *Dictionary of Mythology, Folklore, and Symbols,* 2 Vols. New York: The Scarecrow Press, 1961, 1,736–1,759.

KIRKLAND, EDWIN C. "A Check List of the Titles of Tennessee Folksongs." *JAF,* LIX (October-December 1946), 423–476.

KOCH, FREDERICK HENRY. *American Folk Plays.* New York: D. Appleton-Century, 1939.

LCN: "The Carolina Playmakers: A Selected Bibliography, September, 1931, to September, 1938," 557–570. " 'For a selected bibliography of The Carolina Playmakers from 1918 to 1931 see Appendix I of the Second Series and Appendix I of the Third Series of *Carolina Folk Plays* (Henry Holt & Co.), and Appendix I of *Carolina Plays* (Samuel French).' "

LEACH, MARIA, ed. *Funk and Wagnalls' Standard Dictionary of Folklore, Mythology, and Legend,* 2 Vols. New York: Funk and Wagnalls Co., 1950.

LESSER, ALEXANDER. "Bibliography of American Folklore." *JAF,* XLI (January-March 1928), 1–60.

LIBRARY OF CONGRESS. *Folk Music: A Selection of Folk Songs, Ballads, Dances, Instrumental Pieces, and Folk Tales of the United States and Latin America: Catalog of Phonograph Records.* Washington, 1959, 103 pp.

Revised edition in preparation.

LOMAX, ALAN, and SIDNEY ROBERTSON COWELL, comps. *American Folk Song and Folk Lore: A Regional Bibliography.* New York: Progressive Education Association, 1942, 59 pp.

LUMPKIN, BEN GRAY, and NORMAL L. McNEIL. *Folk-Songs on Records.* Denver: Alan Swallow, 1950, 98 pp.

MUNN, ROBERT F. *The Southern Appalachians: A Bibliography and Guide to Studies.* Morgantown: West Virginia Univ. Library, 1961, 106 pp.

NAESETH, HENRIETTE. "Drama in Early Deadwood (1876–1879)." *AL*, X (November 1938), 289–312.

NEW YORK PUBLIC LIBRARY. "List of Works in the New York Public Library Relating to Folk Songs, Folk Music, Ballads, etc." *BNYPL*, XI (May 1907), 187–226.

PRICE, ROBERT. *John Chapman: A Bibliography of "Johnny Appleseed" in American History, Literature, and Folklore.* Paterson, New Jersey: The Swedenborg Press, 1944, 40 pp.

RANDOLPH, VANCE, ed. *"The Devil's Pretty Daughter" and Other Ozark Folk Tales,* with notes by Herbert Halpert. New York: Columbia Univ. Press, 1955, 231–239.

—————————, ed. *"Sticks in the Knapsack" and Other Ozark Folk Tales,* with notes by Ernest W.

Baughman. New York: Columbia Univ. Press, 1958, 167–171.

—————————, ed. *"The Talking Turtle" and Other Ozark Folk Tales.* New York: Columbia Univ. Press, 1957, 221–226.

—————————, ed. *"Who Blowed Up the Church House?" and Other Ozark Folk Tales,* with notes by Herbert Halpert. New York: Columbia Univ. Press, 1952, 227–232.

RANDOLPH, VANCE, and GEORGE P. WILSON, comps. *Down in the Holler: A Gallery of Ozark Folk Speech.* Norman: Univ. of Oklahoma Press, 1953, 303–314.

THOMPSON, HAROLD W., ed. "Indexes: Country Lore in *NYFQ,* 1954–1955." *NYFQ,* XI (Summer 1955), 152–153.

THOMPSON, STITH. *Motif-Index of Folk-Literature,* revised edition, 6 Vols. Copenhagen: Rosenkilde and Bagger, 1955–1958.

Classifies "narrative elements" in folktales, ballads, myths.

TILLMAN, MARJORIE. *Dictionary of American Folklore.* New York: Philosophical Library, 1959, 324 pp.

UTLEY, ROBERT MARSHALL. *Custer and the Great Controversy: The Origin and Development of a Legend.* Los Angeles: Westernlore Press, 1962, 167–177.

Great West and Indian Series, No. 22.

9. FOREIGN CRITICISM OF AMERICAN LITERATURE

ANDERSON, CARL L. *The Swedish Acceptance of American Literature.* Philadelphia: Univ. of Pennsylvania Press, 1957, 103–152.

"Anglo-French and Franco-American Studies: A Bibliography." *RR.*

Bibliography appears annually in

either April or October issue, 1939—
1948.

ANSERMOZ-DUBOIS, FELIX.
*L'interprétation Française de la
littérature américaine d'entre-deux-
guerres (1919–1939): Essaie de
Bibliographie.* Lausanne: La
Concorde, 1944, 255 pp.

ARNOLD, ARMIN. *D. H. Lawrence and America.* London: Linden
Press, 1958, 231—244.

Also: New York: Philosophical
Library, 1959.

BAGINSKY, PAUL BEN, comp.
*German Works Relating to America,
1493–1800: A List Compiled from
the Collections of the New York
Public Library.* New York: New
York Public Library, 1942, 232 pp.

BALLA-CAYARD, L. "German
Dissertations in American Literature
Accepted between 1900 and 1945."
AL, XXIV (1952), 384—390.

BARCIA CARBALLIDO Y ZUÑIGA,
ANDRÉS GONZÁLEZ DE. "Works
on North America," in *Ensayo Cro-
nólogico para la Historia General de
la Florida,* by G. de Gardenas z Cano.
Madrid: en la Oficina real, y à Costa
de N. Rodriguez Franco, 1723.

CARRIER, JOSEPH M., et al. "Anglo-
French and Franco-American
Studies: A Bibliography." *French
American Review,* II (October-
December 1949), 214—232; III (April-
September 1950), 94—119.

CHAPMAN, ARNOLD. *The Spanish-
American Reception of United States
Fiction, 1920–1940.* Berkeley:
Univ. of California Press, 1966, 226
pp.

*Univ. of California Publications in
Modern Philology,* LXVII.

DUCHARME, JACQUES. "Bibliographie franco-américaine." *Bulletin de
la Societé Historique Franco-Ameri-
caine,* 1942, 97—108.

DURHAM, PHILIP, AND TAUNO
F. MUSTANOJA. "American Fiction in Finland: An Essay and Bibliography." *Mémoires de la Societé
Néophilologique de Helsinke* (Modern
Language Society), XXIV (1960),
121—124.

Bibliography of translations, 125—
171.

EBERHARDT, FRITZ. *Amerika-
Literatur: Die Wichtigsten seit 1900
in Deutscher Sprache erschienenen
Werke über Amerika.* Leipzig:
Koehler and Volckmar, 1926, 335
pp.

ENGLEKIRK, JOHN EUGENE. *A
Literatura Norteamericana no Brasil.*
México: n.p., 1950, 181 pp.

FABIAN, BERNHARD. "Deutsche
Amerikanistische Veröffentli-
chunger." *Jahrbuch fur Amerika-
studien,* I (1956), 184—206; II (1957),
231—282; III (1958), 238—261.

FARIBAULT, GEORGES BARTHE-
LEMI (rédigé par). *Catalogue d'Ouvrages sur l'Histoire de l'Amérique et
en particulier sur celle du Canada, de
la Louisiane, de l'Acadie et autres
lieux, ci-devant connus sous le nom
de la Nouvelle France,* en trois
parties. Quebec: W. Cowan, 1837,
207 pp.

FAŸ, BERNARD. "Bibliographie
critique des ouvrages français relatifs
aux Etats-Unis," in *Revue des
Bibliotheques,* XXXIV. Paris: n.p.,
1924, 180 pp.

Also: E. Champion, 1925, 108 pp.

FERGUSON, JOHN DE LANCEY.
American Literature in Spain. New

York: Columbia Univ. Press, 1916, 203–260.

Columbia Univ. Studies in English and Comparative Literature.

FERRARIO, GUILIO. *Il Costume Antico e Moderno . . . ,* 18 Vols. Milan: printed for the author, 1816–1834, XVI, 65.

Title pages of the first two volumes in French.

FISHER, MARVIN MARK. *Workshops in the Wilderness: The European Response to American Industrialization, 1830–1860.* New York: Oxford Univ. Press, 1967, 189–231.

FRAUWAULLNER, ERICH, et al. *Die Weltliteratur,* 3 Vols. Vienna: Bruden Hollinek, 1951–1954.

GENZEL, PETER. *Kurze Bibliographie für das Studium der Anglistik und Amerikanistik.* Halle: Niemeyer, 1960, 176 pp.

GJELSNESS, RUDOLPH. *The American Book in Mexico.* Ann Arbor: Univ. of Michigan, Dept. of Library Science, 1957, 92 pp.

HANDELMANN, HEINRICH. "Authorities," in *Geschichte der Amerikanischen Kolonisation und Unabbängigkeit.* Kiel: Schwerssche buchhandlung, 1856.

HIBLER, LEO, KARL BRUNNER and HERBERT KOZIOL. "Austrian Dissertations on American Literature." *AL,* XXIV (January 1953), 543–547.

JAHN, JANHEINZ. *A Bibliography of Neo-African Literature from Africa, America, and the Caribbean.* New York: F. A. Praeger, 1965, 359 pp.

LAET, JOANNIS DE. "List of Works on America," in *Nieuwe Wereldt.* Leyden: In de druckerye van I. Elzevier, 1625, 12 pp.

LEARY, LEWIS. *Articles on American Literature, 1900–1950.* Durham: Duke Univ. Press, 1954, 353–364.

"Foreign Influences and Estimates."

LECLERC, CHARLES ALFRED. *Bibliotheca Americana: Catalogue raisonné d'une très-précieuse collection de livres anciens et modernes sur l'Amérique . . . .* Paris: Maisonneuve, 1867, 424 pp.

Prices realized, 409–424. Remainder of collection offered for sale under same title, 1878.

_____. "Publications relative a l'histoire et à la linguistique de l'Amérique," in *Bibliotheca Americana: Histoire, Geographie . . . .* Paris: Maisonneuve et Cie., 1878, 111–127.

LÓPEZ, JOSÉ TIMOTEO, EDGARDO NUÑEZ and ROBERTO LARA VIALPANDO. *Breve Reseña de la Literature Hispana de Nuevo México y Colorado.* Cd. Juárez, Chihuahua: El Alacran, 1959, 91 pp.

LUDEKE, H. "American Literature in Germany: A Report of Recent Research and Criticism, 1931–1933." *AL,* VI (May 1934), 168–175.

MAGYAR, F. "American Literature in Hungary." *BA,* VI (April 1932), 151–152.

MUMMENDEY, RICHARD. *Language and Literature of the Anglo-Saxon Nations as Presented in German Doctoral Dissertations, 1885–1950: A Bibliography.* Charlottesville: Bibliographical Society of the Univ. of Virginia, 1954, 216 pp.

PALMER, PHILIP MOTLEY, comp. "German Works on America, 1492– 1800." *Univ. of California Publications in Modern Philology,* XXXVI (1952), 271–412.

Revue de Littérature Comparée. Paris: E. Champion, 1921–   .

Each issue includes special section on North American influences. Indexed.

The Rising Generation, 1898-   .

A Japanese monthly dealing with English and American literature. In recent years contains an annual bibliography of Japanese books and articles on the two literatures (including translations). Printed in Japanese.

ROBERTSON, WILLIAM. "Catalogue of Spanish Books and Manuscripts Relating to America," in *History of America,* 2 Vols. London: W. Strahan, 1777, II, 523–535.

Also: 1778.

Also: 3 Vols. Leipzig: printed for E. B. Schwickert, 1786.

Also: 4 Vols. Printed for A. Strahan, 1803.

Also: Philadelphia: Johnson and Warner, 1812.

Also: Albany: E. and E. Hosford, 1822.

SMITH, CHARLES ALPHONSO. "Bibliographische Anmerkungen" in *Die amerikanische Literatur,* Berlin: Weidmann, 1912, 369–380.

TAUPIN, RENE. "L'Interprétation americaine de la poésie française contempiraine (essai de bibliographie)." Unpublished doctoral dissertation, Univ. de Paris, Faculté des Lettres, 1930.

TERNAUX-COMPANS, HENRI. *Bibliothèque Américaine, ou Catalogue des Ouvrages relatifs a l'Amérique, qui ont paru depuis sa découverte jusqu'à l'an 1700.* Paris: Arthus-Bertrand, 1837, 192 pp.

VON MUHLENFELS, ASTRID A. "A Bibliography of German Scholarship on Early American Literature: 1850–   ." *EALN,* II (Fall 1967), 32–35.

10. HISTORY: SOCIAL, ECONOMIC, POLITICAL, LEGAL

ADAMS, JAMES TRUSLOW. *Provincial Society, 1690–1763.* New York: Macmillan Co., 1936, 324–356.

ADAMS, RAMON FREDERICK. *Six-Guns and Saddle Leather: A Bibliography of Books and Pamphlets on Western Outlaws and Gunmen.* Norman: Univ. of Oklahoma Press, 1954, 439 pp.

ADAMS, THOMAS RANDOLPH. *American Independence: The Growth of an Idea.* Providence: Brown Univ. Press, 1965, 202 pp.

ALLEN, FREDERICK LEWIS. *Only Yesterday: An Informal History of the Nineteen-Twenties.* New York and London: Harper and Brothers, 1931, 358–361.

AMERICAN HISTORICAL ASSOCIATION. *Guide to Historical Literature.* New York: Macmillan, 1961, 962 pp.

AMERICAN JEWISH HISTORICAL SOCIETY. *Index to the Publications of the American Jewish Historical Society,* Nos. 1–20. New York: American Jewish Historical Society, 1914, 600 pp.

The American Magazine; or, A Monthly View of the Political State of the British Colonies, reproduced from the original edition, Philadelphia, 1741. New York: Facsimile Text Society, 1937.

Bibliographical note by Lyon Norman Richardson.

AMERICAN STUDIES ASSOCIATION, COMMITTEE ON MICROFILM BIBLIOGRAPHY. *Bibliography of American Culture, 1949–1875,* compiled and edited by David R. Weimer. Ann Arbor: University Microfilms, 1957, 244 pp.

ANDERSON, LORENE, and ALAN W. FARLEY, comps. "A Bibliography of Town and County Histories of Kansas." *Kansas Historical Quarterly,* XXI (Autumn 1955), 513–555.

ANDREWS, CHARLES McLEAN. *Guide to the Materials for American History to 1783 in the Public Record Office of Great Britain,* 2 Vols. Washington: Carnegie Institute of Washington, 1912–1914.

AUER, J. JEFFERY. "American Public Address and American Studies: A Bibliography." *American Quarterly,* IX (Winter 1957), 217–222.

BAER, ELIZABETH. *Seventeenth Century Maryland: A Bibliography.* Baltimore: John Work Garret Library, 1949, 248 pp.

BAKER, ERNEST ALBERT. *A Guide to Historical Fiction.* New York: Macmillan Co., 1914, 573 pp.

Also: London: G. Routledge and Sons, Ltd.

BAKER, GEORGE HALL. *Bibliography of Political Science, 1886.* Boston: Ginn and Co., 1887, 55 pp.

Supplement: *Political Science Quarterly,* I.

BARTLETT, IRVING H. *The American Mind in the Mid-Nineteenth Century.* New York: Crowell, 1967, 119–124.

BARTLETT, JOHN RUSSELL. *The Literature of the Rebellion: A Catalogue of Books and Pamphlets Relating to the Civil War in the United States, and on Subjects Growing Out of that Event, together with Works on American Slavery, and Essays from Reviews and Magazines on the Same Subjects.* Boston: Draper and Halliday, 1866, 477 pp.

250 copies printed.

BASLER, ROY PRENTICE, DONALD H. MUGRIDGE and BLANCHE P. McCRUM. *A Guide to the Study of the United States of America.* Washington, 1960, 2,008 pp.

BEERS, HENRY PUTNEY. *Bibliographies in American History: Guide to Materials for Research,* 2nd edition. New York: H. W. Wilson Co., 1942, 502 pp.

Useful for independent index and arrangement, but superseded by *Harvard Guide.*

──────────. *The French in North America: A Bibliographical Guide to French Archives, Reproductions, and Research Missions.* Baton Rouge: Louisiana State Univ. Press, 1957, 424 pp.

BELKNAP, GEORGE N. "Early Oregon Documents: Some Bibliographical Revisions." *Oregon Historical Quarterly,* LVI (June 1955), 107–125.

BILLINGTON, RAY ALLEN. *Guides to American History Manuscript Collections in Libraries of the United States.* New York: P. Smith, 1952, 29 pp.

Reprinted from *Mississippi Valley Historical Review,* XXXVIII (December 1951), 467–496.

BINNS, NORMAN E. *An Introduction to Historical Bibliography,* with a preface by Arundell Esdaile. London: Association of Assistant Librarians, 1953, 370 pp.

BOGART, E. L. "Historical Novels in American History." *History Teachers' Magazine,* VIII (September 1917), 226–230.

BOWERS, DAVID FREDERICK, ed. *Foreign Influences in American Life; Essays and Critical Bibliographies.* New York: Princeton Univ. Press, 1944, 173–254.

Princeton Studies in American Civilization.

BRADFORD, THOMAS LINDSLEY. *Bibliographer's Manual of American History,* 5 Vols. Philadelphia: S. V. Henkels and Co., 1907–1910.

BRADLEY, I. S. "Bibliographies Published by Historical Societies of the United States." *PBSA,* I (1907), 146–157.

BRYAN, WILHELMUS BOGART. *Bibliography of the District of Columbia: Being a List of Books, Maps, and Newspapers, Including Articles in Magazines and Other Publications to 1898,* prepared for the Columbia Historical Society. Washington, 1900, 211 pp.

BUCK, S. J. "The Status of Historical Bibliography in the United States." *PMHB,* LXIII (October 1939), 390–400.

BULL, JACQUELINE. "Writings on Kentucky History, 1955." *Kentucky Historical Society Register,* LV (1957), 237–256.

BUREAU OF RAILWAY ECONOMICS. *List of References on the Use of Railroads in War.* Washington, 1915, 34 leaves.

BUSHEY, GLENN L. "A Bibliography of Controversial Literature Published in the American Revolutionary Period, 1750–1785, Found in the Historical Society of Pennsylvania." Unpublished doctoral dissertation, Temple Univ., 1939.

BUSHNELL, CHARLES IRA. *Catalogue of the Library of Charles I. Bushnell, Esq.: Comprising His Extensive Collections of Rare and Curious Americana of Engravings, Autographs, Historical Relics, Woodblocks Engraved by Dr. Anderson,* compiled by Alexander Denham. New York, 1883, 283 pp.

Sold at auction by Messrs. Bangs and Co.

BUTLER, FREDERICK. *A Complete History of the United States of America . . . down to . . . 1820,* 3 Vols. Hartford: the author, 1821.

Also: Elizabeth-town, New Jersey: M. Hale, 1822.

CADY, EDWIN HARRISON. *The Gentleman in America: A Literary Study in American Culture.* Syracuse: Syracuse Univ. Press, 1949, bibliographical notes.

CALLAHAN, NORTH. *Flight from the Republic: The Tories of the American Revolution.* Indianapolis: Bobbs Merrill, 1967, 189–198.

CARMAN, HARRY JAMES, and ARTHUR W. THOMPSON. *A Guide*

to the Principal Sources for American Civilization, 1800–1900, in the City of New York: Printed Materials. New York: Columbia Univ. Press, 1962, 676 pp.

CHANNING, EDWARD, ALBERT BUSHNELL HART and FREDERICK JACKSON TURNER. Guide to the Study and Reading of American History. Boston and London: Ginn and Co., 1912, 89–102.

Appeared as Guide to the Study of American History, 1896.

CHARLEVOIX, PIERRE FRANÇOIS XAVIER DE. Histoire et Description Générale de la Nouvelle France, avec le Journal historique d'un voyage fait par ordre du roi dans l'Amérique Septentrionnale, 6 Vols. Paris: Chez la veuve Ganeau, 1744, 378–422.

Also: New York: J. G. Shea, 1866.

"A Check List of Papers Read before the Savannah Historical Research Association That Have Appeared in Print: A Guide to the Unpublished Papers in the Files of the Savannah Historical Research Association." Georgia Historical Quarterly, XXVIII (September 1944), 213–223.

"Check List of Works Relating to the Social History of the City of New York – Its Clubs, Charities, Hospitals, etc." BNYPL, V (June 1901), 261–293.

CHURCH, ELIHU DWIGHT. A Catalogue of Books Relating to the Discovery and Early History of North and South America, Forming a Part of the Library of E. D. Church, compiled and annotated by George Watson Cole, 5 Vols. New York: Dodd, Mead and Co., 1907.

Also: Cambridge: Harvard Univ. Press.

150 copies printed.

Also: P. Smith, 1951.

CLARK, CHARLES EDWIN. "The Literature of the New England Earthquake of 1755." PBSA, LIX (3rd Quart. 1965), 295–305.

CLEBSCH, WILLIAM A. "Episcopal and Anglican History, 1966: An Annotated Bibliography." Historical Magazine of the Protestant Episcopal Church, XXXVI (June 1967), 179–206.

COLBURN, JEREMIAH. Bibliography of the Local History of Massachusetts. Boston: W. P. Lunt, 1871, 119 pp.

COLEMAN, JOHN WINSTON, JR. A Bibliography of Kentucky History. Lexington: Univ. of Kentucky Press, 1949, Items 1,707–1,723, 2,345–2,388, 2,433–2,450.

COOPERMAN, STANLEY. World War I and the American Novel. Baltimore: Johns Hopkins Press, 1967, 243–251.

COULTER, EDITH MARGARET, and MELANIE GERSTENFELD. Historical Bibliographies: A Systematic and Annotated Guide, with a foreword by Herbert Eugene Bolton. Berkeley: Univ. of California Press, 1935, 218 pp.

"General Bibliographies," 1–7.

COWAN, ROBERT ERNEST. A Bibliography of the History of California, 3 Vols. San Francisco: J. H. Nash, 1936.

CURTI, MERLE EUGENE. The Growth of American Thought. London: Harper and Brothers, 1943, 755–816.

CUTHBERT, NORMA BARRETT, comp. *American Manuscript Collections in the Huntington Library for the History of the Seventeenth and Eighteenth Centuries.* San Marino, California: Huntington Library, 1941, 101 pp.

DEBRETT, J., et al. *Bibliotheca Americana: or, A Chronological Catalogue of the Most Curious and Interesting Books, Pamphlets, and State Papers, etc., upon the Subject of North and South America, from the Earliest Period to the Present, in Print, and in Manuscript, for which Research Has Been Made in the British Museum.* London: printed for J. Debrett et al., 1789, 271 pp.

Work ascribed to Debrett and others.

DE WITT, FREDERIC M. *California Index Cards: Bibliography of the History and Literature of that Part of the West Coast of North America Known as California . . . ,* Series 1–   . Oakland: DeWitt and Snelling, 1915–   .

DIAZ, ALBERT JAMES. "A Bibliography of Bibliographies Relating to the History and Literature of Arizona and New Mexico." *Arizona Quarterly,* XIV (Autumn 1958), 197–218.

DICK, EVERETT NEWTON. *The Sod-House Frontier, 1854–1890: A Social History of the Northern Plains from the Creation of Kansas and Nebraska to the Admission of the Dakotas.* New York and London: D. Appleton-Century Co., 1937, 519–528.

DICKINSON, ARTHUR TAYLOR. *American Historical Fiction.* New York: Scarecrow Press, 1958, 314 pp.

DONOVAN, FRANK PIERCE. *The Railroad in Literature.* Boston: Railway and Locomotive Historical Society, Baker Library, Harvard Business School, 1940, 138 pp.

DORNBUSCH, CHARLES EMIL, ed. *Regimental Publications and Personal Narratives of the Civil War: A Checklist,* 2 Vols. New York: New York Public Library, 1961–1967.

DOUGHERTY, CHARLES T. "Novels of the Middle Border: A Critical Bibliography for Historians." *Historical Bulletin,* XXV (1947), 77–78, 85–88.

DRAKE, SAMUEL GARDNER. *Annals of Witchcraft in New England and Elsewhere in the United States from Their First Settlement.* Boston: W. E. Woodward, 1869, 306 pp.

275 copies printed.

——————. *Catalogue of the Private Library of Samuel G. Drake of Boston: Chiefly Relating to the Antiquities, History, and Biography of America, and in an Especial Manner to the Indians, Collected and Used by Him in Preparing His Works upon the Aborigines of America.* Boston: S. G. Drake, 1845, 80 pp.

DURRIE, DANIEL STEELE. *Bibliographia Genealogica Americana: An Alphabetical Index to American Genealogies and Pedigrees Contained in State, County, and Town Histories, Printed Genealogies and Kindred Works.* Albany: J. Munsell, 1868, 296 pp.

2nd edition: 1878, 238 pp.

3rd edition: 1886, 245 pp.

FARIBAULT, GEORGES BARTHELEMI (rédigé par). *Catalogue d'Ouvrages sur l'Histoire de l'Amerique et en particulier sur celle du Canada, de la Lousiane, de l'Acadie et autres lieux, ci-devant* connus sus le nom de la Nouvelle France, en trois parties. Quebec: W. Cowan, 1837, 207 pp.

FILLER, LOUIS. *A Dictionary of American Social Reform.* New York: Philosophical Library, 1963, 854 pp.

FINK, RYCHARD. *American Democracy in Mid-Century: A Bibliography of Recent Books in the American Tradition.* Danville, Illinois: Interstate Printers and Publishers, 1954, 85 pp.

FOLEY, PATRICK KEVIN. *American Authors, 1795–1895: A Bibliography.* Boston: The Publishers' Printing Co., 1897, 350 pp.

75 copies printed for subscribers.

FORD, PAUL LEICESTER. . . . *Some Materials for a Bibliography of the Official Publications of the Continental Congress, 1774–1789* . . . . Boston: printed by order of the trustees, Boston Public Library, 1890, 31 pp.

Also issued in *Boston Public Library Bulletin,* 1888–1891.

FRENCH, BENJAMIN FRANKLIN. *Historical Collections of Louisiana, Embracing Many Rare and Valuable Documents, Relating to the Natural, Civil and Political History of That State,* compiled with historical and biographical notes, 5 Vols. New York: Wiley and Putnam, 1846–1853.

GAINES, FRANCIS PENDLETON. *The Southern Plantation: A Study in the Development and the Accuracy of a Tradition.* New York: Columbia Univ. Press, 1924, 237–243.

Columbia Univ. Studies in English and Comparative Literature.

GREEN, SAMUEL ABBOTT. "A Centennial Bibliography of the Massachusetts Historical Society." *PMHS,* 2nd Series, VI (December 1890), 203–249; (February 1891), 343–349.

GREENE, EVARTS BOUTELL, and RICHARD B. MORRIS. *A Guide to the Principal Sources for Early American History (1600–1800) in the City of New York.* New York: Columbia Univ. Press, 1929, 382 pp.

GREENLY, ALBERT HARRY. *A Selective Bibliography of Important Books, Pamphlets, and Broadsides Relating to Michigan History.* Lunenburg, Vermont: Stinehour Press, 1958, 183 pp.

GRIFFIN, APPLETON PRENTISS CLARK. *Index of Articles upon American Local History in the Historical Collections in the Boston Public Library.* Boston: printed by order of the trustees, Boston Public Library, 1889, 225 pp.

Boston Public Library Bibliographies of Special Subjects, No. 3.

GRIFFIN, GRACE B. "Writings on American History, 1930." *Annual Report of the American History Association, 1930,* II (1933), 255–260.

GRISWOLD, WILLIAM McCRILLIS. *Descriptive List of Novels and Tales Dealing with the History of North America.* Cambridge, Massachusetts: W. M. Griswold, 1895, 101–183.

GROLIER CLUB (NEW YORK). *Catalogue of an Exhibit of Historical and Literary Americana, from the Collections of Thomas W. Streeter and C. Waller Barrett* . . . . New York: The Grolier Club, 1960, 47 pp.

HARDING, WALTER. "American History in the Novel: The Period of

Expansion, 1815–1861." *Midwest Journal,* VIII (Spring-Fall 1956), 393–398.

HARKNESS, R. E. E. "America's Heritage of Colonial Culture." *Crozer Quarterly,* XIX (October 1942), 278–291.

HARPER, LATHROP C. *Priced Catalogue of a Remarkable Collection of Scarce and Out-of-print Books Relating to the Discovery, Settlement, and History of the Western Hemisphere* . . . . New York: Harper, 1914, 219 pp.

HART, A. B. "List of Readings on the History of the U.S." *Academy,* II (May 1887), 158, 367.

Superseded by *School and College.*

HAYS, ISAAC MINIS. "A Contribution to the Bibliography of the Declaration of Independence." *PAPS,* XXIX (January 1900), 69–78.

HEARTMAN, CHARLES FREDERICK, comp. *The Cradle of the U U.S., 1765–1798: 500 Contemporary Broadsides, Pamphlets, and a Few Books Pertaining to the Stamp Act, the Boston Massacre, and Other Pre-Revolutionary Troubles,* 2 Vols. Perth Amboy, New Jersey: n.p. 1922–1923.

Title of II varies slightly.

HILDEBURN, CHARLES R. "An Index to the Obituary Notices Published in the *Pennsylvania Gazette,* from 1728–1791." *PMHB,* X (No. 3, 1886), 334–349.

"Historical Notes and References: Bibliographical." *Journal of Southern History,* XVI (November 1950), 577–588.

IRVINE, D. D. "The Fate of Confederate Archives." *AHR,* XLIV (July 1939), 823–841.

JOHNSON, THOMAS HERBERT, and PERRY MILLER. *The Puritans.* New York: American Book Co., 1938, 785–834.

Revised edition: 2 Vols. Harper and Row, 1963.

JONES, HOWARD MUMFORD. "Fifty Guides to American Civilization." *SRL,* XXIX (Oct. 12, 1946), 15–16, 47.

JONES, M. B. "Thomas Maule, the Salem Quaker, and Free Speech in Massachusetts Bay, with Bibliographical Notes." *Essex Institute Historical Collection,* LXXI (January 1936), 1–42.

KAMMAN, WILLIAM FREDERIC. *Socialism in German-American Literature.* Philadelphia: Americana Germanica Press, 1917, 119–124.

KAPLAN, CHARLES. "American History in the Novel: The Period of Development, 1861–1900." *Midwest Journal,* VIII (Spring–Fall 1956), 399–406.

LANGDON, GEORGE D., JR. *Pilgrim Colony: A History of New Plymouth, 1620–1691.* New Haven: Yale Univ. Press, 1966, bibliographical footnotes.

Yale Publications in American Studies, No. 12.

LARKIN, OLIVER W. *Art and Life in America.* New York: Rinehart, 1949, 483–514.

LARNED, JOSEPHUS NELSON, ed. *The Literature of American History: A Bibliographical Guide.* Boston:

Houghton Mifflin for the American Library Association, 1902, 597 pp.

Supplement: 1902, 37 pp. Covers 1900–1901.

Also: Columbus, Ohio: Long's College Book Co., 1953. Includes supplement.

LEARY, LEWIS. *Articles on American Literature, 1900–1950.* Durham: Duke Univ. Press, 1954, 425–427.

"Social Aspects."

——————. *Articles on American Literature, 1900–1950.* Durham: Duke Univ. Press, 1954, 427–428.

"Societies."

LEFLER, HUGH TALMAGE. *A Guide to the Study and Reading of North Carolina Histories,* revised edition. Chapel Hill: Univ. of North Carolina Press, 1963, 30–34.

LEISY, ERNEST ERWIN. *The American Historical Novel.* Norman: Univ. of Oklahoma Press, 1950, 219–259.

LIBRARY OF CONGRESS. *The American Civil War: A Selected Reading List.* Washington, 1960, 24 pp.

——————. *Check List of Collections of Personal Papers in Historical Societies, University and Public Libraries, and Other Learned Institutions in the United States.* Washington, 1918, 87 pp.

——————. *The Civil War in Motion Pictures: A Bibliography of Films Produced in the United States since 1897.* Washington, 1961, 109 pp.

——————. *The Civil War in Pictures, 1861–1961: A Chronological List of Selected Pictorial Works.* Washington, 1961, 30 pp.

——————. *A Guide to the Microfilm Collection of Early State Records,* compiled by William Sumner Jenkins. Washington, 1950, varying pagination.

Supplement: 1951, 130 pp.

——————. *A Guide to the Study of the United States of America: Representative Books Reflecting the Development of American Life and Thought.* Washington, 1960, 1,208 pp.

——————. *Some Bibliographies Which List Works Published in the United States during the War Years.* Washington, 1947, 4 pp.

LIBRARY OF CONGRESS, DIVISION OF BIBLIOGRAPHY. *A Partial List of War Plays in the Library of Congress.* Washington, 1921, 4 leaves.

LIBRARY OF CONGRESS, GENERAL REFERENCE AND BIBLIOGRAPHY DIVISION. *Current National Bibliographies,* compiled by Helen F. Conover. Washington, 1955, 132 pp.

LIBRARY OF CONGRESS, MAP DIVISION. *Civil War Maps: An Annotated List of Maps and Atlases in Map Collections of the Library of Congress.* Washington, 1961, 138 pp.

LIBRARY OF CONGRESS, PRINTS AND PHOTOGRAPHS DIVISION. *Civil War Photographs, 1861–1865: A Catalog of Copy Negatives Made from Originals Selected from the Mathew B. Brady Collection in the Prints and Photographs Division of the Library of Congress.* Washington, 1961, 74 pp.

LINDER, HAROLD LE ROY. *The Rise of Current Complete National Bibliography.* New York: The Scarecrow Press, 1959, 290 pp.

Chapter VI, "The United States from 1846 to 1891," identifies and describes particular bibliographies with historical focus.

LITTLE, BROWN AND COMPANY. *A General Catalogue of Law Books, Including All the Reports, Both English and American, from the Earliest Period.* Boston: Little, Brown and Co., 1856, 149 pp.

LIVELY, ROBERT A. *Fiction Fights the Civil War: An Unfinished Chapter in the Literary History of the American People.* Chapel Hill: Univ. of North Carolina Press, 1957, 197–224.

LUDEWIG, HERMAN ERNST. *The Literature of American Local History: A Bibliographical Essay.* New York: R. Craighead, 1846, 201 pp.

Supplement: 1848, 20 pp.

McMURTRIE, DOUGLAS CRAWFORD. "Locating the Printed Source Materials in United States History; with a Bibliography of Lists of Regional Imprints." *MVHR*, XXXI (December 1944), 369–406.

MARVIN, JOHN GAGE. *Legal Bibliography: or, a Thesaurus of American, English, Irish, and Scotch Law Books, together with Some Continental Treatises, Interspersed with Critical Observations, and a Copious List of Abbreviations.* Philadelphia: T. and J. W. Johnson, 1847, 800 pp.

MARX, ALEXANDER. *Studies in Jewish History and Booklore.* New York: Jewish Theological Seminary of America, 1944, bibliographical footnotes.

MERRITT, RICHARD L. *Symbols of American Community, 1735–1775.* New Haven: Yale Univ. Press, 1966, bibliographical footnotes.

Yale Studies in Political Science, No. 16.

MICHIGAN CIVIL WAR CENTENNIAL OBSERVANCE COMMISSION. *Michigan in the Civil War: A Guide to the Materials in Detroit Newspapers, 1861–1866.* Lansing: Michigan Civil War Centennial Observance Commission, 1965, 404 pp.

MORRISON, HUGH ALEXANDER, ed. *Guide to the Poetry of the World War.* Washington, 1921, 376 leaves.

NETTELS, CURTIS PUTNAM. *The Roots of American Civilization: A History of American Colonial Life.* New York: F. S. Crofts and Co., 1938, bibliographical footnotes, chapter notes.

NEVINS, ALLAN, JAMES I. ROBERTSON JR. and BELL I. WILEY, eds. *Civil War Books: A Critical Bibliography,* I. Baton Rouge: published for the U. S. Civil War Centennial Commission by Louisiana State Univ. Press, 1967, 278 pp.

NEW ENGLAND HISTORIC GENEALOGICAL SOCIETY. *New-England Historical and Genealogical Register.* Boston: S. G. Drake, 1847–   .

Entitled *New-England Historical and Genealogical Register and Antiquarian Journal,* 1923–1927.

NEW YORK PUBLIC LIBRARY,
REFERENCE DEPARTMENT.
*Dictionary Catalogue of the History
of the Americas,* 28 Vols. Boston:
G. K. Hall, 1961.

NEW YORK STATE LIBRARY.
"Contributions to a Bibliography of
Civil War Fiction."

Available only in manuscript.

NIELD, JONATHAN. *A Guide to
the Best Historical Novels and
Tales.* New York: G. P. Putnam's
Sons, 1925, 518 pp.

NORDHOFF, CHARLES. *The
Communistic Societies of the United
States . . . Including Detailed Ac-
counts of the Economists, Zoarites,
Shakers, The Amana, Oneida,
Bethal, Aurora, Icarian . . . .* New
York: Harper and Brothers, 1875,
421–432.

ODUM, HOWARD WASHINGTON,
and HARRY ESTILL MOORE.
*American Regionalism: A Cultural-
Historical Approach to National
Integration.* New York: H. Holt and
Co., 1938, 643–675.

Also: Gloucester, Massachusetts:
P. Smith, 1966.

OGILBY, JOHN. *America: Being
the Latest and Most Accurate
Description of the New World.*
London: printed by the author,
1671, 5.

"A Catalogue of Authors Who Have
Written on America."

PARKER, DAVID W. *Calendar of
Papers in Washington Archives Relating to the Territories of the
United States (to 1873).* Washington: Carnegie Institute of Washington, 1911, 476 pp.

_____. *Guide to the Ma-
terials for the United States History
in Canadian Archives.* Washington:
Carnegie Institute of Washington,
1913, 349 pp.

PETERSON, CLARENCE STEWART.
*Bibliography of County Histories of
the 3,050 Counties in the 48 States.*
Baltimore: n.p., 1944, 49 leaves.

Also: *Bibliography of . . . 3,111
Counties.* 1946, 126 leaves.

Supplement to 1946 edition: 1950,
35 leaves.

PHILLIPS, WILLIAM. "American
History in the Novel: The Colonial
Period, 1585–1775." *Midwest
Journal,* VIII (Spring–Fall 1956),
376–384.

PIERCE, WILLIAM. "A Select
Bibliography of the Pilgrim Fathers
of New England." *Congregational
Historical Society Transactions,*
VIII (February 1920), 16–23;
(August 1920), 59–68.

POCHMANN, HENRY AUGUST,
and ARTHUR R. SCHULTZ.
*Bibliography of German Culture in
America to 1940.* Madison: Univ. of
Wisconsin Press, 1933, 483 pp.

POLLARD, A. F. "American Historical Journals." *TLS,* Nov. 16,
1933, 795.

POORE, BENJAMIN PERLEY.
*A Descriptive Catalogue of the
Government Publications of the
United States, September 5,
1774–March 4, 1881.* Washington,
1885, 1,392 pp.

PRIESTLEY, HERBERT INGRAM.
*The Coming of the White Man,
1492–1848.* New York: Macmillan
Co., 1929, 351–386.

RAFINESQUE, CONSTANTINE SAMUEL. "Catalogue of Authorities," in *Ancient History, or Annals of Kentucky.* Frankfort, Kentucky: printed for the author, 1824, 38 pp.

_____. "Materials for American History," in *The American Nations.* Philadelphia: C. S. Rafinesque, 1836, 35 pp.

REA, ROBERT R. "Anglo-American Parliamentary Reporting: A Case Study in Historical Bibliography." *PBSA*, XLIX (3rd Quart. 1955), 212–229.

REGIER, CORNELIUS, C. *The Era of the Muckrakers.* Chapel Hill: Univ. of North Carolina Press, 1932, 217–241.

RODABAUGH, JAMES H., and S. WINIFRED SMITH. "A Survey of Publications in Ohio History, Archaeology, and Natural History." *Ohio State Archaeological and Historical Quarterly.*

Appears in last number of each volume, beginning with LV (1946). Title changed to *Ohio History,* 1961.

ROSE, LISLE A. "A Bibliographical Survey of Economic and Political Writings, 1865–1900." *AL,* XV (January 1944), 381–410.

_____. "A Descriptive Catalogue of Economic and Politico-Economic Fiction in the United States, 1902–1909." Unpublished doctoral dissertation, Univ. of Chicago, 1936.

ROWLAND, ARTHUR RAY, ed. *A Bibliography of the Writings on Georgia History.* Hamden, Connecticut: Archon Books, 1966, 289 pp.

RUTHERFORD, MILDRED LEWIS. *The South in History and Literature:*

A Handbook of Southern Writers from the Settlement of Jamestown, 1607, to Living Writers. Atlanta: Franklin-Turner Co., 1907, xxxvii–xxxviii.

SAFIRE, WILLIAM. *The New Language of Politics: An Anecdotal Dictionary of Catchwords, Slogans, and Political Usage.* New York: Random House, 1968, 528 pp.

SAMUEL, EDITH. "Index to Deaths Mentioned in *The American Mercury,* 1724–1746." *PMHB,* XVIII (January 1934), 37–60.

SHANNON, FRED ALBERT. *The Farmer's Last Frontier: Agriculture, 1860–1897.* New York and Toronto: Farrar and Rinehart, Inc., 1945, 379–414.

SHEPPERSON, GEORGE. "Scottish-American Cultural Connections: A Bibliographical Note." *British Association for American Studies Bulletin,* No. 8 (1959), 26–28.

SHERMAN, STUART C. *The Voice of the Whalemen, with an Account of the Nicholson Whaling Collection.* Providence: Providence Public Library, 1965, 194–202.

SMITH, CHARLES WESLEY. *Check-list of Books and Pamphlets Relating to the History of the Pacific Northwest.* Olympia, Washington: E. L. Boardman, 1909, 191 pp.

SMITH, REBECCA W., comp. "Catalogue of the Chief Novels and Short Stories by American Authors Dealing with the Civil War and Its Effects, 1861–1899." *BB,* XVI (September–December 1935), 193–194; XVII (January–April 1940), 10–12; (May–August 1940), 33–35; (September–December 1940), 53–55; (January–April 1941), 72–75.

_____. "The Civil War and Its Aftermath in American Fiction, 1861–1899." Unpublished doctoral dissertation, Univ. of Chicago, 1932.

SOCIAL SCIENCE RESEARCH COUNCIL, COMMITTEE ON HISTORIOGRAPHY. *Theory and Practice in Historical Study: A Report of the Committee on Historiography.* New York: Social Science Research Council, 1946, 93–102.

SOUTH CAROLINA HISTORICAL SOCIETY. *South Carolina Historical Magazine.* Charleston: printed for the South Carolina Historical Society by Walker, Evans and Cogswell Co., 1900–   .

Entitled *South Carolina Historical and Genealogical Magazine,* 1900–1952.

SPERBER, HANS, and TRAVIS TRITTSCHUH. *American Political Terms: An Historical Dictionary.* Detroit: Wayne State Univ. Press, 1962, 499–516.

STERN, MADELEINE BETTINA. *Imprints on History, Book Publishers, and American Frontiers.* Bloomington: Indiana Univ. Press, 1956, 389–464.

STEVENS, HENRY. *Bibliotheca Geographica and Historica . . . .* London: H. Stevens, 1872, 361 pp.

_____. *Bibliotheca Historica: A Catalogue of 5,000 Volumes of Books and Manuscripts Relating Chiefly to the History and Literature of North and South America . . . .* Boston: H. O. Houghton and Co., 1870, 234 pp.

_____. *Historical Nuggets: Bibliotheca Americana or a Descriptive Account of My Collection of Rare Books Relating to America,* 2 Vols. London: Whittingham and Wilkins, 1862.

_____. *Schedule of Two Thousand American Historical Nuggets . . . .* London: privately printed, Stevens' Bibliographical Nuggetory, Whittingham and Wilkins, printers, 1870, 20 pp.

STRUVE, BURKHARD GOTTHELF. "List of Works on America," in *Bibliotheca Historica,* 3 Vols. Jena: C. H. Cunonis, 1740.

Also: Lipsiae: n.p., 1782.

SWIFT, LINDSAY. *Brook Farm: Its Members, Scholars, and Visitors.* New York: Macmillan, 1900, 283–292.

THOMAS, WILLIAM S. "American Revolutionary Diaries: Also Journals, Narratives, Autobiographies, Reminiscences and Personal Memoirs, Catalogued and Described with and Index to Places and Events." *NYSQ,* VI (April 1922), 32–35; (July 1922), 61–71; (October 1922), 101–107; (January 1923), 143–147.

THOMPSON, LAWRENCE SIDNEY. "The Civil War in Fiction." *CWH,* II (1956), 83–95.

_____. "The War between the States in Kentucky Novel." *KSHSR,* L (January 1952), 26–34.

TRENT, WILLIAM PETERFIELD, et al. "American Political Writing, 1760–1789," in *Cambridge History of American Literature,* 4 Vols. New York: G. P. Putnam's Sons, 1917–1921, I, 454–457.

_____. "The Historians, 1607–1783," in *Cambridge History of American Literature,* 4 Vols. New

York: G. P. Putnam's Sons, 1917–1921, I, 380–385.

_____. "Later Historians," in *Cambridge History of American Literature*, 4 Vols. New York: G. P. Putnam's Sons, 1917–1921, IV, 728–742.

_____. "Political Writing since 1850," in *Cambridge History of American Literature*, 4 Vols. New York: G. P. Putnam's Sons, 1917–1921, IV, 782–784.

_____. "Writers on American History, 1783–1850," in *Cambridge History of American Literature*, 4 Vols. New York: G. P. Putnam's Sons, 1917–1921, II, 488–499.

TYLER, MOSES COIT. *The Literary History of the American Revolution, 1763–1783*, 2 Vols. New York: Putnam, 1897, II, 429–483.

UNITED STATES, NAVAL HISTORY DIVISION. *Naval Documents of the American Revolution*, edited by William Bell Clark. Washington, 1964–   .

I: 1774–1775. Bibliography, 1,395–1,399.

VAIL, ROBERT WILLIAM GLENROIE. *The Voice of the Old Frontier*. Philadelphia: Univ. of Pennsylvania Press, 1949, 492 pp.

"Frontier" indicates the fringes of civilization, whether Vermont, Kansas or Oregon.

VIRGINIA COMPANY OF LONDON. *The Records of the Virginia Company of London*, 4 Vols. Washington, 1906–1935.

WALLACE, WILLIAM SWILLING. *Bibliography of Published Bibliog-*

raphies on the History of the Eleven Western States, 1941–1947: A Partial Supplement to the Writings on American History. Albuquerque: n.p., 1954, 233 pp.

WAXMAN, JULIA. *Race Relations.* Chicago: Julius Rosenwald Fund, 1945, 47 pp.

WICKERSHAM, JAMES, comp. *Bibliography of Literature, 1724–1924: Containing the Titles of Histories, Travels, Voyages, Newspapers, Periodicals, Public Documents... Relating to ... Alaska.* Cordova, Alaska: Cordova *Daily Times*, 1927, 662 pp.

WILKINSON, NORMAN B., comp. *Bibliography of Pennsylvania History*, edited by S. K. Stevens and Donald H. Kent. Harrisburg: Pennsylvania Historical and Museum Commission, 1957, 856 pp.

WINSOR, JUSTIN. "Literature of Witchcraft in New England." *PAAS*, ns X (October 1895), 351–373.

_____, ed. *Narrative and Critical History of America*, 8 Vols. Boston: Houghton, Mifflin and Co., 1884–1889.

Volumes consist of introductory sections and assorted critical essays, many with bibliographies.

WOODRESS, JAMES. "American History in the Novel: The Revolution and Early National Periods, 1775–1815." *Midwest Journal*, VIII (Spring–Fall 1956), 385–392.

WRIGHT, RICHARDSON. *Forgotten Ladies: Nine Portraits from the American Family Album.* Philadelphia: J. B. Lippincott Co., 1928, 287–294.

Writings on American History, 1902–   .

Title varies slightly. Variously issued by United States Government Printing Office and Carnegie Institution of Washington, and as a House of Representatives Document. A one-volume index covers 1902–1940.

WYCKOFF, ALEXANDER, EDWARD WARWICK and HENRY PITZ. *Early American Dress: The Colonial and Revolutionary Periods.* New York: B. Blom, 1965, bibliographical footnotes.

11. HUMOR, SATIRE

BLAIR, WALTER. *Horse Sense in American Humor from Benjamin Franklin to Ogden Nash.* Chicago: Univ. of Chicago Press, 1942, 319–325.

BLAIR, WALTER. *Native American Humor (1800–1900).* New York: American Book Co., 1931, 163–196.

HALL, WADE. *The Smiling Phoenix: Southern Humor from 1865 to 1914.* Gainesville: Univ. of Florida Press, 1965, 357–368.

JENKINS, JOHN HOLMES. *Cracker Barrel Chronicles: A Bibliography of Texas Town and County Histories.* Austin: Pemberton Press, 1965, 509 pp.

LEARY, LEWIS. *Articles on American Literature, 1900–1950.* Durham: Duke Univ. Press, 1954, 365–367.

"Humor."

LIBRARY OF CONGRESS, DIVISION OF BIBLIOGRAPHY. *List of References on Wit, Humor,*

Laughter, Satire, Etc. Washington, 1912, 21 pp.

Exists only as typescript.

MURRELL, WILLIAM. *A History of American Graphic Humor,* 2 Vols. New York: published for Whitney Museum of American Art by Macmillan Co., 1933–1938, I, 241–242; II, 265–267.

TANDY, JENNETTE REID. *Crackerbox Philosophers in American Humor and Satire.* Port Washington, New York: Kennikat Press, 1964, 20–23, 97–102, 173–175.

TRENT, WILLIAM PETERFIELD, et al. "Early Humorists," in *Cambridge History of American Literature,* 4 Vols. New York: G. P. Putnam's Sons, 1917–1921, II, 503–511.

——————. "Minor Humorists," in *Cambridge History of American Literature,* 4 Vols. New York: G. P. Putnam's Sons, 1917–1921, IV, 639–644.

12. INDIAN LANGUAGE, LITERATURE

BEDER, E. F. "Kingston to Newson to Balke: or, Bibliographical Adventures among the Indians." *BNYPL,* XLVI (June 1942), 525–530.

BRINTON, DANIEL GARRISON. *Aboriginal American Authors and Their Productions, Especially Those*

in the Native Languages. Philadelphia: D. G. Brinton, 1883, 54 pp.

BYINGTON, CYRUS. *A Dictionary of the Choctaw Language,* edited by John R. Swanton and Henry Halbert. Washington, 1915, 611 pp.

Smithsonian Institution Bureau of American Ethnology Bulletin, No. 46.

DRAKE, SAMUEL GARDNER. *Catalogue of the Private Library of Samuel G. Drake of Boston: Chiefly Relating to the Antiquities, History, and Biography of America, and in an Especial Manner to the Indians, Collected and Used by Him in Preparing His Works upon the Aborigines of America.* Boston: S. G. Drake, 1845, 80 pp.

FIELD, THOMAS WARREN, ed. *An Essay Towards an Indian Bibliography: Being a Catalogue of Books, Relating to the History, Antiquities, Languages, Customs, Religion, Wars, Literature, and Origin of American Indians, in the Library of Thomas W. Field.* New York: Scribner, Armstrong, and Co., 1873, 430 pp.

FREEMAN, JOHN F., comp. *A Guide to Manuscripts Relating to the American Indian in the Library of the American Philosophical Society.* Philadelphia: American Philosophical Society, 1966, 491 pp.

Memoirs of the American Philosophical Society, LXV.

HEARN, LAFCADIO. "Bibliography of the Creole Language," in *Gombo Zhèbes.* New York: W. H. Coleman, 1885, 7 leaves.

KEISER, ALBERT. *The Indian in American Literature.* New York: Oxford Univ. Press, 1933, 300–305.

LEARY, LEWIS. *Articles on American Literature, 1900–1950.* Durham: Duke Univ. Press, 1954, 367–368.

"Indian."

LUDEWIG, HERMAN ERNST. *The Literature of American Aboriginal Languages.* London: Trübner and Co., 1858, 258 pp.

NEWBERRY LIBRARY (CHICAGO). *Narratives of Captivity Among the Indians of North America: A List of Books and Manuscripts on the Subject in the Edward E. Ayer Collection of the Newberry Library.* Chicago: Newberry Library, 1912, 120 pp.

Supplement: 1928, 49 pp.

RIGGS, S. R. "Bibliography of the Dakota Language," in *Grammar and Dictionary of the Dakota Language.* Washington: Smithsonian Institution, 1852, xx.

SCHOOLCRAFT, HENRY ROWE. *A Bibliographical Catalogue of Books, Translations of the Scriptures, and Other Publications in the Indian Tongues of the United States.* Washington: C. Alexander, 1849, 28 pp.

Also: *Indian Tribes,* IV (1854), 523.

TRUMBULL, JAMES HAMMOND. *Origin . . . of Indian Missions in New England with a List of Books in the Indian Language Printed at Cambridge and Boston, 1653–1721.* Worcester: for private distribution, 1874, 50 pp.

LCN: "From the report of the Council of the American Antiquarian Society presented at its annual meeting in Worcester, Oct. 22, 1873."

13. LANGUAGE, LINGUISTICS

BARTLETT, JOHN RUSSELL. *Dictionary of Americanisms.* New York: Bartlett and Welford, 1848, 412 pp.

2nd edition: Boston: Little, Brown, 1859, 524 pp.

4th edition: 1877, 813 pp.

BICKLEY, JOHN. "The King and Kingship: An Annotated Bibliography of Studies in the English Language from 1933 to 1953." *BNYPL,* LIX (February 1955), 55–61.

BRENNI, VITO JOSEPH. *American English: A Bibliography.* Philadelphia: Univ. of Pennsylvania Press, 1964, 221 pp.

BYRD, MILTON BRUCE, and ARNOLD L. GOLDSMITH. *Publication Guide for Literary and Linguistic Scholars.* Detroit: Wayne State Univ. Press, 1958, 146 pp.

Wayne State Univ. Studies, Humanities Series, No. 4.

DALE, EDGAR. *Bibliography of Vocabulary Studies.* Columbus: Bureau of Educational Research, Ohio State Univ., 1949, 101 leaves.

DUNCAN, HUGH DALZIEL. *Language and Literature in Society: A Sociological Essay on Theory and Method in the Interpretation of Linguistic Symbols, with a Bibliographical Guide to the Sociology of Literature.* Chicago: Univ. of Chicago Press, 1953, 141–214.

EELLS, WALTER C. "American Doctoral Theses on Modern Languages Written by Women in the Nineteenth Century." *MLJ,* XLI (May 1957), 209–211.

GRANDGENT, J. H. "From Franklin to Lowell: A Century of New England Pronunciation." *PMLA,* XIV (1899), 207–239.

HUNTER, ARIA D. "Bibliography: Dialectical Studies." *The Cue of Theta Alpha Phi,* XV (Spring 1936), 25–27.

KURATH, HANS. "A Bibliography of American Pronunciation, 1888–1928." *Language,* V (1929), 155–162.

OLIVER, ROBERT T. "A Working Bibliography on Conversation." *QJS,* XX (November 1934), 524–535.

SAFIRE, WILLIAM. *The New Language of Politics: An Ancedotal Dictionary of Catchwords, Slogans, and Political Usage.* New York: Random House, 1968, 528 pp.

SAPON, STANLEY M. "The American Library of Recorded Dialect Studies." *AS,* XXXII (October 1957), 205–206.

STEADMAN, J. M., JR. "Articles on the English Language Published during 1937." *EJ,* XXVII (November 1938), 734–741.

TINKER, EDWARD LAROCQUE. "Gombo: The Creole Dialect of Louisiana, with a Bibliography." *PAAS,* XLV (April 1935), 101–142.

—————————. *Les Ecrits de langue française en Louisiane au XIX^{em} siècle: Essais biographiques et Bibliographiques.* Paris: H. Champion, 1933, 502 pp.

TRENT, WILLIAM PETERFIELD, et al. "Dialect Writers," in *Cambridge History of American Literature,* 4 Vols. New York: G. P. Putnam's Sons, 1917–1921, II, 611–615.

—————————. "The English Language in America," in *Cambridge History of American Literature,* 4 Vols. New York: G. P. Putnam's Sons, 1917–1921, IV, 810–813.

TUCKER, GILBERT MILLIGAN. *American English.* New York: A. A. Knopf, 1921, 333–345.

WALSH, S. PADRAIG. *English Language Dictionaries in Print: A Comparative Analysis.* Newark, Delaware: Reference Books Research Publications, Inc., 1965, 56 pp.

14. LIBRARIES: CATALOGS, GUIDES

ACADEMY OF NATURAL SCIENCES OF PHILADELPHIA. *Catalogue of the Library of Natural Sciences of Philadelphia.* Philadelphia: J. Dobson, 1837, 300 pp.

ADAMS, THOMAS RANDOLPH. *A Brief Account of the Origins and Purpose of the Chapin Library at Williams College.* Williamstown, Massachusetts: Williams College Press, 1956, 20 pp.

ALBANY INSTITUTE, LIBRARY. *Catalogue of the Albany Institute Library, Founded 1793,* prepared by George Wood. Albany: J. Munsell, 1855, 454 pp.

ALLEGHENY COLLEGE, LIBRARY. *Catalogus Bibliotheca Collegii Alleghaniensis.* Meadville, Pennsylvania: T. Atkinson and Soc., 1823, 139 pp.

ASH, LEE, and DENIS LORENZ. *Subject Collections and Subject Emphasis as Reported by University, College, Public, and Special Libraries in the United States and Canada.* New York: R. R. Bowker, 1967, 1,221 pp.

ASTOR LIBRARY (NEW YORK). *Alphabetical Index to the Astor Library, or Catalogue with Short Titles of the Books Now Collected and of the Proposed Accessions, as Submitted to the Trustees of the Library for Their Approval, January, 1851.* New York: R. Craighead, printer, 1851, 446 pp.

_____. *Catalogue, or Alphabetical Index, of the Astor Library,* 4 Vols. New York: R. Craighead, 1857—1861.

Part 1: "Authors and Books." Proposed Part 2, "Index of Subjects," not issued in the four volumes, but appeared abridged in the supplement, 1866, 445—605.

AVERY MEMORIAL LIBRARY. *Catalogue of the Avery Architectural Library: A Memorial Library of Architecture, Archeology, and Decorative Art.* New York: Columbia Univ., Avery Memorial Architectural Library, 1895, 1,139 pp.

BAKER, GEORGE H., ed. *List of Books Chiefly on the Drama and Literary Criticism.* New York: privately printed for Columbia Univ., 1897, 64 pp.

BENTON, E. J. "The Western Reserve Historical Society and Its Library." *CRL,* VI (December 1944), 23—29.

BIGELOW, FRANK BARNA. "Early Files of Newspapers in the New York Society Library." *Literary Collector,* V (1902), 38—42.

BOSTON ATHENAEUM, LIBRARY. *Catalogue of the Library of Boston Athenaeum, 1807—1871 . . .,* 5 Vols. Boston: n.p., 1874—1882.

BOSTON MECHANIC APPRENTICES' LIBRARY ASSOCIATION. *Catalogue of Books of the Mechanic Apprentices' Library Association.* Boston: White and Potter, printers, 1847, 68 pp.

Also: Damrell and Moore, 1851,
75 pp.

Also: Brown Type Setting Machine
Co., 1873, 116 pp.

BOSTON MERCANTILE LIBRARY
ASSOCIATION. *Catalogue of
Books of the Boston Mercantile Library Association. . . .* Boston: printed
for the Boston Mercantile Library
Association by Freemen and Bolles,
1844, 100 pp.

Also: Damrell and Moore, 1850,
170 pp.

Also: J. Wilson and Son, 1854,
298 pp.

Supplement: 1858, 52 pp.

BOSTON PUBLIC LIBRARY,
PRINCE COLLECTION. *The Prince
Library: A Catalogue of the Collec-
tion of Books and Manuscripts which
Formerly Belonged to the Reverend
Thomas Prince . . . .* Boston: A.
Mudge and Son, 1870, 160 pp.

BRIGGS, F. ALLEN. "The Sunday-
School Library in the Nineteenth
Century." *LQ,* XXXI (April 1961),
166–177.

BRITISH MUSEUM. *British Museum
Catalogue of Printed Books:
Periodical Publications . . . ,* 7 Parts.
London: printed by W. Clowes and
Sons, Ltd., 1899–1900.

Six parts and index in one volume.

BROWN UNIVERSITY, LIBRARY.
*A Catalogue of the Library of Brown
University, in Providence, Rhode
Island, with an Index of Subjects.*
Providence: n.p., 1843, 586 pp.

——————. *A List of Books
Printed in the Fifteenth Century in
the John Carter Brown Library and*
*the General Library of Brown Uni-
versity, Providence, Rhode Island.*
Oxford: Oxford Univ. Press, 1910,
19 pp.

BUCK, SOLON JUSTUS. *Travel and
Description, 1765–1865: Together
with a List of County Histories,
Atlases, and Biographical Collections
and a List of Territorial and State
Laws.* Springfield: published by the
trustees of the Illinois State Historical Library, 1914, 514 pp.

*Collections of the Illinois State His-
torical Library,* IX; *Bibliographical
Series,* II.

CAHOON, HERBERT. "Virginia's
Barrett Library." *SAB,* XVI (May
1960), 1–5.

CALIFORNIA, UNIVERSITY,
LIBRARY. *Cooperative List of
Periodical Literature in the Libraries
of Central California.* Berkeley:
State Printing Office, 1902, 130 pp.

Univ. of California Library Bulletin,
No. 1.

——————. *List of Serials in
the University of California Library.*
Berkeley: Univ. of California Press,
1913, 266 pp.

Univ. of California Library Bulletin,
No. 18.

CANNONS, HARRY GEORGE
TURNER. *Bibliography of Library
Economy: A Classified Index to the
Professional Periodical Literature
Relating to Library Economy,
Printing, Methods of Publishing,
Copyright, Bibliography, etc.*
London: Stanley Russell and Co.,
1910, 448 pp.

CARRIER, ESTHER JANE. *Fiction
in Public Libraries, 1876–1960.*

New York: The Scarecrow Press, 1965, 458 pp.

Catalogue of the Books on the Masonic Institution, in Public Libraries of 28 States of the Union, Anti-Masonic in Arguments and Conclusions, by Distinguished Literary Gentlemen . . . Boston: n.p., 1852, 270 pp.

"Catalogue of Literary Annuals and Gift Books in the New York Public Library." *BNYPL,* VI (July 1902), 270–275.

Catalogue of the New York State Library, 1872: Subject Index of the General Library. Albany: Van Benthuysen Printing House, 1872, 651 pp.

Also: *Catalogue. . . ., 1882: First Supplement to the Subject Index of the General Library for Ten Years, 1872–1882.* Weed, Parsons and Co., 1882, 414 pp.

"Check List of Brooklyn and Long Island Newspapers in the New York Public Library." *BNYPL,* VI (January 1902), 20–21.

"Check List of Newspapers Published in New York City Contained in the New York Public Library, December 31st, 1900." *BNYPL,* V (January 1901), 20–30.

"Check List of New York City Almanacs in the New York Public Library." *BNYPL,* V (May 1901), 186–189.

CHICAGO LIBRARY CLUB. *A List of Serials in Public Libraries of Chicago and Evanston, Corrected to January, 1901.* Chicago: published for the Chicago Library Club by W. P. Dunn, 1901, 195 pp.

LCN: "Supplement to the first edition issued by John Crerar Library,

appeared 1903, the second (corrected to Nov. 1905), in 1906."

CINCINNATI PUBLIC LIBRARY. *Catalogue of the Dramas and Dramatic Poems Contained in the Public Library of Cincinnati.* Cincinnati: published by the Board of Managers, 1879, 192 pp.

_____. *Finding List of Books in the Public Library of Cincinnati.* Cincinnati: published by the Board of Managers, 1882–1884, 892 pp.

CINCINNATI YOUNG MEN'S MERCANTILE LIBRARY ASSOCIATION. *Catalogue of the Young Men's Mercantile Library in Cincinnati.* Cincinnati: n.p., 1846, 260 pp.

Also: Truman and Spofford, 1855, 307 pp.

Also: 1869, 468 pp.

DRURY, FRANCIS KEESE WYNKOOP. *List of Serials in the University of Illinois Library, together with Those in Other Libraries in Urbana and Champaign.* Urbana-Champaign: Univ. of Illinois Press, 1911, 241 pp.

Univ. of Illinois Bulletin, IX, No. 2.

DUKE UNIVERSITY, LIBRARY. *A Checklist of the United States Newspapers (and Weeklies before 1900) in the General Library,* compiled by Mary Wescott and Allene Ramage, 6 Parts in 3 Vols. Durham: Duke Univ. Press, 1932–1937.

THE EDITORS. "A List of Articles Published in *More Books,* 1906–1935." *More Books,* X (December 1935), 391–395.

EDMONDS, CECIL KAY. "Huntington Library Supplement to the

Record of Its Books in the Short Title Catalogue of English Books, 1475–1640." *Huntington Library Bulletin,* IV (October 1933), 6–152.

Huntington Library Bulletin superseded by *Huntington Library Quarterly.*

ENGLISH, E. D. "Author List of Caroliniana in the University of South Carolina Library." *Bulletin of the Univ. of South Carolina,* CXXXIV (December 1933).

ENGLISH, T. H. "The Treasure Room of Emory University." *SRev,* (August 1943), 30–36.

FARNHAM, LUTHER. *A Glance at Private Libraries.* Boston: Press of Crocker and Brewster, 1855, 79 pp.

FLANDERS, R. B. "Newspapers and Periodicals in the Washington Memorial Library, Macon, Georgia." *North Carolina Historical Review,* VII (April 1930), 220–223.

FRANK, J. C. "Early American Poetry to 1820: A List of Works in the New York Public Library." *BNYPL,* XXI (April 1917), 517–578.

GILLIS, M. R. "Materials for Writers in California State Library." *Overland Monthly,* LXXIX (August–September 1931), 22.

HARRIS, DOROTHY G. "History of Friends' Meeting Libraries." *Bulletin of Friends' Historical Association,* XXXI (Autumn 1942), 52–62.

HARTFORD PUBLIC LIBRARY. *Catalogue of the Library and Reading Room of the Young Men's Institute, Hartford.* Hartford: press of Case, Tiffany and Burnham, 1844, 359 pp.

Also: 1847, 32 pp.

Also: 1852, 35 pp.

Also: Young Men's Institute, 1873, 471 pp.

HARVARD UNIVERSITY, LIBRARY. *A Catalogue of the Library of Harvard University in Cambridge, Massachusetts . . .,* 3 Vols. Cambridge: E. W. Metcalf and Co., 1830–1831.

First supplement: C. Folsom, 1834, 260 pp.

HARVARD UNIVERSITY, LIBRARY, HOUGHTON LIBRARY. *The Houghton Library, 1942–1967: A Selection of Books and Manuscripts in Harvard Collections.* Cambridge: Harvard Univ. Press, 1967, 269 pp.

HASKELL, DANIEL CARL, comp. "A Checklist of Newspapers and Official Gazettes in the New York Public Library." *BNYPL,* XVIII (July 1914), 683–722; (August 1914), 793–826; (September 1914), 905–938; (October 1914), 1,079–1,110; (November 1914), 1,261–1,294; (December 1914), 1,467–1,480; XIX (July 1915), 553–569.

——————. "List of American Dramas in the New York Public Library." *BNYPL,* XIX (October 1915), 739–786.

Also issued as separate pamphlet.

HENRY E. HUNTINGTON LIBRARY AND ART GALLERY. *Incunabula in the Huntington Library,* compiled by Herman Ralph Read. San Marino, California: Henry E. Huntington Library, 1937, 398 pp.

Huntington Library List, No. 3.

HISPANIC SOCIETY OF AMERICA. *Incunabula in the Library of the*

Hispanic Society of America. New York: printed by order of the trustees of the Hispanic Society of America, 1928, 5 pp.

Half-title: "Hispanic Notes and Monographs: Essays, Studies, and Brief Biographies Issued by the Hispanic Society of America."

HISTORICAL SOCIETY OF WESTERN PENNSYLVANIA. *Inventory of Files of American Newspapers in Pittsburgh and Allegheny County, Pennsylvania.* Pittsburgh: n.p., 1933, 41 pp.

Western Pennsylvania Historical Survey, Bibliographical Contributions, No. 2.

"Index to Special Book Lists Found in the Catalogue of the Boston Public Library and Other Libraries, and Also in Periodicals." *Boston Public Library Bulletin,* V (1883), 444 pp.

INDIANA UNIVERSITY, LIBRARY. *Union List of Little Magazines: Showing Holdings of 1,037 Little Magazines in the Libraries of Indiana University, Northwestern University, Ohio State University, State University of Iowa, University of Chicago, University of Illinois.* Chicago: Midwest Inter-Library Center, 1956, 98 pp.

JENNINGS, JOHN MELVILLE. "Notes on the Original Library of the College of William and Mary in Virginia, 1693–1705." *PBSA,* XLI (3rd Quart. 1947), 239–267.

Includes catalog of books of Colonel Francis Nicholson given to the college, 1698.

JEWETT, CHARLES COFFIN. *Notices of Public Libraries in the United States.* Washington: printed for the House of Representatives, 1851, 208 pp.

——————. *On the Construction of Catalogues of Libraries, and of a General Catalogue, and Their Publication by Means of Separate, Stereotyped Titles; with Rules and Examples, by C. C. Jewett, Librarian of the Smithsonian Institution.* Washington: Smithsonian Institution, 1852, 78 pp.

2nd edition: 1853, 96 pp.

JOHN CRERAR LIBRARY (CHICAGO). *A List of Bibliographies of Special Subjects, July, 1902.* Chicago: printed by order of the board of directors, 1902, 504 pp.

"Indexes to Periodicals," 16–26, 35–47, 421–422; "Book Collecting," 50–59, 425–426; "Folklore," 130–132, 436; "Language," 132–144, 437–438; "Literature," 376–380.

KENNETT, (WHITE), BISHOP OF PETERBOROUGH. *Bibliothecae Americanae Primordia: An Attempt Towards Laying the Foundation of an American Library . . . .* London: printed for S. Churchill at the Black Swan, Pater-Noster Row, 1713, 275 pp.

LEARY, LEWIS. *Articles on American Literature, 1900–1950.* Durham: Duke Univ. Press, 1954, 368–372.

"Libraries and Reading."

LIBRARY OF CONGRESS. *Catalogue of Books, Maps, and Charts, Belonging to the Library of the Two Houses of Congress.* Washington: printed by W. Duane, 1802, 10 pp.

The first catalog of the Library of Congress. Supplements and catalogs of additions issued irregularly until

1878. Now replaced by *Library of Congress, Catalogue of Printed Cards,* issued regularly.

_____. *Catalogue of the Library of Congress, in the Capitol of the United States of America, December, 1839.* Washington: printed by order of Congress by Langtree and O'Sullivan, 1840, 747 pp.

_____. *Catalogue of the Library of Congress: Index of Subjects,* 2 Vols. Washington, 1869.

_____. *Writings and Addresses of Luther Harris Evans, Librarian of Congress, 1945–1953.* Washington, 1953, 92 pp.

LIBRARY OF CONGRESS, PERIODICAL DIVISION. *Check List of American Eighteenth Century Newspapers in the Library of Congress,* compiled by John Van Ness Ingram. Washington, 1912, 186 pp.

Revised edition: 1936, 401 pp.

_____. *A Check List of American Newspapers in the Library of Congress.* Washington, 1901, 292 pp.

"Lists of Almanacs, Ephemerides, etc., and of Works Relating to the Calendar, in the New York Public Library." *BNYPL,* VII (July 1903), 246–267; (August 1903), 281–302.

"Literary Periodicals in the New York Public Library and the Columbia University Library." *BNYPL,* III (March 1899), 118–135; (April 1899), 172–186.

LYDENBERG, HARRY MILLER, comp. *History of the New York Public Library: Astor, Lenox and Tilden Foundations.* New York: New York Public Library, 1923, 643 pp.

MARINE HISTORICAL ASSOCIATION. *Inventory of the Logbooks and Journals in the G. W. Blunt White Library.* Mystic, Connecticut: Marine Historical Association, 1965, 60 pp.

Mystic Seaport Manuscripts Inventory, No. 4.

MASSACHUSETTS HISTORICAL SOCIETY. *Catalogue of the Library of the Massachusetts Historical Society,* 2 Vols. Boston: printed for the Massachusetts Historical Society, 1859–1860.

McMULLEN, HAYNES. "Special Libraries in Ante-Bellum Kentucky." *Kentucky Historical Society Register,* LIX (January 1961), 29–46.

MICHIGAN, UNIVERSITY, WILLIAM L. CLEMENTS LIBRARY. *The Clements Library Presents an Exhibition of Early American Drama.* Ann Arbor: William L. Clements Library, 1947, 3 pp.

_____. *Early American Drama: A Guide to an Exhibition in the William L. Clements Library.* Ann Arbor: William L. Clements Library, 1945, 18 pp.

MIDDLEBURY COLLEGE, LIBRARY. *A Check List of Books in the Julian Willis Abernethy Library of American Literature, Middlebury College, Middlebury, Vermont,* compiled by Harriet Smith Potter. Middlebury: Middlebury College Library, 1930, 238 pp.

Middlebury College Bulletin, XXV, No. 2 (October 1930).

Also: 1940, 291 pp.

MINOR, KATE PLEASANTS, and SUSIE B. HARRISON, comps. "A List of Newspapers in the Virginia

State Library, Confederate Museum and Valentine Museum." *Bulletin of the Virginia State Library,* V (1912), 285–425.

MISSOURI STATE HISTORICAL SOCIETY, LIBRARY. *List of Old Newspapers in the Library of the State Historical Society of Missouri.* Columbia: Missouri State Historical Society Library, 1910, 43 pp.

Reprinted from *Missouri Historical Review,* October 1910.

MOORE, JOHN HAMMOND, ed. *Research Materials in South Carolina: A Guide.* Columbia: Univ. of South Carolina Press, 1967, 346 pp.

Compiled for the South Carolina State Library Board with the cooperation of the South Carolina Library Association.

MURPHY, HENRY CRUSE. *A Catalogue of an American Library, Chronologically Arranged.* Brooklyn: I. Van Anden, printer, 1853, 57 pp.

Part 1: description of 589 titles. No more published.

NEW YORK HISTORICAL SOCIETY. *Catalogue of American Portraits in the New York Historical Society.* New York: New York Historical Society, 1941, 374 pp.

NEW YORK HISTORICAL SOCIETY, LIBRARY. *Catalogue of Books, Manuscripts, Maps, etc., Added to the Library of the New York Historical Society, since January, 1839.* New York: J. W. Harrison, printer, 1840, 32 pp.

————————. *A Catalogue of Illinois Newspapers in the New York Historical Society,* compiled by Thomas O. Mabbott and Philip D. Jordan. Springfield: Illinois State Historical Library, 1931, 58 pp.

Reprinted from *Journal of Illinois State Historical Society,* XXIV (July 1931).

————————. *Catalogue of Printed Books in the Library of the New York Historical Society.* New York: printed for the New York Historical Society, 1859, 653 pp.

Collections of the New York Historical Society, 2nd Series, IV.

NEW YORK MERCANTILE LIBRARY ASSOCIATION. *Catalogue of Books in the Mercantile Library of the City of New York, with a Supplement to August 1, 1856.* New York: Baker and Godwin, printers, 1856, 290 pp.

Also: F. T. Taylor, 1866, 699 pp.

Supplement: J. Medole, 1869, 265 pp.

Supplement: J. Sutton and Co., 1872, 296 pp.

NEW YORK STATE LIBRARY. *Catalogue of the New-York State Library, January 1, 1846 . . .,* 2 Parts. Albany: C. Wendell, printer, 1846.

Also: *Thru January 1, 1850,* 1,058 pp.

Also: *General Library, 1856,* 987 pp.

Also: *General Library, 1861,* 1,084 pp.

————————. *Catalogue of the New York State Library, 1872: Subject Index to the General Library.* Albany: Van Benthuysen Printing House, 1872, 651 pp.

Supplement: Weed, Parsons and Co., 1882, 414 pp.

NEWBERRY LIBRARY (CHICAGO). *American Novels with an American Setting Printed before 1880: A Checklist of Books in the Library, August 1941.* Chicago: Newberry Library, 1941, 36 leaves.

NORTH CAROLINA, UNIVERSITY, LIBRARY. *Library Resources of the University of North Carolina: A Summary of Facilities for Study and Research,* edited by Charles E. Rush. Chapel Hill: Univ. of North Carolina Press, 1945, 264 pp.

PATERSON, LEWIS. "Dime Novel Heroes Abound in University's Walter Library." St. Paul (Minn.) *Dispatch,* June 21, 1961.

PEABODY INSTITUTE, LIBRARY (BALTIMORE). *Alphabetical Catalogue of Books Proposed to Be Purchased for the Library of the Peabody Institute, Baltimore.* Baltimore: printed by J. D. Toy, 1861, 415 pp.

Title varies slightly.

Also: 1863, 218 pp.

_____. *Catalogue of the Library of the Peabody Institute of the City of Baltimore,* 5 Vols. Baltimore: I. Friedenwald, 1883–1892.

PENNINGTON, EDGAR LEGARE. "The Beginnings of the Library in Charles Town, South Carolina." *PAAS,* XLIV (April 1935), 159–187.

PENNSYLVANIA HORTI-CULTURAL SOCIETY, LIBRARY (PHILADELPHIA). *Catalogue of the Library of the Pennsylvania Horticultural Society.* Philadelphia:

Stavely and McCalla, printers, 1850, 48 pp.

Also: Pennsylvania Horticultural Society, 1931, 85 pp.

Also: 1941, 161 pp.

PENNSYLVANIA, UNIVERSITY, LIBRARY. *Checklist of American Drama Published in the English Colonies of North America and the United States through 1865 in the Possession of the Library, University of Pennsylvania,* compiled by Albert Von Chorba Jr. Philadelphia: Univ. of Pennsylvania Press, 1951, 92 leaves.

PHILADELPHIA APPRENTICES' LIBRARY COMPANY. *A Catalogue of Books Belonging to the Apprentices' Library Company of Philadelphia.* Philadelphia: Kite and Walton, printers, 1850, 159 pp.

_____. *Catalogue of Books Belonging to the Girls' Department of the Apprentices' Library Company of Philadelphia.* Philadelphia: n.p., 1850, 57 pp.

Also: 1853, 74 pp.

Also: W. H. Pile, 1872, 129 pp.

_____. *Finding List of the Apprentices' Library of Philadelphia.* Philadelphia: press of Globe Printing House, 1892, 97 pp.

Also: T. C. Davis and Sons, 1898, 141 pp.

PHILADELPHIA BIBLIO-GRAPHICAL CENTER AND UNION LIBRARY CATALOGUE, COMMITTEE ON MICRO-PHOTOGRAPHY. *Union List of Microfilms: A Basic List of Holdings in the United States and Canada.* Philadelphia: n.p., 1942, 392 pp.

Reproduced from typewritten copy.

Supplements, I–V: 1942–1947.

Also: Ann Arbor: J. W. Edwards, 1951, 9,661 columns.

PHILADELPHIA FREE LIBRARY. *A List of Serials in the Principal Libraries of Philadelphia and Its Vicinity.* Philadelphia: Allen, Lane and Scott, 1908, 324 pp.

Supplement: 1910, 88 pp.

PHILADELPHIA LIBRARY AS-SOCIATION OF FRIENDS. *Catalogue of Books in Friends' Library, Cherry Street, Below Fifth, Philadelphia.* Philadelphia: printed by J. Rakestraw, 1853, 82 pp.

PHILADELPHIA LIBRARY COM-PANY. *A Catalogue of the Books Belonging to the Library Company of Philadelphia. . . .* Philadelphia: printed by Zachariah Poulson Jr., 1789, 406 pp.

Supplement: 1793, 38 pp.

Supplement: 1796, 38 pp.

Also: Bartram and Reynolds, 1807, 656 pp.

Also: printed for the Philadelphia Library Co., 1856, 2,103 pp.

———————. *Catalogue of Books Belonging to the Library Company of Philadelphia to which is Prefixed a Short Account of the Institution, with the Charter, Laws, and Regulations,* 2 Vols. Philadelphia: C. Sherman and Co., printers, 1835.

———————. *The Charter, Laws, and Catalogue of Books of the Library Company of Philadelphia.* Philadelphia: printed by B. Franklin and D. Hall, 1764, 150 pp.

Also: printed by Joseph Crukshank, 1770, 310 pp.

PHILADELPHIA LIBRARY COM-PANY, LOGANIAN LIBRARY. *Catalogue of Books Belonging to the Loganian Library . . .,* 2 Vols. Philadelphia: printed by Zachariah Poulson Jr., 1795–1829.

Also: C. Sherman and Co., printers, 1837, 450 pp.

PHILADELPHIA MERCANTILE LIBRARY COMPANY. *Alphabetical List (by Title) of the Class of Prose Fiction in the Mercantile Library of Philadelphia.* Philadelphia: printed for the Philadelphia Mercantile Library Co. by Woodruff and Van Horn, 1891, 166 pp.

———————. *Catalogue of a Collection of Books in All Departments of Literature, Many of Them Scarce and Valuable . . . .* Philadelphia: n.p., 1879, 203 pp.

———————. *A Catalogue of the Mercantile Library of Philadelphia,* 2 Vols. Philadelphia: printed for the Philadelphia Library Co., 1850.

Supplement: T. K. and P. G. Collins, printers, 1856, 132 pp.

Supplement: 1860, 139 pp.

Also: 1870, 707 pp.

———————. *Finding List for Novels in the Mercantile Library of Philadelphia.* Philadelphia: printed for the Philadelphia Mercantile Library Co., 1878, 187 pp.

POLISH ROMAN CATHOLIC UNION OF AMERICA, ARCHIVES AND MUSEUM. *Polonica Americana: Annotated Catalogue of the Archives and Museum of the Polish Roman Catholic Union,* by Alphonse S.

Wolanin. Chicago: Polish Roman Catholic Union of America, 1950, 295 pp.

Catalogs several thousand books, pamphlets and broadsides in various languages written by Polish immigrants and their descendants in America.

POOLE, WILLIAM FREDERICK. *Finding List of the Chicago Public Library,* 7th edition. Chicago: Chicago Public Library, 1889–1899.

PRIESTLEY, HERBERT I. "History on File." *Sat R,* XXVI (Oct. 30, 1943), 18–19.

The holdings of Bancroft Library, Univ. of California.

PRINCETON THEOLOGICAL SEMINARY. *Catalogue of the Library of the Princeton Theological School, Part I: Religious Literature.* Princeton: C. S. Robinson and Co., 1886, 453 pp.

PRINCETON UNIVERSITY, LIBRARY. *Subject-Catalogue of the Library of the College of New Jersey, at Princeton.* New York: C. M. Green Printing Co., 1884, 894 pp.

PROVIDENCE ATHENAEUM. *Catalogue of the Athenaeum Library, with an Appendix, Containing the Library Regulations and a List of the Officers and Proprietors.* Providence: Knowles, Vose and Co., 1837, 116 pp.

_____. *Catalogue of the Library of the Providence Athenaeum, to which are Prefixed the Charter, Constitution and By-laws, and an Historical Sketch of the Institution.* Providence: Knowles, Anthony and Co., printers, 1853, 557 pp.

Supplement: 1861, 374 pp.

QUINN, ARTHUR HOBSON. "American Drama at Pennsylvania." *LCUP,* XVIII (Winter 1951–52), 3–6.

QUINN, ARTHUR HOBSON, and E. H. O'NEILL. "The Bibliography of American Literature at Philadelphia." *Journal of Documentation,* III (December 1947), 177–187.

RADDIN, GEORGE GATES, JR. *An Early New York Library of Fiction: With a Checklist of the Fiction in H. Caritat's Circulating Library, No. 1 City Hotel, Broadway, 1804.* New York: H. W. Wilson Co., 1940, 113 pp.

READ, HERMAN RALPH. "Incunabula Medica in the Huntington Library." *HLQ,* I (1931), 107–151.

RUGG, HAROLD G. "Modern Authors in New England Libraries." *CRL,* VI (December 1944), 54–57.

ST. LOUIS MERCANTILE LIBRARY ASSOCIATION. *Catalogue of Books Belonging to the Saint Louis Mercantile Library Association, January, 1850.* St. Louis: St. Louis Mercantile Library Association, 1850, 315 pp.

Supplement: printed at the Republican Office, 1851, 107 pp.

_____. *Catalogue, Systematic and Analytical, of the Books of the Saint Louis Mercantile Library Association, by Edward William Johnston, December 1858.* St. Louis: printed for the St. Louis Mercantile Library Association, 1858, 575 pp.

_____. *Classified Catalogue of St. Louis Mercantile Library, with an Index of Authors.* St. Louis: printed for the St. Louis Mercantile

Library Association by the Democrat Lithographing and Printing Co., 1874, 762 pp.

Supplement: J. McKittrick and Co., printers, 1876, 138 pp.

_____. . . . *1. Missouri and Illinois Newspapers, 1808–1897, Chronologically Arranged. 2. Manuscripts Relating to Louisiana Territory and Missouri.* St. Louis: St. Louis Mercantile Library Association, 1898, 22 pp.

SAN FRANCISCO MERCANTILE LIBRARY ASSOCIATION. *Catalogue of the Library of the Mercantile Library Association of San Francisco.* San Francisco: San Francisco Mercantile Library Association, Francis and Valentine, printers, 1874, 958 pp.

Supplement: 1875, 168 pp.

_____. *Catalogue of the San Francisco Mercantile Library, August, 1854.* San Francisco: San Francisco Mercantile Library Association, printed at *Daily Evening News* Office, 1854, 197 pp.

Supplement: 189–197.

Also: Francis and Valentine, printers, 1874, 958 pp.

Also: 1875, 168 pp.

_____. *Catalogue of Ten Thousand Selected Books in All Branches of Knowledge from the Shelves of the Mercantile Library Association.* San Francisco: San Francisco Mercantile Library Association, 1903, 300 pp.

_____. *A Classified Catalogue of the Mercantile Library of San Francisco, with an Index of Authors and Subjects, Consisting of*

About Fourteen Thousand Volumes. San Francisco: San Francisco Mercantile Library Association, 1861, 145 pp.

SMITH, DOROTHY. "Union List of Serials in Maine Libraries." *Univ. of Maine Studies,* 2nd Series, XL (1937), 257 pp.

STEVENS, HENRY. *Catalogue of the American Books in the Library of the British Museum at Christmas, 1856.* London: printed by C. Whittingham at the Cheswick Press, 1866, 716 pp.

Four parts in one volume.

TEXAS, UNIVERSITY, JOHN HENRY WRENN LIBRARY. *A Catalogue of the Library of the Late John Henry Wrenn,* 5 Vols. Austin: privately printed by E. T. Heron and Co., 1920.

A Union Catalog of Photo Facsimiles in North American Libraries, Material So Far Received by the Library of Congress, compiled by the curator of Union Catalogs of the Library of Congress. Yardley, Pennsylvania: F. S. Cook and Son, 1929, 9 leaves.

UNITED STATES, COPYRIGHT OFFICE. *Catalog of Copyright Entries of Books and Other Articles Entered in the Office of the Librarian of Congress.* Washington, 1891–   .

Title varies. Issued irregularly, combined in segments of various lengths.

UNITED STATES MILITARY ACADEMY, LIBRARY. *Catalogue of the Library of the Military Academy, West Point, New York, Exhibiting Its Condition at the Close of the Year 1852.* New York: J. F. Trow, printer, 1853, 412 pp.

Supplement: printed by G. W. Wood, 1860, 155 pp.

UTAH, UNIVERSITY, UTAH HUMANITIES RESEARCH FOUNDATION. *A Bibliography of the Archives of the Utah Humanities Research Foundation, 1944–1947,* compiled by Hector Lee. Salt Lake City: Utah Humanities Research Foundation, 1947, 41 pp.

Utah Univ. Bulletin, XXXVIII, No. 9.

VAN MALE, JOHN. *Resources of Pacific Northwest Libraries: A Survey of Facilities for Study and Research.* Seattle: Pacific Northwest Library Association, 1943, 404 pp.

VIRGINIA STATE LIBRARY. *Catalogue of the Virginia State Library, 1877.* Richmond: G. W. Gary's Steam Printing House, 1877, 369 pp.

WILSON, LOUIS R. "Resources of Research Libraries." *CRL,* V (June 1944), 259–266.

WING, DONALD G., and MARGARET L. JOHNSON. "The Books Given [to Yale University Library] by Elihu Yale in 1718." *YULG,* XIII (October 1938), 46–67.

WISCONSIN STATE HISTORICAL SOCIETY, LIBRARY. *Annotated Catalogue of Newspaper Files in the Library of the State Historical Society of Wisconsin,* compiled by Emma Helen Blair. Madison: Democrat Printing Co., 1898, 386 pp.

2nd edition: Wisconsin State Historical Society, 1911, 591 pp.

Supplement: 1918, 91 pp.

WYNNE, MARJORIE GRAY. "Bibliographical Files for Research in the Yale University Libraries." *PBSA,* XLIX (3rd Quart. 1955), 199–211.

YOUNG MEN'S ASSOCIATION, LIBRARY (ALBANY). *Catalogue of the Library of the Young Men's Association, Albany.* Albany: C. Van Benthuysen, 1848, 1,202 pp.

Also: 1853, 148 pp.

15. MANUSCRIPTS

ADCOCK, LYNETTE, comp. *Guide to the Manuscript Collections of Colonial Williamsburg.* Williamsburg: Colonial Williamsburg, Inc., 1954, 58 pp.

ANDREWS, CHARLES McLEAN, and FRANCES G. DAVENPORT. *Guide to the Manuscript Materials for the History of the United States to 1783, in the British Museum, in Minor London Archives, and in the Libraries of Oxford and Cambridge.* Washington: Carnegie Institution of Washington, 1908, 514 pp.

Carnegie Institution of Washington Publication, No. 90.

AUSTIN, MARY. "Spanish Manuscripts in the Southwest." *SRev,* (July 1934), 402–409.

BESTERMAN, THEODORE. "Preliminary Short-Title List of Bibliographies, Containing Manuscript Notes." *PBSA,* XLIII (2nd Quart. 1949), 209–226.

BILLINGTON, RAY ALLEN. *Guides to American History Manu-*

script Collections in Libraries of the
United States. New York: P. Smith,
1952, 29 pp.

Reprinted from *Mississippi Valley
Historical Review*, XXXVIII
(December 1951), 467–496.

BOSTON PUBLIC LIBRARY.
*Ships and Sea: A Catalog of an Ex-
hibition of Books and Manuscripts in
Tribute to Boston's Maritime Past,
July 1–September 1966, in the
Boston Public Library.* Boston:
Boston Public Library, 1966, 58 pp.,
unpaginated.

BOYCE, GEORGE K. "Modern
Literary Manuscripts in the Morgan
Library." *PMLA*, LXVII (February
1952), 3–36.

BURKE, FRANK G. "Manuscripts
and Archives." *Library Trends*, XV
(January 1967), 430–445.

BURTON, WILLIAM LESTER, ed.
*Descriptive Bibliography of Civil War
Manuscripts in Illinois.* Evanston:
published for the Civil War Centennial Commission of Illinois by Northwestern Univ. Press, 1966, 393 pp.

CAMERON, KENNETH W. "Literary
Manuscripts in the Trinity College
Library." *ESQ*, XIV (1st Quart.
1959), 18.

CRICK, BERNARD R., and
MIRIAM ALMAN, eds. *A Guide to
Manuscripts Relating to America in
Great Britain and Ireland.* London:
published for the British Association
for American Studies by Oxford
Univ. Press, 1961, 703 pp.

CUTHBERT, NORMA BARRETT,
comp. *American Manuscript Collections in the Huntington Library for
the History of the Seventeenth and
Eighteenth Centuries.* San Marino,
California: Huntington Library,
1941, 101 pp.

DEBRETT, J., et al. *Bibliotheca
Americana: or, A Chronological
Catalogue of the Most Curious and
Interesting Books, Pamphlets, and
State Papers, etc., upon the Subject
of North and South America, from
the Earliest Period to the Present,
in Print, and in Manuscript, for
which Research Has Been Made in
the British Museum.* London: printed
for J. Debrett et al., 1789, 271 pp.

Work ascribed to Debrett and others.

DEDMOND, FRANCIS B. "A
Check List of Manuscripts in the
Huntington Library, the Houghton
Library of Harvard University, and
the Berg Collection of the New York
Public Library." *TSB*, XLIII
(Spring 1953), no pagination.

ELIOT, MARGARET SHERBURNE,
and SYLVESTER K. STEVENS.
*Guide to Depositories of Manuscript
Collections in Pennsylvania.*
Harrisburg: Commonwealth of
Pennsylvania, Dept. of Public Instruc-
tion, Pennsylvania Historical Com-
mission, 1939, 132 pp.

FREEMAN, JOHN F., comp. *A
Guide to Manuscripts Relating to the
American Indian in the Library of
the American Philosophical Society.*
Philadelphia: American Philosophical
Society, 1966, 491 pp.

*Memoirs of the American Philo-
sophical Society*, LXV.

GARRISON, C. W. "List of Manu-
script Collections in the Library of
Congress to July, 1931." *Annual
Report of the American Historical
Association*, I (1931), 123–233.

HAMER, PHILIP MAY, ed. *A Guide
to Archives and Manuscripts in the
United States*, compiled for the
National Historical Publications
Commission. New Haven: Yale
Univ. Press, 1961, 798 pp.

HEPBURN, W. M. "The Charles Major Manuscripts in the Purdue University Libraries." *Indiana Quarterly for Bookmen,* II (July 1946), 71–81.

HISTORICAL RECORDS SURVEY. *Guide to Manuscript Depositories in New York City.* New York: prepared by the Historical Records Survey, Division of Professional and Service Projects, Work Progress Administration, 1941, 161 pp.

KARPINSKI, L. C. "Manuscript Maps of America in European Archives." *Michigan Historical Magazine,* XIV (Winter 1930), 5–14.

LOHF, KENNETH A., comp. *The Collection of the Books, Manuscripts, and Autograph Letters in the Library of Jean and Donald Stralem.* New York: n. p., 1962, 55 pp.

MODERN LANGUAGE ASSOCIATION OF AMERICA, AMERICAN LITERATURE GROUP, COMMITTEE ON MANUSCRIPT HOLDINGS. *American Literary Manuscripts: A Checklist of Holdings in Academic, Historical, and Public Libraries in the United States.* Austin: Univ. of Texas Press, 1961, 449 pp.

Locates manuscripts pertaining to more than 2,300 American authors in more than 250 libraries.

NEW JERSEY HISTORICAL SOCIETY. *A Guide to the Manuscript Collection of the New Jersey Historical Society,* by Fred Shelley. Newark: New Jersey Historical Society, 1957, 84 pp.

New Jersey Historical Society Collections, No. 11.

NEW YORK HISTORICAL SOCIETY, LIBRARY. *Catalogue of Books, Manuscripts, Maps, etc., Added to the Library of the New York Historical Society, since January, 1839.* New York: J. W. Harrison, printer, 1840, 32 pp.

NEW YORK PUBLIC LIBRARY, MANUSCRIPT DIVISION. "Manuscript Collections in the New York Public Library." *BNYPL,* V (July 1901), 306–336.

Additional lists of accessions printed in February issues of *BNYPL* since 1935.

Supplement: XIX (February 1915), 149–165.

—————. "Manuscript Division Accessions during 1943." *BNYPL,* XLVIII (April 1944), 400–408.

PALTSITS, VICTOR HUGO. "Supplement to the List of 'Manuscript Collections,' of 1901, Noted above, Embracing Principal Additions and Accessions to the End of 1914." *BNYPL,* XIX (February 1915), 149–162.

PECKHAM, HOWARD HENRY, comp. *Guide to the Manuscript Collections in the William L. Clements Library.* Ann Arbor: Univ. of Michigan Press, 1942, 419 pp.

POULTNEY, GEORGE W. *An Index of Plays of the American Theatre in Manuscript Form,* from the collection of George W. Poultney, to accompany the exhibit for the Dramatists Alliance of Stanford University. Palo Alto: Stanford Univ. Press, 1939, 21 leaves.

RICH, OBADIAH. *Catalogue of a Collection of Manuscripts, Principally in Spanish, Relating to America in the Possession of O. Rich.* London: W. Bowden, 1845, 48 pp.

—————. *Manuscripts and Printed Books in the Possession of Obadiah Rich, Esq., December 27, 1827.* Washington: printed by order of the House of Representatives, 1827, 24 pp.

ROACH, GEORGE W., comp. "Guide to Depositories of Manuscript Collections in New York State (exclusive of New York City)." *NYH,* XXIV (April 1943), 265–270; (July 1943), 417–422; (October 1943), 560–564; XXV (January 1944), 64–68; (April 1944), 226–227.

ST. LOUIS MERCANTILE LIBRARY ASSOCIATION. . . .*1. Missouri and Illinois Newspapers, 1808–1897, Chronologically Arranged. 2. Manuscripts Relating to Louisiana Territory and Missouri.* St. Louis: St. Louis Mercantile Library Association, 1898, 22 pp.

SARGENT, GEORGE H. "Literary Manuscripts in Boston." *AC,* IV (June 1927), 98–107.

SCHULZ, HERBERT C. "American Literary Manuscripts in the Huntington Library." *HLQ,* XXII (May 1959), 209–250.

SHELLEY, FRED. "Manuscripts in the Library of Congress, 1800–1890." *AA,* XI (January 1948), 3–19.

SMITH, HERBERT FRANKLIN, comp. *A Guide to the Manuscript Collection of the Rutgers University Library.* New Brunswick: Rutgers Univ. Press, 1964, 190 pp.

"Supplement to the Guide to the Manuscript Collections in the Historical Society of Pennsylvania." *PMHB,* LXVIII (January 1944), 98–111.

TAYLOR, ROBERT H. *Authors at Work. . . . : An Address Delivered at the Opening of an Exhibition of Literary Manuscripts at the Grolier Club together with a Catalogue of the Exhibition by Herman W. Liebert and Facsimiles of Many of the Exhibits.* New York: Grolier Club, 1957, 52 pp.

UNITED STATES, NATIONAL HISTORICAL PUBLICATIONS COMMISSION. *A Guide to Archives and Manuscripts in the United States,* edited by Philip M. Hamer. New Haven: Yale Univ. Press, 1961, 775 pp.

16. MUSIC

BARLOW, ROBERT. "Yale and the American Musical Theater." *YULG,* XXVIII (April 1954), 144–149.

BIEBER, ALBERT ALOYSIUS. *The Albert Bieber Collection of American Plays, Poetry and Songsters. . . .* New York: Cooper Square Publishers, 1963, 103 pp.

DAMON, S. FOSTER. "The Negro in Early American Songs-

ters." *PBSA,* XXVIII (1934), 132–163.

DICHTER, HARRY, and ELLIOTT SHAPIRO. *Early American Sheet Music: Its Lure and Its Lore, 1768–1889.* New York: R. R. Bowker Co., 1941, 259.

Includes directory of early American music publishers.

HOWARD, JOHN TASKER. *Our American Music: Three*

Hundred Years of It, 3rd edition, revised. New York: Thomas Y. Crowell Co., 1946, 693–743.

_____. *Our Contemporary Composers: American Music in the Twentieth Century.* New York: Thomas Y. Crowell Co., 1841, 349–350.

JAMES, URIAH PIERSON. *The Negro Melodist: Containing a Great Variety of the Most Popular Airs, Songs, and Melodies, Comic Humorous, Sentimental, and Patriotic.* Cincinnati: H. M. Rulison, 1857, 120 pp.

LOMAX, ALAN, and SIDNEY ROBERTSON COWELL, comps. *American Folk Song and Folk Lore: A Regional Bibliography.* New York: Progressive Education Association, 1942, 59 pp.

LOWENS, IRVING. "Writings about Music in the Periodicals of American Transcendentalism (1835–50)." *JAMS,* X (Summer 1957), 71–85.

MATTFLED, JULIUS. "A Hundred Years of Grand Opera in New York: A List of Records." *BNYPL,* XIX (October 1925), 695–702; (November 1925), 778–814; (December 1925), 873–914.

SCHLESINGER, ARTHUR M. "A Note on Songs as Patriotic Propaganda, 1765–1776." *WMQ,* XI (January 1954), 78–88.

SONNECK, OSCAR GEORGE THEODORE, ed. *A Bibliography of Early Secular American Music, Eighteenth Century,* revised and enlarged by William Treat Upton. New York: De Capo Press, 1964, 616 pp.

_____. "Early American Operas." *Sammelbande der Internationalen Musikgesellschaft,* XI (1904), 428–495.

TRENT, WILLIAM PETERFIELD, et al. "Patriotic Songs and Hymns," in *Cambridge History of American Literature,* 4 Vols. New York: G. P. Putnam's Sons, 1917–1921, IV, 797–799.

WARRINGTON, JAMES. *Short Titles of Books Relating to or Illustrating the History and Practice of Psalmody in the United States, 1620–1820.* Philadelphia: privately printed, 1898, 96 numbered leaves.

WOLFE, RICHARD J. *Secular Music in America, 1801–1825: A Bibliography,* 3 Vols. New York: New York Public Library, 1964.

17. NEGRO

ADULT DEPARTMENT STAFF. "The Negro: A Selected Bibliography." *BNYPL,* LIV (October 1950), 471–485.

BONTEMPS, ARNA. "The James Weldon Johnson Memorial Collection of Negro Arts and Letters." *YULG,* XVIII (October 1943), 19–26.

_____. "Special Collections of Negroana." *LQ,* XIV (July 1944), 187–206.

"Books by and about Negroes— 1943–1944." *A Monthly Summary of Events and Trends in Race Relations,* III (August–September 1945), 64–65.

BRAWLEY, BENJAMIN GRIFFITH. *The Negro in Literature and Art.* New York: Duffield and Co., 1910, 58–60.

Also: 1918, 160–174.

Also: 1921, 180–194.

Also: 1929, 213–228.

_____. *A Short History of the American Negro.* New York: Macmillan Co., 1913, 233–238.

Also: 1919, 265–272.

Also: 1927, 269–276.

Also: 1931, 294–302.

Also: 1939, 275–280.

BUNI, ANDREW. *The Negro in Virginia Politics, 1902–1965.* Charlottesville: Univ. Press of Virginia, 1967, 271–285.

DAMON, S. FOSTER. "The Negro in Early American Songsters." *PBSA,* XXVIII (1934), 132–163.

A list of songsters in the Brown Univ. Harris Collection of American Poetry and Plays, published in or before 1830 and containing Negro songs, 154–163.

DETWEILER, FREDERICK EGERMAN. *The Negro Press in the United States.* Chicago: Univ. of Chicago Press, 1922, 274 pp.

DU BOIS, WILLIAM EDWARD BURGHARDT. *A Select Bibliography of the American Negro.* Atlanta: Atlanta Univ. Press, 1901, 12 pp.

Also: 1905, 71 pp.
DUMOND, DWIGHT LOWELL. *A Bibliography of Anti-Slavery in America.* Ann Arbor: Univ. of Michigan Press, 1961, 119 pp.

DUNLAP, MOLLIE E. "A Selected Annotated List of Books by or about the Negro." *Negro College Quarterly,* III (March 1945), 40–45; (June 1945), 94–96; (September 1945), 153–158.

GREEN, ELIZABETH LAY. *The Negro in Contemporary American Literature: An Outline for Individual and Group Study.* Chapel Hill: Univ. of North Carolina Press, 1928, 94 pp.

GROSS, SEYMOUR LEE, and JOHN EDWARD HARDY, eds. *Images of the Negro in American Literature.* Chicago: Univ. of Chicago Press, 1966, 289–315.

Guide to Negro Periodical Literature, 4 Vols. Winston-Salem, North Carolina: n.p., 1941–1946.

HILL, M. C., and P. B. FOREMAN. "The Negro in the United States: A Bibliography." *Southwestern Journal,* II (Summer 1946), 225–230.

Index to Selected Periodicals. Boston: G. K. Hall and Co., 1950– .

Originally undertaken by the Hallie Q. Brown Library to replace *Guide to Negro Periodical Literature,* 1941–1946. The first 40 quarterly issues have been cumulated and published as *Index to Selected Periodicals: Decennial Cumulation, 1950–1959,* 1961, 501 pp. Because the 18 periodicals were not indexed elsewhere, this cumulation is a particularly valuable guide to Negro materials. Enlarged in 1960 by the Hallie Q. Brown Library and the New

York Public Library to include periodicals indexed by the staff of the Schomburg Collection of Negro Literature and History, and issued as *Annual Cumulation.* With XVII (1966), title changed to *Index to Periodical Articles by and about Negroes.*

JACKSON, BRUCE, ed. *The Negro and His Folklore in Nineteenth-Century Periodicals.* Austin: printed for the American Folklore Society by the Univ. of Texas Press, 1967, 353–367.

JAMES, URIAH PIERSON. *The Negro Melodist: Containing a Great Variety of the Most Popular Airs, Songs, and Melodies, Comic Humorous, Sentimental, and Patriotic.* Cincinnati: H. M. Rulison, 1857, 120 pp.

JARRETT, THOMAS D. "Recent Fiction by Negroes." *CE,* XVI (November 1954), 85–91.

KESSLER, SIDNEY H. "American Negro Literature: A Bibliographic Guide." *BB,* XXI (September-December 1955), 181–185.

LASH, JOHN S. "The American Negro and American Literature: A Checklist of Significant Commentaries." *BB,* XIX (September–December 1946), 12–15; (January–April 1947), 33–36.

LAWSON, HILDA J., comp. "The Negro in American Drama (Bibliography of Contemporary Negro Drama)." *BB,* XVII (January 1940), 7–8; (May 1940), 27–30.

LEARY, LEWIS. *Articles on American Literature, 1900–1950.* Durham: Duke Univ. Press, 1954, 384–386.

"Negro."

LOGGINS, VERNON. *The Negro Author: His Development in America.* New York: Columbia Univ. Press, 1931, 408–457.

MURRAY, DANIEL. *Preliminary List of Books and Pamphlets by Negro Authors for Paris Exposition and Library of Congress.* Washington: U. S. Commission to the Paris Exposition, 1900, 8 pp.

NATIONAL URBAN LEAGUE, DEPARTMENT OF RESEARCH. *Selected Bibliography on the Negro,* 4th edition. New York: National Urban League, 1951, 124 pp.

NELSON, JOHN HERBERT. *The Negro Character in American Literature.* Lawrence: Univ. of Kansas, Dept. of Journalism Press, 1926, bibliographical footnotes.

Bulletin of the Univ. of Kansas, XXVII, No. 15.

NEW YORK PUBLIC LIBRARY. *Dictionary Catalog of the Schomburg Collection of Negro Literature and History,* 9 Vols. New York: New York Public Library, 1962, 177,000 cards.

First Supplement: 2 Vols. 1967, 37,100 cards.

NOBLE, PETER. *The Negro in Films.* London: S. Robinson, 1948, 241–254.

PORTER, DOROTHY BURNETT. "Afro-American Writings Published before 1835, with an Alphabetical List (Tentative) of Imprints Written by American Negroes, 1760–1835." Unpublished master's thesis, Columbia Univ., 1932.

346 BIBLIOGRAPHY OF BIBLIOGRAPHIES

——————. "Early American Negro Writings: A Bibliographical Study." *PBSA*, XXXIX (3rd Quart. 1945), 192–268.

——————. *North American Negro Poets: A Bibliographical Checklist of Their Writings, 1760–1944*. Hattiesburg: The Book Farm, 1945, 90 pp.

SCALLY, SISTER MARY ANTHONY. *Negro Catholic Writers, 1900–1943: A Bio-Bibliography*. Detroit: W. Romig and Co., 1945, 152 pp.

SCHOMBURG, ARTHUR ALFONSO. *A Bibliographical Checklist of American Negro Poetry*. New York: C. F. Heartman, 1916, 57 pp.

WHITEMAN, MAXWELL, ed. *A Century of Fiction by American Negroes, 1853–1952: A Descriptive Bibliography*. Philadelphia: n.p., 1955, 64 pp.

WYETH, OLA M. "Negro Spirituals." *BALA*, XXVI (August 1932), 520–524.

18. PERIODICALS, JOURNALISM, SERIALS

ALDEN, EDWIN, and BROTHER. *Edwin Alden and Bro.'s American Newspaper Catalogue, Including Lists of All Newspapers and Magazines Published in the United States and Canada. . .* Cincinnati: E. Alden and Bro., 1883, 838 pp.

ALLEN, FREDERICK LEWIS. "American Magazines, 1741–1941." *BNYPL*, XLV (June 1941), 439–460.

AMERICAN FOUNDATION FOR THE BLIND. *Directory of Periodicals of Special Interest to the Blind in Braille and Inkprint*, compiled by Helga Lende. New York: American Foundation for the Blind, 1933, 58 pp.

3rd edition: 1938, 66 pp.

The American Magazine; or, A Monthly View of the Political State of the British Colonies, reproduced from the original edition, Philadelphia, 1741. New York: Facsimile Text Society, 1937.

Bibliographical note by Lyon Norman Richardson.

American Newspapers, 1821–1936: A Union List of Files Available in the United States and Canada, edited by Winifred Gregory under the auspices of the Bibliographical Society of America. New York: H. W. Wilson Co., 1937, 791 pp.

AUERBACH, HERBERT S. *Western Americana: Books Newspapers, and Pamphlets, Many Relating to the Mormon Church from the Collection of Herbert S. Auerbach*, 2 Parts. New York: Parke-Bernet Galleries, Inc., 1947–1948.

AYER, N. W., AND SON. *Ayer's Directory of Newspapers and Periodicals: A Guide to Publications Printed in the United States and Possessions, Dominion of Canada, Bermuda, Cuba and the West Indies*. Philadelphia: N. W. Ayer and Son, 1880– .

BEER, WILLIAM. "Checklist of American Periodicals." *PAAS*, ns XXXII (October 1922), 330–345.

BIGELOW, FRANK BARNA.
"Early Files of Newspapers in
the New York Society Library."
Literary Collector, V (1902),
38–42.

BIRD, MARY CAROL, ed.
*International Guide to Liter-
ary and Art Periodicals, 1960.*
London: Villiers Publications,
1960–   .

BLEYER, WILLARD GROS-
VENOR. *Main Currents in the
History of American Journalism.*
Boston: Houghton Mifflin Co.,
1927, 431–441.

BOLTON, H. CARRINGTON.
"Helps for Cataloguers of
Serials: A Short List of Bibliographies Arranged by Countries,
with Special Reference to Periodicals." *BB,* I (October 1897),
37–40.

BRAYER, HERBERT O.
"Preliminary Guide to Indexed
Newspapers in the United
States, 1850–1900." *MVHR,*
XXXIII (September 1946),
237–258.

BRIGHAM, CLARENCE
SAUNDERS. "Additions and
Corrections to History and Bibliog-
raphy of American Newspapers,
1690–1820." *PAAS,* ns LXXI
(April 1961), 15–62.

––––––––––. "Daniel Hewett's
List of Newspapers and Periodicals
in the United States in 1828."
PAAS, ns XLIV (October 1934),
365–396.

––––––––––. *History and
Bibliography of American
Newspapers, 1690–1820,* 2 Vols.
Worchester: American Anti-
quarian Society, 1947.

Published serially in *PAAS,*
October 1913–April 1927.

Also: Hamden, Connecticut:
Archon Books, 1962. Includes
supplement.

*British Union-Catalogue of
Periodicals: A Record of the
Periodicals of the World from
the Seventeenth Century to
the Present Day in British
Libraries,* 4 Vols. London:
Butterworths Scientific Pub-
lications, 1955–1958.

CAIRNS, WILLIAM B.
*On the Development of Ameri-
can Literature from 1815 to
1833, with Special Reference
to Periodicals.* Madison: Univ.
of Wisconsin Press, 1898, 87 pp.

CALIFORNIA, UNIVERSITY,
LIBRARY. *Cooperative List
of Periodical Literature in the
Libraries of Central California.*
Berkeley: State Printing Office,
1902, 130 pp.

*Univ. of California Library
Bulletin,* No. 1.

––––––––––. *List of Serials
in the University of California
Library.* Berkeley: Univ. of
California Press, 1913, 266 pp.

*Univ. of California Library
Bulletin,* No. 18.

CANNON, CARL LESLIE.
Journalism: A Bibliography.
New York: New York Public
Library, 1924, 366 pp.

CAPPON, LESTER JESSE.
*American Genealogical Periodi-
cals: A Bibliography with a
Chronological Finding-List.*
New York: New York Public
Library, 1962, 29 pp.

_____ . "Preparing a Bibliography of American Genealogical Periodicals." *BNYPL*, LXVI (January 1962), 63–66.

_____ . *Virginia Newspapers, 1821–1935: A Bibliography with Historical Introduction and Notes.* New York: D. Appleton-Century Co., 1936, 312 pp.

Univ. of Virginia Institute for Research in the Social Sciences Monograph, No. 22.

CAPPON, LESTER JESSE, and STELLA F. DUFF. *Virginia Gazette Index, 1763–1780,* 2 Vols. Williamsburg: Institute of Early American History and Culture, 1950, 1,323 pp.

CARDWELL, GUY A. "Charleston Periodicals, 1795–1860: A Study in Literary Influences, with a Descriptive Check List of Seventy-five Magazines." Unpublished doctoral dissertation, Univ. of North Carolina, 1937.

Catholic Periodical Index: A Guide to Catholic Magazines, 1930–1931, 2 Vols. New York: H. W. Wilson, 1931.

Catholic Press Directory: Official Media Reference Guide to Catholic Newspapers and Magazines of the United States and Canada. New York: Catholic Press Association, 1923–   .

Issued annually.

CHAMBERS, LENOIR, and JOSEPH E. SHANK. *Salt Water and Printer's Ink: Norfolk and Its Newspapers, 1865–1965.* Chapel Hill: Univ. of North Carolina Press, 1967, 396–398.

CHAMBERS, M. M. "Periodicals Covering Foreign Universities." *School and Society*, LXVIII (Nov. 6, 1948), 321–323.

CHANDLER, KATHERINE. *List of California Periodicals Issued Previous to the Completion of the Transcontinental Telegraph (August 15, 1846–October 24, 1861).* San Francisco: n.p., 1905, 20 pp.

Publications of the Library Association of California, No. 7.

"Check List of Brooklyn and Long Island Newspapers in the New York Public Library." *BNYPL*, VI (January 1902), 20–21.

"Check List of Newspapers Published in New York City Contained in the New York Public Library, December 31st, 1900." *BNYPL*, V (January 1901), 20–30.

CHICAGO LIBRARY CLUB. *A List of Serials in Public Libraries of Chicago and Evanston, Corrected to January, 1901.* Chicago: published for the Chicago Library Club by W. P. Dunn, 1901, 195 pp.

LCN: "Supplement to the first edition issued by John Crerar Library, appeared 1903, the second (corrected to Nov. 1905) in 1906."

COGGESHALL, WILLIAM TURNER. *The Newspaper Record: Containing a Complete List of Newspapers and Periodicals in the United States, Canada, and Great Britain, together with a Sketch of the Origin and Progress of Printing, with Some Facts about Newspapers in Europe and America.*

Philadelphia: Lay and Brother, 1856, 208 pp.

COOK, ELIZABETH CHRISTINE. *Literary Influences in Colonial Newspapers, 1704–50.* New York: Columbia Univ. Press, 1912, 266–272.

COOKE, G. W. *"The Dial:* An Historical and Biographical Introduction, with a List of the Contributors." *Journal of Speculative Philosophy,* XIX (July 1885), 225–265.

CRICK, BERNARD R., and ANNE DALTROP. "List of American Newspapers Up to 1940, Held by Libraries in Great Britain and Ireland." *BAASB,* VII, Supplement (1958), 1–90.

CUSHING, HELEN GRANT, and ADAH V. MORRIS, eds. *Nineteenth Century Reader's Guide to Periodical Literature, 1890–1899,* with supplemental indexing, 1900–1922, 2 Vols. New York: H. W. Wilson, 1944.

DILL, WILLIAM ADELBERT. *The First Century of American Newspapers. . . . A Graphic Check List of Periodicals Published from 1690 to 1790 in What Was to Become the United States.* Lawrence: Univ. of Kansas, 1925, 23 pp.

Univ. of Kansas Department of Journalism Bulletin, September 1925.

DITZION, SIDNEY. "The History of Periodical Literature in the United States: A Bibliography." *BB,* XV (January–April 1935), 110; (May–August 1935), 129–133.

DORNBUSCH, C. E. *"Stars and Stripes:* Check List of Several Editions." *BNYPL,* LII (July 1948), 331–340; LIII (July 1949), 335–338.

DORNBUSCH, C. E., and ANNIE DAVIS WEEKS. *"Yank, the Army Weekly:* A Check List." *BNYPL,* LIV (June 1950), 272–279.

DRURY, FRANCIS KEESE WYNKOOP. *List of Serials in the University of Illinois Library, together with Those in Other Libraries in Urbana and Champaign.* Urbana-Champaign: Univ. of Illinois Press, 1911, 241 pp.

Univ. of Illinois Bulletin, IX, No. 2.

DUKE UNIVERSITY, LIBRARY. *A Checklist of the United States Newspapers (and Weeklies before 1900) in the General Library,* compiled by Mary Wescott and Allene Ramage, 6 Parts in 3 Vols. Durham: Duke Univ. Press, 1932–1937.

"Early Iowa Papers Valuable." *Annals of Iowa,* 3rd Series, XXXIII (July 1955), 57–58.

ELLISON, RHODA COLEMAN. *History and Bibliography of Alabama Newspapers in the Nineteenth Century.* University: Univ. of Alabama Press, 1954, 221 pp.

ELY, MARGARET. *Some Great American Newspaper Editors.* New York: H. W. Wilson, 1916, 9–33.

FARBER, EVAN IRA. *Classified List of Periodicals for the College Library,* 4th edition. Boston: F. W. Faxon Co., 1957, 157 pp.

Useful Reference Series, No. 86.

FLANDERS, R. B. "Newspapers and Periodicals in the Washington Memorial Library, Macon, Georgia." *North Carolina Historical Review,* VII (April 1930), 220–223.

FORD, EDWIN HOPKINS. *History of Journalism in the United States: A Bibliography of Books and Annotated Articles.* Minneapolis: Burgess Publishing Co., 1938, 42 pp., mimeographed.

FORD, PAUL LEICESTER. *Check-List of American Magasiens Printed in the Eighteenth Century.* Brooklyn: n.p., 1889, 12 leaves.

GALBREATH, C. B. "Early Newspapers of Ohio," in *Newspapers and Periodicals in the Ohio State Library. . .* Columbus: F. J. Heer, state printers, 1902, 3–15.

GARNSEY, CAROLINE JOHN. "Ladies' Magazines to 1850: The Beginning of an Industry." *BNYPL,* LVIII (February 1954), 74–88.

GAVIT, JOSEPH, comp. "American Newspaper Reprints." *BNYPL,* XXXV (April 1931), 212–223.

The General Magazine and Historical Chronicle, for All the British Plantations in America, published by Benjamin Franklin, reproduced from the original edition, Philadelphia, 1741, with a bibliographical note by Lyon Norman Richardson. New York: Facsimile Text Society, 1938, 426 pp.

GERSTENBERGER, DONNA, and GEORGE HENDRICK. *Directory of Periodicals Pub-*

lishing Articles in English and American Literature and Language. Denver: Alan Swallow, 1959, 178 pp.

Second Directory. . . . : 1965, 151 pp.

GILMER, GERTRUDE CORDELIA, comp. *Checklist of Southern Periodicals to 1861.* Boston: F. W. Faxon Co., 1934, 128 pp.

Useful Reference Series, No. 49.

_____. "A Critique of Certain Georgia Ante-Bellum Literary Magazines Arranged Chronologically and a Checklist." *Georgia Historical Quarterly,* XVIII (December 1934), 293–334.

_____, comp. "Maryland Magazines—Ante-Bellum, 1793 to 1861." *Maryland Historical Magazines,* XXIX (June 1934), 120–131.

GLEASON, ELSIE CADY. "Newspapers of the Panhandle of Oklahoma, 1886–1940." *Chronicles of Oklahoma,* XIX (June 1941), 141–161.

GOLDWATER, WALTER. "Radical Periodicals in America, 1890–1950." *YULG,* XXXVII (April 1963), 133–177.

Also: New Haven: Yale Univ. Library, 1966, 51 pp.

GOODE, STEPHEN H., comp. *Index to Little Magazines, 1943–1947.* Denver: Alan Swallow, 1965, 281 pp.

Continued under various editors, issued generally biannually, and retrospectively by Goode for 1940–1942.

GRIFFIN, MAX L. "A Bibliography of New Orleans Magazines." *Louisiana Historical Quarterly,* XVIII (July 1935), 493–566.

HAGEMANN, E. R., and JAMES E. MARSH. *"The American Spectator,* 1932–1937: A Selected and Annotated Check List." *BB,* XXII (May–August 1958), 133–137.

_____. "Contributions of Literary Import to *Esquire,* 1933–1941: An Annotated Check-List." *BB,* XXII (January–April 1957),-33–40; (May–August 1957), 69–72.

HAMILTON, MILTON W. "Anti-Masonic Newspapers, 1826–1834." *PBSA,* XXXII (1938), 71–97.

HAMMOND, OTIS GRANT. *Bibliography of the Newspapers and Periodicals of Concord, N.H., 1790–1898.* Concord: Ira C. Evans Co., 1902, 32 pp.

HARRISON, JAMES G. "Nineteenth-Century American Novels on American Journalism." *JQ,* XXII (September 1945), 215–224; (December 1945), 335–345.

HASKELL, DANIEL CARL, comp. "A Checklist of Newspapers and Official Gazettes in the New York Public Library." *BNYPL,* XVIII (July 1914), 683–722; (August 1914), 793–826; (September 1914), 905–938; (October 1914), 1,079–1,110; (November 1914), 1,261–1,294; (December 1914), 1,467–1,480; XIX (July 1915), 553–569.

HENRY, EDWARD A. "The Durrett Collection, Now in the Library of the University of Chicago: I. Its Newspapers." *PBSA,* VIII (1914), 57–94.

HILDEBURN, CHARLES R. "A List of the Issues of the Press in New York, 1693–1784." *PMHB,* XXI (No. 4, 1888), 475–482; XIII (No. 1, 1889), 90–98; (No. 2, 1889), 207–215.

HISTORICAL SOCIETY OF WESTERN PENNSYLVANIA. *Inventory of Files of American Newspapers in Pittsburgh and Allegheny County, Pennsylvania.* Pittsburgh: n.p., 1933, 41 pp.

Western Pennsylvania Historical Survey, Bibliographical Contributions, No. 2.

HOFFMAN, FREDERICK JOHN, CHARLES ALLEN and CAROLYN F. ULRICH. *The Little Magazine: A History and Bibliography.* Princeton: Princeton Univ. Press, 1946, 233–403.

HOLLAND, DOROTHY G. "An Annotated Checklist of Magazines Published in St. Louis before 1900." *Washington Univ. Libraries Studies,* II (1951), 1–53.

HOOLE, WILLIAM STANLEY. *A Check List and Finding List of Charleston Periodicals, 1732–1864.* Durham: Duke Univ. Press, 1936, 84 pp.

HUDSON, FREDERIC. *Journalism in the United States from 1690 to 1872.* New York: Harper and Brothers, 1873, 789 pp.

INDIANA UNIVERSITY, LIBRARY. *Union List of Little Magazines: Showing Holdings of 1,037 Little Magazines in the Libraries of Indiana University, Northwestern University, Ohio State University, State University of Iowa, University of Chicago,*

University of Illinois. Chicago: Midwest Inter-Library Center, 1956, 98 pp.

JAFFE, ADRIAN H. *Bibliography of French Literature in American Magazines in the Eighteenth Century.* East Lansing: Michigan State College Press, 1951, 27 pp.

JAMES, EDMUND JAMES. *A Bibliography of Newspapers Published in Illinois Prior to 1860.* Springfield: Phillips Brothers, state printers, 1899, 94 pp.

Appendix A: chronological list of Missouri and Illinois newspapers, 1808–1897, in the St. Louis Mercantile Library. Appendix B: list of county histories of Illinois.

Illinois State Historical Library Publications, No. 1.

JILLSON, WILLARD ROUSE. *The First Printing in Kentucky: Some Account of Thomas Parvin and John Bradford and the Establishment of the Kentucky Gazette in Lexington in the Year 1787,* with a bibliography of 70 titles. Louisville: C. T. Dearing Printing Co., 1936, 41–54.

JONES, ROBERT WILLIAM. *Journalism in the United States.* New York: E. P. Dutton and Co., Inc., 1947, 705–716.

JOSEPHSON, AKSEL GUSTAV SALOMON. *A Bibliography of Union Lists of Periodicals, 1864–1899.* Chicago: the author, 1899, 8 pp.

50 copies printed.

Also: Kay Printing House.

JOYAUX, GEORGES JULES. "French Press in Michigan: A Bibliography." *Michigan History,* XXXVI (September 1952), 260–278.

KEIDEL, GEORGE C. "Early Maryland Newspapers: A List of Titles." *Maryland Historical Magazine,* XXVIII (June 1933), 119–137; (September 1933), 244–257; (December 1933), 328–344; XXIX (March 1934), 25–34; (June 1934), 132–144; (September 1934), 223–236; (December 1934), 310–332; XXX (June 1935), 149–152.

KELLER, DEAN H. *An Index to The Colophon, New Series; The Colophon, New Graphic Series; and The New Colophon.* Metuchen, New Jersey: The Scarecrow Press, 1968, 139 pp.

KENNERLY, SARAH L. "Confederate Juvenile Imprints: Children's Books and Periodicals Published in the Confederate States of America, 1861–1865." Unpublished doctoral dissertation, Univ. of Michigan, 1957.

LEARY, LEWIS. *Articles on American Literature, 1900–1950.* Durham: Duke Univ. Press, 1954, 335–336.

"Bibliography, Serial."

——————. *Articles on American Literature, 1900–1950.* Durham: Duke Univ. Press, 1954, 386–396.

"Newspapers and Periodicals."

LEE, ALFRED McCLUNG. *The Daily Newspaper in America: The Evolution of a Social Instrument.* New York: Macmillan Co., 1937, 754–765.

LEWIS, BENJAMIN MORGAN.
"A History and Bibliography of
American Magazines, 1800–1810."
Unpublished doctoral dissertation,
Univ. of Michigan, 1956.

LIBRARY OF CONGRESS,
PERIODICAL DIVISION. *Check
List of American Eighteenth Cen-
tury Newspapers in the Library of
Congress,* compiled by John Van
Ness Ingram. Washington, 1912,
186 pp.

Revised edition: 1936, 401 pp.

_____. *A Check List of
American Newspapers in the
Library of Congress.* Washington,
1901, 292 pp.

_____. *Duplicate Periodi-
cals and Serials Available for
Exchange November 1, 1902.*
Washington, 1902, 44 pp.

LIBRARY OF CONGRESS,
PERIODICAL DIVISION. *Want
List of American Eighteenth
Century Newspapers, 1909.*
Washington, 1909, 43 pp.

_____. *Want List of
Periodicals and Serials, Corrected
to September 2, 1902.* Washington,
1902, 102 pp.

Title varies slightly.

Also: 1904, 280 pp.

Also: 1909, 241 pp.

LIBRARY OF CONGRESS,
UNION CATALOG DIVISION.
Newspapers on Microfilm,
6th edition. Washington, 1967,
487 pp.

_____. *Selected List of
United States Newspapers Recommended for Preservation by the*

*ALA Committee on Cooperative
Microfilm Projects.* Washington,
1953, 119 pp.

LINGENFELTER, RICHARD E.
*The Newspaper of Nevada: A
History and Bibliography, 1858–
1958.* San Francisco: John
Howell, 1964, 228 pp.

"Literary Periodicals in the New
York Public Library and the
Columbia University Library."
BNYPL, III (March 1899), 118–
135; (April 1899), 172–186.

LITTLEFIELD, GEORGE
EMERY. *The Early Massa-
chusetts Press, 1638–1711,*
2 Vols. Boston: The Club of
Odd Volumes, 1907.

175 copies printed.

LOWENS, IRVING. "Writings
about Music in the Periodicals
of American Transcendentalism
(1835–50)." *JAMS,* X (Summer
1957), 71–85.

MacCURDY, RAYMOND R.
"A Tentative Bibliography of
the Spanish-Language Press in
Louisiana, 1808–1871." *The
Americans,* X (January 1954),
307–329.

MACMILLAN, ANNABELLE.
"American Journals in the Hu-
manities: A Guide to Scope and
Editorial Policy." *PMLA,*
LXXII (September 1957),
52–65.

MASSACHUSETTS HISTORICAL
SOCIETY. "Continuation of the
Narrative of Newspapers Published
in New England, 1704 to the
Revolution." *Massachusetts
Historical Society Collections,*
VI (1800), 64–77.

_____ . "A Narrative of the Newspapers Printed in New England." *Massachusetts Historical Society Collections,* V (1798), 208–216.

MATTHEWS, ALBERT. "Lists of New England Magazines of the Eighteenth Century." *PCSM,* XIII (January 1910), 69–74.

MICHIGAN CIVIL WAR CENTENNIAL OBSERVANCE COMMISSION. *Michigan in the Civil War: A Guide to the Materials in Detroit Newspapers, 1861–1866.* Lansing: Michigan Civil War Centennial Observance Commission, 1965, 404 pp.

MILLINGTON, YALE O. "A List of Newspapers Published in the District of Columbia, 1820–1850." *PBSA,* XIX (1925), 43–65.

MINOR, KATE PLEASANTS, and SUSIE B. HARRISON, comps. "A List of Newspapers in the Virginia State Library, Confederate Museum and Valentine Museum." *Bulletin of the Virginia State Library,* V (1912), 285–425.

MISSOURI STATE HISTORICAL SOCIETY, LIBRARY. *List of Old Newspapers in the Library of the State Historical Society of Missouri.* Columbia: Missouri State Historical Society Library, 1910, 43 pp.

Reprinted from *Missouri Historical Review,* October 1910.

MOORE, IKE H. "The Earliest Printing and the First Newspaper in Texas." *Southwestern Historical Quarterly,* XXXIX (October 1935), 83–99.

MOTT, FRANK LUTHER. *American Journalism: A History of Newspapers in the United States through 260 Years, 1690–1950.* New York: Macmillan, 1956, bibliographical footnotes.

Also: *American Journalism: A History, 1690–1960,* 3rd edition. 1962.

_____ . *A History of American Magazines,* 5 Vols. Cambridge: Harvard Univ. Press, 1938– .

I: 1741–1850.

II: 1850–1865.

III: 1865–1885.

IV: 1885–1905.

V: 1905–1930.

_____ . "Iowa Magazines— Series 1 and 2." *Palimpest,* XLIV (July 1963), 285–316; (August 1963), 317–380.

_____ . *100 Books on American Journalism.* Columbia: Univ. of Missouri Press, 1949, 15 pp.

NATIONAL RESEARCH BUREAU, INC., DIRECTORY DIVISION. *Blue Book of Magazine Writers,* 3rd edition. Chicago: National Research Bureau, 1960, 145 pp.

NELSON, WILLIAM. *Check-List of the Issues of the Press of New Jersey, 1723, 1728, 1754–1800.* Paterson: Call Printing and Publishing Co., 1899, 42 pp.

NEW YORK HISTORICAL SOCIETY, LIBRARY. *A Catalogue of Illinois Newspapers in the New York Historical Society,* compiled by Thomas O. Mabbott and Philip D. Jordan. Springfield: Illinois State Historical Library, 1931, 58 pp.

Reprinted from *Journal of Illinois State Historical Society*, XXIV (July 1931).

NEW YORK PUBLIC LIBRARY. *Check List of Cumulative Indexes to Individual Periodicals in the New York Public Library*, compiled by Daniel C. Haskell. New York: New York Public Library, 1942, 370 pp.

NORCROSS, GRENVILLE HOWLAND. "Southern Newspapers Printed on Wall Paper." *PMHS*, XLVI (November 1912), 241–243.

PAYNE, GEORGE HENRY. *History of Journalism in the United States.* New York: D. Appleton and Co., 1920, 399–427.

PENCE, JAMES HARRY, comp. *The Magazine and the Drama: An Index.* New York: Dunlap Society, 1896, 190 pp.

From the preface: "A guide to the mass of literature the magazines have published concerning the acted drama and the men and women directly connected with it." 250 copies printed.

PETERSON, THEODORE. *Magazines in the Twentieth Century.* Urbana: Univ. of Illinois Press, 1956, 397–411.

PHILADELPHIA FREE LIBRARY. *A List of Serials in the Principal Libraries of Philadelphia and Its Vicinity.* Philadelphia: Allen, Lane and Scott, 1908, 324 pp.

Supplement: 1910, 88 pp.

POLLARD, A. F. "American Historical Journals." *TLS*, Nov. 16, 1933, 795.

REX, WALLACE HAYDEN, comp. *Colorado Newspapers Bibliography, 1859–1933.* Denver: Bibliographical Center for Research, Rocky Mountain Region, 1939, 69 pp.

RICHARDSON, LYON NORMAN. *A History of Early American Magazines, 1741–1789.* New York: T. Nelson and Sons, 1931, 362–375.

ROWELL, G. P., AND COMPANY. *Rowell's American Newspaper Directory*, 40 Vols. New York: G. P. Rowell and Co., 1869–1908.

RUSK, RALPH L. "Newspapers and Magazines," in *The Literature of the Middle Western Frontier,* 2 Vols. New York: Columbia Univ. Press, I, 131–203; II, 145–184.

ST. LOUIS MERCANTILE LIBRARY ASSOCIATION... *1. Missouri and Illinois Newspapers, 1808–1897, Chronologically Arranged. 2. Manuscripts Relating to Louisiana Territory and Missouri.* St. Louis: St. Louis Mercantile Library Association, 1898, 22 pp.

SCHWEGMANN, GEORGE A., JR. *Newspapers on Microfilm: A Union Check List.* Philadelphia: Office of the Executive Secretary, 1948, 176 pp.

LCN: "Includes all entries of newspapers on microfilm... reported to the National Union Catalog."

SEALOCK, RICHARD BURL, and PAULINE A. SEELEY. *Lists of Newspapers and Periodicals from "Long Island Bibliography."* Washington, 1941?, 71 pp.

Photostat made by Library of Congress.

SEVERANCE, HENRY ORMAL. *A Guide to the Current Periodicals and Serials of the United States and Canada,* 5th edition. Ann Arbor: G. Wahr, 1931, 432 pp.

SHEARER, AUGUSTUS H., et al. "French Newspapers in the United States Before 1800." *PBSA,* XIV (Part 2, 1920), 45–147.

SHELTON, WILMA LOY. "Checklist of New Mexico Publications." *New Mexico Historical Review,* XXIV (April 1949), 130–155; (July 1949), 223–235; (October 1949), 300–331; XXV (January 1950), 57–73; (April 1950), 136–161; (October 1950), 222–241; XXVI (January 1951), 64–67; (April 1951), 137–147; (July 1951), 225–241; (October 1951), 325–331; XXVII (January 1952), 51–63; XXIX (January 1954), 47–70; (April 1954), 124–140.

SMITH, DOROTHY. "Union List of Serials in Maine Libraries." *Univ. of Maine Studies,* 2nd Series, XL (1937), 257 pp.

STEIGER, ERNST. *The Periodical Literature of the United States of America.* New York: Steiger, 1873, 139 pp.

STEPHENS, ETHEL. "American Popular Magazines: A Bibliography." *BB,* IX (January 1916), 7–10; (April 1916), 41–43; (July 1916), 69–70; (October 1916), 95–98.

Also: *Bulletin of Bibliography Pamphlet,* No. 23.

STEWART, GUY HARRY. "History and Bibliography of Middle Tennessee Newspapers, 1799–1876." Unpublished doctoral dissertation, Univ. of Illinois, 1957.

STOCK, LEO FRANCIS. *List of American Periodicals and Serials Publications in the Humanities and Social Sciences.* Washington: Executive Offices, American Council of Learned Societies, 1934, 130 pp.

American Council of Learned Societies Bulletin, No. 21.

STOCKETT, JULIA CARSON. *Masters of American Journalism: A Bibliography.* White Plains and New York: H. W. Wilson Co., 1916, 40 pp.

STOKES, ISSAC NEWTON PHELPS. "Early New York Newspapers," in *The Iconography of Manhattan Island, 1498–1909. . . .,* 6 Vols. New York: R. H. Dodd, 1916, II, 413–452.

SWALLOW, ALAN, et al. *Index to Little Magazines.* Denver: Alan Swallow, 1948–

Annual, 1948–1952, biannual, 1953–1965. Under Stephen H. Goode *Index* covers 1940–1947.

SWINDLER, WILLIAM F. "Graduate Theses in the Field of Journalism, 1936–1945." *JQ,* XXII (September 1945), 231–254.

_____. "Press and Communications: An Annotated Bibliography of Journalism Subjects in American Magazines." *JQ.*

Appeared regularly, XXII–XXVIII, 1945–1951.

TALMADGE, JOHN E. "Savannah's Yankee Newspapers." *GaR,* XII (Spring 1958), 66–73.

THRASH, JAMES R. "New Periodicals of 1962—Part 1." *CRL*, XXIII (September 1962), 410—421.

TINKER, EDWARD LAROCQUE. "Bibliography of the French Newspapers and Periodicals of Louisiana." *PAAS*, XLII (October 1932), 247—370.

TRENT, WILLIAM PETERFIELD, et al. "Colonial Newspapers and Magazines, 1704—1775," in *Cambridge History of American Literature*, 4 Vols. New York: G. P. Putnam's Sons, 1917—1921, I, 111—123, 452—454.

——————. "Later Magazines," in *Cambridge History of American Literature*, 4 Vols. New York: G. P. Putnam's Sons, 1917—1921, IV, 774—779.

——————. "Magazines and Annuals," in *Cambridge History of American Literature*, 4 Vols. New York: G. P. Putnam's Sons, 1917—1921, II, 511—518.

——————. "Newspapers, 1776—1860," in *Cambridge History of American Literature*, 4 Vols. New York: G. P. Putnam's Sons, 1917—1921, II, 518—524.

——————. "Newspapers since 1860," in *Cambridge History of American Literature*, 4 Vols. New York: G. P. Putnam's Sons, 1917—1921, IV, 779—781.

ULRICH, CAROLYN F., and EUGENIA PATTERSON. "Little Magazines (1890—1946)." *BNYPL*, LI (January 1947), 3—25.

WALL, ALEXANDER J. "Early Newspapers, With a List of the New York Historical Society's Collection of Papers Published in California, Oregon, Washington, Montana, and Utah." *NYHSB*, XV (July 1931), 39—66.

WATSON, MELVIN RAY. *Magazine Serials and the Essay Tradition, 1746—1820.* Baton Rouge: Louisiana State Univ. Press, 1956, 107—155.

Louisiana State Univ. Studies, Humanities Series, No. 6.

WICKERSHAM, JAMES. *Alaskan Newspapers and Periodicals: A Preliminary Checklist Prepared for the Use of Hon. James Wickersham, Delegate from Alaska,* by Hugh Morrison. Washington, 1915, 28 pp.

——————, comp. *Bibliography of Literature, 1724—1924: Containing the Titles of Histories, Travels, Voyages, Newspapers, Periodicals, Public Documents. . . . Relating to. . . . Alaska.* Cordova, Alaska: Cordova *Daily Times,* 1927, 662 pp.

WINTHER, OSCAR OSBURN. *A Classified Bibliography of the Periodical Literature of the Trans-Mississippi West (1811— 1957).* Bloomington: Indiana Univ. Press, 1961, 626 pp.

Arranged geographically, with a section of bibliography for each area.

——————. *The Trans-Mississippi West: A Guide to Its Periodical Literature, 1811—1938.* Bloomington: Indiana Univ. Press, 1942, 278 pp.

WISCONSIN STATE HISTORICAL SOCIETY, LIBRARY. *Annotated Catalogue of Newspaper Files in the Library of the State His-*

torical Society of Wisconsin,
compiled by Emma Helen Blair.
Madison: Democrat Printing Co.,
1898, 386 pp.

2nd edition: Wisconsin State
Historical Society, 1911, 591 pp.

Supplement: 1918, 91 pp.

19. PRINTING AND PUBLISHING

The American Book-Circular,
with Notes and Statistics. London
and New York: Wiley and Putnam,
April 1843, 64 pp.

The editor was a German bookseller
in New York. Beyond the prospectus nothing is known of the
circular.

American Book-Prices Current: A
Record of Books, Manuscripts and
Autographs Sold in the Principal
Auction Rooms of the United
States. New York, 1895—

BENNETT, WHITMAN. *A Practical*
Guide to American Book Collect-
ing (1663–1940). . . . New York:
Bennett Book Studios, Inc., 1941,
254 pp.

Publisher varies. Issued annually
and collected into five-year hard-
bound segments.

1,250 copies printed.

Index: New York: E. P. Dutton
and Co., 1925, 1,397 pp. Covers
1916–1922.

BIGMORE, EDWARD CLEMENTS,
and C. W. H. WYMAN. *A Bibliog-*
raphy of Printing with Notes and
Illustrations, 2nd edition, 2 Vols.
New York: P. C. Duschnes, 1945.

ANNMARY BROWN MEMORIAL.
Catalogue of Books Mostly from
the Presses of the First Printers. . . .
Collected by Rush C. Hawkins. . . .
and Deposited in the Annmary
Brown Memorial at Providence,
Rhode Island, compiled by Alfred
William Pollard. Oxford: printed
at the university press at the cost of
Rush C. Hawkins, 1910, 374 pp.

BLAKE, ALEXANDER V., comp.
The American Bookseller's Complete
Reference Trade List, and Alpha-
betical Catalogue of Books Published
in this Country, with the Publish-
ers' and Authors' Names and
Arranged in Classes for Quick and
Convenient Reference, to which
is Added an Article on the Law
of Copyright. Claremont, New
Hampshire: published by Simeon
Ide, 1847, 232 pp.

BATES, ALBERT CARLOS. "The
Work of Hartford's First Printer,"
in *Bibliographical Essays: A Tribute*
to Wilberforce Eames. Cambridge:
Harvard Univ. Press. 1924, 345—
361.

Supplement: Claremont Publishing
Co., 1848, 233–351.

On Thomas Green of the Connecticut
Courant and the *Connecticut*
Journal.

BLANCK, JACOB, ed. *Merle*
Johnson's American First Editions,
4th edition, revised and enlarged.
Waltham, Massachusetts: Mark
Press, 1965, 553 pp.

BEHR, K. VON, ed. *Prospectus*
of an American Book-Circular.
1828.

Some of the material included
appeared serially in *Publishers'*
Weekly.

BLAND, DAVID. *A Bibliography of Book Illustration.* Cambridge: Cambridge Univ. Press, 1955, 16 pp.

The Book Series, No. 4.

BOLTON, THEODORE. *American Book Illustrators: Bibliographic Check Lists of 123 Artists.* New York: R. R. Bowker Co., 1938, 302 pp.

1,000 copies printed.

Book-Auction Records: A Priced and Annotated Record of London Book Auctions. London: H. Stevens, 1902— .

Publishing suspended, July 1903—September 1904.

The Book Buyer: A Monthly Review of American and Foreign Literature. New York: C. Scribner and Co., 1867—1938.

Subtitle varies.

The Book-Buyers' Manual: A Catalogue of Foreign and American Books in Every Branch of Literature, with a classified index. New York: G. P. Putnam, 1852, 235 pp.

Bookman: A Review of Books and Life. New York, 1876—1933.

Publisher varies.

Superseded by *American Review,* 1933—1937.

BOWKER, RICHARD ROGERS. *Copyright: Its Law and Its Literature. . . .,* with a bibliography of literary property by Thorvald Solberg. New York: Publishers' Weekly, 1886, 60 pp.

BOWKER, R. R., COMPANY. *American Booktrade Directory,*
Including Lists of Publishers, Booksellers and Private Book Collectors. New York: R. R. Bowker Co., 1915— .

Title varies: *American Booktrade Manual, 1915—1922; American Booktrade Directory, 1925—* .

Published approximately every three years.

BOYNTON, HENRY WALCOTT. *Annals of American Bookselling, 1638—1850.* New York: J. Wiley and Sons, Inc., 1932, 218 pp.

BRIGHAM, CLARENCE SAUNDERS. "American Booksellers' Catalogues, 1734—18. . ." in *Essays Honoring Lawrence C. Wroth.* Portland, Maine: The Anthoensen Press, 1951, 31—67.

BRISTOL, ROGER PATTRELL. *Index of Printers, Publishers, and Booksellers Indicated by Charles Evans in His American Bibliography.* Charlottesville: Bibliographical Society of the Univ. of Virginia, 1961, 176 pp.

BROWN, HARRY GLENN, and MAUDE O. BROWN, comps. "A Directory of the Book Art and Book Trade in Philadelphia to 1821, Including Printers and Engravers." *BNYPL,* LIII (May 1949), 211—226; (June 1949), 290—298; (July 1949), 339—347; (August 1949), 387—401; (September 1949), 447—458; (October 1949), 492—503; (November 1949), 564—573; (December 1949), 615—622; LIV (January 1950), 25—37; (February 1950), 89—92; (March 1950), 123—145.

——————————, comps. *A Directory of Printing, Publish-*

ing, *Bookselling and Allied Trades in Rhode Island to 1865.* New York: New York Public Library, 1958, 211 pp.

BUTLER, PIERCE, ed. *Librarians, Scholars, and Booksellers at Mid-Century.* Chicago: Univ. of Chicago Press, 1953, bibliographical notes.

CANNONS, HARRY GEORGE TURNER. *Bibliography of Library Economy: A Classified Index to the Professional Periodical Literature Relating to Library Economy, Printing, Methods of Publishing, Copyright, Bibliography, etc.* London: Stanley Russell and Co., 1910, 448 pp.

CASPAR, CARL NICOLAUS. *Caspar's Directory of the American Book, News, and Stationery Trade, Wholesale and Retail. . . .* Milwaukee: C. N. Caspar, 1889, 1,434 pp.

A Catalogue of All the Books Printed in the United States, with the Prices and Places Where Published Annexed. Boston: published by the booksellers in Boston, 1804, 79 pp.

Included in Adolf Growoll's *Booktrade Bibliography in the United States in the Nineteenth Century,* 1898.

CHARVAT, WILLIAM. *Literary Publishing in America, 1790–1850.* Philadelphia: Univ. of Pennsylvania Press, 1959, 94 pp.

CHEEVER, L. O. "The Prairie Press: A Thirty-Year Record." *Books at Iowa,* No. 3 (November 1965), 15–33.

CLARKSON, JOHN W., JR. "Franklin Benjamin Sanborn,

Editor." *PBSA,* LX (1st Quart. 1966), 73–85.

CLEGG, JAMES. "Fictitious Names, Initials, etc., Used by Authors and Book Illustrators," in *The Directory of Second-Hand Booksellers.* Rochdale: J. Clegg, 1891, 157–238.

CLEMENT, SAMFORD C., and JOHN M. HEMPHILL. *Bookbinding in Colonial Virginia.* Williamsburg, Virginia: Colonial Williamsburg, 1966, 185 pp.

COGGESHALL, WILLIAM TURNER. *The Newspaper Record: Containing a Complete List of Newspapers and Periodicals in the United States, Canada, and Great Britain, together with a Sketch of the Origin and Progress of Printing, with Some Facts about Newspapers in Europe and America.* Philadelphia: Lay and Brother, 1856, 208 pp.

COLUMBIA UNIVERSITY, LIBRARY. *Fifty Books about Bookmaking: An Exhibition Prepared by Columbia University Library for the Twelfth Annual Conference on Printing Education, June 26, 27, 28, 1933,* compiled by Hellmut Lehmann-Haupt. New York: Columbia Univ. Press, 1933, 33 pp.

DANIEL, PRICE, JR. *Books Printed and Designed by Jack D. Rittenhouse of the Stagecoach Press: A Bibliography.* Waco, Texas: Stagecoach Press, 1965, 16 pp., unpaginated.

Texas and the West Catalogue, No. 32.

DETWEILER, FREDERICK EGERMAN. *The Negro Press of the United States.* Chicago: Univ. of Chicago Press, 1922, 274 pp.

DIEHL, EDITH. *Bookbinding:
Its Background and Technique,*
2 Vols. New York: Rinehart,
1946, I, 195–219.

DUSCHNES, PHILIP C. *A Com-
plete Catalogue: Thirty-eight
Years of Limited Editions Club
Books, 1929–1967.* New York:
Philip C. Duschnes, 1968, 32 pp.

Includes Series 1–35. Some
60 American titles included.

EAMES, WILBERFORCE. "The
First Year of Printing in New York,
May 1693–April 1694." *BNYPL,*
XXXII (January 1928), 3–24.

ECKERT, ROBERT P., JR.
"A Poet and His Library." *The
Colophon,* Part 15, Series 1, IV
(1933).

The sale of the books of James
Gates Percival by Leonard and
Co., Boston, 1860.

FINCHAM, HENRY WALTER.
*Artists and Engravers of
British and American Book
Plates: A Book of Reference
for Book Plate and Print Col-
lectors.* London: K. Paul,
Trench, Trübner and Co., Ltd.,
1897, 161 pp.

1,050 copies printed.

FREER, PERCY. *Bibliography
and Modern Book Production:
Notes and Sources for Student
Librarians, Printers, Booksellers,
Stationers, Book-collectors,*
foreword by H. R. Raikes. Johan-
nesburg: Witwatersrand Univ.
Press, 1954, 345 pp.

FULLER, GEORGE WASHING-
TON, ed. *A Bibliography of
Bookplate Literature.* Spokane:
Spokane Public Library, 1926,
151 pp.

GINSBERG, LOUIS. *Methodist
Book Prices, 1955–1965: With a
List of Printers, Publishers, Book-
sellers of Methodist-Related
Material Published in America
prior to 1800.* Petersburg,
Virginia: Louis Ginsberg, 1965,
72 pp.

GOFF, FREDERICK R. "The
First Decade of the Federal Act
of Copyright, 1790–1800," in
*Essays Honoring Lawrence C.
Wroth.* Portland, Maine: An-
thoensen Press, 1951, 101–128.

Lists 80 works copyrighted by
Pennsylvania authors, 1790–1794.

GREEN, SAMUEL ABBOTT.
*Ten Facsimile Reproductions
Relating to Old Boston and
Neighborhood.* Boston: J. Wilson
and Son, 1901, 44 pp.

100 copies printed.

GROWOLL, ADOLF. *Book Trade
Bibliography in the United States
in the Nineteenth Century.* New
York: printed for the Dibdin
Club, 1898, 79 pp.

Also: E. B. Hackett, Brick Row
Book Shop, Inc., 1939.

_____. *A Bookseller's
Library and How to Use It.* New
York: Publishers' Weekly, 1891,
76 pp.

HAMILTON, SINCLAIR. *Early
American Book Illustrators and
Wood Engravers, 1670–1870. . .*
Princeton: Princeton Univ.
Library 1958, 312 pp.

HAMMETT, CHARLES EDWARD,
JR. *A Contribution to the Bibliography and Literature of Newport,
Rhode Island: Comprising a List
of Books Published or Printed*

in Newport, with Notes and Additions. Newport: printed for the author by Davis and Pitman, 1887, 185 pp.

200 copies printed.

HARPEL, OSCAR HENRY. *Poets and Poetry of Printerdom: A Collection of Original, Selected and Fugitive Lyrics, Written by Persons Connected with Printing.* Cincinnati: privately printed, 1875, bibliographical notes.

HARRISSE, HENRY. *Introducción de la imprenta en América, con una bibliografía de las obras impresas en aquel hemisfero desde a 1600.* Madrid: Rivadeneyra, 1872, 59 pp.

HEARTMAN, CHARLES FREDERICK. *Checklist of Printers in the United States from Stephen Day to the Close of the War for Independence.* New York: Heartman, 1915, 11–53.

1,060 copies printed.

HEWLETT, LEROY. "James Rivington, Loyalist Printer, Publisher, and Bookseller of the American Revolution, 1724–1802: A Biographical-Bibliographical Study." Unpublished doctoral dissertation, Univ. of Michigan, 1958.

HILDEBURN, CHARLES SWIFT RICHE. *A Century of Printing: The Issues of the Press of Pennsylvania, 1685–1784,* 2 Vols. Philadelphia: press of Matlack and Harvey, 1885–1886.

Includes 4,700 titles, index of authors, chronological list of printers.

——————. *A List of the Press in New York, 1693–1752.* Philadelphia: J. B. Lippincott Co., 1889, 28 pp.

HILL, FRANK PIERCE, and VARNUM LANSING COLLINS. *Books, Pamphlets, and Newspapers Printed at Newark, New Jersey, 1776–1900.* Newark: private press of the *Courier-Citizen* Co., 1902, 296 pp.

HOLT, HENRY. *Garrulities of an Octogenarian Editor.* Boston: Henry Holt, 1923, 460 pp.

JENKS, W. L. "Calendar of Michigan Copyrights." *Michigan Historical Magazine,* XIV (Spring 1930), 150–155; (Winter 1930), 311–313; XV (Winter 1931), 126–129.

JILLSON, WILLARD ROUSE. *The First Printing in Kentucky: Some Account of Thomas Parvin and John Bradford and the Establishment of the Kentucky Gazette in Lexington in the Year 1787,* with a bibliography of 70 titles. Louisville: C. T. Dearing Printing Co., 1936, 41–54.

KASER, DAVID, ed. *The Cost Books of Carey and Lea, 1825–1938.* Philadelphia: Univ. of Pennsylvania Press, 1963, 355 pp.

KELLER, HELEN REX, ed. *The Reader's Digest of Books.* New York: Macmillan, 1948, 947 pp.

KUBLER, GEORGE ADOLF. *Historical Treatises, Abstracts, and Papers on Stereotyping.* New York: J. J. Little and Ives Co., 1936, 169 pp.

LAWLER, THOMAS BONAVENTURE. *Seventy Years of*

Textbook Publishing, 1867–1937.
Boston: Ginn and Co., 1938, 304 pp.

LEARY, LEWIS. *Articles on
American Literature, 1900–1950.*
Durham: Duke Univ. Press,
1954, 405–412.

"Printing."

LEHMANN-HAUPT, HELLMUT,
HANNAH DUSTIN FRENCH and
JOSEPH W. ROGERS. *Bookbinding
in America: Three Essays.* Portland,
Maine: Southworth-Anthoensen
Press, 1941, 312 pp.

LEHMANN-HAUPT, HELLMUT,
LAWRENCE C. WROTH and
ROLLO G. SILVER. *The Book
In America: A History of the
Making and Selling of Books in the
United States,* 2nd edition. New
York: Bowker, 1951, 507 pp.

*The Literary World: A Gazette
for Authors, Readers, and Publishers,* 13 Vols. New York:
Osgood and Co., 1847–1853.

LITTLEFIELD, GEORGE
EMERY. *Early Boston Booksellers, 1642–1711.* Boston: The
Club of Odd Volumes, 1900,
256 pp.

150 copies printed.

LIVINGSTON, L. S. "Two
Little-Known First Editions of
American Authors." *Bibliographer,*
I (1902), 455–459; II (1903),
127–128.

LOVE, WILLIAM DE LOSS.
*Thomas Short: The First Printer
of Connecticut.* Hartford, Connecticut: Case, Lockwood and
Brainard, 1901, 48 pp.

102 copies printed.

LOW, SAMPSON, SON AND
COMPANY. *The American Catalogue of Books: or, English Guide
to American Literature, Giving
the Full Title of Original Works
Published in the United States
since the Year 1800, with
Especial Reference to Books of
Interest to Great Britain.* London:
Sampson Low, Son and Co., 1856,
190 pp.

MacDONALD, ALLAN HOUSTON.
Richard Hovey: Man and Craftsman.
Durham: Duke Univ. Press, 1957,
229–250.

MARTIN, CHARLOTTE M., and
BENJAMIN ELLIS MARTIN.
*The New York Press and Its
Makers in the Eighteenth Century.*
New York: Putnam, 1898, 119–
162.

MASSE, GERTRUDE C. E.
*A Bibliography of First Editions
of Books Illustrated by Walter
Crane.* London: Chelsea Publishing
Co., 1923, 60 pp.

McCORISON, MARCUS ALLEN.
"A Bibliography of Vermont
Bibliography and Printing." *PBSA,*
LV (1st Quart. 1961), 17–33.

McDONALD, GERALD D.
"William Bradford's Book Trade
and John Browne, Long Island
Quaker, as His Book Agent, 1686–
1891," in *Essays Honoring Lawrence
C. Wroth.* Portland, Maine:
Anthoensen Press, 1951, 209–222.

McKAY, GEORGE LESLIE.
*American Book Auction Catalogues,
1713–1934.* New York: New York
Public Library, 1937, 572 pp.

Additions: *BNYPL,* L (1946),
177–184; LII (1948), 401–412.

——————, comp. "A Register
of Artists, Booksellers, Printers

and Publishers in New York City, 1811–1820." *BNYPL,* XLIV (April 1940), 351–357; (May 1940), 415–428; (June 1940), 475–487; XLV (June 1941), 483–489.

McMURTRIE, DOUGLAS CRAWFORD. *A History of Printing in the United States: The Story of the Introduction of the Press and of Its History and Influence during the Pioneer Period in Each State of the Union,* 4 Vols. New York: R. R. Bowker Co., 1936.

Bibliography at end of each volume.

McMURTRIE, DOUGLAS CRAWFORD, and ALBERT H. ALLEN. *Jotham Meeker: Pioneer Printer of Kansas,* with a bibliography of the known issues of the Baptist Mission Press at Shawanoe, Stockbridge and Ottawa, 1834–1854. Chicago: Eyncourt Press, 1930, 129–134.

MILLER, BERTHA E. (MAHONEY), LOUISE PAYSON LATIMER and BEULAH FOLMSBEE, comps. *Illustrators of Children's Books, 1744–1945.* Boston: Horn Book, 1947, 543 pp.

Supplement: 1958, 299 pp. Covers 1946–1956.

MILLER, LEON STUART. *American First Editions: Their Points and Price.* Kansas City, Missouri: Westport Press, 1933, 98 pp.

MOORE, IKE H. "The Earliest Printing and the First Newspaper in Texas." *Southwestern Historical Quarterly,* XXXIX (October 1935), 83–99.

MUMBY, FRANK ARTHUR. *Publishing and Bookselling: A His-*

tory from the Earliest Times to the Present Day, with a bibliography by W. H. Peet. London: J. Cape, 1930, 419–459.

Also: 1934, 419–462.

Published also as *The Romance of Book Selling.* Chapman and Hall, Ltd., 1910, 490 pp.

MUNSELL, CHARLES, comp. *A Collection of Songs of the American Press, and Other Poems Relating to the Art of Printing.* Albany: n.p., 1868, 206 pp.

MUNSELL, JOEL. *Catalogue of a Bibliographical Library, Offered for Sale Complete, at the Prices Affixed.* Albany: J. Munsell, 1856, 38 pp.

——————. *Catalogue of Books on Printing and the Kindred Arts, Embracing Also Works on Copyright, Liberty of the Press, Libel, Literary Property, Bibliography, etc.* Albany: J. Munsell, 1868, 47 pp.

——————. *A Chronology of Paper and Paper-Making.* Albany: J. Munsell, 1856, 58 pp.

Second edition: 1857, 110 pp.

Third edition: 1864, 174 pp.

Fourth edition: 1870, 226 pp.

Fifth edition: 1876, 263 pp.

MURRELL, WILLIAM. *A History of American Graphic Humor,* 2 Vols. New York: published for Whitney Museum of American Art by Macmillan Co., 1933–1938, I, 241–242; II, 265–267.

NEWBERRY LIBRARY (CHICAGO). *Book Arts, Bibliography,*

Printing, Bookbinding, Publishing and Bookselling: National and Local Bibliography, 2 Vols. Chicago: Newberry Library, 1919–1920.

NICHOLS, CHARLES LEMUEL. *Bibliography of Worcester: A List of Books, Pamphlets, Newspapers, and Broadsides Printed in the Town of Worcester, Mass., from 1775 to 1848, with Historical and Explanatory Notes.* Worcester: privately printed at the press of Franklin P. Rice, 1899, 216 pp.

_____. *Isaiah Thomas: Printer, Writer, and Collector,* a paper read Apr. 12, 1911, before the Club of Odd Volumes, with a bibliography of the books printed by Isaiah Thomas. Boston: printed for the Club of Odd Volumes, 1912, 37–144.

NICHOLSON, JAMES B. *A Manual of the Art of Bookbinding: Containing Full Instructions in the Different Branches of Forwarding, Gilding, and Finishing; Also the Art of Marbling Bookedges and Paper, the Whole Designed for the Practical Workman, the Amateur, and the Book-collector.* Philadelphia: H. C. Baird, 1856, 318 pp.

Norton's Literary Gazette and Publishers' Calendar, I–III, May 1851–December 1853; ns I–II, January 1854–August 1855. New York: C. B. Norton, 1851–1855.

Superseded by *American Publishers' Circular and Literary Gazette,* later entitled *American Literary Gazette and Publishers' Circular,* 1855–1872.

Norton's Literary Letter: Comprising American Papers of Interest, and a Catalogue of Rare and Valuable Books Relative to America, Nos. 1–4, 1857–1860; ns Nos. 1–2, 1860. New York: C. B. Norton, 1857–1860.

Norton's Literary Register. . ., I–IV. New York: C. B. Norton, 1852–1856.

1852: *Norton's Literary Almanac.*

1853: *Norton's Literary Register and Book Buyer's Almanac.*

1854: *Norton's Literary and Educational Register.*

1855: not published.

1856: *Norton's Literary Register; or Annual Book List.*

O'NEAL, WILLIAM B. *Charles Smith, His Work in Book Design: A Checklist.* Charlottesville, Virginia: The Cockescraw Press, 1963, 13 pp.

OSWALD, JOHN CLYDE. *A History of Printing: Its Development through Five Hundred Years.* New York: D. Appleton and Co., 1928, 389–391.

_____. *Printing in the Americas.* New York: Gregg Publishing Co., 1937, 565 pp.

PERRIN, WILLIAM HENRY. *The Pioneer Press of Kentucky: From the Printing of the First Paper West of the Alleghenies, August 11, 1787, to the Establishment of the Daily Press in 1830. . .* Louisville: John P. Morton and Co., 1888, 93 pp.

PITZ, HENRY CLARENCE. *Illustrating Children's Books: History, Technique, Production.* New York: Watson-Guptill Publications, 1963, 207 pp.

—————. *A Treasury of American Book Illustrations.* New York: American Studio Books and Watson-Guptill Publications, Inc., 1947, 128 pp.

POWELL, WILLIAM S. "Patrons of the Press: Subscription Book Purchases in North Carolina, 1733–1850," *NCHR,* XXXIX (October 1962), 423–499.

PRATT, JOHN BARNES. *A Century of Book Publishing.* New York: A. S. Barnes and Co., 1938, 43–56.

Publishers' Trade List Annual. New York: R. R. Bowker Co., 1873– .

Books In Print is the index to *Publishers' Trade List Annual.*

Quarterly Bibliography of Books Reviewed in Leading Periodicals, 3 Vols. Bloomington, Indiana: Index Publishing Co., 1901–1903.

1902 volume entitled *Bibliography of Books Reviewed in Leading American Periodicals.*

The Reader's Adviser and Bookman's Annual. New York: R. R. Bowker, 1921– .

REICHMAN, FELIX. "German Printing in Maryland: A Check List, 1768–1950." *Society for the History of Germans in Maryland,* XXVII (1950), 9–70.

RICCI, SEYMOUR DE. *The Book Collector's Guide: A Practical Handbook of British and American Bibliography.* Philadelphia: Rosenbach Co., 1921, 667 pp.

Bibliography, xv–xviii. Locates copies of rare books and collec-

tions. 1,100 numbered copies printed.

RICH, OBADIAH, AND SONS. *Rich and Sons' Catalogue for 1848, Containing Near Two Thousand Books, Relating Principally to America, Now on Sale at No. 12, Red Lion Square, London.* London: printed by W. Bowden, 1848, 127 pp.

Issued as Part 1, but no further parts published.

ROGERS, JOSEPH WILLIAM. *U. S. National Bibliography and the Copyright Law: An Historical Study.* New York: Bowker, 1960, 97–107.

RUGG, HAROLD G. "Printing in Peacham, Vermont: A Bibliography." *Proceedings of the Vermont Historical Society,* XII (April 1944), 125–128.

RUTHERFORD, LIVINGSTON. *John Peter Zenger: His Press, His Trial, and a Bibliography of Zenger Imprints, with a Reprint of the First Edition of the Trial.* New York; 1904. New York: Dodd, 1904, no pagination.

Bibliography of issues of Zenger Press, 113–169; bibliography of Zenger trial, 247–255; list of issues of *New York Weekly Journal,* 257–267.

SCHAPER, JOSEPH. "A Question of 'Firsts' Again." *WMH,* XVI (September 1932), 102–104.

SCHICK, FRANK LEOPOLD. *The Paperbound Book in America: The History of Paperbacks and Their European Background.* New York: R. R. Bowker and Co., 1958, bibliographical notes.

SEINDENSTICKER, OSWALD. *The First Century of German Printing in America, 1728–1830, Preceded by a Notice of the Literary Work of F. D. Pastorius.* Philadelphia: published by the German Pioneer-Verein of Philadelphia, 1893, 263 pp.

SHERA, JESSE H. "The Beginnings of Systematic Bibliography in America, 1647–1799," in *Essays Honoring Lawrence C. Wroth.* Portland, Maine: Anthoensen Press, 1951, 263–278.

SHOVE, RAYMOND HOWARD. *Cheap Book Production in the United States, 1870–1891.* Urbana: Univ. of Illinois Press, 1937, 131–135.

SILVER, ROLLO G. "The Boston Book Trade, 1770–1799," in *Essays Honoring Lawrence C. Wroth.* Portland, Maine: Anthoensen Press, 1951, 279–303.

An annotated list of book sellers.

SPOFFORD, AINSWORTH RAND. *The Copyright System of the United States: Its Origin and Growth.* Washington: press of Gedney and Roberts Co., 1892, 160 pp.

STARKEY, LAWRENCE G. "A Descriptive and Analytical Bibliography of the Cambridge, Massachusetts, Press from Its Beginnings to the Publication of Eliot's Indian Bible in 1663." Unpublished doctoral dissertation, Univ. of Virginia, 1949.

STEIGER, ERNST. *Specimen of an Attempt at a Catalogue of Original American Books, with Index of Subject-Matter.* New York: E. Steiger, 1873, 17 pp.

STONE, HERBERT STUART. *First Editions of American Authors: A Manual for Booklovers,* with an introduction by Eugene Field. Cambridge: Stone and Kimball, 1893, 247 pp.

SUTTON, WALTER. *The Western Book Trade: Cincinnati as a Nineteenth Century Publishing and Book Trade Center.* Columbus: Ohio State Univ. Press for the Ohio Historical Society, 1961, 360 pp.

TANSELLE, G. THOMAS. "The Historiography of American Literary Publishing." *SB,* XVIII (1965), 3–39.

TAYLOR, ARCHER. *Book Catalogues: Their Varieties and Uses.* Chicago: Newberry Library, 1957, 284 pp.

List of early private library catalogs, 223–270.

THOMAS, ISAIAH. *The History of Printing in America: With a Biography of Printers and an Account of Newspapers, to which is Prefixed a Concise view of the Discovery and Progress of the Art in other Parts of the World,* 2 Vols. Worcester, Massachusetts: from the press of Isaiah Thomas, Isaac Sturtevant, printer, 1810.

TRENT, WILLIAM PETERFIELD, et al. "Book Publishers and Publishing," in *Cambridge History of American Literature,* 4 Vols. New York: G. P. Putnam's Sons, 1917–1921, IV, 806–810.

TRYON, WARREN STENSON. *Parnassus Corner: A Life of James T. Fields, Publisher to the Victorians.* Boston: Houghton Mifflin Co., 1963, 413–431.

TURNER, MARY C. *The Book-man's Glossary,* 4th edition. New York: R. R. Bowker Co., 1961, 212 pp.

WATKINS, GEORGE THOMAS, comp. *Bibliography of Printing in America: Books, Pamphlets, and Some Articles in Magazines Relating to the History of Printing in the New World.* Boston: published by the compiler, 1906, 31 pp.

300 copies printed.

WEEKS, STEPHEN BEAURE-GARD. *The Press of North Carolina in the Eighteenth Century.* Brooklyn: Historical Printing Club, 1891, 53–80.

250 copies printed.

WEITENKAMPF, FRANK. *American Graphic Art,* 2nd edition. New York: H. Holt and Co., 1924, 291–298.

WEST, CLARENCE JAY. *Bibliography of Paper Making and United States Patents on Paper Making and Related Subjects, 1931.* New York: Technical Association of

the Pulp and Paper Industry, 1932, 175 pp.

LCN: "Previously issued annually in the Society's Technical Association Papers and in the Paper Trade Journal."

WHEELER, JOSEPH TOWNE. *The Maryland Press, 1777–1790.* Baltimore: Maryland Historical Society, 1938, 226 pp.

WHITLOCK, WILLIAM FRANCIS. *The Story of Book Concerns.* Cincinnati: Jennings and Pye, 1903, 204 pp.

WINSHIP, GEORGE PARKER. "The Literature of the History of Printing in the United States: A Survey." *Library,* 4th Series, III (1922–1923), 288–303.

WROTH, LAWRENCE COUNSEL-MAN. *The Colonial Printer.* New York: The Grolier Club, 1931, 271 pp.

—————— . *Williams Parks: Printer and Journalist of England and Colonial America, with a List of the Issues of His Several Presses. . . .* Richmond: Appeals Press, 1926, 70 pp.

20. BOOK COLLECTIONS, AMERICANA

ALABAMA, UNIVERSITY, LIBRARY. *A Bibliography of Louisiana Books and Pamphlets in the T. P. Thompson Collection of the University of Alabama Library.* University: Univ. of Alabama Press, 1947, 210 pp.

ALOFSEN, SOLOMON. *Catalogue of a Portion of the Library Formed by the Late Mr. S. Alofsen of Jersey City . . . .* New York: n.p., 1877, 130 pp.

The greater part of this collection was sold in Utrecht, 1876.

ANDERSON, JOHN, JR. *Catalogue of the Late Frank R. Burbank's Collection of Books, Autographs, and Playbills (mainly relating to the drama).* New York: John Anderson Jr., 1902, 78 pp.

ANNMARY BROWN MEMORIAL. *Catalogue of Books Mostly from the Presses of the First Printers . . . Col-*

lected by Rush C. Hawkins ... and Deposited in the Annuary Brown Memorial at Providence, Rhode Island, compiled by Alfred William Pollard. Oxford: printed at the Univ. Press at the cost of Rush C. Hawkins, 1910, 374 pp.

AUERBACH, HERBERT S. Western Americana: Books, Newspapers, and Pamphlets, Many Relating to the Mormon Church from the Collection of Herbert S. Auerbach, 2 Parts. New York: Parke-Bernet Galleries, Inc., 1947–1948.

BAGINSKY, PAUL BEN, comp. German Works Relating to America, 1493–1800: A List Complied from the Collections of the New York Public Library. New York: New York Public Library, 1942, 232 pp.

BARLOW, ROBERT. "Yale and the American Musical Theater." YULG, XXVIII (April 1954), 144–149.

BARRETT, CLIFTON WALLER. "Contemporary Collectors X: The Barrett Collection." BC, V (1956), 218–230.

_____. "Some Bibliographical Adventures in Americana." PBSA, XLIV (1st Quart. 1950), 17–28.

"The Beadle Collection of Dime Novels." BNYPL, XXVI (January 1922), 555–628.

"Becks Collection of Prompt Books in the New York Public Library." BNYPL, X (February 1906), 100–148.

BIBLIOGRAPHICAL SOCIETY OF AMERICA. Census of Fifteenth Century Books Owned in America. New York: Bibliographical Society of America, 1919, 269 pp.

Bibliothèque Américaine: Collection d'un Amateur. . . . Paris: Tross, 1873, 124 pp.

BIEBER, ALBERT ALOYSIUS. The Albert Bieber Collection of American Plays, Poetry and Songsters . . . . New York: Cooper Square Publishers, 1963, 103 pp.

BONTEMPS, ARNA. "The James Weldon Johnson Memorial Collection of Negro Arts and Letters." YULG, XVIII (October 1943), 19–26.

_____. "Special Collections of Negroana." LQ, XIV (July 1944), 187–206.

BOSTON PUBLIC LIBRARY. A Catalogue of the Allen A. Brown Collection of Books Relating to the State in the Public Library of the City of Boston. Boston: Boston Public Library, 1919, 952 pp.

_____. Catalogue of a Collection of Early New England Books Made by the Late John Allen Lewis and Now in the Possession of the Boston Public Library. Boston: the trustees of the Boston Public Library, 1892, 31 pp.

_____. Ships and Sea: A Catalog of an Exhibition of Books and Manuscripts in Tribute to Boston's Maritime Past, July 1–September 1966, in the Boston Public Library. Boston: Boston Public Library, 1966, 58 pages, unpaginated.

BRADLEY, VAN ALLEN. The New Gold in Your Attic, 2nd edition. New York: Fleet Press Corp., 1958, 100–280.

BRETT, OLIVER. "The Rare Books of Living Authors." Life and Letters, September 1, 1928, pp. 305–311.

BRIGHAM, CLARENCE
SAUNDERS. *Fifty Years of
Collecting Americana for the Library
of the American Antiquarian Society,
1908–1958.* Worcester, Massachusetts: American Antiquarian Society,
1958, 185 pp.

BRINLEY, GEORGE. *Catalogue of
the American Library of the Late
George Brinley, of Hartford, Connecticut,* 5 Vols. Hartford: press of
the Case, Lockwood and Brainard
Co., 1878–1893.

Auction catalog of extensive collection of early American books. Fletcher's Index, list of prices, V. Special
edition published 1878–1897; I
dated 1878–1897; II–V 1880–1893.
First issued as sale catalog, 1878–
1893.

BROOKS, JEROME E. "The Library
Relating to Tobacco, Collected by
George Arents." *BNYPL,* LXVIII
(January 1944), 3–15.

BROWN UNIVERSITY, JOHN
CARTER BROWN LIBRARY.
*Bibliotheca Americana: Catalogue of
the John Carter Brown Library in
Brown University, Providence, Rhode
Island,* 3 Vols. Providence: John
Carter Brown Library, 1919–1931.

3rd edition: 1961.

BROWN UNIVERSITY, LIBRARY.
*The Anthony Memorial: A Catalogue
of the [C. Fiske] Harris Collection of
American Poetry,* with biographical
and bibliographical notes by J.C.
Stockbridge. Providence, Rhode
Island: Providence Press Co., printers,
1886, 820 pp.

——————. *Colonial Poets,
1609–1760: A Selection from the
Harris Collection of American Poetry
and Plays,* with an introduction by
S. Foster Damon. Providence: friends

of the Library of Brown Univ., 1947,
32 pp.

BUSHNELL, CHARLES IRA. *Catalogue of the Library of Charles I.
Bushnell, Esq.: Comprising His Extensive Collections of Rare and
Curious Americana of Engravings,
Autographs, Historical Relics, Woodblocks Engraved by Dr. Anderson,*
compiled by Alexander Denham.
New York, 1883, 283 pp.

Sold at auction by Messrs. Bangs and
Co.

CHURCH, ELIHU DWIGHT. *A Catalogue of Books Relating to the Discovery and Early History of North
and South America, Forming a Part
of the Library of E. D. Church,* compiled and annotated by George Watson Cole, 5 Vols. New York: Dodd,
Mead and Co., 1907.

Also: Cambridge: Harvard Univ. Press.

150 copies printed.

Also: P. Smith, 1951.

CLARKE, ROBERT, AND COMPA-
NY. *Bibliotheca Americana: Cata-
logue of a Valuable Collection of
Books and Pamphlets Relating to
America.* Cincinnati: Robert Clarke
and Co., 1875, 180 pp.

Also: 1876, 303 pp.

Also: 1878, 326 pp.

Supplement: 1879, 92 pp.

Also: 1883, 308 pp.

Also: 1886, 331 pp.

Supplement: 1887, 56 pp.

Also: 1893, 346 pp.

CLEMENTS, WILLIAM L. *The William L. Clements Library of Americana at the University of Michigan.* Ann Arbor: Univ. of Michigan Press, 1923, 328 pp.

COOKE, JOSEPH JESSE. *Catalogue of the Library of the Late Joseph J. Cooke of Providence, Rhode Island,* 3 Vols. New York: G. A. Leavitt and Co., 1883.

Americana, III.

DEBRETT, J., et al. *Bibliotheca Americana: or, A Chronological Catalogue of the Most Curious and Interesting Books, Pamphlets, and State Papers, etc., upon the Subject of North and South America, from the Earliest Period to the Present, in Print, and in Manuscript, for which Research Has Been Made in the British Museum.* London: printed for J. Debrett et al., 1789, 271 pp.

Work ascribed to Debrett and others.

DRAKE, SAMUEL G. *Catalogue of the Private Library of Samuel G. Drake of Boston: Chiefly Relating to the Antiquities, History, and Biography of America, and in an Especial Manner to the Indians, Collected and Used by Him in Preparing His Works upon the Aborigines of America.* Boston: S. G. Drake, 1845, 80 pp.

EAMES, WILBERFORCE, comp. *Americana Collection of Herschel V. Jones: A Check-List, 1473–1926.* New York: privately printed by William E. Rudge's Sons, 1938, 181 pp.

FARNHAM, LUTHER. *A Glance at Private Libraries.* Boston: press of Crocker and Brewster, 1855, 79 pp.

FORD, WORTHINGTON CHAUNCEY. "The Isaiah Thomas Collection of Ballads." *PAAS,* ns XXXIII (April 1923), 34–112.

FORMAN, HARRY BUXTON. *The Library of the Late H. Buxton Forman . . . Anderson Galleries.* New York: n.p., 1920.

Two volumes in one. Autction catalog of more than 3,500 items. Part 3 priced in pencil.

FREEDLEY, GEORGE. "The 26 Principal Theatre Collections in American Libraries and Museums." *BNYPL,* LXII (July 1958), 319–329.

GARLOCH, LORENA A. "The Hervey Allen Collection." *Pennsylvania Library Association Bulletin,* XIII (Winter 1958), 1–3.

GILDER, ROSAMOND, and GEORGE FREEDLEY. *Theatre Collections in Libraries and Museums: An International Handbook.* New York: Theatre Arts, Inc., 1936, 182 pp.

GILHOFER AND RANSCHBURG. *Catalogue No. 200: Fine Books from the Library of a Friend of A. Durer . . . Incunabula American, French XVIII Century Books, Early MSS, etc.* Vienna: Gilholfer and Ranschburg, 1928, 115 pp.

GORDAN, JOHN D. "First Fruits, an Exhibition of First Editions of First Books by American Authors in the Henry W. and Albert A. Berg Collection." *BNYPL,* LV (December 1951), 581–603.

—————. "New in the Berg Collection: 1952–1958." *BNYPL,* LXI (June 1957), 303–311; (July 1957), 353–363.

GRATTAN, C. HARTLEY. "An American Bookshelf." *PW,* CXXXIV (September 2, 1933), 655–662.

GRIFFIN, APPLETON PRENTISS CLARK. *Index of Articles upon American Local History in the Historical Collections in the Boston Public Library.* Boston: printed by order of the trustees Boston Public Library, 1889, 225 pp.

Boston Public Library Bibliographies of Special Subjects, No. 3.

GROLIER CLUB (NEW YORK). *Catalogue of an Exhibit of Historical and Literary Americana, from the Collections of Thomas W. Streeter and C. Waller Barrett* . . . . New York: the Grolier Club, 1960, 47 pp.

_____. *A Description of the Early Printed Books Owned by the Grolier Club.* New York: printed for the Grolier Club, 1895, 78 pp.

403 copies printed.

_____. *One Hundred Influential American Books Printed before 1900: Catalogue of an Exhibition at the Grolier Club, April 18 – June 16, 1946.* New York: the Grolier Club, 1947, 139 pp.

GROWOLL, ADOLF. *American Book Clubs: Their Beginnings and History, and a Bibliography of Their Publications.* New York: Dodd, Mead and Co., 1897, 423 pp.

GUILD, CHESTER. *Catalogue of the Private Library of Chester Guild, Esq., of Boston* . . . *to Be Sold by Auction* . . . *Feb. 24 and 25, 1881* . . . *Sullivan Brothers & Libbie, Auctioneers.* Boston: W. F. Brown and Co., 1881, 57 pp.

677 entries.

HARPER, FRANCIS P. *Bibliotheca Americana: Priced Catalogue of a Remarkable Collection of Scarce and Out-of-print Books* . . . . New York: Francis P. Harper, 1901, 168 pp.

Also: 1905, 257 pp.

HARPER, LATHROP C. *Priced Catalogue of a Remarkable Collection of Scarce and Out-of-print Books Relating to the Discovery, Settlement, and History of the Western Hemisphere* . . . . New York: Harper, 1914, 219 pp.

HARRIS, CALEB FISKE. *Index to American Poetry and Plays in the Collection of C. Fiske Harris.* Providence: printed for private distribution by Hammond, Angell and Co., 1874, 171 pp.

HEANLEY, HOWELL J. "The Americana Collection of William M. Elkins: A Checklist, 1493–1869." *PBSA,* L (2nd Quart. 1956), 129–168.

HEARD, JOSEPH NORMAN. *Bookman's Guide to Americana,* 2 Vols. Washington: Scarecrow Press, 1953–1956.

3rd edition: New York, 1964, 424 pp.

4th edition: Metuchen, New Jersey, 1967, 394 pp.

HENRY, EDWARD A. "The Durrett Collection, Now in the Library of the University of Chicago: I. Its Newspapers." *PBSA,* VIII (1914), 57–94.

HOLLIDAY, WILLIAM J. *Western Americana, Many of Great Rarity: The Distinguished Collection Formed by William J. Holliday* . . . *Sold by His order, April 20–22, 1954.* New York: Parke-Bernet Galleries, 1954, 266 pp.

HOWES, WRIGHT. *U.S.-iana (1650–1950).* New York: R. R. Bowker, 1963, II, 620 items.

HUNTINGTON, HENRY EDWARD S. *Catalogue of Rare American from the Library of Mr. Henry E. Hunting-*

ton: to Be Sold . . . December 11,
1917. New York: D. Taylor and Co.,
1917, 204 pp.

IRWIN, THEODORE. *Catalogue of
the Library and a Brief List of the
Engravings and Etchings Belonging
to Theodore Irwin, Oswego, New
York.* New York: privately printed
by the press of J. J. Little and Co.,
1887, 534 pp.

100 copies printed.

JONES, HERSCHEL VESPASIAN.
*Adventures in Americana, 1492–
1897: Being a Selection of Books
from the Library of Herschel V.
Jones, Minneapolis, Minnesota,* 2
Vols. New York: W. E. Ridge, 1928.

"The Koopman Collection." *BBr,*
XVIII (March 1958), 133–134.

On books and manuscripts given to
Brown Univ.

LEARY, LEWIS. "Knickerbocker
Literature in the Benjamin Collections." *CLC,* IX (February 1960),
22–27.

LEMON, ROBERT, ed. *Catalogue
of a Collection of Printed Broadsides
in the Possession of the Society of
Antiquaries of London.* London:
published by the Society of Antiquaries of London, 1866, no
pagination.

LIBRARY OF CONGRESS. *The
Rosenwald Collection: A Catalogue
of Illustrated Books and Manuscripts,
of Books from Celebrated Presses,
and of Bindings, and Maps, 1150–
1950.* Washington, 1954, 292 pp.

LOHF, KENNETH A., comp. *The
Collection of the Books, Manuscripts,
and Autograph Letters in the Library
of Jean and Donald Stralem.* New
York: n.p., 1962, 55 pp.

MAGGS BROTHERS (LONDON).
Bibliotheca Americana, 9 Parts.
London: Maggs Bros., Ltd., 1922–
1930.

Maggs Bros. catalog Nos. 429, 432,
442, 465, 479, 496, 502, 546, 549.

_____ . *United States of
America,* London: Maggs Bros., Ltd.,
1956, 56 pp.

Maggs Bros. catalog No. 838.

_____ . *United States of
America: A Selection of Two Hundred and Sixty Books, with 11 Illustrations.* London: Maggs Bros., Ltd.,
1936, 63 pp.

Maggs Bros. catalog No. 625.

MONTGOMERY, CHARLES ALEX-
ANDER. *A Selection of First Edi-
tions of over 150 Representative
American Authors.* New York:
D. Taylor and Co., 1895, 106 pp.

MORRISON, HUGH ALEXANDER,
ed. *The Leiter Library: A Catalogue
of the Books, Manuscripts, and Maps
Relating Principally to America Collected by the Late Levi Ziegler Leiter.*
Washington: privately printed, 1907,
533 pp.

MUGRIDGE, DONALD. "Recent
Americana." *LCQJ,* I (July–September), 42–44.

MULLER, FREDERIK AND
COMPANY. *Catalogue of Books
Relating to America . . . .* Amsterdam:
F. Muller, 1850, 104 pp.

MUMEY, NOLIE. *A Study of Rare
Books, with Special Reference to
Colophons, Press Devices, and Title
Pages of Interest to the Bibliophile
and the Student of Literature.*
Denver: Clason Publishing Co., 1930,
553–560.

MUNSELL, JOEL. *Catalogue of Books from the Library of Joel Munsell of Albany* . . . . New York, 1879, 43 pp.

Sold at auction by Messrs. Geo. A. Leavitt and Co.

_____. *Catalogue of a Library of Rare Books and Pamphlets, Chiefly American and Especially Rich in Local History and Genealogy.* Boston: 1879, 87 pp.

Sold at auction by Charles F. Libbie.

_____. *A List of Historical, Genealogical and Miscellaneous Books.* Albany: J. Munsell, 1871, 16 pp.

_____. *Valuable Private Library: Catalogue of a . . . Collection of Books Principally Relating to America. Comprising a Portion of the Private Library of Joel Munsell.* New York, 1865, 123 pp.

Sold at auction by J. E. Cooley, George A. Leavitt, auctioneer.

MURPHY, HENRY CRUSE. *Catalogue of the Magnificent Library of the Late Hon. Henry C. Murphy . . . Consisting Almost Wholly of Americana or Books Relating to America.* New York: G. A. Leavitt and Co., 1884, 434 pp.

Supplement: 1884, 16 pp.

MURRAY, CHARLES FAIRFAX. *Catalogue of a Collection of Early French Books in the Library of C. Fairfax Murray,* compiled by Hugh William Davies, 2 Vols. London: privately printed, 1910.

NEW YORK PUBLIC LIBRARY. *The Arents Collection of Books in Parts and Associated Literature:* *A Complete Checklist,* with an introductory survey by Sarah Augusta Dickson. New York: New York Public Library, 1957, 88 pp.

Norton's Literary Letter: Comprising American Papers of Interest, and a Catalogue of Rare and Valuable Books Relative to America, Nos. 1–4, 1857–1860; ns Nos. 1–2, 1860. New York: C. B. Norton, 1857–1860.

PALTSITS, VICTOR HUGO. "Proposal of Henry Stevens for a 'Bibliographica Americana' to the Year 1700, to be Published by the Smithsonian Institution." *PBSA,* XXXVI (4th Quart. 1942), 245–266.

PATRICK, WALTON R., and CECIL G. TAYLOR. "A Louisiana French Plantation Library, 1842." *French American Review,* I (January–March 1948), 47–67.

PENNSYLVANIA, UNIVERSITY, LIBRARY. *Check List of Poetry by American Authors Published in the English Colonies of North America and the United States through 1865, in the Possession of the Rare Book Collection, University of Pennsylvania,* compiled by Albert von Chorba, Jr. Philadelphia: Univ. of Pennsylvania Press, 1951, 63 leaves.

PHILLIPS, PHILIP LEE, ed. "List of Books Relating to America in the Register of the London Company of Stationers, from 1562 to 1638," in *Annual Report of the American Historical Association for the Year 1896.* Washington: American Historical Association, 1897, I, 1,249–1,261.

POWELL, LAWRENCE CLARK. *Books in My Baggage.* Cleveland:

World Publishing Co., 1960, 243–247.

POWER, FLORENCE M. "American Private Book Clubs." *BB,* XX (September–December 1952), 216–220; (January–April 1953), 233–236.

RICE, HOWARD C. "Soundings in the Sinclair Hamilton Collection." *PULC,* XX (Autumn 1958), 29–38.

RICH, OBADIAH. *Bibliotheca Americana Nova: A Catalogue of Books Relating to America, in Various Languages; Including Voyages to the Pacific and Around the World, and Collections of Voyages and Travels, Printed since the Year 1700,* 2 Vols. London: Rich and Sons, 1846.

——————. *Bibliotheca Americana Nova: or, A Catalogue of Books in Various Languages Relating to America, Printed since the Year 1700.* London: O. Rich, 1835, 424 pp.

Also: New York: Harper and Brothers.

Supplements: Part 1, Additions and Corrections, 1701–1800. London, 1841, 425–517. Part 2, 1841–1844. 1844–1846, 425 pp.

Also: 2 Vols. New York: Burt Franklin, 1961.

——————. *Bibliotheca Americana Vetus: A Catalogue of Books Relating to America, with Two Supplements, 1493–1700.* London: Hodson, printers, 1846, 154 pp.

——————. *A Catalogue of Books Relating Principally to America, Arranged Under the Years in which They Were*

Printed, 1500–1700, 2 Parts. London: O. Rich, 1832, 129 pp.

——————. *Manuscripts and Printed Books in the Possession of Obadiah Rich, Esq., December 27, 1827.* Washington: printed by order of the House of Representatives, 1827, 24 pp.

RIVET, PAUL, and H. VOSY-BOURBON. *Bibliographie Américaniste.* Paris: Au siège de la Société des Américanistes de Paris, 1928, 150 pp.

Extract from *Journal de la Société des Américanistes de Paris,* ns XVII (1925), 437–584.

ROSENBACH, A. S. W. *Early American Children's Books with Bibliographical Descriptions of the Books in His Private Collection.* Portland, Maine: The Southworth Press, 1933, 354 pp.

SABIN, JOSEPH. *Catalogue of the Books, Manuscripts, and Engravings Belonging to William Menzies of New York.* New York: Albany press of J. Munsell, 1875, 471 pp.

——————. *Catalogue of John A. Rice's Library.* New York: J. Sabin and Sons, 1870.

——————, comp. *Catalogue of the Library Belonging to Thomas Addis Emmet,* New York: Bradstreet Press, 1868, 371 pp.

60 copies printed.

SADLEIR, MICHAEL. *XIX Century Fiction: A Bibliographical Record Based on His Own Collection,* 2 Vols. Berkeley: Univ. of California Press, 1951.

SANZ, CARLOS, ed. *Bibliotheca Americana Vetustissma: A Facsim-*

ile Reprint, with Four Volumes of Additions, etc., and a General Index. Madrid: Libréria Suarez, 1958–1960.

SHAFFER, ELLEN. "The Rosenbach Collection of Early American Children's Books in the Free Library of Philadelphia." *ABC,* VI (March 1956), 3–7.

SHERMAN, STUART C. *The Voice of the Whalemen, with an Account of the Nicholson Whaling Collection.* Providence: Providence Public Library, 1965, 194–202.

Describes a collection of whaling logbooks and related material.

SOUTHERN CONNECTICUT STATE COLLEGE, LIBRARY. *The Carolyn Sherwin Bailey Historical Collection of Children's Books: A Catalogue,* compiled by Dorothy R. Davis. New Haven: Southern Connecticut State College, 1966, 232 pp.

STEVENS, HENRY. *Bibliotheca Americana.* London, 1861, 273 pp.

Sold at auction by Messrs. Puttick and Simpson.

STILLWELL, MARGARET BINGHAM. *Incunabula and Americana, 1450–1800: A Key to Bibliographical Study.* New York: Columbia Univ. Press, 1931, 341–440.

Lists some 550 bibliographies and monographs on Americana.

STODDARD, ROGER E. "C. Fiske Harris, Collector of American Poetry and Plays." *PBSA,* LVII (1st Quart. 1963), 14–32.

_____. "The Harris Collection of American Poetry and Plays: Report of Acquisitions for 1961–1962." *BBr,* XIX (1963), 161–175.

TAYLOR, ROBERT H. *Authors at Work: An Address Delivered at the Opening of an Exhibition of Literary Manuscripts at the Grolier Club together with a Catalogue of the Exhibition by Herman W. Liebert and Facsimiles of Many of the Exhibits.* New York: Grolier Club, 1957, 52 pp.

THACHER, JOHN BOYD. *Catalogue of the John Boyd Thacher Collection of Incunabula,* compiled by Frederick William Ashley. Washington, 1915, 329 pp.

_____. *The Collection of John Boyd Thacher in the Library of Congress,* 3 Vols. Washington, 1931.

THOMPSON, THOMAS PAYNE. *Index to a Collection of Americana (Relating Principally to Louisiana) Art and Miscellanea, All Included in the Private Library of T. P. Thompson.* New Orleans: press of Perry and Buckley Co., 1912, 203 pp.

WAKE FOREST COLLEGE, LIBRARY. *A Catalogue of the Library of Charles Lee Smith,* edited by Edgar Estes Folk. Wake Forest: Wake Forest College Press, 1950, 654 pp.

WAKEMAN, STEPHEN H. *The Stephen H. Wakeman Collections of Books of Nineteenth Century American Writers, . . .* New York: American Art Association, Inc., 1924, 258 pp.

WARDEN, DAVID BAILLIE.
Bibliotheca Americana: Being a
Choice Collection of Books Re-
lating to North and South America,
and the West Indies; Including
Voyages to the Southern Hemis-
phere, Maps, Engravings, and
Medals. Paris: printed by Fain
and Thunot, 1831, 140 pp.

Also: 1840.

WEMYSS, STANLEY. *The*
General Guide to Rare Americana,
1493–1943, 2 Vols. Philadelphia:
the author, 1944.

"General Bibliography," I, ix–xi.
"Check List of Books Printed in
the American Colonies," 1639–1700,
I, 99–114. "Eighteenth Century
Check List," II, 140–156. "A Check
List of Books Printed West of the
Mississippi River," II, 157–172.

WILLIAMS, GEORGE CLINTON
FAIRCHILD. *The Fine Historical*
Library of Dr. George C. F.
Williams . . . Auction May 17th &
18th, 1926. New York: Anderson
Galleries, 1926, 208 pp.

WOODWARD, WILLIAM ELLIOT.
Bibliotheca Americana: Catalogue
of the Library of W. E. Woodward
of Boston Highlands, Massachusetts.
Boston: L. B. Weston, 1869, 668 pp.

YALE UNIVERSITY, LIBRARY.
Catalogue of the William Loring
Andrews Collection of Early Books
in the Library of Yale University,
compiled by Addison Van Name.
New Haven: Yale Univ. Press, 1913,
56 pp.

300 copies printed.

21. IMPRINTS

ALDEN, JOHN ELIOT, ed.
Rhode Island Imprints, 1727–
1800. New York: published for
the Bibliographical Society of
America by R. R. Bowker, 1950,
689 pp.

ALLEN, ALBERT HENRY, ed.
A Check List of Arkansas Imprints,
1821–1876. New York: published
for the Bibliographical Society of
America by R. R. Bowker, 1947,
236 pp.

From the introduction: "Based
upon the original sources from
which *A Check List of Arkansas*
Imprints, 1821–1876 (published
in 1942 by the Arkansas Historical
Records Survey) was compiled."

_____. *Dakota Imprints,*
1858–1889. New York: published for the Bibliographical

Society of America by Bowker,
1947, 242 pp.

AMERICAN ANTIQUARIAN
SOCIETY, LIBRARY (WOR-
CESTER, MASSACHUSETTS).
A List of Early American Im-
prints, 1640–1700, Belonging
to the Library . . . Worcester:
press of C. Hamilton, 1896,
80 pp.

"American Imprints Inventories."
Secretary's News Sheet, Bibliogra-
phy Society of the Univ. of
Virginia, No. 28, 2–3.

BALAS, LESLIE. *A Checklist*
of New Haven, Connecticut, Im-
prints for the Years 1835–1837,
with a Historical Introduction.
Washington, 1965, 14–15.

BRISTOL, ROGER PATTRELL.
Maryland Imprints, 1801–1810.

Charlottesville: published by the Univ. of Virginia Press for the Bibliographical Society of the Univ. of Virginia, 1953, 338 pp.

BYRD, CECIL K. *A Bibliography of Illinois Imprints.* Chicago: Univ. of Chicago Press, 1966, 601 pp.

BYRD, CECIL K., and HOWARD H. PECKHAM. *A Bibliography of Indiana Imprints, 1804–1853.* Indianapolis: Indiana Historical Bureau, 1955, 500 pp.

Indiana Historical Collections, XXXV.

CRANDALL, MARJORIE LYLE. *Confederate Imprints: A Check List Based Principally on the Collection of the Boston Athenaeum,* with an introduction by Walter Muir Whitehill, 2 Vols. Boston: Athenaeum, 1955.

FOREMAN, CAROLYN THOMAS. *Oklahoma Imprints, 1835–1907.* Norman: Univ. of Oklahoma Press, 1936, 499 pp.

Bibliography, 431–436.

GREEN, SAMUEL ABBOTT. "A Further List of Early American Imprints." *PMHS,* XXXVII (January 1903), 13–77.

_____. *A List of Early American Imprints Belonging to the Library of the Massachusetts Historical Society.* Cambridge: J. Wilson and Son, 1895, 137 pp.

Supplement: 1898, 15 pp.

Supplement: 1899, 70 pp.

Supplement: 1903, 67 pp.

HISTORICAL RECORDS SURVEY, ILLINOIS. *A Check List of Utica Imprints, 1799–1830.* Chicago: Illinois Historical Records Survey, 1942, 179 pp.

American Imprints Inventory, No. 36.

HISTORICAL RECORDS SURVEY, WISCONSIN. *Check List of Wisconsin Imprints, 1833–1849–1864–1869,* 5 Vols. Madison: Wisconsin Historical Records Survey, 1942–1953.

I–IV issued as *American Imprints Inventory,* Nos. 23–24, 41–42. V published by the State Historical Society of Wisconsin.

KENNERLY, SARAH L. "Confederate Juvenile Imprints: Children's Books and Periodicals Published in the Confederate States of America, 1861–1865." Unpublished doctoral dissertation, Univ. of Michigan, 1957.

McMURTRIE, DOUGLAS CRAWFORD. "Additional Buffalo (New York) Imprints, 1812–1849." *Grosvernor Library Bulletin,* XVIII (June 1936), 69–91.

_____. "Additional Geneva (New York) Imprints, 1815–1849." *Grosvernor Library Bulletin,* XVIII (June 1936), 93–99.

_____. *A Bibliography of Chicago Imprints, 1835–1850.* Chicago: W. Howes, 1944, 112 pp.

200 copies printed.

_____. "A Bibliography of Morristown Imprints, 1798–1820." *New Jersey Historical*

Society Proceedings, LIV (April 1936), 129–155.

—————————. "A Bibliography of North Carolina Imprints, 1761–1800." *NCHR,* XIII (January 1936), 47–86; (April 1930), 143–166; (July 1936), 219–254.

—————————. "A Bibliography of South Carolina Imprints, 1731–1740." *South Carolina Historical and General Magazine,* XXXIV (July 1933), 117–137.

—————————. "Located Georgia Imprints of the Eighteenth Century Not in the De Renne Catalogue." *Georgia Historical Quarterly,* XVIII (March 1934), 27–65.

—————————. "Locating the Printed Source Materials in United States History; with a Bibliography of Lists of Regional Imprints." *MVHR,* XXXI (December 1944), 369–406.

—————————. *Oregon Imprints, 1847–1870.* Eugene: Univ. of Oregon Press, 1950, 206 pp.

—————————. "Some Supplementary New Mexican Imprints: 1850–1860." *New Mexico Historical Review,* VII (April 1932), 165–175.

McMURTRIE, DOUGLAS CRAWFORD, and A. M. ALLEN. "A Supplementary List of Kentucky Imprints, 1794–1820." *Kentucky Historical Society Register,* XLII (April 1944), 99–119.

MOFFITT, ALEXANDER. "A Checklist of Iowa Imprints, 1837–1860." *Iowa Journal of History and Politics,* XXXVI (January 1938), 3–95; (April 1938), 152–205.

MORSCH, LUCILE M. *Check List of New Jersey Imprints, 1784–1800.* Baltimore: Historical Records Survey, 1939, 189 pp.

American Imprints Inventory, No. 9.

NOYES, REGINALD WEBB. *A Bibliography of Maine Imprints to 1820.* Stonington, Maine: R. Webb Noyes, 1930, 48 pp.

PIERSON, ROSCOE MITCHELL, comp. *A Preliminary Checklist of Lexington, Kentucky, Imprints, 1821–1850.* Charlottesville: Bibliographical Society of the Univ. of Virginia, 1953, 155 leaves.

Bibliography, 123–124.

PORTER, DOROTHY BURNETT. "Afro-American Writings Published before 1835, with an Alphabetical List (Tentative) of Imprints Written by American Negroes, 1760–1835." Unpublished master's thesis, Columbia Univ., 1932.

POWELL, WILLIAM STEVENS. "Eighteenth-Century North Carolina Imprints: A Revision and Supplement to McMurtrie." *NCHR,* XXXV (January 1958), 50–73.

RHODE ISLAND HISTORICAL SOCIETY. *Rhode Island Imprints: A List of Books, Pamphlets, Newspapers and Broadsides Printed at Newport, Providence, Warren, Rhode Island, between 1727 and 1800.* Providence: Rhode Island Historical Society, 1915, 88 pp.

SHOEMAKER, ALFRED LEWIS, comp. *A Check List of Imprints of the German*

Press of Northampton County, Pennsylvania, 1766–1905, with Biographies of the Printers. Easton, Pennsylvania: n.p., 1943, 162 pp.

Also: *Publications of the Northampton Historical and Genealogical Society,* IV.

200 copies printed.

STERN, MADELEINE BETTINA. *Imprints on History, Book Publishers, and American Frontiers.* Bloomington: Indiana Univ. Press, 1956, 389–464.

STREETER, THOMAS WINTHROP. *Bibliography of Texas, 1795–1845,* 5 Vols. in 3 Parts. Cambridge: Harvard Univ. Press, 1955–1960.

Part 1: Texas Imprints, I, 1817–1838; II, 1839–1845.

Part 2: Mexican Imprints Relating to Texas, 1803–1845.

Part 3: United States and European Imprints Relating to Texas, I, 1795–1837; II, 1838–1845.

STUTLER, BOYD B. "Early West Virginia Imprints." *PBSA,* XLV (3rd Quart. 1951), 237–245.

TANSELLE, G. THOMAS. "The Thomas Siltzer Imprint." *PBSA,* LVIII (4th Quart. 1964), 380–448.

TAPLEY, HARRIET SILVESTER. *Salem Imprints, 1768–1824: A History of the First Fifty Years of Printing* . . . Salem, Massachusetts: Essex Institute, 1927, 301–486.

TREMAINE, MARIE. *A Bibliography of Canadian Imprints, 1751–1800.* Toronto: Univ. of Toronto Press, 1952, 732 pp.

Bibliography, 671–680.

YALE UNIVERSITY, LIBRARY. "List of Connecticut and New Haven Imprints."

Available only in manuscript.

22. PRESSES

APPLETON-CENTURY COMPANY. *The House of Appleton-Century.* New York: Appleton-Century, 1936, 48 pp.

BLAKISTON'S SONS AND COMPANY. *One Hundred Years, 1843–1943.* Philadelphia: Blakiston's Sons and Co., 1943, 37 pp.

BURLINGAME, ROGER. *Endless Frontiers: The Story of McGraw-Hill.* New York: McGraw-Hill, 1959, bibliographical footnotes.

CHEEVER, L. O. "The Prairie Press: A Thirty-Year Record." *Books at Iowa,* No. 3 (November 1965), 15–33.

HARPER, JOSEPH HENRY. *The House of Harper: A Century of Publishing in Franklin Square.* New York: Harper Brothers, 1912, 670 pp.

HAWES, GENE R. *To Advance Knowledge: A Handbook on American University Press Publishing.* New York: published for the Association of American Univ. Presses, 1967, 141–142.

HEATH, D. C., COMPANY.
Forty Years of Service. Boston:
D. C. Heath Co., 1925, 61 pp.

HELLER, ELINOR RAAS,
and DAVID MAGEE. *Bibliography of the Grabhorn Press, 1915–
1940.* San Francisco: Graham
Press, 1940, 207 pp.

210 copies printed.

HOUGHTON, MIFFLIN AND
COMPANY. *A Portrait Catalogue
of the Books Published by Houghton,
Mifflin and Company, with a Sketch
of the Firm, Brief Descriptions of
the Various Departments, and
Some Account of the Origin and
Character of the Literary Enter-
prises Undertaken.* Boston: River-
side Press, 1905–1906, 267 pp.

KASER, DAVID. *Messrs. Carey
and Lea of Philadelphia.* Philadelphia: Univ. of Pennsylvania
Press, 1957, 182 pp.

KNOPF, ALFRED A., INC.
The Borzoi 1925. New York:
A. A. Knopf, 1925, 271–351.

KRAMER, SIDNEY. *History
of Stone and Kimball and
Herbert F. Stone and Company.*
Chicago: Univ. of Chicago
Press, 1940, 191–361.

LAWLER, JOHN LAWRENCE.
*The H. W. Wilson Company: Half
a Century of Bibliographic Publishing.* Minneapolis: Univ. of
Minnesota Press, 1950, 207 pp.

NORTH CAROLINA, UNIVERS-
ITY. *Books from Chapel Hill:
A Complete Catalogue, 1923–
1945.* Chapel Hill: Univ. of
North Carolina Press, 1946, 231 pp.

NOYES, EDWARD ALLING,
and HENRY M. SILVER, II.

*Columbia Books 1893–1933: A
Dictionary Catalogue of Columbia
University Press Publications.*
New York: Columbia Univ. Press,
1933, 247 pp.

PILKINGTON, JAMES PENN.
The Methodist Publishing House.
Nashville: Abington Press, 1968,
585 pp.

Appears to be the first of a
series. Covers 1769–1870.

RANSOM, WILL. *Private Presses
and Their Books.* New York:
R. R. Bowker Co., 1929, 493 pp.

A history of the private press
movement in England and America
with detailed checklists of publications, arranged chronologically
under press names.

REYNOLDS, QUENTIN JAMES.
*The Fiction Factory, or, From
Pulp Row to Quality Street: The
Story of 100 Years of Publishing
at Street and Smith.* New York:
Random House, 1955, 283 pp.

RODEN, ROBERT F. *The Cam-
bridge Press, 1638–1692: A
History of the First Printing
Press Established in English Ameri-
ca, together with a Bibliographical
List of the Issues of the Press.*
New York: Dodd, Mead and
Co., 1905, 145–185.

ROLLINS, CARL P. "The
Bibliographical Press at Yale,"
in *Essays Honoring Lawrence C.
Wroth.* Portland, Maine: Anthoensen Press, 1951, 247–261.

*The Roycroft Books: A Catalogue
and Some Comments.* East
Aurora, New York: Roycroft
Shop, 1902, 32 pp.

STOKES COMPANY. *The House of Stokes, 1881–1926.* New York: Frederick A. Stokes Co., 1926, 89 pp.

WILEY AND SONS. *The First Hundred and Fifty Years: A History of John Wiley and Sons.* New York: Wiley and Sons, 1957, 242 pp.

WINSHIP, GEORGE PARKER. *Daniel Berkeley Updike and the Merrymount Press of Boston, Massachusetts, 1860, 1894, 1941.* Rochester: printing house of Leo Hart, 1947, 151 pp.

23. REGIONALISM

BERNARD, HARRY. *Le Roman Régionaliste aux Etats-Unis, 1913–1940.* Montréal: Fides, 1949, 357–364.

DERSHEM, ELSIE. *An Outline of American State Literature.* Lawrence, Kansas: World Co., 1922, 187 pp.

GRAY, GORDON. "A Bibliography of American Regional Novels for the Use of Teachers." Unpublished doctoral dissertation, Teachers College, Columbia Univ.

GRIFFIN, APPLETON PRENTISS CLARK. *Index of Articles upon American Local History in the Historical Collections in the Boston Public Library.* Boston: printed by order of the trustees Boston Public Library 1889, 225 pp.

Boston Public Library Bibliographies of Special Subjects, No. 3.

LEARY, LEWIS. *Articles on American Literature, 1900–1950.* Durham: Duke Univ. Press, 1954, 413–422.

"Regionalism."

LIEBERMAN, ELIAS, ed. *The American Short Story: A Study of the Influence of Locality in Its Development.* Ridgewood, New Jersey: the editor, 1912, 169–175.

LOMAX, ALAN, and SIDNEY ROBERTSON COWELL, comps. *American Folk Song and Folk Lore: A Regional Bibliography.* New York: Progressive Education Association, 1942, 59 pp.

LUDEWIG, HERMAN ERNST. *The Literature of American Local History: A Bibliographical Essay.* New York: R. Craighead, 1846, 201 pp.

Supplement: 1848, 20 pp.

ODUM, HOWARD WASHINGTON, and HARRY ESTILL MOORE. *American Regionalism: A Cultural-Historical Approach to National Integration.* New York: H. Holt and Co., 1938, 643–675.

Also: Gloucester, Massachusetts: P. Smith, 1966.

SPER, FELIX. *From Native Roots: A Panorama of Our Regional Drama.* Caldwell, Idaho: Caxton Printers, 1948, 279–334.

STARKE, AUBREY. "Books in the Wilderness." *Journal of the Illinois State Historical Society,* XXVIII (January 1936), 258–270.

STREETER, THOMAS WINTHROP. "Notes on North American Regional Bibliographies." *PBSA,* XXXVII (3rd Quart, 1942), 171–186.

24. REGIONS

NORTHEAST

ADIRONDACK MOUNTAIN CLUB, INC., BIBLIOGRAPHY COMMITTEE. *Adirondack Bibliography: A List of Books, Pamphlets, and Periodical Articles Published through the Year 1955.* New York: New York Univ. Press, 1958, 372 pp.

ATKESON, MARY MEEK. *A Study of the Local Literature of the Upper Ohio Valley with Special Reference to the Early Pioneer and Indian Tales.* Columbus: Ohio State Univ. Press, 1921, 62 pp.

BOSTON PUBLIC LIBRARY. *Catalogue of a Collection of Early New England Books Made by the Late John Allen Lewis and Now in the Possession of the Boston Public Library.* Boston: the trustees of the Boston Public Library, 1892, 31 pp.

DRAKE, SAMUEL GARDNER. *Annals of Witchcraft in New England and Elsewhere in the United States from Their First Settlement.* Boston: W. E. Woodward, 1869, 306 pp.

275 copies printed.

FORBES, HARRIETTE (MERRIFIELD). *New England Diaries, 1602–1800: A Descriptive Catalogue of Diaries, Orderly Books, and Sea Journals,* Topsfield, Massachusetts: privately printed, 1923, 440 pp.

FORD, PAUL LEICESTER. *The New England Primer: A History of Its Origin and Development . . .* New York: Dodd, Mead, 1897, 354 pp.

GODDARD, HAROLD CLARKE. *Studies in New England Transcendentalism.* New York: Columbia Univ. Press, 1908, 207–212.

GRIFFIN, A. P. C. "Bibliography of the Historical Publications of the New England States." *PCSM,* III (April 1895), 95–139.

HEARTMAN, CHARLES FREDERICK, comp. *The New England Primer Issued prior to 1830: A Bibliographical Checklist for the More Easy Attaining the True Knowledge of This Book.* New York: printed for the compiler, 1915, 190 pp.

110 copies printed.

Also: 1922, 190 pp.

265 copies printed.

Also: R. R. Bowker Co., 1934, 148 pp.

300 copies printed.

JANTZ, HAROLD S. "The First Century of New England Verse." *PAAS,* LIII (October 1943), 219–508.

LEARY, LEWIS. "Knickerbocker Literature in the Benjamin Collections." *CLC,* IX (February 1960), 22–27.

LITTLEFIELD, GEORGE EMERY. *Early Schools and School-Books of New England.* Boston: The Club of Odd Volumes, 1904, 354 pp.

167 copies printed.

MASSACHUSETTS HISTORICAL SOCIETY. "Continuation of

the Narrative of Newspapers Published in New England, 1704 to the Revolution." *Massachusetts Historical Society Collections,* VI (1800), 64–77.

——————. "A Narrative of the Newspapers Printed in New England." *Massachusetts Historical Society Collections,* V (1798), 208–216.

MATTHEWS, ALBERT. "Lists of New England Magazines of the Eighteenth Century." *PCSM,* XIII (January 1910), 69–74.

NEW ENGLAND HISTORIC GENEALOGICAL SOCIETY. *New-England Historical and Genealogical Register.* Boston: S. G. Drake, 1847– .

Entitled *New-England Historical and Genealogical Register and Antiquarian Journal,* 1923–1927.

TAFT, KENDALL B., ed. *Minor Knickerbockers: Representative Selections,* with introduction, bibliography and notes. New York: American Book Co., 1947, cxi–cxxviii.

WILSON, JAMES GRANT. "The Knickerbocker Authors," in *Memorial History of the City of New York,* 4 Vols. New York: New York History Co., 1893, IV, 54–77.

WINSOR, JUSTIN. "Literature of Witchcraft in New England." *PAAS,* ns X (October 1895), 351–373.

SOUTHEAST

AGNEW, JANET MARGARET. *A Southern Bibliography,* 4 Vols. University: Louisiana State Univ. and Agricultural and Mechanical College, 1939–1942.

I: Fiction.

II: Historical Fiction.

III: Poetry.

IV: Biography.

ALDERMAN, EDWIN ANDERSON, et al., eds. *Library of Southern Literature,* 16 Vols. New Orleans and Atlanta: Martin and Hoyt, 1908–1913.

Supplement: Atlanta, 1923.

BAXTER, CHARLES N., and JAMES M. DEARBORN. *Confederate Literature: A List of Books and Newspapers, Maps, Music . . . . Now in the Boston Athenaeum.* Boston: Boston Athenaeum, 1917, 213 pp.

BEATTY, RICHMOND CROOM, and WILLIAM PERRY FIDLER, eds. *Contemporary Southern Prose.* Boston: D. C. Heath and Co., 1940, 313–320.

BOGER, LORISE C. *The Southern Mountaineer in Literature: An Annotated Bibliography.* Morgantown: West Virginia Univ. Library, 1964, 114 pp.

BRADBURY, JOHN M. *The Fugitives: A Critical Account.* Chapel Hill: Univ. of North Carolina Press, 1958, 274–294.

BRADSHAW, SIDNEY ERNEST. *On Southern Poetry Prior to 1860.* Richmond: B. F. Johnson Publishing Co., 1900, 148–157.

BROCKETT, O. G. "The Theatre of the Southern United States from the Beginnings through 1865: A Bibliographical Essay." *Theatre Research,* II (No. 3, 1960), 163–174.

CANTRELL, CLYDE HULL, and WALTON R. PATRICK. *Southern Literary Culture: A Bibliography of Masters' and Doctors' Theses.* Tuscaloosa: Univ. of Alabama Press, 1955, 124 pp.

CARDWELL, GUY A. "On Scholarship and Southern Literature." *SAQ,* XL (January 1941), 60–72.

CHAPMAN, MARISTAN. "Is Our Ink Well?: A Catalogue Comment upon Southern Novelists from 1917 to 1934." *Westminister Magazine,* XXIII (January–March 1935), 259–277.

CLARK, THOMAS DIONYSIUS, ed. *Travels in the New South: A Bibliography,* 2 Vols. Norman: Univ. of Oklahoma Press, 1962.

I: The Postwar South, 1865–1900.

II: The Twentieth Century South, 1900–1955.

_____. *Travels in the Old South: A Bibliography,* 2 Vols. Norman: Univ. of Oklahoma Press, 1956, 662 pp.

COLLINS, CARVEL E., comp. "Nineteenth Century Fiction of the Southern Appalachians." *BB,* XVII (September–December 1942), 186–190; (January–April 1942), 215–218.

COLVILLE, DEREK. "A Rich Store of Southern Tall Tales." Univ. of Virginia Bibliographical Society, *Secretary's News Sheet,* XXXIII (June 1955).

COMBS, JOSIAH H. *Folk-Songs of the Southern United States* (Folk-Songs du Midi des Etats-Unis), edited by Donald Knight Wilgus. Austin: published for the American Folklore Society by the Univ. of Texas Press, 1967, 195–238.

COULTER, ELLIS MERTON. *Travels in the Confederate States: A Bibliography.* Norman: Univ. of Oklahoma Press, 1948, 303 pp.

American Exploration and Travel, No. 11.

COWAN, LOUISE (SHILLINGBURG). *The Fugitive Group: A Literary History.* Baton Rouge: Louisiana State Univ. Press, 1959, bibliographical footnotes.

DAVIDSON, DONALD. "The 43 Best Southern Novels for Readers and Collectors." *PW,* CXXVII (Apr. 27, 1935), 1,675–1,676.

DORMON, JAMES H., JR. *Theater in the Ante Bellum South, 1815–1861.* Chapel Hill: Univ. of North Carolina Press, 1967, 291–309.

ELLINGER, ESTHER PARKER. *The Southern War Poetry of the Civil War.* Philadelphia: The Hershey Press, 1918, 49–55.

GAINES, FRANCIS PENDLETON. *The Southern Plantation: A Study in the Development and the Accuracy of a Tradition.* New York: Columbia Univ. Press, 1924, 237–243.

Columbia Univ. Studies in English and Comparative Literature.

GILMER, GERTRUDE CORDELIA, comp. *Checklist of Southern Periodicals to 1861.* Boston: F. W. Faxon Co., 1934, 128 pp.

Useful Reference Series, No. 49.

HALL, WADE. *The Smiling Phoenix: Southern Humor from 1865 to 1914.* Gainesville: Univ. of Florida Press, 1965, 357—368.

HARTIN, JOHN S. "The Southeastern United States in the Novel through 1950: A Bibliographic Review." Unpublished doctoral dissertation, Univ. of Michigan, 1957.

HARWELL, RICHARD BARKSDALE. "The Cause That Refreshes: Reading, 'Riting, and Rebellion." *CRL,* XX (May 1959), 281—288.

On collections of Confederate materials.

—————. *Confederate Belles-Lettres: A Bibliography and a Finding List of the Fiction, Poetry, Drama, Songsters, and Miscellaneous Literature Published in the Confederate States of America.* Hattiesburg: Book Farm, 1941, 79 pp.

199 copies printed.

—————. *The Confederate Hundred: A Bibliophilic Selection of Confederate Books.* Urbana: Beta Phi Mu, 1964, 58 pp.

HOFFMAN, FREDERICK JOHN. *The Art of Southern Fiction: A Study of Some Modern Novelists.* Carbondale: Southern Illinois Univ. Press, 1967, 170—192.

HUBBELL, JAY B. *The South in American Literature, 1607—1900.* Durham: Duke Univ. Press, 1954, 883—974.

IRVINE, D. D. "The Fate of Confederate Archives." *AHR,* XLIV (July 1939), 823—841.

JOHNSON, JAMES GIBSON. *Southern Fiction Prior to 1860: An Attempt at a First-hand Bibliography.* Charlottesville: Michie Co., printers, 1909, 126 pp.

JONES, HOWARD MUMFORD. "Contemporary Southern Literature." *Univ. of North Carolina Extension Bulletin,* VIII (No. 3, 1928), 56 pp.

KENNERLY, SARAH L. "Confederate Juvenile Imprints: Children's Books and Periodicals Published in the Confederate States of America, 1861—1865." Unpublished doctoral dissertation, Univ. of Michigan, 1957.

MANLY, LOUISE. *Southern Literature from 1579—1895.* Richmond: B. F. Johnson Publishing Co., 1895, 457—514.

MORRISON, HUGH ALEXANDER, ed. "A Bibliography of the Official Publications of the Confederate States of America." *PBSA,* III (1908), 92—132.

MOSES, MONTROSE JONAS. *The Literature of the South.* New York: T. Y. Crowell and Co., 1910, 475—499.

MUNN, ROBERT F. *The Southern Appalachians: A Bibliography and Guide to Studies.* Morgantown: West Virginia Univ. Library, 1961, 106 pp.

Emphasis on social studies with considerable attention given to folklore.

NORCROSS, GRENVILLE HOWLAND. "Southern Newspapers Printed on Wall Paper." *PMHS,* XLVI (November 1912), 241—243.

PAINE, GREGORY LANSING, ed. *Southern Prose Writers: Representative Selections,* with introduction, bibliography and notes. New York: American Book Co., 1947, cxix–cxxiii.

PARKS, EDD WINFIELD, ed. *Southern Poets: Representative Selections,* with introduction, bibliography and notes. New York: American Book Co., 1936, cxxxi–cxlviii.

RUBIN, LOUIS DECIMUS. *The Faraway Country: Writers of the Modern South.* Seattle: Univ. of Washington Press, 1963, 241–247.

RUTHERFORD, MILDRED LEWIS. *The South in History and Literature: A Handbook of Southern Writers from the Settlement of Jamestown, 1607, to Living Writers.* Atlanta: Franklin-Turner Co., 1907, xxxvii–xxxviii.

SIMONINI, RINALDO C. *Southern Writers: Appraisals in Our Time.* Charlottesville: Univ. Press of Virginia, 1964, bibliographical footnotes.

TRENT, WILLIAM PETERFIELD, et al. "The New South," in *Cambridge History of American Literature,* 4 Vols. New York: G. P. Putnam's Sons, 1917–1921, II, 588–611.

WARREN, ROBERT PENN, ed. *A Southern Harvest: Short Stories by Southern Writers.* Boston: Houghton Mifflin, 1937, 353–360.

WEEKS, STEPHEN BEAUREGARD. *Southern Quakers and Slavery.* Baltimore: Johns Hopkins Press, 1898, 345–362.

MIDWEST

CLARK, THOMAS DIONYSIUS. "Arts and Sciences on the Early American Frontier." *Nebraska History.* XXXVII (December 1956), 247–268.

Surveys frontier fiction, travel, literature, textbooks, 1810–1840.

DE MENIL, ALEXANDER NICOLAS. *The Literature of the Louisiana Territory.* St. Louis: St. Louis News Co., 1904, 354 pp.

DICK, EVERETT NEWTON. *The Sod-House Frontier, 1854–1890: A Social History of the Northern Plains from the Creation of Kansas and Nebraska to the Admission of the Dakotas.* New York and London: D. Appleton-Century Co., 1937, 519–528.

DONDORE, DOROTHY ANNE. *The Prairie and the Making of Middle America: Four Centuries of Description.* Cedar Rapids, Iowa: The Torch Press, 1926, 435–451.

DOUGHERTY, CHARLES T. "Novels of the Middle Border: A Critical Bibliography for Historians." *Historical Bulletin,* XXV (1947), 77–78, 85–88.

FLANAGAN, JOHN T., comp. "A Bibliography of Middle Western Farm Novels." *Minnesota History,* XXIII (June 1942), 156–158.

HAFERKORN, HENRY ERNEST. *Mississippi River and Valley: Bibliography, Mostly Non-technical.* Fort Humphreys, Virginia: Engineer School, 1931, 353–365.

HUBACH, ROBERT ROGERS. *Early Midwestern Travel Narratives: An Annotated Bibliography, 1634–1850.* Detroit: Wayne State Univ. Press, 1961, 159 pp.

_____. "They Saw the Early Midwest: A Bibliography of Travel Narratives." *Journal of the Illinois State Historical Society,* XLVI (1953), 283–289; XLVII (1954), 285–297; *Iowa Journal of History,* LII (1954), 223–234.

Covers 1722–1850.

JENNEWEIN, JOHN LEONARD, comp. *Black Hills Booktrails.* Mitchell, South Dakota: Dakota Territory Centennial Commission, 1962, 111 pp.

Lists and annotates 322 books on the Black Hills Region. "A Note on Bibliographical Materials," 103–104.

MEYER, ROY WILLARD. *The Middle Western Farm Novel in the Twentieth Century.* Lincoln: Univ. Of Nebraska Press, 1965, 243–252.

RANDOLPH, VANCE, ed. *"The Devil's Pretty Daughter" and Other Ozark Folk Tales,* with notes by Herbert Halpert. New York: Columbia Univ. Press, 1955, 231–239.

_____, ed. *"Sticks in the Knapsack" and Other Ozark Folk Tales,* with notes by Ernest W. Baughman. New York: Columbia Univ. Press, 1958, 167–171.

_____, ed. *"The Talking Turtle" and Other Ozark Folk Tales.* New York: Columbia Univ. Press, 1957, 221–226.

_____, ed. *"Who Blowed Up the Church House?" and Other Ozark Folk Tales,* with notes by Herbert Halpert. New York: Columbia Univ. Press, 1952, 227–232.

RANDOLPH, VANCE, and GEORGE P. WILSON, comps. *Down in the Holler: A Gallery of Ozark Folk Speech.* Norman: Univ. of Oklahoma Press, 1953, 303–314.

RUSK, RALPH LESLIE. *The Literature of the Middlewestern Frontier,* 2 Vols. New York: Columbia Univ. Press, 1925.

ST. LOUIS MERCANTILE LIBRARY ASSOCIATION.... *1. Missouri and Illinois Newspapers, 1808–1897, Chronologically Arranged. 2. Manuscripts Relating to Louisiana Territory and Missouri.* St. Louis: St. Louis Mercantile Library Association, 1898, 22 pp.

SOUTHWEST

BLOOM, L. B. "Bourke on the Southwest." *New Mexico Historical Review,* VIII (January 1933), 1–30.

CAMPBELL, WALTER S. (STANLEY VESTAL). *The Booklover's Southwest: A Guide to Good Reading.* Norman: Univ. of Oklahoma Press, 1955, 269–272.

COLVILLE, DEREK. "Checklist to Travel Essays Relating to the Southwest Which Appeared in the New Orleans *Daily Picayune,* 1819–1841." *New Mexico Historical Review,* XXXIII (July 1958), 232–235.

DOBIE, JAMES FRANK. *Guide to Life and Literature of the*

Southwest. Austin: Univ. of Texas Press, 1943, 111 pp.

2nd edition: Dallas: Southern Methodist Univ. Press, 1952, 230 pp.

HARRINGTON, MILDRED PRISCILLA. *The Southwest in Children's Books: A Bibliography.* Baton Rouge: Louisiana State Univ. Press, 1952, 143 pp.

KURTZ, KENNETH. *Literature of the American Southwest: A Selective Bibliography.* Los Angeles: Occidental College, 1956, 63 pp.

POWELL, LAWRENCE CLARK. *Heart of the Southwest: A Selected Bibliography of Novels, Stories, and Tales Laid in Arizona and New Mexico and Adjacent Lands.* Los Angeles: Dawson's Book Shop, 1955, 42 pp.

Great Southwest Travels Series, No. 2.

——————. *Southwestern Book Trails: A Reader's Guide to the Heartland of New Mexico and Arizona.* Albuquerque: Horn and Wallace, 1963, bibliographical notes.

——————. *A Southwestern Century: A Bibliography of One Hundred Books of Non-Fiction about the Southwest.* Van Nuys, California: J. E. Reynolds, 1958, 40 pp.

500 copies printed.

RADER, JESSE LEE. *South of Forty, From the Mississippi to the Rio Grande: A Bibliography.* Norman: Univ. of Oklahoma Press, 1947, 347 pp.

SAUNDERS, LYLE. "A Guide to the Literature of the Southwest." *NMQ.*

XII—XXIV, 1942—1954.

TUCKER, MARY. *Books of the Southwest: A General Bibliography.* New York: J. J. Augustin, 1937, 105 pp.

Vestal, Stanley (see Campbell)

WAGNER, HENRY RAUP. *The Spanish Southwest, 1542—1794: An Annotated Bibliography,* 2 Vols. Albuquerque: The Quivira Society, 1937.

NORTHWEST

BROMBERG, ERIK. "A Bibliography of Theses and Dissertations Concerning the Pacific Northwest and Alaska." *Pacific Northwest Quarterly,* XL (July 1949), 203—252.

INLAND EMPIRE COUNCIL OF TEACHERS OF ENGLISH. *Northwest Books, Report of the Committee on Books of the Inland Empire Council of Teachers of English, 1942: Review of over 1,100 Books, Selected Magazine Bibliography. . . .* Portland: Binfords and Mort, 1942, 356 pp.

Supplement: Lincoln: Nebraska Univ. Press, 1949. Covers 1942—1947.

"A Pacific Northwest Bibliography." *Pacific Northwest Quarterly.*

XXXII—XL, 1941—1949.

POLLARD, LANCASTER. "Research Suggestions: A Pacific Northwest Bibliography, 1948." *Pacific Northwest Quarterly,* XL (April 1949), 147—159.

SMITH, CHARLES WESLEY.
*Check-list of Books and
Pamphlets Relating to the
History of the Pacific Northwest.*
Olympia, Washington: E. L.
Boardman, 1909, 191 pp.

WEST

AUERBACH, HERBERT S.
*Western Americana: Books,
Newspapers, and Pamphlets,
Many Relating to the Mormon
Church from the Collection of
Herbert S. Auerbach,* 2 Parts.
New York: Parke-Bernet Galleries,
Inc., 1947–1948.

BAY, JEAN CHRISTIAN.
*A Second Handful of Western
Books.* Cedar Rapids, Iowa:
privately printed for friends of
the Torch Press, 1936, 56 pp.

COLE, WENDELL. "Early
Theatre in America West of the
Rockies: A Bibliographical
Essay." *Theatre Research,* IV
(No. 1, 1962), 36–45.

DAVIDSON, LEVETTE JAY.
*Rocky Mountain Life in Literature:
A Descriptive Bibliography.*
Denver: Univ. of Denver Bookstore,
1936, 25 pp.

DAVIDSON, LEVETTE JAY,
and PRUDENCE BOSTWICK, eds.
*The Literature of the Rocky
Mountain West, 1803–1903.*
Caldwell, Idaho: Caxton Printers,
1939, 449 pp.

FARQUHAR, FRANCIS
PELOUBET. *The Books of the
Colorado River and the Grand*

*Canyon: A Selective Bibliog-
raphy.* Los Angeles: G. Dawson,
1953, 86 pp.

Early California Travels Series,
No. 12.

HOLLIDAY, WILLIAM J.
*Western Americana, Many of
Great Rarity: The Distinguished
Collection Formed by William J.
Holliday. . . Sold by His Order,
April 20–22, 1954.* New York:
Parke-Bernet Galleries, 1954,
266 pp.

SMITH, HENRY NASH.
*Virgin Land: The American West
as Symbol and Myth.* Cambridge:
Harvard Univ. Press, 1950, bibliographical footnotes.

WAGNER, HENRY RAUP.
*The Plains and the Rockies: A
Bibliography of Original Narratives
of Travel and Adventure, 1800–
1865,* 3rd edition. Columbus, Ohio:
Long's College Book Co., 1953,
601 pp.

WINTHER, OSCAR OSBURN.
*A Classified Bibliography of the
Periodical Literature of the Trans-
Mississippi West (1811–1957).*
Bloomington: Indiana Univ.
Press, 1961, 626 pp.

Arranged geographically, with a
section of bibliography for each
area.

—————. *The Trans-
Mississippi West: A Guide to Its
Periodical Literature, 1811–1938.*
Bloomington: Indiana Univ. Press,
1942, 278 pp.

25. STATES

ALABAMA

ELLISON, RHODA COLEMAN. *Early Alabama Publications: A Study in Literary Interests.* University: Univ. of Alabama Press, 1947, 193–204.

_____. *History and Bibliography of Alabama Newspapers in the Nineteenth Century.* University: Univ. of Alabama Press, 1954, 221 pp.

ENGSTFELD, CAROLINE P., comp. *Bibliography of Alabama Authors.* Birmingham: Howard College, 1923, 47 pp.

OWEN, THOMAS McADORY. "Alabama Archives," in *Annual Report of the American Historical Association for 1904.* Washington, 1905, 66 pp.

Includes checklist of Newspaper and periodical files.

ALASKA

WICKERSHAM, JAMES. *Alaskan Newspapers and Periodicals: A Preliminary Checklist Prepared for the Use of Hon. James Wickersham, Delegate from Alaska,* by Hugh Morrison. Washington, 1915, 28 pp.

_____; comp. *Bibliography of Literature, 1724–1924: Containing the Titles of Histories, Travels, Voyages, Newspapers, Periodicals, Public Documents . . . . Relating to , . . . Alaska.* Cordova, Alaska: Cordova *Daily Times,* 1927, 662 pp.

ARIZONA

DIAZ, ALBERT JAMES. "A Bibliography of Bibliographies Relating to the History and Literature of Arizona and New Mexico." *Arizona Quarterly,* XIV (Autumn 1958), 197–218.

MUNK, JOSEPH AMASA. *Bibliography of Arizona Books, Pamphlets and Periodicals in the Library of Dr. J. A. Munk.* Los Angeles: n.p., 1900, 28 pp.

SOUTHWEST MUSEUM, MUNK LIBRARY OF ARIZONIANA (LOS ANGELES). *Bibliography of Arizona. . . .* Los Angeles: Southwest Museum, 1914, 431 pp.

WILLSON, CLAIR EUGENE. *Mimes and Miners: A Historical Study of the Theatre in Tombstone.* Tucson: Univ. of Arizona Press, 1935, 206–207.

ARKANSAS

NOLAN, PAUL T., and AMOS E. SIMPSON. "Arkansas Drama before World War I: An Unexplored Country." *AHQ,* XXII (Spring 1963), 61–75.

CALIFORNIA

ADAMS, JOHN R. *Books and Authors of San Diego: A Check List.* San Diego: San Diego State College Press, 1966, 250 pp.

ARLT, GUSTAVE O., et al. "Bibliography of California Folklore." *CFQ,* II (January 1943), 63–70; (April 1943), 169–175; (July 1943), 245–251; (October 1943), 347–352.

CALIFORNIA STATE LIBRARY. "Fiction in the State Library Having a California Coloring." *News Notes of California Libraries,* IX (1914), 228–242; XIII (1918), 874–878.

_____ . "Fiction in the State Library Having a California Coloring, compiled by the California Department." *News Notes of California Libraries,* XXI (1926), 101–127.

CHANDLER, KATHERINE. *List of California Periodicals Issued Previous to the Completion of the Transcontinental Telegraph (August 15, 1846– October 24, 1861),* San Francisco: n.p., 1905, 20 pp.

Publications of the Library Association of California, No. 7.

COWAN, ROBERT ERNEST. *A Bibliography of the History of California,* 3 Vols. San Francisco: printed by J. H. Nash, 1936.

CUMMINS, ELLA STERLING. *The Story of the Files: A Review of Californian Writers and Literature.* San Francisco: Co-operative Printing Co., 1893, 460 pp.

DE WITT, FREDERIC M. *California Index Cards: Bibliography of the History and Literature of That Part of the West Coast of North America Known as California . . . . ,* Series 1–   . Oakland: DeWitt and Snelling, 1915–

Cards in numbered series of 10 cards each.

HANNA, PHIL TOWNSEND. *Libros Californianos: or, Five Feet of California Books,* revised and enlarged by Lawrence Clark Powell. Los Angeles: Zeitlin and Ver Brugge, 1958, 87 pp.

HENRY E. HUNTINGTON LIBRARY. *A Century of California Literature: An Exhibition Prepared for the California Literary Centennial.* San Marino: Henry E. Huntington Library, 1950, 27 pp.

LELAND STANFORD JUNIOR UNIVERSITY, DRAMATISTS ALLIANCE. *Stanford Writers, 1891–1941.* Palo Alto: Dramatists Alliance, 1941, 141 pp.

ROSS, BASIL. "California Young Writers, Angry and Otherwise." *LJ,* LXXXIII (June 15, 1958), 1850–1854.

Bio-bibliographical notes on Rexroth, Ginsberg, Kerouac, Everson, Ferlinghetti, Duncan and other contemporary writers of California.

WALL, ALEXANDER J. "Early Newspapers, With a List of the New York Historical Society's Collection of Papers Published in California, Oregon, Washington, Montana, and Utah." *NYHSB,* XV (July 1931), 39–66.

COLORADO

REX, WALLACE HAYDEN, comp. *Colorado Newspapers Bibliography, 1859–1933.* Denver: Bibliographical Center for Research, Rocky Mountain Region, 1939, 69 pp.

SCHOBERLIN, MELVIN. *From Candles to Footlights: A Biography of the Pike's Peak Theatre, 1859–1876.* Denver: F. A. Rosenstock, Old West Publishing Co., 1941, 293–300.

WILCOX, VIRGINIA. *Colorado: A Selected Bibliography of Its Literature, 1858–1952.* Denver: Sage Books, 1954, 151 pp.

CONNECTICUT

BATES, ALBERT CARLOS.

"Checklist of Connecticut Almanacs, 1709–1805." *PAAS,* ns XXIV (April 1914), 93–215.

DELAWARE

REED, HENRY CLAY, and MARION BJÖRNSON REED. *A Bibliography of Delaware through 1960.* Newark, Delaware: published for the Institute of Delaware History and Culture by the Univ. of Delaware Press, 1966, Items 4,647–4,703.

500 copies printed.

FLORIDA

McRORY, MARY O. *Florida in Fiction: A Bibliography.* Tallahassee: Florida State Library, 1958, 67 pp.

GEORGIA

AMERICAN LIBRARY ASSOCIATION, JUNIOR MEMBERS ROUND TABLE, ATLANTA CHAPTER. *Georgia Author Bibliography, 1900–1940.* Atlanta, 1942.

Available from T. W. Atkinson, 534 Hurt Building, Atlanta, Georgia.

BONNER, JOHN WYATT, JR. "Bibliography of Georgia Authors, 1949–1950." *Georgia Review,* IV (Winter 1950), 353–367.

Appears biannually in Winter issue, beginning with IV (1950).

_____. *Bibliography of Georgia Authors, 1949–1965.* Athens: Univ. of Georgia Press, 1966, 266 pp.

CANDLER, ALLEN DANIEL, ed. *Colonial Records of the State of Georgia,* 26 Vols. Atlanta: C. P. Byrd, 1904–1916.

Lucian Lamour Knight succeeded Candler as editor. XX never published.

GILMER, GERTRUDE CORDELIA. "A Critique of Certain Georgia Ante-Bellum Literary Magazines Arranged Chronologically and a Checklist." *Georgia Historical Quarterly,* XVIII (December 1934), 293–334.

HORTON, O. E., JR. "A Descriptive Bibliography of Historical and Imaginative Writings in Georgia." Unpublished doctoral dessertation, Vanderbilt Univ., 1933.

MOODY, MINNIE HITE. "Books about Georgia, 1950–1953." *Georgia Review,* VIII (Spring 1954), 70–81.

ROWLAND, ARTHUR RAY, ed. *A Bibliography of the Writings on Georgia History.* Hamden, Connecticut: Archon Books, 1966, 289 pp.

TALMADGE, JOHN E. "Savannah's Yankee Newspapers." *GaR,* XII (Spring 1958), 66–73.

ILLINOIS

DUFFEY, BERNARD I. *The Chicago Renaissance in American Letters: A Critical History.* East Lansing: Michigan State Univ. Press, 1954, bibliographical references.

JAMES, EDMUND JAMES. *A Bibliography of Newspapers Published in Illinois Prior to 1860.* Springfield: Phillips Brothers, state printers, 1899, 94 pp.

Illinois State Historical Library Publications, No. 1.

NEW YORK HISTORICAL SOCIETY, LIBRARY. *A Catalogue of Illinois Newspapers in the New York Historical Society,* compiled by Thomas O. Mabbott and Philip D. Jordan. Springfield: Illinois State Historical Library, 1931, 58 pp.

Reprinted from *Journal of Illinois State Historical Society,* XXIV (July 1931).

ST. LOUIS MERCANTILE LIBRARY ASSOCIATION . . . . *1. Missouri and Illinois Newspapers, 1808–1897, Chronologically Arranged. 2. Manuscripts Relating to Louisiana Térritory and Missouri.* St. Louis: St. Louis Mercantile Library Association, 1898, 22 pp.

SUTCLIFFE, DENHAM. "New Light on the 'Chicago Writers.' " *NLB,* 2nd Series, No. 5 (December 1950), 146–157.

IOWA

COFFEY, WILBUR JOHN, comp. *List of Books and Pamphlets Written by Cedar Rapids Authors.* Dubuque, Iowa: Columbia College Library, 1930, 42 pp.

HANLEY, L. E. "Some Recent Publications by Iowa Authors." *IJHP,* VIII (January 1910), 140–144.

IOWA COMMISSION TO THE LOUISIANA PURCHASE EXPOSITION, 1904. *List of Books by Iowa Authors.* Des Moines: Iowa Library Commission, 1904, 30 pp.

MOTT, FRANK LUTHER. "Iowa Magazines—Series 1 and 2." *Palimpest,* XLIV (July 1963), 285–316; (August 1963), 317–380.

——————. *The Literature of Pioneer Life in Iowa . . . .* Iowa City: State Historical Society of Iowa, 1923, 89 pp.

KANSAS

ANDERSON, LORENE, and ALAN W. FARLEY, comps. "A Bibliography of Town and County Histories of Kansas." *Kansas Historical Quarterly,* XXI (Autumn 1955), 513–551.

McMURTRIE, DOUGLAS CRAW-FORD, and ALBERT H. ALLEN. *Jotham Meeker: Pioneer Printer of Kansas,* with a bibliography of the known issues of the Baptist Mission Press at Shawanoe, Stockbridge and Ottawa, 1834–1854. Chicago: Eyncourt Press, 1930, 129–134.

KENTUCKY

BULL, JACQUELINE. "Writings on Kentucky History, 1955." *Kentucky Historical Society Register,* LV (1957), 237–256.

COLEMAN, JOHN WINSTON, JR. *A Bibliography of Kentucky History.* Lexington: Univ. of Kentucky Press, 1949, Items 1,707–1,723, 2,345–2,388 and 2,433–2,450.

JILLSON, WILLARD ROUSE. *A Bibliography of Early Western Travel in Kentucky, 1674–1824.* Louisville: C. T. Dearing Printing Co., 1944, 24 pp.

——————. "A Bibliography of Lexington, Kentucky. . . ." *Kentucky State Historical Society Register,* XLIV (July 1946), 151–186; XLV (January 1947), 39–70.

_____. "Bibliography of Lincoln County, Chronologically Arranged and Annotated." *Kentucky State Historical Society Register,* XXXV (October 1937), 339–359.

_____. "A Bibliography of the Lower Blue Licks (with Annotations)." *Kentucky State Historical Society Register,* XLII (October 1944), 297–311; XLIII (January 1945), 24–58.

_____. *Books on Kentucky Books and Writers: A Bibliography, 1784–1950.* Frankfort, Kentucky: Roberts Printing Co., 1951, 27 pp.

_____. *The First Printing in Kentucky: Some Account of Thomas Parvin and John Bradford and the Establishment of the Kentucky Gazette in Lexington in the Year 1787,* with a bibliography of 70 titles. Louisville: C. T. Dearing Printing Co., 1936, 41–54.

McMULLEN, HAYNES. "Special Libraries in Ante-Bellum Kentucky." *Kentucky Historical Society Register,* LIX (January 1961), 29–46.

PERRIN, WILLIAM HENRY. *The Pioneer Press of Kentucky: From the Printing of the First Paper West of the Alleghenies, August 11, 1787, to the Establishment of the Daily Press in 1830. . . .* Louisville: John P. Morton and Co., 1888, 93 pp.

THOMPSON, LAWRENCE SIDNEY. "The War between the States in Kentucky Novel." *KSHSR,* L (January 1952), 26–34.

THOMPSON, LAWRENCE SIDNEY, and ALGERNON D. THOMPSON. *The Kentucky Novel.* Lexington: Univ. of Kentucky Press, 1953, 158–160.

TOWNSEND, JOHN WILSON. *Kentucky in American Letters, 1784–1912,* 2 Vols. Cedar Rapids, Iowa: Torch Press, 1913.

1,000 sets printed.

LOUISIANA

ALABAMA, UNIVERSITY, LIBRARY. *A Bibliography of Louisiana Books and Pamphlets in the T. P. Thompson Collection of the University of Alabama Library.* University: Univ. of Alabama Press, 1947, 210 pp.

FRENCH, BENJAMIN FRANKLIN. *Historical Collections of Louisiana, Embracing Many Rare and Valuable Documents, Relating to the Natural, Civil and Political History of That State,* compiled with historical and biographical notes, 5 Vols. New York: Wiley and Putnam, 1846–1853.

GRIFFIN, MAX L. "A Bibliography of New Orleans Magazines." *Louisiana Historical Quarterly,* XVIII (July 1935), 493–566.

HOLLAND, DOROTHY G. "An Annotated Checklist of Magazines Published in St. Louis before 1900." *Washington Univ. Libraries Studies,* II (1951), 1–53.

McCURDY, RAYMOND R. "A Tentative Bibliography of the Spanish-Language Press in Louisiana, 1808–1871." *The Americans,* X (January 1954), 307–329.

McVOY, LIZZIE CARTER, and RUTH BATES CAMPBELL. *A Bibliography of Fiction by Louisianians and on Louisiana Subjects.* Baton Rouge: Louisiana State Univ. Press, 1935, 87 pp.

Also: *Louisiana State Univ. Studies,* XVIII.

PATRICK, WALTON R., and CECIL G. TAYLOR. "A Louisiana French Plantation Library, 1842." *French American Review*, I (January—March 1948), 47—67.

SMITHER, NELLE. *A History of the English Theatre at New Orleans, 1806—1842*, revised edition. New York: B. Blom, 1967, 193—194.

THOMPSON, LAWRENCE SIDNEY. "Books in Foreign Languages about Louisiana, 1900—1950." *Louisiana Historical Quarterly*, XXXIV (1951), 25—27.

THOMPSON, THOMAS PAYNE. *Index to a Collection of Americana (Relating Principally to Louisiana) . . . Art and Miscellanea, All Included in the Private Library of T. P. Thompson.* New Orleans: press of Perry and Buckley Co., 1912, 203 pp.

TINKER, EDWARD LAROCQUE. "Bibliography of the French Newspapers and Periodicals of Louisiana." *PAAS*, XLII (October 1932), 247—370.

——————. "Gombo: The Creole Dialect of Louisiana, with a Bibliography." *PAAS*, XLV (April 1935), 101—142.

——————. *Les Écrits de langue française en Louisiane au XIX^{em} siècle: Essais biographiques et Bibliographiques.* Paris: H. Champion, 1933, 502 pp.

MAINE

HUSTON, A. J. "A List of Maine Novels." *PW*, CXXVIII (July 6, 1935), 12—13.

NICHOLS, CHARLES LEMUEL. *Checklist of Maine, New Hampshire and Vermont Almanacs.* Worcester, Massachusetts: American Antiquarian Society, 1929, 103 pp.

Also: *PAAS,* ns XXXVIII (April 1928), 63—163.

MARYLAND

BAER, ELIZABETH. *Seventeenth Century Maryland: A Bibliography.* Baltimore: John Work Garret Library, 1949, 248 pp.

GILMER, GERTRUDE CORDELIA, comp. "Maryland Magazines—Ante-Bellum, 1793 to 1861." *Maryland Historical Mazazine*, XXIX (June 1934), 120—131.

KEIDEL, GEORGE C. "Early Maryland Newspapers: A List of Titles." *Maryland Historical Magazine*, XXVIII (June 1933), 119—137; (September 1933), 244—257; (December 1933), 328—344; XXIX (March 1934), 25—34;(June 1934), 132—144; (September 1934), 223—236; (December 1934), 310—332; XXX (June 1935), 149—152.

REICHMAN, FELIX. "German Printing in Maryland: A Check List, 1768—1950." *Society for the History of Germans in Maryland*, XXVII (1950), 9—70.

THOMPSON, LAWRENCE SIDNEY. "Foreign Travelers in Maryland, 1900—1950." *Maryland Historical Magazine*, XLVIII (1953), 337—343.

WHEELER, JOSEPH TOWNE. *The Maryland Press, 1777—1790.* Baltimore: Maryland Historical Society, 1938, 226 pp.

——————. "Reading Interests of Maryland Planters and Merchants, 1700—1776." *Maryland Historical Quarterly*, XXXVII (March 1942), 26—41.

MASSACHUSETTS

BOSTON PUBLIC LIBRARY. *A*

Catalogue of the Allen A. Brown Collection of Books Relating to the State in the Public Library of the City of Boston. Boston: Boston Public Library, 1919, 952 pp.

_____. Ships and Sea: A Catalog of an Exhibition of Books and Manuscripts in Tribute to Boston's Maritime Past, July 1– September 1966, in the Boston Public Library. Boston: Boston Public Library, 1966, 58 pages, unpaginated.

COLBURN, JEREMIAH. *Bibliography of the Local History of Massachusetts.* Boston: W. P. Lunt, 1871, 119 pp.

FORD, WORTHINGTON CHAUNCEY. *Broadsides, Ballads, etc., Printed in Massachusetts, 1639–1800.* Boston: Massachusetts Historical Society, 1922, 499 pp.

GREEN, SAMUEL ABBOTT. "A Centennial Bibliography of the Massachusetts Historical Society." *PMHS,* 2nd Series, VI (December 1890), 203–249; (February 1891), 343–349.

_____. *Ten Facsimile Reproductions Relating to Old Boston and Neighborhood.* Boston: J. Wilson and Son, 1901, 44 pp.

100 copies printed.

JONES, M. B. "Thomas Maule, the Salem Quaker, and Free Speech in Massachusetts Bay, with Bibliographical Notes." *Essex Institute Historical Collection,* LXXI (January 1936), 1–42.

LANGDON, GEORGE D., JR. *Pilgrim Colony: A History of New Plymouth, 1620–1691.* New Haven: Yale Univ. Press, 1966, bibliographical footnotes.

Yale Publications in American Studies, No. 12.

NICHOLS, CHARLES LEMUEL. *Bibliography of Worcester: A List of Books, Pamphlets, Newspapers, and Broadsides Printed in the Town of Worcester, Mass., from 1775 to 1848, with Historical and Explanatory Notes.* Worcester: privately printed at the press of Franklin P. Rice, 1899, 216 pp.

_____. "Notes on the Almanacs of Massachusetts." *PAAS,* ns XXII (April 1912), 15–134.

SILVER, ROLLO G. "The Boston Book Trade, 1770–1799," in *Essays Honoring Lawrence C. Wroth.* Portland, Maine: Anthoensen Press, 1951, 279–303.

MICHIGAN

BLACK, ALBERT GEORGE. *Michigan Novels: An Annotated Bibliography.* Ann Arbor: Michigan Council of Teachers of English, 1963, 64 pp.

GOODRICH, MADGE VRIEHUIS (KNEVELS). *A Bibliography of Michigan Authors.* Richmond: Richmond Press, Inc., 1928, 222 pp.

GREENLY, ALBERT HARRY. *A Selective Bibliography of Important Books, Pamphlets, and Broadsides Relating to Michigan History.* Lunenburg, Vermont: Stinehour Press, 1958, 183 pp.

JENKS, W. L. "Calendar of Michigan Copyrights." *Michigan Historical Magazine,* XIV (Spring 1930), 150–155; (Winter 1930), 311–313; XV (Winter 1931), 126–129.

JOYAUX, GEORGES JULES. "French Press in Michigan: A Bibliography." *Michigan History*, XXXVI (September 1952), 260–278.

"Michigan Bibliography." *Michigan History*.

Generally issued annually by various compilers, beginning with XL (1956).

MICHIGAN CIVIL WAR CENTENNIAL OBSERVANCE COMMISSION. *Michigan in the Civil War: A Guide to the Materials in Detroit Newspapers, 1861–1866.* Lansing: Michigan Civil War Centennial Observance Commission, 1965, 404 pp.

STREETER, FLOYD BENJAMIN. *Michigan Bibliography*, 2 Vols. Lansing: Michigan Historical Commission, 1921.

MINNESOTA

WILLIAMS, J. F. "Bibliography of Minnesota." *Minnesota Historical Society Collections*, III (1880), 13–15.

MISSISSIPPI

OWEN, THOMAS McADORY. "A Bibliography of Mississippi," in *Annual Report of the American Historical Association for 1899.* Washington, 1900, 195 pp.

THOMPSON, LAWRENCE SIDNEY. "A Bibliography of Foreign Language Books about Mississippi." *Journal of Mississippi History*, XIV (July 1952), 202–207.

MISSOURI

CARSON, WILLIAM GLASCOW BRUCE. *Managers in Distress: The St. Louis Stage, 1840–1844.* St. Louis: St. Louis Historical Documents Foundation, 1949, 311–313.

——————. *The Theatre on the Frontier: The Early Years of the St. Louis Stage.* New York: B. Blom, 1965, 331–335.

KRAUS, JOE W. "Missouri in Fiction: A Review and a Bibliography." *Missouri Historical Review*, XLII (April–July 1948), 209–225, 310–324.

READ, ALLEN W. "Bibliography of Library Sources for the Study of Place Names of Missouri." *Univ. of Missouri Studies*, IX (1934), 39–59.

ST. LOUIS MERCANTILE LIBRARY ASSOCIATION. . . .*1. Missouri and Illinois Newspapers, 1808–1897, Chronologically Arranged. 2. Manuscripts Relating to Louisiana Territory and Missouri.* St. Louis: St. Louis Mercantile Library Association, 1898, 22 pp.

MONTANA

WALL, ALEXANDER J. "Early Newspapers, With a List of the New York Historical Society's Collection of Papers Published in California, Oregon, Washington, Montana, and Utah." *NYHSB*, XV (July 1931), 39–66.

NEBRASKA

LAMMERS, SOPHIA JOSEPHINE. *A Provisional List of Nebraska Authors.* Lincoln: Univ. of Nebraska Press, 1918, 60 pp.

NEVADA

LINGENFELTER, RICHARD E. *The Newspaper of Nevada: A History and Bibliography, 1858–1958.* San Francisco: John Howell, 1964, 228 pp.

NEW HAMPSHIRE

HAMMOND, OTIS GRANT.
Bibliography of the Newspapers and Periodicals of Concord, N. H., 1790–1898. Concord: Ira C. Evans Co., 1902, 32 pp.

NICHOLS, CHARLES LEMUEL.
Checklist of Maine, New Hampshire, and Vermont Almanacs. Worcester, Massachusetts: American Antiquarian Society, 1929, 103 pp.

Also: *PAAS*, ns XXXVIII (April 1928), 63–163.

NEW JERSEY

ANDREWS, FRANK DeWITTE.
A Bibliography of Vineland: Its Authors and Writers. Vineland, New Jersey: the author, 1916, 21 pp.

56 copies printed.

HEARTMAN, CHARLES FREDERICK. *Preliminary Check List of Almanacs Printed in New Jersey Prior to 1890.* Metuchen, New Jersey: privately printed, 1929, 39 pp.

HILL, FRANK PIERCE, and VARNUM LANSING COLLINS.
Books, Pamphlets, and Newspapers Printed at Newark, New Jersey, 1776–1900. Newark: private press of the *Courier-Citizen* Co., 1902, 296 pp.

NELSON, WILLIAM. *Check-list of the Issues of the Press of New Jersey, 1723, 1728, 1754–1800.* Paterson: Call Printing and Publishing Co., 1899, 42 pp.

NEW MEXICO

DIAZ, ALBERT JAMES. "A Bibliography of Bibliographies Relating to the History and Literature of Arizona and New Mexico."

Arizona Quarterly, XIV (Autumn 1958), 197–218.

"New Mexicana." *NMQ,* II (August 1932), 245–250.

SAUNDERS, LYLE. *A Guide to Materials Bearing on Cultural Relations in New Mexico.* Albuquerque: Univ. of New Mexico Press, 1944, 528 pp.

SHELTON, WILMA LOY. "Checklist of New Mexico Publications." *New Mexico Historical Review,* XXIV (April 1949), 130–155; (July 1949), 223–235; (October 1949), 300–331; XXV (January 1950), 57–73; (April 1950), 136–161; (October 1950), 222–241; XXVI (January 1951), 64–67; (April 1951), 137–147; (July 1951), 225–241; (October 1951), 325–331; XXVII (January 1952), 51–63; XXIX (January 1954), 47–70; (April 1954), 124–140.

NEW YORK

ALBANY INSTITUTE AND HISTORICAL AND ART SOCIETY, LIBRARY. *Albany Authors: A List of Books Written by Albanians . . . .* Albany?: n.p., 1902?, 107 pp.

BROWN, THOMAS ALLSTON.
A History of the New York Stage: From the First Performance in 1732–1901, 3 Vols. New York: Dodd, Mead and Co., 1903.

"Check List of Brooklyn and Long Island Newspapers in the New York Public Library." *BNYPL,* VI (January 1902), 20–21.

"Check List of New York City Almanacs in the New York Public Library." *BNYPL,* V (May 1901), 186–189.

"Check List of Newspapers Published in New York City Contained in the New York Public Library, December 31st, 1900." *BNYPL,* V (January 1901), 20–30.

"Check List of Works Relating to the Social History of the City of New York—Its Clubs, Charities, Hospitals, etc." *BNYPL,* V (June 1901), 261–293.

HILDEBURN, CHARLES R. "A List of the Issues of the Press in New York, 1693–1784." *PMHB,* XXI (No. 4, 1888), 475–482; XIII (No. 1, 1889), 90–98; (No. 2, 1889), 207–215.

IRELAND, JOSEPH NORTON. *Records of the New York Stage, 1750–1860,* 2 Vols. New York: T. H. Morrell, 1866–1867.

2nd edition: B. Blom, 1966.

MUNSELL, FRANK. *Bibliography of Albany: Being a Catalogue of Books and Other Publications Relating to the City and County of Albany in the State of New York.* Albany: J. Munsell's Sons, 1883, 72 pp.

NESTLER, HAROLD. *A Bibliography of New York State Communities.* Port Washington: T. J. Friedman, 1968, no pagination.

ODELL, GEORGE CLINTON DENSMORE. *Annals of the New York Stage,* 15 Vols. New York: Columbia Univ. Press, 1927–1949.

SEVERANCE, FRANK HAYWARD. "Random Notes on the Authors of Buffalo." *Buffalo Historical Society Publications,* IV (1896), 339–379.

STOKES, ISSAC NEWTON PHELPS. "Early New York Newspapers," in *The Iconography of Manhattan Island, 1498–1909. . .,*

6 Vols. New York: R. H. Dodd, 1916, II, 413–452.

WALL, ALEXANDER J. "A List of New York Almanacs, 1649–1850." *BNYPL,* XXIV (May 1920), 287–296; (June 1920), 335–355; (July 1920), 389–413; (August 1920), 443–460; (September 1920), 508–519; (October 1920), 543–559; (November 1920), 620–641.

NORTH CAROLINA

GREEN, C. H. "North Carolina Books and Authors of the Year: A Review." *NCHR,* XXIII (April 1946), 23–29.

LEFLER, HUGH TALMAGE. *A Guide to the Study and Reading of North Carolina Histories,* revised edition. Chapel Hill: Univ. of North Carolina Press, 1963, 30–34.

LEHMER, D. N. "The Literary Material in the Colonial Records of North Carolina." *Univ. of California Chronicle,* XXX (April 1928), 125–139.

POWELL, WILLIAM STEVENS, ed. *North Carolina Fiction, 1734–1957: An Annotated Bibliography.* Chapel Hill: Univ. of North Carolina Library, 1958, 207 pp.

THORNTON, MARY LINDSAY. *A Bibliography of North Carolina, 1589–1956.* Chapel Hill: Univ. of North Carolina Press, 1958, 597 pp.

————————, comp. "North Carolina Bibliography." *NCHR.*

Appears annually in April issue, beginning with XI (1934). With XXXIV (1957), William S. Powell became compiler.

————————, comp. *Official Publications of the Colony and State of*

*North Carolina, 1749–1939: A
Bibliography.* Chapel Hill: Univ. of
North Carolina Press, 1954, 357 pp.

WALSER, RICHARD GAITHER,
and HUGH TALMAGE LEFLER,
comps. *One Hundred Outstanding
Books about North Carolina.*
Chapel Hill: Univ. of North Carolina
Press, 1956, 15 pp.

WEEKS, STEPHEN BEAUREGARD.
*The Press of North Carolina in the
Eighteenth Century.* Brooklyn:
Historical Printing Club, 1891,
53–80.

250 copies printed.

WILSON, LOUIS ROUND. "Fiction
with North Carolina Setting."
North Carolina Review, June 2,
1912, p. 3.

NORTH DAKOTA

NORELL, IRENE P., ed. "Prose
Writers of North Dakota: A Special
Issue." *NDQ,* XXVI (Winter 1958),
37.

SULLIVAN, HELEN J. "North
Dakota Literary Trails: A Literary
Map with Bibliography of Titles."
*Quarterly Journal of the Univ. of
North Dakota,* XXIII (Winter 1933),
99–103.

OHIO

COYLE, WILLIAM, ed. *Ohio Authors
and Their Books: Biographical Data
and Selective Bibliographies for
Ohio Authors, Native and Resident,
1796–1950.* Cleveland: World
Publishing Co., 1962, 762 pp.

EMCH, LUCILLE B. "Ohio in Short
Stories, 1824–1839." *Ohio Archeological and Historical Quarterly,*
LIII (July–September 1944),
209–250.

GALBREATH, C. B. "Early
Newspapers of Ohio," in *Newspapers
and Periodicals in the Ohio State
Library. . . .* Columbus: F. J. Heer,
state printers, 1902, 3–15.

JANEWAY, WILLIAM RALPH.
*A Selected List of Ohio Authors and
Their Books.* Columbus, Ohio:
H. L. Hendrick, 1933, 248 pp.

RODABAUGH, JAMES H., and
S. WINIFRED SMITH. "A Survey
of Publications in Ohio History,
Archaeology, and Natural History."
*Ohio State Archaeological and His-
torical Quarterly.*

Appears in last number of each
volume, beginning with LV (1946).
Title changed to *Ohio History,* 1961.

SUTTON, WALTER. *The Western
Book Trade: Cincinnati as a Nine-
teenth Century Publishing and Book
Trade Center.* Columbus: Ohio State
Univ. Press for the Ohio Historical
Society, 1961, 360 pp.

THOMSON, PETER GIBSON.
*A Bibliography of the State of
Ohio . . . and a Complete Index by
Subjects.* Cincinnati: the author,
1880, 436 pp.

A pioneer local bibliography, citing
some 1,400 books and pamphlets,
many with lengthy notes on contents
and critical comments.

OKLAHOMA

GLEASON, ELSIE CADY. "Newspapers of the Panhandle of Oklahoma,
1886–1940." *Chronicles of Oklahoma,* XIX (June 1941), 141–161.

OREGON

BELKNAP, GEORGE N. "Early
Oregon Documents: Some Bibliographical Revisions." *Oregon His-*

torical Quarterly, LVI (June 1955), 107—125.

——————. "An Oregon Miscellany." *PBSA*, LVII (2nd Quart. 1963), 191—200.

HORNER, JOHN B. *Oregon Literature*, 2nd edition. Portland: J. K. Gill Co., 1902, 255 pp.

WALL, ALEXANDER J. "Early Newspapers, With a List of the New York Historical Society's Collection of Papers Published in California, Oregon, Washington, Montana, and Utah." *NYHSB*, XV (July 1931), 39—66.

PENNSYLVANIA

HISTORICAL SOCIETY OF WESTERN PENNSYLVANIA. *Inventory of Files of American Newspapers in Pittsburgh and Allegheny County, Pennsylvania.* Pittsburgh: n.p., 1933, 41 pp.

Western Pennsylvania Historical Survey, Bibliographical Contributions, No. 2.

WILKINSON, NORMAN B., comp. *Bibliography of Pennsylvania History*, edited by S. K. Stevens and Donald H. Kent. Harrisburg: Pennsylvania Historical and Museum Commission, 1957, 856 pp.

——————, comp. "Current Writings on Pennsylvania." *Pennsylvania History*, XVI (October 1949), 326—330.

RHODE ISLAND

BARTLETT, JOHN RUSSELL. *Bibliography of Rhode Island . . . with Notes, Historical, Biographical, and Critical.* Providence: A. Anthony, printer, 1864, 287 pp.

CHAPIN, H. M. "Check List of Rhode Island Almanacs, 1643—1850." *PAAS*, XXXV (April 1915), 19—54.

HAMMETT, CHARLES EDWARD, JR. *A Contribution to the Bibliography and Literature of Newport, Rhode Island: Comprising a List of Books Published or Printed in Newport, with Notes and Additions.* Newport: printed for the author by Davis and Pitman, 1887, 185 pp.

200 copies printed.

NARRAGANSETT CLUB (PROVIDENCE). *Publications of the Narragansett Club*, 1st Series, I-VI. Providence: Providence Press Co., printers, 1866—1874.

SOUTH CAROLINA

CARDWELL, GUY A. "Charleston Periodicals, 1795—1860: A Study in Literary Influences, with a Descriptive Check List of Seventy-five Magazines." Unpublished doctoral dissertation, Univ. of North Carolina, 1937.

ENGLISH, E. D. "Author List of Caroliniana in the University of South Carolina Library." *Bulletin of the Univ. of South Carolina*, CXXXIV (December 1933).

HOOLE, WILLIAM STANLEY. *The Ante-Bellum Charleston Theatre.* University: Univ. of Alabama Press, 1946, biliographical footnotes.

——————. *A Check List and Finding List of Charleston Periodicals, 1732—1864.* Durham: Duke Univ. Press, 1936, 84 pp.

MOORE, JOHN HAMMOND, ed. *Research Materials in South Carolina: A Guide.* Columbia: Univ.

of South Carolina Press, 1967,
346 pp.

SALLEY, A. S. "A Bibliography of
the Women Writers of South
Carolina." *Publication of the
Southern Historical Association,*
V (March 1902), 143–157.

SOUTH CAROLINA HISTORICAL
SOCIETY. *South Carolina Historical
Magazine.* Charleston: printed for
the South Carolina Historical Society
by Walker, Evans and Cogswell Co.,
1900–   .

Entitled *South Carolina Historical
and Genealogical Magazine,* 1900–
1952.

TURNBULL, ROBERT JAMES.
*Bibliography of South Carolina,
1563–1950,* 5 Vols. Charlottesville:
Univ. of Virginia Press, 1956.

WEBBER, MABEL L. "South
Carolina Almanacs to 1800."
*South Carolina Historical and
General Magazine,* XV (April 1914),
73–81.

TENNESSEE

KIRKLAND, EDWIN C. "A Check
List of the Titles of Tennessee
Folksongs." *JAF,* LIX (October–
December 1946), 423–476.

STEWART, GUY HARRY. "History
and Bibliography of Middle Tennessee Newspapers, 1799–1876."
Unpublished doctoral dissertation,
Univ. of Illinois, 1957.

TEXAS

AGATHA, SISTER M. *Texas Prose
Writings: A Reader's Digest.* Dallas:
B. Upshaw, 1936, xvii–xx.

DANIEL, PRICE, JR. *Books Printed
and Designed by Jack D. Rittenhouse
of the Stagecoach Press: A Bibliography.* Waco, Texas: Stagecoach
Press, 1965, 16 pages, unpaginated.

Texas and the West Catalogue, No. 32.

JENKINS, JOHN HOLMES. *Cracker
Barrel Chronicles: A Bibliography of
Texas Town and County Histories.*
Austin: Pemberton Press, 1965,
509 pp.

MOORE, IKE H. "The Earliest
Printing and the First Newspaper in
Texas." *Southwestern Historical
Quarterly,* XXXIX (October 1935),
83–99.

RAINES, CADWELL WALTON.
*A Bibliography of Texas: Being a
Descriptive List of Books, Pamphlets, and Documents Relating to
Texas in Print and Manuscript since
1536, Including a Complete Collation
of the Laws; with an Introductory
Essay on the Materials of Early
Texan History.* Austin: published
for the author by Gammel Book Co.,
1896, 284 pp.

500 copies printed.

THOMPSON, LAWRENCE SIDNEY.
"Travel Books on Texas Published
in Foreign Countries, 1900–1950."
Southwestern Historical Quarterly,
LVII (October 1953), 202–221.

UTAH

ALTER, J. CECIL. "Bibliographers'
Choice of Books on Utah and the
Mormons." *Utah Historical Quarterly,*
XXIV (July 1956), 215–231.

WALL, ALEXANDER J. "Early
Newspapers, With a List of the
New York Historical Society's Collec-
tion of Papers Published in California,
Oregon, Washington, Montana, and
Utah." *NYHSB,* XV (July 1931),
39–66.

VERMONT

COATES, WALTER J., comp.
*A Bibliography of Vermont Poetry
and Gazetteer of Vermont Poets.*
Montpelier: Vermont Historical
Society, 1942—

Continuing project of the Vermont
Historical Society.

GILMAN, MARCUS DAVIS. *The
Bibliography of Vermont.* Burlington: printed by the Free Press Association, 1897, 349 pp.

McCORISON, MARCUS ALLEN.
"A Bibliography of Vermont Bibliography and Printing." *PBSA,* LV
(1st Quart. 1961), 17—33.

NICHOLS, CHARLES LEMUEL.
*Checklist of Maine, New Hampshire,
and Vermont Almanacs.* Worcester,
Massachusetts: American Antiquarian
Society, 1929, 103 pp.

Also: *PAAS,* ns XXXVIII (April
1928), 63—163.

RUGG, HAROLD G. "Printing in
Peacham, Vermont: A Bibliography."
*Proceedings of the Vermont His-
torical Society,* XII (April 1944),
125—128.

VIRGINIA

BUNI, ANDREW. *The Negro in
Virginia Politics, 1902—1965.*
Charlottesville: Univ. Press of
Virginia, 1967, 271—285.

CAPPON, LESTER JESSE.
*Virginia Newspapers, 1821—1935: A
Bibliography with Historical Intro-
duction and Notes.* New York:
D. Appleton-Century Co., 1936,
312 pp.

*Univ. of Virginia Institute for Re-
search in the Social Sciences
Monograph,* No. 22.

CAPPON, LESTER JESSE, and
STELLA F. DUFF. *Virginia Gazette
Index, 1763—1780,* 2 Vols.
Williamsburg: Institute of Early
American History and Culture, 1950,
1,323 pp.

CHAMBERS, LENOIR, and
JOSEPH E. SHANK. *Salt Water and
Printer's Ink: Norfolk and Its News-
papers, 1865—1965.* Chapel Hill:
Univ. of North Carolina Press, 1967,
396—398.

CLAYTON-TORRENCE, WILLIAM,
comp. "A Trial Bibliography of
Colonial Virginia," in *Annual Reports
of the Library Board of the Virginia
State Library,* 2 Parts. Richmond:
Virginia State Library.

Part 1: *5th Annual Report,* 1907—
1908, 154 pp.

Part 2: *6th Annual Report,* 1908—
1909, 94 pp.

CLEMENT, SAMFORD C., and
JOHN M. HEMPHILL. *Bookbinding
in Colonial Virginia.* Williamsburg,
Virginia: Colonial Williamsburg,
1966, 185 pp.

LANCASTER, EDWIN R. "Books
Read in Virginia in Early 19th
Century, 1806—1823." *VMHB,*
XLVI (January 1938), 56—59.

NEWMAN, CAROL M. "Virginia
Literature: A Catalogue of Authors."
Unpublished doctoral dissertation,
Univ. of Virginia, 1903.

PHILLIPS, PHILIP LEE, ed.
*Virginia Cartography: A Bibliographi-
cal Description.* Washington: published by the Smithsonian Institution,
1896, 85 pp.

WASHINGTON

ELLIOTT, EUGENE CLINTON.

A History of Variety – Vaudeville in Seattle from the Beginning to 1914. Seattle: Univ. of Washington Press, 1944, 81–83, bibliographical footnotes.

HASSELL, SUSAN W. *A Hundred and Sixty Books by Washington Authors.* Seattle: Lowman and Hanford Co., 1916, 40 pp.

POLLARD, LANCASTER. "A Check List of Washington Authors." *Pacific Northwest Quarterly,* XXXI (January 1940), 3–90.

Also: Seattle: n.p., 1940, 96 pp.

——————. "A Check List of Washington Authors: Additions and Corrections." *Pacific Northwest Quarterly,* XXXV (July 1944), 233–266.

STANTON, MARION B. "A Checklist of Washington Authors, 1943–1950." *Pacific Northwest Review,* XLI (July 1950), 245–252.

WALL, ALEXANDER J. "Early Newspapers, With a List of the New York Historical Society's Collection of Papers Published in California, Oregon, Washington, Montana, and Utah." *NYHSB,* XV (July 1931), 39–66.

WASHINGTON, D. C.

BRYAN, WILHELMUS BOGART. *Bibliography of the District of Columbia: Being a List of Books, Maps, and Newspapers, Including Articles in Magazines and Other Publications to 1898,* prepared for the Columbia Historical Society. Washington, 1900, 211 pp.

MILLINGTON, YALE O. "A List of Newspapers Published in the District of Columbia, 1820–1850." *PBSA,* XIX (1925), 43–65.

WEST VIRGINIA

BRENNI, VITO JOSEPH. *West Virginia Authors: A Bibliography.* Morgantown: West Virginia Library Association, 1957, 73 pp.

WISCONSIN

HAWLEY, EMMA A. *Bibliography of Wisconsin Authors . . . .* Madison: Wisconsin State Historical Society, 1893, 263 pp.

WYOMING

WHEELER, EVA FLOY, comp. "A Bibliography of Wyoming Writers." *Univ. of Wyoming Publications,* VI (Feb. 15, 1939), 11–37.

26. RELIGION, THEOLOGY, PHILOSOPHY

ALDIN, JOHN. "American Catholic Poets." *Commonweal,* V (Jan. 19, 1927), 299–300.

ALTER, J. CECIL. "Bibliographers' Choice of Books on Utah and the Mormons." *Utah Historical Quarterly,* XXIV (July 1956), 215–231.

AMERICAN JEWISH HISTORICAL SOCIETY. *Index to the Publications of the American Jewish Historical Society,* 1–20. New York: American Jewish Historical Society, 1914, 600 pp.

ANDERSON, PAUL RUSSELL, and MAX HAROLD FISCH, eds. *Philosophy in America from the Puritans to James, with Representative Selections.* New York: D. Appleton Century Co., Inc., 1939, 583 pp.

AUERBACH, HERBERT S. *Western Americana: Books, Newspapers, and Pamphlets, Many Relating to the Mormon Church from the Collection of Herbert S. Auerbach,* 2 Parts. New York: Parke-Bernet Galleries, Inc., 1947–1948.

"Bibliography of Theological Bibliography," in *Catalogue of the Library of the Princeton Theological School.* Princeton: C. S. Robinson and Co., 1886, 375 pp.

BIBLIOTHECA SACRA. *Index to Bibliotheca Sacra: A Religious and Sociological Quarterly, Volumes I to XXX, Containing a Topical Index, an Index of Scripture Texts, and Lists of Greek and Hebrew Words.* Andover: W. F. Draper, 1874, 293 pp.

BILLINGTON, R. A. "Tentative Bibliography of Anti-Catholic Propaganda in the United States (1800–1860)." *Catholic Historical Review,* XVIII (January 1933), 492–513.

BRIGGS, F. ALLEN. "The Sunday School Library in the Nineteenth Century." *LQ,* XXXI (April 1961), 166–177.

BROWN, STEPHEN JAMES MEREDITH. *Novels and Tales by Catholic Writers.* New York: American Press, 1930, 125 pp.

BURTON, RICHARD FRANCIS. *The City of the Saints.* London: Longman, Green, Longman, and Roberts, 1861, 707 pp.

Also: New York: Harper and Brothers, 1862, 574 pp.

List of works on Mormonism.

CADBURY, H. J. "Quaker Research in Progress or Unpublished." *Bulletin* of the Friends Historical Association, XXXIII (1944), 33–34, 90–91.

CARAYON, AUGUSTE. *Bibliographie historique de la Compagnie de Jesus.* Paris: A. Durand, 1864, 625 pp.

CASE, SHIRLEY JACKSON, et al. *A Bibliographical Guide to the History of Christianity.* Chicago: Univ. of Chicago Press, 1931, 173–207.

Catholic Periodical Index: A Guide to Catholic Magazines, 1930–1931, 2 Vols. New York: H. W. Wilson, 1931.

Catholic Press Directory: Official Media Reference Guide to Catholic Newspapers and Magazines of the United States and Canada. New York: Catholic Press Association, 1923–

Issues annually.

CAVENDER, CURTIS H. (H. C. DECANVER) *Catalogue of Works in Refutation of Methodism, from Its Origin in 1729, to the Present Time.* Philadelphia: J. Penington, 1846, 54 pp.

2nd edition: New York: n.p., 1868.

CLEBSCH, WILLIAM A. "Episcopal and Anglican History, 1966: An Annotated Bibliography." *Historical Magazine of the Protestant Episcopal Church,* XXXVI (June 1967), 179–206.

DEXTER, HENRY MARTYN. "Collections toward a Bibliography of Congregationalism," in *The Congregationalism of the Last 300 Years, as Seen in Its Literature.* New York: Harper, 1880, Appendix.

Arranged chronologically.

_____ . *The Congregational-ism of the Last Three Hundred Years, as Seen in Its Literature: With a Special Reference to Certain Recondite, Neglected, or Disputed Passages.* New York: Harper, 1880, 1,042 pp.

EDDY, RICHARD. *History of Universalism.* New York, 1894, 253–254.

American Church History Series, X.

FAY, JAY WHARTON. *American Psychology before William James.* New Brunswick, New Jersey: Rutgers Univ. Press, 1939, 227–232.

FINOTTI, JOSEPH MARIA. *Bibliographia Catholica Americana: A List of the Works Written by Catholic Authors, and Published in the United States.* New York: Catholic Publication House, 1872, 318 pp.

I: 1784–1820. No more published.

FITCH, GEORGE HAMLIN. *Great Spiritual Writers of America.* San Francisco: P. Elder and Co., 1916, 147–157.

FITZGERALD, JOHN ARTHUR, and LAWRENCE A. FRANK. *A List of 5,000 Catholic Authors.* Ilion, New York: Continental Press, 1941, 101 pp.

GILLETT, E. H. "Bibliography of the Unitarian Controversy." *Historical Magazine,* 2nd Series, IX (April 1871), 316–324.

GINSBERG, LOUIS. *Methodist Book Prices, 1955–1965: With a List of Printers, Publishers, Booksellers of Methodist-Related Material Published in America prior to 1800.* Petersburg, Virginia: Louis Ginsberg, 1965, 72 pp.

GOWANS, WILLIAM. *Catalogue of Books on Freemasonry and Kindred Subjects.* New York: W. Gowans, 1854, 33 pp.

4th edition: 1858, 59 pp.

The Guide to Catholic Literature, 1888–1940. Grosse Pointe, Michigan: Walter Romig, publisher, 1940, 1,240 pp.

Subsequent volumes, under various editors, cover three- and four-year periods. The Catholic Library Association, Haverford, Pennsylvania, publisher, beginning with IV.

HALL, ISAAC HOLLISTER. *American Greek Testaments: A Critical Bibliography of the Greek New Testament as Published in America.* Philadelphia: Pickwick and Co., 1883, 82 pp.

HARRIS, DOROTHY G. "History of Friends' Meeting Libraries." *Bulletin of Friends' Historical Association,* XXXI (Autumn 1942), 52–62.

HINTZ, HOWARD WILLIAM. *The Quaker Influence in American Literature.* New York: F. H. Revell Co., 1940, 96 pp.

HOEHN, MATTHEW, ed. *Catholic Authors: Contemporary Biographical Sketches, 1930–1947,* 2 Vols. Newark: St. Mary's Abbey, 1948–1952.

Also: 1957, 814 pp. One-volume edition.

_____ . ed. *Catholic Authors: Contemporary Biographical Sketches, 1948–1952.* Newark: St. Mary's Abbey, 1952, 633 pp.

HURLEY, LEONARD B. "The American Novel, 1830–1850: Its Reflections of Contemporary

Religious Conditions, with a Bibliography of Fiction." Unpublished doctoral dissertation, Univ. of North Carolina, 1932.

HURST, JOHN FLETCHER. *Bibliotheca Theologica: A Select and Classified Bibliography of Theology and General Religious Literature.* New York: C. Scribner's Sons, 1883, 417 pp.

_____. *Literature of Theology: A Classified Bibliography of Theological and General Religious Literature.* New York: Hunt and Eaton, 1896, 757 pp.

JACKSON, SAMUEL MACAULEY, comp. *A Bibliography of American Church History, 1820–1893.* New York, 1894, 441–513.

American Church History Series, XI.

JOHNSON, THOMAS HERBERT, and PERRY MILLER. *The Puritans.* New York: American Book Co., 1938, 785–834.

Revised edition: 2 Vols. Harper and Row, 1963.

JONES, RUFUS MATTHEW. *The Quakers in the American Colonies.* London: Macmillan and Co., Ltd., 1911, bibliographical footnotes.

Also: New York: W. W. Norton, 1966.

KOHUT, GEORGE A. "Early Jewish Literature in America." *American Jewish Historical Society Publications,* III (1895), 103–147.

LAURIE, THOMAS. *The Ely Volume: or, The Contributions of Our Foreign Missions to Science and Well-Being.* Boston: American Board of Commissioners for Foreign Missions, 1881, 532 pp.

"Home literature of the American Board," 485–494.

LEARY, LEWIS. *Articles on American Literature, 1900–1950.* Durham: Duke Univ. Press, 1954, 396–397.

"Philosophy and Philosophical Trends."

_____. *Articles on American Literature, 1900–1950.* Durham: Duke Univ. Press, 1954, 422–424.

"Religion."

LEHAN, RICHARD. "French and American Philosophical and Literary Existentialism: A Selected Check List." *Wisconsin Studies in Contemporary Literature,* I (Fall 1960), 74–88.

MARX, ALEXANDER. *Studies in Jewish History and Booklore.* New York: Jewish Theological Seminary of America, 1944, bibliographical footnotes.

MODE, PETER G. *Source Book and Bibliographical Guide for American Church History.* Menasha, Wisconsin: George Banta Publishing Co., 1921, 735 pp.

MORRIS, JOHN GOTTLIEB. *Bibliotheca Lutherana: A Complete List of Publications of All the Lutheran Ministers in the United States.* Philadelphia: Lutheran Board of Publication, 1876, 139 pp.

O'CALLAGHAN, EDMUND BAILEY. *List of Editions of the Holy Scriptures Printed in America Previous to 1860.* Albany: Munsell and Rowland, 1861, 415 pp.

OSBORN, GEORGE. *Outlines of Wesleyan Bibliography: or, a Record of Methodist Literature from the Beginning: in Two Parts: The First*

Containing the Publications of John and Charles Wesley . . . the Second, Those of Methodist Preachers . . . . London: Wesleyan Conference Office, 1869, 231 pp.

PETTIT, NORMAN. *The Heart Prepared: Grace and Conversion in Puritan Spiritual Life.* New Haven: Yale Univ. Press, 1966, 223–235.

Yale Publications in American Studies, No. 11.

PIERCE, WILLIAM. "A Select Bibliography of the Pilgrim Fathers of New England." *Congregational Historical Society Transactions,* VIII (February 1920), 16–23; (August 1920), 59–68.

PRINCETON THEOLOGICAL SEMINARY. *Catalogue of the Library of the Princeton Theological School, Part I: Religious Literature.* Princeton: C. S. Robinson and Co., 1886, 453 pp.

REMY, JULES. "Bibliographie Mormonne," in *Voyage au Pays des Mormons,* 2 Vols. Paris: E. Dentu, 1860, II, 499–506.

English edition: London: W. Jeffs, 1861.

Also: Louisville, Kentucky: Lost Cause Press, 1960.

ROSENBACH, ABRAHAM SIMON WOLF. *An American Jewish Bibliography: Being a List of Books and Pamphlets by Jews or Relating to Them Published in the United States from the Establishment of the Press in the Colonies until 1850.* Baltimore: The Lord Baltimore Press, 1926, 486 pp.

SCALLY, SISTER MARY ANTHONY. *Negro Catholic Writers, 1900–1943: A Bio-*

Bibliography. Detroit: W. Romig and Co., 1945, 152 pp.

SCHNEIDER, LOUIS, and SANFORD M. DORNBUSCH. "Inspirational Religious Literature: From Latent to Manifest Functions of Religion." *AJS,* LXII (March 1957), 476–481.

Treats popular inspirational literature of the last 75 years.

SCHNEIDER, REBECCA. *Bibliography of Jewish Life in the Fiction of England and America.* Albany: New York State Library School, 1916, 41 pp.

SHEA, JOHN DAWSON GILMARY. *Bibliographical Account of Catholic Bibles. . . Translated from the Latin Vulgate and Printed in the United States.* New York: Cramoisy Press, 1859, 48 pp.

Reprinted from *New York Freeman's Journal.*

SILBER, MENDEL. *America in Hebrew Literature.* New Orleans: Steeg, 1928, 104 pp.

SMITH, JOSEPH. *Bibliotheca Anti-Quakeriana . . . .* London: J. Smith, 1873, 474 pp.

_____. *Bibliotheca Quakeristica: A Bibliography of Miscellaneous Literature Relating to Friends . . . .* London: Joseph Smith, 1883, 32 pp.

_____. *Catalogue of Books Relating to the Society of Friends.* London, 1883, 32 pp.

Only known copy in the British Museum.

_____. *Descriptive Catalogue of Friends Books . . .,* 2 Vols. London: J. Smith, 1867.

Supplement: London: E. Hicks, June 1893, 364 pp.

SMITH, WILBUR MOOREHEAD. *List of Bibliographies of Theological and Biblical Literature Published in Great Britain and America, 1595–1931,* with critical biographical and bibliographical notes. Coatesville, Pennsylvania, 1931, 62 pp.

STENHOUSE, THOMAS B. H. *The Rocky Mountain Saints.* New York: D. Appleton and Co., 1873.

"Writers on Mormonism," 741–746.

Studies in Bibliography and Booklore. Cincinnati: Library of Union Hebrew College, Jewish Institute of Religion, 1953–   .

THOMAS, ALLEN CLAPP, and RICHARD HENRY THOMAS. *History of the Friends in America,* 4th edition. Philadelphia: Winston, 1905, 229–241.

TOLLES, FREDERICK BARNES. *Meeting House and Counting House: The Quaker Merchants of Colonial Philadelphia, 1682–1763.* Chapel Hill: published for the Institute of Early American History and Culture at Williamsburg, Virginia, by the Univ. of North Carolina Press, 1948, 253–276.

TRENT, WILLIAM PETERFIELD, et al. "Divines and Moralists, 1783–1860," in *Cambridge History of American Literature,* 4 Vols. New York: G. P. Putnam's Sons, 1917–1921, II, 524.

_____. "Later Philosophy," in *Cambridge History of American Literature,* 4 Vols. New York: G. P. Putnam's Sons, 1917–1921, IV, 751–760.

_____. "Later Theology," in *Cambridge History of American Literature,* 4 Vols. New York: G. P. Putnam's Sons, 1917–1921, IV, 742–751.

_____. "Philosophers and Divines, 1720–1789," in *Cambridge History of American Literature,* 4 Vols. New York: G. P. Putnam's Sons, 1917–1921, I, 438–442.

_____. "Popular Bibles," in *Cambridge History of American Literature,* 4 Vols. New York: G. P. Putnam's Sons, 1917–1921, IV, 802–806.

_____."The Puritan Divines, 1620–1720," in *Cambridge History of American Literature,* 4 Vols. New York: G. P. Putnam's Sons, 1917–1921, I, 385–425.

_____. "Transcendentalism," in *Cambridge History of American Literature,* 4 Vols. New York: G. P. Putnam's Sons, 1917–1921, I, 546–551.

VAIL, ROBERT WILLIAM GLENROIE. "A Check List of New England Election Sermons." *PAAS,* XLV (October 1935), 233–266.

WEEKS, STEPHEN BEAUREGARD. *Southern Quakers and Slavery.* Baltimore: Johns Hopkins Press, 1898, 345–362.

WHEELER, BURTON M. "Religious Themes in Contemporary Literature: An Introductory Bibliography." *Journal of Bible and Religion,* XXVII (January 1959), 50–56.

WRIGHT, LUELLA MARGARET. *The Literary Life of the Early Friends, 1650–1725.* New York: Columbia Univ. Press, 1932, 274–294.

Columbia Univ. Studies in English and Comparative Literature.

27. SCIENCE

ACADEMY OF NATURAL
SCIENCES OF PHILADELPHIA.
*Catalogue of the Library of Natural
Sciences of Philadelphia.* Phila-
delphia: J. Dobson, 1837, 300 pp.

BOEHMER, GEORGE HANS.
"Index to Papers on Anthropology
Published by the Smithsonian Insti-
tute, 1847 to 1848," in *Smithsonian
Institute, Annual Report, 1879.*
Washington, 1880, 476–483.

GIRARD, CHARLES. *Bibliographia
Americana Historico-Naturalis, or
Bibliography of American Natural
History, for the Year 1851.* Wash-
ington: Smithsonian Institution,
1852, 64 pp.

HAVEN, SAMUEL FOSTER.
*Archeology of the United States, or
Sketches, Historical and Biblio-
graphical, of the Progress of Informa-
tion and Opinion Respecting
Vestiges of Antiquity in the United
States.* Washington: Smithsonian
Institution, 1856, 168 pp.

*Smithsonian Contributions to
Knowledge,* VIII, Article 2.

HAWLEY, EDITH. "Bibliography of
Literary Geography." *BB,* X (April–
June 1918), 34–38; (July–September
1918), 58–60; (October–December
1918), 76; (January–March 1919),
93–94; (April–June 1919), 104–
105.

JACKSON, JAMES. *List Provisoire
de Bibliographies Géographies
Spéciales.* Paris: C. Delagrave, 1881,
125 pp.

JAFFE, BERNARD. *Men of Science
in America: The Role of Science
in the Growth of Our Country.*
New York: Simon and Schuster,
1944, 640 pp.

Sources and reference material,
555–571.

LEARY, LEWIS. *Articles on
American Literature, 1900–1950.*
Durham: Duke Univ. Press, 1954,
424–425.

"Science."

STRUIK, DIRK JOHN. *Yankee
Science in the Making.* Boston:
Little, Brown, 1948, 387–416.

SVENDSEN, KESTER, SAMUEL
J. MINTZ and LAURIE BOWMAN
ZWICKY. "Relations of Literature
and Science: Selected Bibliography
for 1954." *Symposium,* IX (Spring
1955), 196–201; X (Spring 1956),
182–187; XI (Spring 1957),
178–183; XII (Spring 1958), 256–
262.

28. THEMES AND TYPES

ADAMS, RAMON FREDERICK.
*The Rampaging Herd: A Bibliography
of Books and Pamphlets on Men and
Events in the Cattle Industry.*
Norman: Univ. of Oklahoma Press,
1959, 482 pp.

BOGER, LORISE C. *The Southern
Mountaineer in Literature: An Annotated Bibliography.* Morgantown:
West Virginia Univ. Library, 1964,
114 pp.

"Bibliography of Sources," 94–95.

BUCKLEY, JOHN. "Bibliography of
Ritual." *BB,* XX (April 1953),
236–240.

FENN, WILLIAM PURVIANCE. *Ah Sin and His Brethren in American Literature* . . . . Peking, China: College of Chinese Studies cooperating with California College in China, 1933, 131 pp.

Originally a doctoral dissertation at the Univ. of Iowa, xxxii–xli.

FISHWICK, MARSHALL WILLIAM. *A Bibliography of the American Hero.* Charlottesville: Bibliographical Society of the Univ. of Virginia, 1950, 16 leaves.

GAINES, FRANCIS PENDLETON. *The Southern Plantation: A Study in the Development and the Accuracy of a Tradition.* New York: Columbia Univ. Press, 1924, 237–243.

Columbia Univ. Studies in English and Comparative Literature.

HAZARD, LUCY LOCKWOOD. *The Frontier in American Literature.* New York: Crowell, 1927, 301–304.

"Puritan Frontier," 39–45; "Southern Frontier," 87–93; "Hunter and Trapper," 141–146; "Transcendentalism," 178–180; "Frontier of '49," 207–208; "Industrial Pioneering," 240–242; "Frontier and the Nester," 274–276; "Age of Spiritual Pioneering," 298–300.

HERRON, IMA HONAKER. *The Small Town in American Literature.* Durham: Duke Univ. Press, 1939, 429–468.

KLEIN, MARCUS. "A Fix in the Igloo." *Nation,* CXC (April 23, 1960), 361–364.

A survey of literature about drug addicts.

LANDIS, BENSON Y. "Democracy: A Reading List." *BALA,* XXXIV (January 1940), 55–68.

LEARY, LEWIS. *Articles on American Literature, 1900–1950.* Durham: Duke Univ. Press, 1954, 364–365.

"Frontier."

MERRITT, RICHARD L. *Symbols of American Community, 1735–1775.* New Haven: Yale Univ. Press, 1966, bibliographical footnotes.

Yale Studies in Political Science, No. 16.

MERSAND, JOSEPH. *Traditions in American Literature: A Study of Jewish Characters and Authors.* New York: Modern Chapbooks, 1939, 201–236.

Incomplete account of Jewish authors in 20th-century United States.

MINER, EARL ROY. *The Japanese Tradition in British and American Literature.* Princeton: Princeton Univ. Press, 1958, 281–300.

PARKINSON, THOMAS FRANCIS, ed. *A Casebook on the Beat.* New York: Crowell, 1961, 326 pp.

PARRINGTON, VERNON LOUIS, JR. *American Dreams.* Providence: Brown Univ. Press, 1947, 219–229.

Brown Univ. Studies, XI.

SEALOCK, RICHARD BURL, and PAULINE A. SEELY. *Bibliography of Place Name Literature: United States, Canada, Alaska, and Newfoundland.* Chicago: American Library Association, 1948, 381 pp.

SEELY, PAULINE A., and RICHARD BURL SEALOCK. "Place Name Literature, United States, 1955–1959." *Names,* VII (December 1959), 203–232.

_____. "Place Name Literature, United States and Alaska, 1946–1951." *Names,* VI (March 1958), 26–50.

_____. "Place Name Literature, United States and Canada." *Names,* III (June 1955), 102–116.

SKARD, SIGMUND. "The Use of Color in Literature: A Survey of Research." *PAAS,* XC (July 1946), 163–249.

SMITH, HENRY NASH. *Virgin Land: The American West as Symbol and Myth.* Cambridge: Harvard Univ. Press, 1950, 261–298, bibliographical footnotes.

TINKER, EDWARD LAROCQUE. *The Horsemen of the Americas and the Literature They Inspired.* New York: Hastings House, 1953, 119–149.

TRAVERSO, MARY R. "A Bibliography of Toys in Literature." *More Books,* XVI (October 1941), 355–375.

TRENT, WILLIAM PETERFIELD, et al. "Oral Literature," in *Cambridge History of American Literature,* 4 Vols. New York: G. P. Putnam's Sons, 1917–1921, IV, 799–802.

WEST, THOMAS REED. *Flesh of Steel: Literature and the Machine in American Culture.* Nashville: Vanderbilt Univ. Press, 1967, 137–144.

WHEAT, CARL I. "The Literature of the Gold Rush." *New Colophon,* II (January 1949), 54–67.

A bibliographical account.

WHEELER, BURTON M. "Religious Themes in Contemporary Literature: An Introductory Bibliography." *Journal of Bible and Religion,* XXVII (January 1959), 50–56.

29. TRANSLATIONS

ANDERSON, CARL L. *The Swedish Acceptance of American Literature.* Philadelphia: Univ. of Pennsylvania Press, 1957, 103–152.

BAKER, ERNEST ALBERT, and JAMES PACKMAN. *A Guide to the Best Fiction, English and American, Including Translations from Foreign Languages.* New York: Macmillan Co., 1932, 642 pp.

BELIME, J. "An International Bibliography of Translations." *TLS,* July 7, 1932, p. 499.

BROWN, GLENORA W., and DEMING B. BROWN. *A Guide to*

Soviet Russian Translations of American Literature. New York: King's Crown Press, Columbia Univ., 1954, 243 pp.

Lists books published 1917–1947. Introductory essay on "Soviet Taste in American Literature."

FOSTER, FINLEY MELVILLE KENDALL. *English Translations from the Greek: A Bibliographical Survey.* New York: Columbia Univ. Press, 1918, 175 pp.

Columbia Univ. Studies in English and Comparative Literature.

INDEX TRANSLATIONUM. *Répertoire International des*

Traductions: International Bibliography of Translation. Paris: UNESCO, 1948– .

Issued irregularly.

LUCIANI, VINCENT. "Modern Italian Fiction in America, 1929–1954: An Annotated Bibliography of Translations." *BNYPL*, LX (January 1956), 12–34.

MUMMENDEY, RICHARD. *Die schöne Literatur der Vereinigten*

Staaten von Amerika in Deutschen Übersetzungen. Bonn: H. Bouvier, 1961, 191 pp.

Translations of American literary works.

SINCLAIR, UPTON. *Books of Upton Sinclair in Translations and Foreign Editions: A Bibliography of 525 Titles in 34 Countries.* Pasadena, California: privately printed by the author, 1930, 34 pp.

Also: 1938, 48 pp.

30. TRAVELS

BABEY, ANNA MARY. *Americans in Russia, 1776–1917: A Study of the American Travelers in Russia from the American Revolution to the Russian Revolution.* New York: Comet Press, 1938, 127–169.

BARTLETT, J. R. "Bibliography of Carver's Travels." *Bookmart* (Pittsburgh), IV (1886), 17.

BUCK, SOLON JUSTUS. "The Bibliography of American Travel: A Project." *PBSA*, XXII (1928), 52–59.

_____. *Travel and Description, 1765–1865: Together with a List of County Histories, Atlases, and Biographical Collections and a List of Territorial and State Laws.* Springfield: published by the trustees of the Illinois State Historical Library, 1914, 514 pp.

Collections of the Illinois State Historical Library, IX; Bibliographical Series, II.

CLARK, THOMAS DIONYSIUS. "The Great Visitation to American Democracy." *MVHR*, XLIV (June 1957), 3–28.

A survey of the past three centuries of travel literature by visitors to America.

_____, ed. *Travels in the New South: A Bibliography,* 2 Vols. Norman: Univ. of Oklahoma Press, 1962.

I: The Postwar South, 1865–1900.

II: The Twentieth Century South, 1900–1955.

_____. *Travels in the Old South: A Bibliography,* 2 Vols. Norman: Univ. of Oklahoma Press, 1956, 662 pp.

COLVILLE, DEREK. "Checklist to Travel Essays Relating to the Southwest which Appeared in the New Orleans *Daily Picayune,* 1819–1841." *New Mexico Historical Review,* XXXIII (July 1958), 232–235.

COUES, ELLIOTT. *An Account of the Various Publications Relating to the Travels of Lewis and Clarke, with a Commentary on the Zoological Results of Their Expedition.* Washington, 1876, 417–444.

Extracted from *Bulletin of the Geological and Geographical Survey of the Territories,* No. 6.

COULTER, ELLIS MERTON. *Travels in the Confederate States: A Bibliography.* Norman: Univ. of Oklahoma Press, 1948, 303 pp.

American Exploration and Travel, No. 11.

COX, EDWARD GODFREY. *A Reference Guide to the Literature of Travel, Including Voyages, Geographical Descriptions, Adventures, Shipwrecks and Expeditions.* Seattle: Univ. of Washington Press, 1935– .

FARQUHAR, FRANCIS PELOUBET. *The Books of the Colorado River and the Grand Canyon: A Selective Bibliography.* Los Angeles: G. Dawson, 1953, pp.86.

Early California Travels Series, No. 12.

HENLINE, RUTH. "Travel Literature of Colonists in America, 1754–1783: An Annotated Bibliography." Unpublished doctoral dissertation, Northwestern Univ., 1947.

HUBACH, ROBERT ROGERS. *Early Midwestern Travel Narratives: An Annotated Bibliography, 1634–1850.* Detroit: Wayne State Univ. Press, 1961, 159 pp.

_____. "They Saw the Early Midwest: A Bibliography of Travel Narratives." *Journal of the Illinois State Historical Society,* XLVI (1953), 283–289; XLVII (1954), 285–297; *Iowa Journal of History,* LII (1954), 223–234.

Covers 1722–1850.

JILLSON, WILLARD ROUSE. "A Bibliography of Early Western Travel in Kentucky: 1674–1824." *Kentucky State Historical Society Register,* XLII (April 1945), 99–119.

JONES, HERSCHEL VESPASIAN. *Adventures in Americana, 1492–1897: Being a Selection of Books from the Library of Herschel V. Jones, Minneapolis, Minnesota,* 2 Vols. New York: W. E. Ridge, 1928.

PHILLIPS, PHILIP LEE, ed. *Virginia Cartography: A Bibliographical Description.* Washington: published by the Smithsonian Institution, 1896, 85 pp.

THOMPSON, LAWRENCE SIDNEY. "Foreign Travelers in Maryland, 1900–1950." *Maryland Historical Magazine,* XLVIII (1953), 337–343.

_____. "Travel Books on Texas Published in Foreign Countries, 1900–1950." *Southwestern Historical Quarterly,* LVII (October 1953), 202–221.

TRENT, WILLIAM PETERFIELD, et al. "Travellers and Explorers, 1583–1763," in *Cambridge History of American Literature,* 4 Vols. New York: G. P. Putnam's Sons, 1917–1921, I, 365–380.

_____. "Travellers and Explorers, 1846–1900," in *Cambridge History of American Literature,* 4 Vols. New York: G. P. Putnam's Sons, 1917–1921, IV, 681–728.

_____. "Travellers and Observers, 1763–1846," in *Cambridge History of American Literature,* 4 Vols. New York: G. P. Putnam's Sons, 1917–1921, I, 468–490.

WAGNER, HENRY RAUP. *The Plains and the Rockies: A Bibliography of Original Narratives of Travel and Adventure, 1800–1865,* 3rd edition. Columbus, Ohio: Long's College Book Co., 1593, 601 pp.

WICKERSHAM, JAMES, comp. *Bibliography of Literature, 1724–1924: Containing the Titles of Histories, Travels, Voyages, Newspapers, Periodicals, Public Documents . . . Relating to . . . Alaska.* Cordova, Alaska: Cordova *Daily Times,* 1927, 662 pp.

INDEX